MW01253134

Modeling and Analysis of Communicating Systems

Modeling and Analysis of Communicating Systems

Jan Friso Groote and Mohammad Reza Mousavi

PHI Learning Private Limited
Delhi-110092
2016

This Indian Reprint—₹ 795.00
(Original U.S. Edition—₹ 3430.00)

MODELING AND ANALYSIS OF COMMUNICATING SYSTEMS
by Jan Friso Groote and Mohammad Reza Mousavi

ISBN-978-81-203-5183-7

Original edition published by the MIT Press, Cambridge, MA, U.S.A.

Reprinted in India by special arrangement with MIT Press, Cambridge, MA, U.S.A. Not for sale or shipment outside India, Bangladesh, Burma, Nepal, Sri Lanka, Bhutan, Pakistan and the Maldives.

Published by Asoke K. Ghosh, PHI Learning Private Limited, Rimjhim House, 111, Patparganj Industrial Estate, Delhi-110092 and Printed by Mohan Makhijani at Rekha Printers Private Limited, New Delhi-110020.

Voor papa en mem, en Paula
– Jan Friso

For my mother, my father, and Mona
– Mohammad

Contents

Preface

Robin Milner observed in 1973 that the primary task of computers is to interact with their environment. But the theory of programs and programming at that time ignored this [133, 134]. To remedy this, he set out working on a theory of interaction, leading to his seminal books [135, 137] in which he developed the calculus of communicating systems (CCS). At the same time two other main process calculi were developed, namely the algebra of communicating processes (ACP [25]) and communicating sequential processes (CSP [102, 103]).

Interesting as they were, these process algebras were too bare to be used for the description of actual systems, mainly because they lacked a proper integration of data. In order to solve this, process-algebraic specification languages were designed (most notably LOTOS [108] and PSF [129]) which contained both data and processes. A problem with these languages was that they were too complex to act as a basic carrier for the development of behavioral analysis techniques.

We designed an intermediate language, namely mCRL2 (and its direct predecessor μCRL [76, 85]), as a stripped-down process specification language or an extended process algebra. It contains exactly those ingredients needed to describe the behavior of systems precisely in all aspects, and its (relative) simplicity allows the focus to be on proof and analysis techniques for process behavior.

Throughout the years many of these analysis techniques have been developed. These results include the recursive specification principle (RSP), τ-confluence, invariants, cones and foci, the modal μ-calculus with time and data, abstract interpretation and coordinate transformations, parameterized Boolean equation systems (PBESs), and proof by patterns, to name a few. These results, when combined together, constitute a mathematical framework suitable to launch an attack on several phenomena in the realm of process behavior that are not properly understood. They also form an effective framework to formulate and prove the correctness of complex and intricate protocols.

Prior to now, all these results were lingering around in the literature. We combined them in this book, added exercises and examples to make the developed material suitable for self study and for teaching. The book has been used in recent years as the basis for several graduate-level courses. These include the course on system validation in the Embedded Systems masters program at Eindhoven University of Technology and Delft University of Technology in the Netherlands.

Acknowledgments

The first version of this book appeared as a handbook chapter [87]. This chapter formed the basis of a reader [61] used for courses at several universities (published as [60]). These earlier publications were based on the micro common representation language (μCRL [85, 76]) essentially developed in 1991. In 2003 we decided that it was time for a successor to increase the usability of the μCRL, and we decided to baptize its successor mCRL2. The essential difference is that mCRL2 has richer data types, including standard data types and functions, contrary to μCRL, which contained only a mechanism to define equational data types. This book is solely based on mCRL2, and substantially extends [60].

The development of mCRL2 builds upon the development work on process algebras between 1970 and 1990. Especially the work on CCS by Robin Milner [135] and ACP by Jan Bergstra, Jan Willem Klop, Jos Baeten, Rob van Glabbeek, and Frits Vaandrager [25, 18] form an important basis. An essential step was the EC SPECS project, where an expressive *common representation language* had to be developed to encompass all behavioral description languages that existed at that time (LOTOS, CHILL, SDL, PSF) and that still had to be developed. As a reaction, μCRL was developed, in which Alban Ponse was instrumental. Bert Lisser was the main figure behind the maintenance and development of the tools to support μCRL.

The following people contributed to the development of mCRL2, its tools, and its theory: Sjoerd Cranen, Tom Haenen, Frank van Ham, Jeroen Keiren, Aad Mathijssen, Bas Ploeger, Jaco van de Pol, Hannes Pretorius, Frank Stappers, Carst Tankink, Yaroslav Usenko, Muck van Weerdenburg, Wieger Wesselink, Tim Willemse, and Jeroen van der Wulp.

This book has been used as a reader for several courses among which are the courses Requirements, Analysis, Design and Verification and System Validation at Eindhoven University of Technology and Delft University of Technology. Many thanks go to Sjoerd Cranen, Veronica Gaspes, Jeroen Keiren, Michel Reniers, and Erik de Vink for their careful proofreading. Valuable feedback also came from Michael Adriaansen, Muhammad Atif, Timur Bagautdinov, Ruud Bauhaus, Harsh Beohar, Debjyoti Bera, Dwight Berendse, Anton Bilos, Michiel Bosveld, Gert-Jan van den Braak, Christoph Brandt, Bram Cappers, Mehmet Çubuk, Edin Dudojević, Michiel Fortuin, Joe Ganett, Herman Geuvers, Sven Goossens, Christiaan Hartman, Albert Hofkamp, Hossein Hojjat, Tom Hubregtsen, Femke Jansen, Bas Kloet, Diana Koenraadt, Geert Kwintenberg, Koen van Langen, Tony Larsson, Mattias Lee, Josh Mengerink, Paul Mulders, Gerardo Ochoa, Chidi Okwudire, Mathijs Opdam, Mahboobeh Parsapoor, Eva Ploum, Jagruth

Prassanna Kumar, Sander de Putter, André van Renssen, Marcel Roeloffzen, Koos Rooda, Anson van Rooij, Vikram Saralaya, Frank Stappers, Carst Tankink, Sander Verdonschot, Twan Vermeulen, Maks Verver, Amrita Vikas Sinha, Migiel de Vos, Tim Willemse, Jia Yan, Umar Waqas, and many others.

I

Modeling

1

Introduction

1.1 Motivation

In today's world, virtually all human-made systems contain computers that are connected via data networks. This means that contemporary systems behave in a complex way and are continuously in contact with their environment. For system architects, it is a major aspect of their task to design and understand the behavior of such systems. This book deals with the question of how to model system interaction in a sufficiently abstract way, such that it can be understood and analyzed. In particular, it provides techniques to prove that interaction schemes fulfill their intended purpose.

In order to appreciate this book, it is necessary to understand the complexity of contemporary systems. As an extremely simple example, take the on/off switch of a modern computer. We do not have to go far back in history to find that the power switch had a very simple behavior. After the power switch was turned off, the power to the computer was disconnected, and neither the computer nor the switch would attempt to perform any task, until switched on again.

In a modern computer, the on/off switch is connected to the central processor. If the on/off switch is pressed, the processor is signaled that the computer must switch off. The processor will finish current tasks, shutdown its hardware devices, and inform (or even ask permission from) others via its networks that it intends to go down. So, nowadays, even the simplest system can perform complex, and often counterintuitive behavior. Switching a system off will lead to more activity, although generally only temporarily.

Given the complexity of systems, it is no longer self-evident whether a system will behave as expected. Existing techniques, such as testing to guarantee the quality of such interacting systems, are inadequate. There are too many different runs of the system to inspect and test them all.

A standard engineering approach to contain phenomena with a complexity beyond human grasp is to use mathematical models. State machines appear to be the right mathematical notion to model behavior of computer systems. A system starts in its initial state and whenever something happens it moves to some other state. This something is called an action, which can be any activity such as an internal calculation or a communication with some other system. The act of going from one state to another is called a transition. State machines are also called automata or labeled transition systems.

The core problem of labeled transition systems is that they tend to become large. This is called the *state space explosion problem*. Particularly, the use of data and parallel behavior can easily lead to automata of colossal size.

Modeling a four-byte integer as a state machine, where each value is a state and changing a value is a transition, already leads to a state machine with 4×10^9 states. For parallel systems, the state space of a system is of the same order of magnitude as the product of the sizes of the automata of each component. The numbers indicating the number of states in a labeled transition system are typically 10^{1000} or even $10^{(10^{10})}$ and exceed the well-known astronomical numbers by far. It is completely justified to speak about a whole new class of numbers, that is, the *computer engineering numbers*.

The sheer size of labeled transition systems has two consequences. The first one is that we cannot write transition systems down as a state machine, but require more concise notation. We use the language mCRL2 for this, which was inspired by the process algebra ACP, extended with data and time. And we use the modal mu-calculus, also extended with data and time to denote properties about automata.

The second consequence is that – as in ordinary mathematical modeling – we must restrain ourselves when modeling behavior. If our models have too many states, analysis becomes cumbersome. But of course, the contrary also holds. If our models do not contain sufficient detail, we may not be able to study those phenomena we are interested in.

But mastering the art of behavioral modeling will turn out to be rewarding. If the state space explosion problem can be avoided, it is often very efficient to check a few modal formulas representing correctness requirements of a system. Our own experience is that we found problems in all existing systems that we modeled thoroughly. Several examples of our experiments and the discovered problems are reported in [9, 10, 105, 106, 161]. If these systems, protocols and algorithms were modeled and analyzed using methods and tools available today, many of those problems would have been uncovered easily. Interestingly, some of the faulty protocols and algorithms have been published in scientific venues; it is therefore not much of an exaggeration to say that formal analyses (e.g., model checking) before publication of distributed algorithms and protocols ought to be obligatory.

Without proper mathematical theories, appropriate proof and analysis methods, and adequate computer tools, it is impossible to design correct communicating systems with the complexity that is common today. Using formal modeling and analysis, a far better job is possible. In this book we provide the requisite ingredients.

1.2 The mCRL2 approach

We present a rigorous approach to behavioral specification and verification of concurrent and distributed systems. Our approach builds upon the rich literature of *process algebras* [25, 103, 135], which are algebraic formalisms for compositional specification of concurrent systems. More specifically, we propose a formalism, called *mCRL2*, which extends the algebra of communicating processes (ACP) [25] with various features including notions of data, time, and multi-actions.

Specifications in mCRL2 are built upon atomic (inter)actions, which can be composed using various algebraic operators. The specified behavior can then be simulated, visualized or verified against its requirements. Requirements are defined by using a rich logic, namely the modal mu-calculus with data and time. This logic is very suitable to express patterns of (dis)allowed behavior. In order to mechanically verify the requirements, an extensive tool set has been developed for mCRL2. It can be downloaded from `www.mcrl2.org`.

1.3 An overview of the book

In chapter 2, our basic building block, namely an action, is introduced. Using transition systems, it is explained how actions can be combined into behavior. The circumstances under which behaviors can be considered the same are also investigated.

In chapter 3, data types are explained. In particular it is explained how data types are built upon constructors, mappings, and functions using equations. Appendix B gives the exact definition of all predefined data types.

In chapter 4, sequential and nondeterministic behavior is described in an algebraic way. This means that there are a number of composition operators, of which the properties are characterized by axioms. In chapter 5, it is shown how parallel and communication components are specified, again including the required axioms.

The next chapter explains how to describe behavioral properties in a very expressive logic, called the modal mu-calculus. By integrating data in this calculus, we not only can state simple properties, such as that a system is deadlock-free, but also very complex properties that depend on fair behavior or require data storage and computation in the modal formula.

Chapter 7 contains a number of example descriptions of the behavior of some simple systems. In chapter 8, all components of the framework are extended with time. This chapter concludes the first part of the book.

The second part of the book deals with process manipulation. Chapter 9 provides basic technologies to transform one process into another. Typical techniques are induction, the recursive specification principle, and the expansion theorem.

Chapter 10 describes how to transform processes to the so-called linear form, which will play an important role in all subsequent manipulations. Moreover, recursive specifications and different methods of reasoning about them are presented in this chapter.

Chapter 11 deals with confluence, which is a typical behavioral pattern that originates from the parallel composition of two processes. If a process is found to be confluent, we can reduce it using so-called τ-priority. By giving priority to certain τ-actions, the state space can be reduced considerably.

In chapter 12, the cones and foci technique is explained, which allows for a proof that a specification and an implementation of some system are equivalent. In chapter 13, the verification techniques are used to validate some complex distributed algorithms. In chapter 14, parameterized Boolean equations are used to verify modal formulas on processes in the linear form.

In chapter 15, the formal semantics of mCRL2 and the related formalisms are described. In essence, this provides a mapping between syntactically or algebraically described processes on the one hand and a transition system on the other hand. Using this mapping, it is possible to establish the relationship between the process equivalences given in chapter 2 and the axioms in the subsequent chapters.

In appendix B, the equations characterizing data types are given. In appendix C, the notation used in the book is related to the notation used in the tools. Appendix D provides an overview of the syntaxes of all different formalisms. Appendix E summarizes all process-algebraic axioms. Appendix F contains answers to the exercises.

1.4 Audience and suggested method of reading

The authors have used this book for several years to teach graduate courses on formal specification and verification. It is suitable for graduate (or upper level undergraduate) students of computer science and related fields (e.g., embedded systems and software engineering) with some background in logic and the theory of formal languages and automata.

For a short course (of 7 to 10 lectures) chapters 2 to 6 can be used to treat the theory of parallel processes together with a small project on specification and verification of a small system controller or a protocol (examples of such systems and protocols can be found in chapters 7, although students can deal with more complex systems). For larger modules, chapters 8 to 12 and chapter 14 can also be included. Chapter 13 gives examples of verifications of more complex protocols, while chapter 15 provides formal background material, such as type-checking rules and the semantics of various formalisms.

More advanced material and more difficult exercises in each chapter are designated by a black star (★) and can be skipped for shorter and/or undergraduate courses.

2

Actions, Behavior, Equivalence, and Abstraction

In this chapter the basic notions of (inter)action and behavior are explained in terms of transition systems. It is discussed when different transition systems can behave the same and it is indicated how complex behavior can be abstracted by hiding actions.

2.1 Actions

Interaction is everywhere. Computer systems, humans, machines, animals, plants, molecules, planets, and stars are all interacting with their environment. The classical view is that such interactions are continuous, such as gravity pulling stellar objects toward each other. There is a long mathematical tradition in researching such continuous communication.

But many systems communicate by having infrequent, short interactions. We use the term discrete interactions to contrast such communications with the classical continuous interaction. Human communication is a typical example. People meet, shake hands, exchange messages and proceed to communicate with others. The communication in and especially among computers has the same pattern. The whole nature of computers seems to be to receive, process, and send messages. And as many of the systems that we make these days contain computers inside, they can be viewed as discretely interacting systems.

The complexity of message exchanges among computerized systems is steadily increasing and has reached a level where it is very hard to understand. This complexity needs to be tamed by making models and having the mathematical means to understand these models. The first purpose of this book is to provide the modeling means and mathematical analysis techniques to understand interacting systems. The second derived purpose is to provide the means to design these systems such that we know for sure that they work in the way we want.

Basic actions, also called interactions, represent the elementary communications and are the main ingredients of such models. We denote them abstractly by letters a,

b, c, or more descriptively by names such as $read$, $deliver$, and $timeout$. They are generally referred to as *actions* and they represent some observable atomic event. For instance, action *deliver* can represent the event of a letter being dropped in a mailbox. Action *read* can consist of reading a message on a computer screen.

Actions can be parameterized with data; an action a taking data parameter d is denoted by $a(d)$; examples of such actions are $read(1)$, $write(true, 2)$ and $draw(1.5, 2.5, sqrt(2))$, where $sqrt(2)$ is a data expression denoting the square root of 2. This feature is essential in modeling reactive systems that communicate data and make decisions based on the values of communicated data.

The fact that an action is atomic means that actions do not have distinct start and end moments, and hence, they cannot overlap each other. For every pair of actions a and b, the one happens before the other, or vice versa. Only in rare cases can a and b happen exactly at the same moment. We write this as $a|b$ and call this a *multi-action*. It is possible to indicate that an action can take place at a specific time. For example, $a\text{‘}3$ denotes that action a must take place at time 3. For the moment, multi-actions and time are ignored. We come back to these topics in chapters 4 and 8, respectively.

We use an alarm clock as our running example throughout this chapter. Our simple alarm clock has three basic actions, namely, *set*, *reset* and *alarm*. Also, we specify a variant of alarm clock in which the number of alarms can be given to the clock; in this variant we use actions of the form $set(n)$, where n is a natural number denoting the number of times the alarm should go off.

Exercise 2.1.1. What are the actions of a CD player? What are the actions of a text editor? And what of a data-transfer channel?

2.2 Labeled transition systems

The order in which actions can take place is called behavior. Behavior is generally depicted as a labeled transition system that consists of a set of states and a set of transitions labeled with actions that connect the states. Labeled transition systems have an initial state that is depicted by a small incoming arrow. They may have terminating states, generally indicated with a tick (✓). In figure 2.1, the behaviors of two simple processes are depicted. Both can perform the actions a, b, c, and d. At the end, the lower one can terminate, whereas the upper one can no longer do anything; it is said to be in a *deadlock*, that is, in a reachable state that does not terminate and has no outgoing transitions.

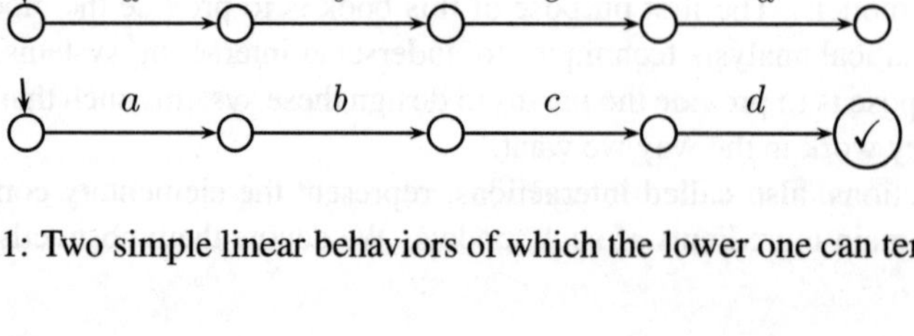

Figure 2.1: Two simple linear behaviors of which the lower one can terminate

Such simple diagrams are already useful to illustrate different behaviors. In figure 2.2, the behaviors of two alarm clocks are drawn. The behavior at the left allows for repeated alarms, whereas the behavior at the right only signals the alarm once. Note also that the behavior at the left only allows a strict alternation between the set and the $reset$ actions, whereas this is not the case in the right diagram, as for instance the trace $set\ alarm\ set$ is possible.

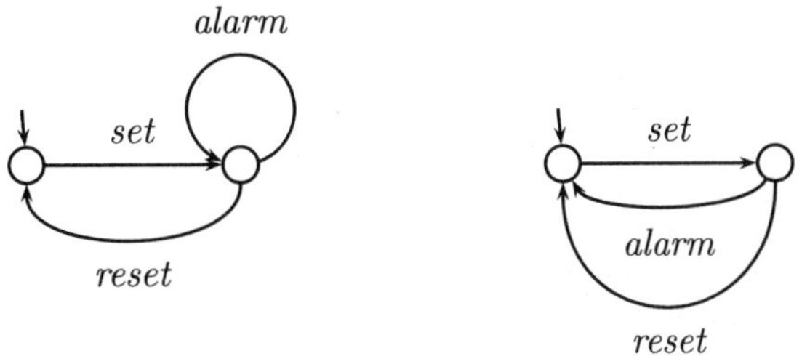

Figure 2.2: Two possible behaviors of an alarm clock

Our model of the alarm clock can be extended with a feature for specifying the number of alarms to go off. This is achieved by parameterizing the action set, with a natural number as depicted in figure 2.3. In this diagram, we assume that the pattern of behavior is repeated and hence, we have an infinite labeled transition system.

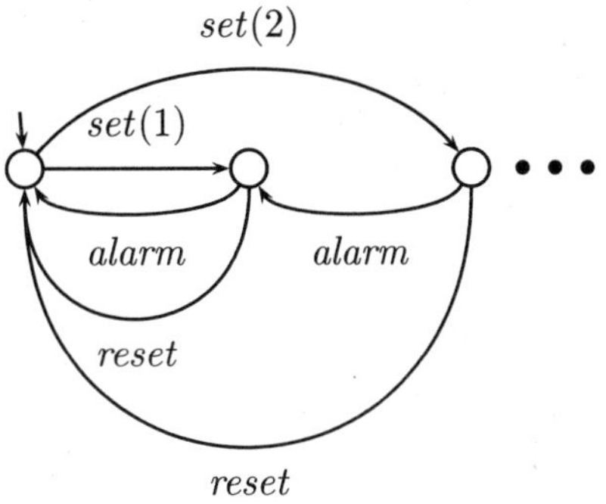

Figure 2.3: An alarm clock with a multiple alarm feature

A state can have more than one outgoing transition with the same label to different states. The state is then called *nondeterministic*. A deterministic transition system contains no reachable nondeterministic states. Nondeterminism is a very strong modeling aid. It allows for modeling behaviors of which the details are not completely known, or are too complex to be modeled fully. The first use of nondeterminism is called underspecification. The second use is called abstraction, allowing for simple models of complex phenomena.

In figure 2.4, sounding the alarm is modeled using nondeterminism. If an alarm sounds, it is not possible to know whether it is the final one, or whether there are more to follow. This can be intentionally underspecified, allowing an implementer to build an alarm clock that can sound the alarm a fixed (yet arbitrary) number of times. But

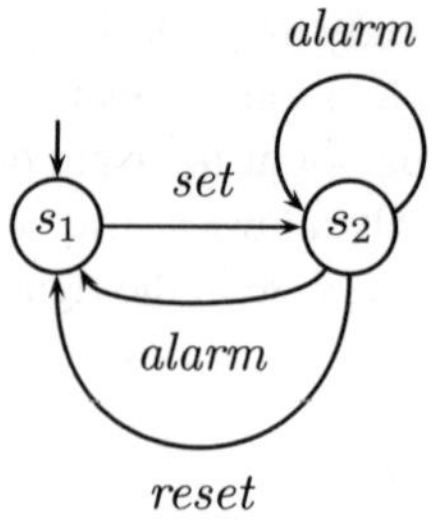

Figure 2.4: Nondeterministic behavior of an alarm clock

figure 2.4 can also represent that the alarm sounds exactly 714 times before stopping. When the fact that the alarm sounds exactly 714 times does not outweigh the increased complexity of the model, this abstract nondeterministic transition system is a good model.

Robin Milner[1] was one of the early defenders of the use of nondeterminism [133, 135]. He called it the weather condition. The weather determines the temperature. The temperature influences the speed of processors and clocks in a computer. This may mean that a timeout may come just too late, or just too early for some behavior to happen. It generally is not effective to include a weather model to predict which behavior will happen. It is much more convenient to describe behavior in a nondeterministic way.

The formal definition of a labeled transition system is the following.

Definition 2.2.1 (Labeled transition system). A *labeled transition system* (LTS) is a five tuple $A = (S, Act, \longrightarrow, s, T)$ where

- S is a set of *states*.
- Act is a set of actions, possibly multi-actions.
- $\longrightarrow \subseteq S \times Act \times S$ is a *transition relation*.
- $s \in S$ is the *initial state*.
- $T \subseteq S$ is the set of *terminating states*.

It is common to write $t \xrightarrow{a} t'$ for $(t, a, t') \in \longrightarrow$.

Often, when not relevant or clear from the context, the set T of terminating states and/or the initial state are omitted from the definition of an *LTS*.

Exercise 2.2.2. Make the following extensions to the alarm clock.

1. Draw the behavior of an alarm clock where it is always possible to do a *set* or a *reset* action.

[1] Robin Milner (1934–2010) was the developer of the theorem prover LCF and the programming language ML. He is also the founding father of process calculi. In 1991 he received the Turing Award.

2. Draw the behavior of an alarm clock with unreliable buttons. When pressing the *set* button, the alarm clock can be set, but this does not need to be the case. Similarly for the *reset* button. Pressing it can reset the alarm clock, but the clock can also stay in a state where an alarm is still possible.

3. Draw the behavior of an alarm clock where the alarm sounds at most three times when no other action interferes.

Exercise 2.2.3. Describe the transition system in figure 2.4 in the form of a labeled transition system conforming to definition 2.2.1.

2.3 Equivalence of behaviors

When do two systems have the same behavior? Or stated differently, when are two labeled transition systems behaviorally equivalent? The initial answer to this question is simple. Whenever the difference in behavior cannot be observed, we say that the behavior is the same. The obvious next question is how behavior is observed. The answer to this latter question is that there are many ways to observe behavior and consequently many different behavioral equivalences exist. We present only the most important ones here.

2.3.1 Trace equivalence

One of the coarsest (most unifying) notions of behavioral equivalence is *trace equivalence*. The essential idea is that two transition systems are equivalent if the same sequences of actions can be performed from their respective initial states. This corresponds to observing that actions can happen without interacting with them. It is not even possible to tell whether a system is deadlocked or whether more actions will come.

Traces are sequences of actions, typically denoted as $a_1 a_2 a_3 \ldots a_n$. We typically use letters σ and ρ to represent traces. The termination symbol $\checkmark$ can also be part of a trace (usually appearing at its end). The symbol ϵ represents the empty trace.

Definition 2.3.1 (Trace equivalence). Let $A = (S, Act, \longrightarrow, s, T)$ be a labeled transition system. The set of *traces* (*runs*, *sequences*) $\mathit{Traces}(t)$ for a state $t \in S$ is the minimal set satisfying:

1. $\epsilon \in \mathit{Traces}(t)$, that is, the empty trace is a member of $\mathit{Traces}(t)$,

2. $\checkmark \in \mathit{Traces}(t)$ iff $t \in T$, and

3. if there is a state $t' \in S$ such that $t \xrightarrow{a} t'$ and $\sigma \in \mathit{Traces}(t')$ then $a\sigma \in \mathit{Traces}(t)$.

The set of traces of the labeled transition system is $\mathit{Traces}(s_0)$. Two states $t, u \in S$ are *trace equivalent* if and only if (iff) $\mathit{Traces}(t) = \mathit{Traces}(u)$. Two transition systems are *trace equivalent* iff their initial states are trace equivalent.

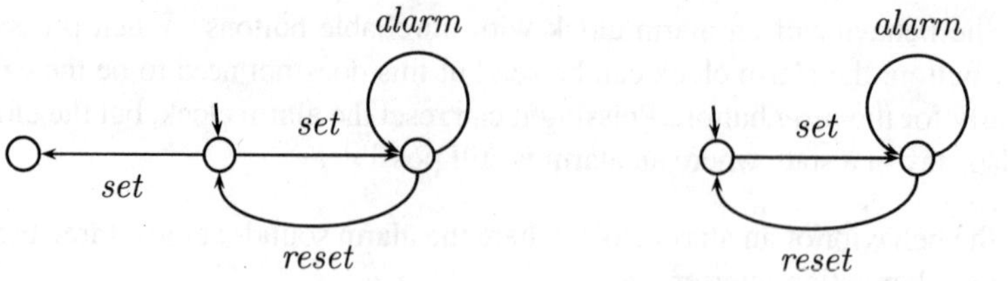

Figure 2.5: Two trace-equivalent alarm clocks

The sets of traces of the two transition systems in figure 2.1 are respectively $\{\epsilon, a, ab, abc, abcd\}$ and $\{\epsilon, a, ab, abc, abcd, abcd\checkmark\}$. The two transition systems are not trace equivalent.

Consider the labeled transition systems for the two alarm clocks depicted in figure 2.5. These two systems are trace equivalent: the set of traces for both labeled transition systems is: $\{set,\ set\ alarm^\star,\ (set\ alarm^\star\ reset)^\star\}$, where * is the so-called Kleene star and denotes zero-time or more times repetition (zero-time repetition results in the empty trace).

The alarm clock at the left-hand side has a nondeterministic choice between the two transitions labeled with *set*: if it moves with the *set* transition to the left, it deadlocks. At the right, there is no deadlock after the *set* action. As one can generally observe a deadlock, the observational behavior of the two transition systems is different. This is the reason why trace equivalence is not used very often and finer notions of equivalence are used that take deadlocks into account.

However, there are cases where trace equivalence is useful, especially when studying properties that only regard the traces of processes. A property can for instance be that before every *reset* a *set* action must be done. This property is preserved by trace equivalence. In order to determine this for the transition system at the left in figure 2.5, it is perfectly valid to first transform it into the transition system on the right of this figure, and then determine the property for this last transition system.

Exercise 2.3.2. Determine which of the following labeled transition systems are trace equivalent.

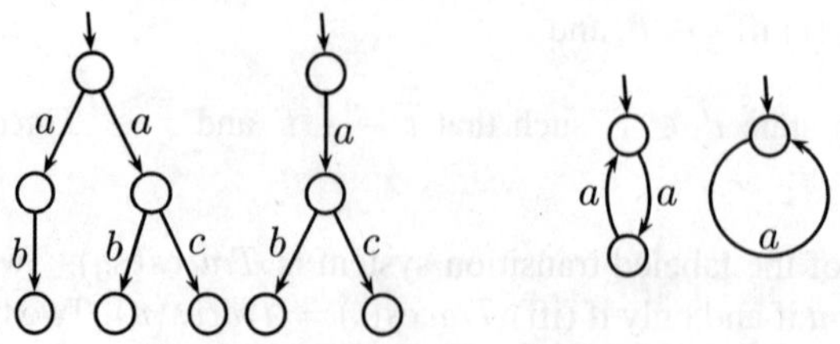

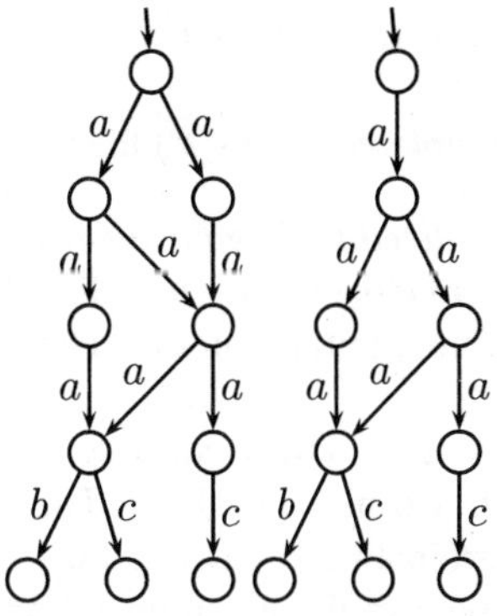

2.3.2 ★Language and completed trace equivalence

In language theory, labeled transition systems are commonly used to help in parsing languages. Generally, the word automaton is used for labeled transition systems in that context. Process theory, as described here, and language theory have a lot in common. For instance, grammars to describe languages are essentially the same as process expressions, described in the chapter 4.

There is, however, one difference. In the process world, there are many different behavioral equivalences, whereas in the language world, *language equivalence* is essentially the only one. Every trace that ends in a successful state is a sentence. Such a sentence is said to be accepted by the language. Two processes are language equivalent if their sets of sentences are the same. This can be stated more formally, as in definition 2.3.3.

Definition 2.3.3 (Language equivalence). Let $A = (S, Act, \longrightarrow, s, T)$ be a labeled transition system. We define the language $Lang(t)$ of a state $t \in S$ as the minimal set satisfying:

- $\epsilon \in Lang(t)$ if $t \in T$, and
- if $t \overset{a}{\longrightarrow} t'$ and $\sigma \in Lang(t')$ then $a\sigma \in Lang(t)$.

Two states $t, u \in S$ are *language equivalent* iff $Lang(t) = Lang(u)$. Two labeled transition systems are *language equivalent* iff their initial states are language equivalent.

The language of the first automaton in figure 2.1 is the empty set. That of the second transition system is $\{abcd\}$.

The closest pendant in the process world is *completed trace equivalence*. A completed trace is a sequence of actions that ends in a deadlocked or a terminating state (and the difference between these states can be observed).

Definition 2.3.4 (Completed trace equivalence). Let $A = (S, Act, \longrightarrow, s, T)$ be a labeled transition system. We define the completed traces $CompletedTraces(t)$ of a state $t \in S$ as the minimal set satisfying:

- $\epsilon \in CompletedTraces(t)$ if $t \notin T$ and there are no $t' \in S$ and $a \in Act$ such that $t \overset{a}{\longrightarrow} t'$,

- $\checkmark \in \mathit{CompletedTraces}(t)$ if $t \in T$, and
- if $t \xrightarrow{a} t'$ and $\sigma \in \mathit{CompletedTraces}(t')$ then $a\sigma \in \mathit{CompletedTraces}(t)$.

Two states $t, u \in S$ are *completed trace equivalent* iff $\mathit{Traces}(t) = \mathit{Traces}(u)$ and $\mathit{CompletedTraces}(t) = \mathit{CompletedTraces}(u)$. Two labeled transition systems are *complete trace equivalent* iff their initial states are completed trace equivalent.

Note that our notion of completed trace equivalence has as an additional constraint that the set of traces should also be equivalent. This is essential for distinguishing systems with infinite, nonterminating behavior. Take, for example, an a-loop and a b-loop. The observable behavior of these two transition systems is very different, but their sets of completed traces are both empty. By including the sets of traces in the definition of completed trace equivalence, they are distinguished again.

Consider the labeled transition systems depicted in figure 2.6. They are trace equivalent. They are also completed trace equivalent since their completed trace sets are both empty. However, when it would be possible to block the $reset$ action, they are no longer completed trace equivalent. Blocking the $reset$ transition boils down to removing $reset$ transitions. Then the transition system at the left has set as a completed trace, which the transition system at the right does not have. Completed trace equivalence is not compositional, i.e., it can be jeopardized when equivalent systems are placed in a context that can influence their behavior. Compositionality, also called congruence, is a much desired property and is the cornerstone of the algebraic approach to system description (see chapter 4). Fortunately, we have good alternatives for language and completed trace equivalence that are compositional, which will be introduced in the next sections.

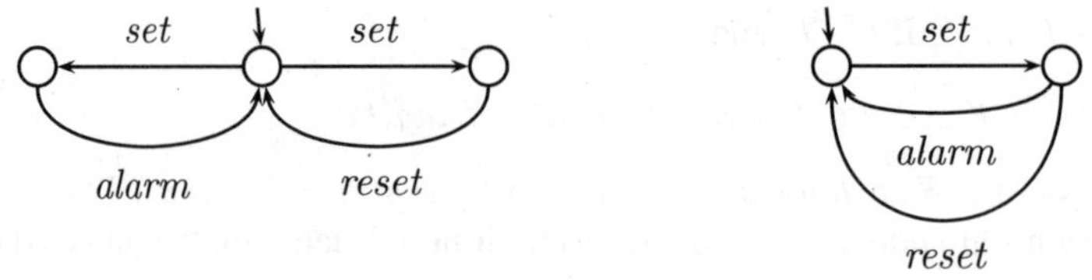

Figure 2.6: Two completed trace equivalent alarm clocks

2.3.3 ★Failures equivalence

The equivalence that is closest to completed trace equivalence and that is a congruence when blocking of actions allowed, is *failures equivalence*. The typical property of failure equivalence is that it relates as many behaviors as possible, while preserving traces and deadlocks, even if the behaviors are placed in an environment constructed of common process operators (see chapters 4 and 5).

The definition of failures equivalence has two steps. First a refusal set of a state t is defined to contain those actions that cannot be performed in t. Then a failure pair is defined to be a trace ending in some refusal set.

Definition 2.3.5 (Failures equivalence). Let $A = (S, Act, \longrightarrow, s, T)$ be a labeled transition system. A set $F \subseteq Act \cup \{\checkmark\}$ is called a *refusal set* of a state $t \in S$,

- If for all actions $a \in F$ there is no $t' \in S$ such that $t \xrightarrow{a} t'$, and
- If $\checkmark \in F$, then $t \notin T$, i.e., t cannot terminate.

The *set of failure pairs*, $FailurePairs(t)$, of a state $t \in S$ is inductively defined as follows

- $(\epsilon, F) \in FailurePairs(t)$ if F is a refusal set of t.
- $(\checkmark, F) \in FailurePairs(t)$ iff $t \in T$ and F is a refusal set of t, and
- If $t \xrightarrow{a} t'$ and $(\sigma, F) \in FailurePairs(t')$ then $(a\sigma, F) \in FailurePairs(t)$.

Two states $t, u \in S$ are *failures equivalent* iff $FailurePairs(t) = FailurePairs(u)$. Two transition systems are *failures equivalent* iff their initial states are failures equivalent.

The labeled transition systems depicted in figure 2.7 are failures equivalent. Initial states of both labeled transition systems refuse the set $\{alarm, reset\}$; hence $(\epsilon, \{alarm, reset\})$ is a failure pair for both initial states. The lower state in the figure at the right has, for instance, failure pairs $(set, \{set\})$ and $(set, \emptyset)$. But these are also failure pairs of the left and right states of both figures. These transitions systems show that behavior demonstrating a lack of choice at the left is equal to behavior at the right with the possibility to choose between a $reset$, or an $alarm$ action. We say that failures equivalence does not preserve the branching structure of behavior.

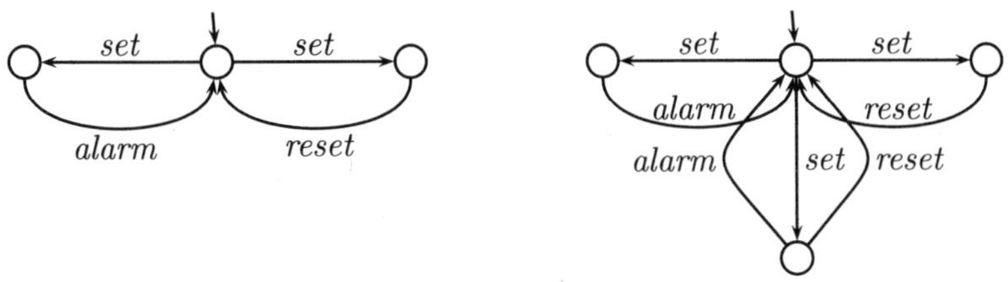

Figure 2.7: Two failure-equivalent alarm clocks

Exercise 2.3.6. State whether the following pairs of transition systems are language and/or failures equivalent.

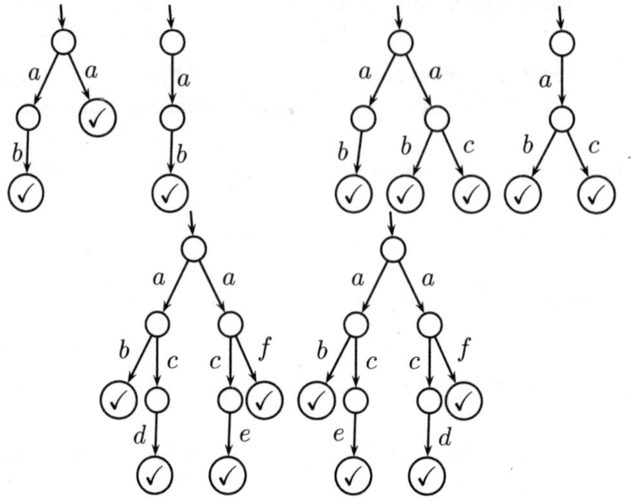

2.3.4 Strong bisimulation equivalence

Bisimulation equivalence, also referred to as strong bisimulation equivalence, or strong bisimilarity, is the most important process equivalence although its definition is far more complex than trace equivalence.

One reason for its importance is that if two processes are bisimulation equivalent, they cannot be distinguished by any realistic form of behavioral observation. This includes, for instance, observations where performed actions can be undone, where copies of the system under observation are made that are tested separately, where it can be observed that actions are not possible, and where it can be observed that arbitrarily long sequences of actions are possible in a certain state. Hence, if two processes are bisimilar, they can certainly be considered indistinguishable under observation.

Another reason is that the algorithms for checking bisimulation equivalence are efficient, contrary to the algorithms for checking any equivalence based on a form of traces, which are generally PSPACE-complete or worse.

The idea behind bisimulation is that two states are related if the actions that can be done in one state, can be done in the other, as well. We say that the second state simulates the first. Moreover, if one action is simulated by another, the resulting states must be related also.

Definition 2.3.7 (Bisimulation). Let $A=(S, Act, \longrightarrow, s, T)$ be a labeled transition system. A binary relation $R \subseteq S \times S$ is called a *strong bisimulation relation* iff for all $s, t \in S$ such that sRt holds, it also holds for all actions $a \in Act$ that:

1. if $s \xrightarrow{a} s'$, then there is a $t' \in S$ such that $t \xrightarrow{a} t'$ with $s'Rt'$,

2. if $t \xrightarrow{a} t'$, then there is a $s' \in S$ such that $s \xrightarrow{a} s'$ with $s'Rt'$, and

3. $s \in T$ if and only if $t \in T$.

Two states s and t are *strongly bisimilar*, denoted by $s \leftrightarrow t$, iff there is a strong bisimulation relation R such that sRt. Two labeled transition systems are *strongly bisimilar* iff their initial states are bisimilar.

Often the adjective *strong* is dropped, speaking about bisimulation rather than strong bisimulation. However, we will see several other variants of bisimulation and in those cases the use of "strong" helps us stress the difference.

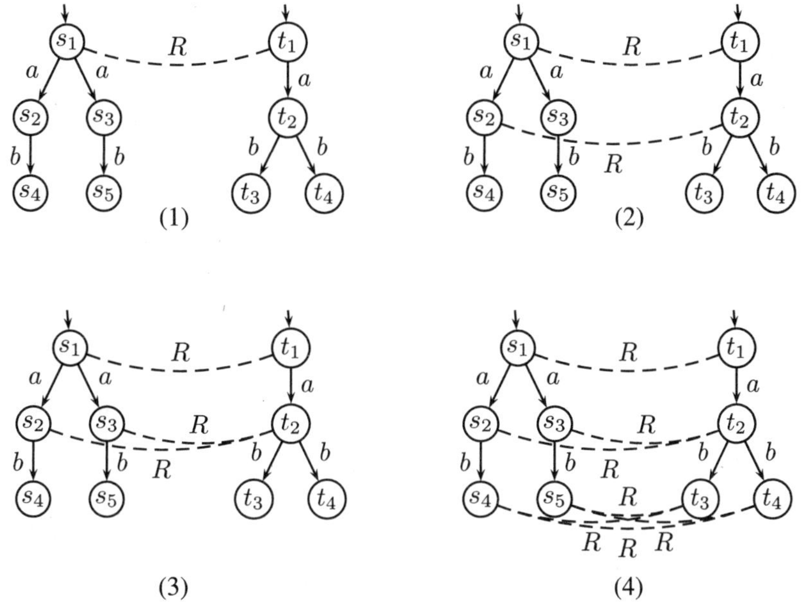

Figure 2.8: Showing two LTSs bisimilar

There are several techniques to show that two labeled transition systems are bisimilar. Computer algorithms generally use partition refinement for the relation coarsest partitioning problem [113, 149]. For small transition systems, a more straightforward technique is generally adequate. Consider the transition systems in figure 2.8. In order to show that the initial states s_1 and t_1 are bisimilar, a bisimulation relation R must be constructed to relate these two states. We assume that this can be done. Hence, we draw an arc between s_1 and t_1 and label it with R. If R is a bisimulation, then every transition from s_1 must be mimicked by a similarly labeled transition from t_1. More concretely, the a-transition from s_1 to s_2 can only be mimicked by an a-transition from t_1 to t_2. Therefore, s_2 and t_2 must be related, too. We also draw an arc to indicate this (see the second picture in figure 2.8). Now we can proceed by showing that the transition from s_1 to s_3 must also be mimicked by the a-transition from t_1 to t_2. Hence, s_3 is related to t_2 (see the third picture). As a rule of thumb, it generally pays off to first choose a transition from the side with more choices in order to force the other side to perform a certain transition. Otherwise, there might be a choice, and several possibilities need to be considered. For example, the a-transition t_1 to t_2 can be simulated by either the transition from s_1 to s_2, or the one from s_1 to s_3.

The relation R needs to be extended to all reachable nodes. Therefore, we consider the relation between s_2 and t_2. We continue the process sketched before, but now let the transitions from the right transition system be simulated by the left one, because the states s_2 and s_3 are deterministic. The relation R is extended as indicated in the fourth picture of figure 2.8. It needs to be checked that all related states satisfy all the requirements in definition 2.3.7. As this is the case, R is a bisimulation relation, the initial states are bisimilar and therefore the systems are bisimilar.

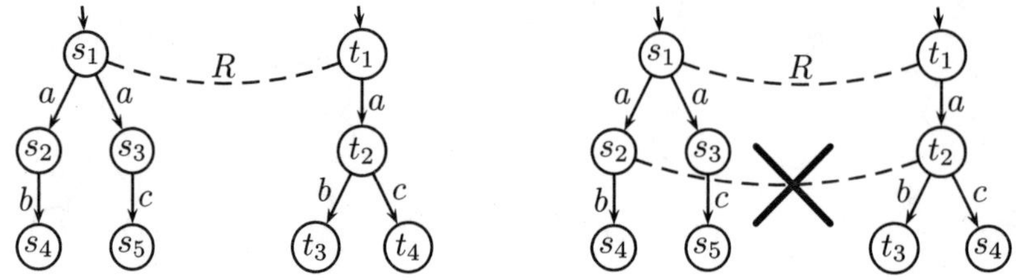

Figure 2.9: Two nonbisimilar labeled transition systems

Now consider the transition systems in figure 2.9. There are three actions a, b, and c. These two transition systems are not bisimilar.

Before showing this formally, we first give an intuitive argument why these two processes are different. Let actions a, b, and c stand for pressing one of three buttons. If a transition is possible, the corresponding button can be pressed. If a transition is not possible, the button is blocked.

Now suppose a customer ordered the transition system at the right (with initial state t_1) and a malicious supplier delivered a box with the behavior of the transition system at the left. If the customer cannot experience the difference, the supplier did an adequate job. However, the customer can first press an a button such that the box ends up being in state s_3. Now the customer, thinking that she is in state t_2, expects that both b and c can be pressed. She, however, finds out that b is blocked, from which she can conclude that she has been deceived and has an argument to sue the supplier.

Now note that in both behaviors in figure 2.9, the same sequence of actions can be performed, namely $a\,b$ and $a\,c$; in other words, they are (completed) trace equivalent. Yet, the behavior of both systems can be experienced to be different!

If one tries to show both transition systems bisimilar using the method outlined above, then in the same way as before, state s_2 must be related to state t_2. However, a c transition is possible from state t_2 that cannot be mimicked by state s_2, which has no outgoing c transition. Hence, s_2 cannot be related to t_2, and consequently, s_1 cannot be bisimilar to t_1.

A pleasant property of bisimulation is that for any labeled transition system, there is a unique minimal transition system (up to graph isomorphism) which is bisimilar to it.

Exercise 2.3.8. State for each pair of transition systems from exercise 2.3.2 whether they are bisimilar.

Exercise 2.3.9. Show that the following transition systems are not bisimilar, where the transition system to the left consists of sequences of a-transitions with length n for each $n \in \mathbb{N}$. The transition system to the right is the same except that it can additionally do an infinite sequence of a-transitions.

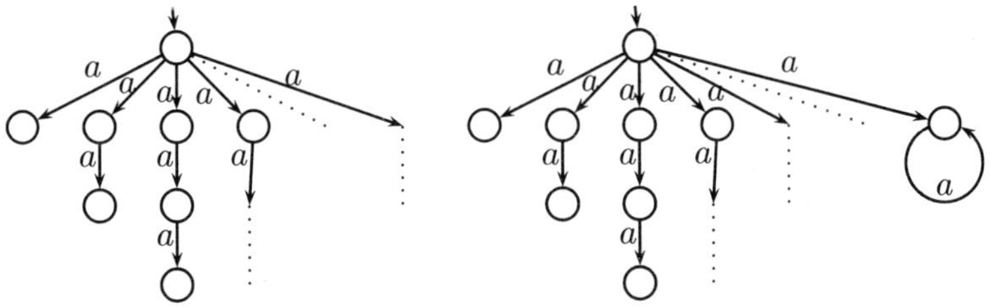

Exercise 2.3.10. Give the unique minimal labeled transition system that is bisimilar to the following one:

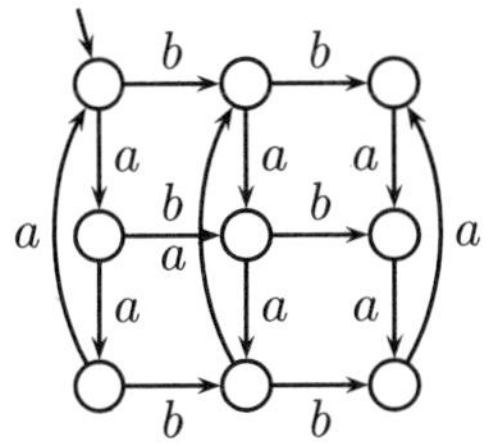

2.3.5 The Van Glabbeek linear time–branching time spectrum

As stated before, there are a myriad of process equivalences. A nice classification of some of these has been given by Van Glabbeek[72].[2] He produced the so-called linear time-branching time spectrum of which a part is depicted in figure 2.10. At the top, the finest equivalence, relating the fewest states, is depicted and at the bottom, the coarsest equivalence, relating the most states, is found. The arrows indicate that an equivalence is strictly coarser. For example, if processes are bisimulation equivalent, then they are also two-nested simulation equivalent. Bisimulation equivalence is the finest equivalence and trace equivalence the coarsest. If two processes are bisimilar then they are equivalent with respect to all equivalences depicted in the spectrum. If processes are not bisimilar, then it makes sense to investigate whether they are equal with respect to another equivalence.

Each equivalence has its own properties, and it goes too far to treat them all. As an illustration we relate a few types of observations to some equivalences. Suppose that we can interact with a machine that is equipped with an undo button. After doing some actions, we can go back to where we came from. Using this metaphor, we can devise tests that precisely distinguish between processes that are not ready simulation equivalent. This tells us that ready simulation is tightly connected to the capability of

[2]Rob van Glabbeek (1960–) classified thousands of process equivalences. He contributed to various areas in mathematics and theoretical computer science, including concurrency theory, linear logic, and protocols for wireless networks. He ran for the Dutch parliament in 2012 for the Libertarian Party.

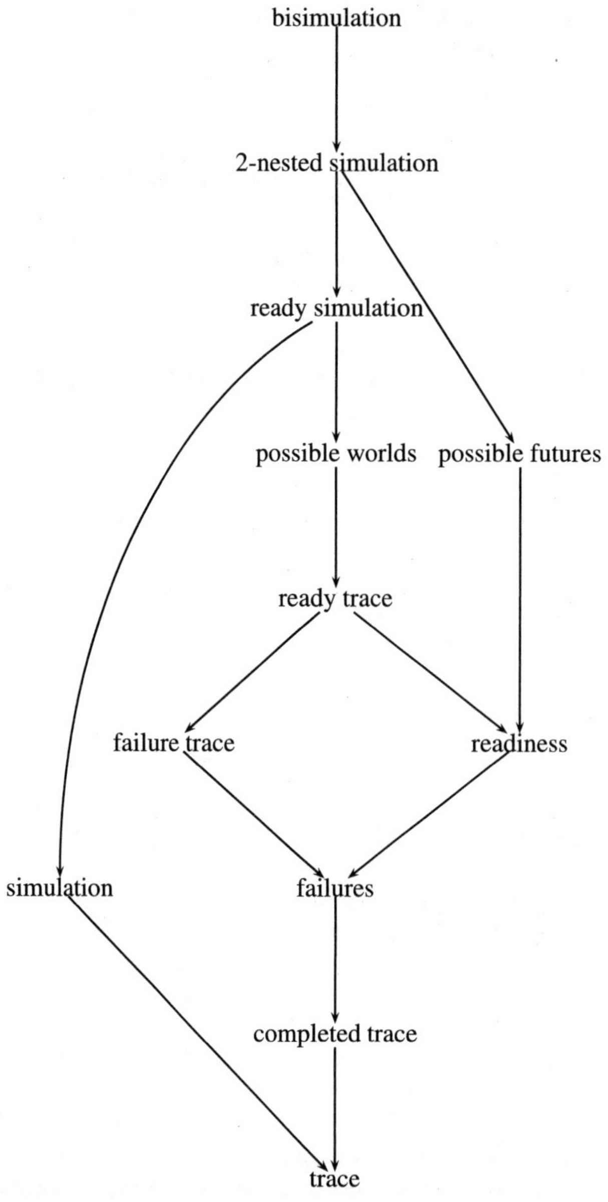

Figure 2.10: The Van Glabbeek linear time–branching time spectrum

undoing actions. In a similar way, possible futures equivalence is strongly connected to the capability of predicting which actions are possible in the future; two-nested simulation equivalence combines them both.

The Van Glabbeek spectrum owes its existence to nondeterminism. If transition systems are deterministic, then the whole spectrum collapses. In that case, two states are bisimulation equivalent if and only if they are trace equivalent. We state this theorem precisely here and provide the proof as an example of how properties of bisimulation are proven.

Definition 2.3.11. We call a labeled transition system $A = (S, Act, \longrightarrow, s, T)$ *deterministic* iff for all reachable states $t, t', t'' \in S$ and action $a \in Act$ it holds that if $t \xrightarrow{a} t'$ and $t \xrightarrow{a} t''$ then $t' = t''$.

Theorem 2.3.12. Let $A = (S, Act, \longrightarrow, s, T)$ be a deterministic transition system. For all states $t, t' \in S$ it holds that

$$Traces(t) = Traces(t') \text{ iff } t \leftrightarrow t'.$$

Proof. We only prove the case from left to right. The proof from right to left is much easier.

In order to show that $t \leftrightarrow t'$, we need to show the existence of a bisimulation relation R such that tRt'. We coin the following relation for all states $u, u' \in S$:

$$u\,R\,u' \text{ iff } Traces(u) = Traces(u').$$

Finding the right relation R is generally the crux in such proofs. Note that R is indeed suitable, as R relates t and t'.

At this point, we are only left with showing that R is indeed a bisimulation relation. This boils down to checking the properties in definition 2.3.7 (strong bisimulation). Assume that for states u and v we have uRv. Then

1. Suppose $u \xrightarrow{a} u'$. According to definition 2.3.1 (trace equivalence) $a\sigma \in Traces(u)$ for all traces $\sigma \in Traces(u')$. Furthermore, as $Traces(u) = Traces(v)$, it holds that $a\sigma \in Traces(v)$ or in other words, $v \xrightarrow{a} v'$ for some state $v' \in S$. We are left to show that $u'Rv'$, or in other words:

   $$Traces(u') = Traces(v').$$

   We prove this by mutual set inclusion, restricting ourselves to only one case, as both are almost identical. Thus, we prove $Traces(u') \subseteq Traces(v')$. Consider a trace $\sigma \in Traces(u')$. It holds that $a\sigma \in Traces(u)$, and consequently $a\sigma \in Traces(v)$. Hence, there is a v'' such that $v \xrightarrow{a} v''$ and $\sigma \in Traces(v'')$. As the transition system A is deterministic, $v \xrightarrow{a} v'$ and $v \xrightarrow{a} v''$, we can conclude $v' = v''$. Ergo, $\sigma \in Traces(v')$.

2. This case is symmetric to the first case and is therefore omitted.

3. If $u \in T$, then $\checkmark \in Traces(u)$. As u and v are related, it follows by definition of R that $\checkmark \in Traces(v)$. Therefore, $v \in T$. Similarly, it can be shown that if $v \in T$ then $u \in T$ must hold.

Figure 2.11: The internal action τ is not visible

□

Exercise 2.3.13. Prove that bisimilarity on a given labeled transition system is an equivalence relation, i.e., it is reflexive ($s \leftrightarrow s$ for any $s \in S$), symmetric (if $s \leftrightarrow t$ then $t \leftrightarrow s$ for all states s and t) and transitive (if $s \leftrightarrow t$ and $t \leftrightarrow u$, then $s \leftrightarrow u$ for all states s, t, u).

2.4 Behavioral abstraction

Although the examples given hitherto may give a different impression, the behavior of systems can be utterly complex. The only way to obtain insight in such behavior is to use abstraction. The most common abstraction mechanism is to declare an action as internal and hence, unobservable and adapt the notions of equivalence such that the unobservable nature of such internal actions is taken into account.

2.4.1 The internal action τ

We say that an action is internal if we have no way of observing it directly. We use the special symbol τ to denote internal actions collectively. We generally assume that internal action is available in every labeled transition system, i.e., $\tau \in Act$. Typical for an internal action is that if it follows another action, it is impossible to say whether it is there. For example, the transition systems in figure 2.11 cannot be distinguished, because the τ after the a cannot be observed. Such internal actions are called *inert*.

However, in certain cases the presence of an internal action can be indirectly observed, although the action by itself cannot be seen. Suppose one expects the behavior of the transition system at the right of figure 2.12. It is always possible to do an a-action, as long as neither an a nor a b have been done. Now suppose the actual behavior is that of the transition system at the left of figure 2.12 and one insists on doing an action a. If the internal action silently happens, a deadlock is observed, because it is impossible to do action a anymore. Hence, when actions can be chosen and deadlocks observed, it can be determined by observations alone that the behavior at the left is not the same as that of the transition system at the right.

With the internal action present, equivalences for processes must take into account that we cannot observe the internal action directly. Next, the most important ones among such equivalences are given.

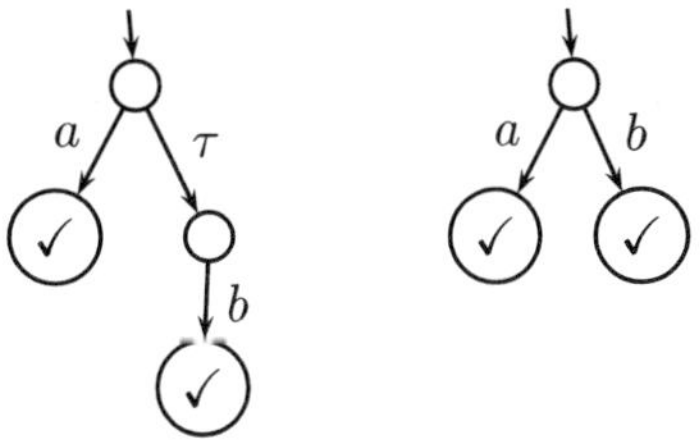

Figure 2.12: The internal action τ is indirectly visible

2.4.2 Weak trace equivalence

Weak traces are obtained by absorbing the internal action in a trace. This is the natural notion if we can observe all but the internal action, and we cannot interact with the system or observe that it is in a deadlock. Formally, two processes are weak trace equivalent if their sets of weak traces (i.e., traces in which τ-transitions are ignored) are the same.

Definition 2.4.1 (Weak trace equivalence). Let $A = (S, Act, \longrightarrow, s, T)$ be a labeled transition system. The set of *weak traces* $WTraces(t)$ for a state $t \in S$ is the minimal set satisfying:

1. $\epsilon \in WTraces(t)$,
2. $\checkmark \in WTraces(t)$ iff $t \in T$,
3. If there is a state $t' \in S$ such that $t \xrightarrow{a} t'$ $(a \neq \tau)$ and $\sigma \in WTraces(t')$ then $a\sigma \in WTraces(t)$, and
4. If there is a state $t' \in S$ such that $t \xrightarrow{\tau} t'$ and $\sigma \in WTraces(t')$ then $\sigma \in WTraces(t)$.

Two states $t, u \in S$ are called *weak trace equivalent* iff $WTraces(t) = WTraces(u)$. Two transition systems are *weak trace equivalent* iff their initial states are weak trace equivalent.

Weak trace equivalence is the weakest of all behavioral equivalences. It does not preserve deadlocks, nor any other branching behavior. Weak trace equivalence is hard to calculate for a given transition system, and it is much harder to obtain a smallest transition system preserving weak trace equivalence. There is in general no unique smallest transition system modulo weak trace equivalence.

However, in practice, transition systems modulo weak trace equivalence can be much smaller than those obtained with any other equivalence. Although one should always be aware of the properties not preserved by weak trace equivalence, those small transition systems expose behavior more clearly, which is of great value for our understanding.

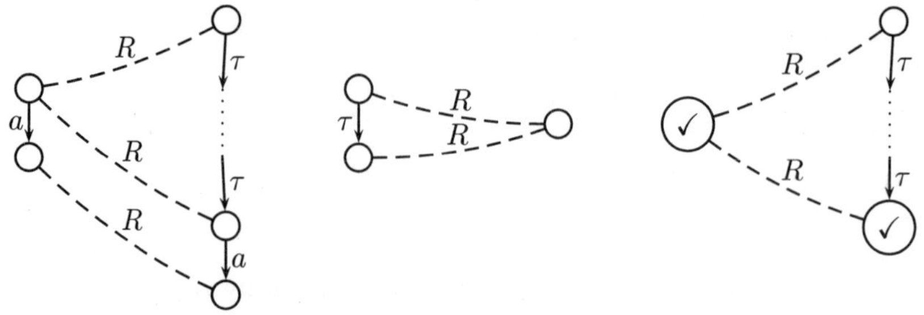

Figure 2.13: Branching bisimulation

2.4.3 (Rooted) branching bisimulation

The definition of branching bisimulation is very similar to that of strong bisimulation. But now, instead of letting a single action be simulated by a single action, an action can be simulated by a sequence of internal transitions, followed by that single action. See the diagram at the left of figure 2.13. It can be shown that all states that are visited via the τ-actions in this diagram are branching bisimilar.

If the action to be simulated is a τ, then it can be simulated by any number of internal transitions, or even by no transition at all, as the diagram in the middle of figure 2.13 shows.

If a state can terminate, it does not need to be related to a terminating state. It suffices if a terminating state can be reached after a number of internal transitions, as shown at the right of figure 2.13.

Definition 2.4.2 (Branching bisimulation). Consider the labeled transition system $A = (S, Act, \longrightarrow, s, T)$. We call a relation $R \subseteq S \times S$ a *branching bisimulation relation* iff for all $s, t \in S$ such that sRt, the following conditions hold for all actions $a \in Act$:

1. If $s \xrightarrow{a} s'$, then
   - Either $a = \tau$ and $s'Rt$, or
   - There is a sequence $t \xrightarrow{\tau} \cdots \xrightarrow{\tau} t'$ of (zero or more) τ-transitions such that sRt' and $t' \xrightarrow{a} t''$ with $s'Rt''$.
2. Symmetrically, if $t \xrightarrow{a} t'$, then
   - Either $a = \tau$ and sRt', or
   - There is a sequence $s \xrightarrow{\tau} \cdots \xrightarrow{\tau} s'$ of (zero or more) τ-transitions such that $s'Rt$ and $s' \xrightarrow{a} s''$ with $s''Rt'$.
3. If $s \in T$, then there is a sequence of (zero or more) τ-transitions $t \xrightarrow{\tau} \cdots \xrightarrow{\tau} t'$ such that sRt' and $t' \in T$.
4. Again, symmetrically, if $t \in T$, then there is a sequence of (zero or more) τ-transitions $s \xrightarrow{\tau} \cdots \xrightarrow{\tau} s'$ such that $s'Rt$ and $s' \in T$.

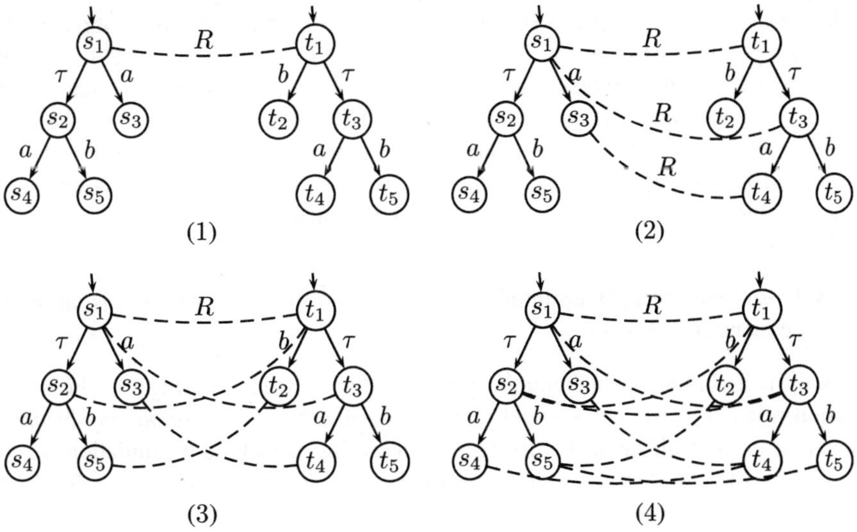

Figure 2.14: Two branching bisimilar transition systems

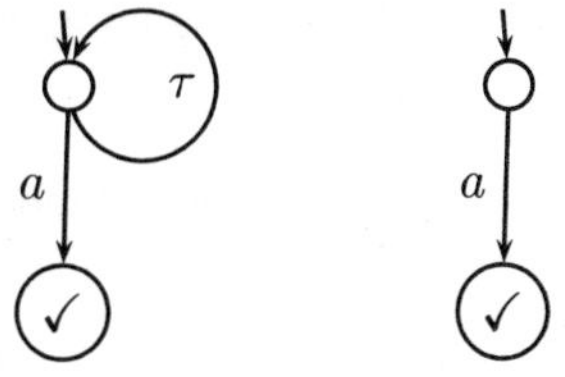

Figure 2.15: Branching bisimulation does not preserve τ-loops

Two states s and t are *branching bisimilar*, denoted by $s \leftrightarrow_b t$, if there is a branching bisimulation relation R such that sRt. Two labeled transition systems are *branching bisimilar* if their initial states are branching bisimilar.

Example 2.4.3. In figure 2.14 two transition systems are depicted. We can determine that they are branching bisimilar in the same way as for strong bisimulation. We first assume that the initial states must be related via some relation R. For R to be a branching bisimulation, the transition $s_1 \xrightarrow{a} s_3$ must be mimicked. This can only be done by two transitions $t_1 \xrightarrow{\tau} t_3 \xrightarrow{a} t_4$. As depicted in the second diagram, s_1 must be related to the intermediate state t_3 and s_3 must be related to t_4. By letting the transition $t_1 \xrightarrow{b} t_2$ be simulated by $s_1 \xrightarrow{\tau} s_2 \xrightarrow{b} s_5$, the relation is extended as indicated in the third diagram. Ultimately, the relation R must be extended as indicated in the fourth diagram. It requires a careful check that this relation is indeed a branching bisimulation relation.

Branching bisimulation equivalence has a built-in notion of *fairness*. That is, if a

τ-loop exists, then no infinite execution sequence will remain in this τ-loop forever if there is a possibility to leave it. The intuition is that there is zero chance that any exit from the τ-loop will ever be chosen. It is straightforward to show that the initial states in the two labeled transition systems in figure 2.15 are branching bisimilar.

A state with a τ-loop is also called a *divergent* state. There are times when it is desired to distinguish divergent states from nondivergent states. This distinction can be achieved by requiring that a branching bisimulation relation has the following additional property.

- If sRt then there is an infinite sequence $s \xrightarrow{\tau}\xrightarrow{\tau} \cdots$ iff there is an infinite sequence $t \xrightarrow{\tau}\xrightarrow{\tau} \cdots$.

We call such a branching bisimulation relation a divergence preserving branching bisimulation relation. Two states s and t are *divergence preserving branching bisimilar*, notation $s \leftrightarrow_{db} t$, iff there is a divergence preserving branching bisimulation R relating them. The initial states of the transition systems in figure 2.15 are not divergence preserving branching bisimilar.

Branching bisimulation (with or without divergence) has an unpleasant property, namely, it is not compositional. If an alternative is added to the initial state, then the resulting processes may cease to be bisimilar. This is illustrated in the following example. In chapter 4, we will see that adding an alternative to the initial state is a common operation.

Example 2.4.4. Consider the following two pairs of labeled transition systems.

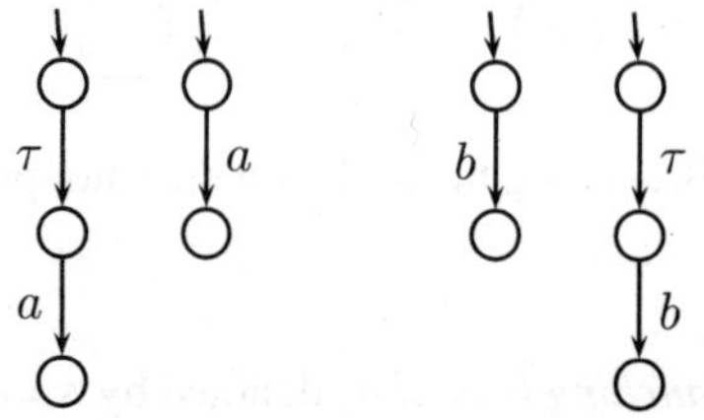

These labeled transition systems are branching bisimilar. However, their pairwise compositions with a choice at their initial states, depicted in figure 2.16, are not branching bisimilar. Assuming that they were branching bisimilar, then there should be a branching bisimulation relation relating their initial states. Since the labeled transition system at the right affords an a-transition from the initial state, the labeled transition system at the left should mimic it by performing a τ-transition followed by an a-transition. This means that the intermediate state after performing the τ-transition and before performing the a-transition should be related by the same relation to the initial state of the right-hand-side labeled transition system, as depicted in the lower part of figure 2.16. But this is impossible since the initial state of labeled transition system at the right allows a b-transition, while the related state at the left cannot mimic this b transition.

The problem explained in example 2.4.4 (and depicted in figure 2.16) is known as the rootedness problem. It is caused because doing a τ means that the option to do an observable action (e.g., a) disappears. Milner [137] showed that this problem can

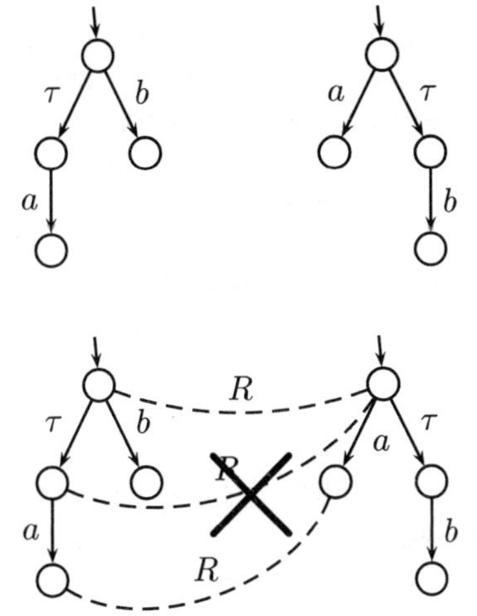

Figure 2.16: Root problem in branching bisimulation

be overcome by adding a rootedness condition: two processes are considered equivalent if they can simulate each other's initial transitions (including τ-transitions), such that the resulting processes are branching bisimilar. This leads to the notion of *rooted branching bisimulation*, which is presented below.

Definition 2.4.5 (Rooted branching bisimulation). Let $A = (S, Act, \longrightarrow, s, T)$ be a labeled transition system. A relation $R \subseteq S \times S$ is called a *rooted branching bisimulation relation* iff it is a branching bisimulation relation and it satisfies for all $s \in S$ and $t \in S$ such that sRt:

1. If $s \xrightarrow{a} s'$, then there is a $t' \in S$ such that $t \xrightarrow{a} t'$ and $s' \underline{\leftrightarrow}_b t'$,

2. Symmetrically, if $t \xrightarrow{a} t'$, then there is an $s' \in S$ such that $s \xrightarrow{a} s'$ and $s' \underline{\leftrightarrow}_b t'$.

Two states $s \in S$ and $t \in S$ are *rooted branching bisimilar*, denoted by $s \underline{\leftrightarrow}_{rb} t$, iff there is a rooted branching bisimulation relation R such that sRt. Two transition systems are *rooted branching bisimilar* iff their initial states are rooted branching bisimilar.

Rooted divergence preserving branching bisimulation can be defined in exactly the same way. We write $s \underline{\leftrightarrow}_{rdb} t$ to express that states s and t are rooted divergence preserving branching bisimilar.

Branching bisimulation equivalence strictly includes rooted branching bisimulation equivalence, which in turn strictly includes bisimulation equivalence. A similar set of strict inclusions can be given for divergence preserving bisimulation.

$$\underline{\leftrightarrow} \subset \underline{\leftrightarrow}_{rb} \subset \underline{\leftrightarrow}_b, \qquad \underline{\leftrightarrow} \subset \underline{\leftrightarrow}_{rdb} \subset \underline{\leftrightarrow}_{db} \subset \underline{\leftrightarrow}_b .$$

Note that in the absence of τ, strong bisimulation and all variants of branching bisimulation coincide.

When behaviors such as those in figure 2.11 are equivalent, which is generally accepted as a reasonable minimal requirement for internal actions, and when processes can be put in parallel, rooted branching bisimulation is the natural finest equivalence. The argument for this goes beyond the scope of this chapter, but it stresses that branching bisimulation is a very natural notion.

Exercise 2.4.6. Show using the definition of rooted branching bisimulation that the two labeled transition systems in figure 2.11 are rooted branching bisimilar. Show also that the two transition systems in figure 2.12 are neither rooted branching bisimilar nor branching bisimilar.

Exercise 2.4.7. Which of the following pairs of transition systems are branching and/or rooted branching bisimilar?

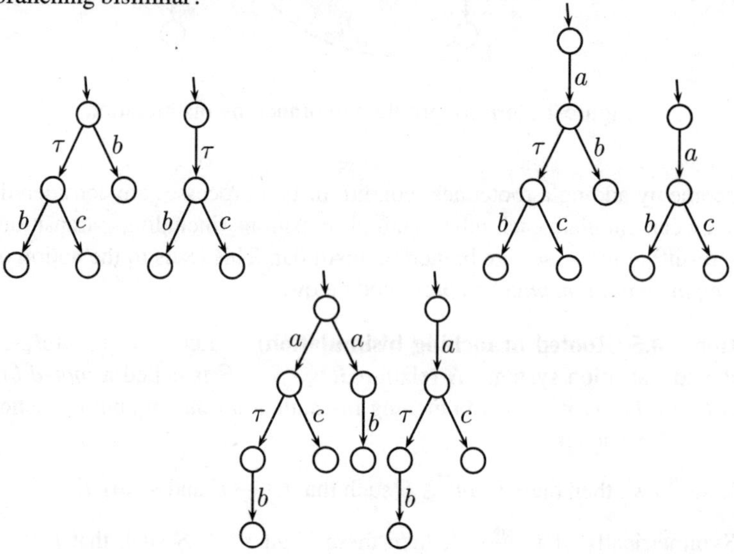

Exercise 2.4.8. With regard to the examples in exercise 2.4.7, which τ-transitions are *inert* with respect to branching bisimulation, i.e., for which τ-transitions $s \xrightarrow{\tau} s'$ are the states s and s' branching bisimilar?

2.4.4 ★(Rooted) weak bisimulation

A slight variation of branching bisimulation is weak bisimulation. We give its definition here, because weak bisimulation was defined well before branching bisimulation was invented, and therefore weak bisimulation is much more commonly used in the literature.

The primary difference between branching and weak bisimulation is that branching bisimulation preserves the branching structure of processes. For instance, the last pair of transition systems in exercise 2.4.7 are weakly bisimilar, although the initial a in the transition system at the left can make a choice that cannot be mimicked in the transition system at the right. The branching structure is not respected.

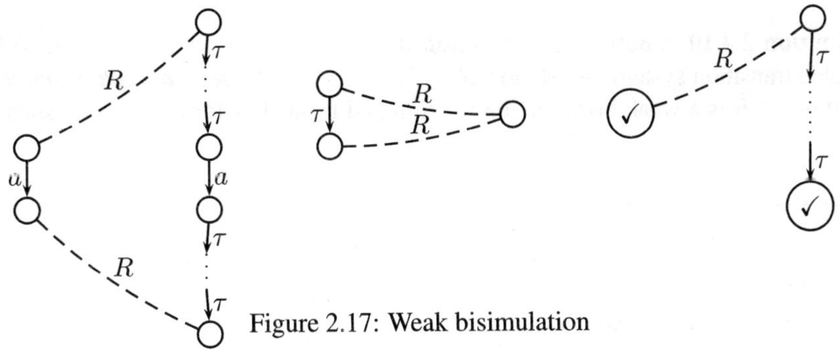

Figure 2.17: Weak bisimulation

It is useful to know that (rooted) branching bisimilar processes are also (rooted) weakly bisimilar. Furthermore, from a practical perspective, it hardly ever matters whether branching or weak bisimulation is used, except that the algorithms to calculate branching bisimulation on large graphs are more efficient than those for weak bisimulation.

Definition 2.4.9 (Weak bisimulation). Consider the labeled transition system $A = (S, Act, \longrightarrow, s, T)$. We call a relation $R \subseteq S \times S$ a *weak bisimulation relation* iff for all $s, t \in S$ such that sRt, the following conditions hold:

1. If $s \xrightarrow{a} s'$, then
   - Either $a = \tau$ and $s'Rt$, or
   - There is a sequence $t \xrightarrow{\tau} \cdots \xrightarrow{\tau}\xrightarrow{a}\xrightarrow{\tau} \cdots \xrightarrow{\tau} t'$ such that $s'Rt'$.
2. Symmetrically, if $t \xrightarrow{a} t'$, then
   - Either $a = \tau$ and sRt', or
   - There is a sequence $s \xrightarrow{\tau} \cdots \xrightarrow{\tau}\xrightarrow{a}\xrightarrow{\tau} \cdots \xrightarrow{\tau} s'$ such that $s'Rt'$.
3. If $s \in T$, then there is a sequence $t \xrightarrow{\tau} \cdots \xrightarrow{\tau} t'$ such that $t' \in T$.
4. Again, symmetrically, if $t \in T$, then there is a sequence $s \xrightarrow{\tau} \cdots \xrightarrow{\tau} s'$ such that $s' \in T$.

Two states s and t are *weakly bisimilar*, denoted by $s \leftrightarroweq_w t$, iff there is a weak bisimulation relation R such that sRt. Two labeled transition systems are *weakly bisimilar* iff their initial states are weakly bisimilar.

In figure 2.17 weak bisimulation is illustrated. Compare this figure with figure 2.13 for branching bisimulation. Note that weak bisimulation is more relaxed in the sense that the weak bisimulation relation R does not have to relate that many states.

The notion of rooted weak bisimulation is defined along the same lines as rooted branching bisimulation. The underlying motivation is exactly the same.

Definition 2.4.10 (Rooted weak bisimulation). Let $A = (S, Act, \longrightarrow, s, T)$ be a labeled transition system. A relation $R \subseteq S \times S$ is called a *rooted weak bisimulation relation* iff R is a weak bisimulation relation and it satisfies for all $s, t \in S$ such that sRt:

1. If $s \xrightarrow{\tau} s'$, then there is a sequence $t \xrightarrow{\tau}\xrightarrow{\tau} \cdots \xrightarrow{\tau} t'$ of at least length 1 and $s' \leftrightarrow_w t'$, and

2. Symmetrically, if $t \xrightarrow{\tau} t'$, then there is sequence of at least length 1 of τ-steps $s \xrightarrow{\tau}\xrightarrow{\tau} \cdots \xrightarrow{\tau} s'$ and $s' \leftrightarrow_w t'$.

Two states $s \in S$ and $t \in S$ are *rooted weakly bisimilar*, denoted by $s \leftrightarrow_{rw} t$, iff there is a rooted weak bisimulation relation R such that sRt. Two transition systems are *rooted weakly bisimilar* iff their initial states are rooted weakly bisimilar.

We conclude this section by showing the relationships between weak and branching bisimulation, where $\subset$ denotes strict set inclusion.

$$\leftrightarrow \subset \leftrightarrow_{rb} \subset \leftrightarrow_b \subset \leftrightarrow_w, \qquad \leftrightarrow \subset \leftrightarrow_{rb} \subset \leftrightarrow_{rw} \subset \leftrightarrow_w .$$

Note that rooted weak bisimulation and branching bisimulation are incomparable. Note also that we can define divergence preserving weak bisimulation, but as this notion is hardly used and its definition is exactly the same as that for divergence preserving branching bisimulation, we do not do this explicitly here.

Exercise 2.4.11. Determine which of the pairs of transition systems of figures 2.11 and 2.12 are (rooted) weakly bisimilar.

Exercise 2.4.12. Determine which of the pairs of transition systems of exercise 2.4.7 are (rooted) weakly bisimilar. Also determine which τ-transitions are inert with respect to weak bisimulation (cf. exercise 2.4.8).

Exercise 2.4.13. Prove that branching bisimulation is a weak bisimulation relation.

2.5 Historical notes

State machines have been used historically to describe programs. They already occur in Turing machines to formalize the concept of computation. Subsequently, they were heavily used in language theory, especially for compiler construction [5].

The idea of capturing the abstract behavior of computer programs by automata has been the cornerstone of the operational approach to semantics (meaning of programs) advocated by McCarthy [131] and Plotkin [154].

However, adding the notion of interaction with the environment was required to develop an abstract theory of system behavior, which was proposed by pioneers such as Petri [153], Bekič [24], and Milner [137]. This led to various theories of process calculi, exemplified by CCS [137], CSP [103], ACP [18], and an early formal and standardized behavioral specification language LOTOS [108]. We refer to [11, 55] for more detailed historical accounts and to [3, 12, 163] for excellent textbook introductions to the field.

Regarding fundamental models of behavior, there are various alternatives to labeled transition systems. Instead of labeled transition systems, one can use sets of traces, if necessary decorated to represent parallel behavior (Mazurkiewicz traces) [50] and even sets representing behavioral trees. A fundamental problem with such traces and trees is that sets cannot contain themselves (axiom of foundation). In other words, a loop cannot be represented in such sets as this would require a set that contains itself. This led to the use of projective limit models and metric spaces where the existence of an object representing a loop could be proven to exist [20]. It was also the motivation to start the work on ACP [26] and led to research into non-well-founded sets [4].

Rather independently and originally invented to describe chemical processes, Petri nets can be viewed as a higher level description of automata, especially suitable to describe data processing [109], and as such are becoming a basis for the description of business information systems [1].

Partly in reaction to the atomic nature of actions as proposed by Milner, a field baptized "true concurrency semantics" arose, stating that events are not atomic and should therefore not be treated as such. The history of the term goes back to 1988 (and possibly before) where a group of prominent researchers on concurrency theory got together for a workshop in Königswinter, Germany. We cite the following interesting anecdote from a report of this meeting [157]:

> Partial order semantics were popular at the conference (Köningswinter 1988). Some of its adherents have taken to calling p.o. [(partial order)] semantics true concurrency, prompting Robin Milner to start his talk by speaking up for "false concurrency."

Event structures [181] are a typical instance of models with a true concurrency semantics. Some regard Petri nets to fall into this category as well [141]. In response Milner referred to process calculi as "false concurrency."

The idea that two objects are the same if they have exactly the same properties is rather old, and is sometimes referred to as Leibniz equality. In the context of behavior, this is translated to the statement that two systems are equal if the difference cannot be observed. Although self evident in retrospect, it came as a surprise that there are very many different ways to observe processes. This led to a myriad of behavioral equivalences, of which [71, 72] provide compact overviews, in the settings with and without internal actions, respectively. The notion of strong bisimulation first proposed by Park [151] and Milner [135] was inspired by earlier automata-theoretic notions, which were in turn explored by Milner and adopted in this context. The same notion has been developed in various other contexts, including in the context of modal logics and non-well-founded sets, of which [166] gives a detailed historical account and [165] provides an excellent textbook introduction. The notion of internal action and weak bisimulation was proposed by Milner [135]. Branching bisimulation was defined by Van Glabbeek and Weijland [70, 73].

3

Data Types

Components of reactive systems often exchange messages containing data items among themselves and with the environment. For example, recall the alarm clock with multiple alarms from chapter 2, of which the labeled transition system is reproduced in figure 3.1. In this figure, the data parameter of action *set* is to be used by the environment to communicate the number of times the alarm should sound. We need a language to describe data types and their elements to be used in specifying behavior.

In this section we first describe a basic equational data type specification mechanism. One may define data types (called sorts), by defining their elements (constructors), their operations (maps) and the rules (equations) defining the operations. Function types are also allowed to be used in this setting.

As there are a number of data types that are commonly used in behavioral specifications, these have been predefined. These are, for example, common data types such as natural numbers, Booleans, and real numbers. These data types are designed to be as close as possible to their mathematical counterpart. This means that there are an unbounded number of natural and real numbers. The full specification of all built-in data types is given in appendix B. There are also mechanisms to compactly define more elaborate data types without giving a full equational data type specification. Typical examples are structured data types (specified by enumerating their members), lists, and sets. This chapter is dedicated to the data type specification language and in the next chapter we study how data types can be attached to actions and how data expressions can influence the behavior of processes.

3.1 Data type definition mechanism

In mCRL2, we have a straightforward data definition mechanism from which all data sorts can be built. One can declare arbitrary sorts using the keyword **sort**. Sorts are nonempty, possibly infinite sets with data elements. For a sort one can define constructor functions using the keyword **cons**. These are functions by which exactly all elements in the sort can be denoted. For instance

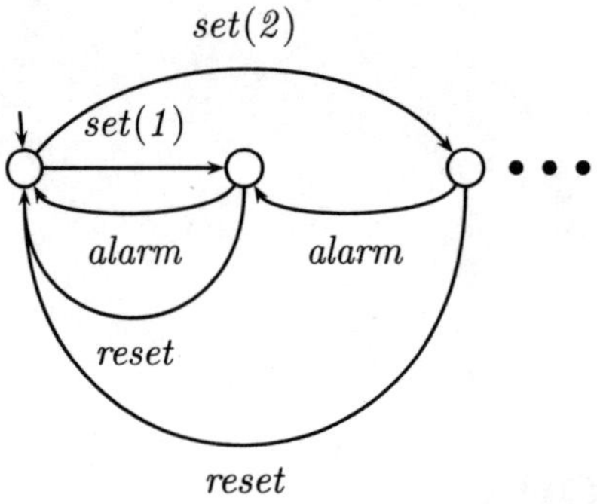

Figure 3.1: An alarm clock of which the number of alarms can be set

sort D;
cons $c, d : D$;

declares sort D in which all elements can be denoted by either c or d. Thus, D has either two elements, or in case c and d are the same, it has one element.

Using constructor functions, it is possible to declare a sort *Nat* representing the natural numbers. This is not the actual built-in sort $\mathbb{N}$ in mCRL2, which for efficiency purposes has a different internal structure. The definition of the built-in data type can be found in appendix B.

sort Nat;
cons $zero : Nat$;
$successor : Nat \to Nat$;

In this case we have a domain Nat of which all elements can be denoted by $zero$, or an expression of the form:

$$successor(successor(\ldots successor(zero)\ldots)).$$

Without explicitly indicating so, these elements are not necessarily different. Below, it is shown how it can be guaranteed that all elements of the sort *Nat* must differ.

Similarly to the definition of sort *Nat*, a sort $\mathbb{B}$ of Booleans can be defined. The standard definition for $\mathbb{B}$ is as follows:

sort $\mathbb{B}$;
cons $true, false : \mathbb{B}$;

The sort $\mathbb{B}$ plays a special role. In the first place the semantics of the language prescribes that the constructors $true$ and $false$ must be different. This is the only exception to the rule that constructors are not presumed to be different. Using this exception one can build sorts with necessarily different elements. Thus, there are exactly two Booleans. In the second place, Booleans are used to connect data specification with behavior, namely, conditions in processes and conditional equations must be of sort $\mathbb{B}$. In appendix B, additional operators for $\mathbb{B}$ are defined.

The following example does not define a proper sort, because it can only be empty. All data elements in D must be denoted as a term consisting of applications of the function f only. But as there is no constant, i.e., a function symbol with no argument, such a term cannot be constructed, and hence the sort D must be empty. However, empty sorts are not permitted and therefore there is no data type satisfying this specification. We say that such a data type is inconsistent.

sort $D;$
cons $f : D \to D;$

It is possible to declare sorts without constructor functions. In this case the sort can contain an arbitrary number of elements. In particular, the sort can contain elements that cannot be denoted by a term. As an example it is possible to declare a sort *Message* without constructors. In this way, one can model, for instance, data transfer protocols without assuming anything about the messages being transferred.

sort $Message;$

Auxiliary functions can be declared using the keyword **map**. For instance, the equality, addition, and multiplication operators on natural numbers are not necessary to construct all the numbers, but they are just useful operations. They can be declared as follows:

map $eq : Nat \times Nat \to \mathbb{B};$
$\quad plus, times : Nat \times Nat \to Nat;$

Here the notation $eq : Nat \times Nat \to \mathbb{B}$ says that eq is a function with two arguments of sort Nat yielding an element of sort $\mathbb{B}$. The symbol $\times$ is called the Cartesian product operator.

But it is not sufficient to only declare the type of an operator. It must also be defined how the operator calculates a value. This can be done by introducing equations using the keyword **eqn**. Two terms are equal if they can be transformed into each other using the equations. It does not matter if the equations are applied from left to right, or from right to left. However, for efficiency reasons, most tools strictly apply the equations from left to right, which is generally called term rewriting. This directed view of equations is an informal convention, but it has a profound effect on the equations.

For addition and multiplication, the equations are given below. Using the keyword **var**, the variables needed in the next equation section are declared.

var $n, m : Nat;$
eqn $eq(n, n) = true;$
$\quad eq(zero, successor(n)) = false;$
$\quad eq(successor(n), zero) = false;$
$\quad eq(successor(n), successor(m)) = eq(n, m);$
$\quad plus(n, zero) = n;$
$\quad plus(n, successor(m)) = successor(plus(n, m));$
$\quad times(n, zero) = zero;$
$\quad times(n, successor(m)) = plus(n, times(n, m));$

By applying these equations, one can show which terms are equal to others. For instance, showing that $2 \cdot 2 = 4$ goes as follows (where the numbers 2 and 4 represent $successor(successor(zero))$ and $successor(successor(successor(successor(zero))))$, respectively):

$$
\begin{array}{l}
times(successor(successor(zero)), successor(successor(zero))) = \\
plus(successor(successor(zero)), \\
\qquad times(successor(successor(zero)), successor(zero))) = \\
plus(successor(successor(zero)), plus(successor(successor(zero)), \\
\qquad times(successor(successor(zero)), zero))) = \\
plus(successor(successor(zero)), plus(successor(successor(zero)), zero)) = \\
plus(successor(successor(zero)), successor(successor(zero))) = \\
successor(plus(successor(successor(zero)), successor(zero))) = \\
successor(successor(plus(successor(successor(zero)), zero))) = \\
successor(successor(successor(successor(zero))))
\end{array}
$$

There is much to say about whether these equations suffice or whether their symmetric variants (e.g., $plus(zero, n)$) should be included, too. These equations are essentially sufficient to prove properties, but for the tools, adding more equations can make a huge difference in performance.

When defining functions, it is a good strategy to define them based on terms consisting of the constructors applied to variables. In the case above, these constructors are $zero$ and $successor(n)$ and the constructor patterns are only used in one argument. But sometimes such patterns are required in more arguments, and it can even be necessary that the patterns be more complex. As an example, consider the definition of the function $even$ below which in this form requires patterns $zero$, $successor(zero)$ and $successor(successor(n))$.

map $even : Nat \to \mathbb{B}$;
var $n : Nat$;
eqn $even(zero) = true$;
$even(successor(zero)) = false$;
$even(successor(successor(n))) = even(n)$;

It is very well possible to only partly define a function. Suppose the function $even$ should yield $true$ for even numbers, and it is immaterial whether it should deliver $true$ or $false$ for odd numbers. Then the second equation can be omitted. This does not mean that $even(successor(zero))$ is undefined. It has a fixed value (either $true$ or $false$), except that we do not know what it is.

The equations can have conditions that must be valid before they can be applied. The definition above can be rephrased as:

var $n : Nat$;
eqn $eq(n, zero) \to even(n) = true$;
$eq(n, successor(zero)) \to even(n) = false$;
$even(successor(successor(n))) = even(n)$;

Apart from equational reasoning, there are two major proof principles to be used in the context of equational data types, namely proof by contradiction and proof by induction, which are explained below.

The equations in an equation section can only be used to show that certain data elements are equal. In order to show that $zero$ and $successor(zero)$ are not equal another mechanism is required. We know that $true$ and $false$ are different. Within this basic data definition mechanism, this is the only assumption about terms not being equal. In order to show that other data elements are not equal, we assume that they are equal and then derive $true = false$, from which we conclude that the assumption is not true. This is called proof by contradiction or reductio ad absurdum. Note that such a reduction always requires an auxiliary function from such a data sort to Booleans. In the case of the sort Nat, we can define the function $less$ to do the job:

map $less : Nat \times Nat \to \mathbb{B};$
var $n, m : Nat;$
eqn $less(n, zero) = false;$
$less(zero, successor(n)) = true;$
$less(successor(n), successor(m)) = less(n, m);$

Now assume that $zero$ and $successor(zero)$ are equal, more precisely,

$$zero = successor(zero).$$

Then, we can derive:

$$true = less(zero, successor(zero)) \overset{\text{assumption}}{=} less(zero, zero) = false.$$

Under this assumption, $true$ and $false$ coincide, leading to the conclusion that $zero$ and $successor(zero)$ must be different. In a similar way, it can be proven that any pair of different natural numbers are indeed different when the function $less$ is present.

When constructors are present, we know that all terms have a particular shape and we can use that to prove properties about all terms. For instance, to prove a property $\phi(b)$ for a Boolean variable b, it suffices to prove that $\phi(false)$ and $\phi(true)$ hold. This proof principle is called *induction* on the structure of Booleans.

When there is a constructor f of a data type D that depends on D, we can assume that a property $\phi(x)$ holds for a variable of sort D to prove $\phi(f(x))$. Here $\phi(x)$ is called the induction hypothesis. In this way, we have shown that if property ϕ holds for smaller terms, it also holds for larger terms, and by simply repeating this, ϕ holds for all terms. A precise formulation of induction on the basis of constructors can be found in section 9.5.

Example 3.1.1. Consider the data type Nat as defined above. There are constructors $zero$ and $successor$. Therefore, in order to prove that a property $\phi(n)$ holds for n a variable of sort Nat, it must be shown that $\phi(zero)$ holds, and $\phi(n)$ implies $\phi(successor(n))$. This form of induction is sometimes referred to as mathematical induction.

Concretely, we can prove that $plus(zero, n) = n$. Next, we must show:

$$plus(zero, zero) = zero, \text{ and}$$
$$plus(zero, n) = n \text{ implies } plus(zero, successor(n)) = successor(n).$$

The first equation is easy to prove with the equations for *plus*. The second equations follows by

$$plus(zero, successor(n)) =$$
$$successor(plus(zero, n)) \overset{\text{induction hypothesis}}{=}$$
$$successor(n).$$

Thus, we can conclude by induction on *Nat* that $plus(zero, n) = n$.

Exercise 3.1.2. Give equational specifications of greater than or equal, $\geq$, and greater than, $>$, on the natural numbers.

Exercise 3.1.3. Give specifications of $max{:}Nat \times Nat \to Nat$, $minus{:}\ Nat \times Nat \to Nat$ and $power{:}Nat \times Nat \to Nat$ where $power(m, n)$ denotes m^n.

Exercise 3.1.4. Explain why any of the following equations is not wrong, but unpleasant or problematic, when using term rewriting tools.

var $n : Nat;$
eqn $true = even(zero);$
$false = even(successor(zero));$
$even(n) = even(successor(successor(n)));$

Exercise 3.1.5. Prove using the mapping *eq* that *zero* and $successor(zero)$ represent different data elements.

Exercise 3.1.6. Prove using induction that

$$plus(successor(n), m) = successor(plus(n, m)).$$

Use this result to prove, again with induction on *Nat*, that $plus(n, m) = plus(m, n)$.

Exercise 3.1.7. Prove for variables n, m of sort *Nat* that if $less(n, m) = true$, then $n \neq m$.

Exercise 3.1.8. Define a sort *List* on an arbitrary nonempty domain D, with as constructors the empty list $[]{:}List$ and $in{:}D \times List \to List$ to insert an element of D at the beginning of a list. Extend this with the following nonconstructor functions: $append{:}D \times List \to List$ to insert an element of D at the end of a list; $top{:}List \to D$ and $toe{:}List \to D$ to obtain the first and the last element of a list; $tail{:}List \to List$ and $untoe{:}List \to List$ to remove the first and the last element from a list, respectively; $nonempty{:}List \to \mathbb{B}$ to check whether a list is empty, $length{:}List \to Nat$ to compute the length of a list, and $+\!\!+{:}List \times List \to List$ to concatenate two lists.

Sort	*Rich notation*
Booleans	$\mathbb{B}$
Positive numbers	$\mathbb{N}^+$
Natural numbers	$\mathbb{N}$
Integers	$\mathbb{Z}$
Real numbers	$\mathbb{R}$
Structured types	$\mathbf{struct}\ldots\mid\ldots\mid\ldots.$
Functions	$D_1 \times \cdots \times D_n \to E$
Lists	$List(D)$
Sets	$Set(D)$
Bags	$Bag(D)$

Table 3.1: The predefined sorts (D, D_i, and E are sorts)

3.2 Standard data types

When modeling communicating systems, often the same data types are used, namely, Booleans, numbers, structured types, lists, functions, and sets. Therefore, these are predefined. For these data types we use common mathematical notation. The sorts are summarized in table 3.1.

Each sort (both user-defined and built-in) has automatically generated built-in functions for if-then-else ($if(\_,\_,\_)$), equality ($\approx$), inequality ($\not\approx$) and ordering operators ($\leq, <, >, \geq$). These functions are functions from their respective data domains to Booleans. Most predefined functions are denoted using infix notation, instead of the somewhat cumbersome prefix notation used in the previous section.

The equality function should not be confused with equality among terms ($=$), which indicates which terms are equal. It is the strength of the defining equations for data equality that allows us to use term equality and data equality interchangeably.

The defining equations for $\approx$, $\not\approx$, and $if(\_,\_,\_)$ are as follows (the equations for missing operators can be found in appendix B). Note that for a specific sort D, the user may specify more equations for calculating functions such as $\approx$ by exploiting the structure of D.

map $\approx, \not\approx, \leq, <, >, \geq : D \times D \to \mathbb{B}$;
  $if : \mathbb{B} \times D \times D \to D$;
var $x, y : D$;
  $b : \mathbb{B}$;
eqn $x{\approx}x = true$; $\quad x{<}x = false$;
  $x{\not\approx}y = \neg(x{\approx}y)$; $\quad x{\leq}x = true$;
  $if(true, x, y) = x$; $\quad x{>}y = y{<}x$;
  $if(false, x, y) = y$; $\quad x{\geq}y = y{\leq}x$;
  $if(b, x, x) = x$;
  $if(x{\approx}y, x, y) = y$;

The last equation is called *Bergstra's axiom.*[1] As stated above, equality on terms is

[1] Jan Bergstra (1951–) is the founding father of process algebra in the Amsterdam style (ACP). He con-

strongly related to data equality $\approx$. More precisely, the following lemma holds:

Lemma 3.2.1. For any data sort D for which the equations above are defined, it holds that:

$$x \approx y = \mathit{true} \text{ iff } x = y.$$

Proof. For the direction from left to right, we derive:

$$x = \mathit{if}(\mathit{true}, x, y) = \mathit{if}(x \approx y, x, y) = y.$$

For the direction from right to left, we derive:

$$x \approx y = x \approx x = \mathit{true}.$$

□

Bergstra's axiom is generally not used by tools since the shape of the axiom is not very convenient for term rewriting.

Exercise 3.2.2. Consider the specification

sort D;
map $d_1, d_2{:}D$;

Which of the following expressions are equal to *true* or *false*: $d_1 \approx d_1$, $d_1 \approx d_2$, $d_1 > d_2$, $d_2 \not\approx d_1$ and $d_2 \geq d_2$.

3.2.1 Booleans

The sort for Boolean has already been introduced as $\mathbb{B}$. It consists of exactly two different constructors, *true* and *false*. For this sort, the operations are listed in table 3.2. The syntax used by the tools in the mCRL2 language can be found in appendix C. The equations with which the operators on Booleans are defined are found in appendix B.

Most functions on $\mathbb{B}$ are standard and do not need an explanation. In Boolean expressions, it is possible to use quantifiers $\forall$ and $\exists$. They add a substantial amount of expressiveness to the language. This is important because compact and insightful behavioral specifications reduce the number of errors, increase the comprehensibility, and in general lead to better balanced behavior of designs.

We illustrate the expressiveness of the specification language with quantifiers with an example.

Example 3.2.3. Fermat's Last Theorem was an open problem for more than three centuries. It states that there is no positive number $n > 2$ such that $a^n + b^n = c^n$ for natural number a, b, and c.

map $\mathit{fermat} : \mathbb{B}$;
eqn $\mathit{fermat} = \forall a, b, c, n{:}\mathbb{N}^+.(n \leq 2 \vee a^n + b^n \not\approx c^n)$;

tributed to many other topics, such as the theory of abstract data types and modules and program algebras.

Operator	*Rich notation*
True	$true$
False	$false$
Negation	$\neg\_$
Conjunction	$\_\wedge\_$
Disjunction	$\_\vee\_$
Implication	$\_\Rightarrow\_$
Equality	$\_\approx\_$
Inequality	$\_\not\approx\_$
Conditional	$if(\_,\_,\_)$
Universal quantification	$\forall\_:\_.\_$
Existential quantification	$\exists\_:\_.\_$

Table 3.2: Operators on Booleans

As the conjecture holds, $fermat$ is equal to $true$, but any tool that wants to figure this out must be sufficiently strong to prove Fermat's Last Theorem.

As demonstrated by the example given above, the downside of the expressiveness of quantifiers is that tools can have difficulties to handle them. This may mean that a specification with quantifiers cannot even be simulated. It is the subject of continuous research to make the tools more effective in dealing with these primitives. It requires experience to know which expressions can and which cannot be handled effectively by the tools in their current state.

3.2.2 Numbers

Positive numbers, natural numbers, integers, and reals are represented by the sorts $\mathbb{N}^+$, $\mathbb{N}$, $\mathbb{Z}$, and $\mathbb{R}$, respectively. Numbers are denoted in the common way, for example, 1, 2, $45978, 0, -1$. There is no special notation for reals, but these can be constructed using, for instance, the division operator.

The common notation for numbers is there just for convenience. Each number is immediately translated to a number as an element of an abstract data type as defined in appendix B. All data types in this appendix have been designed such that each constructor term uniquely defines a data element and has an efficient representation. For instance, there is only one constructor term representing 0 in the integers (and not for instance -0 and $+0$) and the internal representation uses a binary encoding (and not zero and successor).

For positive numbers there are two constructors, namely $@c1 : \mathbb{N}^+$ and $@cDub : \mathbb{B} \times \mathbb{N}^+ \to \mathbb{N}^+$. The constructor $@c1$ represents 1 and $@cDub(b, p)$ equals $2p$ if b is false, and $2p + 1$ if b is true. Thus, 2 is represented by $@cDub(false, p)$ and 3 is represented by $@cDub(true, p)$. A natural number is either 0 or a positive number. An integer is either a natural number representing 0, 1, etc., or a positive number, representing $-1, -2, \ldots$.

Generally, we will not refer to the representation of numbers in their internal format and use their common denotation. The numbers satisfy all properties that we expect from ordinary mathematical numbers. In particular, the numbers are unbounded, which means that there is no largest natural number, and there are no smallest and largest integers. Real numbers are exact, so there is no issue regarding precision.

But the internal representation and the equations in appendix B can become relevant if a more detailed scrutiny of the data types is required. It can be that a certain equality between data terms cannot be proven, and in order to understand why, the precise defining equations are required. Also, the induction on numbers that is defined by the constructors is not ordinary mathematical induction, which uses zero and successor. In order to understand that mathematical induction on natural numbers is sound, the precise definitions are also required. The relation between constructors and induction is an issue that we address in chapter 9.

There is an implicit type conversion between numbers. Any positive number can become a natural number, which in turn can become an integer, which can become a real number. These automatic conversions apply to any object, not only to constants, but also to variables and terms.

The operators on numbers are given in table 3.3. They are all well known. Most operators are defined for all possible types of numbers. This means that there are additional operators for $\mathbb{N}^+ \times \mathbb{N}^+$, $\mathbb{N} \times \mathbb{N}$, $\mathbb{Z} \times \mathbb{Z}$, and $\mathbb{R} \times \mathbb{R}$. The resulting type is the most restrictive sort possible. Addition on $\mathbb{N}^+ \times \mathbb{N}^+$ has as resulting sort $\mathbb{N}^+$, but subtraction on $\mathbb{N}^+ \times \mathbb{N}^+$ has as resulting sort $\mathbb{Z}$, as the second number can be larger than the first. Some operators have restricted sorts. For instance, for the modulo operator the sort of the second operator must be $\mathbb{N}^+$ as $x|_0$ is generally not defined. In accordance with common usage, we write multiplication as a dot, or leave it out completely, although in the tools we write $*$ for multiplication.

In some cases, the sort of the result must be upgraded. For numbers, we have the explicit type conversion operations $A2B$ (pronounced A to B) where $A, B \in \{\mathit{Pos}, \mathit{Nat}, \mathit{Int}, \mathit{Real}\}$. For instance, the expression $n{-}1$ has sort $\mathbb{Z}$, because n can be zero. However, if it is known that n is larger than 0, it can be retyped to $\mathbb{N}$ by writing $\mathit{Int2Nat}(n{-}1)$. These operators are generally only written in specifications intended for tools. In textual specifications we typically leave them out.

The reals $\mathbb{R}$ are a complex data type, because the number of reals that exist is uncountably infinite. Without going into detail, this means that we cannot describe reals with constructors, and that means that we do not have an induction principle on reals. The definition of reals that we give allows for the denotation of the rational numbers only, although it would be possible to extend this data type to include operators such as the square root or the logarithm. Reals are important for timed behavior as the moment an action can take place is expressed by a real.

Exercise 3.2.4. Determine what are the sorts of the successor function $succ(\_)$, and what are the sorts of the predecessor function $pred(\_)$.

Exercise 3.2.5. Prove using the equations in appendix B that the numbers 0 and 1 are different.

Exercise 3.2.6. Calculate using the axioms in appendix B that $2|_1 = 0$.

Operator	*Rich notation*
Positive numbers	$\mathbb{N}^+\ (1, 2, 3, \ldots)$
Natural numbers	$\mathbb{N}\ (0, 1, 2, \ldots)$
Integers	$\mathbb{Z}\ (\ldots, -2, -1, 0, 1, 2, \ldots)$
Reals	$\mathbb{R}$
Equality	$\_ \approx \_$
Inequality	$\_ \not\approx \_$
Conditional	$\mathit{if}(\_, \_, \_)$
Conversion	$A2B(\_)$
Less than or equal	$\_ \leq \_$
Less than	$\_ < \_$
Greater than or equal	$\_ \geq \_$
Greater than	$\_ > \_$
Maximum	$\max(\_, \_)$
Minimum	$\min(\_, \_)$
Absolute value	$\mathrm{abs}(\_)$
Negation	$-\_$
Successor	$succ(\_)$
Predecessor	$pred(\_)$
Addition	$\_ + \_$
Subtraction	$\_ - \_$
Multiplication	$\_ \cdot \_$
Integer div	$\_ \mathrm{\ div\ } \_$
Integer mod	$\_ \mid \_$
Exponentiation	$\_^{\_}$
Real division	$\_ / \_$
Rounding operators	$\mathit{floor}(\_), ceil(\_), round(\_)$

Table 3.3: Operations on numbers

Operator	*Rich notation*
Function application	$\_(\_, \ldots, \_)$
Lambda abstraction	$\lambda\_{:}D_0, \ldots, \_{:}D_n.\_$
Equality	$\_\approx\_$
Inequality	$\_\not\approx\_$
Less than or equal	$\_ \leq \_$
Less than	$\_ < \_$
Greater than or equal	$\_ \geq \_$
Greater than	$\_ > \_$
Conditional	$\mathit{if}(\_, \_, \_)$
Function update	$\_[\_ \rightarrow \_]$

Table 3.4: Lambda abstraction and function application

3.3 Function data types

Functions are objects in common mathematical use and they are very convenient for abstract modeling of data in behavior. Therefore, it is possible to use function sorts in specifications. For example,

$$\begin{array}{ll}\textbf{sort} & F = \mathbb{N} \rightarrow \mathbb{N};\\ & G = \mathbb{R} \times \mathbb{N} \rightarrow \mathbb{R};\\ & H = \mathbb{R} \rightarrow F \rightarrow G;\end{array}$$

declares that F is the sort of functions from natural numbers to natural numbers and G is the sort of functions from $\mathbb{R}$ and $\mathbb{N}$ to $\mathbb{R}$. Functions of the complex sort H map reals to functions from F to G. Function types associate to the right. Hence, the sort H equals $\mathbb{R} \rightarrow (F \rightarrow G)$. If the sort $(\mathbb{R} \rightarrow F) \rightarrow G$ were required, explicit bracketing is needed.

Functions can be made using lambda abstraction and application (see table 3.4). Lambda abstraction is used to denote functions. For example,

$$\lambda n{:}\mathbb{N}.n^2$$

represents a function of sort $\mathbb{N}$ to $\mathbb{N}$ that yields for each argument n its square. The variable n is said to be *bound* by lambda abstraction . A variable that is bound does not occur freely in a term. For example, the variable n is free in n^2, bound in $\lambda n{:}\mathbb{N}.n^2$ and both free and bound in $n^2 + \lambda n{:}\mathbb{N}.n^2$. In this last case the bound and free variables n are different.

The function defined above can be applied to an argument by putting it directly behind the function. For instance

$$(\lambda n{:}\mathbb{N}.n^2)(4)$$

equals 16. It is common to drop the brackets around the argument of such a function as follows

$$(\lambda n{:}\mathbb{N}.n^2)4.$$

However, the syntax of mCRL2 requires these brackets. When functions require more arguments, brackets associate to the left. For example, consider a function f and terms t and u, then the application $f(t)(u)$ is parsed as $(f(t))(u)$, and not as $f(t(u))$.

Lambda terms can have more variables. For example, the function f defined as $\lambda x, y{:}\mathbb{N}, b{:}\mathbb{B}.\ \mathit{if}(b, x, x{+}y)$ is a function of sort $\mathbb{N} \times \mathbb{N} \times \mathbb{B} \to \mathbb{N}$. The function f must always be applied to three arguments simultaneously. It is not allowed to feed it with only a partial number of arguments, as in $f(3, 4)$. When it should be possible to provide the arguments one at a time, three lambdas are necessary, as in $g = \lambda x{:}\mathbb{N}.\lambda y{:}\mathbb{N}.\lambda b{:}\mathbb{B}.\mathit{if}(b, x, x{+}y)$. The type of this function is $\mathbb{N}{\to}\mathbb{N}{\to}\mathbb{B}{\to}\mathbb{N}$. In this case $g(3)$ is a function from $\mathbb{N}{\to}\mathbb{B}{\to}\mathbb{N}$, and $g(3)(4)(\mathit{true})$ is an expression of sort $\mathbb{N}$.

There are two conversion rules for lambda expressions. A lambda term $\lambda x{:}\mathbb{N}.t$ binds the variable x in t and the variable y has exactly the same role in $\lambda y{:}\mathbb{N}.t[x{:=}y]$, if y does not appear freely in t. Here, $t[x{:=}y]$ is the substitution operator that replaces each free occurrence of x in t by y. Renaming a bound variable is called α-conversion, and it is generally denoted as

$$\lambda x{:}\mathbb{N}.t =_\alpha \lambda y{:}\mathbb{N}.t[x{:=}y].$$

If a lambda expression has more bound variables, then renaming any subset of these is also called α-conversion.

When applying substitutions to lambda terms, care must be taken that substituted variables do not accidentally get bound. Consider the term $\lambda x{:}D.y$ to which the substitution $[y{:=}x]$ is applied. We see $(\lambda x{:}D.y)[y{:=}x] = (\lambda x{:}D.x)$. The unbound y is replaced by x and becomes bound. This is wrong. Therefore, it is necessary when applying a substitution to a lambda term to first α-convert the term such that there is no conflict between the bound variables and the variables in the substitution. In the case above, the correct sequence should be $(\lambda x{:}D.y)[y{:=}x] =_\alpha (\lambda z{:}D.y)[y{:=}x] = \lambda z{:}D.x$.

The second conversion is called β-conversion. It corresponds to function application. A term $\lambda x{:}D.t$ applied to a term u is equal to $t[x{:=}u]$, namely t where u is substituted for all occurrences of x. It is generally denoted by

$$(\lambda x{:}D.t)(u) =_\beta t[x{:=}u].$$

If there are more bound variables in a lambda expression, then β-conversion has the following shape requiring multiple substitutions of variables.

$$(\lambda x_1{:}D_1, \ldots, x_n{:}D_n.t)(u_1, \ldots, u_n) =_\beta t[x_1{:=}u_1, \ldots, x_n{:=}u_n].$$

Example 3.3.1. ★ Lambda abstraction and application are far more powerful than they may seem. They can be used to specify fundamental mathematical and computational concepts. Alonzo Church represented numbers by lambda terms. The number n is represented by a lambda term that applies a function n times to an argument.[2]

$$
\begin{array}{ll}
0 & \lambda f{:}D{\to}D.\lambda x{:}D.x \\
1 & \lambda f{:}D{\to}D.\lambda x{:}D.f(x) \\
2 & \lambda f{:}D{\to}D.\lambda x{:}D.f(f(x)) \\
3 & \lambda f{:}D{\to}D.\lambda x{:}D.f(f(f(x))) \\
 & \dots \\
n & \lambda f{:}D{\to}D.\lambda x{:}D.f^n(x)
\end{array}
$$

Adding two Church numerals can be done by the lambda term

$$\lambda g_1, g_2{:}D{\to}D.\lambda f{:}D{\to}D.\lambda x{:}D.g_1(f)(g_2(f)(x)).$$

Evaluation is represented by β-conversion. Thus, adding one and two looks like:

$$
\begin{array}{l}
\lambda g_1, g_2{:}D{\to}D.\lambda f{:}D{\to}D.\lambda x{:}D. \\
\qquad g_1(f)(g_2(f)(x))(\lambda f{:}D{\to}D.\lambda x{:}D.f(x), \lambda f{:}D{\to}D.\lambda x{:}D.f(f(x))) =_\beta \\
\lambda f{:}D{\to}D.\lambda x{:}D. \\
\qquad g_1(f)(g_2(f)(x))[g_1{:=}\lambda f{:}D{\to}D.\lambda x{:}D.f(x), g_2{:=}\lambda f{:}D{\to}D.\lambda x{:}D.f(f(x))] = \\
\lambda f'{:}D{\to}D.\lambda x'{:}D. \\
\qquad g_1(f')(g_2(f')(x'))[g_1{:=}\lambda f{:}D{\to}D.\lambda x{:}D.f(x), g_2{:=}\lambda f{:}D{\to}D.\lambda x{:}D.f(f(x))] = \\
\lambda f'{:}D{\to}D.\lambda x'{:}D.(\lambda f{:}D{\to}D.\lambda x{:}D.f(x))(f')((\lambda f{:}D{\to}D.\lambda x{:}D.f(f(x)))(f')(x')) =_\beta \\
\lambda f'{:}D{\to}D.\lambda x'{:}D.(\lambda x{:}D.f(x)[f{:=}f'])((\lambda x{:}D.f(f(x))[f{:=}f'])(x')) = \\
\lambda f'{:}D{\to}D.\lambda x'{:}D.(\lambda x{:}D.f'(x))((\lambda x{:}D.f'(f'(x)))(x')) =_\beta \\
\lambda f'{:}D{\to}D.\lambda x'{:}D.f'(x)[x{:=}(\lambda x{:}D.f'(f'(x)))(x')] = \\
\lambda f'{:}D{\to}D.\lambda x'{:}D.f'((\lambda x{:}D.f'(f'(x)))(x')) =_\beta \\
\lambda f'{:}D{\to}D.\lambda x'{:}D.(f'(f'(f'(x)))[x{:=}x']) = \\
\lambda f'{:}D{\to}D.\lambda x'{:}D.f'(f'(f'(x'))).
\end{array}
$$

Function sorts are sorts like any other. This means that equality, its negation, comparison operators and an if-then-else function are also available for function sorts.

There is one specific operator for unary function sorts, namely the *function update operator*. For a function $f : D \to E$ it is written as $f[d{\to}e]$. It represents the function f except if applied to value d it must yield e. Using lambda notation, the update operator can be defined by

$$f[d{\to}e] = \lambda x{:}D.\mathit{if}(x{\approx}d, e, f(x)).$$

The advantage of using a function update over explicit lambda notation is that the equations for function updates allow for effectively determining whether two functions after a number of updates represent the same function. This is not always possible when using explicit lambda notation. Apart from that, the function update notation is easier to read.

Example 3.3.2. Suppose we want to specify a possibly infinite buffer containing elements of some sort D where the elements are stored at specific positions. This can be done by declaring the buffer to be a function $\mathbb{N} \to D$. The definitions of the empty buffer, an insert function, and a get function are straightforward.

[2]Alonzo Church (1903–1995) developed the lambda calculus as a basic mechanism for calculations and showed the existence of undecidable problems.

sort $\mathit{Buffer} = \mathbb{N} \to D$;
map $\mathit{default\_buffer} : \mathit{Buffer}$;
$\mathit{insert} : \mathbb{N} \times D \times \mathit{Buffer} \to \mathit{Buffer}$;
$\mathit{get} : \mathbb{N} \times \mathit{Buffer} \to D$;
var $n{:}\mathbb{N}; d{:}D; B{:}\mathit{Buffer}$;
eqn $\mathit{default\_buffer}(n) = d_0$;
$\mathit{insert}(n, d, B) = B[n{\to}d]$;
$\mathit{get}(n, B) = B(n)$;

Exercise 3.3.3. Consider arrays containing Booleans as a function from $\mathbb{N}$ to $\mathbb{B}$. Specify a function get to get the Boolean at index i and another function $assign$ that assigns a Boolean value to a certain position i in the array.

Exercise 3.3.4.★ The Booleans *true* and *false* can be represented by the lambda expressions $\lambda x, y{:}D.x$ and $\lambda x, y{:}D.y$. Give a lambda term for an if-then-else function on Church numerals. Also provide a function is_zero that tests whether a Church numeral is equal to zero. Show that is_zero applied to zero is true, and is_zero applied to one is false.

3.4 Structured data types

Structured types, also called functional or recursive types, find their origin in functional programming. The idea is that the elements of a data type are explicitly characterized. For instance, an enumerated type *Direction* with elements *up*, *down*, *left*, and *right* can be characterized as follows:

sort *Direction* $=$ **struct** *up?isUp* | *down?isDown* | *left?isLeft* | *right?isRight*;

This says the sort *Direction* has four constructors characterizing different elements. The optional recognizers such as *isUp* are functions from *Direction* to $\mathbb{B}$ and yield true iff they are applied to the constructor to which they belong. For example, $\mathit{isUp}(\mathit{up}) = \mathit{true}$ and $\mathit{isUp}(\mathit{down}) = \mathit{false}$.

It is possible to let the constructors in a structured sort depend on other sorts. Hence, pairs of elements of fixed sorts A and B can be declared as follows:

sort *Pair* $=$ **struct** $\mathit{pair}(\mathit{fst}{:}A, \mathit{snd}{:}B)$;

This says that any term of sort *Pair* can be denoted as $\mathit{pair}(a, b)$ where a and b are data elements of sort A and B. The functions *fst* and *snd* are so-called projection functions. They allow for the extraction of the first and second element out of a pair. They satisfy the equations:

$$\mathit{fst}(\mathit{pair}(a, b)) = a;$$
$$\mathit{snd}(\mathit{pair}(a, b)) = b;$$

Projection functions are optional, and can be omitted.

In structured sorts, it is even possible to let a sort depend on itself. Using this, well-known recursive data types such as lists and trees can be constructed. A sort *Tree* for binary trees has the following minimal definition:

Operator	*Rich notation*
Constructor i	$c_i(\_, \ldots, \_)$
Recognizer for c_i	$is\_c_i(\_)$
Projection (i, j), if declared	$pr_{i,j}(\_)$
Equality	$\_\approx\_$
Inequality	$\_\not\approx\_$
Less than or equal	$\_\leq\_$
Less than	$\_<\_$
Greater than or equal	$\_\geq\_$
Greater than	$\_>\_$
Conditional	$if(\_, \_, \_)$

Table 3.5: Operators for structured types

sort $Tree = $ **struct** $leaf(A) \mid node(Tree, Tree)$;

By adding projection and recognizer functions, this looks like:

sort $Tree = $ **struct** $leaf(val{:}A)?isLeaf \mid node(left{:}Tree, right{:}Tree)?isNode$;

As an example we define a function HE, short for holds everywhere, that gets a function of sort $A \to \mathbb{B}$ and checks whether the function yields true in every leaf of the tree.

map $HE : (A \to \mathbb{B}) \times Tree \to \mathbb{B}$;
var $f : A \to \mathbb{B}$;
$t, u : Tree$;
$a : A$;
eqn $HE(f, leaf(a)) = f(a)$;
$HE(f, node(t, u)) = HE(f, t) \wedge HE(f, u)$;

The following definition of sort *Tree* allows the definition of operation *HE* without pattern matching.

var $f : A \to \mathbb{B}$;
$t : Tree$;
eqn $HE(f, t) = if(isLeaf(t), f(val(t)), HE(f, left(t)) \wedge HE(f, right(t)))$;

This last definition has the disadvantage that the equation is not a terminating rewrite rule. Under certain circumstances, tools will have difficulties dealing with such an equation.

The general form of a structured type is the following, where $n \in \mathbb{N}^+$ and $k_i \in \mathbb{N}$ with $1 \leq i \leq n$:

$$
\begin{aligned}
\textbf{struct}\ & c_1(pr_{1,1} : A_{1,1}, \ldots, pr_{1,k_1} : A_{1,k_1})?isC_1 \\
\mid\ & c_2(pr_{2,1} : A_{2,1}, \ldots, pr_{2,k_2} : A_{2,k_2})?isC_2 \\
& \vdots \\
\mid\ & c_n(pr_{n,1} : A_{n,1}, \ldots, pr_{n,k_n} : A_{n,k_n})?isC_n;
\end{aligned}
$$

Operator	*Rich notation*
Construction	$[\_, \ldots, \_]$
Element test	$\_ \in \_$
Length	$\#\_$
Cons	$\_ \triangleright \_$
Snoc	$\_ \triangleleft \_$
Concatenation	$\_ +\!\!+ \_$
Element at position	$\_ . \_$
The first element of a list	$head(\_)$
List without its first element	$tail(\_)$
The last element of a list	$rhead(\_)$
List without its last element	$rtail(\_)$
Equality	$\_ \approx \_$
Inequality	$\_ \not\approx \_$
Less than or equal	$\_ \leq \_$
Less than	$\_ < \_$
Greater than or equal	$\_ \geq \_$
Greater than	$\_ > \_$
Conditional	$if(\_, \_, \_)$

Table 3.6: Operations on lists

This declares n constructors c_i, projection functions $pr_{i,j}$ and recognizers isC_i. All names have to be chosen such that no ambiguity can arise. The operations in table 3.5 are available after declaring the sort above. For the comparison operators, the first function in a struct is the smallest and the arguments are compared from left to right. The precise definition of structured sorts is given in appendix B.10.

Exercise 3.4.1. Define the sort *Message* that contains message frames with a header containing the type of the message (ack, $ctrl$, mes), a checksum field, and optionally a data field. Typical instances of messages are $frame(ack, cs)$ and $frame(mes, cs, d)$ where cs is a checksum and d some data element. Leave the data and checksums unspecified.

3.5 Lists

Lists, where all elements are of sort A, are declared by the sort expression $List(A)$. The operations in table 3.6 are predefined for this sort. Lists consist of constructors $[\,]$, the empty list, and $\triangleright$, putting an element in front of a list. All other functions on lists are internally declared as mappings.

Lists can also be denoted explicitly, by putting the elements between square brackets. For instance, for lists of natural numbers $[1, 5, 0, 234, 2]$ is a valid list. Using the . operator, an element at a certain position can be obtained where the first element has index 0 (e.g., $[2, 4, 1].1$ equals 4). The concatenation operator $+\!\!+$ can be used to ap-

Operator	*Rich notation*
Set enumeration	$\{\_, \ldots, \_\}$
Bag enumeration	$\{\_ : \_, \ldots, \_ : \_\}$
Comprehension	$\{\_ {:} \_ \mid \_\}$
Element test	$\_ \in \_$
Bag multiplicity	$count(\_, \_)$
Subset/subbag	$\_ \subseteq \_$
Proper subset/subbag	$\_ \subset \_$
Union	$\_ \cup \_$
Difference	$\_ - \_$
Intersection	$\_ \cap \_$
Set complement	$\overline{\_}$
Convert set to bag	$Set2Bag(\_)$
Convert bag to set	$Bag2Set(\_)$
Equality	$\_ \approx \_$
Inequality	$\_ \not\approx \_$
Less than or equal	$\_ \leq \_$
Less than	$\_ < \_$
Greater than or equal	$\_ \geq \_$
Greater than	$\_ > \_$
Conditional	$if(\_, \_, \_)$

Table 3.7: Operations on sets and bags

pend one list to the end of another. The $\triangleleft$ operator can be used to add an element to the end of a list. Thus, the lists $[a, b]$, $a \triangleright [b]$, $[a] \triangleleft b$ and $[a] \mathbin{+\!\!+} [] \triangleleft b$ are all equivalent. The precise equations for lists are given in appendix B.

Exercise 3.5.1. Specify a function *map* that gets a function $f : D \to D$ and applies it to all elements of a given list of sort $List(D)$ for some arbitrary sort D.

Exercise 3.5.2. Specify a function *stretch* that given a list of lists of some sort D, concatenates all these lists to one single list.

Exercise 3.5.3. Define an *insert* operator on lists of some sort D such that the elements in the list occur at most once. Give a proof that the insert operation is indeed correct.

3.6 Sets and bags

Mathematical specifications often use sets or bags. These are declared as shown in table 3.7. For example, consider the following simple specification which defines sorts D and B as sets and bags of sort A, respectively:

sort $D = Set(A)$;
$\quad B = Bag(A)$;

An important difference between lists and sets (or bags) is that lists are inherently finite structures. It is impossible to build a list of all natural numbers, whereas the set of all natural numbers can easily be denoted as $\{n{:}\mathbb{N} \mid \mathit{true}\}$. Similarly, the infinite set of all even numbers is easily denoted as $\{n{:}\mathbb{N} \mid n|_2{\approx}0\}$. The difference between bags and sets is that elements can occur at most once in a set, whereas they can occur with any multiplicity in a bag.

The empty set is represented by an empty set enumeration $\{\}$. A set enumeration declares a set where each element can occur at most once. So, $\{a, b, c\}$ declares the same set as $\{a, b, c, c, a, c\}$. In a bag enumeration, the number of times an element occurs has to be declared explicitly. So, for example, $\{a{:}2, b{:}1\}$ declares a bag consisting of two a's and one b. Also $\{a{:}1, b{:}1, a{:}1\}$ declares the same bag. The empty bag is represented by the empty bag enumeration $\{:\}$.

A set comprehension $\{\, x{:}A \mid P(x)\, \}$ declares the set consisting of all elements x of sort A for which predicate $P(x)$ holds, that is, $P(x)$ is an expression of sort $\mathbb{B}$. A bag comprehension $\{\, x{:}A \mid f(x)\, \}$ declares the bag in which each element x occurs $f(x)$ times, that is, $f(x)$ is an expression of sort $\mathbb{N}$.

Exercise 3.6.1. Specify the set of all prime numbers.

Exercise 3.6.2. Specify the set of all lists of natural numbers that only contain the number 0. This is the set $\{[], [0], [0, 0], \ldots\}$. Also specify the set of all lists with length 2.

3.7 Where expressions and priorities

Where expressions are an abbreviation mechanism in data expressions. They have the form e **whr** $a_1{=}e_1, \ldots, a_n{=}e_n$ **end**, with $n \in \mathbb{N}$. Here, e is a data expression, and for all $1 \leq i \leq n$, a_i is an identifier and e_i is a data expression. Expression e is called the body and each equation $a_i = e_i$ is called a *definition*. Each identifier a_i is used as an abbreviation for e_i in e, even if a_i is already defined in the context. An identifier a_i is not used in any of the expressions e_j, $1 \leq j \leq n$. As a consequence, the order in which the definitions in a where expression occur is irrelevant.

Example 3.7.1. The expression (n **whr** $n{=}m, m{=}3$ **end**) **whr** $m{=}255$ **end** is equal to 255. The expression ($f(n, n)$ **whr** $n{=}g(m, m)$ **end**) **whr** $m{=}h(p, p)$ **end** is equal to $f(g(h(p, p), h(p, p)), g(h(p, p), h(p, p)))$.

For the construction of data terms, the following priority rules apply. The prefix operators have the highest priority, followed by the infix operators, followed by the lambda operator together with universal and existential quantification, followed by the where clause. The precise priority rules can be found in appendix D where the syntax of constructs in mcrl2 are given, including data expressions, together with priority and associativity rules.

3.8 Historical notes

Our approach to data type specification has its root in the field of universal algebra, to which [41] gives a good introduction. Universal algebra has been adopted extensively for formalization of abstract data types. A standard textbook for abstract data types is [120]. The data type specification language developed for mCRL2 is rather complex and contains ingredients (e.g., multi-sorted signature with subsorting and higher-order functions) that do not occur simultaneously in other formalisms for abstract data types.

Earlier data type specification languages in the context of process calculi, such as those of PSF [129], μCRL [34], and LOTOS [108], lacked the practicality of built-in standard data types as in mCRL2. A modern data type specification language that has some of these features is CASL [142], which is incorporated in the process-algebraic language CSP-CASL [162]. Other examples are the data type languages of E-LOTOS [53] and LOTOS-NT [169]. We defer the discussion on the historical developments in the semantics of abstract data types to chapter 15, where the semantics of all formalisms used in this book, including the data specification language, are defined precisely.

4

Sequential Processes

In chapter 2 we described behavior by labeled transition systems. If behavior becomes more complex, this technique falls short and we need a higher-level syntax to concisely describe larger labeled transition systems. In this chapter, we describe processes using an extended process algebra. The basic building blocks of our process algebra are (multi-)actions with data. We provide operators to combine behavior in both a sequential and nondeterministic way and allow it to be controlled by data parameters. Axioms are used to characterize the meaning of the various constructs.

The language that we introduce allows for the description of all reactive behavior. In the next chapter we define operators to combine behavior in a more complex way, especially using the parallel operator. But these operators do not add to the expressiveness of the language.

The sort of all processes defined in this and the next chapter is $\mathbb{P}$.

4.1 Actions

As in chapter 2, actions are the basic ingredients of processes. More precisely, every action is an elementary process. Actions can carry data. For example, a *receive* action can carry a message, and an *error* action can carry a natural number, for instance indicating its severity. Actions can have any number of parameters. They are declared as follows:

act $timeout;$
$\quad error : \mathbb{N};$
$\quad receive : \mathbb{B} \times \mathbb{N}^+;$

This declares parameterless action name *timeout*, action name *error* with a data parameter of sort $\mathbb{N}$ (natural numbers), and action name *receive* with two parameters of sort $\mathbb{B}$ (Booleans) and $\mathbb{N}^+$ (positive numbers), respectively. For the above action name declaration, *timeout*, *error*(0), and *receive*$(\mathit{false}, 6)$ are valid actions. Processes cannot appear as parameters of actions.

Actions are events that happen atomically in time. They have no duration. In case duration of activity is important, it is most convenient to think of an action as the

MA1	$\alpha\|\beta = \beta\|\alpha$
MA2	$(\alpha\|\beta)\|\gamma = \alpha\|(\beta\|\gamma)$
MA3	$\alpha\|\tau = \alpha$
MD1	$\tau \setminus \alpha = \tau$
MD2	$\alpha \setminus \tau = \alpha$
MD3	$\alpha \setminus (\beta\|\gamma) = (\alpha \setminus \beta) \setminus \gamma$
MD4	$(a(d)\|\alpha) \setminus a(d) = \alpha$
MD5	$(a(d)\|\alpha) \setminus b(e) = a(d)\|(\alpha \setminus b(e))$ if $a \not\equiv b$ or $d \not\approx e$
MS1	$\tau \sqsubseteq \alpha = \mathit{true}$
MS2	$a(d) \sqsubseteq \tau = \mathit{false}$
MS3	$a(d)\|\alpha \sqsubseteq a(d)\|\beta = \alpha \sqsubseteq \beta$
MS4	$a(d)\|\alpha \sqsubseteq b(e)\|\beta = a(d)\|(\alpha \setminus b(e)) \sqsubseteq \beta$ if $a \not\equiv b$ or $d \not\approx e$
MAN1	$\underline{\tau} = \tau$
MAN2	$\underline{a(d)} = a$
MAN3	$\underline{\alpha\|\beta} = \underline{\alpha}\|\underline{\beta}$

Table 4.1: Axioms for multi-actions

beginning of the activity. If that does not suffice, activity can be modeled by two actions that mark its beginning and end. A declaration of actions describing the beginning and end of an activity a could look like:

act a_{begin}, a_{end};

From now on, we write $a, b, \ldots$ to denote both actions and action names. In concrete models we attach the required number of data arguments to an action name in accordance with the declaration, for example, $a(1, \mathit{true})$. In more abstract treatments we let actions have only a single parameter, and we typically write $a(d)$ or $a(e)$. If we want to stress that there can be zero or more parameters, we sometimes write $a(\vec{d}), a(\vec{e}), \ldots$.

4.2 Multi-actions

Multi-actions represent a collection of actions that occur at the same time instant. Multi-actions are constructed according to the following BNF grammar. BNF stands for Backus-Naur Form which is a popular notation to denote context-free grammars.[1]

$$\alpha ::= \tau \mid a(\vec{d}) \mid \alpha|\beta,$$

[1]John Backus (1924–2007) developed the first higher level programming language Fortran. Peter Naur (1928-) worked on the development of the very influential programming language Algol 60 for which he received the Turing award.

where, as indicated above, $a(\vec{d})$ is used to stress that the action name can have zero or more data parameters, but in general we leave the small arrow denoting the vector symbol out. See for instance the axioms in table 4.1.

The term τ represents the empty multi-action, which contains no actions and as such cannot be observed. It is exactly the internal action introduced in chapter 2. The multi-action $\alpha|\beta$ consists of the actions from both the multi-actions α and β, which all must happen simultaneously.

Typical examples of multi-actions are the following: τ, $\mathit{error}|\mathit{error}|\mathit{send}(\mathit{true})$, $\mathit{send}(\mathit{true})|\mathit{receive}(\mathit{false}, 6)$, and $\tau|\mathit{error}$. We generally write $\alpha, \beta, \ldots$ as variables for multi-actions. Multi-actions are particularly interesting for parallel behavior. If sequential behavior is described, multi-actions generally do not occur.

In table 4.1 the basic properties about multi-actions are listed by defining which multi-actions are equal to each other using the equality symbol ($=$). In particular the first three are interesting, as they express that multi-actions are associative, commutative, and have τ as unit element. This structure is called a monoid.

The rest of the axioms are about three auxiliary operators. The operation $\alpha \setminus \beta$ represents the multi-action α from which all those occurring in β have been removed. Typically $(a(1)|a(2)|a(2)) \setminus a(2) = a(1)|a(2)$. The predicate $\alpha \sqsubseteq \beta$ is true iff all multi-actions in α also occur in β. The operation $\underline{\alpha}$ removes all data from the individual actions in the multi-action α.

Because multi-actions are given by the BNF above, we know the shape of all multi-actions and can use induction on the structure of multi-actions to prove properties of all multi-actions. This form of induction is in general called *structural induction*, illustrated in example 4.2.1 below. This is not always the most convenient form of induction to prove properties on multi-actions. An alternative is induction on the number of actions in a multi-action, which is illustrated in example 4.2.2.

Example 4.2.1. The following lemma $(\alpha|\beta) \setminus \beta = \alpha$ holds for all multi-actions α and β. We prove for any multi-action α that $(\alpha|\beta) \setminus \beta = \alpha$ with induction on the structure of β. Thus, there are two base cases:

$$\begin{aligned}&(\alpha|\tau) \setminus \tau = \alpha,\\ &(\alpha|a(d)) \setminus a(d) = \alpha.\end{aligned}$$

The former equation follows directly from MA3 and MD2, and the latter follows from MA1 and MD4, respectively. For the induction case we can assume that the lemma holds for smaller multi-actions and prove it for larger ones. Concretely, if we know that the induction hypotheses $(\alpha'|\beta_1)\setminus\beta_1 = \alpha'$ and $(\alpha'|\beta_2)\setminus\beta_2 = \alpha'$ for any multi-action α' hold, $(\alpha|\beta_1|\beta_2)\setminus(\beta_1|\beta_2) = \alpha$ must be proven. This can be shown as follows:

$$(\alpha|\beta_1|\beta_2) \setminus (\beta_1|\beta_2) \overset{\text{MA1, MA2, MD3}}{=} ((\alpha|\beta_2|\beta_1) \setminus \beta_1) \setminus \beta_2 \overset{i.h.}{=} (\alpha|\beta_2) \setminus \beta_2 \overset{i.h.}{=} \alpha.$$

As we have proven all induction steps, we can conclude that in general $(\alpha|\beta)\setminus\beta = \alpha$.

Example 4.2.2. It is obvious that $\alpha\setminus\alpha = \tau$. This can be most conveniently be proven by induction on the number of actions in α. If α has no actions, it must be equal to τ: $\tau\setminus\tau \overset{\text{MD2}}{=} \tau$ (cf., exercise 4.2.4 (2)). If α has at least one action, α can be written as $a(d)|\beta$ where β has less actions. So, the induction hypothesis allows us to use $\beta\backslash\beta = \tau$. Now the proof of the inductive case becomes

$$\alpha \setminus \alpha = (a(d)|\beta) \setminus (a(d)|\beta) \overset{\text{MD3}}{=} ((a(d)|\beta) \setminus a(d)) \setminus \beta \overset{\text{MD4}}{=} \beta \setminus \beta \overset{\text{i.h.}}{=} \tau.$$

As $\alpha\backslash\alpha = \tau$ has been proven for α's containing any number of actions, we can conclude it holds for all α.

There are a few operators on multi-actions that turn out to be useful. There is an operator $\underline{\alpha}$ that associates with a multi-action α the multi-set of action names that is obtained by omitting all data parameters that occur in α. We also define operators $\backslash$ and $\sqsubseteq$ on multi-actions that represents removal and inclusion of multi-actions. Here $\equiv$ denotes syntactic equality on action names and $\approx$ denotes equality on data.

Exercise 4.2.3. Simplify the following expressions using the equations in table 4.1.

1. $(a(1)|b(2))\backslash(b(2)|a(1))$.
2. $(a(1)|b(2))\backslash(b(3)|c(2))$.
3. $a(1)|b(2) \sqsubseteq b(2)$.

Exercise 4.2.4. Prove (1) and (2) below using induction on the structure of multi-actions and (3) using induction on the number of actions in α for all multi-actions α, β, and γ:

1. $(\alpha|\beta|\gamma)\backslash\beta = \alpha|\gamma$.
2. Every multi-action α can be written as either τ or $a(d)|\beta$.
3. $\alpha \sqsubseteq \alpha = \mathit{true}$.

4.3 Sequential and alternative composition

There are two main operators to combine multi-actions into behavior. These are the sequential and alternative composition operators. For processes p and q we write $p{\cdot}q$ to indicate the process that first performs the behavior of p and after p terminates, continues to behave as q. Note that the dot is often omitted when denoting concrete processes.

If a, b, and c are actions, the action a is the process that can do an a-action and then terminate. The process $a{\cdot}b$ can do an a followed by a b and then terminate. The process $a{\cdot}b{\cdot}c$ can do three actions in a row before terminating. The three processes are depicted in figure 4.1.

The process $p{+}q$ is the alternative composition of processes p and q. This expresses that either the behavior of p or that of q can be chosen. The actual choice is made by the first action in either p or q. Therefore, the process $a+b$ is the process that can either do an a or a b, and the process $a{\cdot}b + c{\cdot}d$ can either do a followed by b, or c followed by d as shown in figure 4.2. The alternative composition operator $+$ is also called the choice

A1	$x + y = y + x$
A2	$x + (y + z) = (x + y) + z$
A3	$x + x = x$
A4	$(x + y)\cdot z = x\cdot z + y\cdot z$
A5	$(x\cdot y)\cdot z = x\cdot(y\cdot z)$
A6‡	$x + \delta = x$
A7	$\delta\cdot x = \delta$
Cond1	$\mathit{true}{\rightarrow}x \diamond y = x$
Cond2	$\mathit{false}{\rightarrow}x \diamond y = y$
THEN‡	$c{\rightarrow}x = c{\rightarrow}x \diamond \delta$
SUM1	$\sum_{d:D} x = x$
SUM3	$\sum_{d:D} X(d) = X(e) + \sum_{d:D} X(d)$
SUM4	$\sum_{d:D}(X(d) + Y(d)) = \sum_{d:D} X(d) + \sum_{d:D} Y(d)$
SUM5	$(\sum_{d:D} X(d))\cdot y = \sum_{d:D} X(d)\cdot y$

Table 4.2: Axioms for the basic operators

operator. In table 4.2 some axioms are given that indicate which processes are equal to other processes. In the axioms symbols x and y are variables that can be substituted by processes. For the alternative and sequential composition, axioms A1 to A5 are particularly important. A1 and A2 say that alternative composition is commutative and associative. Practically, this means that is does not matter whether behavior stands at the left or right of the choice, and that brackets to group more than one choice operator can be omitted. An interesting axiom is A3, which says that the choice is idempotent. If a choice can be made between two identical processes, there is no choice to make at all.

Axiom A4 says that sequential composition right distributes over the choice. The left distribution, namely $x\cdot(y + z) = x\cdot y + x\cdot z$, is not valid, as it would imply that $a\cdot(b+c)$ would be equal to $a\cdot b + a\cdot c$, which are in general not behaviorally equivalent, as argued in the previous chapter (see figure 2.9). Axiom A5 says that sequential composition is associative. As such, we can as well write $a\cdot b\cdot c$ instead of $(a\cdot b)\cdot c$, as the position of the brackets is immaterial.

The axioms listed in table 4.2 and elsewhere are valid for strong bisimulation. If we provide axioms that hold for other process equivalences, this will be explicitly stated. Using the axioms, we can show that the process $a\cdot b + a\cdot b$ is equal to $a\cdot(b + b)$. This goes as follows:

$$a\cdot(b + b) \stackrel{\text{A3}}{=} a\cdot b \stackrel{\text{A3}}{=} a\cdot b + a\cdot b.$$

In the first step we take the subexpression $b + b$. It is reduced to b using axiom A3 by substituting b for x. Henceforth b is used to replace $b + b$. In the second step, axiom

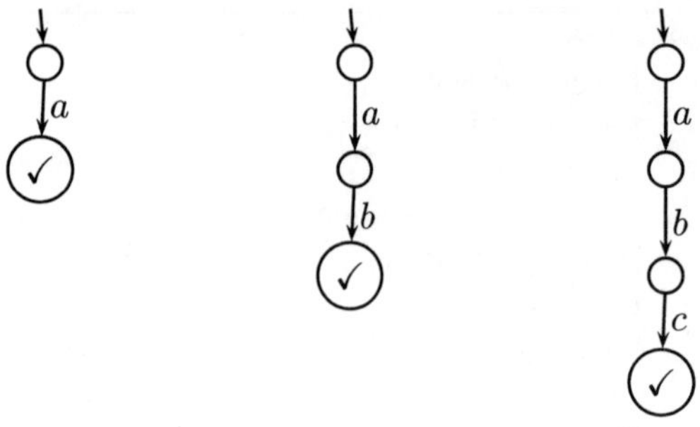

Figure 4.1: Three sequential processes

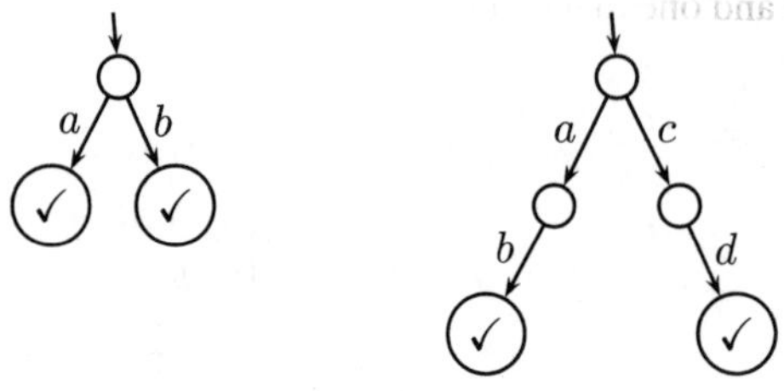

Figure 4.2: Two processes with a choice

A3 is used again, but now by taking $a{\cdot}b$ for x. Compare this to the proof in figure 2.8.

As a more elaborate example, we show that $((a+b){\cdot}c + a{\cdot}c){\cdot}d$ and $(b+a){\cdot}(c{\cdot}d)$ are equal.

$$((a+b){\cdot}c + a{\cdot}c){\cdot}d \stackrel{\text{A4}}{=} (a{\cdot}c + b{\cdot}c + a{\cdot}c){\cdot}d \stackrel{\text{A1,A3}}{=} (a{\cdot}c + b{\cdot}c){\cdot}d \stackrel{\text{A4}}{=} ((a+b){\cdot}c){\cdot}d \stackrel{\text{A5}}{=} (b+a){\cdot}(c{\cdot}d).$$

Exercise 4.3.1. Derive the following equations from axioms A1–A5:

1. $((a+a){\cdot}(b+b)){\cdot}(c+c) = a{\cdot}(b{\cdot}c)$,
2. $(a+a){\cdot}(b{\cdot}c) + (a{\cdot}b){\cdot}(c+c) = (a{\cdot}(b+b)){\cdot}(c+c)$.

We use the shorthand $x \subseteq y$ for $x+y=y$, and write $x \supseteq y$ for $y \subseteq x$. This notation is called *summand inclusion*. It is possible to divide the proof of an equation into proving two inclusions, as the following exercise shows.

Exercise 4.3.2. Prove that if $x \subseteq y$ and $y \subseteq x$, then $x = y$.

4.4 Deadlock

A remarkable but very essential process is *deadlock*, also called *inaction*. It is denoted as δ and cannot do any action. In particular, it cannot terminate. The properties of deadlock are best illustrated by the axioms A6‡ and A7 in table 4.2. Axiom A7 says that it is impossible to go beyond a deadlock. So, the x in $\delta \cdot x$ can be omitted because it cannot be reached.

The axiom A6‡ says that if we can choose between a process x and δ, we must choose x because δ has no first action that would cause the δ to be chosen. The axiom A6‡ is designated with ‡ to indicate that it is only sound in an untimed setting, i.e., in case x represents a process in which no explicit reference to time is made. If one restricts this axiom to multi-actions, i.e., $\alpha + \delta = \alpha$ with α a multi-action, one obtains a weaker axiom, called A6. Axiom A6 also holds in the timed settings as presented in chapter 8.

The deadlock can be used to prevent processes from terminating. As such, the process $a + b$ can terminate, whereas the process $a \cdot \delta + b \cdot \delta$ cannot, and $a + b \cdot \delta$ has both a terminating branch and one that cannot terminate. The tree graphs belonging to these processes are depicted below.

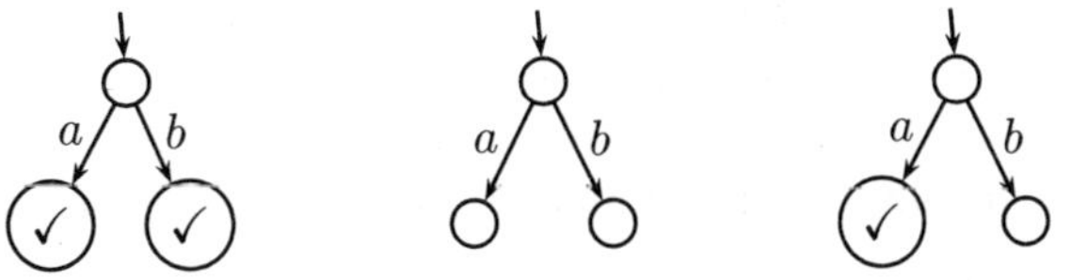

Deadlock is not used very often as a specification primitive, as specifying that a system has a deadlock is strange because this is undesired behavior. The deadlock is generally the result of some communicating parallel processes. It shows that there is some incompatibility in these processes such that at a certain moment no actions can be done anymore.

The most common use of deadlock in a specification is to prevent a process from terminating. For instance, an action *error* can be added to a specification to indicate a state that should never be reached. By generating the state space and by inspecting that the error action does not occur in it, it can be shown that the undesired state cannot indeed be reached. But often, the behavior after the *error* action is of no concern. This behavior is made unreachable by putting a deadlock after the error: $error \cdot \delta$.

Later when we introduce time, it will turn out that a stronger deadlock than δ exists. One feature of δ is that it lets time pass. The stronger variant can even let time come to a halt.

Exercise 4.4.1. Prove the following implication, assuming that x represents an untimed process.

$$x + y = \delta \text{ implies } x = \delta.$$

This implication is known as *Fer-Jan's lemma*.[2] It was the first process-algebraic identity verified using proof checkers.

[2]Fer-Jan de Vries (1956–) is a researcher in logic and semantics with a strong interest in infinitary systems.

4.5 The conditional operator

Data influences the run of processes using the conditional operator. For a condition c of sort $\mathbb{B}$ (Boolean) and processes p and q we write $c \to p \diamond q$ to express *if c then p else q*. The condition c must consist of data, and it is not allowed to use processes in c. The axioms Cond1 and Cond2 in table 4.2 are obvious. If c is $true$, then the behavior is p, and otherwise it is q.

The else part of the condition can be omitted, meaning that nothing can be done in the else part. This is expressed by the axiom THEN‡, also only valid when x does not refer to time. When x contains time, the else part must be a timed deadlock.

To say that if the water level is too high, an alarm is sounded, and otherwise an OK message is sent, is described as follows:

$$(\mathit{waterLevel}{>}\mathit{limit}) \to \mathit{soundAlarm} \diamond \mathit{sendOK}.$$

Here, $\mathit{waterLevel}$ is a local variable representing the water level.

Case distinction can also be described neatly. Suppose there is a data variable *desiredColor* which indicates which color a signal should get. Using actions such as *setSignalToRed*, the desire is transformed in actions to set the signal to the required color:

$$\begin{array}{l} \quad(\mathit{desiredColor}{\approx}\mathit{Red}) \to \mathit{setSignalToRed} \\ +\,(\mathit{desiredColor}{\approx}\mathit{Yellow}) \to \mathit{setSignalToYellow} \\ +\,(\mathit{desiredColor}{\approx}\mathit{Green}) \to \mathit{setSignalToGreen}. \end{array}$$

The axioms Cond1 and Cond2 are very handy, when used in combination with *case distinction* or *induction* on Booleans. There are exactly two Booleans, $true$ and $false$, which means that to prove a property for all Booleans, it suffices to prove it only for $true$ and $false$. More concretely, in order to show $c \to x \diamond x = x$ we must show $true \to x \diamond x = x$, which follows directly from Cond1, and $false \to x \diamond x = x$ which follows directly from Cond2.

Exercise 4.5.1. Describe a process that if a given natural number n is larger than 0, can do a $down$ action, if n is larger than 100 can perform a $too\_large\_warning$ and that can always do an up action.

Exercise 4.5.2. Derive the following equations:

1. $c \to x \diamond y = \neg c \to y \diamond x$;

2. $c \vee c' \to x \diamond y = c \to x \diamond (c' \to x \diamond y)$;

3. $x{+}y \supseteq c{\to}x{\diamond}y$;

4. if, assuming that c holds, we can prove that $x = y$, then $c \to x \diamond z = c \to y \diamond z$.

4.6 The sum operator

The sum operator $\sum_{d:D} p(d)$ is a generalization of the choice operator. The notation $p(d)$ is used to stress that d can occur in the process p. Where $p + q$ allows a choice among processes p and q, $\sum_{d:D} p(d)$ allows for a choice of $p(d)$ for any value d from D. If D is finite, for example, equal to $\mathbb{B}$, then the sum operator can be expressed using the choice. In this case the following is valid:

$$\sum_{c:\mathbb{B}} p(c) = p(true) + p(false).$$

For sums over infinite domains, for example, $\sum_{n:\mathbb{N}} p(n)$, it is no longer possible to expand the sum operator using the choice operator.

The sum operator can be used for many purposes, but the most important one is to model reading data values. Modeling a (one time usable) buffer that can read a message to be forwarded at a later moment, yields the following:

$$\textstyle\sum_{m:Message} read(m)\cdot forward(m).$$

A commonly made mistake is to not place the sum operator directly around the action in which the reading takes place. Compare the following two processes, where reading takes place with actions $read_1$ and $read_2$.

$$\textstyle\sum_{m_1:Message} read_1(m_1)\cdot \sum_{m_2:Message} read_2(m_2)\cdot forward(m_1, m_2).$$
$$\textstyle\sum_{m_1,m_2:Message} read_1(m_1)\cdot read_2(m_2)\cdot forward(m_1, m_2).$$

In the first (correct) process, the message m_2 is chosen when the action $read_2$ takes place. In the second process, the message m_2 to be read is chosen when action $read_1$ takes place. When doing $read_2$, the value to be read is already fixed. If this fixed value is not equal to the value to be read, a deadlock occurs.

The axioms for the sum operator given in table 4.2 are quite subtle. The axiom SUM2 did exist, but turned out to be a reformulation of general logic principles and has therefore been omitted. We defer full treatment of these axioms to chapter 9. In order to use them it is necessary that data variables that occur in the sum operator must not bind variables in terms that are substituted for process variables as x, y, and z. For variables written as $X(d)$ it is allowed to substitute a term with a data variable d even if d becomes bound by a surrounding sum.

Therefore, for the axiom SUM112 no process containing the variable d can be substituted for x. This is another way of saying that d does not occur in x (or more precisely, any process substituted for x). Therefore, the sum operator can be omitted, as no real choice needs to be made. This is essentially the same as what axiom A3 expresses.

Exercise 4.6.1. Specify a (one time usable) buffer that reads a natural number, and forwards it if the number is smaller than 100. Otherwise it should flag an overflow.

Exercise 4.6.2. Axioms SUM1 and SUM3 resemble the axiom A3 in the sense that if the sum ranges over a finite domain SUM1 and SUM3 can be proven using A3. With which axioms do SUM4 and SUM5 correspond?

4.7 Recursive processes

With the description of one time usable buffers in the previous section, it was already apparent that continuing behavior must also be described. This is done by introducing process variables and defining their behavior by equations. Consider the following specification, which describes the alarm clock at the left, in figure 2.2:

act $set, alarm, reset;$
proc $P = set{\cdot}Q;$
$Q = reset{\cdot}P + alarm{\cdot}Q;$

This declares process variables P and Q (often just called processes, which explains the use of the keyword **proc**). The process variable P corresponds to the situation where the alarm clock is switched off, and the process variable Q corresponds to the state where the alarm clock is set.

If in a set of equations defining a process there are only single variables at the left we speak of a *recursive specification.* The variables at the left are called the defined process variables. If every occurrence of a defined process variable at the right is preceded by an action, we speak about a *guarded recursive specification.* A guarded recursive specification defines the behavior of the process variables that occur in it. In the example given above, the behavior of P and Q is neatly defined.

The keyword **init** can be used to indicated the initial behavior. In accordance with figure 2.2, this ought to be variable P.

init $P;$

While interacting with their environment, processes store information that can later influence their behavior. For this purpose, process variables can contain parameters in which this information can be stored. Data and processes are strictly distinguished. This means that there cannot be any reference to processes in data parameters.

We can transform the alarm clock such that it sounds its alarm after a specified number of *tick* actions have happened.

act $set{:}\mathbb{N};\ alarm, reset, tick;$
proc $P = \sum_{n:\mathbb{N}} set(n){\cdot}Q(n) + tick{\cdot}P;$
$Q(n{:}\mathbb{N}) = reset{\cdot}P + (n{\approx}0) \rightarrow alarm{\cdot}Q(0) \diamond tick{\cdot}Q(n{-}1);$
init $P;$

Note that the value of n is used in process Q to determine whether an alarm must sound or whether a *tick* action is still possible.

A guarded recursive specification with data also uniquely defines a process. More precisely, it defines a function from the data parameters to processes. For example, the process Q above is actually a function from natural numbers to processes. The equation must be understood to hold for any concrete value for the parameters. Therefore, given the equation for Q above, the following are also valid by taking for n respectively 0, m, $n+1$, and $23k+7$ and simplifying the result.

$$Q(0) = reset{\cdot}P + alarm{\cdot}Q(0);$$
$$Q(m) = reset{\cdot}P + (m{\approx}0) \rightarrow alarm{\cdot}Q(0) \diamond tick{\cdot}Q(m{-}1);$$
$$Q(n{+}1) = reset{\cdot}P + tick{\cdot}Q(n);$$
$$Q(23k+7) = reset{\cdot}P + tick{\cdot}Q(23k+6).$$

Below, we describe a process that maintains an unbounded array in which natural numbers can be stored. There are actions set, get, and $show$. The action $set(n, m)$ sets the nth entry of the array to value m using the function update operator. After an action $get(n)$, an action $show(m)$ shows the value m stored at position n in the array.

act $set : \mathbb{N} \times \mathbb{N};$
$get, show : \mathbb{N};$
proc $P(a{:}\mathbb{N}\to\mathbb{N})$
$= \sum_{n,m:\mathbb{N}} set(n, m)\cdot P(a[n\to m])$
$+ \sum_{n:\mathbb{N}} get(n)\cdot show(a(n))\cdot P(a);$

Another example is the specification of a sorting machine. This machine reads arrays of natural numbers and delivers sorted arrays with exactly the same numbers. The predicate *sorted* expresses that the numbers in an array are increasing and the predicate *equalcontents* expresses that each of the arrays a and a' contain the same elements. But note that *equalcontents* does not necessarily preserve the number of occurrences of numbers.

act $read, deliver : \mathbb{N} \to \mathbb{N};$
map $sorted, equalcontents, includes : (\mathbb{N} \to \mathbb{N}) \to \mathbb{B};$
var $a, a' : \mathbb{N} \to \mathbb{N};$
eqn $sorted(a) = \forall i{:}\mathbb{N}.a(i) \leq a(i{+}1);$
$equalcontents(a, a') = includes(a, a') \wedge includes(a', a);$
$includes(a, a') = \forall i{:}\mathbb{N}.\exists j{:}\mathbb{N}.a(i) \approx a'(j);$
proc $P = \sum_{a:\mathbb{N}\to\mathbb{N}} read(a)\cdot$
$\sum_{a':\mathbb{N}\to\mathbb{N}}(sorted(a') \wedge equalcontents(a, a')) \to deliver(a')\cdot P;$

Sometimes processes have a large number of parameters. In that case it is convenient to only write changing parameters in the right-hand side of processes by an explicit assignment. The following example shows how that can be done.

proc $P(n_1, n_2, n_3{:}\mathbb{N})$
$= \sum_{m:\mathbb{N}} change\_par_1(m)\cdot P(n_1{=}m)$
$+ \sum_{m:\mathbb{N}} change\_par_2(m)\cdot P(n_2{=}m)$
$+ \sum_{m:\mathbb{N}} change\_par_3(m)\cdot P(n_3{=}m)$
$+ change\_no\_par\cdot P();$

The parameters that are not mentioned at the right side remain unchanged. Note in particular $P()$ at the end, which describes that no value of any parameters is changed.

We only allow the process assignment notation in recursive invocations at the right-hand side if the process variable of this invocation is equal to the one at the right-hand side. So, $P(n{:}\mathbb{N}) = a.Q()$ is not allowed. The reason is that the parameters of Q and P can differ making it unclear how the assignments must be interpreted.

There is a ugly snag in the use of use of assignments. Consider the process

$$P(x{:}\mathbb{N}) = \sum_{x:\mathbb{N}} a\cdot P(x{=}x)$$

To which x's do the x's in $x{=}x$ refer? The answer is that the first x in $x{=}x$ is a placeholder for a variable in the left-hand side of the equation. The second x in $x{=}x$

is an ordinary variable which is bound by its closest binder, i.e., the x in the sum. As such, the equation above must be read as

$$P(x{:}\mathbb{N}) = \sum_{y:\mathbb{N}} a{\cdot}P(x{=}y)$$

Note that this also indicates that an assignment $x{=}x$ cannot always be removed from a right-hand side. This is only possible if the x at the right-hand side refers to the parameter x of the equation.

This finishes the treatment of sequential processes. We have now seen all the operators to specify sequential behavior. Using recursion we can specify iterative behavior and by using data parameters in these equations they are suitable to describe even the most complex real-life systems.

Exercise 4.7.1. Describe the behavior of a buffer with capacity 1 that iteratively reads and forwards a message. Add the option to empty the buffer when it is full, by a specific *empty* action.

Exercise 4.7.2. Describe a simple coffee machine that accepts 5 and 10 cent coins. After receiving at least 10 cents, it asks whether cream and sugar needs to be added and then serves the desired coffee, after which it repeats itself.

Exercise 4.7.3. Adapt the predicate $\mathit{equalcontents}(a, a')$ such that it also preserves the number of occurrences of data elements, assuming that the arrays contain at most n elements. The requested predicate has the shape $\mathit{equalcontents}(a, a', n)$ with the extra element n.

★Exercise 4.7.4. Describe a coffee and tea machine that accepts coins (1 cent, 5 cents, 10 cents, 20 cents, 50 cents, 1 euro and 2 euros). Coffee costs 45 cents, tea costs 25 cents. The machine can give change, but there is a limited amount of coins (it knows exactly how many). Develop a way to accept coins, return change, and deliver beverages when the machine is low on cash.

4.8 Axioms for the internal action

The axioms provided hitherto in this chapter are valid for strong bisimulation. If we want to remove internal actions while transforming and simplifying processes, we need axioms to get rid of the internal action. These are provided in this section.

In the context of rooted branching bisimulation, the axioms in table 4.3 can be used, provided no time is used in x, y, and z, which as elsewhere is indicated by the use of ‡. The axiom W‡ is pretty obvious. It says that a trailing τ after a process can be omitted. The axiom BRANCH‡ is more intriguing and is generally seen as the typical axiom for branching bisimulation. It says that behavior does not have to be apparent at once, but may gradually become visible. Concretely, instead of seeing $y + z$ at once, it is possible to first see the behavior of y, and after some internal rumble (read τ), the total behavior of $y + z$ becomes visible.

W‡	$x \cdot \tau = x$
BRANCH‡	$x \cdot (\tau \cdot (y + z) + y) = x \cdot (y + z)$

Table 4.3: Axioms for τ valid in rooted branching bisimulation for untimed processes

W‡	$x \cdot \tau = x$
W2‡	$\tau \cdot x = \tau \cdot x + x$
W3‡	$x \cdot (\tau \cdot y + z) = x \cdot (\tau \cdot y + z) + x \cdot y$

Table 4.4: Axioms for τ valid in rooted weak bisimulation for untimed processes

The characterizing axioms for rooted weak bisimulation are found in table 4.4. These are also only valid in an untimed setting.

All equivalences in the Van Glabbeek spectrum have their equational characterization. In table 4.5, axiomatic characterizations are provided for failures equivalence, trace equivalence, language equivalence, and weak trace equivalence. Note that the axioms for trace and weak trace equivalence also hold for timed processes.

Failures equivalence	F1‡	$a \cdot (b \cdot x + u) + a \cdot (b \cdot y + v) = a \cdot (b \cdot x + b \cdot y + u) + a \cdot (b \cdot x + b \cdot y + v)$
	F2‡	$a \cdot x + a \cdot (y + z) = a \cdot x + a \cdot (x + y) + a \cdot (y + z)$
Trace equivalence	RDIS	$x \cdot (y + z) = x \cdot y + x \cdot z$
Language equivalence	Lang1‡	$x \cdot \delta = \delta$
	RDIS	$x \cdot (y + z) = x \cdot y + x \cdot z$
Weak trace equivalence	RDIS	$x \cdot (y + z) = x \cdot y + x \cdot z$
	WT‡	$\tau \cdot x = x$
	W‡	$x \cdot \tau = x$

Table 4.5: Axioms for some other equivalences for untimed processes

Exercise 4.8.1. Derive the following equations using the axioms valid in rooted branching bisimulation.

1. $a \cdot (\tau \cdot b + b) = a \cdot b$;
2. $a \cdot (\tau \cdot (b + c) + b) = a \cdot (\tau \cdot (b + c) + c)$;
3. If $y \subseteq x$, then $\tau \cdot (\tau \cdot x + y) = \tau \cdot x$.

See exercise 4.3.2 for the definition of $\subseteq$.

Exercise 4.8.2. Derive the axioms for rooted branching bisimulation from those for rooted weak bisimulation. Similarly, derive the axioms for rooted weak and branching bisimulation from those of weak trace equivalence.

4.9 Historical notes

Our notation for sequential processes stems from the algebra of communicating processes [25] (for an overview see [18, 59]). We essentially presented here basic process algebra (BPA), also called context-free process algebra, consisting of actions and the alternative- and sequential-composition operator. Basic process algebra is interesting because it strongly resembles context-free grammars. Remarkably, all bisimulations are (efficiently) decidable for such processes, whereas all other equivalences are undecidable [78] (cf. section 10.4). Note that the use of a general sequential composition is not common. Most process algebras use an action prefix operator $a{:}p$ which is theoretically much simpler.

To this basic language the constant δ was added (denoted as NIL, $STOP$, or **0** elsewhere [12, 103, 135, 137]). As the axioms A6 and A7 suggest, the constant δ in process algebra has similar properties to the number 0 in number theory, and hence, investigations started to add a constant behaving like 1. This constant is denoted as ϵ or **1** and satisfies equations $\epsilon{\cdot}x{=}x$ and $x{\cdot}\epsilon{=}x$ [177]. It has even been tried to merge the properties of δ and ϵ but that has never been very successful [138]. We have not added ϵ because it combines badly with time. With a constant ϵ it would be easy to write $c{\to}p \diamond \epsilon$, saying that if c holds, then p must be executed, and otherwise the process must terminate to continue with subsequent behavior. This is not that easily possible without this constant.

Combining data and processes was generally done in an ad hoc way in the early days of process algebras. Exceptions were process-algebraic specification languages, such as LOTOS [69, 108] and PSF [129]. The use of some form of conditional or if-then-else operator has been very common. The notation that we use looks quite like the one used in the guarded command language [112]. In μCRL, and several languages related to CSP, the conditional was denoted as $p \lhd c \rhd q$ [85].

The use of a sum operator over possibly infinite domains is relatively rare. More often the sum is restricted to finite domains only [69, 129]. The generality of our operator allows it to be used for several purposes, in particular for reading inputs from unbounded domains. A popular alternative for this is the use of input and output actions, often written as $a!3$ and $a?x{:}\mathbb{N}$, meaning that the value 3 is sent via channel a, and a value received via channel a is put into variable x [93]. In [121] it was proven that the expressivity of input/output actions is strictly less than that of the sum operator, which coincides with our experience that the unbounded sum operator is far more versatile. In combination with only the conditional operator it is straightforward to describe input and output with constraints, select minimal or maximal values from the input, or describe detailed timed behavior. The axioms that we provide here were first proposed in [84] and strongly influenced by the encoding of μCRL in Coq [29].

There are completely different approaches to incorporate data in processes. As one particular curiosity we mention process algebras with signals and state operators [14].

In mCRL2 there is a strict distinction between data and processes. Processes cannot be used in data, especially not in conditions; processes cannot be sent around through channels either. This restriction can be relaxed, leading to a whole new family of higher order process calculi such as CHOCS [171] and the higher order π-calculus [164]. In such process calculi, not only can processes be sent around; but they can also be run by receiving processes.

The axioms for weak bisimulation were provided in [135], those for branching bisimulation stem from [73]. An abundance of axioms for weaker equivalences can be found in [71, 72]. The use of guarded recursive equations with unique solutions is typical for ACP [18, 25].

5

Parallel Processes

In chapter 4, we showed how it is possible to describe sequential processes that can interact with their environment. In this chapter we describe how to put these in parallel to describe and study the interaction between different processes.

The actions in two parallel processes happen independently of each other. Recall that we consider actions as atomic events in time. Hence, an action from the first process can happen before, after, or simultaneously with an action of the second process. This view on how parallel actions happen is called interleaving. Below we first discuss processes that do not interact. In the subsequent sections, we show how actions that happen simultaneously can be synchronized. By synchronizing data values, they can pass information to each other. In this way, communication of data values is modeled.

5.1 The parallel operator

The parallel composition of two processes p and q is denoted by $p \parallel q$, and the binary (infix) operator $\parallel$ is called the *parallel operator*. This means that the actions in p happen independently of those in q. The process $p \parallel q$ terminates if both p and q can terminate. Three processes can simply be put in parallel by writing $p \parallel q \parallel r$. We require the parallel operator to be commutative and associative, and hence, the brackets around the parallel composition of several processes can be omitted. Typically, parallel processes are depicted as follows, where the arrows indicate how processes communicate.

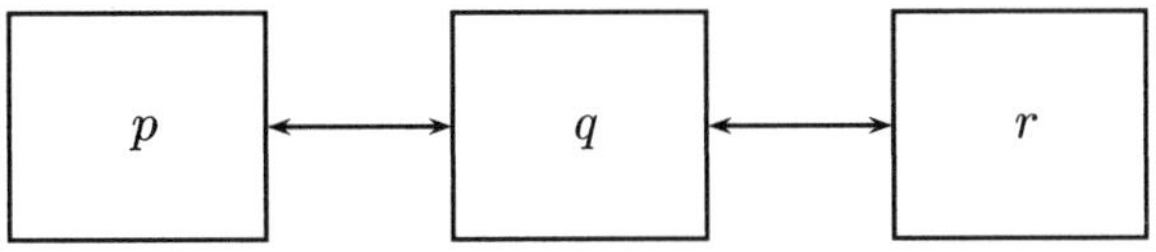

In table 5.1 the axioms governing the behavior of processes are found. It turns out that it is only possible to give a finite set of axioms, if auxiliary operators are introduced. The necessary operators are the leftmerge ($\lfloor\!\lfloor$) and the synchronization merge ($|$).

The process $p \lfloor\!\lfloor q$ (say p left merge q) is almost the same as the process $p \parallel q$ except that the first action must come from p.

M	$x \parallel y = x \mathbin{⌊\!⌊} y + y \mathbin{⌊\!⌊} x + x \mid y$
LM1‡	$\alpha \mathbin{⌊\!⌊} x = \alpha \cdot x$
LM2‡	$\delta \mathbin{⌊\!⌊} x = \delta$
LM3‡	$\alpha \cdot x \mathbin{⌊\!⌊} y = \alpha \cdot (x \parallel y)$
LM4	$(x + y) \mathbin{⌊\!⌊} z = x \mathbin{⌊\!⌊} z + y \mathbin{⌊\!⌊} z$
LM5	$(\sum_{d:D} X(d)) \mathbin{⌊\!⌊} y = \sum_{d:D} X(d) \mathbin{⌊\!⌊} y$
S1	$x \mid y = y \mid x$
S2	$(x \mid y) \mid z = x \mid (y \mid z)$
S3	$x \mid \tau = x$
S4	$\alpha \mid \delta = \delta$
S5	$(\alpha \cdot x) \mid \beta = \alpha \mid \beta \cdot x$
S6	$(\alpha \cdot x) \mid (\beta \cdot y) = \alpha \mid \beta \cdot (x \parallel y)$
S7	$(x + y) \mid z = x \mid z + y \mid z$
S8	$(\sum_{d:D} X(d)) \mid y = \sum_{d:D} X(d) \mid y$
TC1	$(x \mathbin{⌊\!⌊} y) \mathbin{⌊\!⌊} z = x \mathbin{⌊\!⌊} (y \parallel z)$
TC2	$x \mathbin{⌊\!⌊} \delta = x \cdot \delta$
TC3	$(x \mid y) \mathbin{⌊\!⌊} z = x \mid (y \mathbin{⌊\!⌊} z)$

Table 5.1: Axioms for the parallel composition operators

The process $p|q$ (say p synchronizes with q) is also the same as the process $p \parallel q$, except that the first action must happen simultaneously in p and q. Note that the symbol that we use for synchronization between processes, is the same as the symbol used for combination of actions to multi-actions. Although these are two different operators, we use them interchangeably as their meaning in both cases is the same. More concretely, $a|b$ both represents a multi-action and a synchronization of two processes both consisting of a single action.

The axiom marked M in table 5.1 characterizes our view on parallelism. The first action in $x \parallel y$ can come from x, come from y, or can be an action that happens simultaneously in both of them. Axioms LM1‡ and LM3‡ state that the multi-action α must happen before any in the process x (and y) must do an action. Axiom LM2‡ expresses that a first action cannot come from δ. LM4 and LM5 indicate how parallel composition distributes over the sum and choice operator. The axioms that start with S allow the communication merge to be eliminated.

As done elsewhere, the axioms that are only valid in an untimed setting are marked with a ‡. The variants valid in a timed setting can be found in chapter 8.

Consider the following process $a{\cdot}b \parallel c{\cdot}d$. Using the axioms in table 5.1, except TC1, TC2, and TC3, it is possible to remove parallel operators from expressions without variables and recursive behavior in favor of the operators from chapter 4. This is called parallel expansion. We get:

$$
\begin{aligned}
& a{\cdot}b \parallel c{\cdot}d \overset{\text{M}}{=} \\
& a{\cdot}b \mathbin{⌊\!⌊} c{\cdot}d + c{\cdot}d \mathbin{⌊\!⌊} a{\cdot}b + a{\cdot}b|c{\cdot}d \overset{\text{LM3‡,S6}}{=} \\
& a{\cdot}(b \parallel c{\cdot}d) + c{\cdot}(a{\cdot}b \parallel d) + a{\cdot}b|c{\cdot}d \overset{\text{M}}{=} \\
& a{\cdot}(b \mathbin{⌊\!⌊} c{\cdot}d + c{\cdot}d \mathbin{⌊\!⌊} b + b|c{\cdot}d) + c{\cdot}(a{\cdot}b \mathbin{⌊\!⌊} d + d \mathbin{⌊\!⌊} a{\cdot}b + a{\cdot}b|d) + \\
& \qquad (a|c){\cdot}(b \parallel d) \overset{\text{LM1‡,LM3‡,S6,M}}{=} \\
& a{\cdot}(b{\cdot}c{\cdot}d + c{\cdot}(b \parallel d) + (b|c){\cdot}d) + c{\cdot}(a{\cdot}(b \parallel d) + \\
& \qquad d{\cdot}a{\cdot}b + (a|d){\cdot}b) + (a|c){\cdot}(b \mathbin{⌊\!⌊} d + d \mathbin{⌊\!⌊} b + b|d) \overset{\text{M,LM1‡}}{=} \\
& a{\cdot}(b{\cdot}c{\cdot}d + c{\cdot}(b{\cdot}d + d{\cdot}b + b|d) + (b|c){\cdot}d) + c{\cdot}(a{\cdot}(b{\cdot}d + d{\cdot}b + b|d) + \\
& \qquad d{\cdot}a{\cdot}b + (a|d){\cdot}b) + (a|c){\cdot}(b{\cdot}d + d{\cdot}b + b|d)
\end{aligned}
$$

In this expansion quite a number of axioms have been applied each time. Expansion is a very time-consuming activity that shows how many options are possible when parallel behavior is involved. Later on, we treat ways to get rid of the parallel operator, without getting entangled in an axiomatic parallel expansion. Although not evident from the expansion above, parallel processes have a very typical structure, which becomes clear if the behavior is plotted in a labeled transition system (see figure 5.1).

The axioms TC1, TC2, and TC3 are called axioms of true concurrency. They are useful to simplify expressions with parallel operators and variables.

The synchronization operator binds stronger than all other binary operators. The parallel composition and left merge bind stronger than the sum and choice operator but weaker than the conditional operator.

Exercise 5.1.1. Expand the process $a{\cdot}b \parallel c$. Indicate precisely which axioms have been used.

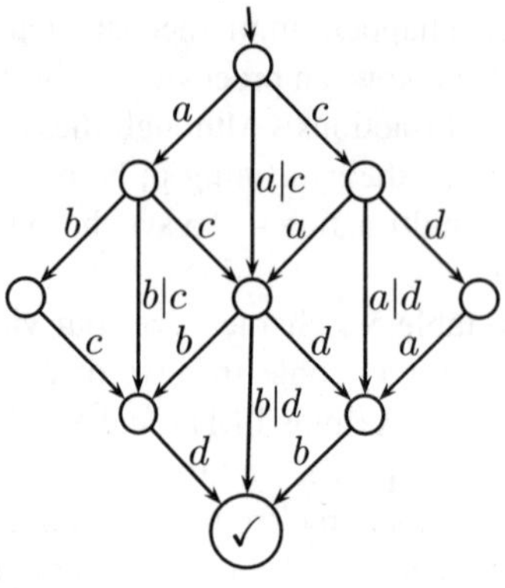

Figure 5.1: The behavior of $a \cdot b \parallel c \cdot d$

Exercise 5.1.2. Give a rough estimate the size of the expansion of $a \cdot a \cdot a \parallel b \cdot b \cdot b \parallel c \cdot c \cdot c$.

Exercise 5.1.3. Prove that the parallel operator is both commutative and associative, i.e., $x \parallel y = y \parallel x$ and $x \parallel (y \parallel z) = (x \parallel y) \parallel z$.

5.2 Communication among parallel processes

Processes that are put in parallel can execute actions simultaneously, resulting in multi-actions. The communication operator $\Gamma_C(p)$ takes some actions out of a multi-action and replaces them with a single action, provided their data is equal. In this way it is made clear that these actions communicate or synchronize. Here C is a set of allowed communications of the form $a_1|\cdots|a_n \rightarrow c$, with $n > 1$ and a_i and c are action names. For each communication $a_1|\cdots|a_n \rightarrow c$, the part of a multi-action consisting of $a_1(d)|\cdots|a_n(d)$ (for some d) in p is replaced by $c(d)$. Note that the data parameter must be equal for all communicating actions, and this data parameter is retained in action c. For example

$$\Gamma_{\{a|b \rightarrow c\}}(a(0)|b(0)) = c(0) \text{ and}$$
$$\Gamma_{\{a|b \rightarrow c\}}(a(0)|b(0)|d(0)) = c(0)|d(0).$$

If data parameters of synchronizing actions are not equal, no communication takes place: $\Gamma_{\{a|b \rightarrow c\}}(a(0)|b(1)) = a(0)|b(1)$. The axioms for the communication operator are given in table 5.2.

The function $\gamma_C(\alpha)$ applies the communications described by C to a multi-action α. It replaces every occurrence of a left-hand side of a communication it can find in α

C1 $\Gamma_C(\alpha) = \gamma_C(\alpha)$	C4 $\Gamma_C(x \cdot y) = \Gamma_C(x) \cdot \Gamma_C(y)$
C2 $\Gamma_C(\delta) = \delta$	C5 $\Gamma_C(\sum_{d:D} X(d)) = \sum_{d:D} \Gamma_C(X(d))$
C3 $\Gamma_C(x+y) = \Gamma_C(x)+\Gamma_C(y)$	

Table 5.2: Axioms for the communication operator

with the appropriate result. More precisely:

$$\begin{array}{lcl}
\gamma_\emptyset(\alpha) & = & \alpha \\
\gamma_{C_1 \cup C_2}(\alpha) & = & \gamma_{C_1}(\gamma_{C_2}(\alpha)) \\
\gamma_{\{a_1 \mid \cdots \mid a_n \to b\}}(\alpha) & = & \left\{ \begin{array}{ll} b(d) \mid \gamma_{\{a_1 \mid \cdots \mid a_n \to b\}}(\alpha \setminus (a_1(d)| \cdots |a_n(d))) & \\ \quad \text{if } a_1(d)| \cdots |a_n(d) \sqsubseteq \alpha \text{ for some } d. & \\ \alpha \quad \text{otherwise.} & \end{array} \right.
\end{array}$$

For example, $\gamma_{\{a|b \to c\}}(a|a|b|c) = a|c|c$ and $\gamma_{\{a|a \to a, b|c|d \to e\}}(a|b|a|d|c|a) = a|a|e$.

An action cannot occur in two left-hand sides of allowed communications (e.g., $C = \{a|b \to c, a|d \to e\}$ is not allowed) and a right-hand side of a communication cannot occur in a left-hand side. Otherwise, $\gamma_{C_1}(\gamma_{C_2}(\alpha)) = \gamma_{C_2}(\gamma_{C_1}(\alpha))$ would not necessarily hold. In that case, $\gamma_{C_1 \cup C_2}(\alpha)$ is not uniquely defined and γ_C would not be a properly defined function.

When there are variables being used in actions, it cannot always directly be determined whether communication can take place. Consider

$$\Gamma_{\{a|b \to c\}}(a(d)|b(e)). \tag{5.1}$$

In order to determine whether a and b can communicate, it must be determined whether d and e are equal. Using $x = c' \to x \diamond x$ (see section 4.5) with $c' = d \approx e$, we rewrite process (5.1) to

$$\Gamma_{\{a|b \to c\}}((d \approx e) \to (a(d)|b(e)) \diamond (a(d)|b(e))).$$

Now the communication can be applied to both sides, obtaining

$$(d \approx e) \to c(d) \diamond (a(d)|b(e)),$$

which can also be written as

$$(d \approx e) \to c(d) + (d \not\approx e) \to (a(d)|b(e)).$$

Exercise 5.2.1. Use the axioms for the communication operator to simplify the following process expressions.

1. $\Gamma_{\{a|b \to c\}}(a(1)|b(1)|d)$.
2. $\Gamma_{\{a|b \to c\}}(a(1)|b(2)|b(1))$.
3. $\Gamma_{\{a|b \to c\}}(a(d_1, d_2)|b(e_1, e_2))$.

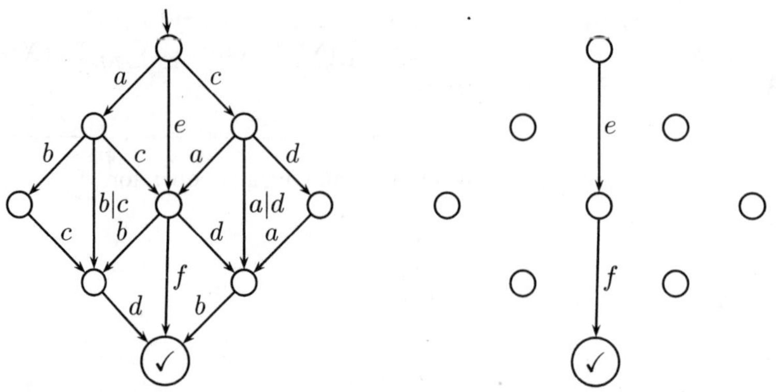

Figure 5.2: The behavior of $\Gamma_{\{a|c\to e, b|d\to f\}}(a{\cdot}b \| c{\cdot}d)$, also with application of $\nabla_{\{e,f\}}$

Exercise 5.2.2. If the communications in the communication operator use the same actions in the left-hand sides, then the communication operator is not well defined. Show that

$$\Gamma_{\{a|b\to c, a|d\to e\}}(a|b|d)$$

can be simplified to two nonbisimilar processes. Similarly, if the right-hand side of a communication overlaps with a left-hand side, more outcomes are possible. Show also that

$$\Gamma_{\{a|b\to c, c|d\to e\}}(a|b|d)$$

can be simplified to nonbisimilar processes.

5.3 The allow operator

The communication operator lets actions communicate when their data parameters are equal. However, it cannot enforce communication. In order to enforce communication, we must explicitly allow those actions the result of communications, and implicitly block other actions.

The *allow operator* $\nabla_V(p)$ is used for this purpose, where V is a set of multi-action names that specifies exactly which multi-actions from p are allowed to occur. For example $\nabla_{\{a,a|b\}}(a|b + a + b) = a + a|b$. The operator $\nabla_V(p)$ ignores the data parameters of the multi-actions in p, for example, $\nabla_{\{b|c\}}(b(\mathit{true}, 5)|c) = b(\mathit{true}, 5)|c$. The empty multi-action τ is not allowed to occur in the set V because it cannot be blocked.

The axioms are given in table 5.3. Axioms V1 and V2 express how actions are allowed and blocked. Axiom TV1 allows complex constellations of allow expressions to be simplified. All other axioms say that the allow operator distributes through a process expression.

Consider again the process $a{\cdot}b \| c{\cdot}d$ as depicted in figure 5.1. Assume that we want to ensure that action a communicates with c to e and b communicates with d to f. Then

V1	$\nabla_V(\alpha) = \alpha$ if $\underline{\alpha}\in V\cup\{\tau\}$	V4	$\nabla_V(x+y) = \nabla_V(x) + \nabla_V(y)$
V2	$\nabla_V(\alpha) = \delta$ if $\underline{\alpha}\notin V\cup\{\tau\}$	V5	$\nabla_V(x{\cdot}y) = \nabla_V(x){\cdot}\nabla_V(y)$
V3	$\nabla_V(\delta) = \delta$	V6	$\nabla_V(\sum_{d:D} X(d)) = \sum_{d:D} \nabla_V(X(d))$
TV1	$\nabla_V(\nabla_W(x)) = \nabla_{V\cap W}(x)$		

Table 5.3: Axioms for the allow operator

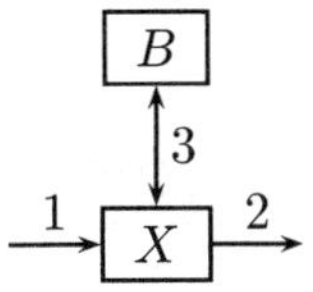

Figure 5.3: A buffer with a temporary store

we can first apply the operator $\Gamma_{\{a|c\to e, b|d\to f\}}$ to this process. We get the state space as depicted in figure 5.2 at the left. As a next operation, we say that we only allow communications e and f to occur, effectively blocking all (multi-)actions in which an a, b, c, or d occurs. The labeled transition system in figure 5.2 at the right belongs to the expression $\nabla_{\{e,f\}}(\Gamma_{\{a|c\to e, b|d\to f\}}(a{\cdot}b \parallel c{\cdot}d))$.

As a more realistic example, we describe a system with a switching buffer X and a temporary store B, depicted in figure 5.3. Data elements can be received by X via gate 1. An incoming datum is either sent on via gate 2, or stored in a one-place buffer B via gate 3. For sending an action via gate i, we use the action s_i, and for receiving data via gate i, we use r_i.

The processes X and B are defined as follows:

act $r_1, s_2, s_3, r_3, c_3{:}D;$
proc $X = \sum_{d:D}(r_1(d) + r_3(d)){\cdot}(s_2(d) + s_3(d)){\cdot}X;$
$\quad B = \sum_{d:D} r_3(d){\cdot}s_3(d){\cdot}B;$

Consider the behavior $S = \nabla_{\{r_1,s_2,c_3\}}(\Gamma_{\{r_3|s_3\to c_3\}}(X \parallel B))$. In order to depict the labeled transition system, we let D be equal to $\{d_1, d_2\}$. In figure 5.4, the behavior of the processes X, B, and S are drawn. Note that it is somewhat tedious to combine the behavior of X and B and apply the communication and allow operator. In subsequent chapters we will provide different techniques to do this.

As we have the transition system of S, we can answer a few questions about its behavior. For instance, it is obvious that there are no deadlocks. It is also easy to see that reading at gate 1 and delivery at gate 2 does not necessarily have to take place in sequence. Reading more than two times at gate 1 without any intermediate delivery at gate 2 is also not possible. The system S can store at most two data elements.

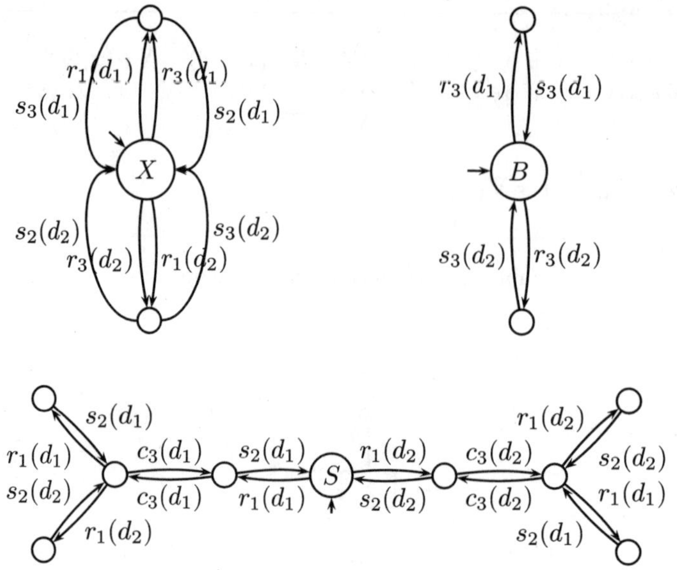

Figure 5.4: The LTSs of X, B, and $\nabla_{\{r_1,s_2,c_3\}}(\Gamma_{\{r_3|s_3\to c_3\}}(X \parallel B))$

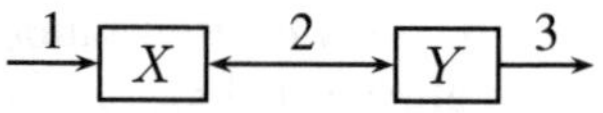

Figure 5.5: Two one-place buffers

Exercise 5.3.1. Consider the architecture depicted in figure 5.5. Data elements (from a set D) can be received by a one-place buffer X via gate 1, in which case they are sent on to a one-place buffer Y via gate 2. Y either forwards an incoming datum via gate 3, or it returns this datum to X via gate 2. In the latter case, X returns the datum to Y via gate 2.

X and Y are defined by the following recursive specification:

act $r_1, s_2, r_2, c_2, s_3{:}D;$
proc $X = \sum_{d:D}(r_1(d) + r_2(d))\cdot s_2(d)\cdot X;$
$\quad Y = \sum_{d:D} r_2(d)\cdot(s_3(d) + s_2(d))\cdot Y;$

Let S denote $\nabla_{\{r_1,c_2,s_3\}}(\Gamma_{\{s_2|r_2\to c_2\}}(X \parallel Y))$, and let D consist of $\{d_1, d_2\}$.

1. Draw the state space of S.
2. Are data elements read via gate 1 and sent in the same order via gate 3?
3. Does $\nabla_{\{r_1,c_2\}}(S)$ contain a deadlock? If yes, give an execution trace to a deadlock state.

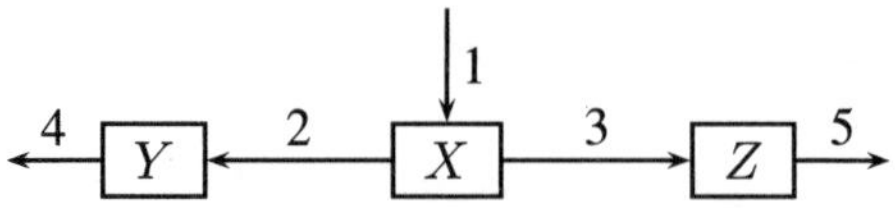

Figure 5.6: Three one place buffers

Exercise 5.3.2. Consider the architecture in figure 5.6. Data elements (from a set D) can be received by a one-place buffer X via gate 1, in which case they are sent on in an alternating fashion to one-place buffers Y and Z via gates 2 and 3, respectively. So the first received datum is sent to Y, the second to Z, the third to Y, etc. Y and Z send on incoming data elements via gates 4 and 5, respectively.

1. Specify the independent processes X, Y, and Z and the parallel composition with the right communication and allow functions around it.

2. Let D consist of a single element. Draw the state space.

5.4 Blocking and renaming

The *blocking operator* $\partial_B(p)$ (also known as the *encapsulation operator*) has the opposite effect of the allow operator. The set B contains action names that are not allowed. Any multi-action containing an action name in B is blocked. Blocking $\partial_B(p)$ does not have an effect on the data parameters of the actions in p when determining whether an action should be blocked. For example, $\partial_{\{b\}}(a(0) + b(\mathit{true}, 5)|c) = a(0)$. The blocking operator is sometimes used as an auxiliary operator, by blocking certain actions when analyzing processes. For instance blocking the possibility to lose messages allows to get insight into the good weather behavior of a communication protocol more easily. The blocking operator is characterized by the axioms in table 5.4.

E1	$\partial_B(\tau) = \tau$	E5	$\partial_B(\delta) = \delta$
E2	$\partial_B(a(d)) = a(d)$ if $a \notin B$	E6	$\partial_B(x + y) = \partial_B(x) + \partial_B(y)$
E3	$\partial_B(a(d)) = \delta$ if $a \in B$	E7	$\partial_B(x \cdot y) = \partial_B(x) \cdot \partial_B(y)$
E4	$\partial_B(\alpha\|\beta) = \partial_B(\alpha)\|\partial_B(\beta)$	E8	$\partial_B(\sum_{d:D} X(d)) = \sum_{d:D} \partial_B(X(d))$
E10	$\partial_H(\partial_{H'}(x)) = \partial_{H \cup H'}(x)$		

Table 5.4: Axioms for the blocking operator

The *Renaming operator* ρ_R is used to rename action names. The set R contains renamings of the form $a \rightarrow b$. For a process $\rho_R(p)$, this means that every occurrence of action name a in p is replaced by action name b. Renaming $\rho_R(p)$ also disregards the data parameters. When a renaming is applied, then the data parameters are retained, for example, $\rho_{\{a \to b\}}(a(0) + a) = b(0) + b$. To avoid ambiguities, every action name may only occur once as a left-hand side of $a \to b$ in R. All renamings are applied simultaneously, i.e., a renamed action cannot be renamed twice in one application of the renaming operator. Thus, $\rho_{\{a \to b, b \to c\}}$ renames action label a to b, not to c. The axioms are given in table 5.5.

R1	$\rho_R(\tau) = \tau$	
R2	$\rho_R(a(d)) = b(d)$	if $a \to b \in R$ for some b
R3	$\rho_R(a(d)) = a(d)$	if $a \to b \notin R$ for all b
R4	$\rho_R(\alpha \mid \beta) = \rho_R(\alpha) \mid \rho_R(\beta)$	
R5	$\rho_R(\delta) = \delta$	
R6	$\rho_R(x + y) = \rho_R(x) + \rho_R(y)$	
R7	$\rho_R(x \cdot y) = \rho_R(x) \cdot \rho_R(y)$	
R8	$\rho_R(\sum_{d:D} X(d)) = \sum_{d:D} \rho_R(X(d))$	

Table 5.5: Axioms for the renaming operator

Exercise 5.4.1. Simplify the following expressions.

1. $\partial_{\{a\}}(a + b + a \mid b)$.
2. $\rho_{\{a \to b\}}(a + b + a \mid b)$.
3. $\rho_{\{a \to b\}}(\partial_{\{a,b\}}(a + b + a \mid b))$.

5.5 Hiding internal behavior

As indicated in the previous chapter, hiding information is very important to obtain insight in the behavior of processes. For this purpose the *hiding operator* τ_I is used. The action names in the set I are removed from multi-actions. Therefore, $\tau_{\{a\}}(a \mid b) = b$ and $\tau_{\{a\}}(a) = \tau$. The axioms for hiding are listed in table 5.6.

It is convenient to be able to postpone hiding of actions, by first renaming them to a special visible action int which is subsequently renamed to τ. For this purpose, the straightforward *prehide operator* Υ_U is defined, where U is a set of action labels. All actions with labels in U are renamed to the action int and the data is removed. The important property of the prehide operator is that $\tau_{I \cup \{int\}}(x) = \tau_{\{int\}}(\Upsilon_I(x))$. The axioms for the prehide operator are given in table 5.7.

As an example we apply hiding to the example in section 5.2 with a switching buffer and a temporary store. We may be interested in the communication at gates 1 and 2, but we are not interested how X and B exchange information on gate 3. Therefore, we hide the action c_3. Thus, we are interested in the behavior of $\tau_{\{c_3\}}(S)$. In the first labeled transition system in figure 5.7, the hiding operator has been applied to the

H1	$\tau_I(\tau) = \tau$	H5	$\tau_I(\delta) = \delta$
H2	$\tau_I(a(d)) = \tau$ if $a \in I$	H6	$\tau_I(x+y) = \tau_I(x) + \tau_I(y)$
H3	$\tau_I(a(d)) = a(d)$ if $a \notin I$	H7	$\tau_I(x \cdot y) = \tau_I(x) \cdot \tau_I(y)$
H4	$\tau_I(\alpha\|\beta) = \tau_I(\alpha)\|\tau_I(\beta)$	H8	$\tau_I(\sum_{d:D} X(d)) = \sum_{d:D} \tau_I(X(d))$
H10	$\tau_I(\tau_{I'}(x)) = \tau_{I \cup I'}(x)$		

Table 5.6: Axioms for the hiding operator

U1	$\Upsilon_U(\tau) = \tau$	U5	$\Upsilon_U(\delta) = \delta$
U2	$\Upsilon_U(a(d)) = int$ if $a \in U$	U6	$\Upsilon_U(x+y) = \Upsilon_U(x) + \Upsilon_U(y)$
U3	$\Upsilon_U(a(d)) = a(d)$ if $a \notin U$	U7	$\Upsilon_U(x \cdot y) = \Upsilon_U(x) \cdot \Upsilon_U(y)$
U4	$\Upsilon_U(\alpha\|\beta) = \Upsilon_U(\alpha)\|\Upsilon_U(\beta)$	U8	$\Upsilon_U(\sum_{d:D} X(d)) = \sum_{d:D} \Upsilon_U(X(d))$
U10	$\Upsilon_U(\Upsilon_{U'}(x)) = \Upsilon_{U \cup U'}(x)$		

Table 5.7: Axioms for the prehiding operator

behavior as given in figure 5.4. In the second transition system, the states connected with τ's have been joined, because they are branching bisimilar.

Exercise 5.5.1. Consider the labeled transition system drawn for the system in exercise 5.3.1 where c_2 is hidden. Draw this transition system modulo branching bisimulation. Would it make sense to reduce this transition system further using weak bisimulation or weak trace equivalence?

5.6 ★Alphabet axioms

The parallel operator and its associated operators such as the hiding and the allow operator have many relations that can fruitfully be exploited. These are for instance useful when performing a parallel expansion. By distributing the communication and allow operator as far as possible over the parallel operator, the generation of many multi-actions that will be blocked anyhow can be avoided, substantially reducing the size of the calculation.

These relations are characterized by the so-called alphabet axioms. The reason is that they are very dependent on the action labels that occur in a process. The set of action names in a process p is often called its alphabet and denoted by $\alpha(p)$ and is defined as follows on basic processes.

VL1	$\nabla_V(x)=x$	if $\alpha(x)\subseteq V$
VL2	$\nabla_V(x\|y)=\nabla_V(x\|\nabla_{V'}(y))$	if $\Downarrow(V)\subseteq V'$
DL1	$\partial_H(x)=x$	if $H\cap\mathcal{N}(\alpha(x))=\emptyset$
DL2	$\partial_H(x\|y)=\partial_H(x)\|\partial_H(y)$	
TL1	$\tau_I(x)=x$	if $I\cap\mathcal{N}(\alpha(x))=\emptyset$
TL2	$\tau_I(x\|y)=\tau_I(x)\|\tau_I(y)$	
CL1	$\Gamma_C(x)=x$	if $\mathit{dom}(C)\cap\Downarrow(\alpha(x))=\emptyset$
CL2	$\Gamma_C(\Gamma_{C'}(x))=\Gamma_{C\cup C'}(x)$	if $\mathcal{N}(\mathit{dom}(C))\cap\mathcal{N}(\mathit{dom}(C'))=\emptyset\wedge$ $\mathcal{N}(\mathit{dom}(C))\cap\mathit{rng}(C')=\emptyset$
CL3	$\Gamma_C(x\|y)=x\|\Gamma_C(y)$	if $\Downarrow(\mathit{dom}(C))\cap\Downarrow(\alpha(x))=\emptyset$
CL4	$\Gamma_C(x\|y)=\Gamma_C(x\|\Gamma_C(y))$	if $\mathcal{N}(\mathit{dom}(C))\cap\mathit{rng}(C)=\emptyset$
RL1	$\rho_R(x)=x$	if $\mathit{dom}(R)\cap\mathcal{N}(\alpha(x))=\emptyset$
RL2	$\rho_R(\rho_{R'}(x))=\rho_{R\cup R'}(x)$	if $\mathit{dom}(R)\cap\mathit{dom}(R')=\emptyset\wedge$ $\mathit{dom}(R)\cap\mathit{rng}(R')=\emptyset$
RL3	$\rho_R(\rho_{R'}(x))=\rho_{R''}(x)$	if $R''=\{a\to b \mid (a\to b\in R\wedge$ $a\notin(\mathit{dom}(R')\cup\mathit{rng}(R')))\vee$ $(c\to b\in R\wedge a\to c\in R')\vee$ $(a\to b\in R'\wedge b\notin\mathit{dom}(R))\}$
RL4	$\rho_R(x\|y)=\rho_R(x)\|\rho_R(y)$	
VC1	$\nabla_V(\Gamma_C(x))=\nabla_V(\Gamma_C(\nabla_{V'}(x)))$	if $V'=\{\alpha\|\beta \mid C(\alpha)\|\beta\in V\}$
VC2	$\Gamma_C(\nabla_V(x))=\nabla_V(x)$	if $\mathit{dom}\|(C)\cap\Downarrow(V)=\emptyset$
VD1	$\nabla_V(\partial_H(x))=\partial_H(\nabla_V(x))$	
VD2	$\nabla_V(\partial_H(x))=\nabla_{V'}(x)$	if $V'=\{\alpha \mid \alpha\in V\wedge\mathcal{N}(\{\alpha\})\cap H=\emptyset\}$
VD3	$\partial_H(\nabla_V(x))=\nabla_{V'}(x)$	if $V'=\{\alpha \mid \alpha\in V\wedge\mathcal{N}(\{\alpha\})\cap H=\emptyset\}$
VR	$\nabla_V(\rho_R(x))=\rho_R(\nabla_{V'}(x))$	if $V'=\{\alpha \mid R(\alpha)\in V\}$
CD1	$\partial_H(\Gamma_C(x))=\Gamma_C(\partial_H(x))$	if $(\mathcal{N}(\mathit{dom}(C))\cup\mathit{rng}(C))\cap H=\emptyset$
CD2	$\Gamma_C(\partial_H(x))=\partial_H(x)$	if $\mathcal{N}(\mathit{dom}(C))\subseteq H$
CT1	$\tau_I(\Gamma_C(x))=\Gamma_C(\tau_I(x))$	if $(\mathcal{N}(\mathit{dom}(C))\cup\mathit{rng}(C))\cap I=\emptyset$
CT2	$\Gamma_C(\tau_I(x))=\tau_I(x)$	if $\mathcal{N}(\mathit{dom}(C))\subseteq I$
CR1	$\rho_R(\Gamma_C(x))=\Gamma_C(\rho_R(x))$.	if $\mathit{dom}(R)\cap\mathit{rng}(C)=\mathit{dom}(R)\wedge$ $\mathcal{N}(\mathit{dom}(C))=\mathit{rng}(R)\wedge$ $\mathcal{N}(\mathit{dom}(C))=\emptyset$
CR2	$\Gamma_C(\rho_R(x))=\rho_R(x)$	if $\mathcal{N}(\mathit{dom}(C))\subseteq\mathit{dom}(R)\wedge$ $\mathcal{N}(\mathit{dom}(C))\cap\mathit{rng}(R)=\emptyset$
DT	$\partial_H(\tau_I(x))=\tau_I(\partial_H(x))$	if $I\cap H=\emptyset$
DR	$\partial_H(\rho_R(x))=\rho_R(\partial_{H'}(x))$	if $H'=\{\alpha\|R(\alpha)\in H\}$
TR	$\tau_I(\rho_R(x))=\rho_R(\tau_{I'}(x))$	if $I=\{R(a)\|a\in I'\}$

Table 5.8: Alphabet axioms

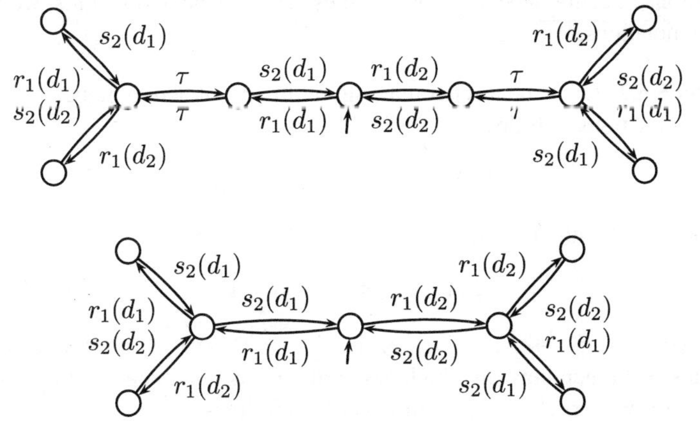

Figure 5.7: The full and reduced LTSs of $\tau_{\{c_3\}}(\nabla_{\{r_1,s_2,c_3\}}(\Gamma_{\{r_3|s_3\to c_3\}}(X \parallel B)))$

Definition 5.6.1. Let p be a process expression. We define the alphabet of p, notation $\alpha(p)$ inductively by:

- $\alpha(\alpha) = \{\underline{\alpha}\}$ if $\alpha \not\equiv \tau$.
- $\alpha(\tau) = \alpha(\delta) = \emptyset$.
- $\alpha(p + q) = \alpha(c \to p \diamond q) = \alpha(p \cdot q) = \alpha(p) \cup \alpha(q)$.
- $\alpha(\sum_{d:D} p(d)) = \alpha(p(d))$.
- $\alpha(p \parallel q) = \alpha(p \mathbin{⌊\!⌊} q) = \alpha(p) \cup \alpha(q) \cup \{\beta_1|\beta_2 \mid \beta_1 \in \alpha(p), \beta_2 \in \alpha(q)\}$.
- $\alpha(p \mid q) = \{\beta_1|\beta_2 \mid \beta_1 \in \alpha(p), \beta_2 \in \alpha(q)\}$.
- $\alpha(\Gamma_C(p)) = \alpha(p) \cup \{b|\beta_1 \mid \beta_2 \to b \in C$ and $\beta_1|\beta_2 \in \alpha(p)\}$.
- $\alpha(\nabla_V(p)) = V \cap \alpha(p)$.
- $\alpha(\partial_B(p)) = \{\beta \mid \beta \in \alpha(p)$ and no action in B occurs in $\beta\}$.
- $\alpha(\rho_R(p)) = \{\rho_R(\beta) \mid \beta \in \alpha(p)\}$.
- $\alpha(\tau_I(p)) = \{\tau_I(\beta) \mid \beta \in \alpha(p)\}$.
- $\alpha(\Upsilon_I(p)) = \{\Upsilon_I(\beta) \mid \beta \in \alpha(p)\}$.

Here $\rho_R(\beta)$ is defined by $\rho_R(\tau) = \tau$, $\rho_R(a) = b$ if $a \to b \in R$ for some action name b. Otherwise, $\rho_R(a) = a$. Furthermore, $\rho_R(\beta_1|\beta_2) = \rho_R(\beta_1)|\rho_R(\beta_2)$. Similarly, $\tau_I(\beta)$ is defined by $\tau_I(\tau) = \tau$, $\tau_I(a) = \tau$ if $a \in I$, otherwise, $\tau_I(a) = a$, and $\tau_I(\beta_1|\beta_2) = \tau_I(\beta_1)|\tau_I(\beta_2)$. The definition of $\Upsilon_I(\beta)$ is exactly the same as $\tau_I(\beta)$ except that $\Upsilon_I(a) = \mathit{int}$ if $a \in I$.

In table 5.8 the alphabet axioms are given (inspired by [179]). They depend heavily on operations of action labels. To phrase these action label constraints, we require the following notations.

Definition 5.6.2. Let V be a set containing multi-sets of action names. We define the set $\mathcal{N}(V)$ of actions as follows:

$$\mathcal{N}(V) = \{a \mid a \in \alpha \wedge \alpha \in V\}.$$

We define the set with multi-sets of action names $\Downarrow(V)$ by

$$\Downarrow(V) = \{\beta \sqsubseteq \alpha \mid \alpha \in V\}.$$

Let $C = \{a_1^1|\ldots|a_{m_1}^1 \rightarrow a^1, \ldots, a_1^n|\ldots|a_{m_n}^n \rightarrow a^n\}$ be a set of allowed communications or a set of renamings (in which case only one action occurs at the left-hand side of the arrow). We write $dom(C)$ and $rng(C)$ as follows:

$$\begin{array}{rcl} dom(C) & = & \{a_1^1|\ldots|a_{m_1}^1, \ldots, a_1^n|\ldots|a_{m_n}^n\}, \text{ and} \\ rng(C) & = & \{a^1, \ldots, a^n\}. \end{array}$$

If R is a renaming we write $R(a(d_1, \ldots, d_n)) = b(d_1, \ldots, d_n)$ if $a \rightarrow b \in R$. If α is a multi-action, we apply R to all individual action names. That is, if α is an action then $R(\alpha)$ is as indicated above. If $\alpha = \alpha_1|\alpha_2$, then $R(\alpha_1|\alpha_2) = R(\alpha_1)|R(\alpha_2)$. For C a set of communications, we write $C(\alpha) = b$ if $\underline{\alpha} \rightarrow b \in C$.

Example 5.6.3. We show how the alphabet axioms can be used to reduce the number of multi-actions when simplifying a process. Consider

$$\nabla_{\{a,d\}}(\Gamma_{\{b|c \rightarrow d\}}(a \parallel b \parallel c)). \tag{5.2}$$

Straightforward expansion of the parallel operators yields the following term:

$$\nabla_{\{a,d\}}(\Gamma_{\{b|c \rightarrow d\}}(a \cdot (b \cdot c + c \cdot b + b|c) + b \cdot (a \cdot c + c \cdot a + a|c) + c \cdot (a \cdot b + b \cdot a + a|b) + (a|b) \cdot c + (a|c) \cdot b + (b|c) \cdot a + (a|b|c))).$$

Via a straightforward but laborious series of applications of axioms this term can be shown to be equal to $a \cdot d + d \cdot a$. But using the alphabet axioms CL3 and VL2 we can rewrite equation (5.2) to:

$$\nabla_{\{a,d\}}(a \parallel \nabla_{\{a,d\}}(\Gamma_{\{b|c \rightarrow d\}}(b \parallel c))).$$

Expansion of the innermost $b \parallel c$ yields $b \cdot c + c \cdot d + b|c$ and application of the communication and allow operator shows that process (5.2) is equal to

$$\nabla_{\{a,d\}}(a \parallel d).$$

This is easily shown to be equal to $a \cdot d + d \cdot a$, too.

Exercise 5.6.4. Simplify $\nabla_{\{e,f\}}(\Gamma_{\{a|b \rightarrow e, c|d \rightarrow f\}}(a \parallel b \parallel c \parallel d))$.

5.7 Historical notes

The history of parallel composition, as we know it in process algebra, goes back to the seminal work of Bekič [24] and Milner [137]. Various process algebras defined different variants of parallel composition, particularly with respect to synchronization. In CCS [137], there is a hand-shaking (send and single receive) tied with hiding. In CSP [103], multi-party synchronization is possible, together with an implicit block operator disallowing individual happening of common actions.

In ACP [18, 25] (and later in TCP [12]) there is a generic synchronization scheme which allows, among others, for both hand-shaking and multi-party synchronization. Moreover, hiding and blocking (also called encapsulation) are separated from parallel composition. The synchronization scheme introduced in this chapter is an extension of ACP synchronization scheme, which enforces common data parameters; this is essential for communicating data values among processes.

6

The Modal μ-calculus

In this chapter we discuss how to denote properties of a reactive system. A property describes some aspect of the behavior of a system. For instance, deadlock freedom is a simple, but a generally very desired property. Also, the property that every message that is sent will ultimately be received, is a typical behavioral property.

There are three main reasons to formulate properties of systems:

- Communicating systems are often so complex that its behavior cannot neatly be characterized by a description of its external behavior. Only certain properties can be formulated. For instance, in a leader election protocol processes can negotiate to select one, and only one, leader. In the more advanced versions of this protocol it is almost impossible to predict which process will become the leader [52]. Hence, describing the external behavior of the protocol is hard. But in this case it is relatively easy to denote the property that exactly one leader will be chosen.

- In the early design stages, it is unclear what the behavior of a system will be. Hence, writing down basic properties can help to establish some of the essential aspects of the system behavior before commencing a detailed behavioral design. In UML, *use cases* are used for this purpose. These are examples of potential runs of the system. The property language described in this chapter allows use cases to be denoted, but also allows far more complex properties to be denoted.

- It is very common that behavioral descriptions contain mistakes. By checking that a behavioral specification satisfies desirable properties, an extra safeguard is built in to guarantee the correctness of the specification.

Although properties address only aspects of the behavior, it turns out that it is not easy to formulate them precisely. The reason for this is that most people are used to think rather sloppily about behavior. They are often only thinking about normal behavior, and not taking all possibilities into account: It is too simplistic that a light can only go off by turning the switch. Power failure, a blown fuse, a cut wire, on a broken lightbulb are also potential causes. Computer systems allow even more complexity.

Because it is hard to imagine all behavior, properties must be checked precisely, either by mathematical reasoning or via tools. Techniques to do so are treated in chapter 14. It will be quite amazing to find out how often an obviously valid modal property of a system does not turn out to be true.

Instead of making modal formulas more and more complex to make them valid, a reverse approach can be taken, namely, to try to design systems such that their behavior can be characterized by only simple modal requirements. Then the behavior of a system becomes simpler to understand, which means that its usability will increase.

6.1 Hennessy-Milner logic

Hennessy-Milner logic is the underlying modal logic for our property language [96].[1] Its syntax is given by the following BNF grammar:

$$\phi ::= true \mid false \mid \neg\phi \mid \phi \wedge \phi \mid \phi \vee \phi \mid \phi \rightarrow \phi \mid \langle a \rangle \phi \mid [a]\phi.$$

A modal formula is either valid or invalid in a state. A modal formula is considered to be valid for a transition system iff it is valid in its initial state.

The modal formula $true$ is valid in each state of a process and the modal formula $false$ is never valid. The connectives $\wedge$ (and), $\vee$ (or), $\neg$ (not), and $\rightarrow$ (implication) have their usual meaning. For example, the formula $\phi_1 \wedge \phi_2$ is valid wherever both ϕ_1 and ϕ_2 hold.

The diamond modality $\langle a \rangle \phi$ is valid whenever an a-action can be performed such that ϕ is valid after this a has been done. For example, the formula $\langle a \rangle \langle b \rangle \langle c \rangle true$ expresses that a process can do an a followed by a b followed by a c.

Using the connectives, more complex properties can be formulated. Expressing that after doing an a action both a b and a c *must* be possible is done by the formula $\langle a \rangle (\langle b \rangle true \wedge \langle c \rangle true)$. Expressing that after an a action, no b is possible can be done by $\langle a \rangle \neg \langle b \rangle true$.

The box modality $[a]\phi$ is more involved. It is valid when for every action a that can be done, ϕ holds after doing that a. The formula $[a]\langle b \rangle true$ says that whenever an a can be done, a b action is possible afterward. The formula $[a]false$ says that whenever an action a is done, a situation is reached where $false$ is valid. As this cannot be, the formula expresses that an action a is not possible. Likewise, $[a][b]false$ holds when a trace $a\,b$ does not exist.

Clearly, $[a]\phi$ and $\langle a \rangle \phi$ express different properties. A good way to understand the differences is by giving two transition systems, one where $\langle a \rangle \phi$ holds and $[a]\phi$ is invalid, and vice versa, one where $[a]\phi$ is valid, and $\langle a \rangle \phi$ is invalid. In the leftmost transition system of figure 6.1, $\langle a \rangle \phi$ is valid, and $[a]\phi$ is not. In the second transition system the situation is reversed, namely $[a]\phi$ is valid, and $\langle a \rangle \phi$ is not. Both formulas are true in the third transition system and both are invalid in the fourth (i.e., the rightmost) one.

In the labeled transition system at the left of figure 6.1, an a action is possible to a state where ϕ holds, and one to a state where ϕ does not hold. Therefore, $\langle a \rangle \phi$ is

[1] Matthew Hennessy (1949–) is an Irish researcher in the theory of concurrency and one of the pioneers of concurrency theory. He is currently a professor at Trinity College Dublin.

Figure 6.1: Four labeled transition systems distinguishing box and diamond formulas

valid, and $[a]\phi$ is not. In the second labeled transition diagram there is no a-transition at all, so certainly not one to a state where ϕ is valid. Hence, $\langle a\rangle\phi$ is not valid. But all a-transitions (which are none) go to a state where ϕ is valid. So, $[a]\phi$ holds. In the third, all a-transitions go to a state where ϕ is valid, and in the fourth, all a-transitions go to a state where ϕ does not hold.

The following identities are valid for Hennessy-Milner formulas. These identities are not only useful to simplify formulas, but can also help to reformulate a modal formula to check whether its meaning matches intuition. For instance, the formula $\neg\langle a\rangle[b]\mathit{false}$ can be hard to comprehend. Yet the equivalent $[a]\langle b\rangle \mathit{true}$ clearly says that whenever an action a can be done, an action b must be possible after that a. Note that the equations show that the box and diamond modalities are dual to each other, just like the $\wedge$ and the $\vee$ are duals of each other.

$$\begin{array}{ll}
\neg\langle a\rangle\phi = [a]\neg\phi & \neg[a]\phi = \langle a\rangle\neg\phi \\
\langle a\rangle \mathit{false} = \mathit{false} & [a]\mathit{true} = \mathit{true} \\
\langle a\rangle(\phi\vee\psi) = \langle a\rangle\phi\vee\langle a\rangle\psi & [a](\phi\wedge\psi) = [a]\phi\wedge[a]\psi \\
\langle a\rangle\phi\wedge[a]\psi \Rightarrow \langle a\rangle(\phi\wedge\psi) &
\end{array}$$

Besides these identities, the ordinary identities of propositional logic are also valid. A list of identities for modal formulas is given in tables 6.1 and 6.2 at the end of this chapter.

Exercise 6.1.1.

1. Give a modal formula that says that in the current state an a can be done, followed by a b. Moreover, after the a no c is allowed.

2. Give a modal formula that expresses that whenever an a action is possible in the current state, it cannot be followed by an action b or an action c.

3. Give a modal formula that expresses that whenever in the current state an a action can be done when a b is also possible, the a cannot be followed by a b. In other words, the action a cancels a b.

Exercise 6.1.2. Give an argument why the following two formulas are equivalent.

$$\langle a\rangle\,(\langle b\rangle \mathit{true}\vee\langle c_1\rangle \mathit{false}), \qquad \neg[a]\,([b]\mathit{false}\wedge[c_2]\mathit{true}).$$

Exercise 6.1.3. Consider formulas $\phi_1 = \langle a\rangle\langle b\rangle \mathit{true}$ and $\phi_2 = [a](\langle b\rangle \mathit{true}\wedge[c]\mathit{false})$. Give process expressions or transition systems where ϕ_1 is valid and ϕ_2 is invalid and vice versa.

6.2 Regular formulas

It is often useful to allow more than just a single action in a modality. For instance, to express that after two arbitrary actions, a specific action must happen. Or to say that after observing one or more *receive* actions, a deliver must follow.

A very convenient way to do this, as put forward by [127], is the use of *regular formulas* within modalities. Regular formulas are based on action formulas, which we define first:

Action formulas have the following syntax:

$$af \ ::= \ \alpha \mid true \mid false \mid \overline{af} \mid af \cap af \mid af \cup af.$$

Action formulas define a set of multi-actions. A multi-action α represents the set with exactly the multi-action α. The formula $true$ stands for the set of all multi-actions and the formula *false* is the empty set. Note that this notation is rather confusing, as in this place $true$ and *false* are not Booleans. This set of multi-actions can be used instead of an action in a Hennessy-Milner formula. For example, the modal formula $\langle true\rangle\langle a\rangle true$ expresses that an arbitrary multi-action followed by an action a can be performed. The formula $[true]false$ expresses that no multi-action can be done.

The connectives $\cap$ and $\cup$ in action formulas denote intersection and union of sets of multi-actions. The notation $\overline{af}$ denotes the complement of the set af with respect to the set of all multi-actions. The formula $\langle\overline{a}\rangle\langle b \cup c\rangle true$ says that an action other than an a can be done, followed by either a b or a c. The formula $[\overline{a}]false$ says that only an a action is allowed.

The precise definitions of modalities with action formulas in them is the following. Let af be a set of multi-actions then:

$$\langle af\rangle\phi = \bigvee_{\alpha\in af} \langle\alpha\rangle\phi \qquad\qquad [af]\phi = \bigwedge_{\alpha\in af} [\alpha]\phi.$$

Regular formulas extend the action formulas to allow the use of sequences of actions in modalities. The syntax of regular formulas, with af an action formula, is:

$$R ::= \ \varepsilon \mid af \mid R{\cdot}R \mid R{+}R \mid R^{\star} \mid R^{+}.$$

The formula ε represents the empty sequence of actions. So, $[\varepsilon]\phi = \langle\varepsilon\rangle\phi = \phi$. In other words, it is always possible to perform no action and by doing so, one stays in the same state.

The regular formula $R_1{\cdot}R_2$ represents the concatenation of the sequences of actions in R_1 and R_2. For instance, $\langle a{\cdot}b{\cdot}c\rangle true$ is the same as $\langle a\rangle\langle b\rangle\langle c\rangle true$ expressing that a sequence of actions a, b, and c can be performed. The regular formula $R_1{+}R_2$ denotes the union of the sequences in R_1 and R_2. Therefore, $[a{\cdot}b + c{\cdot}d]false$ expresses that neither the sequence $a\,b$ nor the sequence $c\,d$ is possible.

The definitions of both operators is the following:

$$\langle R_1{+}R_2\rangle\phi = \langle R_1\rangle\phi \vee \langle R_2\rangle\phi, \qquad [R_1{+}R_2]\phi = [R_1]\phi \wedge [R_2]\phi,$$
$$\langle R_1{\cdot}R_2\rangle\phi = \langle R_1\rangle\langle R_2\rangle\phi, \qquad [R_1{\cdot}R_2]\phi = [R_1][R_2]\phi.$$

All the modal formulas described up to now are rather elementary, and not of much use to formulate requirements of real system behavior. By allowing $R^{\star}$ and R^{+}, this improves substantially, because they allow iterative behavior.

The regular formula $R^{\star}$ denotes zero or more repetitions of the sequences in R. Similarly, the formula R^{+} stands for one or more repetitions. Thus, $\langle a^{\star}\rangle true$ expresses that any sequence of a actions is possible. And $[a^{+}]\phi$ expresses that the formula ϕ must hold in any state reachable by doing one or more actions a.

Two formulas, the *always* and *eventually* modalities, are commonly used. The always modality is often denoted as $\Box\phi$ and expresses that ϕ holds in all reachable states. The eventually modality is written as $\Diamond\phi$ and expresses that there is a sequence of actions that leads to a state in which ϕ holds. Using regular formulas these can be written as follows:

$$\Box\phi = [true^{\star}]\phi, \qquad\qquad \Diamond\phi = \langle true^{\star}\rangle\phi.$$

The always modality is a typical instance of a so-called safety property. Such properties typically say that something bad will never happen. A typical example is that two processes cannot be in a critical region at the same time. Entering the critical region is modeled by the action $enter$ and leaving the critical region is modeled by an action $leave$. In a modal formula we want to say that it is impossible to do two consecutive $enter$s without a $leave$ action in between:

$$[true^{\star}\cdot enter\cdot \overline{leave}^{\star}\cdot enter]\mathit{false}.$$

A similar safety requirement, which occurs quite often, is that between an action a and a consecutive action b, an action c must happen. This is expressed by saying that if an a happens followed by a b without a c in between, falsum has to hold in the state that is reached.

$$[true^{\star}\cdot a\cdot \overline{c}^{\star}\cdot b]\mathit{false}.$$

A very similar property is the following. Namely, between an action a and a subsequent action b an action c is not allowed to happen. This can be rephrased by saying that between an action c that follows an action a an action b must happen. With this, we get a similar formula to the one above:

$$[true^{\star}\cdot a\cdot \overline{b}^{\star}\cdot c]\mathit{false}.$$

There is one safety property that gives rise to a very particular shaped formula. It says that there is no deadlock in any reachable state:

$$[true^{\star}]\langle true\rangle true.$$

The eventuality modality $\Diamond\phi$ is a typical example of a liveness property stating that something good will happen. For instance, the following formula expresses that after sending a message, it can eventually be received:

$$[true^{\star}\cdot send]\langle true^{\star}\cdot receive\rangle true.$$

Compare this to the following formula

$$[\mathit{true}^{\star}\cdot \mathit{send}\cdot \overline{\mathit{receive}}^{\star}]\langle \mathit{true}^{\star}\cdot \mathit{receive}\rangle \mathit{true}$$

which states that after a *send*, a *receive* is possible as long as it has not happened.

Exercise 6.2.1. Give modal formulas for the following properties:

1. As long as no *error* happens, a deadlock will not occur.
2. Whenever an a can happen in any reachable state, a b action can subsequently be done unless a c happens canceling the need to do the b.
3. Whenever an a action happens, it must always be possible to do a b after that, although doing the b can infinitely be postponed.

Exercise 6.2.2. What is the difference between the following two formulas? Which one is used more often?

$$[\mathit{send}]\langle \mathit{true}^{\star}\cdot \mathit{receive}\rangle \mathit{true}.$$
$$[\mathit{true}^{\star}\cdot \mathit{send}]\langle \mathit{true}^{\star}\cdot \mathit{receive}\rangle \mathit{true}.$$

Exercise 6.2.3. Show that the identities $[R_1\cdot(R_2 + R_3)]\phi = [R_1\cdot R_2 + R_1\cdot R_3]\phi$ and $\langle R_1\cdot(R_2 + R_3)\rangle\phi = \langle R_1\cdot R_2 + R_1\cdot R_3\rangle\phi$ hold. This shows that regular formulas satisfy the left distribution of sequential composition over choice, which justifies saying that regular formulas represent sequences.

6.3 Fixed point modalities

Although regular expressions are very expressive and suitable for stating most behavioral properties, they do not suit every purpose. By adding explicit minimal and maximal fixed point operators to Hennessy-Milner logic, a much more expressive language is obtained. This language is called the modal μ-calculus. As a sign of its expressiveness, it is possible to translate regular formulas to the modal μ-calculus. However, the expressiveness comes at a price. Formulating properties using the modal μ-calculus requires experience.

The modal μ-calculus in its basic form is given by the following syntax. Note that Hennessy-Milner logic is included in this language.

$$\phi ::= \mathit{true} \mid \mathit{false} \mid \neg\phi \mid \phi \wedge \phi \mid \phi \vee \phi \mid \phi \rightarrow \phi \mid \langle a\rangle\phi \mid [a]\phi \mid \mu X.\phi \mid \nu X.\phi \mid X.$$

The formula $\mu X.\phi$ is the minimal fixed point and $\nu X.\phi$ stands for the maximal fixed point. Typically, the variable X is used in fixed points, but other capitals, such as Y and Z are used as well.

A good way to understand fixed point modalities is by considering X as a set of states. The formula $\mu X.\phi$ is valid for all those states in the smallest set X that satisfies the equation $X{=}\phi$, where X generally occurs in ϕ. Here we abuse notation, by thinking of X and ϕ as the sets of states where both are valid. Similarly, $\nu X.\phi$ is valid for the states in the largest set X that satisfies $X{=}\phi$.

We can illustrate this by looking at two simple fixed point formulas, namely $\mu X.X$ and $\nu X.X$. Thus, we are interested in respectively the smallest and largest sets of states X that satisfy the equation $X{=}X$. Now, any set satisfies this equation. The smallest set to satisfy it is the empty set. This means that $\mu X.X$ is not valid for any state. This is equivalent to saying that $\mu X.X{=}\mathit{false}$. The largest set to satisfy the equation $X{=}X$ is the set of all states. Therefore, $\nu X.X$ is valid everywhere. In other words, $\nu X.X{=}\mathit{true}$.

As another example consider the formulas $\mu X.\langle a\rangle X$ and $\nu X.\langle a\rangle X$. One may wonder whether these hold for state s in the following transition system:

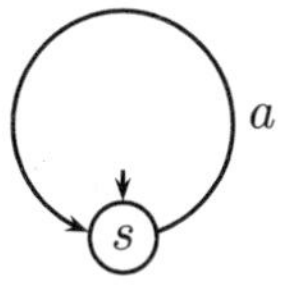

The only sets of states to be considered are the empty set $X{=}\emptyset$ and the set of all states $X{=}\{s\}$. Both satisfy the fixed point equation $X = \langle a\rangle X$. Namely, if $X{=}\emptyset$, then the equation reduces to $\mathit{false}{=}\langle a\rangle \mathit{false}$, which is valid. If $X{=}\{s\}$ it is also clear that this equation holds.

Thus, $\mu X.\langle a\rangle X$ is valid for all states in the empty set. Hence, this formula is not valid in s. However, $\nu X.\langle a\rangle X$ is valid for all states in the largest set, being $\{s\}$ in this case. Therefore, $\nu X.\langle a\rangle X$ is valid.

An effective intuition to understand whether or not a fixed point formula holds is by thinking of it as a graph to be traversed, where the fixed point variables are states and the modalities $\langle a\rangle$ and $[a]$ are seen as transitions. A formula is true when it can be made true by passing a finite number of times through the minimal fixed point variables, whereas it is allowed to traverse an infinite number of times through the maximal fixed point variables. In the example with a single a-loop above, the formulas $\mu X.\langle a\rangle X$ and $\nu X.\langle a\rangle X$ can only be made true by passing an infinite number of times through X and/or s. Thus, the minimal fixed point formula does not hold, and the maximal one is valid.

Safety properties express that some undesired behavior will never happen. These properties are generally formulated using the maximal fixed point operator. Dually, liveness properties say that something good will happen within a finite number of steps. These are formulated using the minimal fixed point operator.

Consider the formulas $\mu X.\phi$ and $\nu X.\phi$. As the maximal fixed point formula is valid for the largest set of states satisfying $X{=}\phi$ and the minimal fixed point only for the smallest set, $\nu X.\phi$ is valid whenever $\mu X.\phi$ is. This can concisely be formulated as follows:

$$\mu X.\phi \Rightarrow \nu X.\phi.$$

We use here a double implication arrow to stress that we are dealing with two formulas. If the first is true, then the second is true.

In order to be sure that a fixed point $\mu X.\phi$ or $\nu X.\phi$ exists, X must occur positively in ϕ. This means that X in ϕ must be preceded by an even number of negations. For counting negations $\phi_1{\rightarrow}\phi_2$ ought to be read as $\neg\phi_1{\vee}\phi_2$. For instance, $\mu X.\neg X$ and $\nu X.\neg([a]\neg X{\vee}X)$ are not allowed. In the first case, the variable X is preceded by one negation. But there is no set of states that is equal to its complement. Therefore there is no solution for the fixed point equation $X{=}\neg X$, and certainly no minimal solution. Hence, $\mu X.\neg X$ is not properly defined. In the second formula the first occurrence of X is preceded by two negations, which is fine, but the second is preceded by only one. The formula $\nu X.\neg([a]\neg X \vee \neg X)$ is well defined as both occurrences of the variable X are preceded by an even number of negations.

The minimal and maximal fixed point operators are each other's duals. This boils down to the following two equations:

$$\neg\nu X.\phi = \mu X.\neg\phi[X{:=}\neg X],$$
$$\neg\mu X.\phi = \nu X.\neg\phi[X{:=}\neg X].$$

The notation $\phi[X{:=}\neg X]$ stands for ϕ where each X is replaced by $\neg X$. Note that using these equations, it is always possible to remove the negations from modal formulas, provided they have solutions (i.e., variables occur in the scope of an even number of negations).

Regular formulas containing a $\star$ or a $+$ are straightforwardly translated to fixed point formulas. The translation is:

$$\langle R^\star\rangle\phi = \mu X.(\langle R\rangle X \vee \phi), \quad [R^\star]\phi = \nu X.([R]X \wedge \phi),$$
$$\langle R^+\rangle\phi = \langle R\rangle\langle R^\star\rangle\phi, \quad [R^+]\phi = [R][R^\star]\phi.$$

Note that with the rules given above, every regular formula can be translated to a fixed point modal formula. From a strictly formal standpoint, regular formulas are unnecessary. However, they turn out to be very practical to formulate many commonly occurring requirements.

In the previous section we have seen that $\Diamond\phi$ means that ϕ can eventually become valid. More precisely, there is a run starting in the current state on which ϕ becomes valid. Very often a stronger property is required, namely that ϕ will eventually become valid along every path. The formula to express this is:

$$\mu X.([\mathit{true}]X \vee \phi).$$

Strictly speaking, this formula will also become true for paths ending in a deadlock, because in such a state $[\mathit{true}]X$ becomes valid. In order to avoid this anomaly, the absence of a deadlock must explicitly be mentioned:

$$\mu X.(([\mathit{true}]X \wedge \langle \mathit{true}\rangle \mathit{true}) \vee \phi).$$

A variation of this is that an a action must inevitably be done, provided there is no deadlock before the action a.

$$\mu X.[\overline{a}]X.$$

In order to express that a must be done anyhow, the possibility for a deadlock before an action a must explicitly be excluded. This can be expressed by the following formula:

$$\mu X.([\overline{a}]X \wedge \langle \mathit{true}\rangle \mathit{true}).$$

The last two formulas are not valid for the following transition system. The reason is that the b can infinitely often be done, and hence, an a action can be avoided.

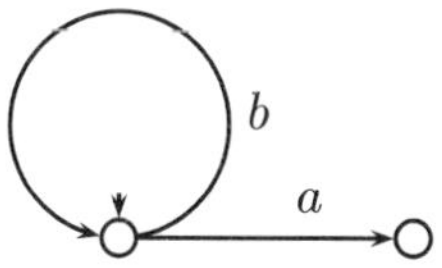

The formula $\mu X.([\overline{a}]X \vee \langle a\rangle true)$ is valid in the initial state of the previous transition system. This transition system distinguishes between the last formula and the two before that.

Until now, we have only addressed fixed point formulas where the fixed point operators are used in a straightforward way. However, by nesting different fixed point operators, a whole new class of properties can be stated. In these formulas one can reach a minimal fixed point variable from a maximal fixed point variable and vice versa. Consider, for instance variables, X and Y in formula (6.1) below. These properties are often called *fairness* properties, because these can express that some action must happen, provided it is unboundedly often enabled, or because some other action happens only a bounded number of times.

Consider for instance the formula

$$\mu X.\nu Y.((\langle a\rangle true \wedge [b]X) \vee (\neg\langle a\rangle true \wedge [b]Y)). \tag{6.1}$$

It says that from the states on each infinite b-trail, there are only a finite number of states where a-transitions are possible. This is caused by the minimal fixed point operator before the X. The X can only finitely often be traversed, and this exactly occurs in a state where an a action is possible. The variable Y can be traversed infinitely often, as it is preceded by a maximal fixed point, meaning that infinite b sequences where no a is possible are allowed.

By exchanging the minimal and maximal fixed point symbol, the meaning of the formula can become quite different. The formula

$$\nu X.\mu Y.((\langle a\rangle true \wedge [b]X) \vee (\neg\langle a\rangle true \wedge [b]Y)) \tag{6.2}$$

says that on each sequence of states reachable via b actions, only finite substretches of states cannot have an outgoing a transition. If an infinite sequence of b's is possible where a is enabled in every state, as shown below, this formula holds. This shows that this formula is not equal to formula (6.1), which is invalid if a is always enabled.

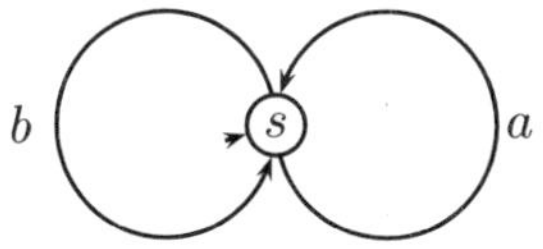

Exercise 6.3.1. Consider the formulas $\phi_1 = \mu X.[a]X$ and $\phi_2 = \nu X.[a]X$. If possible, give transition systems where ϕ_1 is valid in the initial state and ϕ_2 is not valid and vice versa.

Exercise 6.3.2. Give a labeled transition system that distinguishes between the following formulas

$$\mu X.([\overline{a}]X \vee \langle true^{\star}{\cdot}a\rangle true) \quad\text{and}\quad \mu X.[\overline{a}]X.$$

Exercise 6.3.3. Explain the difference between the following two formulas

$$[true^{\star}{\cdot}a]\mu X.([\overline{b}]X \wedge \langle true\rangle true).$$
$$[true^{\star}{\cdot}a]\mu X.(([true]X \wedge \langle true\rangle true) \vee \langle b\rangle true).$$

Exercise 6.3.4. Why is the formula $[true^{\star}{\cdot}a]\langle true^{*}{\cdot}b\rangle true$ not a fairness formula?

Exercise 6.3.5. Are the following formulas equivalent, and if not, explain why:

$$[send{\cdot}\overline{receive}^{\star}]\langle true^{\star}{\cdot}receive\rangle true \quad \text{and} \quad [send]\mu X.([\overline{receive}]X \wedge \langle true\rangle true).$$

Exercise 6.3.6. Explain what the following formulas express:

$$\mu X.\nu Y.([a]Y \wedge [b]X) \quad \text{and} \quad \nu X.\mu Y.([a]Y \wedge [b]X).$$

Is there a process that shows that these formulas are not equivalent?

6.4 Modal formulas and labeled transition systems

How can one establish whether a modal formula is valid in the initial state of a labeled transition system? In chapter 15 the semantics of a modal formula is given, using which the validity can be calculated, and in chapter 14, it is explained how one can calculate this using parameterized Boolean equation systems. In this section a more direct method is sketched to verify a modal formula on a transition system.

For Hennessy-Milner formulas, the procedure is straightforward. Consider a formula ϕ and a labeled transition system. Label each state with all subformulas of ϕ that hold in that state. This should be done by working from the smaller to the larger subformulas.

As a first step, each state is labeled with $true$, and none with $false$. Subsequently, the following steps are repeatedly executed, until all subformulas are considered. Each state is labeled with a formula $\neg\phi$, if it is not labeled with ϕ. A state is labeled with $\phi \wedge \psi$ if it is labeled with ϕ and ψ. Similarly, a state is labeled with $\phi \vee \psi$ if it is labeled with ϕ or ψ. A state is labeled with $\langle a\rangle\phi$ if there is an outgoing a transition to a state where ϕ holds. Similarly, a state is labeled with $[a]\phi$ if all outgoing a transitions go to states where ϕ holds. Note that as the number of subformulas is linear in the size of the formula, the complexity of this procedure is linear in the product of the size of the transition system and that of the formula.

Note that procedure terminates, as there are only a finite number of possible labelings. At some point, the labeling cannot be extended anymore. At termination, the initial state is labeled with ϕ iff ϕ is valid in the initial state.

Consider the transition systems in figure 6.2. At the left the formula $\langle a\rangle\langle b\rangle true$ is verified, and at the right the formula $[a]\langle b\rangle true$. It is clear that in the initial states, the first formula holds, and the second does not.

In the case where there are fixed point symbols, the procedure is slightly more complicated. We only sketch an algorithm for formulas with only one fixed point symbol. For a minimal fixed point $\mu X.\phi$, we do not label the diagram with $\mu X.\phi$, but we use all other subformulas of ϕ, including X. It is initially assumed that X does not

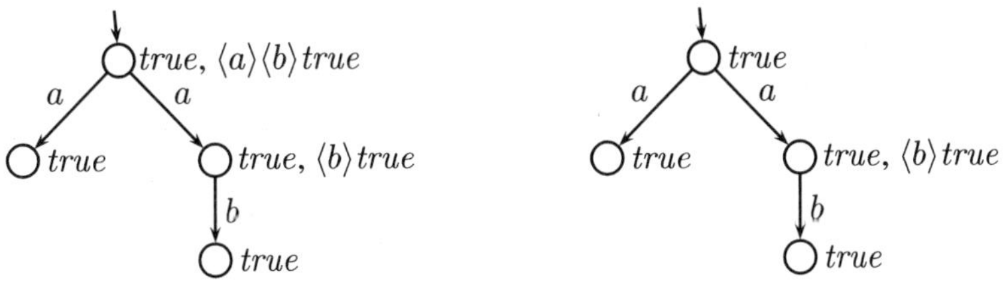

Figure 6.2: Labeling an LTS with subformulas

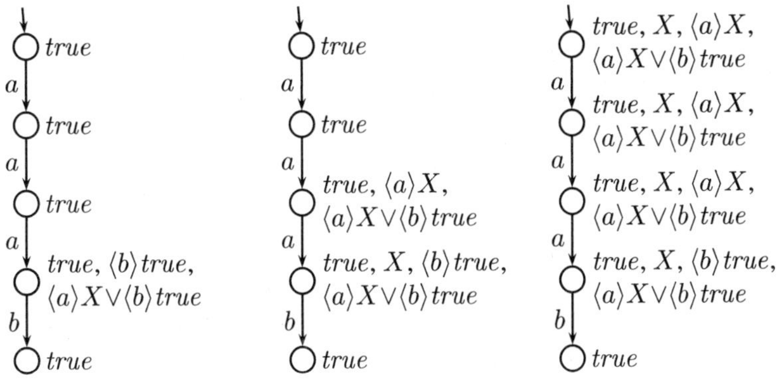

Figure 6.3: Labeling an LTS with subformulas

hold, i.e., no state is initially labeled with X. Then states are labeled by valid formulas, as is done above. When a state is labeled with ϕ, it is also labeled with X. When labeling is ready, the formula $\mu X.\phi$ holds in the initial state iff it is labeled with X.

As an example consider figure 6.3 and the formula $\mu X.(\langle a\rangle X \vee \langle b\rangle \mathit{true})$, which expresses that there is a finite sequence of a actions after which a b is possible. After two rounds of labeling we arrive at the situation at the left, where no state is labeled with X. Note that the one but last state gets the labeling $\langle a\rangle X \vee \langle b\rangle \mathit{true}$, but this is because it is also labeled with $\langle b\rangle \mathit{true}$. As the one but last state is labeled with $\langle a\rangle X \vee \langle b\rangle \mathit{true}$, it will also be labeled with X. After a next round of updating the labels, one obtains the diagram in the middle of figure 6.3. Now, it can be observed that $\langle a\rangle X \vee \langle b\rangle \mathit{true}$ holds in the third state. So, it is labeled with X, too. After repeating this procedure two more steps, it can be seen in the diagram at the right that X and therefore $\mu X.(\langle a\rangle X \vee \langle b\rangle \mathit{true})$ holds in the initial state.

For a maximal fixed point $\nu X.\phi$ it is assumed that X holds initially in all states, and therefore all states are initially labeled with X. The same procedure as for the minimal fixed point is followed, except that X is removed from a state if ϕ does not hold when the labeling process stabilizes. If X is removed, it might be that other formulas must be removed also, as they were present due to the existence of X. If removing of labels stabilizes again, it can be that more X's must be removed as ϕ is not a label of that state anymore. Hence more formulas must be removed, etc. As there are only a finite number of X's, this process also terminates. If the initial state is labeled with X, the

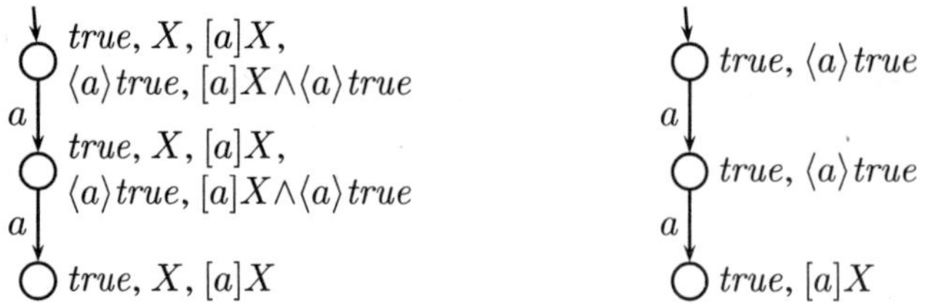

Figure 6.4: Labeling an LTS with subformulas

formula $\nu X.\phi$ is valid.

The formula $[a^\star]\langle a\rangle true$ or equivalently $\nu X.([a]X\wedge\langle a\rangle true)$ says that always one more a can be done after an arbitrary a-sequence. It is checked in figure 6.4. Note that in the last state, $[a]X\wedge\langle a\rangle true$ is not true and therefore X must be removed. Subsequently, X must be removed from the second and finally also from the initial state. Therefore, the formula $\nu X.([a]X\wedge\langle a\rangle true)$ does not hold in the initial state. The final labeling is shown in the figure at the right.

This procedure can also be used for nested fixed points. For a maximal fixed point variable, assume initially that it holds in all states, and for a minimal fixed point variable assume it holds in no state. Approximate the fixed point variables as sketched above from the inner to the outer variables. A fixed point variable has a stable solution when all variables in it scope also have a stable solution.

Consider as an example formulas (6.1) and (6.2) and the transition diagram directly below these. The initial approximation in (6.1) is that X holds in no state (minimal fixed point) and Y holds everywhere (maximal fixed point), especially in s. Using the algorithm above quickly shows that Y cannot be valid in s, which is stable for Y. As X and Y are valid in the same states, X is not valid in s, which is also a stable solution. So, formula (6.1) does not hold in s.

In formula (6.2), the initial approximation is that X is valid in s, and Y is nowhere valid. But then it becomes clear that Y holds in s via the labeling procedure above, which is the stable solution. This is also the stable solution for X. Formula (6.2) is valid in s.

In all states in a labeled transition system that are strongly bisimilar the same modal formulas hold. Therefore, it can be useful to first reduce a transition system modulo strong bisimulation, before calculating the modal formula.

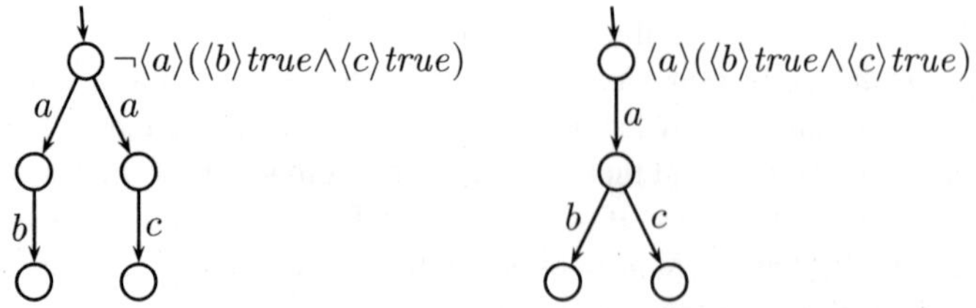

Figure 6.5: Two nonbisimilar transition systems with distinguishing formulas

The reverse also holds provided that the transition system has a finite number of transitions leaving each state. When the initial states of two transition systems are not bisimilar, there is a modal formula that is valid in one state and invalid in the other. This formula is called the *distinguishing formula*. It can be helpful to understand why two transition systems are not bisimilar. For instance, the well-known nonbisimilar transition systems in figure 6.5 have $\phi{=}\langle a\rangle(\langle b\rangle true{\wedge}\langle c\rangle true)$ as their distinguishing formula. The formula ϕ holds at the right, but not at the left.

Exercise 6.4.1. Prove by applying the algorithm from this section that the formula $\langle a\rangle(\langle b\rangle true{\wedge}\langle c\rangle true)$ does not hold in the transition system at the left of figure 6.5 and holds at the right.

Exercise 6.4.2. Provide distinguishing formulas for the three pairs of transition systems in exercise 2.3.6.

6.5 Modal formulas with data

Similar to the situation with processes, we also need data, and sometimes time in modal formulas to describe real world phenomena. Modal formulas are extended with data in three ways, similar to processes. In the first place, modal variables can have arguments. Secondly, actions can carry data arguments and time stamps, which are introduced in chapter 8. Moreover, existential and universal quantification is possible. The extensions lead to the following extensions of the syntax, where α stands for a multi-action, R represents a regular formula, ϕ stands for a modal formula, and af stands for an action formula. In appendix C the translation of the operators to plain ASCII notation is provided, which is used in the tools. For parsing reasons, the ASCII notation requires `val` to be written around some Boolean data expressions in modal formulas.

$$\begin{array}{lcl}
\alpha & ::= & \tau \mid a(t_1,\ldots,t_n) \mid \alpha|\alpha. \\
af & ::= & t \mid true \mid false \mid \alpha \mid \overline{af} \mid af \cap af \mid af \cup af \mid \forall d{:}D.af \mid \exists d{:}D.af. \\
R & ::= & \varepsilon \mid af \mid R{\cdot}R \mid R{+}R \mid R^\star \mid R^+. \\
\phi & ::= & true \mid false \mid t \mid \neg\phi \mid \phi{\wedge}\phi \mid \phi{\vee}\phi \mid \phi{\rightarrow}\phi \mid \forall d{:}D.\phi \mid \exists d{:}D.\phi \mid \langle R\rangle\phi \mid [R]\phi \mid \\
 & & \mu X(d_1{:}D_1{:=}t_1,\ldots,d_n{:}D_n{:=}t_n).\phi \mid \nu X(d_1{:}D_1{:=}t_1,\ldots,d_n{:}D_n{:=}t_n).\phi \mid \\
 & & X(t_1,\ldots,t_n).
\end{array}$$

Any expression t of sort $\mathbb{B}$ is an action formula. If t is $true$, it represents the set of all actions, and if $false$, it represents the empty set. The action formula $\exists n{:}\mathbb{N}.a(n)$ represents the set of actions $\{a(n) \mid n{\in}\mathbb{N}\}$. More generally, the action formula $\exists d{:}D.af$ represents $\bigcup_{d:D} af$. Dually, $\forall d{:}D.af$ represents $\bigcap_{d:D} af$.

These quantifications are useful to express properties involving certain subclasses of actions. For example, the formula

$$[true^\star{\cdot}\exists n{:}\mathbb{N}.error(n)]\mu X.([\overline{shutdown}]X \wedge \langle true\rangle true)$$

says that whenever an error with some number n is observed, a shutdown is inevitable.

There can be a side condition on the error, for instance, using a predicate *fatal*. A shutdown should only occur if the error is fatal:

$$[true^{\star}\cdot\exists n{:}\mathbb{N}.(fatal(n)\cap error(n))]\mu X.([\overline{shutdown}]X \wedge \langle true\rangle true).$$

If $fatal(n)$ holds, $fatal(n)$ is $true$ and represents the set of all actions. The expression $fatal(n)\cap error(n)$ represents the set with exactly the action $error(n)$, provided $fatal(n)$ is valid. Thus, $\exists n{:}\mathbb{N}.(fatal(n)\cap error(n))$ is exactly the set of all those $error(n)$ actions which are fatal. Note that *fatal*, being a predicate, and *error*, being an action, are very different objects.

Conversely, one may be interested in stating that as long as no fatal error occurs, there will be no deadlock.

$$[(\forall n{:}\mathbb{N}.\overline{(fatal(n)\cap error(n))})^{\star}]\langle true\rangle true.$$

In such cases the universal quantifier can be used in action formulas.

In modal formulas, it is also allowed to use universal and existential quantifications over data with the standard meaning. Thus, $\forall d{:}D.\phi$ is true if ϕ holds for all values from the domain D substituted for d in ϕ. For the existential quantifier, ϕ only needs to hold for some value in D substituted for d. Quantification allows for the use of data that stretches throughout a formula. For instance, stating that the same value is never delivered twice can be done as follows:

$$\forall n{:}\mathbb{N}.[true^{\star}\cdot deliver(n)\cdot true^{\star}\cdot deliver(n)]false.$$

Note that this is not possible using the quantifiers of action formulas, as their scope is only limited to a single action formula.

Using the existential quantifier we can express that some action takes place, about which we do not have all information. For instance, after sending a message, the message can eventually be delivered with some error code n. The error code is irrelevant for this requirement, but as it is a parameter of the action *deliver*, it must be included in the formula.

$$\forall m{:}Message.[true^{\star}\cdot send(m)]\langle true^{\star}\cdot\exists n{:}\mathbb{N}.deliver(m,n)\rangle true.$$

Note that it does not really matter where the quantifiers are put. That is,

$$\forall d{:}D.[true^{\star}\cdot a(d)]false = [true^{\star}]\forall d{:}D.[a(d)]false = [true^{\star}\cdot\exists d{:}D.a(d)]false$$

but it is good practice to put quantifiers as close as possible around the place where they are used.

A very powerful feature is the ability of allowing data in fixed point variables as parameters. Using this feature, it is possible, for instance, to count the number of events. Saying that a buffer may never deliver more messages than it received can be done as follows:

$$\nu X(n{:}\mathbb{N}{:=}0).[\overline{deliver\cup receive}]X(n)\wedge[receive]X(n{+}1)\wedge[deliver](n{>}0\wedge X(n{-}1)).$$

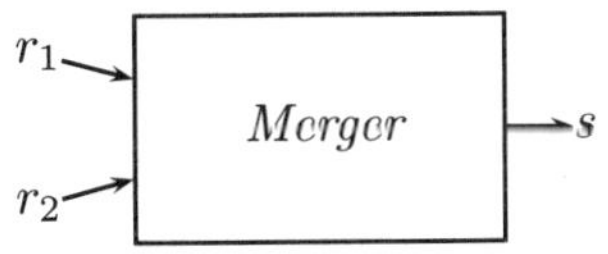

Figure 6.6: A merger reading natural numbers at r_1 and r_2 and delivering at s

Here n counts the number of received messages that have not been delivered. The notation n:N:=0 says that n is a natural number that is initially set to 0. The core of the formula is in its last conjunct, which is false if a deliver is possible while n=0. This conjunct then becomes false, turning the whole modal formula into false.

Note that the fixed point variables that depend on data, are effectively variables ranging over functions from data elements to sets of states. Although this turns modal formulas into rather advanced mathematical objects, the use of data in variables is generally quite intuitive and straightforward.

Another example consists of a merger process (see figure 6.6). It reads two streams of natural numbers, and delivers a merged stream. Reading goes via actions r_1 and r_2 and data is delivered via stream s. The property that the merger must satisfy is that as long as the input streams at r_1 and r_2 are ascending, the output must be ascending too. This can be formulated as follows. The variables in_1, in_2, and out contain the last numbers read and delivered.

$$\begin{aligned}\nu X(in_1{:}\mathbb{N}{:=}0, in_2{:}\mathbb{N}{:=}0, out{:}\mathbb{N}{:=}0).\forall l{:}\mathbb{N}.(&[r_1(l)](l{\geq}in_1{\rightarrow}X(l, in_2, out))\wedge\\ &[r_2(l)](l{\geq}in_2{\rightarrow}X(in_1, l, out))\wedge\\ &[s(l)](l{\geq}out{\wedge}X(in_1, in_2, l))).\end{aligned}$$

It does not appear to be possible to phrase this property without using data in the fixed point variables.

Exercise 6.5.1. Specify an increasing number generator that works properly if it generates a strictly increasing sequence of numbers.

Exercise 6.5.2. Express the property that a sorting machine only delivers sorted arrays. Arrays are represented by a function $f : \mathbb{N} \rightarrow \mathbb{N}$.

Exercise 6.5.3. Specify that a store with product types of sort *Prod* is guaranteed to refresh each product. For each product type, there can be more instances in the store. The only way to see this is that the difference in the number of $enter(p)$ and $leave(p)$ is always guaranteed to become zero within a finite number of steps.

6.6 Equations

In tables 6.1 and 6.2, identities are enumerated that hold between modal formulas. Although most valid equations are contained in the list it is not known whether it is complete in the sense that all valid identities between logic formulas can be derived from them.

Proposition logic	
$\phi \wedge \psi = \psi \wedge \phi$	$\phi \vee \psi = \psi \vee \phi$
$(\phi \wedge \psi) \wedge \chi = \phi \wedge (\psi \wedge \chi)$	$(\phi \vee \psi) \vee \chi = \phi \vee (\psi \vee \chi)$
$\phi \wedge \phi = \phi$	$\phi \vee \phi = \phi$
$\neg true = false$	$\neg false = true$
$\phi \wedge true = \phi$	$\phi \vee true = true$
$\phi \wedge false = false$	$\phi \vee false = \phi$
$\phi \wedge (\psi \vee \chi) = (\phi \wedge \psi) \vee (\phi \wedge \chi)$	$\phi \vee (\psi \wedge \chi) = (\phi \vee \psi) \wedge (\phi \vee \chi)$
$\neg(\phi \wedge \psi) = \neg\phi \vee \neg\psi$	$\neg(\phi \vee \psi) = \neg\phi \wedge \neg\psi$
$\neg\neg\phi = \phi$	$\phi \rightarrow \psi = \neg\phi \vee \psi$
Predicate logic	
$\forall d{:}D.\phi = \phi$	$\exists d{:}D.\phi = \phi$
$\neg\forall d{:}D.\Phi(d) = \exists d{:}D.\neg\Phi(d)$	$\neg\exists d{:}D.\Phi(d) = \forall d{:}D.\neg\Phi(d)$
$\forall d{:}D.(\Phi(d) \wedge \Psi(d)) = \forall d{:}D.\Phi(d) \wedge \forall d{:}D.\Psi(d)$	$\exists d{:}D.(\Phi(d) \vee \Psi(d)) = \exists d{:}D.\Phi(d) \vee \exists d{:}D.\Psi(d)$
$\forall d{:}D.(\Phi(d) \vee \psi) = \forall d{:}D.\Phi(d) \vee \psi$	$\exists d{:}D.(\Phi(d) \wedge \psi) = \exists d{:}D.\Phi(d) \wedge \psi$
$\forall d{:}D.\Phi(d) \Rightarrow \Phi(e)$	$\Phi(e) \Rightarrow \exists d{:}D.\Phi(d)$
Action formulas	
$\overline{true} = false$	$\overline{false} = true$
$\overline{\alpha_1 \cup \alpha_2} = \overline{\alpha_1} \cap \overline{\alpha_2}$	$\overline{\alpha_1 \cap \alpha_2} = \overline{\alpha_1} \cup \overline{\alpha_2}$
$\overline{\exists d{:}D.A(d)} = \forall d{:}D.\overline{A(d)}$	$\overline{\forall d{:}D.A(d)} = \exists d{:}D.\overline{A(d)}$
Hennessy-Milner logic	
$\neg\langle a\rangle\phi = [a]\neg\phi$	$\neg[a]\phi = \langle a\rangle\neg\phi$
$\langle a\rangle false = false$	$[a] true = true$
$\langle a\rangle(\phi \vee \psi) = \langle a\rangle\phi \vee \langle a\rangle\psi$	$[a](\phi \wedge \psi) = [a]\phi \wedge [a]\psi$
$\langle a\rangle\phi \wedge [a]\psi \Rightarrow \langle a\rangle(\phi \wedge \psi)$	$[a](\phi \vee \psi) \Rightarrow \langle a\rangle\phi \vee [a]\psi$

Table 6.1: Equivalences between modal formulas (part I)

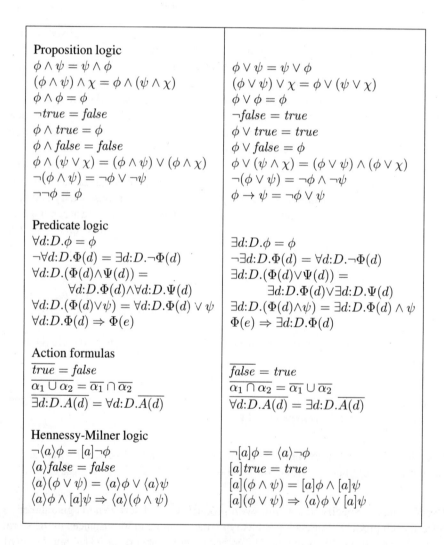

Fixed point equations	
$\mu X.\phi(X) \Rightarrow \nu X.\phi(X)$	
$\mu X.\phi = \phi$	$\nu X.\phi = \phi$
$\mu X.X = \mathit{false}$	$\nu X.X = \mathit{true}$
$\mu X.\langle R\rangle X = \mathit{false}$	$\nu X.[R]X = \mathit{true}$
$\neg\mu X.\phi = \nu X.\neg\phi[X{:=}\neg X]$	$\neg\nu X.\phi = \mu X.\neg\phi[X{:=}\neg X]$
$\mu X.\phi = \phi[X{:=}\mu X.\phi(X)]$	$\nu X.\phi = \phi[X{:=}\nu X.\phi(X)]$
if $\phi[X{:=}\psi] \Rightarrow \psi$ then $\mu X.\phi \Rightarrow \psi$	if $\psi \Rightarrow \phi[X{:=}\psi]$ then $\psi \Rightarrow \nu X.\phi$
Regular formulas	
$\langle\varepsilon\rangle\phi = \phi$	$[\varepsilon]\phi = \phi$
$\langle\mathit{false}\rangle\phi = \mathit{false}$	$[\mathit{false}]\phi = \mathit{true}$
$\langle af_1 \cup af_2\rangle\phi = \langle af_1\rangle\phi \vee \langle af_2\rangle\phi$	$[af_1 \cup af_2]\phi = [af_1]\phi \wedge [af_2]\phi$
$\langle af_1 \cap af_2\rangle\phi \Rightarrow \langle af_1\rangle\phi \wedge \langle af_2\rangle\phi$	$[af_1 \cap af_2]\phi \Leftarrow [af_1]\phi \vee [af_2]\phi$
$\langle\exists d{:}D.AF(d)\rangle\phi = \exists d{:}D.\langle AF(d)\rangle\phi$	$[\exists d{:}D.AF(d)]\phi = \forall d{:}D.[AF(d)]\phi$
$\langle\forall d{:}D.AF(d)\rangle\phi \Rightarrow \forall d{:}D.\langle AF(d)\rangle\phi$	$[\forall d{:}D.AF(d)]\phi \Leftarrow \exists d{:}D.[AF(d)]\phi$
$\langle R_1{+}R_2\rangle\phi = \langle R_1\rangle\phi \vee \langle R_2\rangle\phi$	$[R_1{+}R_2]\phi = [R_1]\phi \wedge [R_2]\phi$
$\langle R_1{\cdot}R_2\rangle\phi = \langle R_1\rangle\langle R_2\rangle\phi$	$[R_1{\cdot}R_2]\phi = [R_1][R_2]\phi$
$\langle R^\star\rangle\phi = \mu X.(\langle R\rangle X \vee \phi)$	$[R^\star]\phi = \nu X.([R]X \wedge \phi)$
$\langle R^+\rangle\phi = \langle R\rangle\langle R^\star\rangle\phi$	$[R^+]\phi = [R][R^\star]\phi$
$\neg\langle R\rangle\phi = [R]\neg\phi$	$\neg[R]\phi = \langle R\rangle\neg\phi$
$\langle R\rangle\mathit{false} = \mathit{false}$	$[R]\mathit{true} = \mathit{true}$
$\langle R\rangle(\phi \vee \psi) = \langle R\rangle\phi \vee \langle R\rangle\psi$	$[R](\phi \wedge \psi) = [R]\phi \wedge [R]\psi$
$\langle R\rangle\phi \wedge [R]\psi \Rightarrow \langle R\rangle(\phi \wedge \psi)$	$[R](\phi \vee \psi) \Rightarrow \langle R\rangle\phi \vee [R]\psi$

Table 6.2: Equivalences between modal formulas (part II)

Note that the identity $\langle a \cap b\rangle\phi = \langle a\rangle\phi \wedge \langle b\rangle\phi$ is *not* valid. This is caused by the fact that $a \cap b$ is the empty action formula, i.e., *false*. The formula $\langle \mathit{false}\rangle\phi$ equals *false* as it says that in the current state a step can be done, not carrying any action label. Such a step does not exist. The formula $\langle a\rangle\phi \wedge \langle b\rangle\phi$ is not equal to false. It, for instance, holds for the process $a + b$.

A weaker version, in this case $\langle a \cap b\rangle\phi \Rightarrow \langle a\rangle\phi \wedge \langle b\rangle\phi$, is valid. Here we cannot use equality, but use implication between formulas, denoted as $\Rightarrow$, instead. Note that implication in formulas $\rightarrow$ and $\Rightarrow$ relate in the same way as data equality $\approx$ and $=$. We also write $\phi \Leftarrow \psi$ for $\psi \Rightarrow \phi$. In chapter 9 we give a proof system that deals with, among other things, implication between formulas.

The following implications cannot be formulated as identities, too:

$$[af_1 \cap af_2]\phi \Leftarrow [af_1]\phi \vee [af_2]\phi,$$
$$\langle\forall d{:}D.AF(d)\rangle\phi \Rightarrow \forall d{:}D.\langle AF(d)\rangle\phi,$$
$$[\forall d{:}D.AF(d)]\phi \Leftarrow \exists d{:}D.[AF(d)]\phi.$$

6.7 Historical notes

Modal logic is the extension of ordinary logic with modalities, such as to which extent a statement is necessary or possible, will or has happened, is wished, believed, or known. For example, epistemic modalities deal with which facts are known and deontic logic contains modalities about what ought to be the case [8, 56]. Logic, including various modalities, goes back to Aristotle [22],[2] although independently and at approximately the same time forms of logic were developed in India and China.

The work of Aristotle was translated by Ibn Sĩnã and he formulated the first formal modal logical system of reasoning.[3] In late Medieval Europe, logic slowly developed as rules for proper verbal reasoning, until the development of symbolic logic in the late 19th and early 20th century [66, 119, 180]. Temporal logic was developed in [159] where the modal operators $[F]$ (eventually) and $[P]$ (previously) were introduced.

The relation between transition systems and modal logics (with the modalities for possibility and necessity) was formulated in Kripke structures [118].[4] Kripke structures were later widely used for the semantics of intuitionistic logic [48].

Pnueli recognized the applicability to the verification of concurrent programs [155].[5] At this time the rather different Floyd-Hoare-logic had been developed for program verification as an annotation of programs with pre-condition and postcondition [58, 101].[6,7] Two major branches of logic were developed, namely linear temporal logic (LTL) and computational tree logic on the one hand [19] and Hennessy-Milner logic [95] on the other hand. All properties expressible in any of these logics can efficiently be expressed the modal mu-calculus with data, as presented here. The original purpose of Hennessy-Milner logic was to find an alternative characterization of bisimulation. This logic was based on dynamic logic by Pratt [156].[8] Kozen [117] introduced the modal μ-calculus in and added fixed point constructions to modal logic.[9]

An excellent textbook on these logics is [19]. In [37] a detailed historical account and an accessible presentation of the modal μ-calculus is presented.

[2]Aristotle (384BC–322BC) was a Greek philosopher and mathematician who worked on logic. In some of his writings he indicates that his work on logic stems "neither as a whole, nor in part from other authors."

[3]Ibn Sĩnã (980–1037), also called Avicenna in Latin, was a Persian philosopher, mathematician, and physician, who lived in what is now contemporary Uzbekistan, Turkmenistan, and Iran and whose books were used as regular educational material at universities up to 1860, for instance, in Leuven, Belgium.

[4]Saul Kripke (1940–) is an American philosopher and logician. He is considered to belong to the top ten of most influential philosophers of the last 200 years.

[5]Amir Pnueli (1941–2009) was an Israeli computer scientist contributing to formal verification techniques. He received the Turing award in 1996.

[6]Robert Floyd (1936–2001) was an American computer scientist working on algorithms and program verification. He received the Turing Award in 1978.

[7]Tony Hoare (1934–) worked on computer translation while studying Russian. He developed several algorithms, among them quicksort, programming logics, and later the process calculus CSP. He received the Turing award in 1980.

[8]Vaughan Pratt (1944–) was raised in Australia. He became a faculty member at MIT and Stanford University and contributed to very diverse areas such as computer science, geometry, and algebra. He was among the founders of Sun Microsystems.

[9]Dexter Kozen (1951–) is an American computer scientist working on algorithms, complexity, logic, and semantics.

7

Modeling System Behavior

Modeling system behavior is generally not too difficult. However, making compact and insightful models that can serve as a means of communication and that can be shown to satisfy all desirable properties, is generally not so easy. This craftsmanship can only be obtained by making and analyzing many models. There is no other way to learn this than by trying. This chapter provides a number of examples of what such models could look like. But every situation is unique, requiring a model with its own characteristics.

The examples in this chapter are used throughout the rest of this book where we provide techniques to verify correctness. Note that the examples given here are minimal in the sense that realistic systems often have many more features. Advanced modeling skills are required to find the right balance between making the model as close as possible to the real system, and keeping it sufficiently simple such that the model is understandable. Ideally, the model and the real system coincide, and the model fits on a single page.

7.1 Alternating bit protocol

We start out by providing a model of a protocol that is used when a simple mechanism for reliable data transfer is required. We are speaking about the alternating bit protocol (ABP) [23, 123]. The alternating bit protocol ensures successful transmission of data through lossy channels. The protocol is depicted in figure 7.1. Processes K and L are channels that transfer messages from gate 2 to gate 3 and from gate 5 to gate 6, respectively. However, the data can be lost in transmission, in which case the processes K and L deliver an error. The sender process S and receiver R must take care that despite this loss of data, transfer between gate 1 and gate 4 is reliable, in the sense that messages sent at 1 are received at 4 exactly once in the same order in which they were sent.

In order to model the protocol, we assume some sort D with data elements to be transferred. We model the external behavior of the ABP using the following process equation which defines a simple buffer B and we expect that the modeled protocol is branching bisimulation equivalent to this buffer:

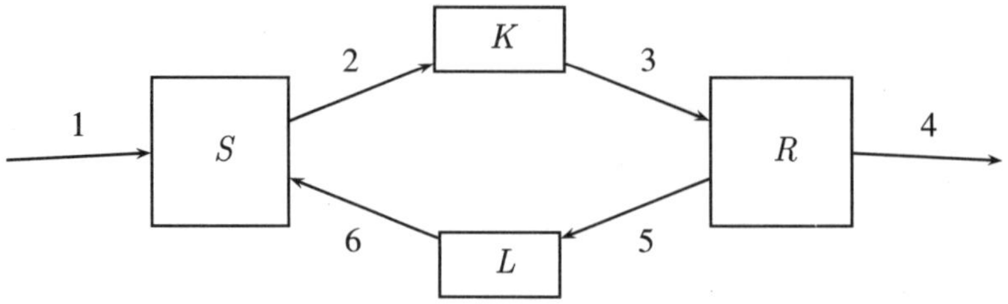

Figure 7.1: Alternating bit protocol

proc $B \;=\; \sum_{d:D} r_1(d)\cdot s_4(d)\cdot B.$

Action $r_1(d)$ represents "read datum d at gate 1," and action $s_4(d)$ represents "deliver datum d at gate 4." Strictly speaking, B is a process variable that satisfies the equation above.

In order to develop the sender and the receiver we must have a good understanding of the exact behavior of channels K and L. As modeled below, process K sends pairs of a message and a bit, and process L only forwards bits. We can introduce a data sort *Bits*, but it is easier to use the Booleans to represent bits. The processes choose internally whether data is delivered or lost using the action i. If it is lost, an error message $\perp$ is delivered:

$$\textbf{proc}\ K \;=\; \sum_{d:D,b:\mathbb{B}} r_2(d,b)\cdot(i\cdot s_3(d,b) + i\cdot s_3(\perp))\cdot K$$
$$L \;=\; \sum_{b:\mathbb{B}} r_5(b)\cdot(i\cdot s_6(b) + i\cdot s_6(\perp))\cdot L$$

Note that the action i cannot be omitted. If it would be removed, the choice between delivering the correct datum or the error is made while interacting with the receiver of the message. The receiver can henceforth determine whether the data will be lost or not. This is not what we want to model here. We want to model that it is determined internally in K and L whether or not data is lost. Because the factors that cause the message to be lost are outside our model, we use a nondeterministic choice to model data loss.

We model the sender and receiver using the protocol proposed in [23, 123]. The first aspect of the protocol is that the sender must guarantee that despite data loss in K, data eventually arrives at the receiver. For this purpose, it iteratively sends the same message to the sender. The receiver responds with an acknowledgment to the sender, whenever it receives a message. If a message is acknowledged, the sender knows that the message is received and it can proceed with the next message.

One problem of this protocol is that data may be sent more than once, and the receiver has no way of telling whether the data stems from a single message which is resent, or whether it stems from two messages that contain the same data. In order to resolve this, extra control information must be added to the message. Adding a single bit already suffices for the job [23, 123]. For consecutive messages, the bit is alternated for each subsequent datum to be transferred, which allows the receiver to tell them apart. If data is resent, the old bit is used. This explains the name alternating bit protocol.

After receiving a message at the receiver's side, its accompanying bit is sent back in the acknowledgment. When the bit differs from the bit associated with the last message, the receiver knows that this concerns new data and delivers it at gate 4. If an error $\perp$ arrives at the receiver, it does not know whether this regards an old or new message, and it sends the old bit to indicate that resending is necessary.

Whenever an unexpected bit or an error message arrives at the sender, it knows that the old data must be resent. Otherwise, it can proceed to read new data from 1 and forward it.

First, we specify the sender S in the state that it is going to send out a datum with the bit b attached to it, represented by the process name $S(b)$:

$$\textbf{proc } S(b{:}\mathbb{B}) = \sum_{d:D} r_1(d)\cdot T(d,b);$$
$$T(d{:}D, b{:}\mathbb{B}) = s_2(d,b)\cdot(r_6(b)\cdot S(\neg b) \;+\; (r_6(\neg b) + r_6(\perp))\cdot T(d,b));$$

In state $S(b)$, the sender reads a datum d at gate 1. Next, the system proceeds to state $T(d,b)$, in which it sends this datum via gate 2 with the bit/Boolean b attached to it. Then it expects to receive the acknowledgment b via gate 6, ensuring that the pair (d,b) has reached the receiver unscathed. If the correct acknowledgment b is received, then the system proceeds to state $S(\neg b)$, in which it is going to send out a datum with the bit $\neg b$ attached to it. If the acknowledgment is either the wrong bit $\neg b$ or the error message $\perp$, then the system sends the pair (d,b) into gate 2 once more.

Next, we specify the receiver in the state that it is expecting to receive a datum with the bit b attached to it, represented by the process name $R(b)$:

$$\textbf{proc } R(b{:}\mathbb{B}) = \sum_{d:D} r_3(d,b)\cdot s_4(d)\cdot s_5(b)\cdot R(\neg b) + (\sum_{d:D} r_3(d,\neg b) + r_3(\perp))\cdot s_5(\neg b)\cdot R(b).$$

In state $R(b)$ there are two possibilities.

1. If in $R(b)$ the receiver reads a pair (d,b) at gate 3, then this constitutes new information, so the datum d is sent via gate 4, after which acknowledgment b is sent to the sender via gate 5. Next, the receiver proceeds to state $R(\neg b)$, in which it is expecting to receive a datum with the bit $\neg b$ attached to it.

2. If in $R(b)$ the receiver reads a pair $(d,\neg b)$ or an error message $\perp$ via gate 3, then this does not constitute new information. So the receiver sends acknowledgment $\neg b$ to the sender via gate 5 and remains in state $R(b)$.

The desired concurrent system is obtained by putting $S(\mathit{true})$, $R(\mathit{true})$, K, and L in parallel, enforcing communication between sends and reads, blocking single send and read actions along internal gates, and abstracting away from communication actions over these gates and from the action i. That is, the alternating bit protocol is defined by the process term

proc $ABP = \nabla_I(\Gamma_C(S(true) \parallel K \parallel L \parallel R(true)))$

with $I=\{r_1, s_4, c_2, c_3, c_5, c_6, i\}$ and $C=\{r_2|s_2 \to c_2, r_3|s_3 \to c_3, r_5|s_5 \to c_5, r_6|s_6 \to c_6\}$.

Does the scheme with alternating bits work correctly? Or in other words, do the buffer process B and the process ABP behave the same when only the actions r_1 and s_4 are visible? This question is concisely stated by the following equation to hold in branching bisimulation:

$$B = \tau_{\{c_2,c_3,c_5,c_6,i\}}(ABP) \tag{7.1}$$

In section 12.2.3 the proof of this equation is given, using the explicit assumption that i is fair, meaning that the channels do not always lose messages. Note that with the equation above, it is possible to use B when proving the correctness of a system employing the alternating bit protocol. This makes reasoning about such systems considerably simpler.

Exercise 7.1.1. In the mCRL2 tool set a description of the alternating bit protocol can be found in the directory `examples/academic/abp/abp.mcrl2`. Take care that all communications and i are hidden. Use the tool `mcrl22lps abp.mcrl2 abp.lps` to transform it into linear process. This linear process can be simulated using the `lpsxsim` tool. Transfer several data items from the sender to the receiver and convince yourself that the observed actions indeed match with the specified behavior in this section. Use the command `lps2lts abp.mcrl2 abp.lts` to generate a state space. Visualize the state space using the `ltsgraph` tool. Use the auto-layout option to obtain a reasonable layout. Use `ltsconvert -ebranching-bisim abp.lts abp-red.lts` to reduce the transition system modulo branching bisimulation. Inspect the result using `ltsgraph`. Is the reduced behavior that of a one place buffer?

Exercise 7.1.2. Make a copy of the file `abp.mcrl2` from exercise 7.1.1 and make a change in the bits, for instance, by removing a negation `(!)` or changing the initial value of the bit in for instance S. Show on the one hand with the simulator `lpsxsim` and on the other hand using `lps2lts`, `ltsconvert` combined with `ltsgraph` that the behavior is not correct anymore. Observe that simulation is far less efficient than behavioral reduction to find behavioral anomalies.

7.2 Sliding window protocol

In the ABP, the sender sends out a datum and then waits for an acknowledgment before it sends the next datum. In situations where transmission of data is relatively time-consuming, this procedure tends to be unacceptably slow. In sliding window protocols (SWPs) [43] (see also [170]), this situation was resolved as the sender can send out multiple data elements before it requires an acknowledgment. This protocol is so effective that it is one of the core protocols of the internet.

The most complex sliding window protocol (SWP) described in [170] was modeled in 1991 using techniques as described in this book [38]. This model revealed a deadlock. When confronted with this, the author of [170] indicated that this problem remained undetected for a whole decade, despite the fact that the protocol had been implemented quite a number of times. There is some evidence, that this particular deadlock occurs in actual implementations of internet protocols, but this has never been systematically investigated. In recent editions of [170], the cause of the deadlock has been removed. In our models the deadlock does not occur either.

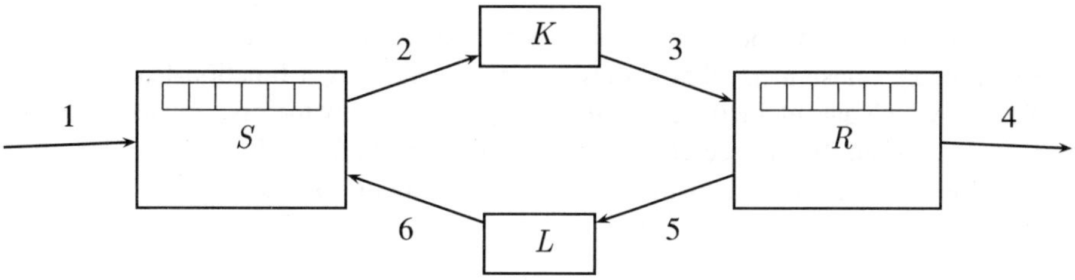

Figure 7.2: Sliding window protocol

We concentrate on a variant of the sliding window protocol which is unidirectional, to keep the model to its essential minimum. The essential feature of the sliding window protocol is that it contains buffers in the sender and the receiver to keep copies of the data in transit. This is needed to be able to resend this data if it turns out after a while that the data did not arrive correctly. Both buffers have size n. This means that there can be at most $2n$ data elements under way, i.e., there can at most be $2n$ data elements that have been received at gate 1, but have not been delivered at gate 4. From this it is natural to conclude that the external behavior of the sliding window protocol is a bounded first-in-first-out (FIFO) queue of length $2n$.

As in the ABP elements from a nonempty data domain D are sent from a sender to a receiver. The FIFO queue representing the external behavior of the sliding window protocol is defined by the following equation:

$$
\begin{aligned}
&\textbf{proc } \mathit{FIFO}(l{:}\mathit{List}(D), m{:}\mathbb{N}^+) \\
&\qquad = \textstyle\sum_{d:D} \#(l){<}m \rightarrow r_1(d)\cdot \mathit{FIFO}(l{\lhd}d, m) \\
&\qquad\ + \#(l) > 0 \rightarrow s_4(\mathit{head}(l))\cdot \mathit{FIFO}(\mathit{tail}(l), m);
\end{aligned}
$$

Note that $r_1(d)$ can be performed until the list l contains m elements, because in that situation the sending and receiving buffers will be filled. Furthermore, $s_4(\mathit{head}(l))$ can only be performed if l is not empty.

We now give a model of the sliding window protocol which implements the bounded buffer on top of two unreliable channels K and L. The setup is similar to that of the alternating bit protocol. See figure 7.2.

The channels differ from those of the ABP because they do not deliver an error in case of data loss. An indication of an error is necessary for the ABP to work correctly, but it is not very realistic. A better model of a channel is one where data is lost without an explicit indication. In this case we still assume that the channels can only carry a single item, and have no buffer capacity. However, the channels can be replaced by others, for instance, with bounded, or even unbounded capacity. As long as the channels transfer a message every now and then and do not reorder messages, the sliding window protocol can be used to transform all these unreliable channels into a reliable fifo queue.

$$\textbf{proc } K = \textstyle\sum_{d:D,k:\mathbb{N}} r_2(d,k)\cdot(i\cdot s_3(d,k) + i)\cdot K;$$
$$L = \textstyle\sum_{k:\mathbb{N}} r_5(k)\cdot(i\cdot s_6(k) + i)\cdot L;$$

Both the sender and the receiver in the SWP maintain a buffer of size n containing the data being transmitted. The buffers are represented by a function from $\mathbb{N}$ to D indicating which data element occurs at which position. Only the first n places of these functions are used. In the receiver we additionally use a buffer of Booleans of length n to recall which of the first n positions in the buffer contain valid data.

$$\textbf{sort } \mathit{DBuf} = \mathbb{N} \to D;$$
$$\mathit{BBuf} = \mathbb{N} \to \mathbb{B};$$

The sliding window protocol uses a numbering scheme to number the messages that are sent via the channels. It turns out that if the sequence numbers are issued modulo $2n$, messages are not confused and are transferred in order. Each message with sequence number j is put at position $j|_n$ in the buffers.

We use the following auxiliary functions to describe the sliding window protocol. The function *empty* below represents a Boolean buffer that is false everywhere, indicating that there is no valid data in the buffer. We use a function update $q[i\to d]$ to say that position i of buffer q is filled with datum d.

The most involved function is $\mathit{nextempty}_{mod}(i,b,m,n)$. It yields the first position (modulo $2n$) in buffer b starting at $i|_n$ that contains *false*. If the first m positions from $i|_n$ of b are all *true*, it yields the value $(i+m)|_{2n}$. The variable m is used to guarantee that the function *nextempty* is well defined if b is false at all its first n positions. The variables have the following sorts: $d{:}D$, $i, j, m{:}\mathbb{N}$, $n{:}\mathbb{N}^+$, $q{:}\mathit{DBuf}$, $c{:}\mathbb{B}$, and $b{:}\mathit{BBuf}$.

$$\textbf{eqn } \mathit{empty}(m) = \mathit{false};$$
$$\mathit{nextempty}_{mod}(i,b,m,n) =$$
$$\mathit{if}\,(b(i|_n) \wedge m{>}0, \mathit{nextempty}_{mod}((i{+}1)|_{2n}, b, m{-}1, n), i|_{2n});$$

Below we model the sender process S. The variable ℓ contains the sequence number of the oldest message in sending buffer q and m is the number of items in the sending buffer. If data arrives via gate 1, it is put in the sending buffer q, provided there is a place. There is the possibility to send the kth datum via gate 2 with sequence number $(\ell{+}k)|_{2n}$ and an acknowledgment can arrive via gate 6. This acknowledgment is the index of the first message that has not yet been received by the receiver.

$$\textbf{proc } S(\ell, m{:}\mathbb{N}, q{:}\mathit{DBuf}, n{:}\mathbb{N}^+)$$
$$= \textstyle\sum_{d:D} m{<}n \to r_1(d)\cdot S(\ell, m{+}1, q[((\ell{+}m)|_n)\to d], n)$$
$$+ \textstyle\sum_{k:\mathbb{N}} k{<}m \to s_2(q((\ell{+}k)|_n), (\ell{+}k)|_{2n})\cdot S(\ell, m, q, n)$$
$$+ \textstyle\sum_{k:\mathbb{N}} r_6(k)\cdot S(k, (m{-}k{+}\ell)|_{2n}, q, n);$$

The receiver R is modeled by the process $R(\ell', q', b, n)$ where ℓ' is the sequence number of the oldest message in the receiving buffer q'. Data can be received via gate 3 from channel K and is only put in the receiving buffer q' if its sequence number k is in the receiving window. If sequence numbers and buffer positions would not be considered modulo $2n$ and n this could be stated by $\ell' \leq k < \ell' + n$. The condition $(k - \ell')|_{2n} < n$ states exactly this, taking the modulo boundaries into account.

The second summand in the receiver says that if the oldest message position is valid (i.e., $b(\ell'|_n)$ holds), then this message can be delivered via gate 4. Moreover, the oldest message is now $(\ell'{+}1)|_{2n}$ and the message at position $\ell'|_n$ becomes invalid.

The last summand says that the index of the first message that has not been received at the receiver is sent back to the sender as an acknowledgment that all lower numbered messages have been received.

$$
\begin{aligned}
\textbf{proc } R(\ell'{:}\mathbb{N}, q'{:}\mathit{DBuf}, b{:}\mathit{BBuf}, n{:}\mathbb{N}^+)\\
= \textstyle\sum_{d:D,k:\mathbb{N}} r_3(d,k)\cdot(((k{-}\ell')|_{2n} < n)\\
\rightarrow R(\ell', q'[(k|_n)\rightarrow d], b[(k|_n)\rightarrow \mathit{true}], n)\\
\diamond\ R(\ell', q', b, n))\\
+\ b(\ell'|_n)\rightarrow s_4(q'(\ell'|_n))\cdot R((\ell'{+}1)|_{2n}, q', b[(\ell'|_n)\rightarrow \mathit{false}], n)\\
+\ s_5(\mathit{nextempty}_{mod}(\ell', b, n, n))\cdot R(\ell', q', b, n);
\end{aligned}
$$

The behavior of the SWP is characterized by:

$$\textbf{proc } SWP(q, q'{:}\mathit{DBuf}, n{:}\mathbb{N}^+) = \nabla_H(\Gamma_C(S(0,0,q,n) \| K \| L \| R(0, q', \mathit{empty}, n)));$$

where we define the sets H and C by

$$
\begin{aligned}
H &= \{c_2, c_3, c_5, c_6, i, r_1, s_4\} \text{ and}\\
C &= \{r_2|s_2\rightarrow c_2, r_3|s_3\rightarrow c_3, r_5|s_5\rightarrow c_5, r_6|s_6\rightarrow c_6\}.
\end{aligned}
$$

The contents of the buffers q and q' can be chosen arbitrarily without affecting the correctness of the protocol. This is stressed by not instantiating these variables below. The sliding window protocol behaves as a bounded FIFO buffer for any $n{:}\mathbb{N}^+$ and $q, q'{:}\mathit{DBuf}$:

$$\tau.\mathit{FIFO}([], 2n) = \tau.\tau_I(SWP(q, q', n))$$

where $I = \{c_2, c_3, c_4, c_5, i\}$. To make the equivalence valid in rooted branching bisimulation τ's are put before the processes at the left and right side. In section 13.2 it is proven that this equation holds. Due to the tricky nature of modulo calculation, this proof is quite involved.

Exercise 7.2.1. Suppose the buffer size is two and messages are sent modulo 4 (see `swp_func.mcrl2` in the directory `examples/academic/swp`). Give an execution trace of $SWP(q, q', n)$ where a single datum is read at gate 1 and delivered at 4. Verify that this trace is indeed a correct execution trace using the simulator of mCRL2.

Now make a copy of the file with the sliding window protocol and adapt it such that messages are sent modulo 2. Find a trace where a datum d_1 is sent first, and d_2 is received first.

In the *two-way* SWP [35, 42], not only does the sender read data elements from gate 1 and pass them on to the receiver, but the receiver also reads data elements from gate 4 and passes them on to the sender (see figure 7.3). In the two-way SWP, the sender has two buffers, one to store incoming data elements from gate 1, and one to store incoming data elements from gate 4; likewise for the receiver. Note that in the two-way SWP, the sender and the receiver are symmetric identities, and likewise for the channels K and L.

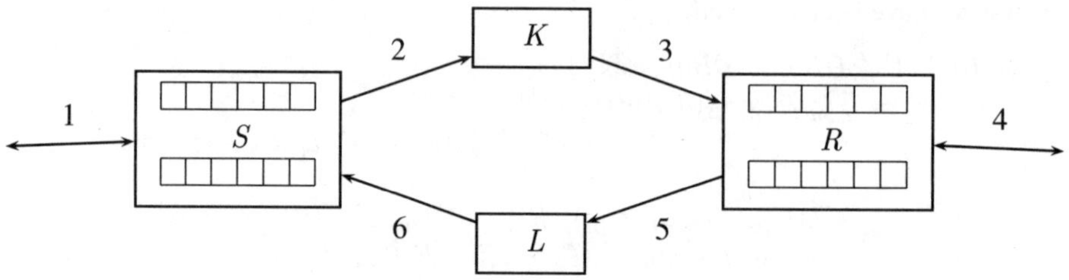

Figure 7.3: Two-way SWP

Exercise 7.2.2. Give a specification of the two-way SWP. Note that due to symmetry, the sender and the receiver and also the channels K and L are equal, except for a renaming of the input and output gates. So, you can use renaming to extract the receiver and L from the process declarations of the sender and K, respectively.

In the two-way SWP, acknowledgments that are sent from the sender to the receiver, and vice versa, can get a free ride by attaching them to data packets. This technique, which is commonly known as *piggybacking* (as the acknowledgment gets a free ride), helps to achieve a better use of available channel bandwidth.

Exercise 7.2.3. Give a specification of the sender in the two-way SWP where all acknowledgments are sent using piggybacking.

Piggybacking as described in exercise 7.2.3 slows down the two-way SWP, since an acknowledgment may have to wait for a long time before it can be attached to a data packet. Therefore, the sender and the receiver ought to be supplied with a timer, which sends a time-out message if an acknowledgment must be sent out without further delay; see [170] for more details.

Exercise 7.2.4. Model the two-way SWP with piggybacking supplied with timers. Note that there are two ways to do this. The first one is by using explicit time (see chapter 8). But in this case, analysis of the protocol might be harder. It is also possible to model time-outs as actions that can take place at any time after the timer has been set. This avoids the use of explicit time and makes the model much easier to analyze.

7.3 A patient support platform

We show how to develop a controller for a typical embedded system. The system given here is much simpler than its original, but it will still give a flavor of how such a system can be modeled.

The system is a movable patient support unit that is used to move patients into magnetic-resonance (MR) scanners. These scanners are used to look inside a patient using magnetic radiation. They consist of a huge bore with very strong magnets. The patient is put on the gurney, the gurney is docked into the MR scanner, and using a motor on the gurney, the patient is moved into the bore of the scanner.

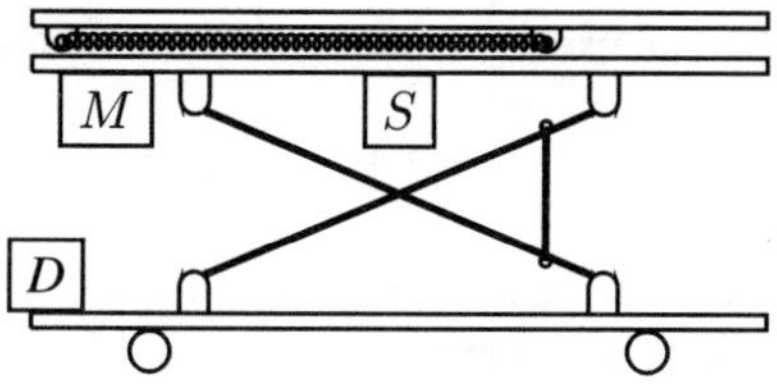

Figure 7.4: A movable patient support unit

The patient support unit is depicted in figure 7.4. The motor M has a brake that is applied when the patient support is undocked, or when the bed is not moving in nonemergency mode.

There is a sensor S that senses the position of the movable bed. It can sense whether the bed is at the left, at the right, or somewhere in between.

The bed contains a docking station D which can sense whether the bed is docked onto the MR scanner. Furthermore, it has a mechanical lock which applies automatically when the bed is docked. If the unit must be undocked, the docking unit must first get a signal to unlock.

The bed is controlled using a panel, which is depicted in figure 7.5. This interface has five buttons. The stop button puts the patient support unit in emergency mode. In this mode no movement of the bed is allowed. In case the bed is docked, the brakes must be released to allow to move the patient out of the scanner manually. In case the unit is undocked, the brakes must be applied. The resume button is used to return the bed back to normal mode.

The buttons marked with the arrows are used to move the bed to the left and to the right. They only have an effect if the bed is docked and not already completely moved to the left or right.

The undock button is used to unlock the docking unit. This can only be done when the bed has moved completely on top of the support unit. In order to allow a patient to be removed in case of an emergency, the undock button can be applied when the platform is in emergency mode. Also in this case, the bed must be on top of the unit. When the lock of the docking unit is released, the brakes must be applied.

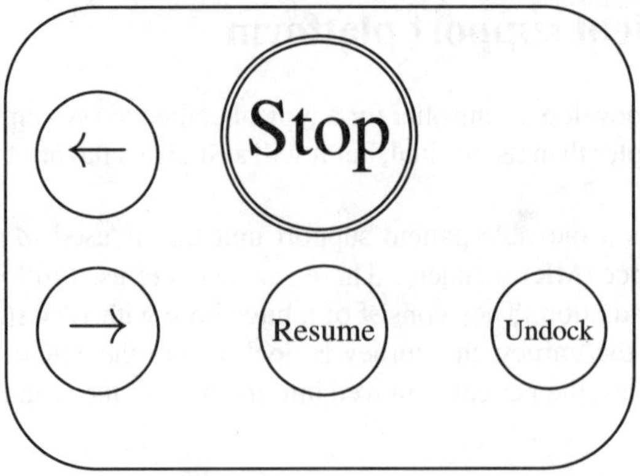

Figure 7.5: The user console on the patient support unit

As indicated above, actual docking units are much more complex. They can also move up and down, and often have means of moving sideways. Generally, such platforms can be remotely controlled, either from the scanner or from an operating room. Apart from normal and emergency modes, such platforms have other modes, such as a manual mode where the bed can be moved manually, without the need to press the emergency buttons. There are also means for logging and remote maintenance. For the exposition here, we keep our setup relatively simple. We also ignore the possibilities of errors, such as nonfunctioning sensors and broken motors.

The first question to address is what we must model. In this case we must develop a controller for the patient support platform. Therefore, it makes sense to identify the actions by which the controller communicates with the outside world. These actions are listed in table 7.1. Note that there are fundamentally two ways of communication. The controller can poll the devices continuously, or the devices can inform the controller on an interrupt basis. For the design here, we choose the latter. Before detailing the behavior of the controller it is a good habit to first list all behavioral requirements or properties on the behavior. Alternatively, the external behavior could be made explicit as done with the alternating bit protocol (section 7.1) and the sliding window protocol (section 7.2). There are three reasons not to do this. The first one is that the behavior of embedded systems is often quite complex, which makes it very hard to give a neat description of the external behavior. The second one is that such controllers are not really used as part of a more complex behavioral description and therefore there is little use in detailing the external behavior as a process expression. The last one is that the actual external behavior is not of real interest, as long as a number of essential properties are satisfied.

Finding the list of such properties is generally one of the more difficult tasks of behavioral modeling. The reason is that properties must be formulated on the basis of general understanding of the problem domain. There is no way to check whether the properties cover all relevant aspects, and are correct. It is very common that properties must be rephrased or extended in a later phase of the project because they turn out to

pressStop	The stop button is pressed
pressResume	The resume button is pressed
pressUndock	The undock button is pressed
pressLeft	The button marked with a left arrow is pressed
pressRight	The button with a right arrow is pressed
motorLeft	The motor is switched on and makes an inward movement
motorRight	The motor is switched on and makes an outward movement
motorOff	The motor is switched off
applyBrake	Apply the brake of the motor
releaseBrake	Release the brake of the motor
isDocked	Indicates that the platform has been docked
unlockDock	Unlock the lock in the docking unit, to enable undocking
atInnermost	An indication that the bed is completely inside the bore of the MR scanner
atOutermost	Indicates that the bed is completely on top of the patient support unit

Table 7.1: The interactions of the MPSU controller

be incorrect or incomplete.

It is helpful to formulate the behavioral requirements by distinguishing the following groups of properties.

- Safety properties. What must absolutely not happen! It is useful to first formulate this for the whole system, and later translate this into concrete requirements on the interactions of the controller to be designed.

- Liveness properties. What should happen! Here the basic question is what the purpose of an interaction from the outside world with the system is. For example, if the *pressStop* button is pressed, the system must go to emergency mode.

As a rule of thumb, each interaction should at least occur once in a property. This is a practical way to check the completeness of the requirements.

The requirement must ultimately be stated in terms of the interactions of the system to be designed. The way to achieve this is to state the properties at increased levels of detail. Below, we state the requirements in three stages, indicated with **a**, **b**, and **c**. At **a**, the property is stated in ordinary English referring to intuitive notions such as "emergency mode" and "being undocked." At **b**, the properties are reformulated in terms of interactions only. Instead of speaking about emergency mode, we must now speak about "having pressed the stop button, without having pressed the release button yet." At **c** we translate a property to a modal formula. It is good habit to at least describe the properties informally (as done under **a**) and describe them at least once precisely as under **b** or **c**. The informal description is needed for quick human understanding, whereas the other is required as the first description is often ambiguous.

We have the following requirements for the patient platform. We intentionally provide the list of requirements that sprang to our mind at the initial design of the platform.

We also provide a model of the controller as we initially thought the controller should behave. The purpose of not giving a definitive list of requirements is to show how deceptive initial ideas about system behavior are.

For each, we list the **a**, **b**, and **c** formulations grouped together, but for first reading, it is best to skip **b** and **c**.

1**a**. For the patient platform we want that the platform cannot tumble over. Concretely this means that when undocked, the bed is in the rightmost position, the brakes are applied and the motor is off (safety).

1**b**. Before sending an *unlockDock* action, the following actions must happen: An *applyBrake* without a *releaseBrake* in between, an *atOutermost* without a *motorLeft* in between, and a *motorOff* action without a *motorLeft* or *motorRight* in between. Furthermore, between an *unlockDock* and the subsequent *isDocked*, the actions *releaseBrake*, *motorLeft*, and *motorRight* action are not allowed.

1**c**. We can formulate this requirement as six separate modal formulas. As smaller formulas are easier to check, it is always wise to make the formulas as compact as possible.

- $[\overline{applyBrake}^{\star} \cdot unlockDock]false.$
- $[true^{\star} \cdot releaseBrake \cdot \overline{applyBrake}^{\star} \cdot unlockDock]false.$
- $[\overline{atOutermost}^{\star} \cdot unlockDock]false.$
- $[true^{\star} \cdot motorLeft \cdot \overline{atOutermost}^{\star} \cdot unlockDock]false.$
- $[\overline{motorOff}^{\star} \cdot unlockDock]false.$
- $[true^{\star} \cdot (motorLeft + motorRight) \cdot \overline{motorOff}^{\star} \cdot unlockDock]false.$
- $[true^{\star} \cdot unlockDock \cdot \overline{isDocked} \cdot (releaseBrake + motorLeft + motorRight)]false.$

2**a**. After pressing the stop button, a patient on the platform can manually be moved out of the scanner and scanning room (liveness).

2**b**. After a *pressStop* event takes place, a *motorOff*, a *releaseBrake*, and an *unlockDock* action must inevitably follow.

2**c**. We can write this requirement as three compact modal formulas.

- $[true^{\star} \cdot pressStop]\mu X.([\overline{motorOff}]X \wedge \langle true \rangle true).$
- $[true^{\star} \cdot pressStop]\mu X.([\overline{releaseBrake}]X \wedge \langle true \rangle true).$
- $[true^{\star} \cdot pressStop]\mu X.([\overline{unlockDock}]X \wedge \langle true \rangle true).$

3**a**. In order to protect the motor, the motor will not attempt to push the bed beyond its outermost and innermost positions.

3**b**. If an *atOutermost* or an *atInnermost* action takes place, a *motorOff* event will follow.

3c. $[\mathit{true}^\star\cdot(\mathit{atOutermost}+\mathit{atInnermost})]\mu X.([\overline{\mathit{motorOff}}]X\wedge\langle\mathit{true}\rangle\mathit{true})$.

4a. If *pressUndock* takes place, and the patient platform is in rightmost position, an *unlockDock* event takes place.

4b. After a *pressUndock*, if there has been a preceding *atInnermost*, and between those no *motorLeft* and *releaseBrake* has taken place, then an *unlockDock* will take place, except if there is a prior *motorLeft* or *releaseBrake*.

4c. $[\mathit{true}^\star\cdot\mathit{atInnermost}\cdot\overline{\mathit{motorLeft}\cup\mathit{releaseBrake}}^\star\cdot\mathit{pressUndock}]$

$$\mu X.([\overline{\mathit{unlockDock}}\cap\overline{\mathit{motorLeft}}\cap\overline{\mathit{releaseBrake}}]X\wedge\langle\mathit{true}\rangle\mathit{true}).$$

5a. If *pressLeft* takes place, the platform is docked, not in emergency mode, the bed is not completely inside the bore and not already moving to the left, the motor is switched on to move the bed inside the bore.

5b. If a *pressLeft* takes place, with a preceding *isDocked* without an intermediary *unlockDock*, no preceding *pressStop* without an intermediary *pressResume* took place, no *atInnermost* took place without intermediary *motorRight*, and no *motorLeft* happened without any *motorOff* or *motorRight* in between, then a *motorLeft* will take place, unless an *unlockDock*, a *pressStop*, or an *atInnermost* takes place before that.

5c. In the Booleans b_1, b_2, b_3, and b_4 we record that the four conditions that must hold before the *pressLeft* to lead to a *motorLeft* are favorable. Then the formula becomes:

$$
\begin{array}{l}
\nu X(b_1{:}\mathbb{B}{\rightarrow}\mathit{false}, b_2{:}\mathbb{B}{:=}\mathit{true}, b_3{:}\mathbb{B}{:=}\mathit{true}, b_4{:}\mathbb{B}{:=}\mathit{true}).\\
\quad[\mathit{isDocked}]X(\mathit{true}, b_2, b_3, b_4)\wedge\\
\quad[\mathit{unlockDock}]X(\mathit{false}, b_2, b_3, b_4)\wedge\\
\quad[\mathit{pressResume}]X(b_1, \mathit{true}, b_3, b_4)\wedge\\
\quad[\mathit{pressStop}]X(b_1, \mathit{false}, b_3, b_4)\wedge\\
\quad[\mathit{atInnermost}]X(b_1, b_2, \mathit{true}, b_4)\wedge\\
\quad[\mathit{motorRight}]X(b_1, b_2, \mathit{false}, b_4)\wedge\\
\quad[\mathit{motorOff}\cup\mathit{motorRight}]X(b_1, b_2, b_3, \mathit{true})\wedge\\
\quad[\mathit{motorLeft}]X(b_1, b_2, b_3, \mathit{false})\wedge\\
\qquad(b_1\wedge b_2\wedge b_3\wedge b_4\Rightarrow[\mathit{pressLeft}]\\
\qquad\quad\mu Y.([\overline{\mathit{motorLeft}}\cap\overline{\mathit{unlockDock}}\cap\overline{\mathit{pressStop}}\cap\overline{\mathit{atInnermost}}]Y\wedge\\
\qquad\qquad\langle\mathit{true}\rangle\mathit{true}))\ .
\end{array}
$$

6a. If *pressRight* happens, the platform is docked, not in emergency mode and the bed is not completely on top of the platform, not already moving to the right, the motor is switched on for an outward movement.

6b. This requirement is completely similar to requirement 5. We reformulate it into actions and into a modal formula along exactly the same lines. If a *pressRight* takes place, with a preceding *isDocked* without an intermediary *unlockDock*, no preceding *pressStop* without an intermediary *pressResume* took place, no *atOutermost* took place without an intermediary *motorLeft*, and no *motorRight* happened without any *motorOff* or *motorLeft* in between, then a *motorRight* will take place, unless an *unlockDock*, a *pressStop*, or an *atInnermost* takes place before that.

6c. This formula very much resembles the formula at 5c.

$$
\begin{array}{l}
\nu X(b_1{:}\mathbb{B}{:=}\mathit{false}, b_2{:}\mathbb{B}{:=}\mathit{true}, b_3{:}\mathbb{B}{:=}\mathit{true}, b_4{:}\mathbb{B}{:=}\mathit{true}).\\
\quad [\mathit{isDocked}]X(\mathit{true}, b_2, b_3, b_4)\wedge\\
\quad [\mathit{unlockDock}]X(\mathit{false}, b_2, b_3, b_4)\wedge\\
\quad [\mathit{pressResume}]X(b_1, \mathit{true}, b_3, b_4)\wedge\\
\quad [\mathit{pressStop}]X(b_1, \mathit{false}, b_3, b_4)\wedge\\
\quad [\mathit{atOutermost}]X(b_1, b_2, \mathit{true}, b_4)\wedge\\
\quad [\mathit{motorLeft}]X(b_1, b_2, \mathit{false}, b_4)\wedge\\
\quad [\mathit{motorOff} \cup \mathit{motorLeft}]X(b_1, b_2, b_3, \mathit{true})\wedge\\
\quad [\mathit{motorRight}]X(b_1, b_2, b_3, \mathit{false})\wedge\\
\qquad (b_1 \wedge b_2 \wedge b_3 \wedge b_4 \Rightarrow [\mathit{pressRight}]\\
\qquad\quad \mu Y.([\overline{\mathit{motorRight}} \cap \overline{\mathit{unlockDock}} \cap \overline{\mathit{pressStop}} \cap \overline{\mathit{atOutermost}}]Y \wedge\\
\qquad\qquad \langle \mathit{true}\rangle \mathit{true})).
\end{array}
$$

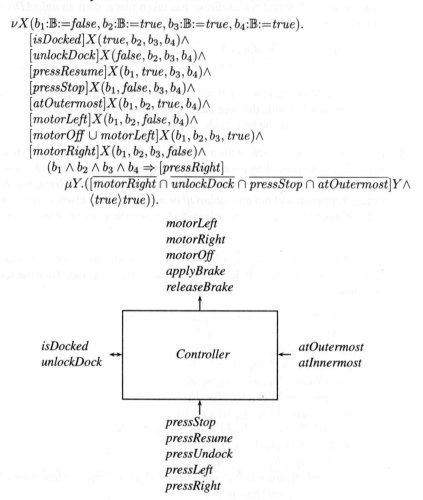

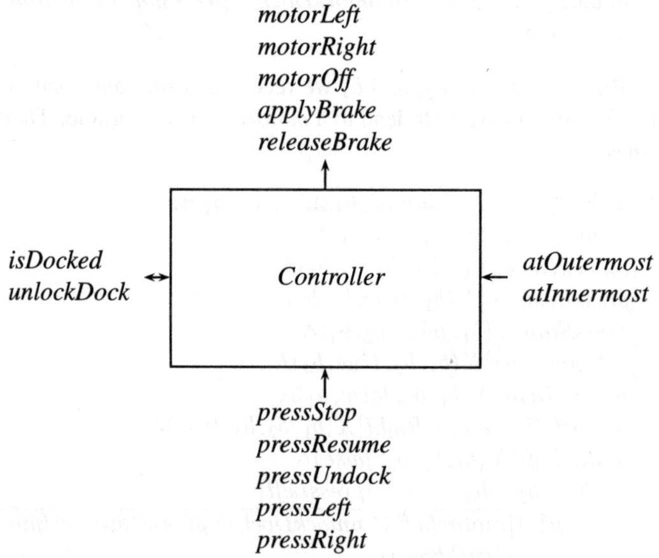

Figure 7.6: Input/output diagram of the MPSU controller

A possible behavior of the controller is given below. The idea is that there are two primary modes, namely *Normal* and *Emergency*. In *Emergency* mode the bed the brakes are released and the motors are off and the bed only responds to pressing the resume button. In *Normal* mode, all functions operate normally. Within the controller it is recalled whether the unit is *docked*, and whether it is signaled to be at the *leftmost* or *rightmost* position. Also the status of the motor is recalled to be *moveleft*, *moveright*, and *stopped*. The process itself is rather straightforward and is therefore not explained.

$$
\begin{array}{ll}
\mathbf{sort} & \mathit{Mode} = \mathbf{struct}\ \mathit{Normal} \mid \mathit{Emergency};\\
& \mathit{MotorStatus} = \mathbf{struct}\ \mathit{moveleft} \mid \mathit{moveright} \mid \mathit{stopped};
\end{array}
$$

$$
\begin{array}{l}
\mathbf{proc}\ \mathit{Controller}(m{:}\mathit{Mode}, \mathit{docked}, \mathit{rightmost}, \mathit{leftmost}{:}\mathbb{B}, \mathit{ms}{:}\mathit{MotorStatus})\\
\quad = \mathit{pressStop}\cdot \mathit{releaseBrake}\cdot \mathit{motorOff}\cdot\\
\qquad\quad \mathit{Controller}(\mathit{Emergency}, \mathit{docked}, \mathit{rightmost}, \mathit{leftmost}, \mathit{stopped})\\
\qquad + \mathit{pressResume}\cdot \mathit{Controller}(\mathit{Normal}, \mathit{docked}, \mathit{rightmost}, \mathit{leftmost}, \mathit{ms})\\
\qquad + \mathit{pressUndock}\cdot\\
\qquad\quad (\mathit{docked} \wedge \mathit{rightmost})\\
\qquad\qquad \rightarrow \mathit{applyBrake}\cdot \mathit{unlockDock}\cdot\\
\qquad\qquad\quad \mathit{Controller}(m, \mathit{false}, \mathit{rightmost}, \mathit{leftmost}, \mathit{ms})\\
\qquad\qquad \diamond\ \mathit{Controller}(m, \mathit{docked}, \mathit{rightmost}, \mathit{leftmost}, \mathit{ms})\\
\qquad + \mathit{pressLeft}\cdot\\
\qquad\quad (\mathit{docked} \wedge \mathit{ms}{\not\approx}\mathit{moveleft} \wedge \neg \mathit{leftmost} \wedge m{\approx}\mathit{Normal})\\
\qquad\qquad \rightarrow \mathit{releaseBrake}\cdot \mathit{motorLeft}\cdot\\
\qquad\qquad\quad \mathit{Controller}(m, \mathit{docked}, \mathit{false}, \mathit{leftmost}, \mathit{moveleft})\\
\qquad\qquad \diamond\ \mathit{Controller}(m, \mathit{docked}, \mathit{rightmost}, \mathit{leftmost}, \mathit{ms})\\
\qquad + \mathit{pressRight}\cdot\\
\qquad\quad (\mathit{docked} \wedge \mathit{ms}{\not\approx}\mathit{moveright} \wedge \neg \mathit{rightmost} \wedge m{\approx}\mathit{Normal})\\
\qquad\qquad \rightarrow \mathit{releaseBrake}\cdot \mathit{motorRight}\cdot\\
\qquad\qquad\quad \mathit{Controller}(m, \mathit{docked}, \mathit{rightmost}, \mathit{false}, \mathit{moveright})\\
\qquad\qquad \diamond\ \mathit{Controller}(m, \mathit{docked}, \mathit{rightmost}, \mathit{leftmost}, \mathit{ms})\\
\qquad + \mathit{isDocked}\cdot \mathit{Controller}(m, \mathit{true}, \mathit{rightmost}, \mathit{leftmost}, \mathit{ms})\\
\qquad + \mathit{atInnermost}\cdot \mathit{motorOff}\cdot \mathit{applyBrake}\cdot\\
\qquad\quad \mathit{Controller}(m, \mathit{docked}, \mathit{true}, \mathit{false}, \mathit{stopped})\\
\qquad + \mathit{atOutermost}\cdot \mathit{motorOff}\cdot \mathit{applyBrake}\cdot\\
\qquad\quad \mathit{Controller}(m, \mathit{docked}, \mathit{false}, \mathit{true}, \mathit{stopped}).
\end{array}
$$

Initially, the support unit starts in *Normal* mode, the motor is stopped, and the position of the bed is not known. It is assumed that when the unit is switched on, it is always docked.

$$\mathbf{init}\quad \mathit{Controller}(\mathit{Normal}, \mathit{true}, \mathit{false}, \mathit{false}, \mathit{stopped});$$

Controllers are generally much more complex than the one above, and are often distributed over different computing units. So, in general controllers consist of a number of parallel components that all have a well defined task. Between the components communication takes place to keep the components in par with each other. This parallel structure generally makes it much harder to understand the behavior, than in the case above.

Exercise 7.3.1. Which of the modal formulas are valid for the given model of the patient support platform? You may want to use the tools `mcrl22lps`, `lps2pbes`, and `pbes2bool` to verify the modal formulas automatically. Also, the state space generation tool `lps2lts` and the visualization tools `ltsgraph` and `ltsview` can be used to understand whether the patient support platform works properly.

Exercise 7.3.2. Are the requirements consistent in the sense that there exists a behavioral description such that all requirements are valid?

Exercise 7.3.3. In parallel programming synchronization operators can become costly. In order to avoid the problems, synchronization free programming has been invented. Unfortunately, without synchronization operators and with only the possibility to read from and write to memory, the *consensus problem* cannot be solved, where several parallel processes must agree on a common value [122].

In order to overcome this problem, extra hardware primitives are available, such as *LoadLock* and *Compare&Swap* (*CMPSWP*). In *LoadLock* a memory location is read and locked. When this memory location is written by the same process, it can see whether this location has been written by another process in the mean time. *Compare&Swap* is an atomic instruction that can be used to write a value to a memory location if this location has an expected value. More precisely:

$$
\begin{array}{l}
\mathit{CMPSWP}(n, m_1, m_2) = \\
\quad \textbf{if } M[n] \approx m_1 \\
\quad \textbf{then } M[n] := m_2;\ \textbf{return } \mathit{true} \\
\quad \textbf{else return } \mathit{false}
\end{array}
$$

Here the array M represents the memory. It says that if memory location $M[n]$ equals m_1, then m_2 is written to this location and success is reported. Otherwise, nothing is written and false is returned.

Using the *Compare&Swap* instruction it is possible to construct a list of free nodes that can be accessed by several processes in parallel. The parallelism is on the level of instructions, so all reads, writes, and *Compare&Swaps* can be executed in an interleaved manner.

Lists of free nodes typically have two operations, namely release and get. Release puts a node on the list, effectively making this node available to others. The get operation allows a process to claim a node for its own use. Typically, nodes may not be given to more than one process without being released in the mean time, and nodes that are released become available at some later time.

A straightforward way of doing this is by implementing the following procedures to access the list. The description is in some pseudocode programming language. There is some globally accessible head of the list *hd*. Furthermore, there is a sort **node** of objects to be stored on the list. For each **node** n there is a **node** $n.next$ indicating the next node in the list. The special node *NULL* is used as an end marker of the list. $NULL.next$ is not defined.

```
list hd = NULL;

void release(node n) =
  bool b;
  repeat
    n.next := hd;
    b := CMPSWP(hd, n.next, n);
  until b;
```

```
node get(node n) =
  bool b; node n;
  repeat
    n := hd;
    if n≈NULL return NULL;
    b := CMPSWP(hd, n, n.next);
  until b;
  return n;
```

This implementation is incorrect. The question is to find out why. A systematic technique is to model the memory in mCRL2, together with multiple release and get processes. Verifying the properties for a limited memory size and a limited set of processes should reveal the problem. In the literature, this problem is known as the false positive, or ABA problem. Due to this problem, several microprocessors contain a double compare and swap instruction.

7.4 Historical notes

With the advent of process calculi and modal logics, models of behavior have been made for various systems and protocols. A first notable example was Milner's scheduler [135] described in example 10.2.16. The purpose of this scheduler is to start and stop processes in sequence. It is widely used as a small but typical example, especially because it is τ-confluent and can therefore easily and automatically be verified for thousands of parallel processes.

The alternating bit protocol is also a typical simple example that is often used as an illustration. First described in [23], it has been used as a prototypical example in the Amsterdam school of process algebra [18]. There are all kinds of variations, for example, where the channel does not report message loss, but where timers are used (concurrent alternating bit protocol) or where messages are transmitted in chunks and the number of retransmissions is limited (bounded retransmission protocol [82]). Sliding window protocols are a generalization of the alternating bit protocol in the sense messages are tagged with numbers instead of bits. A good informal introduction of such protocols is found in [170]. A nice collection of process-algebraic descriptions of such distributed systems and protocols is [130].

Scattered in the literature there are very many applications of process algebras and modal logics, but there are very little comprehensive overviews. The patient platform is a typical example stemming from the redesign of a patient platform, which has never been published. The overviews that exist generally describe the state of the art and provide a forward outlook [68], or they contain applications in a certain domain [47].

There are overviews of applications using nonalgebraic formal methods, such as Z, VDM, and B [99, 183]. There are also articles with advice on how to use formal methods [36]. Especially interesting is [79] containing guidelines how to write models such that the state space explosion is being avoided. There are also a few papers investigating the impact of the use of formal methods generally indicating a very substantial increase in quality and even a slight decrease in development time [32, 147, 183].

8

Timed Process Behavior

The labeled transition systems as presented in the previous chapter can easily be transformed into timed transition systems by making it explicit at which time an action can take place. This chapter introduces timed transition systems and extends the theory of the previous chapter to a setting with time.

8.1 Timed actions and time deadlocks

Timed actions are actions with a time tag. Time tags are positive real numbers. Timed process behavior starts at time 0, which means that the first action must take place after time 0. We typically write

$$a^{\varsigma}t$$

for action a that takes place at time t. Graphically, this is denoted by process (a) in figure 8.1. Just as in the transition systems in chapter 2, the initial state is marked with a small incoming arrow, and the terminating state is marked with a small ✓ symbol. In process (b) in the same figure, we see a process that performs an action a at time 2 followed by a b at time 4. In a timed transition system all outgoing transitions have higher time tags than all incoming transitions to indicate that time is progressing. Hence, a transition system as in figure 8.1(c) is not allowed. An action a is just an action that can happen at any time, as depicted in figure 8.1(d). As we can only draw a finite number of transitions, the diagram can only be suggestive, using shades of gray to suggest an infinite number of transitions and using dots between timed actions to suggest that there are many.

An important aspect of time is idling. This means that no action is done while time is proceeding. If an action a can be done at time t, it is self evident that idling is possible until time t. But it can be that action a is ignored if idling beyond time t is also possible. In figure 8.2 the situations are depicted, where in (a) an action a must happen at time 3. In figure 8.2(b), an action a can happen at time 3 but it is also possible to idle until time 4. Idling is indicated by the wavy arrow with a time label. Note that the idle arrow does not have an end state.

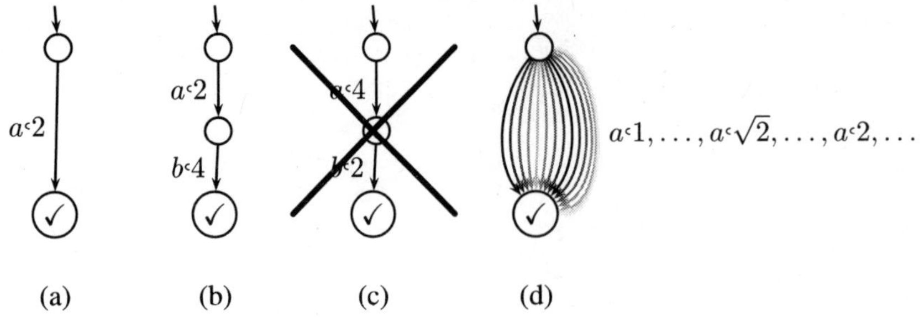

Figure 8.1: Timed transition systems

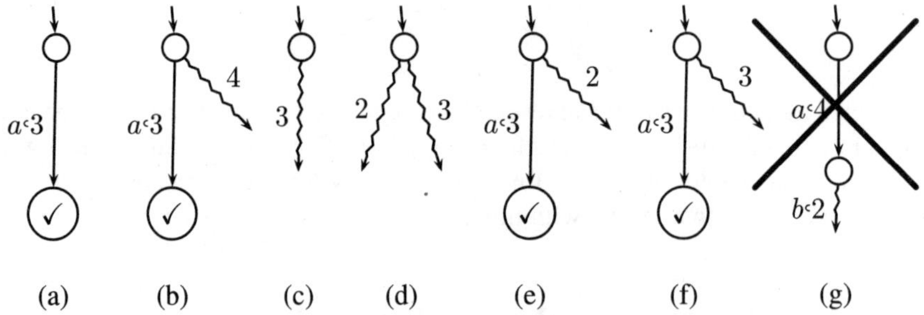

Figure 8.2: Timed transition systems with idling arrows

What if the action a in figure 8.2(a) cannot be performed for whatever reason, for instance, if an action with which a must immediately communicate is not available at time 3? Then at time 3 there is no alternative. We resolve this situation by introducing the notion of a *time deadlock* at time 3. Time cannot proceed. Clearly, a process that has a time deadlock does not represent a real life process, as time cannot stop. A good check to find out whether a timed process can be built, is to prove that it is free of time deadlocks.

A process that only has a time deadlock at time 3 is represented in figure 8.2(c). If it is possible to idle in a state until time t, it is also possible to idle to any earlier moment in time. This means that the process in figure 8.2(d) is equivalent to the process in figure 8.2(c), as the idle transition with time 2 is redundant. Redundant idle transitions are generally not drawn. If an action can be done at some time t, then it is possible to idle until t. Hence, the process in figure 8.2(e) is equivalent to the process in figure 8.2(a). The process in figure 8.2(f) is not equivalent to those in figure 8.2(a) and figure 8.2(e). It is possible to idle until exactly time 3, not doing a‘3.

In figure 8.2(g) the situation is drawn where it is possible to idle to a moment before arriving in a state. This is not allowed. We say that this transition system is not properly timed.

Exercise 8.1.1. Which of the timed transition systems in figure 8.3 are properly timed labeled transition systems and which have time deadlocks?

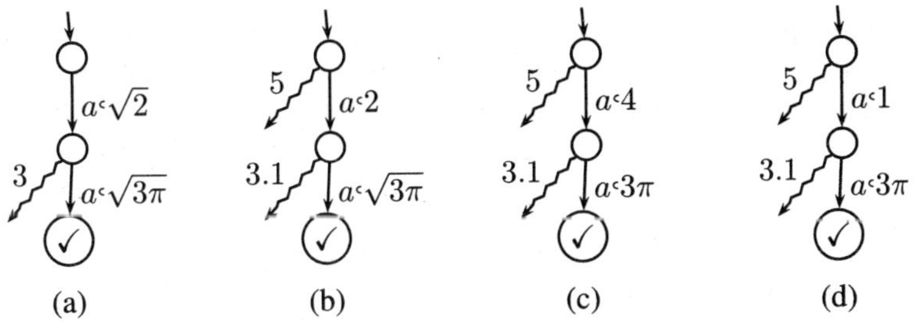

Figure 8.3: Timed transition systems belonging to exercise 8.1.1

Exercise 8.1.2. Draw a timed labeled transition system that represents a process that ticks every second using a timed *tick* action.

8.2 Timed transition systems

We now give the definition of a general timed transition system. It differs from a normal transition system in that there is an extra idle relation, and transitions additionally carry a positive real number indicating when the transition occurs. Moreover, as sketched in the previous section, there are some restrictions on which transitions and idle relations are allowed. We use $\mathbb{R}^{>0}$ for the set of the real numbers larger than or equal to 0.

Definition 8.2.1 (Timed transition system). A *timed transition system* is a six tuple $A = (S, Act, \longrightarrow, \rightsquigarrow, s_0, T)$ where

- S is a set of states.
- Act is a set of actions.
- $\longrightarrow \subseteq S \times Act \times \mathbb{R}^{>0} \times S$ is a *transition relation*. The expression $s \xrightarrow{a}_t s'$ says that a transition is made from state s to state s' by executing action a at time t.
- $\rightsquigarrow \subseteq S \times \mathbb{R}^{>0}$ is the *idle relation*. The predicate $s \rightsquigarrow_t$ expresses that it is possible to idle up to and including time t in state s.
- s_0 is the *initial state*.
- $T \subseteq S$ is the set of *terminating states*.

Every timed transition system must satisfy the *progress* and *density* requirements. The progress requirement says that if

$$s \xrightarrow{a}_t s' \xrightarrow{a'}_{t'} s''$$

for states s, s', s'', actions a and a' and times t and t', then $t' > t$. The density requirement expresses that for any action a, states s, s', and time t

$$\text{if } s \xrightarrow{a}_t s' \text{ or } s \rightsquigarrow_t, \text{ then } s \rightsquigarrow_{t'}$$

for any $0 < t' < t$.

Every labeled transition system can easily be transformed into a timed transition system. Let $A = (S, Act, \longrightarrow, s_0, T)$ be a labeled transition system. The timed transition system that describes the same process is

$$(S \times \mathbb{R}^{\geq 0}, Act, \longmapsto, \rightsquigarrow, \langle s_0, 0\rangle, T \times \mathbb{R}^{\geq 0}).$$

As states, we take all states of S paired with a nonnegative real number indicating when this state was entered. The initial state gets 0 as the starting time, and all termination states are paired with an arbitrary nonnegative real number. The new timed transition relation is defined as follows:

$$\langle s, t\rangle \longmapsto_u \langle s', t'\rangle \text{ iff } s \xrightarrow{a} s', u>t \text{ and } t'=u.$$

The idle relation expresses that in any state it is possible to idle indefinitely:

$$\langle s, t\rangle \rightsquigarrow_{t'} \text{ iff } t'>t.$$

Note that the progress and density requirements are satisfied, and also observe that in general most states of the timed transition system are not reachable.

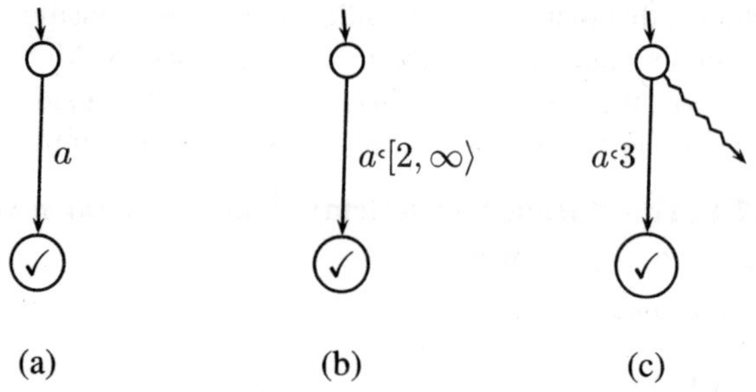

Figure 8.4: Suggestive drawings of timed transition systems

Drawing timed transition systems is generally quite impossible, because of the density requirement. This is the main reason why redundant idle transitions are not drawn. In figure 8.4, three suggestive drawing conventions are given. If an action can happen at any time, then generally the action is drawn without any time stamp (see figure 8.4(a)). In figure 8.4(b), the action a can take place in the time interval $[2, \infty\rangle$. We use the common notation of open and closed intervals to replace time stamps, whenever convenient. In figure 8.4(c), the wavy arrow without a time label indicates that idling is possible until infinity.

A somewhat larger example is depicted in figure 8.5. It describes a process that can send at times 1, 2, and 3 using an s action, but if nothing is sent at time 4 a *timeout* takes place. After sending, it can receive a message using action r from time 4 to time 100 but it can also idle up to infinity.

Exercise 8.2.2. Draw a timed transition system where if an alarm is sounded between time 0 and 10, a response will come at time 11.

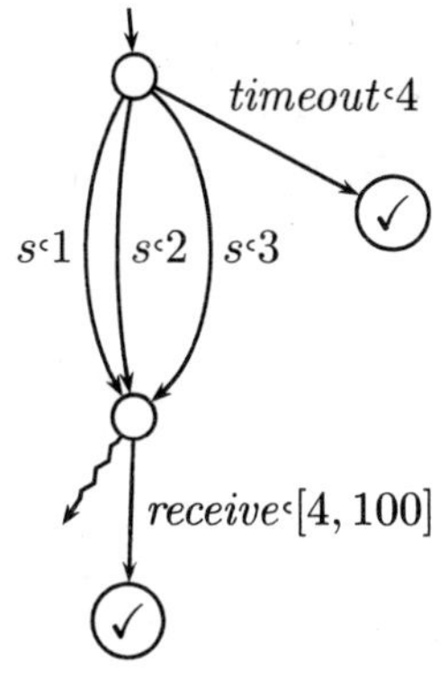

Figure 8.5: A simple timeout process

Exercise 8.2.3. Give explicit definitions of two timed transition systems that both have only one single state, which is also the initial state. In the first transition system it is possible to wait until time 2, whereas in the second transition system it is possible to wait up until and including time 2. Which of the two transition systems is hard to depict using idle transitions?

8.3 Timed process equivalences

The equivalences defined in section 2.3 can been lifted to the setting with time. We treat strong and branching bisimulation, and trace and weak trace equivalence.

8.3.1 Timed (strong) bisimulation

We start out with the definition of timed strong bisimulation. The difference with untimed bisimulation is that actions that simulate each other must have the same time. Moreover, if idling to time t is possible in a state, idling up to t is also possible in its related state.

Definition 8.3.1 (Timed strong bisimulation). Let $A = (S, Act, \longrightarrow, \rightsquigarrow, s_0, T)$ be a timed transition system. A binary relation $R \subseteq S \times S$ is called a timed (strong) *bisimulation relation* iff for all $s, u \in S$ such that sRu holds, it also holds for all actions $a \in Act$ and $t \in \mathbb{R}^{>0}$ that:

1. If $s \xrightarrow{a}_t s'$ for some $s' \in S$, then there is a $u' \in S$ such that $u \xrightarrow{a}_t u'$ with $s'Ru'$,
2. If $u \xrightarrow{a}_t u'$ for some $u' \in S$, then there is a $s' \in S$ such that $s \xrightarrow{a}_t s'$ with $s'Ru'$,
3. $s \rightsquigarrow_t$ if and only if $u \rightsquigarrow_t$, and
4. $s \in T$ if and only if $u \in T$.

Two states s and u are *timed (strongly) bisimilar*, denoted by $s \leftrightarrow u$, iff there is a timed strong bisimulation relation R such that sRu. Two timed transition systems are *timed (strongly) bisimilar* iff their initial states are timed bisimilar.

Note that the symbol $\leftrightarrow$ for timed strong bisimulation is the same as the symbol for ordinary bisimulation. As the two notions coincide for untimed processes, this does not cause confusion. Timed strong branching bisimulation is a congruence for all process-algebraic operators.

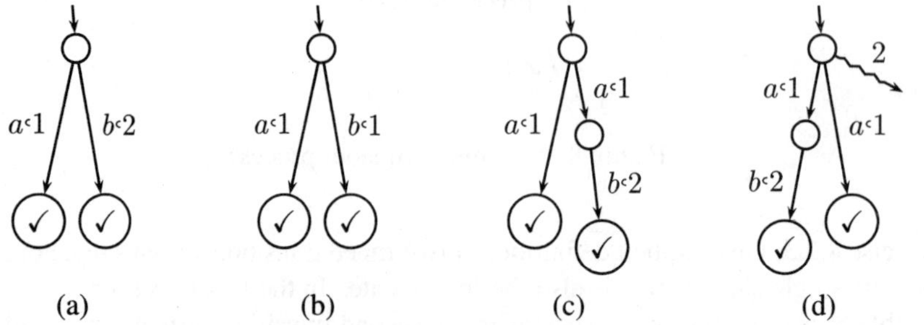

Figure 8.6: Timed and untimed choices are different

From a technical perspective timed strong bisimulation and timed bisimulation are very similar. Intuitively, there is a big difference, best shown in figure 8.6(a). Here there is a process where at time 1 it is chosen to either do the aᐧ1 or not. If not, the b at time 2 must be done. In the untimed setting we choose among actions. In a timed setting we often choose either to do an action or not. But as the LTS in figure 8.6(b) shows, it is also possible to choose among actions in a timed setting.

Exercise 8.3.2. Which of the timed transition systems in figure 8.6 are timed bisimilar?

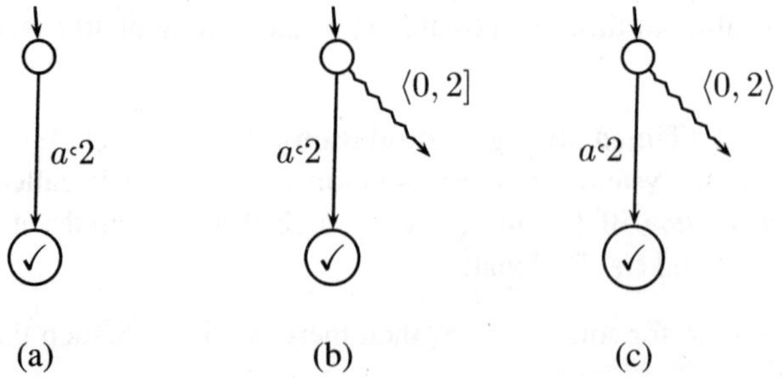

Figure 8.7: Three simple timed transition systems

Exercise 8.3.3. Which of the three timed transition systems in figure 8.7 are strongly bisimilar?

8.3.2 Timed branching bisimulation

We provide here the definition of timed branching bisimulation inspired by [63]. The definition is quite complex. Not only does each timed branching bisimulation relation have an associated time t where processes are considered to be related starting from time t. Beyond this, after a simulating step, states must also be related at all intermediate times. This is necessary to guarantee that timed branching bisimulation relations are associative.

Definition 8.3.4 (Timed branching bisimulation). Let $A = (S, Act, \longrightarrow, \rightsquigarrow, s_0, T)$ be a timed transition system. We call relations $R_t \subseteq S \times S$ with $t \in \mathbb{R}^{\geq 0}$ a *collection of timed branching bisimulation relations* iff for all states $s, u \in S$ such that sR_tu, the following conditions hold for all actions $a \in Act$ and $t' \in \mathbb{R}^{>0}$:

1. If $s \xrightarrow{a}_{t'} s'$ with $t'>t$, then
   (a) Either $a = \tau$, and there are $t = t_0 < t_1 < \cdots < t_n < t_{n+1} = t'$ $(n \geq 0)$ such that $u = u_0 \xrightarrow{\tau}_{t_1} u_1 \xrightarrow{\tau}_{t_2} \cdots \xrightarrow{\tau}_{t_n} u_n \rightsquigarrow_{t'}$, sR_wu_i for all $t_i \leq w < t_{i+1}$ and $0 \leq i \leq n$, and $s'R_{t'}u_n$, or
   (b) There are $t = t_0 < t_1 < \cdots < t_n < t_{n+1} = t'$ $(n \geq 0)$ such that $u = u_0 \xrightarrow{\tau}_{t_1} u_1 \xrightarrow{\tau}_{t_2} \cdots \xrightarrow{\tau}_{t_n} u_n \xrightarrow{a}_{t'} u'$, sR_wu_i for all $t_i \leq w < t_{i+1}$ and $0 \leq i \leq n$, and $s'R_{t'}u'$.
2. The case where $u \xrightarrow{a}_{t'} u'$ with $t'>t$ is symmetric to the case above.
3. If $s \rightsquigarrow_{t'}$ then there are $t = t_0 < t_1 < \cdots < t_n < t_{n+1} = t'$ $(n \geq 0)$ such that $u = u_0 \xrightarrow{\tau}_{t_1} u_1 \xrightarrow{\tau}_{t_2} \cdots \xrightarrow{\tau}_{t_{n-1}} u_{n-1} \xrightarrow{\tau}_{t_n} u_n \rightsquigarrow_{t'}$, sR_wu_i for all $t_i \leq w < t_{i+1}$ and $0 \leq i \leq n$, and $sR_{t'}u_n$.
4. Again, the case where $u \rightsquigarrow_{t'}$ with $t'>t$ is symmetric to the previous case.
5. If $s \in T$, then $u \in T$.
6. Finally, the case where $u \in T$ is symmetric to the case above.

Two states s and u are *timed branching bisimilar at time* t', denoted by $s \leftrightarrow_b^{t'} u$, iff there is a collection of timed branching bisimulation relations R_t such that $sR_{t'}u$. Two states s and u are timed branching bisimilar, notation $s \leftrightarrow_b u$ iff $s \leftrightarrow_b^t u$ for all $t \geq 0$. Two timed transition systems are *timed branching bisimilar* iff their initial states are timed branching bisimilar.

We feel justified to use the same notation for untimed and timed branching bisimulation as they coincide on processes that do not use explicit time.

Contrary to timed strong bisimulation, timed branching bisimulation is very subtle. This is shown in figure 8.8. The transition systems in figure 8.8(a) and figure 8.8(b) are not branching bisimilar, as they are not branching bisimilar at time 2. In that case the left process can do a step at time 3. The right one cannot. The process in figure 8.8(c) is timed branching bisimilar to the one in figure 8.8(a). No matter how close one is to time 3 in figure 8.8(c), a τ is possible before the a^c3.

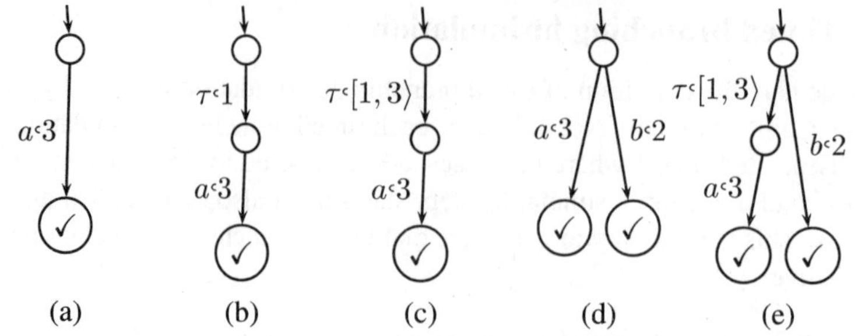

Figure 8.8: Timed branching bisimulation for timed transition systems

If one puts $b^{\backprime}2$ as an alternative to the processes in figure 8.8(a) and figure 8.8(c), we obtain figure 8.8(d) and figure 8.8(e), respectively. But the processes in figure 8.8(d) and figure 8.8(e) are not timed branching bisimilar as the process in figure 8.8(e) can choose the τ at for instance time 1, only leaving the $a^{\backprime}3$ and disabling the possibility to do a $b^{\backprime}2$. In figure 8.8(d) this behavior cannot be mimicked. Until time 2 the $b^{\backprime}2$ remains a possible alternative. Note that similar to untimed branching bisimulation, this shows that timed branching bisimulation is not a congruence for the $+$ operator, which we resolve by introducing a rooted variant below. Fortunately, $\underline{\leftrightarrow}^{t}_{b}$ and $\underline{\leftrightarrow}_{b}$ are equivalence relations.

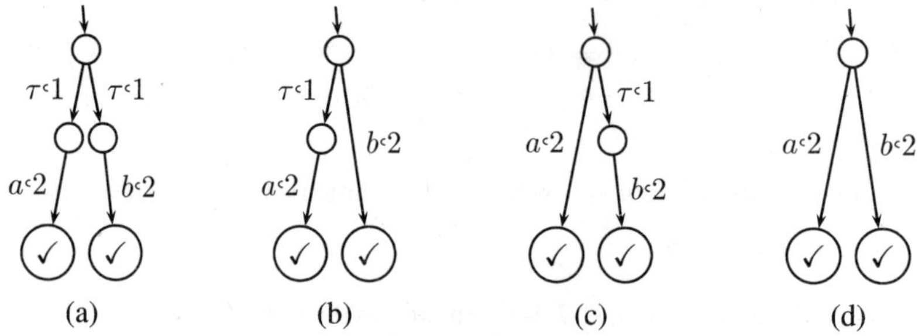

Figure 8.9: In timed processes choices can be implicit

A typical phenomenon for timed processes is that behavioral choices can be made by letting time proceed while ignoring behavior. Such ignoring can either be made explicit using a τ-action or be left implicit, but modulo timed branching bisimulation it makes no difference. This is illustrated in figure 8.9. The processes in figure 8.9(a), (b), and (c) are timed branching bisimilar. Only in figure 8.9(a) it is made explicit that at time 1 the choice for either $a^{\backprime}2$ or $b^{\backprime}2$ is made. In figure 8.9(b) the choice for $b^{\backprime}2$ is left implicit, but is of course made when the $\tau^{\backprime}1$ is not chosen. A similar situation arises in figure 8.9(c). The process depicted in figure 8.9(d) is not timed branching bisimilar as the choice between a and b can be made after time 1.

We saw that timed internal actions can determine a choice even if they are not taken. Under very special conditions it does not matter whether such internal actions

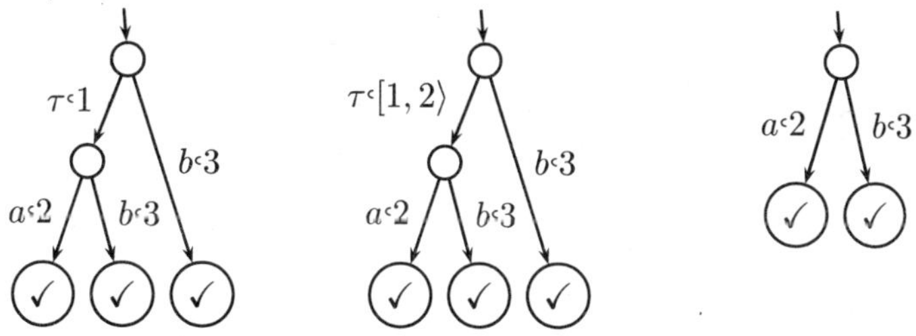

Figure 8.10: Unobservable timed τ's

are chosen or not. This happens when ignoring an internal action can be made up for. This is illustrated in figure 8.10. In the LTS in figure 8.10(a) not taking the τ^c1 determines at time 1 that the a^c2 is not possible. Clearly, the LTS in figure 8.10(a) is not timed branching bisimulation equivalent with the one in figure 8.10(c). But those in figure 8.10(b) and figure 8.10(c) are timed branching bisimilar. The reason is that for any time t up to time 2 there is always a τ that can be taken to enable the a^c2, even if all τ's before or at time t were ignored.

Because timed branching bisimulation is not a congruence, as motivated by figure 8.8, we define rooted timed branching bisimulation.

Definition 8.3.5 (Rooted timed branching bisimulation). Let $A = (S, Act, \longrightarrow, \rightsquigarrow, s_0, T)$ be a timed transition system. A relation $R \subseteq S \times S$ is called a *rooted timed branching bisimulation relation* iff for all states $s, u \in S$ such that sRu, it satisfies the conditions below for all actions $a \in Act$ and $t \in \mathbb{R}^{>0}$:

1. If $s \xrightarrow{a}_t s'$ for some $s' \in S$, then there is a $u' \in S$ such that $u \xrightarrow{a}_t u'$ and $s' \underline{\leftrightarrow}^t_b u'$,

2. Symmetrically, if $u \xrightarrow{a}_t u'$ for some $u' \in S$, then there is an $s' \in S$ such that $s \xrightarrow{a}_t s'$ and $s' \underline{\leftrightarrow}^t_b u'$,

3. $s \rightsquigarrow_t$ if and only if $u \rightsquigarrow_t$, and

4. $s \in T$ if and only if $u \in T$.

Two states $s, u \in S$ are *rooted timed branching bisimilar*, denoted by $s \underline{\leftrightarrow}_{rb} u$, iff there is a rooted timed branching bisimulation relation R such that sRu. Two transition systems are *rooted timed branching bisimilar* iff their initial states are rooted timed branching bisimilar.

Rooted timed branching bisimulation $\underline{\leftrightarrow}_b$ is a congruence relation for all process algebraic operators.

Theorem 8.3.6. $\underline{\leftrightarrow} \subseteq \underline{\leftrightarrow}_{rb} \subseteq \underline{\leftrightarrow}_b$.

Exercise 8.3.7. Give intuitive arguments why the branching bisimulation law for untimed systems $a \cdot (\tau \cdot (x + y) + x) = a \cdot (x + y)$ is valid in rooted timed branching bisimulation, where x and y are processes not referring to time.

8.3.3 Timed trace and timed weak trace equivalence

Other equivalences from the untimed setting can also be translated to the timed setting. We restrict ourselves to the definition of timed trace equivalence and timed weak trace equivalence.

Definition 8.3.8 (Timed trace equivalence). Let $A = (S, Act, \longrightarrow, \rightsquigarrow, s_0, T)$ be a timed labeled transition system. The set of *timed traces* $TTraces(s)$ for a state $s \in S$ is the minimal set satisfying:

1. $\epsilon \in TTraces(s)$, i.e., the empty trace is a member of $TTraces(s)$,
2. $\checkmark \in TTraces(s)$ iff $s \in T$,
3. If $s \rightsquigarrow_t$ then $t \in TTraces(s)$, and
4. If there is a state $s' \in S$ such that $s \xrightarrow{a}_t s'$ and $\sigma \in TTraces(s')$ then $a^{\varsigma}t\,\sigma \in TTraces(s)$.

Two states $s, u \in S$ are called *timed trace equivalent* iff $TTraces(s) = TTraces(u)$. Two transition systems are *timed trace equivalent* iff their initial states are timed trace equivalent.

Definition 8.3.9 (Timed weak trace equivalence). Let $A = (S, Act, \longrightarrow, \rightsquigarrow, s_0, T)$ be a timed labeled transition system. The set of *timed weak traces* $WTTraces(s)$ for a state $s \in S$ is the minimal set satisfying:

1. $\epsilon \in WTTraces(s)$,
2. $\checkmark \in WTTraces(s)$ iff $s \in T$,
3. If $s \rightsquigarrow_t$ then $t \in WTTraces(s)$,
4. If there is a state $s' \in S$ such that $s \xrightarrow{\tau}_t s'$ and $\sigma \in WTTraces(s')$ then $\sigma \in WTTraces(s)$, and
5. If there is a state $s' \in S$ such that $s \xrightarrow{a}_t s'$ with $a \neq \tau$ and $\sigma \in WTTraces(s')$ then $a^{\varsigma}t\,\sigma \in WTTraces(s)$.

Two states $s, u \in S$ are called *timed weak trace equivalent* iff $WTTraces(s) = WTTraces(u)$. Two transition systems are *timed weak trace equivalent* iff their initial states are timed weak trace equivalent.

Example 8.3.10. The timed weak traces of all three labeled transition systems in figure 8.10 are

$$\{\epsilon, a^{\varsigma}2, b^{\varsigma}2, a^{\varsigma}2\surd, b^{\varsigma}2\surd\} \cup \{t \mid 0<t<2\}$$

and therefore they are timed weak trace equivalent. This shows that timed weak trace equivalence relates more processes than timed branching bisimulation.

8.4 Timed processes

The process algebra can be extended with time by adding essentially the at-operator, denoted as $p{}^{\varsigma}t$, expressing that the first action of p must take place at time t, where t is a real number. In particular, we write $a{}^{\varsigma}t$ to indicate that action a takes place at exactly time t. As $p{}^{\varsigma}t$ can do an action at t, it can idle until t, but it cannot idle up to and including t.

A process without explicit time indication can start at any time. Therefore, $a = \sum_{t:\mathbb{R}} a{}^{\varsigma}t$, and more generally $p = \sum_{t:\mathbb{R}} p{}^{\varsigma}t$.

This simple extension with the at-operator turns out to be very expressive. Due to the availability of conditions and the sum operator, it is straightforward to describe complex behavior. But do not be deceived by this simplicity. Timed processes are far more intricate than untimed processes.

Consecutive actions must take place in the right order in time. Thus, $a{}^{\varsigma}1{\cdot}b{}^{\varsigma}2{\cdot}c{}^{\varsigma}3$ indicates a perfectly executable sequence of actions. But in $a{}^{\varsigma}1{\cdot}b{}^{\varsigma}2{\cdot}c{}^{\varsigma}1$, the last c cannot be executed without reversing time. This is an instance of a timing inconsistency. We avoid this inconsistency by stating that time cannot proceed after the b action. We do not let time proceed beyond time 2. This is a *time deadlock* at time 2, which is denoted by $\delta{}^{\varsigma}2$. The process $a{}^{\varsigma}1{\cdot}b{}^{\varsigma}2{\cdot}c{}^{\varsigma}1$ is equivalent to $a{}^{\varsigma}1{\cdot}b{}^{\varsigma}2{\cdot}\delta{}^{\varsigma}2$. It is assumed that processes start at time 0 and actions happen only after time 0. Therefore, $a{}^{\varsigma}0 = \delta{}^{\varsigma}0$.

Time deadlocks typically occur when the interaction of parallel processes is studied, and both processes have incompatible time constraints. Characteristically, one process wants to interact before a certain time t while the other only wants to join in at a later time instant. In this case the system will deadlock at time t. As the time constraints of the individual processes are not to be violated, time cannot proceed beyond t.

Using time we can describe typical processes such as a very precise clock that ticks every time unit:

act tick;
proc $\mathit{Clock}(t{:}\mathbb{R}) = \mathit{tick}{}^{\varsigma}(t{+}1){\cdot}\mathit{Clock}(t{+}1)$;

For a any $u{>}0$ of sort $\mathbb{R}$, the process $\mathit{Clock}(u)$ exhibits sequence

$$\mathit{tick}{}^{\varsigma}(u{+}1){\cdot}\mathit{tick}{}^{\varsigma}(u{+}2){\cdot}\mathit{tick}{}^{\varsigma}(u{+}3){\cdot}\cdots.$$

For $u{\le}-1$, the first action of the sequence takes place at time ≤ 0. As actions must take place after time 0, the process deadlocks at time 0 in that case, equaling $\delta{}^{\varsigma}0$.

It is also possible to model a *drifting* clock. This is a clock where each subsequent tick can happen ϵ too early or too late.

act tick;
proc $\mathit{DriftingClock}(t{:}\mathbb{R}) = \sum_{u:\mathbb{R}}(t{+}1{-}\epsilon{\le}u{\le}t{+}1{+}\epsilon){\rightarrow}\mathit{tick}{}^{\varsigma}u{\cdot}\mathit{DriftingClock}(u)$;

There are two views on describing time constraints. The first one is the specifiers view, where it is prescribing that something must happen before a certain time. Thus, we can describe that after an a action, b must happen within 5 time units:

$$\sum_{t:\mathbb{R}} a{}^{\varsigma}t{\cdot}\sum_{u:\mathbb{R}}(u{\le}t{+}5) \rightarrow b{}^{\varsigma}u.$$

A6	$\alpha + \delta = \alpha$	LM1	$\alpha \mathbin{\|\!\lfloor} x = (\alpha \ll x)\cdot x$
		LM2	$\delta \mathbin{\|\!\lfloor} x = \delta \ll x$
THEN	$c \rightarrow x = c \rightarrow x \diamond \delta{}^{\backprime}0$	LM3	$\alpha\cdot x \mathbin{\|\!\lfloor} y = (\alpha \ll y)\cdot(x \parallel y)$
		S9	$x{}^{\backprime}t \mid y = (x \mid y){}^{\backprime}t$
T1	$x + \delta{}^{\backprime}0 = x$	LM6	$x{}^{\backprime}t \mathbin{\|\!\lfloor} y = (x \mathbin{\|\!\lfloor} y){}^{\backprime}t$
T2	$\delta{}^{\backprime}t = \sum_{t':\mathbb{R}}(t'<t) \rightarrow \delta{}^{\backprime}t'$		
T3	$x = \sum_{t:\mathbb{R}} x{}^{\backprime}t$	C6	$\Gamma_C(x{}^{\backprime}t) = \Gamma_C(x){}^{\backprime}t$
T4	$x{}^{\backprime}t\cdot y = x{}^{\backprime}t\cdot(t \gg y)$	V7	$\nabla_V(x{}^{\backprime}t) = \nabla_V(x){}^{\backprime}t$
T5	$x{}^{\backprime}t = t>0 \rightarrow x{}^{\backprime}t$	E9	$\partial_B(x{}^{\backprime}t) = \partial_B(x){}^{\backprime}t$
		R9	$\rho_R(x{}^{\backprime}t) = \rho_R(x){}^{\backprime}t$
TA1	$\alpha{}^{\backprime}t{}^{\backprime}u = (t \approx u) \rightarrow \alpha{}^{\backprime}t \diamond \delta{}^{\backprime}\min(t,u)$	H9	$\tau_I(x{}^{\backprime}t) = \tau_I(x){}^{\backprime}t$
TA2	$\delta{}^{\backprime}t{}^{\backprime}u = \delta{}^{\backprime}\min(t,u)$	U9	$\Upsilon_U(x{}^{\backprime}t) = \Upsilon_U(x){}^{\backprime}t$
TA3	$(x+y){}^{\backprime}t = x{}^{\backprime}t + y{}^{\backprime}t$		
TA4	$(x\cdot y){}^{\backprime}t = x{}^{\backprime}t\cdot y$	TI	$t \gg x = \sum_{u:\mathbb{R}} u>t \rightarrow (x{}^{\backprime}u) + \delta{}^{\backprime}t$
TA5	$(\sum_{d:D} X(d)){}^{\backprime}t = \sum_{d:D} X(d){}^{\backprime}t$	TB	$x \ll t = \sum_{u:\mathbb{R}} u<t \rightarrow (x{}^{\backprime}u)$
TB1	$x \ll \alpha = x$	TB4	$x \ll (y+z) = x \ll y + x \ll z$
TB2	$x \ll \delta = x$	TB5	$x \ll y\cdot z = x \ll y$
TB3	$x \ll y{}^{\backprime}t = \sum_{u:\mathbb{R}} u<t \rightarrow (x{}^{\backprime}u) \ll y$	TB6	$x \ll \sum_{d:D} Y(d) = \sum_{d:D} x \ll Y(d)$

Table 8.1: Axioms for timed processes valid in strong bisimulation

The implementation oriented view is to describe that if the action b does not happen in time, some time-out action must take place:

$$\sum_{t:\mathbb{R}} a^{\text{c}}t \cdot \sum_{u:\mathbb{R}} (u \leq t+5) \to b^{\text{c}}u \diamond timeOut^{\text{c}}u.$$

The first view can lead to time deadlocks, if the process is put into a noncooperative context. The second view can lead to the action $b^{\text{c}}u$ never happening. The challenge of course is to specify behavior with the first kind of processes, and subsequently implement it using the second kind of processes, showing that implementation and specification behave in an equivalent way.

In table 8.1 all time related axioms for strong bisimulation are provided. In some cases these replace the axioms given earlier, which only apply to untimed processes, and were marked with the symbol ‡.

The axiom T1 says that $\delta^{\text{c}}0$ is not a selectable alternative. Note that $x + \delta^{\text{c}}1$ and x are not equal. It might be that x is a process where an action must be done before time 1. For instance, x can be equal to $a^{\text{c}}0.5$. Thus, the process $x + \delta^{\text{c}}1$ has an option to wait until time 1, whereas in x an action must be done at time 0.5. This is also the reason why the processes $x + \delta$ and x are not the same in a timed setting. The deadlock δ can wait until eternity, and hence can $x + \delta$, whereas x could have to do an action before a certain time.

The axiom THEN indicates that the if-then is an abbreviated form of the if-then-else. It replaces $c \to x = c \to x \diamond \delta$ (THEN‡) which is perfectly valid if x does not refer to time. But in case there is a reference to time, THEN‡ would equate the following two processes:

$$\sum_{t:\mathbb{R}} (t \approx 2) \to a^{\text{c}}t \diamond \delta, \qquad\qquad \sum_{t:\mathbb{R}} (t \approx 2) \to a^{\text{c}}t \diamond \delta^{\text{c}}0.$$

However, the left process equals $a^{\text{c}}2 + \delta$, whereas the right process is equal to $a^{\text{c}}2$. So, in the first process doing an action a at time 2 is an option, whereas in the second process it is unavoidable. Clearly, these processes have different behavior.

The axiom T2 finds its origin in the fact that $\delta^{\text{c}}t$ can idle up to t, but not up to and including t. Idling up to t is equivalent to idling up to any t' arbitrarily close to t.

The axiom T3 shows that any process equals itself where the first action occurs at an arbitrary time. The axiom T4 indicates that consecutive actions happen at strictly increasing moments in time, using the bounded initialization operator $\gg$ explained below. It says that if process x has performed an action at time t, the actions of y must come after time t.

The axiom T5 expresses that all actions must take place after time 0. This is clearly illustrated in the following identity, which is derivable using T5 and T3.

$$x = \sum_{t:\mathbb{R}} (t > 0) \to x^{\text{c}}t.$$

The axioms TA1-TA5 express how the at-operator distributes over basic processes. The axiom TA1 indicates that multiple time tags of a multi-action must coincide. Inconsistent time tags lead to a timed deadlock at the earliest convenience. TA2 is similar to TA1, but then for deadlock.

In order to axiomatize timed processes, we require three auxiliary operators. The process $t{\gg}q$ expresses that part of q taking place after time t. This operator is called the *bounded initialization* operator. So, typically $t{\gg}a{\cdot}3$ equals $a{\cdot}3$ if $t{<}3$. Otherwise it equals $\delta{\cdot}t$. The bounded initialization operator is typically used in axiom T4 in table 8.1. It is characterized by axiom TI.

The process $p{\ll}q$ (pronounce p *before* q) describes the part of process p that can happen before q is forced to perform an action. It is required to guarantee that time proceeds properly when eliminating the parallel operators. As an example consider $a{\cdot}3\|b{\cdot}2$ which using axiom M can be expanded into, among others, $a{\cdot}3 \mathbin{⌊\!⌊} b{\cdot}2$. The first action cannot be $a{\cdot}3$, as $b{\cdot}2$ happens first. Using the axiom LM1 only that part of the left-hand side is allowed that happens before the last action of the right-hand side can happen.

The axioms LM1, LM2, and LM3 are the replacement axioms for LM1‡, LM2‡, and LM3‡, the latter only being valid for untimed processes. In untimed processes the process at the right-hand side is not forced to do any action at a particular time. It can idle forever. Therefore, actions at the left of the left merge always have the possibility of happening, and therefore, we do not need the before operator to remove any of them. The axioms TB1,...,TB6 are provided to manipulate with the before operator.

There is also a before operator that uses an explicit time at the right-hand side, i.e., $p{\ll}t$. It represents the behavior p where the initial actions must take place before time t. This operator is used for the axioms for timed branching bisimulation in table 8.2. The axiom TB describes it.

All other axioms reflect that the at-operator can be distributed over most operators.

BT1	$a{\cdot}t{\cdot}(x{+}\delta{\cdot}t'') = a{\cdot}t{\cdot}(x{\ll}t' + x{\cdot}t' + \tau{\cdot}t'{\cdot}(x{+}\delta{\cdot}t''))$ if $t{<}t'{<}t''$
BT2	Let $M = \sup_{d:D}(t(d)\|b(d))$. If $t'{>}M$ and $\forall u{\in}\mathit{ActionTimes}(y).\, \sup_{d:D}(t(d) \mid t(d){<}u \wedge b(d)) = u$ then $a{\cdot}t{\cdot}\,(\sum_{d:D} b(d) \rightarrow \tau{\cdot}t(d){\cdot}(x{+}y{+}\delta{\cdot}t') + x) = a{\cdot}t{\cdot}(x{+}y{+}\delta{\cdot}t')$

Table 8.2: Axioms for rooted timed branching bisimulation

The axioms characterizing time look quite straightforward, but it can still be tricky to derive expected properties. For instance one may want to show that there is no real choice between an early timed deadlock and a late action. In an equation (with $t{\geq}u$):

$$a{\cdot}t = a{\cdot}t + \delta{\cdot}u.$$

We can prove this equation by distinguishing between $t > u$ and $t{=}u$, respectively:

$$\begin{aligned} a{}^{\varsigma}t &\overset{\text{T3}}{=} (\textstyle\sum_{v:\mathbb{R}} a{}^{\varsigma}v){}^{\varsigma}t \overset{\text{SUM3}}{=} (\textstyle\sum_{v:\mathbb{R}} a{}^{\varsigma}v + a{}^{\varsigma}u){}^{\varsigma}t \overset{\text{T3}}{=} \\ &\quad (a + a{}^{\varsigma}u){}^{\varsigma}t \overset{\text{TA3}}{=} a{}^{\varsigma}t + a{}^{\varsigma}u{}^{\varsigma}t \overset{t>u,\text{TA1}}{=} a{}^{\varsigma}t + \delta{}^{\varsigma}u, \\ a{}^{\varsigma}t &\overset{\text{A6}}{=} (a \mid \delta){}^{\varsigma}t \overset{\text{TA3}}{=} a{}^{\varsigma}t + \delta{}^{\varsigma}t. \end{aligned}$$

In table 8.2 two axioms are provided for rooted timed branching bisimulation. BT1 expresses that the behavioral choices by letting time progress can be made explicit by adding a $\tau{}^{\varsigma}t'$, assuming that the process can at least reach t', which is indicated by the $\delta{}^{\varsigma}t''$ summand. Axiom BT2 is the pendant of the untimed law for branching bisimulation. It uses the supremum of a set of time instances $M = \sup_{d:D}(t(d)|b(d))$. This is the smallest number larger than any $t(d)$ for which $b(d)$ holds. Note that M itself does not need to be equal to any $t(d)$. Take for instance $M{=}\sup_{t:\mathbb{R}}(t|t{<}2)$ where $M{=}2$. It can also be that M is infinite. Consider for instance $M = \sup_{t:\mathbb{R}}(t|t > 0)$. In this case the condition $t'{>}M$ can be dropped.

Axiom BT2 also uses the set $\mathit{ActionTimes}(y)$. This is the set of all times an action can take place in y. It has the following definition.

Definition 8.4.1. Let p be a process expression. We define $\mathit{ActionTimes}(p)$ as a set of positive real numbers as follows:

- $\mathit{ActionTimes}(a) = \mathbb{R}^{>0}$.
- $\mathit{ActionTimes}(\delta) = \emptyset$.
- $\mathit{ActionTimes}(p{}^{\varsigma}u) = \{u\} \cap \mathit{ActionTimes}(p)$.
- $\mathit{ActionTimes}(p_1{+}p_2) = \mathit{ActionTimes}(p_1) \cup \mathit{ActionTimes}(p_2)$.
- $\mathit{ActionTimes}(p_1{\cdot}p_2) = \mathit{ActionTimes}(p_1)$.
- $\mathit{ActionTimes}(b{\rightarrow}p) = \begin{cases} \mathit{ActionTimes}(p) & \text{if } b, \\ \emptyset & \text{otherwise.} \end{cases}$
- $\mathit{ActionTimes}(\sum_{d:D} p) = \bigcup_{d:D} \mathit{ActionTimes}(p)$.
- $\mathit{ActionTimes}(t{\gg}p) = \{r{\in}\mathit{ActionTimes}(p) \mid r{>}t\}$.
- $\mathit{ActionTimes}(p{\ll}t) = \{r{\in}\mathit{ActionTimes}(p) \mid r{<}t\}$.

The condition that uses $\mathit{ActionTimes}$ essentially expresses that for each action in y taking place at some time t and for each time t' before t a τ-action must exist between t' and t. Consider the following three process expressions

$$\begin{aligned} &a{}^{\varsigma}1{\cdot}(b{}^{\varsigma}3 + c{}^{\varsigma}4) \\ &a{}^{\varsigma}1{\cdot}(\tau{}^{\varsigma}2{\cdot}(b{}^{\varsigma}3 + c{}^{\varsigma}4) + c{}^{\varsigma}4) \\ &a{}^{\varsigma}1{\cdot}(\textstyle\sum_{t:\mathbb{R}}(2{\leq}t{<}3){\rightarrow}\tau{}^{\varsigma}t{\cdot}(b{}^{\varsigma}3 + c{}^{\varsigma}4) + c{}^{\varsigma}4) \end{aligned}$$

The second process is not rooted branching bisimilar to the first. In the second it can be decided that at time 2 the action b at time 3 cannot be taken, by ignoring the $\tau{}^{\varsigma}2$. This is not possible in the first process. The third process is branching bisimilar. Ignoring a τ before the $b{}^{\varsigma}3$ can be made up for by taking one of the other available τ's. Note that this example is very similar to the one in figure 8.10.

Exercise 8.4.2. Specify a drifting clock where the drifting influences when $tick$ happens, but which does not influence the accuracy of the clock.

Exercise 8.4.3. Describe the behavior of a coffee machine that returns tea or coffee after entering a coin. If after entering a coin no choice is made in 10 seconds, the coin is returned. Furthermore, after making a choice, coffee or tea is served within 5 seconds.

Exercise 8.4.4. Prove the following equations that are strongly timed bisimilar.

1. $b \rightarrow x \diamond y = b \rightarrow x \diamond \delta{}^{\varsigma}0 + \neg b \rightarrow y \diamond \delta{}^{\varsigma}0$.
2. $a = a + \delta{}^{\varsigma}t$.
3. $\delta{}^{\varsigma}2 + \delta{}^{\varsigma}4 = \delta{}^{\varsigma}4$.

Exercise 8.4.5. Prove that $x{}^{\varsigma}t \cdot a{}^{\varsigma}t = x{}^{\varsigma}t \cdot \delta{}^{\varsigma}t$.

Exercise 8.4.6. Expand the process $a{}^{\varsigma}1 \cdot b{}^{\varsigma}3 \parallel c{}^{\varsigma}2$.

Exercise 8.4.7. Prove that $x \ll (c \rightarrow y) = c \rightarrow (x \ll y)$.

Exercise 8.4.8. Prove using branching bisimulation axioms that $a{}^{\varsigma}1 \cdot (b{}^{\varsigma}3 + \tau{}^{\varsigma}2 \cdot c{}^{\varsigma}4)$ is equal to $a{}^{\varsigma}1 \cdot (\tau{}^{\varsigma}2 \cdot b{}^{\varsigma}3 + c{}^{\varsigma}4)$.

8.5 Modal formulas with time

In order to express time in modal formulas its syntax is extended with the following constructs, namely timed action formulas and the timed/untimed delay (Δ) and yaled (∇).

$$\begin{array}{rcl} af & ::= & \ldots \mid af{}^{\varsigma}u \\ \phi & ::= & \ldots \mid \Delta \mid \Delta{}^{\varsigma}u \mid \nabla \mid \nabla{}^{\varsigma}u \end{array}$$

Similar to its use in the algebra, it is also possible to use the at-operator in modal formulas. The action formulas $\alpha{}^{\varsigma}u$, where u is of sort $\mathbb{R}$, expresses that the multi-action α must take place at time u. More generally, for a set of multi-actions A, $A{}^{\varsigma}u$ expresses that all multi-actions in the set take place at time u. The following formula says that whenever an a action takes place at time 2, an arbitrary subsequent action happening at time 3 is possible:

$$[true^{\star} \cdot a{}^{\varsigma}2]\langle true{}^{\varsigma}3\rangle true.$$

If actions do not have a time stamp, they can take place at any time. So, for instance, $\langle a\rangle\phi = \exists t{:}\mathbb{R}.\langle a{}^{\varsigma}t\rangle\phi$.

In combination with a quantifier, it is possible to express that actions must take place within a certain time interval. For instance, after an emergency call, an ambulance can arrive within 10 minutes:

$$[true^{\star}]\forall t{:}\mathbb{R}.[call{}^{\varsigma}t]\langle true^{\star}\rangle\exists u{:}\mathbb{R}.(u\leq t+10 \wedge \langle ambulance{}^{\varsigma}u\rangle true).$$

A slightly stronger, and very common real-time requirement is that some action must be performed within a certain time interval. After switching the system on, an LED must light up within 0.1 second:

$$\forall u_1{:}\mathbb{R}.[true^{\star}\cdot on{}^{\varsigma}u_1]\mu X.([\forall u_2{:}\mathbb{R}.\overline{u_2\leq u_1+0.1 \cap led{}^{\varsigma}u_2}]X\wedge\langle true\rangle true).$$

As an illustration, we provide yet another commonly used example. If after a *standstill* action, no action is allowed to be done for 5 seconds, the formula can look like this:

$$\forall u_1, u_2{:}\mathbb{R}.[true^{\star}\cdot standstill{}^{\varsigma}u_1\cdot true{}^{\varsigma}u_2](u_2>u_1+5).$$

If time is involved in processes, a requirement can be that it is possible to wait indefinitely, without having to perform an action. Such properties cannot be expressed using the at-operator, as no action is involved. For this the *delay*, denoted as Δ, can be used. It simply expresses that time can proceed eternally. The timed delay $\Delta{}^{\varsigma}u$ says that time can go on up to and including time u without necessarily having to perform an action. Delay can straightforwardly be expressed in terms of timed delays by $\Delta = \forall t{:}\mathbb{R}.\Delta{}^{\varsigma}t$.

Therefore, the requirement that after going to standby mode, it is possible to idle indefinitely, is expressed by:

$$[true^{\star}\cdot standby]\Delta.$$

The requirement that after a standby, one must be able to wait for at least 5 seconds is formulated as follows:

$$\forall u{:}\mathbb{R}.[true^{\star}\cdot standby{}^{\varsigma}u]\Delta{}^{\varsigma}(u+5).$$

The dual of the delay formula, $\neg\Delta{}^{\varsigma}t$, is denoted as $\nabla{}^{\varsigma}t$. We call ∇ *yaled* and $\nabla{}^{\varsigma}t$ *timed yaled*, lacking a better term (yaled is the reverse of delay). The formula $\nabla{}^{\varsigma}t$ says that before time t some action must be done, or time cannot proceed to time t. In the latter case we have a time deadlock before time t. The duality of timed delay and timed yaled is expressed by:

$$\neg\Delta{}^{\varsigma}t = \nabla{}^{\varsigma}t \quad\text{and}\quad \neg\nabla{}^{\varsigma}t = \Delta{}^{\varsigma}t.$$

(Untimed) yaled ∇ says that at some time in the future an action (or a time deadlock) must happen: $\nabla = \exists t{:}\mathbb{R}.\nabla{}^{\varsigma}t$.

Thus, we can express that after an *emergency* action, there must be some response before time t or time must deadlock before time t, using the following formula

$$[true^{*}\cdot emergency]\nabla{}^{\varsigma}t.$$

In table 8.3 some identities about timed modal formulas are listed.

$\langle af\rangle\phi = \exists t{:}\mathbb{R}.\langle af{}^{\backprime}t\rangle\phi$	$[af]\phi = \forall t{:}\mathbb{R}.[af{}^{\backprime}t]\phi$
$\Delta = \forall t{:}\mathbb{R}.\Delta{}^{\backprime}t$	$\nabla = \exists t{:}\mathbb{R}.\nabla{}^{\backprime}t$
$\neg\Delta = \nabla$	$\neg\nabla = \Delta$

Table 8.3: Equivalences between timed modal formulas

Exercise 8.5.1. Specify that a process cannot have a time deadlock and conversely that it must have a time deadlock.

Exercise 8.5.2. Specify a requirement on a machine that sequentially processes products. Each product entering the machine must leave within five time units. In addition, specify that in the long run the time needed to process a product is on average at most three time units.

8.6 Historical notes

Following the advent of process algebras and process calculi that only dealt with the relative order of actions, it was a natural step to extend the processes with an explicit notion of time [13, 140, 143, 160]. An overview of timed calculi is given in [17]. Note that we follow the concepts laid out in [13] (although with somewhat different notation). The most notable non-process-algebraic approach to timed systems are timed automata [115].

There were debates on whether time should be integer, rational, or real valued, whether time should be used as a tag to actions, or as separate wait or delay statements. With time tagged actions there were proponents of interpreting the tags as relative to the previous action, or as an absolute moment in time.

Also the desirability of time deadlocks was heavily debated. Some argued that allowing time deadlocks gives rise to simple theories and semantics. A time deadlock is an indication of inconsistent time requirements and therefore a useful mathematical concept. Others argued that time deadlocks do not have a physical counterpart, and therefore should not be allowed to be written down. They offered the concept of *maximal progress* saying that timed processes must always immediately perform their actions as soon as they can happen. These debates have not really been settled, leaving the particular choice of concepts to be used in a process algebra largely a matter of taste.

Although there are modal logics that use an explicit notion of time, it was never as vividly or polemically debated as timed process theories. Early logics with explicit time can be found in [116]. Another development was the duration calculus [45]. There are straightforward extensions of timed LTL and CTL [6] as well as timed variants of Hennessy-Milner logic [98].

II

Analysis

9

Basic Manipulation of Processes

In this chapter we elaborate on how the axioms given in chapter 4 can be used to prove that different process expressions have the same behavior. Due to the existence of data, some of the variables in the axioms range over functions from data to processes. In order to denote such functions, we introduce the lambda calculus here as a means to denote meta objects. In chapter 3, lambda abstraction was introduced as a way to construct functions within our data language. Although reasoning with the axioms is generally quite intuitive, there are situations, due to bound variables and implicit universal quantification, where it is very subtle to know which reasoning steps are correct. Therefore, in this chapter we define precisely what we mean by a logical derivation. But such a precise derivation is only needed when there is doubt about the validity of a derivation. Generally, common equational reasoning as we already applied in the previous chapters is more than adequate.

There are three principles necessary to prove that processes are equal, of which only induction has been mentioned in the previous chapters. We discuss all these in this chapter. The first one is induction on data types. The second one is the recursive specification principle (RSP) to equate infinite processes. The last one is Koomen's fair abstraction rule, which we need to handle fair behavior. We also show the parallel expansion technique, which within the context of process algebras has long been the primary technique to prove equality of parallel behaviors. This technique has severe limitations when it comes to applicability, which we overcome in later chapters.

9.1 Derivation rules for equations

In table 9.1 we give rules that say how we can prove that two terms are equal. These rules may look like overkill, especially because almost everywhere in this book we do not use this strictly logical proof system but instead use the more verbal, suggestive mathematical style to prove equations. Proofs that strictly adhere to the rules in table 9.1 tend to become unreadable and hard to comprehend.

But all proofs of equalities are ultimately based on the rules in table 9.1. That means that, with some work, they can be completely translated into a derivation sequence

$\dfrac{}{\Gamma \cup \{p = q\} \vdash p = q}$	start
$\dfrac{}{\Gamma \vdash p = p}$	reflexivity
$\dfrac{\Gamma \vdash p = q}{\Gamma \vdash q = p}$	symmetry
$\dfrac{\Gamma \vdash p = q \quad \Gamma \vdash q = r}{\Gamma \vdash p = r}$	transitivity
$\dfrac{\Gamma \vdash p_1 = q_1 \quad \Gamma \vdash p_2 = q_2}{\Gamma \vdash p_1\, p_2 = q_1\, q_2}$	congruence
$\dfrac{\Gamma \vdash p\, x = q\, x}{\Gamma \vdash p = q},\ x \notin \Gamma$	extensionality
$\dfrac{\Gamma \vdash p = q}{\Gamma \vdash \lambda x{:}D.p = \lambda x{:}D.q},\ x \notin \Gamma$	abstraction
$\dfrac{}{\Gamma \vdash \lambda x{:}D.p = \lambda y{:}D.(p[x{:=}y])}$	α-conversion
$\dfrac{}{\Gamma \vdash (\lambda x{:}D.p)\, q = p[x{:=}q]}$	β-conversion

Table 9.1: Derivation rules for equations

consisting of these rules (and some others that we provide later). This is a fallback in those cases when it is unclear whether a verbose proof is actually correct. If the verbose proof can be translated to a logical proof tree, it is valid.

In table 9.1 the letters p, q, and r stand for expressions, x and y for variables, and D is a sort. The letter Γ stands for a context, which is a set of equations. The rules in table 9.1 are schemas. This means that for each context, expression, variable, and sort, there is an instance of a rule.

The notation $p[x{:=}q]$ is a substitution that replaces each occurrence of x in p by q. It was introduced in section 3.3, where it was also explained that care has to be taken when substituting in terms with bound variables. In order to be safe when substituting in a term with a bound variable, the bound variable must be α-converted to a variable neither occurring in the term in which the substitution is taking place, nor in a term that is substituted. A precise definition of substitution of a term is given in chapter 15.

Each rule must be read as follows. If the equation(s) above the line can be proven from the context, then we can prove the equation below the line in this context. In case the set of premises above the line is empty, we have no proof obligation and can consider the conclusion proven straightaway. Some rules can only be applied if a variable x does not occur as a free variable in this context. This is indicated by $x \notin \Gamma$.

The context contains the assumptions upon which we base our proof. The assumptions can contain additional information, such as, for instance, the definition of certain processes. For example, we can say that P is a process variable that satisfies the equation $P = a{\cdot}P$. This equation is put in the context, such that we can use it to derive facts about P. We can, for instance, conclude that $P = a{\cdot}(a{\cdot}P)$ is provable, formally showing that

$$\{P = a{\cdot}P\} \vdash P = a{\cdot}(a{\cdot}P).$$

The brackets are used to indicate explicitly that we do not intend an application of the axiom A5 in this example. In example 9.1.2 we give an exact derivation of this.

The proof rules we provide are a mixture of equational logic and rules taken from typed lambda calculus [21]. It is useful to define exactly what it means for an expression $\Gamma \vdash p = q$ to be provable.

Definition 9.1.1. Let p, q be expressions and Γ be a context. We inductively define that $\Gamma \vdash p = q$ is *provable* iff $\Gamma \vdash p = q$ is the conclusion of some rule in table 9.1 and all premises of this rule are provable.

Generally, we write a proof as a sequence of formulas, such that each formula is provable by a rule of which the premises occur earlier in the sequence.

Example 9.1.2. As an example we show that $\{P = a{\cdot}P\} \vdash P = a{\cdot}(a{\cdot}P)$ is provable. We give the proof as a numbered list. First we provide the formula that is proven, and subsequently the name of the employed rule, followed by the indices of the premises that were used.

1. $\{P = a{\cdot}P\} \vdash P = a{\cdot}P$ by start;
2. $\{P = a{\cdot}P\} \vdash (\lambda y{:}\mathbb{P}.a{\cdot}y) = (\lambda y{:}\mathbb{P}.a{\cdot}y)$ by reflexivity;
3. $\{P = a{\cdot}P\} \vdash (\lambda y{:}\mathbb{P}.a{\cdot}y)\,(a{\cdot}P) = a{\cdot}(a{\cdot}P)$ by β-conversion;

4. $\{P = a{\cdot}P\} \vdash (\lambda y{:}\mathbb{P}.a{\cdot}y)\, P = (\lambda y{:}\mathbb{P}.a{\cdot}y)\, (a{\cdot}P)$ by congruence using 2 and 1;
5. $\{P = a{\cdot}P\} \vdash (\lambda y{:}\mathbb{P}.a{\cdot}y)\, P = a{\cdot}(a{\cdot}P)$ by transitivity using 4 and 3;
6. $\{P = a{\cdot}P\} \vdash (\lambda y{:}\mathbb{P}.a{\cdot}y)\, P = a{\cdot}P$ by β-conversion;
7. $\{P = a{\cdot}P\} \vdash a{\cdot}P = (\lambda y{:}\mathbb{P}.a{\cdot}y)\, P$ by symmetry using 6;
8. $\{P = a{\cdot}P\} \vdash a{\cdot}P = a{\cdot}(a{\cdot}P)$ by transitivity using 7 and 5;
9. $\{P = a{\cdot}P\} \vdash P = a{\cdot}(a{\cdot}P)$ by transitivity using 1 and 8.

If we want to use axioms in a proof, we can also add these to the context. We may want to add axiom A1 ($x + y = y + x$). But with axioms, we want to express that they hold for instantiations of variables; we mean to say *for all* x and y: $x + y = y + x$. Lacking a universal quantifier, which will be introduced later, we can encode this using lambda notation by adding $\lambda x, y{:}\mathbb{P}.x{+}y = \lambda x, y{:}\mathbb{P}.y{+}x$. The sort $\mathbb{P}$ contains the processes. In section 9.2 we will see that this is provably equivalent to $\forall x, y{:}\mathbb{P}.(x{+}y = y{+}x)$. This last form is more natural for an axiom that is added to the context.

In our case the axioms for untimed strong bisimulation are always assumed to be part of the context, and identities are always assumed to be valid for the data types. Aside from that we can have additional axioms valid for branching or trace equivalence, but this is always made clear explicitly.

For actual proofs a linear style for proofs is much more convenient than the derivational style presented here. Suppose we want to prove that $p_1 = p_n$ for expressions p_1 and p_n ($n \geq 0$) in some context Γ. As Γ is generally quite stable, we do not mention it explicitly in the proof, but only indicate what is in Γ. We prove $p_1 = p_n$ using a sequence of the form:

$$p_1 = p_2 = p_3 = \cdots = p_{n-1} = p_n.$$

Each equation $p_i = p_{i+1}$ consists of the application of one axiom or assumption in Γ. More concretely, let $\lambda y{:}D.p = \lambda y{:}D.q$ be this axiom or assumption. For ease of explanation we assume only one bound variable y. Now p_i has the form $r[x := p[y := t]]$ and p_{i+1} has the form $r[x := q[y := t]]$, where t is an arbitrary term. We can derive that $p_i = p_{i+1}$ as follows. Note that using symmetry we can also apply the axiom from right to left, instead of from left to right.

1. $\Gamma \vdash (\lambda x{:}D.r)\, q[y{:=}t] = r[x{:=}q[y{:=}t]]$ by β-conversion;
2. $\Gamma \vdash \lambda y{:}D.p = \lambda y{:}D.q$ by start;
3. $\Gamma \vdash t = t$ by reflexivity;
4. $\Gamma \vdash (\lambda y{:}D.p)t = (\lambda y{:}D.q)t$ by congruence using 2 and 3;
5. $\Gamma \vdash (\lambda y{:}D.p)t = p[y{:=}t]$ by β-conversion
6. $\Gamma \vdash (\lambda y{:}D.q)t = q[y{:=}t]$ by β-conversion
7. $\Gamma \vdash p[y{:=}t] = (\lambda y{:}D.p)t$ by symmetry and 5

8. $\Gamma \vdash p[y{:=}t] = (\lambda y{:}D.q)t$ by transitivity using 7 and 4
9. $\Gamma \vdash p[y{:=}t] = q[y{:=}t]$ by transitivity using 8 and 6
10. $\Gamma \vdash (\lambda x{:}D).r = (\lambda x{:}D).r$ by reflexivity;
11. $\Gamma \vdash (\lambda x{:}D.r)p[y{:=}t] = (\lambda x{:}D.r)q[y{:=}t]$ by congruence using 10 and 9;
12. $\Gamma \vdash (\lambda x{:}D.r)p[y{:=}t] = r[x{:=}q[y{:=}t]]$ by transitivity using 11 and 1;
13. $\Gamma \vdash (\lambda x{:}D.r)p[y{:=}t] = r[x{:=}p[y{:=}t]]$ by β-conversion;
14. $\Gamma \vdash r[x{:=}p[y{:=}t]] = (\lambda x{:}D.r)p[y{:=}t]$ by symmetry using 13;
15. $\Gamma \vdash r[x{:=}p[y{:=}t]] = r[x{:=}q[y{:=}t]]$ by transitivity using 14 and 12.

As we know how to translate such a linear proof to a formal proof derivation, it suffices to give the linear proof. The essential ingredient is the axiom or assumption that has been used. As a service to those that check a proof, a hint is often written above the equation sign. This can be the name of the axiom, the indication that an assumption is used (e.g., using the abbreviation "ass.") or the essential equation itself. Possible forms for the equation above would be:

$$p_i \overset{p=q}{=} p_{i+1} \qquad p_i \overset{\text{ass.}}{=} p_{i+1} \qquad p_i \overset{\text{AX}}{=} p_{i+1}$$

assuming AX is the name of the axiom $p = q$.

Example 9.1.3. We give a linear proof as a replacement of the proof of example 9.1.2. We assume that $P = a{\cdot}P$ (now it is in Γ):

$$P \overset{\text{ass.}}{=} a{\cdot}P \overset{\text{ass.}}{=} a{\cdot}(a{\cdot}P).$$

It is a common mathematical style to derive auxiliary theorems (also called lemmas) from some context. Subsequently, these theorems are added to the context as a help to prove subsequent theorems. This can help to split a complex proof into simpler ones. The question is whether we can conclude that the theorems proven in this way are also provable using the derivation rules as a coherent whole. The following rephrases this symbolically:

$$\left.\begin{array}{l}\Gamma \vdash p_1 = q_1 \text{ is provable}\\ \Gamma \cup \{p_1 = q_1\} \vdash p_2 = q_2 \text{ is provable}\end{array}\right\} \implies \Gamma \vdash p_2 = q_2 \text{ is provable.}$$

This is called the *cut theorem*, because it allows to cut proofs in smaller parts. We can easily see that the cut theorem is valid. Namely, because $\Gamma \vdash p_1 = q_1$ and $\Gamma \cup \{p_1 = q_1\} \vdash p_2 = q_2$ are provable, there are proof sequences for both. Now concatenate both proof sequences with the one for $\Gamma \vdash p_1 = q_1$ occurring first. Moreover, remove all occurrences of $\{p_1 = q_1\}$ from the contexts in the second proof sequence. Now the conclusion of the sequence is $\Gamma \vdash p_2 = q_2$ as we require. The total sequence is still a proof sequence except for applications of the start rule in the second sequence where $\Gamma \vdash p_1 = q_1$ should be proven. But as $p_1 = q_1$ is removed from the context this is not a valid application of start. Fortunately, $p_1 = q_1$ is already proven in the first sequence, and hence this application of the start rule in the proof can be omitted. Thus, we have a valid proof with the conclusion $\Gamma \vdash p_2 = q_2$.

A common rule from the lambda calculus is η-conversion, which is derivable in the current setting. It says that $(\lambda x{:}D.p\,x) = p$, namely the lambda abstraction to the left is superfluous provided x does not occur in p. We can prove it for any context Γ.

1. $\Gamma \vdash (\lambda x{:}D.p\,x)\,y = p\,y$ by β-conversion, where y is chosen not to occur in Γ;

2. $\Gamma \vdash (\lambda x{:}D.p\,x) = p$ by extensionality using 1;

Another useful mechanism is the *weakening lemma*. Suppose we can prove $\Gamma \vdash p = q$. Then we can also prove $\Gamma \cup \Delta \vdash p = q$. This is useful, because it allows for the derivation of facts in their minimal context, and apply them in a much wider context. The construction of a proof sequence for $\Gamma \cup \Delta \vdash p = q$ out of $\Gamma \vdash p = q$ is straightforward. Just replace each context Γ by the context $\Gamma \cup \Delta$ and verify that application of each rule in table 9.1 is still valid. The only complexity is found with the extensionality and abstraction rules as x may occur in Δ. In case of the extensionality rule we can replace x by a fresh variable y not occurring in the existing proof and the new context Δ, and we replace the proof with x with a proof in which all relevant occurrences of x are replaced by y. Note that x does not occur in the start rule, as otherwise x would have occurred in the context.

If there is a problem with the application of the abstraction rule, because x is in the context Δ, then one applies the abstraction rule with a variable not occurring in the Δ. In this way we derive $\lambda y{:}D.p[x{:=}y] = \lambda y{:}D.q[x{:=}y]$ instead of $\lambda x{:}D.p = \lambda x{:}D.q$. By applying α-conversion, $\lambda x{:}D.p = \lambda x{:}D.q$ can be derived again.

Thus, the cut theorem allows for the formulation of useful general lemmas and the weakening lemma allows for these to be proved in a minimal setting without hampering its applicability.

Exercise 9.1.4. The normal rule for congruence is the following. If $p_1 = q_1, \ldots, p_n = q_n$, then $f(p_1, \ldots, p_n) = f(q_1, \ldots, q_n)$ for some function symbol f. Show that this can be proven using the congruence rule in table 9.1.

Exercise 9.1.5. Show that the following slightly weakened form of α-conversion is derivable from the rules in table 9.1, of course without using the rule for alpha conversion:

$$\frac{}{\Gamma \vdash \lambda x{:}D.p = \lambda y{:}D.p[x{:=}y]},\quad y \notin \Gamma.$$

9.2 Derivation rules for formulas

It is not sufficient to only derive equations between data and processes. Sometimes it is necessary to conclude that expressions are not equal, or that they are only equal under certain conditions. Additionally, universal quantification is also useful. Therefore, we introduce *formulas* that allow for expressing these.

Definition 9.2.1. We inductively define formulas as follows:

- If p and q are expressions of the same sort, then $p = q$ is a formula,
- If ϕ and ψ are formulas, then $\phi \Rightarrow \psi$ is a formula, and
- If ϕ is a formula and x is a variable symbol of sort D, then $\forall x{:}D.\phi$ is a formula.

We use the following abbreviations that allow us to use other connectives in formulas.

- $\neg\phi$ stands for $\phi \Rightarrow (\mathit{true} = \mathit{false})$;
- $\phi \vee \psi$ stands for $\neg\phi \Rightarrow \psi$;
- $\phi \wedge \psi$ stands for $\neg(\phi \Rightarrow \neg\psi)$;
- $\exists x{:}D.\phi$ stands for $\neg\forall x{:}D.\neg\phi$.

The derivation rules for formulas are given in table 9.2. Note that we also use substitutions on formulas. These substitutions distribute over the formulas, but just as with lambda abstraction, α-conversion must be performed when substituting terms in the scope of a universal quantifier.

$\dfrac{}{\Gamma \cup \{\phi\} \vdash \phi}$	generalized start
$\dfrac{\Gamma \vdash \mathit{true} = \mathit{false}}{\Gamma \vdash \phi}$	ex falso sequitur quod libet
$\dfrac{\Gamma \cup \{\phi\} \vdash \psi}{\Gamma \vdash \phi \Rightarrow \psi}$	$\Rightarrow$ introduction
$\dfrac{\Gamma \vdash \phi \Rightarrow \psi \quad \Gamma \vdash \phi}{\Gamma \vdash \psi}$	$\Rightarrow$ elimination, or modus ponens
$\dfrac{\Gamma \vdash \phi}{\Gamma \vdash \forall x{:}D.\phi},\ x \notin \Gamma$	$\forall$ introduction
$\dfrac{\Gamma \vdash \forall x{:}D.\phi}{\Gamma \vdash \phi[x{:=}p]}$	$\forall$ elimination (p is of sort D)
$\dfrac{}{\Gamma \vdash \forall x{:}D.\phi = \forall y{:}D.(\phi[x{:=}y])}$	α-conversion for $\forall$

Table 9.2: Derivation rules for formulas

If we have an axiom that is valid for all instantiations of its variables, we saw in the previous section that we can encode it using a lambda operator, for example, $\lambda x, y{:}\mathbb{P}.x{+}y = \lambda x, y{:}\mathbb{P}.y{+}x$. From this it is possible to derive $\forall x, y{:}\mathbb{P}.x{+}y{=}y{+}x$. The derivation is done as follows. Apply the left-hand and right-hand sides of the equation with lambdas to variables not occurring in the context using the reflexivity and congruence rules. Using β-conversion the lambdas can be removed from the equation. Using the $\forall$ introduction rule, which can be applied as the variables are not in the context, put the required universal quantifier in front of the equation. By α-conversion for $\forall$, rename the variables back to x and y.

The reverse is also possible. From an equation preceded by a universal quantifier, the variant with lambdas in front can be derived.

Example 9.2.2. This example contains a proof of the invalid equation $a(d) = a(e)$ as an illustration how easy it is to "prove" a wrong statement. Here a is an arbitrary action and D is some data type. Of course this proof cannot be formalized.

We want to use the lemma that $d'{=}e$ implies $\lambda d{:}D.a(d){=}\lambda d{:}D.a(e)$. Note that from this lemma our result follows by taking d' equal to e making the premise true. We obtain $\lambda d{:}D.a(d){=}\lambda d{:}D.a(e)$. Using the congruence rule the left-hand and right-hand sides of this equation can be applied to d, obtaining using β-conversion $a(d) = a(e)$.

We can prove the lemma as follows. Assume $d'{=}e$. Hence, $a(d'){=}a(e)$. So, $\lambda d'{:}D.a(d'){=}\lambda d'{:}D.a(e)$. By applying α-conversion, which is possible because the variable d does not occur in the context, this is equivalent to $\lambda d{:}D.a(d){=}\lambda d{:}D.a(e)$, which we had to prove.

Two very enjoyable books are [39, 145] describing wrong proofs for almost every imaginable field in mathematics. After reading them, it will be clear that mathematics without underlying proof systems has limited reliability.

Exercise 9.2.3. What goes wrong in the proof in example 9.2.2?

9.3 The sum operator

With the lambda notation available, it is possible to write the sum operator Σ using lambda notation. The sum operator is just an operator that works on functions from data to a process, and yields a process. That is, $\sum_{d:D} p$ is a shorthand for $\sum \lambda d{:}D.p$.

Thus, in order to prove $\sum_{d:D} p = \sum_{d:D} q$ given that $p = q$ is proven, formally requires proving $\lambda d{:}D.p = \lambda d{:}D.q$ using abstraction (so d must not occur in the context). Subsequently, a straightforward application of the congruence rule allows for the proof of $\sum_{d:D} p = \sum_{d:D} q$.

The following lemma provides a very useful fact. Even more importantly, the proof shows how to use the axioms to derive such facts. Recall that the notation $x{\subseteq}y$ stands for $x{+}y{=}y$ with the property that if $x{\subseteq}y$ and $y{\subseteq}x$, then $x{=}y$.

Lemma 9.3.1 (Exchange of sum operators).

$$\sum_{d:D}\sum_{e:E} X(d,e) = \sum_{e:E}\sum_{d:D} X(d,e).$$

Proof. To prove this theorem it is sufficient to show that for all X

$$\sum_{d:D}\sum_{e:E} X(d,e) \subseteq \sum_{e:E}\sum_{d:D} X(d,e) \tag{9.1}$$

because we can substitute $\lambda d{:}D, e{:}E.X(e,d)$ for X in formula (9.1). We obtain

$$\sum_{d:D}\sum_{e:E} X(e,d) \subseteq \sum_{e:E}\sum_{d:D} X(e,d).$$

As we prove this for any sorts D and E, we can exchange d and e:

$$\sum_{e:E}\sum_{d:D} X(d,e) \subseteq \sum_{d:D}\sum_{e:E} X(d,e).$$

Together, with formula (9.1) this implies the theorem.

Thus, we must prove formula (9.1). Using SUM3 twice we derive:

$$\sum_{e:E}\sum_{d:D} X(d,e) \supseteq \sum_{d:D} X(d,e) \supseteq X(d,e).$$

Using abstraction, congruence for Σ, as well as two applications of SUM4 we derive:

$$\sum_{d:D}\sum_{e:E}\sum_{e:E}\sum_{d:D} X(d,e) \supseteq \sum_{d:D}\sum_{e:E} X(d,e). \tag{9.2}$$

Using SUM1 we can derive

$$\sum_{d:D}\sum_{e:E}\sum_{e:E}\sum_{d:D} X(d,e) = \sum_{e:E}\sum_{d:D} X(d,e).$$

Together with formula (9.2), this proves formula (9.1) as desired. □

Exercise 9.3.2. Prove that $\sum_{d:D} X(d) = \sum_{e:D} X(e)$. This is alpha-conversion for the sum operator. In a setting without the lambda calculus, this equality is generally added to table 4.2 as an axiom under the name SUM2.

Exercise 9.3.3. Derive $\sum_{e:E}\sum_{d:D}\sum_{d:D}\sum_{e:E} X(d,e) = \sum_{d:D}\sum_{e:E} X(d,e)$ using the rules of table 9.1 and SUM1.

9.4 The sum elimination lemma

Using the material provided so far, we can prove the following important sum elimination lemma. This lemma is not only applied very frequently when calculating with parallel processes that exchange data, but its proof is also typical for many proofs involving the sum operator.

Lemma 9.4.1 (Sum elimination).

$$\sum_{d:D} d{\approx}e{\to}X(d) = X(e).$$

Proof. We split the proof in two cases:

$\supseteq$. We must show that $X(e) \subseteq \sum_{d:D} d{\approx}e{\rightarrow}X(d)$. This follows by a direct application of SUM3, which yields

$$e{\approx}e{\rightarrow}X(e) \subseteq \sum_{d:D} d{\approx}e{\rightarrow}X(d).$$

Using that $e{\approx}e = \mathit{true}$ and axiom Cond1 yields the result.

$\subseteq$. We must show that $\sum_{d:D} d{\approx}e{\rightarrow}X(d) \subseteq X(e)$. In order to do so, we prove $X(e) = (d{\approx}e){\rightarrow}X(e) + X(e)$. By induction on the Boolean c we derive that $X(e) = c{\rightarrow}X(e){+}X(e)$. If we take c to be $d{\approx}e$, this equation becomes $X(e) = (d{\approx}e){\rightarrow}X(e) + X(e)$. By using the equation $x{\approx}y{\rightarrow}Z(x) = (x{\approx}y){\rightarrow}Z(y)$ derived directly following equation (9.4) in the next section, we can show this equal to

$$X(e) = (d{\approx}e){\rightarrow}X(d) + X(e).$$

Using the rules for abstraction (see table 9.1), it follows that

$$\lambda d{:}D.X(e) = \lambda d{:}D.((d{\approx}e){\rightarrow}X(d) + X(e)).$$

Note that this is allowed, because there are no assumptions on d; d does not occur in the context. Subsequently applying the congruence rule with the sum operator from table 9.1 we obtain

$$\sum_{d:D} X(e) = \sum_{d:D}((d{\approx}e){\rightarrow}X(d) + X(e)).$$

By applying SUM1 (twice) and SUM4 we get:

$$X(e) = \sum_{d:D} d{\approx}e{\rightarrow}X(d) + X(e).$$

This is equivalent to $\sum_{d:D} d{\approx}e{\rightarrow}X(d) \subseteq X(e)$ which we had to prove.

□

Exercise 9.4.2. Prove $x = \sum_{t:\mathbb{R}} (t > 0) \rightarrow x{}^{c}t$.

Exercise 9.4.3. Show for arbitrary sort D, variables $c : D \rightarrow \mathbb{B}$ and $x : \mathbb{P}$.

$$(\exists d{:}D.c(d) = \mathit{true}) \;\Rightarrow\; x = \sum_{d:D} c(d){\rightarrow}x.$$

9.5 Induction for constructor sorts

If D is a constructor sort, i.e., if there is at least one declared constructor $f{:}D_1 \times \cdots \times D_n \rightarrow D$, then elements of D can all be written as an application of a constructor function to smaller elements. This yields a well-known proof principle, namely induction, also referred to as term induction. The idea is that a formula ϕ can be proven for all elements of a constructor sort D if it can be proven for all expressions of the form

$c_i(p_1, \ldots, p_{n_i})$ where c_i is a constructor and n_i the arity of the constructor. Moreover, as those expressions p_i of sort D are smaller than $c_i(p_1, \ldots, p_{n_i})$, the formula ϕ can be used with p_i to prove ϕ with $c_i(p_1, \ldots, p_{n_i})$. The following induction rule summarizes this, where variables x_i are taken, instead of expressions p_i. Here, D_i is the sort of variable x_i.

$$\frac{\{\Gamma \vdash \bigwedge_{D_i=D} \phi[x := x_i] \Rightarrow \phi[x{:=}c_i(x_1, \ldots, x_{n_i})] \mid c_i \text{ is a constructor of } D\}}{\Gamma \vdash \phi} \text{ induction}$$

As an example we show what this general rule looks like if the constructor sort is $\mathbb{B}$. There are two constructors *true* and *false*, which do not have arguments. The induction rule is of the following form:

$$\frac{\Gamma \vdash \phi[x{:=}\mathit{true}] \quad \Gamma \vdash \phi[x{:=}\mathit{false}]}{\Gamma \vdash \phi} \text{ induction on } \mathbb{B}$$

Using this rule we can prove $c \to p \diamond p = p$ with induction on c. Induction on Booleans says that we must prove $\mathit{true} \to p \diamond p = p$ and $\mathit{false} \to p \diamond p = p$. By applying process axioms Cond1 and Cond2 we can easily show both equations to hold.

A useful process identity is $x{\approx}y{\to}Z(x) = x{\approx}y{\to}Z(y)$. Here, x and y are variables over some sort D and Z is a variable ranging over functions from $D{\to}\mathbb{P}$.

In order to prove this, we first prove the auxiliary

$$(c = \mathit{true} \Rightarrow x = y) \Rightarrow (c{\to}x = c{\to}y). \tag{9.3}$$

Note that x and y are of sort $\mathbb{P}$ and c is of sort $\mathbb{B}$. The equation is proven with induction on $\mathbb{B}$. Thus, we need to show:

1. $(\mathit{true} = \mathit{true} \Rightarrow x = y) \Rightarrow \mathit{true}{\to}x = \mathit{true}{\to}y$, and
2. $(\mathit{false} = \mathit{true} \Rightarrow x = y) \Rightarrow \mathit{false}{\to}x = \mathit{false}{\to}y$.

In the first case, using axiom Cond1 we must prove $x = y$ from $\mathit{true} = \mathit{true}{\Rightarrow}x = y$. As $\mathit{true} = \mathit{true}$ is always valid (by reflexivity), this is trivial. In the second case, using axiom T2 and Cond2 it is necessary to show $\delta{\cdot}0 = \delta{\cdot}0$, which also follows directly from reflexivity.

From equation (9.3) we derive the following by taking $x{\approx}y$ for c and $Z(x)$ and $Z(y)$ for x and y.

$$(x{\approx}y = \mathit{true} \Rightarrow Z(x) = Z(y)) \Rightarrow x{\approx}y{\to}Z(x) = x{\approx}y{\to}Z(y). \tag{9.4}$$

Now, using Bergstra's axiom, $x{\approx}y = \mathit{true}$ implies that $x = y$. Using congruence, it follows that $Z(x) = Z(y)$. Hence, using equation (9.4) we can conclude $x{\approx}y{\to}Z(x) = x{\approx}y{\to}Z(y)$.

The constructors for lists are the empty list $[]$ and list prefix $d \triangleright l$ (see appendix B). Using the induction principle this immediately gives the following concrete induction rule:

$$\frac{\Gamma \vdash \phi[x{:=}[]] \quad \Gamma \vdash \phi[x{:=}l] \;\Rightarrow\; \phi[x{:=}d \triangleright l]}{\Gamma \vdash \phi} \quad \text{induction on } List(D)$$

Note that the reals, sets, and bags do not have constructors, and therefore do not have an induction principle.

Exercise 9.5.1. Give a precise formal derivation of the following formula, which is needed for the proof of formula (9.3).

$$\Gamma \vdash (true = true \Rightarrow x = y) \Rightarrow true{\rightarrow}x = true{\rightarrow}y.$$

Exercise 9.5.2. Prove that $c_1{\rightarrow}c_2{\rightarrow}x = (c_1 \wedge c_2){\rightarrow}x$.

Exercise 9.5.3. Formulate the induction principles for positive numbers, natural numbers, and integers, based on the definitions in appendix B.

Exercise 9.5.4. Prove that

$$\sum_{b:\mathbb{B}} b \rightarrow x \diamond y = x + y.$$

Exercise 9.5.5. Prove that

$$\sum_{n:\mathbb{N}} n \leq 2 \rightarrow X(n) = X(0) + X(1) + X(2).$$

★**Exercise 9.5.6.** Mathematical induction on the positive numbers is given by the rule:

$$\frac{\Gamma \vdash \phi(1) \quad \Gamma \vdash \phi(n) \Rightarrow \phi(n{+}1)}{\Gamma \vdash \phi(n)}.$$

The constructors in appendix B suggests the induction principle

$$\frac{\Gamma \vdash \phi(1) \quad \Gamma \vdash \phi(n) \Rightarrow \phi(2n) \quad \Gamma \vdash \phi(n) \Rightarrow \phi(2n{+}1)}{\Gamma \vdash \phi(n)}.$$

Show that both induction rules are equivalent.

9.6 Recursive specification principle

In this section we explain the recursive specification principle (RSP), which allows the proof that recursive processes are equal. Before doing so, we first introduce process operators.

A process operator maps a process to a process. We typically use letters Φ and Ψ for process operators. For example, if we define $\Psi = \lambda X{:}\mathbb{P}.a{\cdot}X$, then $\Psi\,(b + c{\cdot}d)$ is the process $a{\cdot}(b + c{\cdot}d)$.

Process operators can also operate on processes with data. For example, the process operator

$$\Psi' = \lambda X{:}\mathbb{N}{\rightarrow}\mathbb{P}.\lambda n{:}\mathbb{N}.a{\cdot}X(n{+}1)$$

maps a process X which depends on a natural number to another process that depends on such a number. The type of Ψ' is $(\mathbb{N}\to\mathbb{P})\to(\mathbb{N}\to\mathbb{P})$.

Process operators can even be applied to processes with more than one data parameter. For example, the following operator works on processes with a parameter of sort $\mathbb{B}$ and one of sort $\mathbb{N}$: $\Psi'' = \lambda X{:}\mathbb{B} \times \mathbb{N}\to\mathbb{P}.\lambda b{:}\mathbb{B}, n{:}\mathbb{N}.b\to up\cdot X(\mathit{false}, n+1) \diamond \mathit{twice}\cdot X(\mathit{true}, 2n)$ where up and twice are actions. The type of Ψ'' is $(\mathbb{B}\to\mathbb{N}\to\mathbb{P}) \to (\mathbb{B}\to\mathbb{N}\to\mathbb{P})$.

Process operators have a direct link with equations. If Φ is a process operator, then $X = \Phi\, X$ is the equation associated with it. And vice versa, if $X(d_1{:}D_1, \ldots, d_n{:}D_n) = p$ is an equation, then $\lambda X{:}D_1 \times \cdots \times D_n, d_1{:}D_1, \ldots, d_n{:}D_n.p$ is the associated operator. Thus, for the operators Ψ, Ψ' and Ψ'' above the associated equations are $X{=}a\cdot X$, $X(n{:}\mathbb{N}){=}a\cdot X(n{+}1)$ and $X(b{:}\mathbb{B}, n{:}\mathbb{N}) = b\to up\cdot X(\mathit{false}, n{+}1) \diamond \mathit{twice}\cdot X(\mathit{true}, 2n)$.

In chapter 4 we indicated that guarded recursive equations, such as $X = a\cdot X$, define a process because there is only one process that is a solution of this equation, namely the process that can do a actions infinitely. The essential ingredient of this equation is that at the left-hand side X only occurs once and at the right-hand side X only occurs in a guarded position. We make this last notion precise. In the definition below, we assume X has one argument of sort D, in line with our habit to provide formal definitions only for processes with one argument.

Definition 9.6.1 (Guarded). We inductively define that a process variable $X{:}D\to\mathbb{P}$ is *guarded* in a process p iff

- If p equals δ or a nonempty multi-action, then X occurs guarded in p,
- If $p = p_1 + p_2$, $p = p_1 \parallel p_2$, $p = p_1 \mid p_2$, $p = c\to p_1 \diamond p_2$ or $p = p_1 \ll p_2$ then X occurs guarded in p iff X occurs guarded in p_1 and p_2,
- If $p = \sum_{d:D} p_1$, $p = p_1{}^{c}t$, $p = c\to p_1$, $p = t\gg p_1$, $p = p_1 \ll t$, $p = \Gamma_C(p_1)$, $p = \nabla_V(p_1)$, $p = \partial_B(p_1)$ or $p = \rho_R(p_1)$, then X occurs guarded in p iff it occurs guarded in p_1, and
- If $p = p_1\cdot p_2$ or $p = p_1 \mathbin{⌊\!⌊} p_2$ then X occurs guarded in p if X occurs guarded in p_1.

The recursive specification principle says that in any guarded recursive equation, i.e., an equation of the form $X = p$ where X occurs guarded in p, there is at most one process that is a solution for X. In terms of a process operator, if $\Phi = \lambda X{:}D\to\mathbb{P}, \lambda d{:}D.p$ and X occurs guarded in p, then we say that Φ is a guarded process operator and Φ has only one fixed point. Therefore, there is only one process Y satisfying $Y = \Phi Y$.

The following derivation rule compactly characterizes the uniqueness of solutions:

$$\frac{\Gamma \vdash X = \Psi X \quad \Gamma \vdash Y = \Psi Y}{\Gamma \vdash X = Y} \quad \Psi \text{ guarded process operator (RSP)}$$

Example 9.6.2. As a simple example, consider the following definitions for X and Y.

proc $X = a{\cdot}X;$
$Y = a{\cdot}a{\cdot}Y;$

Both X and Y are fixed points of the guarded process operator $\Phi = \lambda Z{:}\mathbb{P}.a{\cdot}a{\cdot}Z$. In order to prove this, we must show $X = \Phi X$ and $Y = \Phi Y$. Or in other words, $X = a{\cdot}a{\cdot}X$ and $Y = a{\cdot}a{\cdot}Y$. It is easy to derive that $X = a{\cdot}X = a{\cdot}a{\cdot}X$ using two applications of the defining equation for X. The defining equation for Y already says that $Y = a{\cdot}a{\cdot}Y$. Thus, we can apply the rule RSP, and conclude that X and Y are equal, i.e., $X = Y$.

Example 9.6.3. A slightly more elaborate example is the following. Assume that the following equations define X and Y.

proc $X(b{:}\mathbb{B}) = a(b){\cdot}X(\neg b);$
$Y(n{:}\mathbb{N}) = a(n|_2{\approx}0){\cdot}Y(n{+}1);$

The first process clearly has behavior $\ldots a(\mathit{true})\,a(\mathit{false})\,a(\mathit{true})\,a(\mathit{false})\ldots$. The second process has the same behavior. It indicates whether n is even, by calculating whether n modulo 2 equals 0. Subsequently, n is increased by one. We show that $X(\mathit{true}) = Y(0)$.

In order to show that $X(\mathit{true}) = Y(0)$ we must show a more general equation from which it follows directly. Finding such a more general statement is often one of the more difficult steps in a proof and is called *property lifting*. In this concrete case we show that $X(n|_2{\approx}0) = Y(n)$ for $n{:}\mathbb{N}$. By taking $n = 0$, the desired result follows.

We prove $X(n|_2{\approx}0) = Y(n)$ by showing that both sides of the equation are a fixed point of the guarded process operator

$$\Psi = \lambda Z{:}\mathbb{N} \to \mathbb{P}, n{:}\mathbb{N}.a(n|_2{\approx}0){\cdot}Z(n{+}1).$$

A problem is that both sides of the equation are not yet of the right type to apply the operator Ψ to it. Therefore we apply lambda abstraction to both sides and get $\lambda n{:}\mathbb{N}.X(n|_2{\approx}0) = Y$. To prove that both sides are a fixed point of the operator we must show (we apply both sides to n, to get more decent equations):

1. For the left-hand side we get:

$$\lambda n{:}\mathbb{N}.X(n|_2{\approx}0)(n) = (\lambda Z{:}\mathbb{N} \to \mathbb{P}, m{:}\mathbb{N}.a(m|_2{\approx}0){\cdot}Z(m{+}1))(\lambda n{:}\mathbb{N}.X(n|_2{\approx}0))(n).$$

This reduces by β-conversion to

$$X(n|_2{\approx}0) = a(n|_2{\approx}0){\cdot}X(n{+}1|_2{\approx}0).$$

Using that $n{+}1|_2{\approx}0 = \neg(n|_2{\approx}0)$ we must show that

$$X(n|_2{\approx}0) = a(n|_2{\approx}0){\cdot}X(\neg(n|_2{\approx}0)).$$

If we now look at the definition for the process X, we see that $X(b{:}\mathbb{B}) = a(b){\cdot}X(\neg b)$ for any Boolean b. Therefore, in particular for $b = n|_2{\approx}0$, this yields exactly the last equation that we had to prove.

2. For the right-hand side we must show that

$$Y(n) = (\lambda Z{:}\mathbb{N} \rightarrow \mathbb{P}, m{:}\mathbb{N}.a(m|_2{\approx}0){\cdot}Z(m{+}1))\, Y\, n.$$

By β-conversion this is equivalent to

$$Y(n) = a(n|_2{\approx}0){\cdot}Y(n{+}1).$$

This is exactly equal to the equation defining Y. Therefore, this equation holds also.

We have shown using RSP that $X(n|_2{\approx}0) = Y(n)$, as required.

It is not always straightforward to find the right guarded process operator. A good guideline is to take the process with the largest state space and transform that one into the operator.

There is another principle which is called the recursive definition principle (RDP). It says that any recursive equation has a solution. We use this principle implicitly, by acting as if X refers to an existing process if it is defined by an equation of the form $X = p$ where X can occur in p. We do not pay further attention to this.

A derived rule is RSP for a set of guarded recursive equations, also called a guarded recursive specification. So, consider the sequence of process operators $\Phi_1, \ldots, \Phi_n$. Assume that $X_1, \ldots, X_n$ and $Y_1, \ldots, Y_n$ are both fixed points of Φ_i, all with type $D{\rightarrow}\mathbb{P}$. If the types of the variables are not equal, it is a simple operation to generalize the types of the variables to harmonize them. Then we can conclude that $X_1 = Y_1, \ldots, X_n = Y_n$. As an inference rule:

$$\frac{\begin{array}{c}\Gamma \vdash X_1 = \Phi_1 X_1,\ \ldots,\ \Gamma \vdash X_n = \Phi_n X_n \\ \Gamma \vdash Y_1 = \Phi_1 Y_1,\ \ldots,\ \Gamma \vdash Y_n = \Phi_n Y_n\end{array}}{\Gamma \vdash X_1 = Y_1, \ldots, \Gamma \vdash X_n = Y_n}.$$

We prove this rule from RSP as follows. Define the operator Ψ by

$$\begin{aligned}\Psi = \lambda Z{:}D{\rightarrow}\mathbb{N}, d{:}D, i{:}\mathbb{N}.(i{\approx}1){\rightarrow}\Phi(d,1) \diamond (i{\approx}2){\rightarrow}\Phi(d,2) \diamond \ldots \\ \ldots (i{\approx}n{-}1)P{\rightarrow}\Phi(d,n{-}1) \diamond \phi(d,n).\end{aligned}$$

Now define the two processes

$$\begin{aligned}X(d{:}D, i{:}\mathbb{N}) &= (i{\approx}1){\rightarrow}X_1(d) \diamond \cdots (i{\approx}n{-}1){\rightarrow}X_{n-1}(n) \diamond X_n(d) \text{ and} \\ Y(d{:}D, i{:}\mathbb{N}) &= (i{\approx}1) \rightarrow Y_1(d) \diamond \cdots (i{\approx}n{-}1){\rightarrow}Y_{n-1}(n) \diamond Y_n(d).\end{aligned}$$

It is now easy to show that X and Y are fixed points of Ψ. So, $X(d,i) = Y(d,i)$. In particular $X_i(d) = X(d,i) = Y(d,i) = Y_i(d)$, which we had to prove.

Exercise 9.6.4. Prove that $X = Y$, where X and Y are given by $X = a{\cdot}X$ and $Y = a{\cdot}a{\cdot}a{\cdot}Y + a{\cdot}a{\cdot}Y$.

Exercise 9.6.5. Prove using RSP that the processes X and Y defined by

proc $X = a{\cdot}X;$
$\quad Y = a{\cdot}Y{\cdot}\delta;$

are equal.

Exercise 9.6.6. Show that $X(0) = Y([])$ for the following two processes

proc $X(n{:}\mathbb{N}) = a(n)\cdot X(n+1);$
$\quad Y(l{:}List(\mathbb{N})) = \sum_{d:\mathbb{N}} a(\#l)\cdot Y(d\triangleright l);$

Exercise 9.6.7. Show that $X(0) = Y(0)$ where $N{:}\mathbb{N}^+$ for the following two processes

proc $X(n{:}\mathbb{N}) = a(n)\cdot X((n+1)|_N);$
$\quad Y(m{:}\mathbb{N}) = a(m|_N)\cdot Y(m+1);$

Exercise 9.6.8. Consider the process $X = a\cdot b\cdot c\cdot X$ and the process $Y(n{:}\mathbb{N}^+) = n{\approx}1{\rightarrow}a\cdot Y(2) + n{\approx}2{\rightarrow}b\cdot Y(3) + n{\approx}3{\rightarrow}c\cdot Y(1)$. Prove using RSP that $X = Y(1)$.

★**Exercise 9.6.9.** Consider the following processes:

proc $X = a\cdot\nabla_{\{a,b\}}(b\|X);$
$\quad Y(n{:}\mathbb{N}) = a\cdot Y(n+1) + n{>}0{\rightarrow}b\cdot Y(n-1);$

Show that $X = Y(0)$ using RSP.

9.7 Koomen's fair abstraction rule

Most processes can perform many different interactions simultaneously, and we only want to study some of them. For instance, a buffer can forward data from gate 1 to 2, or vice versa, from gate 2 to gate 1. In a picture and as a process:

proc $Buffer = read_1\cdot deliver_2\cdot Buffer + read_2\cdot deliver_1\cdot Buffer;$

We may be interested in studying the data transfer from gate 1 to gate 2, hiding the transfer of data from 2 to 1, under the assumption that the amount of data being transferred from 2 to 1 is not so large that it prevents data from being transferred in the other direction. In other words, we assume that data transfer from 2 to 1 is *fair*, in the sense that it allows other events to happen also.

Thus, we expect $\tau_{\{deliver_1,read_2\}}(Buffer)$ to satisfy the equation

$$\tau_{\{deliver_1,read_2\}}(Buffer) = read_1\cdot deliver_2\cdot\tau_{\{deliver_1,read_2\}}(Buffer).$$

What we can prove however, by directly applying the axioms for hiding is:

$$\begin{array}{rcl}\tau_{\{deliver_1,read_2\}}(Buffer) & = & read_1\cdot deliver_2\cdot\tau_{\{deliver_1,read_2\}}(Buffer)\\ & & +\ \tau\cdot\tau\cdot\tau_{\{deliver_1,read_2\}}(Buffer).\end{array}$$

With the rules given hitherto, we will not be able to prove both equations equal. We first introduce a rule that can do the job, and will come back to this example after that.

Koomen's fair abstraction rule (KFAR) is suited for the job. It is valid in branching bisimulation, not in strong bisimulation, and it has the following form:

$$\frac{\Gamma \vdash X = i{\cdot}X + Y}{\Gamma \vdash \tau{\cdot}\tau_{\{i\}}(X) = \tau{\cdot}\tau_{\{i\}}(Y)} \quad \text{KFAR (branching bisimulation)}$$

It says that in the process X, where the behavior of Y is always enabled as long as it is not chosen, the behavior of Y will be chosen. In this way, it is expressed that i is a fair action. Of course the action i is hidden in Y.

The formulation of Koomen's fair abstraction rule looks somewhat complex, and tends to stimulate to investigate the following simplified formulation, which is wrong:

$$\frac{\Gamma \vdash X = \tau{\cdot}X + Y}{\Gamma \vdash X = \tau{\cdot}Y} \tag{9.5}$$

This can be seen as follows. Consider the process $x = \tau{\cdot}y$ where y can be any process. Using axioms T1 and W‡, it follows that $x = \tau{\cdot}x + \delta{\lessdot}0$. Using the faulty version of KFAR, we can conclude that $x = \tau{\cdot}\delta{\lessdot}0$. Or in other words, any process of the form $\tau{\cdot}y$ equals $\tau{\cdot}\delta{\lessdot}0$. This is clearly undesirable.

If we consider the buffer example above, we can prove using the axioms for hiding and the first τ law that:

$$\tau_{\{deliver_1\}}(Buffer) = read_1{\cdot}deliver_2{\cdot}\tau_{\{deliver_1\}}(Buffer) + read_2{\cdot}\tau_{\{deliver_1\}}(Buffer).$$

If we let $read_2$ match i and $\tau_{\{deliver_1\}}(Buffer)$ match X in the KFAR rule, then we can conclude:

$$\tau{\cdot}\tau_{\{read_2, deliver_1\}}(Buffer) = \tau{\cdot}read_1{\cdot}deliver_2{\cdot}\tau_{\{deliver_1, read_2\}}(Buffer).$$

Except for initial internal steps, this is what we would like to prove. It is not possible to remove the initial τ's, as they reflect that initially some hidden messages travel from gate 2 to 1.

For completeness, we also formulate Koomen's fair abstraction rule for weak bisimulation. This differs in the sense that there is no initial τ at the left-hand side of the conclusion.

$$\frac{\Gamma \vdash X = i{\cdot}X + Y}{\Gamma \vdash \tau_{\{i\}}(X) = \tau{\cdot}\tau_{\{i\}}(Y)} \quad \text{KFAR (weak bisimulation)}$$

Exercise 9.7.1. Define $X{=}head{\cdot}X{+}tail$. Prove by KFAR that $\tau{\cdot}\tau_{\{head\}}(X){=}\tau{\cdot}tail$.

Exercise 9.7.2. Show that the wrong KFAR deduction in rule (9.5) is also invalid in an untimed setting.

★Exercise 9.7.3. Consider the process $X_1 = i{\cdot}X_2 + a_1$, $X_2 = i{\cdot}X_1 + a_2$. Prove using KFAR for weak bisimulation that $\tau_{\{i\}}(X_1) = \tau{\cdot}(a_1 + a_2)$. Also show that this cannot be proven using KFAR for branching bisimulation.

9.8 Parallel expansion

Up to now we have not really discussed how to calculate with parallel processes. But real difficulties with behavior come with parallelism. There are so many actions that can take place in so many different orders, that it is impossible to understand what is happening by just imagining the traces.

The universal technique that we apply to understand parallel processes, is by eliminating the parallel operator and by translating it to sequential behavior. In this section we explain how this can be done, directly using the axioms. This technique is very common in process algebra, and generally called *parallel expansion*. We also show how to prove parallel processes equal to simplified counterparts, where internal actions are hidden.

In the first two sections below we explain expansion in a setting without time. The third section illustrates timed expansion. Keeping track of time in the parallel expansion is a tedious procedure.

Parallel expansion falls short if processes become more complex. Therefore, in the next chapter, we explain linearization as an advanced form of parallel expansion.

9.8.1 Basic parallel expansion

The description of a system S of n communicating parallel components $X_1, \ldots, X_n$ is generally as follows:

$$S = \nabla_V(\Gamma_\Gamma(X_1 \parallel \cdots \parallel X_n))$$

where the behavior of the individual components X_i are given by a guarded recursive specification. By systematically applying the axioms in table 5.1 to eliminate the parallel operator, the axioms in table 5.2 to eliminate the communication operator and 5.3 to remove the allow operator, a set of simple process equations results. The axioms are such that they can strictly be used from left to right.

As an example, consider the system $S = \nabla_{\{c,d\}}(\Gamma_{\{a|b\to d\}}(X_1 \parallel X_2))$ where $X_1 = a{\cdot}X_1$ and $X_2 = b{\cdot}c{\cdot}X_2$. Applying the axioms yields:

$$\begin{aligned}
S &\stackrel{\text{def}}{=} \nabla_{\{c,d\}}(\Gamma_{\{a|b\to d\}}(X_1 \| X_2)) \\
&\stackrel{\text{def}}{=} \nabla_{\{c,d\}}(\Gamma_{\{a|b\to d\}}(a{\cdot}X_1 \| b{\cdot}c{\cdot}X_2)) \\
&\stackrel{\text{M}}{=} \nabla_{\{c,d\}}(\Gamma_{\{a|b\to d\}}(a{\cdot}X_1 \lfloor\!\lfloor b{\cdot}c{\cdot}X_2 + b{\cdot}c{\cdot}X_2 \lfloor\!\lfloor a{\cdot}X_1 + a{\cdot}X_1 | b{\cdot}c{\cdot}X_2)) \\
&\stackrel{\text{LM3}\ddagger\text{,S6}}{=} \nabla_{\{c,d\}}(\Gamma_{\{a|b\to d\}}(a{\cdot}(X_1 \| b{\cdot}c{\cdot}X_2) + b{\cdot}(c{\cdot}X_2 \| a{\cdot}X_1) \\
&\qquad\qquad + (a|b){\cdot}(X_1 \| c{\cdot}X_2))) \\
&\stackrel{\substack{\text{C1,C3,C4,}\\ \text{V1,V2,V4,V5}}}{=} d{\cdot}\nabla_{\{c,d\}}(\Gamma_{\{a|b\to d\}}(X_1 \| c{\cdot}X_2)).
\end{aligned}$$

At such a state, it is handy to introduce a new name for the expressions after the initial actions. In this case, it is only one. We define:

$$S_1 = \nabla_{\{c,d\}}(\Gamma_{\{a|b\to d\}}(X_1 \| c{\cdot}X_2)).$$

We can apply the same expansion technique and derive

$$S_1 = c \cdot \nabla_{\{c,d\}}(\Gamma_{\{a|b \to d\}}(X_1 \| X_2)).$$

In other words, we have shown that S satisfies the following recursive specification:

$$S = d \cdot S_1, \qquad S_1 = c \cdot S.$$

Exercise 9.8.1. Take X_1 and X_2 as above and calculate the parallel expansion for

$$\nabla_{\{a,c,d\}}(\Gamma_{\{a|b \to d\}}(X_1 \parallel X_2)).$$

9.8.2 Parallel expansion with data: two one-place buffers

Two actions can only communicate if their data are the same. In this section we carry out a parallel expansion of two sequentially connected one place buffers. This shows how expansion of actions with data is carried out. We also see the sum elimination theorem in action.

We consider two buffers of capacity one that are put in sequence: buffer B_1 reads a datum from gate 1 and sends this datum into gate 3, while buffer B_2 reads a datum from gate 3 and sends this datum via gate 2. This system can be depicted as follows:

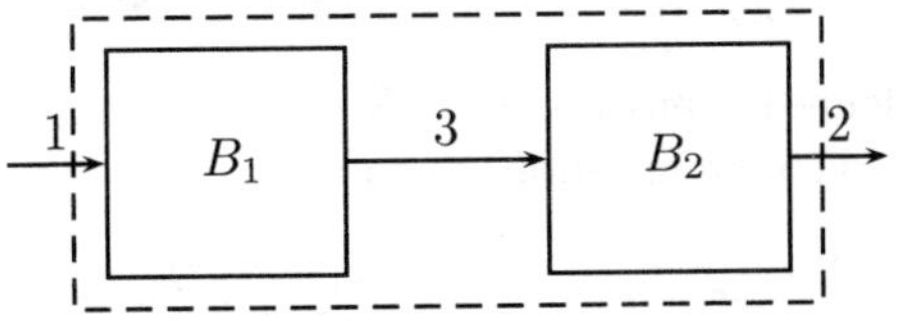

Let D denote a data domain. Action $r_i(d)$ represents reading datum d from gate i, while action $s_i(d)$ represents sending datum d into gate i. Moreover, action $c_3(d)$ denotes communication of datum d through gate 3. We let actions r_3 and s_3 communicate to c_3 and only allow actions r_1, s_2, and c_3. On top of this, we hide c_3. Thus, action c_3 can happen, but we cannot observe it directly.

The buffers B_1 and B_2 are defined by the process declaration

proc $B_1 = \sum_{d:D} r_1(d) \cdot s_3(d) \cdot B_1;$
$\quad B_2 = \sum_{d:D} r_3(d) \cdot s_2(d) \cdot B_2;$

The behavior of the whole system is characterized by the process X consisting of the buffers B_1 and B_2 in parallel:

proc $X = \tau_{\{c_3\}}(\nabla_{\{r_1,s_2,c_3\}}(\Gamma_{\{r_3|s_3 \to c_3\}}(B_1 \parallel B_2)));$

We show that X behaves as a queue of capacity two, which can read two data elements from gate 1 before sending them in the same order into gate 2. That is, X satisfies the following equations:

$$\begin{aligned} X &= \textstyle\sum_{d:D} r_1(d) \cdot Y(d); \\ Y(d{:}D) &= \textstyle\sum_{d':D} r_1(d') \cdot Z(d,d') + s_2(d) \cdot X; \\ Z(d,d'{:}D) &= s_2(d) \cdot Y(d'). \end{aligned} \tag{9.6}$$

In state X, the queue of capacity two is empty, so that it can only read a datum d from gate 1 and proceed to the state $Y(d)$ where the queue contains d. In $Y(d)$, the queue can either read a second datum d' from gate 1 and proceed to the state $Z(d,d')$ where the queue contains d and d', or send datum d into gate 2 and proceed to the state X where the queue is empty. Finally, in state $Z(d,d')$ the queue is full, so that it can only send datum d into gate 2 and proceed to the state $Y(d')$ where it contains d'.

Below we provide the derivation in substantial detail. In each derivation step, the subexpressions that are reduced are underlined. First we expand $B_1 \parallel B_2$:

$$
\begin{array}{rcl}
\underline{B_1 \parallel B_2} & \overset{\text{M}}{=} & \underline{B_1} \mathbin{\lfloor\!\lfloor} B_2 + \underline{B_2} \mathbin{\lfloor\!\lfloor} B_1 + \underline{B_1}|\underline{B_2} \\
& \overset{\text{def}}{=} & \underline{(\sum_{d:D} r_1(d)\cdot s_3(d)\cdot B_1) \mathbin{\lfloor\!\lfloor} B_2} \\
& + & \underline{(\sum_{d:D} r_3(d)\cdot s_2(d)\cdot B_2) \mathbin{\lfloor\!\lfloor} B_1} \\
& + & \underline{(\sum_{d:D} r_1(d)\cdot s_3(d)\cdot B_1)|(\sum_{d':D} r_3(d')\cdot s_2(d')\cdot B_2)} \\
& \overset{\text{LM5,S8}}{=} & \sum_{d:D} \underline{(r_1(d)\cdot s_3(d)\cdot B_1) \mathbin{\lfloor\!\lfloor} B_2} \\
& + & \sum_{d:D} \underline{(r_3(d)\cdot s_2(d)\cdot B_2) \mathbin{\lfloor\!\lfloor} B_1} \\
& + & \sum_{d:D} \sum_{d':D} \underline{(r_1(d)\cdot s_3(d)\cdot B_1)|(r_3(d')\cdot s_2(d')\cdot B_2)} \\
& \overset{\text{LM3,S6,def}}{=} & \sum_{d:D} r_1(d)\cdot(s_3(d)\cdot B_1 \| B_2) \\
& + & \sum_{d:D} r_3(d)\cdot(s_2(d)\cdot B_2 \| B_1) \\
& + & \sum_{d:D} \sum_{d':D}(r_1(d)|r_3(d'))\cdot((s_3(d)\cdot B_1)\|(s_2(d')\cdot B_2)).
\end{array}
$$

For convenience, we define the process $X_1 = \nabla_{\{r_1,s_2,c_3\}}(\Gamma_{\{r_3|s_3\to c_3\}}(\underline{B_1 \parallel B_2}))$. We now apply the allow and communication operator:

$$
\begin{array}{rcl}
X_1 & = & \nabla_{\{r_1,s_2,c_3\}}(\Gamma_{\{r_3|s_3\to c_3\}}(B_1 \parallel B_2)) \\
& = & \underline{\nabla_{\{r_1,s_2,c_3\}}(\Gamma_{\{r_3|s_3\to c_3\}}(\sum_{d:D} r_1(d)\cdot(s_3(d)\cdot B_1)\|B_2)} \\
& + & \underline{\sum_{d:D} r_3(d)\cdot(s_2(d)\cdot B_2)\|B_1)} \\
& + & \underline{\sum_{d:D} \sum_{d':D}(r_1(d)|r_3(d'))\cdot(s_3(d)\cdot B_1\|s_2(d')\cdot B_2)} \\
& \overset{\text{C3,C5,V3,V6}}{=} & \sum_{d:D} \underline{\nabla_{\{r_1,s_2,c_3\}}(\Gamma_{\{r_3|s_3\to c_3\}}(r_1(d)\cdot(s_3(d)\cdot B_1\|B_2)))} \\
& + & \sum_{d:D} \underline{\nabla_{\{r_1,s_2,c_3\}}(\Gamma_{\{r_3|s_3\to c_3\}}(r_3(d)\cdot(s_2(d)\cdot B_2\|B_1)))} \\
& + & \sum_{d:D} \sum_{d':D} \underline{\nabla_{\{r_1,s_2,c_3\}}(\Gamma_{\{r_3|s_3\to c_3\}}((r_1(d)|r_3(d'))\cdot} \\
& & \underline{(s_3(d)\cdot B_1\|s_2(d')\cdot B_2)))} \\
& \overset{\text{C1,C4,V1,V2,V5}}{=} & \sum_{d:D} r_1(d)\cdot\nabla_{\{r_1,s_2,c_3\}}(\Gamma_{\{r_3|s_3\to c_3\}}(s_3(d)\cdot B_1\|B_2))\underline{+\delta+\delta} \\
& \overset{\text{A6}}{=} & \sum_{d:D} r_1(d)\cdot\nabla_{\{r_1,s_2,c_3\}}(\Gamma_{\{r_3|s_3\to c_3\}}(s_3(d)\cdot B_1\|B_2)).
\end{array}
$$

Summarizing, we have derived

$$X_1 = \sum_{d:D} r_1(d)\cdot\nabla_{\{r_1,s_2,c_3\}}(\Gamma_{\{r_3|s_3\to c_3\}}(s_3(d)\cdot B_1 \parallel B_2)). \tag{9.7}$$

We define a new process

$$X_2(d{:}D) = \nabla_{\{r_1,s_2,c_3\}}(\Gamma_{\{r_3|s_3\to c_3\}}(s_3(d)\cdot B_1 \parallel B_2))$$

and we proceed to expand $X_1(d)$. At the first equation we apply the same expansion as above, and block the single s_3 and r_3 actions. Only the communication between s_3

and r_3 survives.

$$X_2(d) \quad = \quad \sum_{d':D} \nabla_{\{r_1,s_2,c_3\}}(\Gamma_{\{r_3|s_3\to c_3\}}(s_3(d)|r_3(d'))\cdot(B_1 \parallel s_2(d')\cdot B_2))$$

Now the communication operator is only effective if $d = d'$. So we split the condition and see that the right-hand side of the last equation is equal to:

$$\begin{aligned}\sum_{d':D} \nabla_{\{r_1,s_2,c_3\}}(\Gamma_{\{r_3|s_3\to c_3\}}(d{\approx}d' \quad &\to \quad (s_3(d)|r_3(d'))\cdot(B_1 \parallel s_2(d')\cdot B_2) \\ &\diamond \quad (s_3(d)|r_3(d'))\cdot(B_1 \parallel s_2(d')\cdot B_2))).\end{aligned}$$

Distribution of the allow and communication operators over the condition and the action yields:

$$\sum_{d':D} d{\approx}d' \to c_3(d)\cdot\nabla_{\{r_1,s_2,c_3\}}(\Gamma_{\{r_3|s_3\to c_3\}}(B_1 \parallel s_2(d')\cdot B_2)) \diamond \delta.$$

To this expression we can apply the sum elimination lemma (lemma 9.4.1) and obtain

$$c_3(d)\cdot\nabla_{\{r_1,s_2,c_3\}}(\Gamma_{\{r_3|s_3\to c_3\}}(B_1 \parallel s_2(d)\cdot B_2)) \diamond \delta.$$

Summarizing, we get

$$X_2(d{:}D) = c_3(d)\cdot\nabla_{\{r_1,s_2,c_3\}}(\Gamma_{\{r_3|s_3\to c_3\}}(B_1 \parallel s_2(d)\cdot B_2)) \diamond \delta.$$

We can now repeat this process, by iteratively introducing new definitions and expanding these. This is a very mechanical procedure that quite often terminates. But if it does not, other, more intricate ways need to be found to eliminate the parallel operators. For the two parallel buffers we need the following auxiliary definitions:

$$\begin{aligned}&X_3(d{:}D) = \nabla_{\{r_1,s_2,c_3\}}(\Gamma_{\{r_3|s_3\to c_3\}}(B_1 \parallel s_2(d)\cdot B_2));\\ &X_4(d,d'{:}D) = \nabla_{\{r_1,s_2,c_3\}}(\Gamma_{\{r_3|s_3\to c_3\}}(s_3(d)\cdot B_1 \parallel s_2(d')\cdot B_2)).\end{aligned}$$

We get the following set of equations, including the two derived above:

$$\begin{aligned}&X_1 = \textstyle\sum_{d:D} r_1(d)\cdot X_2(d);\\ &X_2(d) = c_3(d)\cdot X_3(d);\\ &X_3(d) = \textstyle\sum_{d':D}(r_1(d')\cdot X_4(d',d) + s_2(d)\cdot X_1);\\ &X_4(d,d') = s_2(d')\cdot X_2(d).\end{aligned}$$

The only task that remains to be done is to show that $\tau_{\{c_3\}}(X)$ is a solution for X in equation (9.6). We actually prove that $\tau_{\{c_3\}}(X_1)$ is a solution for X, $\lambda d{:}D.\tau_{\{c_3\}}(X_3(d))$ is a solution for Y and $\lambda d,d'{:}D.\tau_{\{c_3\}}(X_4(d',d))$ is a solution for Z in equation (9.6). This boils down to:

$$\begin{aligned}&\tau_{\{c_3\}}(X_1) = \textstyle\sum_{d:D} r_1(d)\cdot\tau_{\{c_3\}}(X_3(d));\\ &\tau_{\{c_3\}}(X_3(d)) = \textstyle\sum_{d':D} r_1(d')\cdot\tau_{\{c_3\}}(X_4(d',d)) + s_2(d)\cdot\tau_{\{c_3\}}(X_1);\\ &\tau_{\{c_3\}}(X_4(d',d)) = s_2(d)\cdot\tau_{\{c_3\}}(X_3(d')).\end{aligned}$$

The first equation follows directly using the equation for X_1, X_2, and the axioms, among which W‡:

$$\begin{array}{rcl}\tau_{\{c_3\}}(X_1) & = & \tau_{\{c_3\}}(\sum_{d:D} r_1(d)\cdot X_2(d)) \\ & = & \sum_{d:D} r_1(d)\cdot\tau_{\{c_3\}}(X_2(d)) \\ & = & \sum_{d:D} r_1(d)\cdot\tau_{\{c_3\}}(c_3(d)\cdot X_3(d)) \\ & = & \sum_{d:D} r_1(d)\cdot\tau\cdot\tau_{\{c_3\}}(X_3(d)) \\ & \overset{\text{W‡}}{=} & \sum_{d:D} r_1(d)\cdot\tau_{\{c_3\}}(X_3(d)).\end{array}$$

The second equation can be proven as follows:

$$\begin{array}{rcl}\tau_{\{c_3\}}(X_3(d)) & = & \tau_{\{c_3\}}(\sum_{d':D}(r_1(d')\cdot X_4(d',d)+s_2(d)\cdot X_1)) \\ & = & \sum_{d':D} r_1(d')\cdot\tau_{\{c_3\}}(X_4(d',d))+s_2(d)\cdot\tau_{\{c_3\}}(X_1).\end{array}$$

The third equation is then proven as follows:

$$\begin{array}{rcl}\tau_{\{c_3\}}(X_4(d,d')) & = & \tau_{\{c_3\}}(s_2(d')\cdot X_2(d)) \\ & = & \tau_{\{c_3\}}(s_2(d')\cdot c_3(d)\cdot X_3(d)) \\ & = & s_2(d')\cdot\tau\cdot\tau_{\{c_3\}}(X_3(d)) \\ & = & s_2(d')\cdot\tau_{\{c_3\}}(X_3(d)).\end{array}$$

Exercise 9.8.2. Consider the following system (already described on page 75). Expand the definition of S. Compare this to the transition system of figure 5.7.

proc $X = \sum_{d:D}(r_1(d) + r_3(d))\cdot(s_2(d) + s_3(d))\cdot X;$
$B = \sum_{d:D} r_3(d)\cdot s_3(d)\cdot B;$
$S = \tau_{\{c_3\}}(\nabla_{\{r_1,s_2,c_3\}}(\Gamma_{\{r_3|s_3\to c_3\}}(X\|B))).$

9.8.3 Parallel expansion with time

In this section we look at the parallel composition of timed processes. One process X must perform an a action, every other second, whereas a second process Y must perform a b action, only half a second later. See figure 9.1. Now assume that action a and b must synchronize, resulting in the action c. The moments when c must take place are indicated in figure 9.1. We show how the individual processes are specified and how the moments where c must take place are calculated.

The processes X and Y can be specified as follows. The process S is the parallel composition of X and Y, where a and b must synchronize to c:

proc $X(n{:}\mathbb{N}^+) = \sum_{t:\mathbb{R}}(n{\le}t{\le}n{+}1)\to a{\cdot}t\cdot X(n{+}2);$
$Y(n{:}\mathbb{N}^+) = \sum_{u:\mathbb{R}}(n{+}0.5{\le}u{\le}n{+}1.5)\to b{\cdot}u\cdot Y(n{+}2);$
$S = \nabla_{\{c\}}(\Gamma_{\{a|b\to c\}}(X(1)\|Y(1)));$

First, we define a generalized process $S(n{:}\mathbb{N}^+) = \nabla_{\{c\}}(\Gamma_{\{a|b\to c\}}(X(n)\|Y(n)))$. Clearly, $S = S(1)$. We expand the parallel operator in $X(n)\|Y(n)$ using the axioms.

$$X(n)\|Y(n) \overset{\text{M}}{=} X(n) \,⌊\!⌊\, Y(n) + Y(n) \,⌊\!⌊\, X(n) + X(n)|Y(n) \qquad (9.8)$$

We treat the summands separately. We prove the first one in detail.

$$
\begin{aligned}
& X(n) \mathbin{\lfloor\!\lfloor} Y(n) \\
\stackrel{\text{def}}{=}\quad & \textstyle\sum_{t:\mathbb{R}}(n \leq t \leq n+1) \rightarrow a^{\varsigma}t \cdot X(n+2) \mathbin{\lfloor\!\lfloor} Y(n) \\
\stackrel{\text{LM5}}{=}\quad & \textstyle\sum_{t:\mathbb{R}}(n \leq t \leq n+1) \rightarrow (a^{\varsigma}t \cdot X(n+2) \mathbin{\lfloor\!\lfloor} Y(n)) \\
\stackrel{\text{TA4,LM6}}{=}\quad & \textstyle\sum_{t:\mathbb{R}}(n \leq t \leq n+1) \rightarrow (a \cdot X(n+2) \mathbin{\lfloor\!\lfloor} Y(n))^{\varsigma}t \\
\stackrel{\text{LM3}\ddagger}{=}\quad & \textstyle\sum_{t:\mathbb{R}}(n \leq t \leq n+1) \rightarrow (a \ll Y(n)) \cdot (X(n+2) \parallel Y(n))^{\varsigma}t \\
\stackrel{\text{def}}{=}\quad & \textstyle\sum_{t:\mathbb{R}}(n \leq t \leq n+1) \rightarrow (a \ll \sum_{u:\mathbb{R}}(n+0.5 \leq u \leq n+1.5) \\
& \qquad \rightarrow b^{\varsigma}u \cdot Y(n+2)) \cdot (X(n+2) \parallel Y(n))^{\varsigma}t \\
\stackrel{\text{TB6}}{=}\quad & \textstyle\sum_{u,t:\mathbb{R}}(n \leq t \leq n+1 \wedge n+0.5 \leq u \leq n+1.5) \\
& \qquad \rightarrow (a \ll b^{\varsigma}u \cdot Y(n+2)) \cdot (X(n+2) \parallel Y(n))^{\varsigma}t \\
\stackrel{\text{TB5}}{=}\quad & \textstyle\sum_{u,t:\mathbb{R}}(n \leq t \leq n+1 \wedge n+0.5 \leq u \leq n+1.5) \\
& \qquad \rightarrow (a \ll b^{\varsigma}u) \cdot (X(n+2) \parallel Y(n))^{\varsigma}t \\
\stackrel{\text{TB3,TB1}}{=}\quad & \textstyle\sum_{u,t:\mathbb{R}}(n \leq t \leq n+1 \wedge n+0.5 \leq u \leq n+1.5) \rightarrow \\
& \qquad (\textstyle\sum_{v:\mathbb{R}} v < u \rightarrow (a^{\varsigma}v)) \cdot (X(n+2) \parallel Y(n))^{\varsigma}t \\
=\quad & \textstyle\sum_{u,t,v:\mathbb{R}}(n \leq t \leq n+1 \wedge n+0.5 \leq u \leq n+1.5 \wedge v < u) \rightarrow \\
& \qquad a^{\varsigma}v \cdot (X(n+2) \parallel Y(n))^{\varsigma}t \\
\stackrel{\text{TA4}}{=}\quad & \textstyle\sum_{u,t,v:\mathbb{R}}(n \leq t \leq n+1 \wedge n+0.5 \leq u \leq n+1.5 \wedge v < u) \rightarrow \\
& \qquad a^{\varsigma}t^{\varsigma}v \cdot (X(n+2) \parallel Y(n)).
\end{aligned}
$$

In the same way we derive:

$$
\begin{aligned}
Y(n) \mathbin{\lfloor\!\lfloor} X(n) \;=\; & \textstyle\sum_{t,u,v:\mathbb{R}}(n+0.5 \leq u \leq n+1.5 \wedge n \leq t \leq n+1 \wedge v < t) \\
& \qquad \rightarrow b^{\varsigma}u^{\varsigma}v(X(n) \parallel Y(n+2)).
\end{aligned}
$$

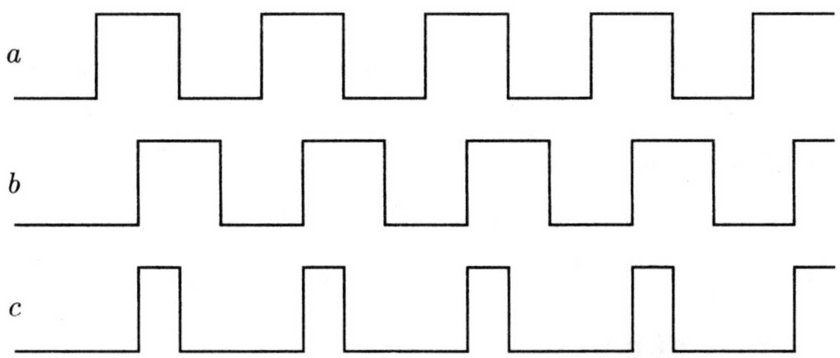

Figure 9.1: Two simple timed processes

The communication summand can be expanded as follows:

$$
\begin{array}{rl}
\underline{X(n)}|\underline{Y(n)} \overset{\text{def}}{=} & \underline{(\sum_{t:\mathbb{R}}(n{\leq}t{\leq}n{+}1){\rightarrow}a{}^{\varsigma}t{\cdot}X(n{+}2))} \\
| & \underline{(\sum_{u:\mathbb{R}}(n{+}0.5{\leq}u{\leq}n{+}1.5){\rightarrow}b{}^{\varsigma}u{\cdot}Y(n{+}2))} \\
\overset{\text{S8}}{=} & \sum_{t,u:\mathbb{R}}(n{\leq}t{\leq}n{+}1{\wedge}n{+}0.5{\leq}u{\leq}n{+}1.5) \\
& \qquad {\rightarrow}\underline{(a{}^{\varsigma}t{\cdot}X(n{+}2)|b{}^{\varsigma}u{\cdot}Y(n{+}2))} \\
\overset{\text{S9}}{=} & \sum_{t,u:\mathbb{R}}(n{\leq}t{\leq}n{+}1{\wedge}n{+}0.5{\leq}u{\leq}n{+}1.5) \\
& \qquad {\rightarrow}\underline{(a{\cdot}X(n{+}2)|b{\cdot}Y(n{+}2))}{}^{\varsigma}t{}^{\varsigma}u \\
\overset{\text{S6}}{=} & \sum_{t,u:\mathbb{R}}(n{\leq}t{\leq}n{+}1{\wedge}n{+}0.5{\leq}u{\leq}n{+}1.5) \\
& \qquad {\rightarrow}\underline{((a|b){\cdot}(X(n{+}2)\|Y(n{+}2))){}^{\varsigma}t{}^{\varsigma}u} \\
\overset{\text{TA4}}{=} & \sum_{t,u:\mathbb{R}}(n{\leq}t{\leq}n{+}1{\wedge}n{+}0.5{\leq}u{\leq}n{+}1.5) \\
& \qquad {\rightarrow}(a|b)\underline{{}^{\varsigma}t{}^{\varsigma}u}{\cdot}(X(n{+}2)\|Y(n{+}2)) \\
\overset{\text{TA1,sum elim}}{=} & \sum_{t:\mathbb{R}}\underline{(n{\leq}t{\leq}n{+}1{\wedge}n{+}0.5{\leq}t{\leq}n{+}1.5)} \\
& \qquad {\rightarrow}(a|b){}^{\varsigma}t{\cdot}(X(n{+}2)\|Y(n{+}2)) \\
+ & \sum_{t,u:\mathbb{R}}\underline{(n{\leq}t{\leq}n{+}1{\wedge}n{+}0.5{\leq}u{\leq}n{+}1.5 \wedge t{\not\approx}u)} \\
& \qquad {\rightarrow}\delta{}^{\varsigma}\min(t,u) \\
\overset{\text{simplify}}{=} & \sum_{t:\mathbb{R}}(n{+}0.5{\leq}t{\leq}n{+}1){\rightarrow}(a|b){}^{\varsigma}t{\cdot}(X(n{+}2)\|Y(n{+}2)) \\
+ & \underline{\sum_{v:\mathbb{R}}(n{\leq}v{\leq}n{+}1){\rightarrow}\delta{}^{\varsigma}v} \\
\overset{\text{delta incl.}}{=} & \sum_{t:\mathbb{R}}(n{+}0.5{\leq}t{\leq}n{+}1){\rightarrow}(a|b){}^{\varsigma}t{\cdot}(X(n{+}2)\|Y(n{+}2)).
\end{array}
$$

Applying the communication and allow operator is now pretty standard. It yields:

$$
\begin{array}{l}
S(n{:}\mathbb{N}^{+}) = \\
\quad \nabla_{\{c\}}(\Gamma_{\{a|b\rightarrow c\}}(X(n)\|Y(n))) = \\
\quad \sum_{t,u,v:\mathbb{R}}(n{\leq}t{\leq}n{+}1 \wedge n{+}0.5{\leq}u{\leq}n{+}1.5{\wedge}v{<}u){\rightarrow}\delta{}^{\varsigma}\min(t,v){+} \\
\quad \sum_{t,u,v:\mathbb{R}}(n{+}0.5{\leq}u{\leq}n{+}1.5{\wedge}n{\leq}t{\leq}n{+}1{\wedge}v{<}t){\rightarrow}\delta{}^{\varsigma}\min(u,v){+} \\
\quad \sum_{t:\mathbb{R}}(n{+}0.5{\leq}t{\leq}n{+}1){\rightarrow}c{}^{\varsigma}t{\cdot}\nabla_{\{c\}}(\Gamma_{\{a|b\rightarrow c\}}(X(n{+}2)\|Y(n{+}2))) = \\
\quad \sum_{t:\mathbb{R}}(t{\leq}n{+}1){\rightarrow}\delta{}^{\varsigma}t{+} \\
\quad \sum_{t:\mathbb{R}}(t{\leq}n{+}1){\rightarrow}\delta{}^{\varsigma}t{+} \\
\quad \sum_{t:\mathbb{R}}(n{+}0.5{\leq}t{\leq}n{+}1){\rightarrow}c{}^{\varsigma}t{\cdot}S(n{+}2) = \\
\quad \sum_{t:\mathbb{R}}(n{+}0.5{\leq}t{\leq}n{+}1){\rightarrow}c{}^{\varsigma}t{\cdot}S(n{+}2).
\end{array}
$$

Note that c can exactly take place at those moments where the third block diagram in figure 9.1 is high.

Exercise 9.8.3. Prove that

$$
\begin{array}{l}
\sum_{t,u:\mathbb{R}}(n{\leq}t{\leq}n{+}1 \wedge n{+}0.5{\leq}u{\leq}n{+}1.5{\wedge}t{\not\approx}u){\rightarrow}\delta{}^{\varsigma}\min(t,u) = \\
\sum_{v:\mathbb{R}}(n{\leq}v{\leq}n{+}1){\rightarrow}\delta{}^{\varsigma}v.
\end{array}
$$

9.9 Historical notes

The desire for an exact proof system has two causes. The first is the uncertainty that comes with informal algebraical reasoning, especially in the context of variable binders such as the sum operator. Within logic there is a long tradition of establishing the exact rules of reasoning [48]. A cumulation of this research is found in the Barendregt cube [21], which encompasses higher order proof systems with flexible type systems and functions strong enough to encode virtually all existing mathematical theories.

The other desire came from the use of proof checkers such as PVS [28, 144, 148] as tools to support and verify reasoning about processes. These tools require that the underlying theory is precisely formulated. The verification of the alternating bit protocol in Coq [29] had a profound influence on the formulation of axioms and rules in this book. In [10] a proof of the sliding window protocol has been verified completely in PVS.

The recursive specification principle (RSP) was first formulated in [27]. Hennessy and Lin [94] introduced a similar derivation rule called UFI-O. It is typical for the algebraic view on processes. In CCS recursive processes are defined using fixed point operators, giving rise to a different proof system [136]. Other process formalisms generally use the semantics as the basic notion to equate recursive processes.

The Koomen's fair abstraction rule is a rather crude but effective way to deal with fairness in processes. It was formulated in [15]. There is a whole plethora of approaches to fairness, varying from putting fairness constraints on program runs, to encoding fairness in modal logics. For an excellent overview, see [64].

The expansion of parallel processes to transform them to sequential processes, was one of the immediate points of attention for any process theory. Milner formulated it using his famous expansion theorem which was a complex but effective scheme to eliminate the parallel operator [135]. The attempt to replace this scheme by a set of finite axioms led to the landmark result that auxiliary operators are required [139]. The leftmerge and the communication merge are motivated by this. Expansion of processes with time turned out to be a delicate matter, which can easily go wrong [90].

10

Linear Process Equations and Linearization

The technique of parallel expansion in the last sections of the previous chapter is cumbersome. Yet, the basic technique, namely, elimination of the parallel composition operators in favor of the alternative and sequential composition operator, is the only effective technique when it comes to analyzing parallel systems. By introducing the explicit notion of a *linear process equation*, we standardize the form of processes, and make it possible to formulate generic parallel expansion laws. We can also formulate certain rules, such as CL-RSP and the invariant rule, much easier on linear processes than on processes in general.

10.1 Linear process equations

We define a *linear process equation* (LPE) as a process of a restricted form. It comes in three equivalent flavors, namely (general) linear process equations, clustered linear process equations, and linear process operators. The two essential properties of linear processes are that each process can be transformed to linear form and that the linear form is so simple that it is relatively easy to manipulate it.

10.1.1 General linear process equations

The most important characteristics of a linear process equation are that the process variable from the left-hand side is the only one used in the right-hand side and that there is precisely one action in front of the recursive invocation of the process variable at the right-hand side.

Definition 10.1.1 (Linear process equation). An LPE is a process of the following form

$$\begin{aligned} X(d{:}D) = & \textstyle\sum_{i \in I} \sum_{e_i:E_i} c_i(d,e_i) \to \alpha_i(d,e_i) {}^{\varsigma} t_i(d,e_i) \cdot X(g_i(d,e_i)) \\ & + \textstyle\sum_{j \in J} \sum_{e_j:E_j} c_j(d,e_j) \to \alpha_{\delta j}(d,e_j) {}^{\varsigma} t_j(d,e_j) \end{aligned}$$

where I and J are disjoint and finite index sets, and for $i \in I$ and $j \in J$:

- E_i and E_j are data sorts over which the variables e_i and e_j range,
- $c_i : D \times E_i \rightarrow \mathbb{B}$ and $c_j : D \times E_j \rightarrow \mathbb{B}$ are conditions,
- $\alpha_i(d, e_i)$ is a multi-action $a_i^1(f_i^1(d, e_i))|\cdots|a_i^{n_i}(f_i^{n_i}(d, e_i))$, where $f_i^k(d, e_i)$ (for $1 \leq k \leq n_i$) gives the parameters of action name a_i^k,
- $\alpha_{\delta j}(d, e_j)$ is either δ or a multi-action $a_j^1(f_j^1(d, e_j))|\cdots|a_j^{n_j}(f_j^{n_j}(d, e_j))$, where $f_j^k(d, e_j)$ (for $1 \leq k \leq n_j$) gives the parameters of action name a_j^k,
- $t_i : D \times E_i \rightarrow \mathbb{R}$ and $t_j : D \times E_j \rightarrow \mathbb{R}$ are the time stamps of multi-actions $\alpha_i(d, e_i)$ and $\alpha_{\delta j}(d, e_j)$,
- $g_i : D \times E_i \rightarrow D$ is the next state.

Note that the summands $\sum_{i \in I}$ and $\sum_{j \in J}$ are *meta-level* operations: $\sum_{i \in I} p_i$ is a shorthand for $p_1 + \cdots + p_n$, assuming $I = \{1, \ldots, n\}$. If the index set I is empty, $\sum_{i \in I} p_i$ is equal to δ0.

We call data parameter d the *state* parameter. Recall that we only use one state parameter d and one sum variable e_i per summand in the definitions to keep the formulas concise. In examples, we generally employ more than one (or sometimes 0) of such parameters.

The form as described above is also referred to as the *condition-action-effect* rule. In a particular state d, the multi-action α_i can be done at time t_i if condition c_i holds. The effect of the action is given by the function g_i.

There is an important theorem that says that any guarded recursive specification can be transformed into a linear process [172]. The proof of this theorem is rather involved, and we only show how to linearize subclasses of processes in this section. In many cases linearizing a given process is so straightforward that it can be done without the help of the theorems or lemmas provided below.

Observe that the α_δ summands, in case α_δ is not equal to δ, indicate the possibility of termination after doing an α_δ-action. In most cases that we encounter, we find that α_δ is equal to δ. Therefore, we simplify the definition of a linear process below by assuming that α_δ always equals δ. This simplifies many of the definitions and theorems. If α_δ could be a multi-action, we generally have to treat a few more case distinctions that do not provide new insight. If necessary, all that follows can be redone using the more general definition of a linear process.

Example 10.1.2. As a first example, consider the following simple process

proc $X = a \cdot b \cdot c \cdot X$;

This is not a linear process because there is more than one action preceding variable X at the right-hand side. We must encode the state of this process in an explicit data variable. For this purpose we can take a positive number $s : \mathbb{N}^+$. We let $s = 1$ equal the state where the a can be done, $s = 2$ equal the state where b is possible, and $s = 3$

represent the state where c can be done. The linearized version of this process then becomes

$$Y(s{:}\mathbb{N}^+) = (s{\approx}1){\to}a{\cdot}Y(2){+}(s{\approx}2){\to}b{\cdot}Y(3){+}(s{\approx}3){\to}c{\cdot}Y(1) \tag{10.1}$$

and $X = Y(1)$. Note that the linearized version of X is much less readable than the original version, which is a strong argument not to specify in linear equations, but to use the full expressiveness of the language.

Formally, we can prove that $X = Y(1)$ using RSP. To do so, one can show that

$$\lambda n{:}\mathbb{N}^+.(n{\approx}1){\to}X + (n{\approx}2){\to}b{\cdot}c{\cdot}X + (n{\approx}3){\to}c{\cdot}X \tag{10.2}$$

is a solution for Y in equation (10.1). If the expression (10.2) is indeed a solution, it is equal to Y, and it immediately follows that $X = Y(1)$. So, we substitute the expression (10.2) for Y in equation (10.1) and we obtain the following proof obligation (after β-conversion and simplification of conditions):

$$\begin{array}{l}(s{\approx}1){\to}X + (s{\approx}2){\to}b{\cdot}c{\cdot}X + (s{\approx}3){\to}c{\cdot}X = \\ (s{\approx}1){\to}a{\cdot}b{\cdot}c{\cdot}X + (s{\approx}2){\to}b{\cdot}c{\cdot}X + (s{\approx}3){\to}c{\cdot}X,\end{array}$$

which easily follows using the definition of X.

Example 10.1.3. Consider as another example a buffer that reads natural numbers via gate 1 and delivers them via gate 2. It is described by:

proc $X = \sum_{n:\mathbb{N}} r_1(n){\cdot}s_2(n){\cdot}X;$

For linearization, we can use a similar technique as above, by numbering the states in the process. As there are two, we encode them using a variable of sort $\mathbb{B}$. But note that between the action r_1 and the action s_2, the process must also recall the value of n. Therefore, n must be added to the parameters of the linear process. Apart from this, linearization is straightforward and yields:

$$Y(n{:}\mathbb{N}, b{:}\mathbb{B}) = \sum_{m:\mathbb{N}} b{\to}r_1(m){\cdot}Y(m, \neg b) + \neg b{\to}s_2(n){\cdot}Y(n, \neg b).$$

It holds that $Y(n, \mathit{true}) = X$ for any $n{:}\mathbb{N}$. Note that sum operators over empty sequences of variables are simply omitted.

Just as for ordinary process equations, linear processes can be denoted as process operators. Reformulated as a linear process operator, the linear process equation of definition 10.1.1 becomes the following where the terminating summands have been left out.

$$\Psi = \lambda X{:}D{\to}\ \mathbb{P}.\lambda d{:}D.\sum_{i\in I}\sum_{e_i:E_i} c_i(d, e_i){\to}\alpha_i(d, e_i){}^{\varsigma}t_i(d, e_i){\cdot}X(g_i(d, e_i)).$$

Exercise 10.1.4. Prove that the linearization of the buffer is indeed equal to the buffer.

Exercise 10.1.5. Linearize the process $X = a{\cdot}b{\cdot}X + b{\cdot}a{\cdot}Y, Y = a{\cdot}b{\cdot}X + a{\cdot}X$. Idem for $X = a{\cdot}b{\cdot}X + b{\cdot}a{\cdot}Y, Y = a{\cdot}b{\cdot}X + X$, and for $X = \sum_{n:\mathbb{N}} a(n){\cdot}(b(n){+}b(n^2)){\cdot}X$. Why is it not possible to linearize $X = a{\cdot}b{\cdot}X + b{\cdot}a{\cdot}Y, Y = a{\cdot}b{\cdot}X + Y$?

10.1.2 Clustered linear process equations

For the concise presentation of theory, for example, τ-confluence in chapter 11, it is useful to group the actions in a linear process by the label of an action. For convenience we avoid multi-actions here. The resulting linear process has a single summand for each action label. Such a linear process is called a clustered linear process equation.

Definition 10.1.6 (Clustered LPE). A *clustered linear process equation* is a process of the following form

$$\begin{aligned} X(d{:}D) = &\textstyle\sum_{a\in Act}\sum_{e_a:E_a} c_a(d,e_a)\rightarrow a(f_a(d,e_a))^{\varsigma} t_a(d,e_a)\cdot X(g_a(d,e_a)) \\ &+ \textstyle\sum_{e_\delta:E_\delta} c_\delta(d,e_\delta)\rightarrow \delta^{\varsigma} t_\delta(d,e_\delta) \end{aligned}$$

where Act is a finite set of action labels possibly containing τ as a special element. The other elements in the definition are just as in definition 10.1.1.

Every linear process can straightforwardly be transformed to a clustered linear process as illustrated in the following example.

Example 10.1.7. Consider the linear process

$$\begin{aligned} X(d{:}D) = &\textstyle\sum_{e_1:E_1} c_1(d,e_1)\rightarrow a(f_1(d,e_1))\cdot X(g_1(d,e_1)) \\ &+ \textstyle\sum_{e_2:E_2} c_2(d,e_2)\rightarrow a(f_2(d,e_2))\cdot X(g_2(d,e_2)) \\ &+ \textstyle\sum_{e_3:E_3} c_3(d,e_3)\rightarrow a(f_3(d,e_3))\cdot X(g_3(d,e_3)). \end{aligned}$$

By introducing a new domain E with three elements, this linear process can be translated to a clustered linear process. In addition, we define a number of case functions C_S for some sort S where S is $\mathbb{B}$, F (the sort of the argument of action a), or D. The expression $C(e,t_1,t_2,t_3)$ equals t_i if e is equal to e_i.

$$\begin{aligned} &\textbf{sort}\ \ E = \textbf{struct}\ \mathit{enum}_1 \mid \mathit{enum}_2 \mid \mathit{enum}_3; \\ &\textbf{map}\ \ C_S : E\times S\times S\times S\rightarrow S; \\ &\textbf{var}\ \ t_1,t_2,t_3 : S; \\ &\textbf{eqn}\ \ C_S(\mathit{enum}_1,t_1,t_2,t_3) = t_1; \\ &\qquad\ C_S(\mathit{enum}_2,t_1,t_2,t_3) = t_2; \\ &\qquad\ C_S(\mathit{enum}_3,t_1,t_2,t_3) = t_3; \end{aligned}$$

The clustered linear process that is equivalent to X has the following shape:

$$\begin{aligned} Y(d{:}D) = &\textstyle\sum_{e:E,e_1:E_1,e_2:E_2,e_3:E_3} C_{\mathbb{B}}(e,c_1(d,e_1),c_2(d,e_2),c_3(d,e_3))\rightarrow \\ &\quad a(C_F(e,f_1(d,e_1),f_2(d,e_2),f_3(d,e_3)))\cdot \\ &\qquad Y(C_D(e,g_1(d,e_1),g_2(d,e_2),g_3(d,e_3))). \end{aligned}$$

Exercise 10.1.8. Give a clustered linear process for $X = a\cdot a\cdot b\cdot X$.

10.2 Linearization

We provide several systematic ways to linearize processes. First we explain how processes without parallelism can be linearized. Then we explain how two linear processes can be put in parallel. Finally, we show how a process can be put in parallel with itself n times. In [172] it is explained how processes can be linearized in general.

10.2.1 Linearization of sequential processes

Assume we have a guarded recursive specification with multi-actions, sum operators, conditions, time, and the alternative and sequential composition operators. We call these sequential processes. We first observe that such a process can be transformed to *Greibach normal form* (GNF).[1] We use it here in adapted form, due to our slightly different setting. The transformation to GNF goes via a *pre-Greibach normal form* (pre-GNF).

Definition 10.2.1 ((pre-)Greibach normal form). A set of recursive equations is said to be in pre-Greibach normal form iff for each $i \in I$ the ith equation has the shape:

$$\begin{aligned} X_i(d_i{:}D_i) =& \textstyle\sum_{j\in J_i}\sum_{e_{ij}:E_{ij}} c_{ij}(d_i,e_{ij}) \rightarrow p^1_{ij}(d_i,e_{ij})\cdot p^2_{ij}(d_i,e_{ij})\cdot\cdots\cdot p^{n_{ij}}_{ij}(d_i,e_{ij}) \\ &+ \textstyle\sum_{k\in K_i}\sum_{e_{ik}:E_{ik}} c_{ik}(d_i,e_{ik}) \rightarrow \delta{}^{c}t_{ik}(d_i,e_{ik}). \end{aligned}$$

Here I, J_i, and K_i are finite index sets. Each expression $p^\ell_{ij}(d_i,e_{ij})$ is a process variable of the form $X_{m(i,j,\ell)}(g_{ij\ell}(d_i,e_{ij}))$ where $m(i,j,\ell) \in I$. The only exception is $p^1_{ij}(d_i,e_{ij})$ which can also be a (possibly timed) multi-action containing $n_{ij1} \geq 0$ actions:

$$(a^1_{ij1}(f^1_{ij1}(d_i,e_{ij}))|\cdots|a^{n_{ij1}}_{ij1}(f^{n_{ij1}}_{ij1}(d_i,e_{ij})))[{}^{c}t_{ij1}(d_i,e_{ij})].$$

If all $p^1_{ij}(d_i,e_{ij})$ are multi-actions, we say that the recursive equation is in Greibach normal form.

If all equations in a recursive specification are in (pre-)Greibach normal form, the recursive specification is in (pre-)Greibach normal form.

The translation to pre-Greibach normal form can be done in linear space and time for every sequential recursive specification. The procedure is rather straightforward. Consider an equation $X(d : D) = p$ in a recursive specification. Then the right-hand side can have such a form that the equation is in Greibach normal form. Or, there is a strict subexpression in p, say q, which violates the pre-Greibach normal form. We can replace q by a fresh process variable $Y(d, e_i)$ and add a new equation $Y(d, e_i) = q$, to that part of the recursive specification that still has to be transformed.

Example 10.2.2.

proc $X = a\cdot(X + Y)$;
$\quad Y = b\cdot Y$;

The equation for Y is in pre-Greibach normal form. But the equation for X has the subexpression $X + Y$. As a $+$ is only allowed as the outermost symbol of a GNF, this subexpression violates the property of being in GNF. Therefore, we replace $X + Y$ by Z and obtain

$$\begin{aligned} X &= a\cdot Z; \\ Y &= b\cdot Y; \\ Z &= X + Y; \end{aligned}$$

This set of equations is in pre-Greibach normal form.

---

[1]Sheila Greibach (1939–) is an American computer scientist contributing especially to the theory of formal languages.

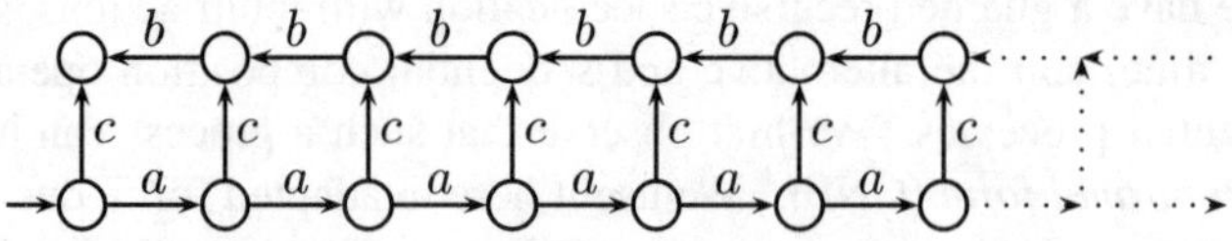

Figure 10.1: The behavior of a stack or counter

The translation from pre-GNF to GNF is more involved, as it can cause an exponential blowup of the specification. Fortunately, in practical cases this potential blowup does not appear to occur.

The only difference between a pre-GNF and a GNF is that in a GNF the $p^1_{ij}(d_i, e_{ij})$ must always be a multi-action. Consider the example above where we have the equation $Z = X + Y$ that is not in GNF. However, the equations for X and Y are. So, by substituting the bodies of X and Y in the right-hand side of Z we obtain

$$Z = a{\cdot}Z + b{\cdot}Y,$$

which is in Greibach normal form. This is the general procedure. Find an equation that is not in GNF of which all equations belonging to the process variables occurring at the front in the right-hand side are in GNF. Substitute these and apply axiom A4 to the result. The equation for which we carried out the substitution is now also in GNF.

An important property is that if the original recursive specification is guarded, the procedure above terminates and leads to a guarded recursive specification in normal form.

Example 10.2.3. As an example, consider the following recursive specification, that models the behavior of a counter. If a c-action is done after doing n a-actions, exactly n b-actions must be executed. See figure 10.1:

proc $X = a{\cdot}X{\cdot}b + c;$
$\quad\;\; Y = X{\cdot}\delta;$

First we must bring this specification in pre-Greibach normal form. The problems are the action b and the δ. We introduce two new variables B and Z with as bodies b and δ. We get:

$$\begin{aligned} X &= a{\cdot}X{\cdot}B + c;\\ Y &= X{\cdot}Z;\\ B &= b;\\ Z &= \delta. \end{aligned}$$

In order to bring this into GNF, we must substitute the body of X for X in the body of Y. We obtain for Y:

$$Y = (a{\cdot}X{\cdot}B + c){\cdot}Z.$$

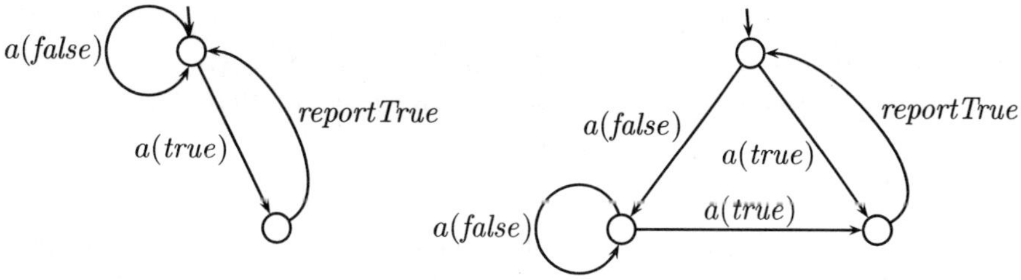

Figure 10.2: The transition system for two linearized processes

Using the axiom A4 we distribute Z over the choice operator and obtain:

$$\begin{aligned} X &= a \cdot X \cdot B + c; \\ Y &= a \cdot X \cdot B \cdot Z + c \cdot Z; \\ B &= b; \\ Z &= \delta. \end{aligned}$$

This set of process equations is in Greibach normal form.

If data plays a role, the exact formulation of a process can influence the size of the state space generated via linearization. The following two examples illustrate this.

Example 10.2.4. Consider the following formulations of the same process:

proc $X = \sum_{b:\mathbb{B}} b \rightarrow a(b) \cdot \mathit{reportTrue} \cdot X \diamond a(b) \cdot X;$
$\quad Y = \sum_{b:\mathbb{B}} a(b) \cdot (b \rightarrow \mathit{reportTrue} \cdot Y \diamond Y);$

The second process Y appears more attractive, as action $a(b)$ is only used once. However, when linearizing, the first one turns out to have a smaller state space. We translate both processes to Greibach normal form in a straightforward way:

proc $X = \sum_{b:\mathbb{B}} b \rightarrow a(b) \cdot R \cdot X + \sum_{b:\mathbb{B}} \neg b \rightarrow a(b) \cdot X;$
$\quad R = \mathit{reportTrue};$
$\quad Y = \sum_{b:\mathbb{B}} a(b) \cdot Z(b);$
$\quad Z(b{:}\mathbb{B}) = b \rightarrow \mathit{reportTrue} \cdot Y + \sum_{b':\mathbb{B}} \neg b \rightarrow a(b') \cdot Z(b');$

The state spaces are drawn in figure 10.2. The figure to the left corresponds to X, and the figure to the right to Y. It is clear that the newly introduced $Z(b{:}\mathbb{B})$ gives rise to one extra state.

Example 10.2.5. The type of data passed on in processes can also have an influence on the number of states. Consider the following two processes:

proc $X = \sum_{n:\mathbb{N}} r(n) \cdot ((n{<}4) \rightarrow \mathit{reportOk} \cdot X \diamond \mathit{reportNotOk} \cdot X);$
$\quad Y = \sum_{n:\mathbb{N}} (n{<}4) \rightarrow r(n) \cdot \mathit{reportOk} \cdot Y \diamond r(n) \cdot \mathit{reportNotOk} \cdot Y;$

Transforming both processes to Greibach normal form yields the following result:

proc $X = \sum_{n:\mathbb{N}} r(n)\cdot X'(n);$
$X'(n{:}\mathbb{N}) = (n<4)\rightarrow reportOk\cdot X + (n\geq 4)\rightarrow reportNotOk\cdot X;$
$Y = \sum_{n:\mathbb{N}}(n<4)\rightarrow r(n)\cdot OK\cdot Y + \sum_{n:\mathbb{N}}(n\geq 4)\rightarrow r(n)\cdot NOK\cdot Y;$
$OK = reportOk;$
$NOK = reportNotOk;$

The linearized process for X has an infinite number of states; one for X and one for $X'(n)$, for each natural number n. The linearized process for Y has only three states, namely one for Y, one corresponding to all cases where $n<4$, and one more where $n\geq 4$.

Example 10.2.6. Consider the following process that is in pre-Greibach normal form.

proc $X_1 = X_2\cdot Y_1 + X_2;$
$X_2 = X_3\cdot Y_2 + X_3;$
$\ldots$
$X_n = X_{n+1}\cdot Y_n + X_{n+1};$
$X_{n+1} = a;$

If we transform this process to Greibach normal form, it grows exponentially. We transform this process to GNF by substituting variables X_i upward. The result is that the equation for variable X_i has summands $a\cdot\sigma$ at the right-hand side for any σ being an ordered subsequence of $Y_n \cdots Y_i$. More concretely:

$$\begin{aligned}
X_{n+1} &= a,\\
X_n &= a\cdot Y_n + a,\\
X_{n-1} &= a\cdot Y_n\cdot Y_{n-1} + a\cdot Y_{n-1} + a\cdot Y_n + a,\\
X_{n-2} &= a\cdot Y_n\cdot Y_{n-1}\cdot Y_{n-2} + a\cdot Y_{n-1}\cdot Y_{n-2} + a\cdot Y_n\cdot Y_{n-2} + a\cdot Y_{n-2}\\
&\qquad + a\cdot Y_n\cdot Y_{n-1} + a\cdot Y_{n-1} + a\cdot Y_n + a,\\
X_{n-4} &= \ldots
\end{aligned}$$

Thus, X_i has 2^{n-i+1} summands. In particular, X_1 has 2^n summands. This shows that the transformation from pre-Greibach normal form to Greibach normal form can cause an exponential blowup of the process. As stated above, we hardly encounter this, when transforming models of the behavior of real systems. Therefore, in practice this blowup does not turn out to be a problem.

Now we assume that we have a set of process equations in GNF as indicated in definition 10.2.1. We must transform this set to a linear process equation. The essential observation is that the state of the process can be represented as a sequential composition of process variables. This sequence is represented using a *Stack* data type. By inspecting the right-hand side of the equation of the first variable in this sequence, it is easy to determine what the initial actions are. The first variable is subsequently replaced by the sequence of process variables following this action.

First we introduce a data type *PA* to contain the individual process variables, together with their arguments. We base ourselves on definition 10.2.1 where we let $I = \{1, \ldots, n\}$. Furthermore, we declare the required stack.

$$\begin{aligned}
\textbf{sort}\ \ & PA = \textbf{struct}\ pr_1(data_1{:}D_1)?isPr_1 \mid \\
& \qquad\qquad\quad pr_2(data_2{:}D_2)?isPr_2 \mid \\
& \qquad\qquad\quad \dots \\
& \qquad\qquad\quad pr_n(data_n{:}D_n)?isPr_n; \\
& Stack = \textbf{struct}\ empty?isEmpty \mid push(top{:}PA, pop{:}Stack);
\end{aligned}$$

The translation of the process in definition 10.2.1 now becomes:

$$\begin{aligned}
\textbf{proc}\ & X(s{:}Stack) = \\
& \textstyle\sum_{i\in I, j\in J_i} \sum_{e_{ij}:E_{ij}} isPr_i(top(s)) \wedge c_{ij}(data_i(top_i(s)), e_{ij}) \rightarrow \\
& \quad p^1_{ij}(data_i(top_i(s)), e_{ij})\cdot \\
& \qquad X(push(pr_{m(i,j,2)}(data_i(top_i(s)), e_{ij}), \dots, \\
& \qquad\qquad push(pr_{m(i,j,n_{ij})}(data_i(top_i(s)), e_{ij}), pop(s)))) + \\
& \textstyle\sum_{i\in I, k\in K_i} \sum_{e_{ik}:E_{ik}} isPr_i(top(s)) \wedge c_{ik}(data_i(top_i(s)), e_{ik}) \rightarrow \\
& \delta{\cdot}t_{ik}(data_i(top_i(s)), e_{ik});
\end{aligned}$$

Note that $p^1_{ij}(data_i(top_i(s)), e_{ij})$ is an action, and $m(i, j, \ell)$ is defined in definition 10.2.1.

Example 10.2.7. The Greibach normal form in example 10.2.3 gives rise to the following.

$$\begin{aligned}
\textbf{sort}\ \ & PA = \textbf{struct}\ prX?isX \mid prY?isY \mid prB?isB \mid prZ?isZ; \\
& Stack = \textbf{struct}\ empty?isEmpty \mid push(top{:}PA, pop{:}Stack); \\
\textbf{proc}\ \ & X(s{:}Stack) = \\
& \qquad isX(top(s)) \rightarrow a{\cdot}X(push(prX, push(prB, pop(s)))) + \\
& \qquad isX(top(s)) \rightarrow c{\cdot}X(pop(s)) + \\
& \qquad isY(top(s)) \rightarrow a{\cdot}X(push(prX, push(prB, push(prZ, pop(s))))) + \\
& \qquad isY(top(s)) \rightarrow c{\cdot}X(push(prZ, pop(s))) + \\
& \qquad isB(top(s)) \rightarrow b{\cdot}X(pop(s)).
\end{aligned}$$

Note that there is no summand for Z, because it cannot perform any action. If the initial state of the process is Y, the initial state of the linear process is $X(push(prY, empty))$.

The use of a stack in linear processes has a substantial disadvantage. It is hard to investigate and use properties of individual data variables in the original process, because their values are stored in the stack structure. In [128] it has been shown that it is decidable for processes in GNF whether the stack can maximally grow to a limited size (the result is shown in a setting without data). In this case, each stack configuration can get an explicit index, which we can call the program counter. Consider for example the following process in Greibach normal form:

$$\begin{aligned}
\textbf{proc}\ \ & X = a{\cdot}Y{\cdot}Y{\cdot}Z + b{\cdot}Z{\cdot}Z; \\
& Y = a; \\
& Z = b{\cdot}Z + c{\cdot}Y{\cdot}Y{\cdot}X;
\end{aligned}$$

First note that Z cannot terminate, so, $Z{\cdot}Z = Z$. Now a quick investigation teaches us that there are a finite number of stack frames which we can number as follows:

1:	X	4:	Z
2:	$Y{\cdot}Z$	5:	$Y{\cdot}X$
3:	$Y{\cdot}Y{\cdot}Z$	6:	$Y{\cdot}Y{\cdot}X$

The linearized process can be formulated using the program counter. The result looks like this:

$$\begin{aligned}\textbf{proc } X(pc{:}\mathbb{N}^+) = {} & pc{\approx}1 \to a{\cdot}X(3)\\ & + pc{\approx}1 \to b{\cdot}X(4)\\ & + pc{\approx}2 \to a{\cdot}X(4)\\ & + pc{\approx}3 \to a{\cdot}X(2)\\ & + pc{\approx}4 \to b{\cdot}X(4)\\ & + pc{\approx}4 \to c{\cdot}X(6)\\ & + pc{\approx}5 \to a{\cdot}X(1)\\ & + pc{\approx}6 \to a{\cdot}X(5);\end{aligned}$$

This result does not require the more complex stack, and therefore the data can more easily be used, for instance, for data flow analysis.

Example 10.2.8. The definition of a buffer is:

proc $X = \sum_{d:D} r(d){\cdot}s(d){\cdot}X;$

This process is already in Greibach normal form except that a process for $s(d)$ should be introduced. But as we can easily linearize without this step, we omit it here. A quick inspection reveals that there are only two interesting states. So, this process can be linearized using a variable with two values. Apart from the program counter, the value of d must also be recalled between an r and an s action.

proc $X(pc{:}\mathbb{N}^+, d{:}D) = \sum_{d':D} pc{\approx}1{\to}r(d'){\cdot}X(2, d') + pc{\approx}2{\to}s(d){\cdot}X(1, d);$

Note that the value of d in $X(1, d)$ in the last summand is irrelevant. To avoid unnecessary growth of the resulting transition system, it would be better to set it to some default value.

Exercise 10.2.9. Give an LPE representing the following process:

$$X = (a + b){\cdot}d{\cdot}X.$$

Exercise 10.2.10. Give an LPE representing the following process:

$$\begin{aligned} X &= a{\cdot}(a{\cdot}X + Y),\\ Y &= b{\cdot}(X + Y).\end{aligned}$$

Exercise 10.2.11. Linearize the following three processes:

$$\begin{aligned}\textbf{proc } X_1 &= \textstyle\sum_{n:\mathbb{N}} a(n){\cdot}(X_1 + c(n)){\cdot}X_1;\\ X_2 &= \textstyle\sum_{n:\mathbb{N}} a(n){\cdot}X_2{\cdot}c(n){\cdot}X_2;\\ X_3 &= \textstyle\sum_{n:\mathbb{N}} a(n){\cdot}(X_3{\cdot}c(n) + c(n));\end{aligned}$$

Exercise 10.2.12. Linearization of sequential timed processes is in essence not different from linearizing sequential processes. Linearize:

$$\begin{aligned}\textbf{proc } X &= a{}^{\varsigma}3{\cdot}c{}^{\varsigma}4{\cdot}X;\\ Y &= \textstyle\sum_{n:\mathbb{N}} r(n){\cdot}((n{>}10) \to a{}^{\varsigma}n{\cdot}Y);\end{aligned}$$

10.2.2 Parallelization of linear processes

Assume that we have two linear processes X and Y that we want to put in parallel. This is a straightforward operation, where in general the size of the result is linear in the size of the components. This is *the* huge advantage of linear processes, namely, that parallel composition does not tend to blow up. This contrasts with calculating the parallel composition of two labeled transition systems, where in general the size of the result is proportional to the product of the sizes of the constituents. At the end of this section we indicate situations where the parallel composition of two linear processes grows more than linearly.

We first look at putting two untimed linear processes in parallel. We consider processes X and Y given by the following linear process equations:

$$\begin{aligned} X(d{:}D) &= \textstyle\sum_{i\in I}\sum_{e_i:E_i} c_i(d,e_i) \rightarrow \alpha_i(d,e_i)\cdot X(g_i(d,e_i)),\\ Y(d'{:}D') &= \textstyle\sum_{j\in J}\sum_{e'_j:E'_j} c'_j(d',e'_j) \rightarrow \alpha_j(d',e'_j)\cdot Y(g'_j(d',e'_j)). \end{aligned}$$

The parallel composition consists of concatenating the parameters of X and Y and by listing all the noncommunicating summands of X and of Y and subsequently all pairs of communicating summands of X and Y. The result is the process XY characterized by the following equation:

$$\begin{aligned} XY(d{:}D,d'{:}D') = {} & \textstyle\sum_{i\in I}\sum_{e_i:E_i} c_i(d,e_i) \rightarrow \alpha_i(d,e_i)\cdot XY(g_i(d,e_i),d')\\ & + \textstyle\sum_{j\in J}\sum_{e'_j:E'_j} c'_j(d',e'_j) \rightarrow \alpha_j(d',e'_j)\cdot XY(d,g'_j(d',e'_j))\\ & + \textstyle\sum_{i\in I}\sum_{j\in J}\sum_{e_i:E_i}\sum_{e'_j:E'_j} c_i(d,e_i)\wedge c'_j(d',e'_j) \rightarrow\\ & \qquad \alpha_i(d,e_i)|\alpha_j(d',e'_j)\cdot XY(g_i(d,e_i),g'_j(d',e'_j)). \end{aligned}$$

Note that when actions of X happen on their own, the parameter d' remains untouched. Similarly, when actions from Y happen without synchronizing with those of X, the data of process X is not touched either.

With time, the linearization is only slightly trickier. When actions synchronize, their time stamps must be equal. Furthermore, if actions of one process must happen before a certain time, the other process cannot do any action at a later time. Thus, consider the following timed linear equations:

$$\begin{aligned} X(d{:}D) = {} & \textstyle\sum_{i\in I}\sum_{e_i:E_i} c_i(d,e_i) \rightarrow \alpha_i(d,e_i){}^{c}t_i(d,e_i)\cdot X(g_i(d,e_i))\\ & + \textstyle\sum_{j\in J}\sum_{e_j:E_j} c_j(d,e_j) \rightarrow \delta_j(d,e_j){}^{c}t_j(d,e_j),\\ Y(d'{:}D') = {} & \textstyle\sum_{i\in I'}\sum_{e'_i:E'_i} c'_i(d',e'_i) \rightarrow \alpha'_i(d',e'_i){}^{c}t'_i(d',e'_i)\cdot Y(g'_i(d',e'_i))\\ & + \textstyle\sum_{j\in J'}\sum_{e'_j:E'_j} c'_j(d',e'_j) \rightarrow \delta{}^{c}t'_j(d',e'_j). \end{aligned}$$

The parallel composition of X and Y has the behavior of the process XY given by the following equation

$$
\begin{array}{l}
XY(d{:}D, d'{:}D') \\
= \sum_{i\in I}\sum_{e_i:E_i} c_i(d,e_i) \land \\
\qquad ((\bigvee_{i'\in I'} \exists e'_{i'}{:}E_{i'}.c'(d',e'_{i'}) \land t_i(d,e_i) < t'_{i'}(d',e'_{i'})) \lor \\
\qquad (\bigvee_{j'\in J'} \exists e'_{j'}{:}E_{j'}.c'(d',e'_{j'}) \land t_i(d,e_i) < t'_{j'}(d',e'_{j'}))) \to \\
\quad \alpha_i(d,e_i){}^{\varsigma} t_i(d,e_i) \cdot XY(g_i(d,e_i),d') \\
\; + \sum_{i\in I'}\sum_{e_i:E'_i} c'_i(d',e_i) \land \\
\qquad ((\bigvee_{i'\in I} \exists e'_{i'}{:}E_{i'}.c(d,e'_{i'}) \land t'_i(d',e_i) < t_{i'}(d,e'_{i'})) \lor \\
\qquad (\bigvee_{j'\in J} \exists e'_{j'}{:}E_{j'}.c(d,e'_{i'}) \land t'_i(d',e_i) < t_{j'}(d,e'_{j'}))) \to \\
\quad \alpha'_i(d',e_i){}^{\varsigma} t_i(d,e_i) \cdot XY(d, g'_i(d',e_i)) \\
\; + \sum_{i\in I}\sum_{i\in I'}\sum_{e_i:E_i}\sum_{e'_i:E'_i} c_i(d,e_i) \land c'_{i'}(d',e'_{i'}) \land t_i(d,e_i) \approx t'_{i'}(d',e'_{i'}) \to \\
\quad \alpha_i(d,e_i) | \alpha'_{i'}(d',e'_i){}^{\varsigma} t_i(d,e_i) \cdot XY(g_i(d,e_i), g'_{i'}(d',e'_{i'})) \\
\; + \sum_{j\in J}\sum_{j'\in J'}\sum_{e_j:E_j}\sum_{e'_{j'}:E'_{j'}} c_j(d,e_j) \land c'_{j'}(d',e'_{j'}) \land \\
\quad t_j(d,e_j) \approx t'_{j'}(d',e'_{j'}) \to \delta{}^{\varsigma} t_j(d,e_j)
\end{array}
$$

The first and second set of summands are the multi-actions of one of the processes that happens on its own. Expressions of the form

$$
\begin{array}{l}
((\bigvee_{i'\in I'} \exists e'_{i'}{:}E_{i'}.c'(d',e'_{i'}) \land t_i(d,e_i) < t'_{i'}(d',e'_{i'})) \lor \\
\qquad (\bigvee_{j'\in J'} \exists e'_{j'}{:}E_{j'}.c'(d',e'_{i'}) \land t_i(d,e_i) < t'_{j'}(d',e'_{j'})))
\end{array}
$$

express that actions in one process must happen either before the latest action in the other process can occur, or before the other process encounters a timed deadlock.

The third set of summands are the synchronizations between the actions of both processes; and the fourth set of summands records the combined timed deadlocks of both processes.

Example 10.2.13. Consider two timed processes. One throws a ball every second, which must be caught by the other process. However, that process is only willing to catch a ball every 2 seconds. They start throwing and catching at time 1.

$$
\begin{array}{l}
\textbf{proc } X(t_1{:}\mathbb{R}) = \mathit{throw}{}^{\varsigma} t_1 \cdot X(t_1{+}1); \\
\qquad Y(t_2{:}\mathbb{R}) = \mathit{catch}{}^{\varsigma} t_2 \cdot Y(t_2{+}2); \\
\qquad \mathit{Sys} = \nabla_{\{c\}}(\Gamma_{\{\mathit{throw}|\mathit{catch}\to c\}}(X(1) || Y(1)));
\end{array}
$$

Linearizing the parallel composition, without the allow and communication operators, yields

$$
\begin{array}{l}
Z_1(t_1,t_2{:}\mathbb{R}) = t_1 < t_2 \to \mathit{throw}{}^{\varsigma} t_1 \cdot Z_1(t_1{+}1, t_2) \\
\qquad + t_2 < t_1 \to \mathit{catch}{}^{\varsigma} t_2 \cdot Z_1(t_1, t_2{+}2) \\
\qquad + t_1 \approx t_2 \to \mathit{throw}|\mathit{catch}{}^{\varsigma} t_1 \cdot Z_1(t_1{+}1, t_2{+}2).
\end{array}
$$

If we apply the allow operator $\nabla_{\{c\}}$ and communication operator $\Gamma_{\{\mathit{throw}|\mathit{catch}\to c\}}$ to this linear equation we obtain

$$
\begin{array}{l}
Z_2(t_1,t_2{:}\mathbb{R}) = t_1 < t_2 \to \delta{}^{\varsigma} t_1 \\
\qquad + t_2 < t_1 \to \delta{}^{\varsigma} t_2 \\
\qquad + t_1 \approx t_2 \to c{}^{\varsigma} t_1 \cdot Z_2(t_1{+}1, t_2{+}2)
\end{array}
$$

where Sys is equal to $Z_2(1,1)$. We can see that $Z_2(1,1)$ can perform a $c^{\text{c}}1$ action, ending up in $Z_2(2,3)$. As $2 \neq 3$, the behavior of $Z_2(2,3)$ reduces to $\delta^{\text{c}}2$. And indeed, the process X wants to throw a second ball at time 2, which process Y is only willing to catch at time 3. Clearly, time cannot proceed up to and beyond time 2 without invalidating a time constraint of one of the processes.

Exercise 10.2.14. Consider the example in section 9.8.2 where two buffers are put in parallel. Calculate a linear equations for B_1, B_2 and for their parallel combination X.

Exercise 10.2.15. Calculate a linear process equations for the process S from section 9.8.3.

10.2.3 Linearization of n parallel processes

When studying distributed algorithms, often n processes are put in parallel, for an arbitrary positive number n. For example, we are interested in the behavior of

$$\nabla_V(\Gamma_C(X(1,f(1)) \parallel \cdots \parallel X(n,f(n)))) \tag{10.3}$$

where X is given by the following linear process equation

$$X(id{:}\mathbb{N}^+, d{:}D) = \sum_{i \in I} \sum_{e_i:E_i} c_i(id,d,e_i) \rightarrow a_i(f_i(id,d,e_i)) \cdot X(g_i(id,d,e_i)).$$

and $f{:}\mathbb{N}^+ \rightarrow D$ is a function that gives for each process i its initial state $f(i)$. Thus, $X(i,f(i))$ is process i with initial value $f(i)$.

For simplicity, we leave out time and let the multi-actions consist of a single action and only allow two actions to communicate in Γ. Furthermore, we assume that the index set I is ordered. A precise way of describing process (10.3) is the following:

$$\begin{aligned}
&Y(n{:}\mathbb{N}^+, f{:}\mathbb{N}^+ \rightarrow D) = \nabla_V(\Gamma_C(Z(f,n))),\\
&Z(n{:}\mathbb{N}^+, f{:}\mathbb{N}^+ \rightarrow D) = (n \approx 1) \rightarrow X(1,f(1)) \diamond (Z(n-1,f) \parallel X(n,f(n))).
\end{aligned}$$

Although the equation for Z is unguarded, it has been proven that it defines a unique process. Moreover, process Y also satisfies the following linear equation. This equation has a regular structure, and therefore, it is useful to eliminate the parallel operator from n parallel linear processes in concrete cases [77].

$$\begin{aligned}
&Y(n{:}\mathbb{N}^+, f{:}\mathbb{N}^+ \rightarrow D) =\\
&\quad \sum_{i \in I, a_i \in V} \; \sum_{k:\mathbb{N}^+, e_i:E_i} (c_i(k,f(k),e_i) \land k \leq n) \rightarrow\\
&\qquad\qquad a_i(f_i(k,f(k),e_i)) \cdot Y(n, f[k \rightarrow g_i(k,f(k),e_i)]) +\\
&\quad \sum_{i,j \in I, i \leq j, C(a_i|a_j) \in V} \; \sum_{k,\ell:\mathbb{N}^+, e_i:E_i, e_j:E_j} (c_i(k,f(k),e_i) \land c_j(\ell,f(\ell),e_j) \land\\
&\qquad f_i(k,f(k),e_i) \approx f_j(\ell,f(\ell),e_j) \land k \not\approx \ell \land k \leq n \land \ell \leq n) \rightarrow\\
&\qquad\quad C(a_i|a_j)(f_k(k,f(k),e_i)) \cdot Y(n, f[k \rightarrow g_i(k,f(k),e_i)][\ell \rightarrow f(\ell,f(\ell),e_j)]).
\end{aligned}$$

Here we use $C(a_i|a_j)$ for the action a such that $a_i|a_j \rightarrow a \in C$. If no such communication occurs in C, we let $C(a_i|a_j)$ be equal to τ.

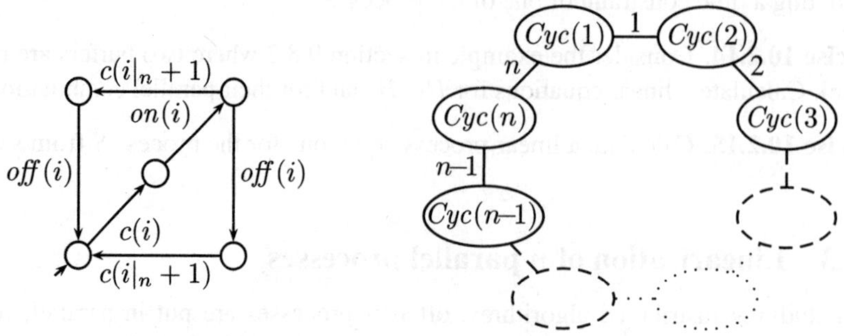

Figure 10.3: Behavior of a cycler and overall process structure in Milner's scheduler

Example 10.2.16. As an example we consider *Milner's scheduler*, as depicted in figure 10.3. This process was used as an example in [135]. The scheduler controls $n{>}1$ production machines. Each machine i can be switched on (using an action $on(i)$) and off (using $\mathit{off}(i)$). The requirements are that each machine must alternately be switched on and off, and all machines must be started in sequence. Milner defined one control process per machine which he called a cycler:

$$Cyc(id{:}\mathbb{N}^+) = c(id)\cdot on(id)(\mathit{off}(id) \parallel c(id|_n + 1))\cdot Cyc(id).$$

The actions $c(id)$ are used to signal the next process that it can start the machine it controls. The process $C(1)$ must initially skip the initial $c(1)$ action, as otherwise the whole system will not start up.

Linearizing the behavior of a cycler is straightforward. The process $C(id)$ is equal to $C(id, 1)$ where the behavior of $C(id, 1)$ is given by the following equation

$$\begin{aligned} C(id, state{:}\mathbb{N}^+) = {} & (state{\approx}1)\to c(id)\cdot C(id, 2)\\ & + (state{\approx}2)\to on(id)\cdot C(id, 3)\\ & + (state{\approx}3)\to c(id|_n{+}1)\cdot C(id, 4)\\ & + (state{\approx}3)\to \mathit{off}(id)\cdot C(id, 5)\\ & + (state{\approx}4)\to \mathit{off}(id)\cdot C(id, 1)\\ & + (state{\approx}5)\to c(id|_n{+}1)\cdot C(id, 1). \end{aligned}$$

The behavior of the scheduler is defined by

$$\begin{aligned} Scheduler(n{:}\mathbb{N}^+) &= \nabla_{\{on,\mathit{off},d\}}(\Gamma_{\{c|c\to d\}}(Sched(n))),\\ Sched(n{:}\mathbb{N}^+) &= (n{\approx}1)\to C(n, 2) \diamond (Sched(n{-}1) \parallel C(n, 1)). \end{aligned}$$

Note that we do not use the function f in this definition explicitly to indicate the initial values of each process. Using the linearization result above as a guideline, it can directly be seen that the scheduler $Scheduler(n)$ is equal to $Scheduler(n, f_{init})$ of which the defining equation is given below. The function $f_{init} : \mathbb{N}^+ \to \mathbb{N}^+$ is defined as $f_{init} = \lambda n{:}\mathbb{N}^+.\mathit{if}(n{\approx}1, 2, 1)$.

$$\begin{array}{l}
\mathit{Scheduler}(n{:}\mathbb{N}^+, f{:}\mathbb{N}^+{\to}\mathbb{N}^+) = \\
\quad \sum_{k:\mathbb{N}^+}(f(k){\approx}2){\to}on(k){\cdot}\mathit{Scheduler}(k, f[k{\to}3])+ \\
\quad \sum_{k:\mathbb{N}^+}(f(k){\approx}3){\to}\mathit{off}(k){\cdot}\mathit{Scheduler}(k, f[k{\to}5])+ \\
\quad \sum_{k:\mathbb{N}^+}(f(k){\approx}4){\to}\mathit{off}(k){\cdot}\mathit{Scheduler}(k, f[k{\to}1])+ \\
\quad \sum_{k:\mathbb{N}^+}(f(k|_n{+}1){\approx}1 \wedge f(k){\approx}3 \wedge k{\leq}n){\to} \\
\qquad\qquad d(k|_n{+}1){\cdot}\mathit{Scheduler}(n, f[k|_n{+}1{\to}2][k{\to}4])+ \\
\quad \sum_{k:\mathbb{N}^+}(f(k|_n{+}1){\approx}1 \wedge f(k){\approx}5 \wedge k{\leq}n){\to} \\
\qquad\qquad d(k|_n{+}1){\cdot}\mathit{Scheduler}(n, f[k|_n{+}1{\to}2][k{\to}1]).
\end{array} \tag{10.4}$$

In section 12.2.2 we show how to reduce this equation further.

Exercise 10.2.17. Derive equation (10.4) in detail. Note that in order to do this it is required that $n{>}1$. What is the behavior of the scheduler if $n{=}1$?

10.3 Proof rules for linear processes

In this section we introduce two proof rules for linear process equations, namely the rule convergent linear recursive specification principle (CL-RSP) and CL-RSP with invariants. Both rules are derivable from RSP, and as such do not add proof strength. However, they are more convenient if it comes to proving the correctness of concrete processes.

10.3.1 τ-convergence

We first introduce the notion of τ-convergence that says that from no state of a linear process can an infinite number of τ's be performed.

Definition 10.3.1 (τ-convergent LPE). An LPE is *τ-convergent* iff it cannot exhibit an infinite sequence of τ-transitions from any state.

An alternative formulation uses well-founded orderings. This formulation allows a straightforward proof technique to show that there are no infinite τ-sequences.

Lemma 10.3.2. An LPE written as in definition 10.1.1 is τ-convergent iff for all $i \in I$ such that $a_i = \tau$, there is a well-founded ordering $<$ on D such that for all $e_i{:}E_i$ and $d{:}D$, $c_i(d, e_i)$ implies $g_i(d, e_i) < d$.

A well-known well-founded ordering is the smaller than ("<") relation on natural numbers. For a wealth of other well-founded relations we refer to [31, chapter 6].

Example 10.3.3. Consider the following linear process, where first an arbitrary number n is selected, and then n τ-steps can be performed.

$$\begin{array}{rl}
X(n{:}\mathbb{N}) = & \sum\limits_{m:\mathbb{N}}(n{\approx}0) \to \mathit{select}(m){\cdot}X(m) \\
& +\ (n{>}0){\to}\tau{\cdot}X(n{-}1).
\end{array}$$

Observe that with each τ-step, n decreases according to the well-founded ordering relation $<$ on natural numbers. More precisely, we find for the second summand of the linear process that:

$$n > 0 \text{ implies } n - 1 < n$$

which is undeniably true. We can conclude that this linear process is τ-convergent. Note that this linear process illustrates that for a τ-convergent linear process there is no upper bound on the number of consecutive τ-steps that can be performed. In the first summand m can be set to any (finite) number.

Example 10.3.4. An alternative technique to show τ-convergence is to map the data state to some domain (generally the natural numbers), and show that in this domain τ-steps are decreasing according to some well-founded relation.

Consider for instance two unbounded queues (see figure 10.4). The queues Q_1 and

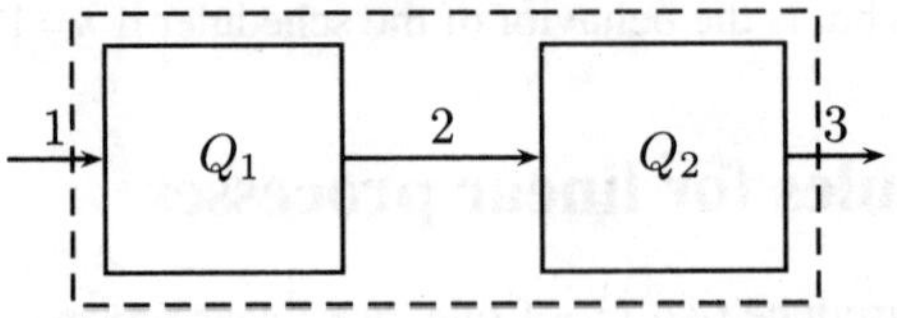

Figure 10.4: Two connected unbounded queues

Q_2 contain data elements of some sort D and are defined as follows:

$$\begin{aligned}
&Q_1(q_1{:}List(D)){=}\sum_{d:D} r_1(d){\cdot}Q_1(d{\triangleright}q_1) + (q_1{\not\approx}[])\to s_2(rhead(q_1)){\cdot}Q_1(rtail(q_1))\\
&Q_2(q_2{:}List(D)){=}\sum_{d:D} r_2(d){\cdot}Q_2(d{\triangleright}q_2) + (q_2{\not\approx}[])\to s_3(rhead(q_2)){\cdot}Q_2(rtail(q_2))\\
&System = \tau_{\{c_2\}}(\nabla_{\{r_1,c_2,s_3\}}(\Gamma_{\{s_2|r_2\to c_2\}}(Q_1([]) \parallel Q_2([])))).
\end{aligned}$$

Linearizing these equations and applying sum elimination yields the following linear process where $System$ is equal to the process $X([],[])$.

$$\begin{aligned}
X(q_1, q_2{:}List(D)) = &\textstyle\sum_{d:D} r_1(d){\cdot}X(d \triangleright q_1, q_2)\\
&+ (q_2{\not\approx}[])\to s_3(rhead(q_2)){\cdot}X(q_1, rtail(q_2))\\
&+ (q_1{\not\approx}[])\to \tau{\cdot}X(rtail(q_1), rhead(q_1) \triangleright q_2).
\end{aligned} \tag{10.5}$$

In order to show that this is a τ-convergent linear process equation, we prove that when doing τ-steps, the length of the first queue decreases. Formally we define a *variant function* f from the state of the linear process to the natural numbers as follows:

$$f(q_1, q_2) = \#q_1.$$

Now expressing that the variant function decreases with every τ-step is expressed by the following condition:

$$(q_1{\not\approx}[]) \to f(rtail(q_1), rhead(q_1) \triangleright q_2) < f(q_1, q_2).$$

Applying the definition of f leads to the following that obviously holds:

$$(q_1 \not\approx []) \rightarrow \#rtail(q_1) < \#q_1.$$

From this we conclude that linear process equation (10.5) is τ-convergent.

The notion of a variant function is coined in [51] but as it is commonly used, other names for it also occur in the literature (e.g., bounded functions). It generally suffices to let variant functions map to the natural numbers to prove τ-convergence. However, sometimes it is convenient or even necessary to consider richer well-founded domains.

10.3.2 The convergent linear recursive specification principle (CL-RSP)

The convergent linear recursive specification principle (CL-RSP) is essentially the same as RSP, except that the guardedness condition is replaced by τ-convergence. We define CL-RSP as follows:

Definition 10.3.5 (CL-RSP).

$$\frac{\Gamma \vdash X = \Psi X \quad \Gamma \vdash Y = \Psi Y}{\Gamma \vdash X = Y} \quad \Psi \text{ is a } \tau\text{-convergent process operator} \quad \text{(CL-RSP)}$$

Note that when τ-actions occur in a linear process, the process is not guarded anymore. Actually, CL-RSP is stronger than RSP, in the sense that RSP is only applicable to processes with a bounded number of τ's. As we have seen in example 10.3.3, τ-convergent linear processes do not allow such an a priori bound.

Example 10.3.6. We prove process $X(n)$ of example 10.3.3 rooted branching bisimilar to the process $Y(n{>}0)$ defined by

$$Y(b{:}\mathbb{B}) = \sum_{m:\mathbb{N}} b \rightarrow select(m) \cdot Y(true) + \neg b \rightarrow \tau \cdot Y(true).$$

Note that contrary to X, the process Y has no unbounded sequences of τ's. We show that $\lambda n{:}\mathbb{N}.Y(n{\approx}0)$ is a fixed point for the linear process operator induced by the equation for X. Hence, we must show:

$$\begin{aligned} Y(n{\approx}0) = {} & \textstyle\sum_{m:\mathbb{N}} (n{\approx}0) \rightarrow select(m) \cdot Y(m{\approx}0) \\ & + \neg(n{\approx}0) \rightarrow \tau \cdot Y(n{-}1{\approx}0). \end{aligned} \tag{10.6}$$

In order to prove this, we observe that $a \cdot Y(false) = a \cdot Y(true)$ for any action a. The proof relies on the use of the first τ-law W‡:

$$a \cdot Y(false) \;=\; a \cdot \tau \cdot Y(true) \overset{\text{W‡}}{=} a \cdot Y(true).$$

Using this observation, equation (10.6) can be transformed to the equivalent:

$$\begin{aligned} Y(n{\approx}0) = {} & \textstyle\sum_{m:\mathbb{N}} (n{\approx}0) \rightarrow select(m) \cdot Y(true) \\ & + \neg(n{\approx}0) \rightarrow \tau \cdot Y(true). \end{aligned}$$

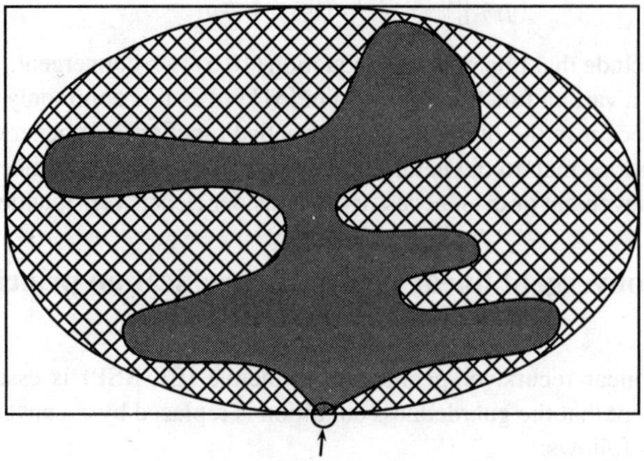

Figure 10.5: An invariant, the total, and the reachable state space

But this is exactly the defining equation for Y where $n{\approx}0$ has been substituted for b. Therefore, it holds, and so we have shown that $\lambda n{:}\mathbb{N}.Y(n{\approx}0)$ is a fixed point of a τ-convergent linear process operator induced by the defining equation of X. Naturally, X itself is also a fixed point. Therefore, we conclude that $Y(n{\approx}0) = X(n)$, or more specifically $Y(true)$ equals $X(0)$.

10.3.3 CL-RSP with invariants

An invariant for a linear process is a property, i.e., a function from the state variable D to Booleans, which once it is valid can never be invalidated by any step of the process. In particular, if the invariant holds in the initial state, it must also hold for all reachable states.

Definition 10.3.7 (Invariant). A mapping $\mathcal{I} : D \to \mathbb{B}$ is an *invariant* for an LPE as in definition 10.1.1 iff, for all $i \in I$, $d{:}D$ and $e_i{:}E_i$,

$$\mathcal{I}(d) \wedge c_i(d, e_i) \Rightarrow \mathcal{I}(g_i(d, e_i)) \tag{10.7}$$

Example 10.3.8. Consider the LPE $X(n{:}\mathbb{N}) = a(n){\cdot}X(n{+}2)$. Two invariants for this LPE are

$$\mathcal{I}_1(n) = \begin{cases} true & \text{if } n \text{ is even} \\ false & \text{if } n \text{ is odd} \end{cases} \qquad \mathcal{I}_2(n) = \begin{cases} false & \text{if } n \text{ is even} \\ true & \text{if } n \text{ is odd} \end{cases}$$

The relation between the total state space, an invariant, and the reachable state space can neatly be depicted as in figure 10.5. At the bottom there is an initial state. The total state space is represented by the rectangle. The reachable state space is characterized by the gray area and contains all states reachable from the initial state. Not only is the reachable state space generally much smaller than the total state space, it also is usually irregular and as such hard to understand and model. But often it is possible to find a nice characterization of an outer boundary that includes the reachable state space and that satisfies the invariant property. This property is generally chosen as the invariant and it is depicted as the hashed oval in figure 10.5.

The following lemma makes it easier to prove that predicates are invariants. It says that to prove that a set of predicates are invariants, each predicate can be shown to satisfy the invariant property separately, using all other predicates.

Lemma 10.3.9. Consider a linear process operator Ψ. If for all $1 \leq k \leq n$, $i{\in}I$ $d{:}D$ and $e_i{:}E_i$, it holds that $(\bigwedge_{\ell=1}^{n} \mathcal{I}_\ell(d)) \wedge c_i(d, e_i) \Rightarrow \mathcal{I}_k(g_i(d, e_i))$, then $\lambda d{:}D. \bigwedge_{k=1}^{n} \mathcal{I}_k(d)$ is an invariant of Ψ.

Note that the conjunction and disjunction of invariants is also an invariant. However, the negation of an invariant is not necessarily an invariant.

Invariants tend to play a crucial role in algebraic verifications of system behavior that involve data. The reason for this is that it allows separation of concerns. Before commencing with the proof that two processes behave the same, invariants can be proven that can be employed in the verification later on. This does not mean that finding invariants is easy. On the contrary, finding proper and useful invariants is one of the harder jobs in any verification.

The following adaptation of CL-RSP allows the use of invariants when proving two processes equivalent.

Definition 10.3.10 (CL-RSP with invariants). Let Ψ be a τ-convergent linear process operator and $\mathcal{I} : D \to \mathbb{B}$ be an invariant of Ψ.

$$\frac{\Gamma \vdash \forall d{:}D.(\mathcal{I}(d) \Rightarrow Xd = \Psi Xd) \qquad \Gamma \vdash \forall d{:}D.(\mathcal{I}(d) \Rightarrow Yd = \Psi Yd)}{\Gamma \vdash \forall d{:}D.(\mathcal{I}(d) \Rightarrow Xd = Yd)} \quad \text{CL-RSP with invariants}$$

The following theorem says that CL-RSP with invariants is not essential. Any proof that uses CL-RSP with invariants can be transformed to a proof without the explicit use of invariants.

Theorem 10.3.11. Every proof using CL-RSP with invariants can be replaced by a proof using CL-RSP.

Proof. For conciseness we give this proof omitting time and terminating summands. Consider a proof in which CL-RSP with invariants is used. We replace each occurrence of CL-RSP with invariants one by one. Consider a single application of CL-RSP with invariants. This means there is a τ-convergent linear process operator Ψ with shape

$$\Psi = \lambda X{:}D{\to}\, \mathbb{P}.\lambda d{:}D. \sum_{i \in I} \sum_{e_i : E_i} c_i(d, e_i) {\to} \alpha_i(d, e_i) {\cdot} X(g_i(d, e_i))$$

with invariant $\mathcal{I}$ and processes X and Y such that

$$\Gamma \vdash \forall d{:}D.\mathcal{I}(d) \Rightarrow Xd = \Psi Xd \text{ and}$$
$$\Gamma \vdash \forall d{:}D.\mathcal{I}(d) \Rightarrow Yd = \Psi Yd$$

are proven. Now consider process operator $\Phi = \lambda Z{:}D{\rightarrow}\mathbb{P}, d{:}D.\mathcal{I}(d){\rightarrow}\Psi Zd$. We show that the processes $\lambda d{:}D.\mathcal{I}(d){\rightarrow}X(d)$ and $\lambda d{:}D.\mathcal{I}(d){\rightarrow}Y(d)$ are solutions of Φ. As both cases are symmetric, we only show the first. We must prove that

$$\Gamma \vdash \lambda d{:}D.\mathcal{I}(d){\rightarrow}X(d) = \Phi(\lambda d{:}D.\mathcal{I}(d){\rightarrow}X(d)).$$

Expanding the definition of Φ and applying β-conversion yields the equivalent equation:

$$\Gamma \vdash \lambda d{:}D.\mathcal{I}(d){\rightarrow}X(d) = \lambda d{:}D.\mathcal{I}(d){\rightarrow}\Psi(\lambda d{:}D.\mathcal{I}(d){\rightarrow}X(d)).$$

Now we expand the definition of Ψ.

$$\begin{aligned}\Gamma \vdash \lambda d{:}D.\mathcal{I}(d){\rightarrow}X(d) = \lambda d{:}D.\mathcal{I}(d){\rightarrow}(&\textstyle\sum_{i:I}\sum_{e_i:E_i} c_i(d,e_i){\rightarrow}\\ &\alpha_i(d,e_i){\cdot}(\mathcal{I}(g_i(d,e_i)){\rightarrow}X(g_i(d,e_i))))).\end{aligned} \tag{10.8}$$

As $\mathcal{I}(d){\wedge}c_i(d,e_i)$ and $\mathcal{I}$ is an invariant, we can show that $\mathcal{I}(g_i(d,e_i)) = \mathit{true}$. Equation (10.8) then becomes:

$$\Gamma \vdash \lambda d{:}D.\mathcal{I}(d){\rightarrow}X(d) = \lambda d{:}D.\mathcal{I}(d){\rightarrow}(\sum_{i:I}\sum_{e_i:E_i} c_i(d,e_i){\rightarrow}\alpha_i(d,e_i){\cdot}X(g_i(d,e_i))).$$

Now, as X is a solution for Ψ, this in turn reduces to

$$\Gamma \vdash \lambda d{:}D.\mathcal{I}(d){\rightarrow}X(d) = \lambda d{:}D.\mathcal{I}(d){\rightarrow}X(d),$$

which is obviously true.

As Ψ is τ-convergent, Φ is τ-convergent, and so we can conclude using CL-RSP that

$$\lambda d{:}D.\mathcal{I}(d){\rightarrow}X(d) \;=\; \lambda d{:}D.\mathcal{I}(d){\rightarrow}Y(d)$$

or in other words

$$\mathcal{I}(d) \;\Rightarrow\; X(d) = Y(d)$$

for all $d{:}D$. □

Example 10.3.12. Consider the following two LPEs:

$$\begin{aligned} X(n{:}\mathbb{N}) &= a(\mathit{even}(n)){\cdot}X(n{+}2),\\ Y &= a(\mathit{true}){\cdot}Y. \end{aligned}$$

We want to show that $X(0)$ equals Y using an application of CL-RSP with invariants. We use the invariant $\mathit{even}{:}\mathbb{N}{\rightarrow}\mathbb{B}$ for X that maps even numbers to *true* and odd numbers to *false* (cf., example 10.3.8).

Substituting $\lambda n{:}\mathbb{N}.Y$ for X in the LPE defining X yields $Y{=}a(\mathit{even}(n)){\cdot}Y$ which we must prove. Using the invariant we know $\mathit{even}(n) = \mathit{true}$ meaning that our proof obligation is equivalent to $Y = a(true)\cdot Y$. And this holds, as it is equal to the defining equation for Y. Clearly, X is a solution for the defining equation of X. So, CL-RSP with invariants allows us to conclude

$$even(n) \Rightarrow X(n) = Y.$$

From this it follows immediately that $X(0) = Y$.

Exercise 10.3.13. Show that the mappings $\mathcal{I}_1(d) = true$ for all $d{:}D$ and $\mathcal{I}_2(d) = false$ for all $d{:}D$ are invariants for all LPEs.

Exercise 10.3.14. Consider the process equations

$$X(b_1, b_2{:}\mathbb{B}) = a(b_1 \vee b_2)\cdot X(b_2, b_1)$$

and

$$Y = a(true)\cdot Y.$$

Prove, using CL-RSP with invariants, that $X(true, false) = Y$.

10.4 Historical notes

The use of linear processes is typical and does not really occur in other process algebras. Although recently it was proposed to extend the use to stochastic processes [114]. However, similar ideas are found in Unity [44] and I/O-automata [115]. An alternative approach is found in the CADP tool set [69] where processes are first translated to Petri nets, where the primary goal is to ease processing in tools.

As a contrast, there is a natural tendency to go for compositional methods. This can mean generating state spaces while reducing intermediate results [110], or it can mean that proofs employ properties of the parallel operator [7, 49].

The notion of a Greibach normal form was introduced in the process-algebraic setting to prove that strong bisimulation is decidable for context-free processes, i.e., processes with actions, and the alternative and sequential composition operators [16]. Later it was even proven that it is polynomial to decide this [100]. In [128] it was shown that it is decidable whether a context-free process is actually a regular process, allowing linearization without a stack. It was shown in [172] that every process can be linearized, by introducing the right data structures, namely recursive stacks of bags. The linearization technique described in this chapter is outlined in [86].

Invariants are an essential proof technique if it comes to proving the correctness of programs. Within the process-algebraic community they are largely ignored except for [30], which introduces and proves CL-RSP with invariants. It turns out that for proofs of actual protocols invariants are very essential tools, especially because they allow for the construction and presentation of proofs in a piecewise manner. Unfortunately, invariants alone are not enough to effectively prove complex distributed systems correct, especially the cones and foci method from chapter 12.

11

Confluence and τ-prioritization

When studying the state spaces of parallel systems, the pattern seen in figure 11.1 may catch your eyes. Here we depicted the behavior of the process $\tau_{\{b,c\}}(\nabla_{\{a,b,c,d\}}(a{\cdot}b \parallel c{\cdot}d))$, i.e., the parallel composition of the processes $a{\cdot}b$ and $c{\cdot}d$ where neither communication nor multi-actions are allowed. The reason for these patterns is that actions in parallel components act independently, meaning that executing the two actions consecutively leads to the same state, irrespective of the fact which of the two transitions is executed first. This phenomenon is generally referred to as *confluence*.

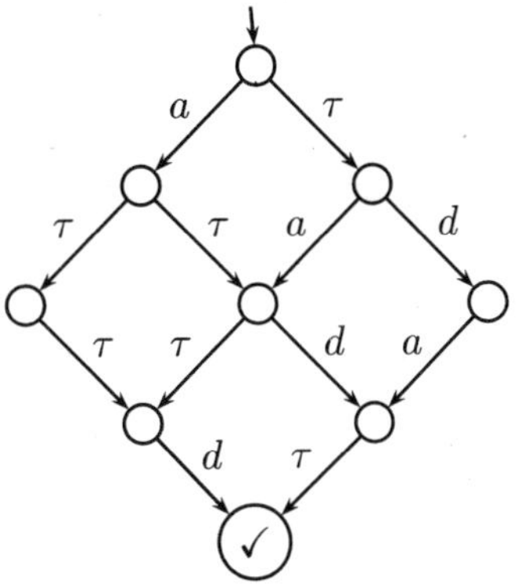

Figure 11.1: Typical confluent behavioral pattern

The independence of actions that happen in parallel is a major cause of the state space explosion problem. But by employing confluence we can sometimes circumvent this problem using what we call τ-prioritization. This means that in any state an outgoing confluent τ can be chosen and all other outgoing actions can be removed.

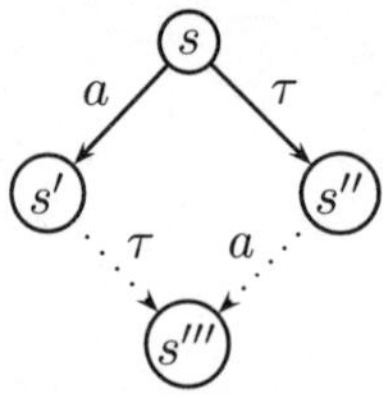

Figure 11.2: The confluence pattern

11.1 τ-confluence on labeled transition systems

First we define confluence on labeled transition systems. We consider a subset U of τ-transitions to be τ-confluent (or confluent for short) as depicted in figure 11.2. For every state s, which is the state on top in figure 11.2, with outgoing τ-transition in U and outgoing a transition, it must be possible to finish the diamond shape. The diagram must be interpreted in such a way that if the solid arrows are present, the dotted arrows must be shown to exist. The definition below makes this precise. Note that it is required that the dotted τ-transition is a member of U.

Definition 11.1.1 (Confluence). Let $A = (S, Act, \longrightarrow, s_0, T)$ be a labeled transition system. A set U of τ-transitions is called τ-*confluent* if for all transitions $s \xrightarrow{a} s' \in \rightarrow$ and $s \xrightarrow{\tau} s'' \in U$:

(1) Either $s' \xrightarrow{\tau} s''' \in U$ and $s'' \xrightarrow{a} s''' \in \rightarrow$, for some state $s''' \in S$;

(2) Or $a = \tau$ and $s' = s''$.

The union of confluent sets of τ-transitions is again confluent, so there is a maximal confluent set of τ-transitions.

There are many variations of τ-confluence. For instance, it is possible to require that s' goes to s''' with zero or more τ-transitions (all in U). It can also be required that from s'' the state s''' can be reached via a sequence of τ's, an a and again a number of τ's. It can even be required that $s' \xrightarrow{\tau} s'''$ and $s'' \xrightarrow{a} s''''$ where s''' and s'''' are related via for instance branching bisimulation. We do not consider these extended versions here. See [88] for the treatment of some of these cases.

Example 11.1.2. Note that in figure 11.1 the maximal set of confluent τ-transitions is the set of all τ-transitions. However, by removing a single τ-transition the confluence property can be destroyed. For instance, the removal of the τ-transition to the terminating state, implies that all other τ-transitions that originate from hiding the action b, violate the confluence property.

Exercise 11.1.3. Give the maximal τ-confluent sets of τ-transitions of the following four state spaces:

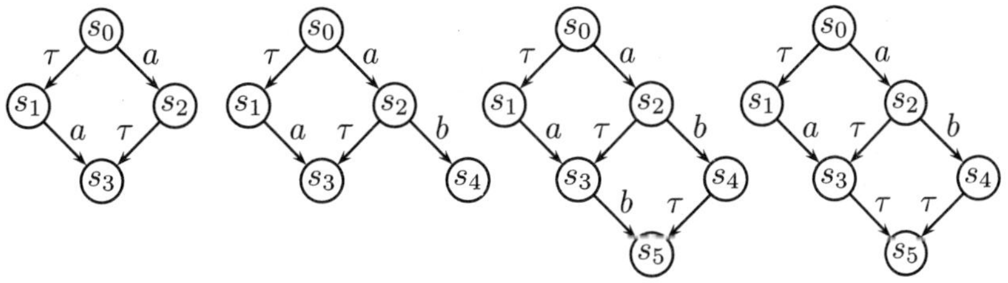

Exercise 11.1.4. Give the maximal τ-confluent sets for the following three state spaces:

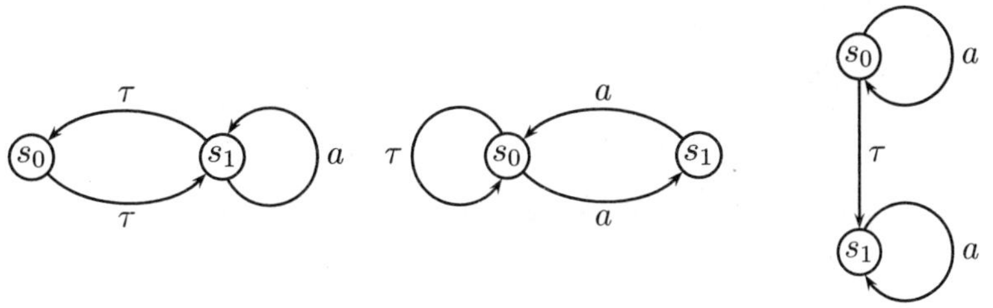

Exercise 11.1.5. Consider a transition system A with a finite number of states and transitions. Let U and U' be τ-confluent sets of τ-transitions. Show that $U \cup U'$ is also a τ-confluent set of τ-transitions. Argue that this shows the existence of a unique maximal τ-confluent set of τ-transitions for A.

Exercise 11.1.6. Prove that in a transition system A with a τ-confluent set of transitions U, every transition $s \xrightarrow{\tau} s'$ in U is *inert*, i.e., s and s' are branching bisimilar. Note that we do not need τ-convergence to prove this.

★Exercise 11.1.7. Show that any LTS has a unique maximal τ-confluent set of τ-transitions.

11.2 τ-prioritization of labeled transition systems

If a transition system is τ-confluent and τ-convergent, then τ-prioritization preserves branching bisimulation. The τ-prioritization means that in any state with an outgoing τ that occurs in a τ-confluent set of transitions, this transition can be taken, and the others can be omitted. For the transition system in figure 11.1 there are two ways to prioritize. Both are depicted in figure 11.3. Note that in both cases the reachable state space is the same. After applying the first τ-law, the state space reduces to that of $\tau \cdot (a \parallel d)$.

The following definition formulates that τ-prioritization is not an operation on state spaces, but rather a relation between them.

Definition 11.2.1. Let $A_1 = (S, Act, \longrightarrow_1, s_0, T)$ and $A_2 = (S, Act, \longrightarrow_2, s_0, T)$ be two transition systems. Let $U \subseteq \longrightarrow_1$ be a set of τ-transitions. We call A_2 a τ-prioritization of A_1 with respect to U iff for all states $s, s' \in S$

- If $s \xrightarrow{a}_2 s'$ then $s \xrightarrow{a}_1 s'$, and
- If $s \xrightarrow{a}_1 s'$, then $s \xrightarrow{a}_2 s'$ or $s \xrightarrow{\tau}_2 s'' \in U$ for some state $s'' \in S$.

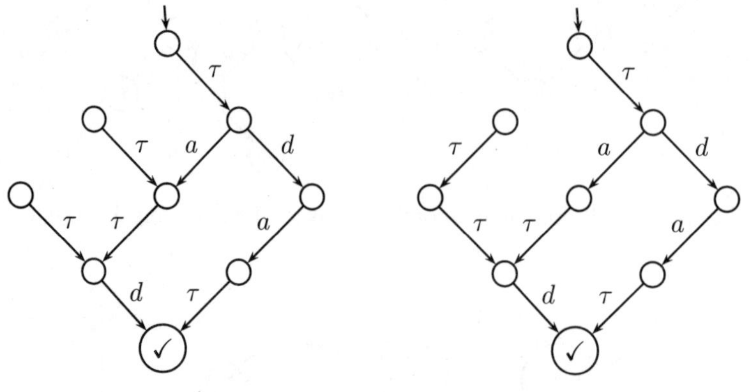

Figure 11.3: The state space of figure 11.1 after prioritization

Theorem 11.2.2. Let $A_1 = (S, Act, \longrightarrow_1, s_0, T)$ and $A_2 = (S, Act, \longrightarrow_2, s_0, T)$ be transition systems. Let $U \subseteq \longrightarrow_1$ be a τ-confluent set of τ-transitions, A_2 a τ-prioritization of A_1 with respect to U and let A_2 be τ-convergent. Then A_1 and A_2 are branching bisimilar.

Proof. Consider the relation $R \subseteq S \times S$ defined by

$$R = \{\langle s_1, s_n\rangle \in S \times S \mid s_i \xrightarrow{\tau}_1 s_{i+1} \text{ is a transition in } U \text{ for all } 1 \le i < n\}.$$

We show that R is a branching bisimulation relation between the states of A_1 and A_2.

Consider a pair of states $\langle s, s'\rangle \in R$. By definition of R it holds that $s = s_1 \xrightarrow{\tau}_1 s_2 \xrightarrow{\tau}_1 \cdots \xrightarrow{\tau}_1 s_n = s'$ and all these τ-transitions occur in U.

First suppose that $s' \xrightarrow{a}_2 t'$. Hence, this step is mimicked in A_1 by the sequence $s \xrightarrow{\tau}_1 \cdots \xrightarrow{\tau}_1 s' \xrightarrow{a}_1 t'$. For all s_i it holds that $\langle s_i, s'\rangle \in R$ and moreover $\langle t', t'\rangle \in R$.

Now suppose $s \xrightarrow{a}_1 t$. Observe that there is a longest finite sequence $s' \xrightarrow{\tau}_2 \ldots \xrightarrow{\tau}_2 t'$ of τ-transitions in U to some t' from which no outgoing τ-transition in U is possible as A_2 is τ-convergent. As A_2 is a τ-prioritization of A_1, such a τ-transition is also not possible in A_1. Figure 11.4 depicts the situation. The solid arrows may occur in A_2. The dashed arrows must occur in A_2.

If $a = \tau$ and $t = s_i$ for some $1 \le i \le n+1$ we mimic this step by staying in s'. Obviously, $\langle s_i, s'\rangle \in R$ as $s_i \xrightarrow{\tau}_1 \cdots \xrightarrow{\tau}_1 s'$ are transitions in U.

If $a = \tau$ and t resides on the τ-path between s' and t'. Then, the transition $s \xrightarrow{\tau}_1 t$ can be mimicked by $s' \xrightarrow{\tau}_2 \cdots \xrightarrow{\tau}_2 t$. Note that for any s'' not equal to t on this τ-path $\langle s, s''\rangle \in R$, as $s \xrightarrow{\tau}_1 \cdots \xrightarrow{\tau}_1 s''$ are transitions in U, and furthermore, $\langle t, t\rangle \in R$.

If $a \neq \tau$ or t is not on the τ-path from s to t', it follows using τ-confluence that $t \xrightarrow{\tau}_1 \cdots \xrightarrow{\tau}_1 t''$ are transitions in U, and $t' \xrightarrow{a}_1 t''$. As t' has no outgoing τ-transition in U, it follows via τ-prioritization that $t' \xrightarrow{a}_2 t''$. From this, we observe

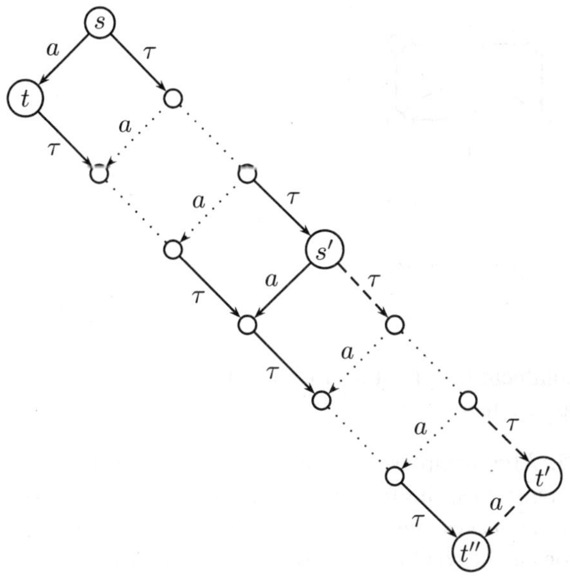

Figure 11.4: Proof that τ-prioritization preserves branching bisimulation

that if $s \xrightarrow{a}_1 t$, then $s' \xrightarrow{\tau}_2 \cdots \xrightarrow{\tau}_2 t' \xrightarrow{a}_2 t''$. Moreover, for all states s'' on the τ-path from s' to t' in A_2 it holds that $\langle s, s'' \rangle \in R$. Furthermore, $\langle t, t'' \rangle \in R$ as there is a τ-path in U between t and t'' in A_1.

Therefore, we can conclude that R is a branching bisimulation relation. In particular, as the initial states $\langle s_0, s_0 \rangle \in R$ both transition systems A_1 and A_2 are bisimilar.
□

Example 11.2.3. This example shows that τ-convergence is essential for the soundness of prioritization of confluent τ-transitions.

Consider the state space defined by the process declaration $X = (\tau + a)\cdot X$; note that it contains a τ-loop. The τ-transition in this state space is confluent. If the a-transition is eliminated from this state space using τ-prioritization, then the resulting state space is defined by the process declaration $Y = \tau \cdot Y$. Clearly the state belonging to X and the state belonging to Y are not branching bisimilar.

Example 11.2.4. In general, not every inert τ-transition needs to be τ-confluent. Consider the state space

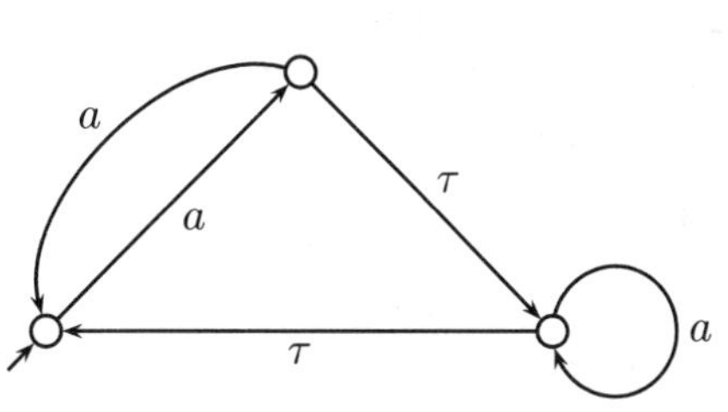

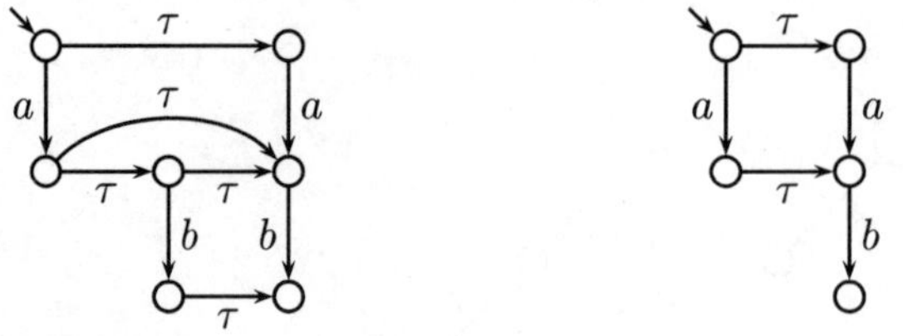

Figure 11.5: Repeated τ-prioritization makes sense

The maximal confluent set of τ-transitions of this state space is empty, but the two τ-transitions are both inert.

Example 11.2.5. After compression of a state space on the basis of its maximal confluent set of τ-transitions, the resulting state space may again contain confluent τ-transitions. Hence, it makes sense to iterate τ-prioritization until the maximal confluent set of τ-transitions in the resulting state space has become empty.

In figure 11.5 we provide a state space before and after compression with respect to the confluent τ-transitions. Compression with respect to the confluent τ-transitions in the latter state space produces the state space belonging to $a \cdot b \cdot \delta$.

Exercise 11.2.6. Apply τ-prioritization to all transition systems in examples 11.1.3 and 11.1.4. Which prioritized transition systems are branching bisimilar to their original? Is this in accordance with the theory?

11.3 Confluence and linear processes

The application of τ-confluence and τ-prioritization can give rise to tremendous reduction of a transition system while maintaining branching bisimulation equivalence. However, the techniques as presented up to now can only be applied if the transition system has been obtained first.

In this section we show how to define and prove τ-confluence on linear processes. When generating a state space from a linear process, τ-prioritization can be applied on the fly and consequently the generated state space can be much smaller than that generated without the use of confluence. We define τ-confluence in terms of linear processes that do not contain time as the use of time adds little. In figure 11.6 the situation is depicted.

Definition 11.3.1 (τ-confluence for LPEs). Consider a clustered LPE as defined in definition 10.1.6 without time. We call this LPE τ-confluent iff for all actions $a \in Act$, for all $d{:}D$, $e_a{:}E_a$, $e_\tau{:}E_\tau$ it holds that if $c_a(d, e_a) \wedge c_\tau(d, e_\tau)$ then

- Either $a = \tau$ and $g_a(d, e_a) = g_\tau(d, e_\tau)$,
- Or $c_a(g_\tau(d, e_\tau), e_a) \wedge c_\tau(g_a(d, e_a), e_\tau) \wedge$
  $f_a(d, e_a) = f_a(g_\tau(d, e_\tau), e_a) \wedge g_a(g_\tau(d, e_\tau), e_a) {=} g_\tau(g_a(d, e_a), e_\tau)$.

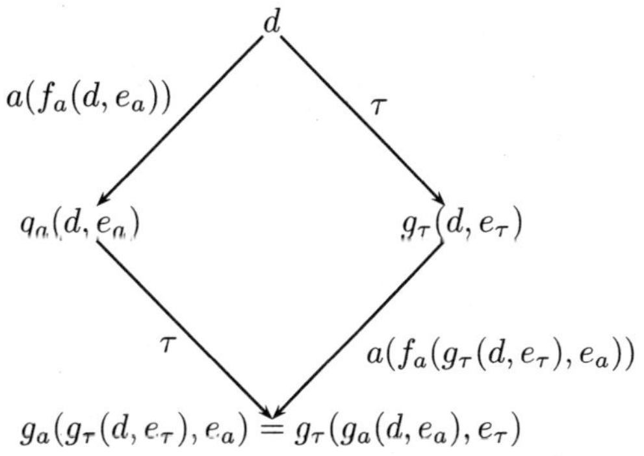

Figure 11.6: τ-confluence for a linear process

The conditions above are called the confluence formulas.

Example 11.3.2. We consider two unbounded queues in sequence of example 10.3.4 where the following process equation was derived:

$$\begin{aligned} X(q_1, q_2{:}List(D)) = & \textstyle\sum_{d:D} r_1(d)\cdot X(d \triangleright q_1, q_2) \\ & + (q_2 \not\approx [])\rightarrow s_3(rhead(q_2))\cdot X(q_1, rtail(q_2)) \\ & + (q_1 \not\approx [])\rightarrow \tau\cdot X(rtail(q_1), rhead(q_1) \triangleright q_2). \end{aligned}$$

We compute the confluence formulas.

1. Confluence for $a = \tau$. In this case we only write down the first part of the confluence formula, namely where $a = \tau$. Note that because this process has state variables q_1 and q_2, the conditions for the next state function g_a are split in two cases.

$$q_1 \not\approx [] \wedge q_1 \not\approx [] \Rightarrow (rtail(q_1) = rtail(q_1) \wedge rhead(q_1) \triangleright q_2 = rhead(q_1) \triangleright q_2).$$

2. Confluence for $r_1(d)$:

$$\begin{aligned} \forall d{:}D.(q_1 \not\approx [] \Rightarrow (& d \triangleright q_1 \not\approx [] \wedge \\ & d = d \wedge \\ & d \triangleright rtail(q_1) = rtail(d \triangleright q_1) \wedge \\ & rhead(q_1) \triangleright q_2 = rhead(d \triangleright q_1) \triangleright q_2)). \end{aligned}$$

3. Confluence for $s_3(rhead(q_2))$ yields the following formula:

$$\begin{aligned} q_1 \not\approx [] \wedge q_2 \not\approx [] \Rightarrow & \; rhead(q_1) \triangleright q_2 \not\approx [] \wedge \\ & q_1 \not\approx [] \wedge \\ & rhead(q_2) = rhead(rhead(q_1) \triangleright q_2) \wedge \\ & rtail(q_1) = rtail(q_1) \wedge \\ & rtail(rhead(q_1) \triangleright q_2) = rhead(q_1) \triangleright rtail(q_2). \end{aligned}$$

Using the definitions of the standard operators on lists, these formulas can be proven either straightforwardly or by induction. In example 11.4.1, we show how we can employ the confluence of these concatenated queues.

Exercise 11.3.3. Consider the following LPEs. In each case, show whether or not the confluence formulas for the τ-summand are true. If not, show a part of the generated transition system that is not τ-confluent.

1. $$\begin{aligned} X(n{:}\mathbb{N}) = {} & \mathit{even}(n) \to \tau\cdot X(n) \\ & + \mathit{true} \to a(n)\cdot X(n{+}2) \end{aligned}$$

2. $$\begin{aligned} X(n{:}\mathbb{N}) = {} & \mathit{even}(n) \to \tau\cdot X(n{+}1) \\ & + \mathit{true} \to a(n)\cdot X(n{+}2) \end{aligned}$$

3. $$\begin{aligned} X(n{:}\mathbb{N}) = {} & \mathit{true} \to \tau\cdot X(n{+}1) \\ & + \mathit{even}(n) \to a\cdot X(n{+}2) \end{aligned}$$

11.4 τ-prioritization for linear processes

If a linear process is τ-confluent, there are several ways to employ this information. The first one is by adding conditions to the linear process such that if a τ-action is possible, other actions are blocked. Concretely consider the following clustered linear process, which does not have time.

$$X(d{:}D) = \textstyle\sum_{a\in Act}\sum_{e_a:E_a} c_a(d,e_a){\to}a(d,e_a)\cdot X(g_a(d,e_a)).$$

We apply τ-prioritization to this process by adding the negation of $c_\tau(d,e_\tau)$ to every non τ-summand:

$$\begin{aligned} X(d{:}D) = {} & \textstyle\sum_{a\in Act\setminus\{\tau\}}\sum_{e_a:E_a} c_a(d,e_a)\wedge \\ & \qquad \neg\exists e_\tau{:}E_\tau.c_\tau(d,e_\tau){\to}a(d,e_a)\cdot X(g_a(d,e_a)) \\ & + \textstyle\sum_{e_\tau:E_\tau} c_\tau(d,e_\tau){\to}\tau\cdot X(g_\tau(d,e_a)). \end{aligned}$$

Just as with τ-prioritization for transition systems, this transformation of processes maintains branching bisimulation if the resulting transition system is τ-convergent.

Example 11.4.1. Consider the linear process from example 11.3.2 which was shown to be τ-confluent. Also note that this process is τ-convergent because the number of consecutive τ's that can be done is bounded by the size of q_1.

$$\begin{aligned} X(q_1,q_2{:}List(D)) = {} & \textstyle\sum_{d:D} r_1(d)\cdot X(d\triangleright q_1,q_2) \\ & + (q_2{\not\approx}[\,]){\to}s_3(\mathit{rhead}(q_2))\cdot X(q_1,\mathit{rtail}(q_2)) \\ & + (q_1{\not\approx}[\,]){\to}\tau\cdot X(\mathit{rtail}(q_1),\mathit{rhead}(q_1)\triangleright q_2). \end{aligned}$$

If we add conditions to apply τ-prioritization we obtain:

$$\begin{aligned} X(q_1,q_2{:}List(D)) = {} & (q_1{\approx}[\,]) \to \textstyle\sum_{d:D} r_1(d)\cdot X(d\triangleright q_1,q_2) \\ & + (q_2{\not\approx}[\,]\wedge q_1{\approx}[\,]){\to}s_3(\mathit{rhead}(q_2))\cdot X(q_1,\mathit{rtail}(q_2)) \\ & + (q_1{\not\approx}[\,]){\to}\tau\cdot X(\mathit{rtail}(q_1),\mathit{rhead}(q_1)\triangleright q_2). \end{aligned} \tag{11.1}$$

In other words, if q_1 is not empty, it is only possible to transfer data from the first queue to the second. Therefore, if data is received via r_1, it must immediately be forwarded using an internal action to the second queue. More concretely, the expression in equation (11.1):

$$(q_1 \approx []) \to \sum_{d:D} r_1(d) \cdot X(d \triangleright q_1, q_2)$$

is equal to (using equation (11.1)):

$$\begin{aligned}(q_1 \approx []) \to \textstyle\sum_{d:D} r_1(d) \cdot (d \triangleright q_1 \approx []) \to \textstyle\sum_{d':D} r_1(d) \cdot X(d' \triangleright d \triangleright q_1, q_2) + \\ (q_2 \not\approx [] \wedge d \triangleright q_1 \approx []) \to s_3(\mathit{rhead}(q_2)) \cdot X(d \triangleright q_1, \mathit{rtail}(q_2)) + \\ (d \triangleright q_1 \not\approx []) \to \tau \cdot X(\mathit{rtail}(d \triangleright q_1), \mathit{rhead}(d \triangleright q_1) \triangleright q_2).\end{aligned}$$

This simplifies to:

$$(q_1 \approx []) \to \sum_{d:D} r_1(d) \cdot \tau \cdot X(\mathit{rtail}(d \triangleright q_1), \mathit{rhead}(d \triangleright q_1) \triangleright q_2).$$

We can apply the first τ-law to this equation and substitute this back in equation (11.1), yielding:

$$\begin{aligned}X(q_1, q_2{:}\mathit{List}(D)) = {} & (q_1 \approx []) \to \textstyle\sum_{d:D} r_1(d) \cdot X(\mathit{rtail}(d \triangleright q_1), \mathit{rhead}(d \triangleright q_1) \triangleright q_2) \\ & + (q_2 \not\approx [] \wedge q_1 \approx []) \to s_3(\mathit{rhead}(q_2)) \cdot X(q_1, \mathit{rtail}(q_2)) \\ & + (q_1 \not\approx []) \to \tau \cdot X(\mathit{rtail}(q_1), \mathit{rhead}(q_1) \triangleright q_2).\end{aligned} \tag{11.2}$$

Thus, modulo branching bisimulation, the behavior of the process X in equation (11.1) is also characterized by the previous equation. Now note that for this equation the simple invariant $q_1 = []$ holds. Using this invariant we can show using CL-RSP with invariants that $\lambda q_1, q_2{:}\mathit{List}(D).Y(q_1 {+\!\!+} q_2)$ is a solution for X in equation (11.2) where Y is defined by

$$\begin{aligned}Y(q{:}\mathit{List}(D)) = {} & \textstyle\sum_{d:D} r_1(d) \cdot Y(d \triangleright q) \\ & + (q \not\approx []) \to s_3(\mathit{rhead}(q)) \cdot Y(\mathit{rtail}(q)).\end{aligned}$$

Therefore, we can conclude $Y([]) = X([], [])$. In section 12.2.1 we give an alternative proof of this equation using the cones and foci method.

11.4.1 Using confluence for state space generation

An effective way to use τ-confluence is to establish that a linear process is τ-confluent. Following an algorithm by Blom [33], it is then possible to generate a τ-prioritized state space, implicitly checking τ-convergence. If the linear process is not τ-convergent but has a finite state space, there is a τ-loop on which all the states are branching bisimilar. While generating the state space, all those states are taken together.

The algorithm of Blom applies the following three reductions when generating a state space.

1. It prioritizes confluent τ's. Thus, if a state s has confluent outgoing τ's, it selects one of them and ignores all other outgoing transitions.

2. The target state s' of the confluent transition found above is substituted for s (except if s is the initial state), which is allowed by Milner's first τ-law W‡. Note that the τ-transition is removed altogether in this operation. In order to detect the outgoing transitions of s, the outgoing transitions of s' are immediately investigated.

3. Note that the step above can be repeated indefinitely, if s' has an outgoing confluent τ-transition to a state with an outgoing confluent τ-transition. If the state space is finite, this must ultimately lead to a loop of τ-transitions. All the states on this loop are branching bisimilar, and hence can be taken together to one single state.

If this state space generation algorithm terminates, it yields a reduced state space which is branching bisimilar to the state space that would directly be generated from the linear process.

11.5 Historical notes

Confluence in process behavior has almost immediately been recognized as an important concept. It already occurs in Milner's seminal book [135]. In the context of verifying modal properties, τ-confluence is often called partial order reduction and it considers those actions that are not explicitly referred to in the modal properties as internal. It goes back to [175] calling it stubborn sets, [152] using the phrase ample set, and [74] using the phrase persistent set method. One of the earlier tools to employ partial order reduction is the SPIN model checker [104].

The approach followed in this chapter stems from [83, 88]. It differs from the partial order reduction technique in the sense that it does not require associated properties or modal formulas, but can be used directly on process behavior.

12

Cones and Foci

In this chapter we explain the cones and foci technique to prove an implementation of some system branching bisimilar to its external behavior. The main motivation behind the cones and foci technique is that it eases making such verifications. Alternative techniques such as applying RSP or establishing an explicit branching bisimulation relation between specification and implementation are not very feasible if it comes to actual system verification. It is often too hard to come up with the required process operator or relation. In this chapter we only consider processes without time.

12.1 Cones and foci

The main idea of the cones and foci technique is that in most implementations hidden events progress toward a state in which no useful internal calculations are possible anymore. We call such a state a *focus point*, as it is the focus toward which internal activity is directed.

The *cone* of a focus point consists of the states from which this focus point can be reached by a sequence of hidden actions, as shown in figure 12.1. Note that there are external actions a, b, c, and d at the edge of the depicted cone. These are used to leave the cone to some state in another cone. Once such an external action can take place, they can be executed in every subsequent state reachable by an internal step. In particular they can also be executed in the ultimate focus point; this is essential if one wants to apply the cones and foci technique, as otherwise the hidden actions in the cone would not be inert.

For the cones and foci method, an implementation is viewed as a set of cones, as depicted in figure 12.2. All states in each cone are related to some state in the specification. One can move from cone to cone using externally visible actions that directly match the actions in the external behavior.

We assume that an implementation and a specification of some system are given by clustered linear process equations. The process X is the implementation given by the following linear process equation. The set Act of actions does not contain the special internal action int. The reason for taking int instead of the internal action τ is that a

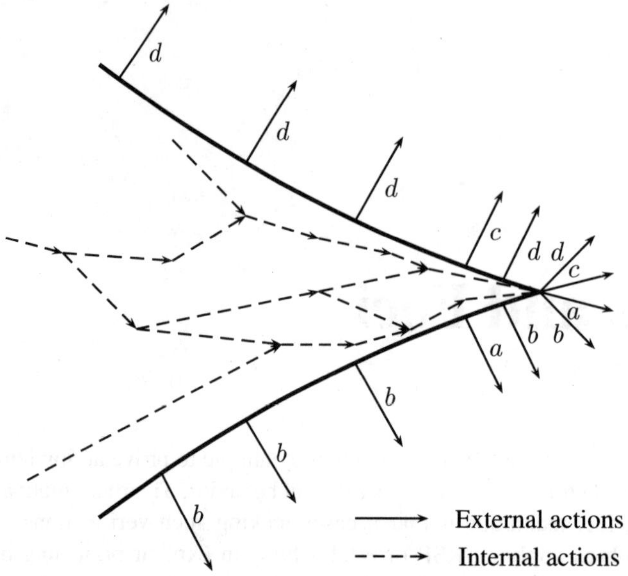

Figure 12.1: A cone with a focus point

linear process with τ-loops is not guarded, and does not have a unique solution.

$$X(d{:}D) = \sum_{a \in Act \cup \{int\}} \sum_{e_a : E_a} c_a(d, e_a) \rightarrow a(f_a(d, e_a)) \cdot X(g_a(d, e_a)) \tag{12.1}$$

The following equation gives the specification. Note that this process does not contain any *int*'s.

$$Y(d'{:}D') = \sum_{a \in Act} \sum_{e_a : E_a} c'_a(d', e_a) \rightarrow a(f'_a(d', e_a)) \cdot Y(g'_a(d', e_a)) \tag{12.2}$$

The process equations both have the same number of summands (except for the *int*-summand in the implementation), and in each summand the same sum operator is used. This is not a real restriction, as it is always possible to align the implementation and specification in this respect, but in concrete cases, it may require some work to do so.

In order to relate the states of the implementation D to the states of the specification D' we introduce a *state mapping* $h : D \rightarrow D'$. It maps all the states in a cone to a corresponding (bisimilar) state in the specification. For concrete examples this state mapping is generally quite easy to define, because it reflects the intuition of how the implementation and specification are related. In order to show that the state mapping is indeed a proper branching bisimulation relation, matching criteria must be proven, which are given below.

The endpoint of a cone is its focus point. We let a predicate $FC : D \rightarrow \mathbb{B}$ (*the focus condition*) indicate whether a state is a focus point or not. If there are no infinite

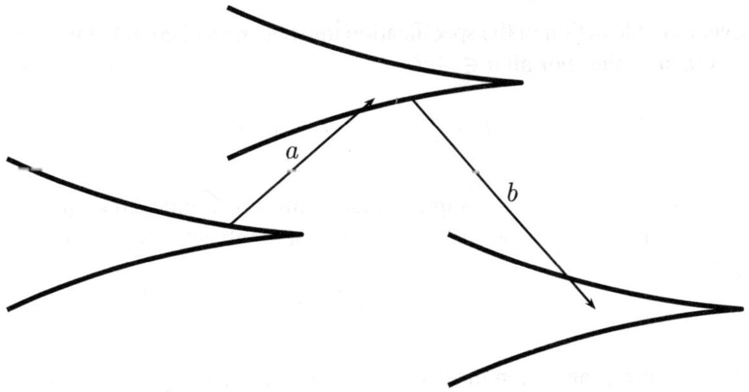

Figure 12.2: An implementation is a set of cones

sequences of internal actions, it suffices to let the focus points be exactly those states where no internal actions can be done. In this case it holds that

$$FC(d) = \forall e_{int}{:}E_{int}.\neg c_{int}(d, e_{int}).$$

If there are infinite internal sequences, the focus points must be chosen such that it can be shown that in every state that is not a focus point there is one internal transition that brings one closer to a focus point.

Generally, not all the states of the implementation are relevant (cf. figure 10.5). An invariant $\mathcal{I}$ can be used to restrict the state space of the implementation to the relevant part. Contrary to formulating the state mapping, finding the necessary invariants is often tedious and cumbersome. Fortunately, if the right invariants are found, it is straightforward to prove that the invariants satisfy the invariant property.

The state mapping h must satisfy a number of *matching criteria*, which ensure that the mapping establishes a branching bisimulation relation between the two LPEs in question, and moreover that all states in a cone of X are mapped to the same state in Y.

A state mapping $h : D \to D'$ satisfies the *matching criteria* if for all for $d \in D$:

1. If not in a focus point, there is at least one internal step such that the target state is closer to the focus point:

   $$\exists e_{int}{:}E_{int}.(\mathcal{I}(d) \wedge \neg FC(d)) \Rightarrow c_{int}(d, e_{int}) \wedge M(d){>}M(g_{int}(d, e_{int}))$$

   where M is a well-founded measure on D.

2. For every internal step, the state mapping h maps source and target state to the same state in the specification:

   $$\forall e_{int}{:}E_{int}.(\mathcal{I}(d) \wedge c_{int}(d, e_{int})) \Rightarrow h(d) = h(g_{int}(d, e_{int})).$$

3. Every visible action in the specification must be mimicked in the implementation in a focus point. For all $a \in Act$

$$\forall e_a{:}E_a.(\mathcal{I}(d) \wedge FC(d) \wedge c'_a(h(d), e_a) \Rightarrow c_a(d, e_a)).$$

4. Every visible action in the implementation must be mimicked in the corresponding state in the specification. This means that for all actions $a \in Act$ it must hold that

$$\forall e_a{:}E_a.(\mathcal{I}(d) \wedge c_a(d, e_a)) \Rightarrow c'_a(h(d), e_a).$$

5. When a matching action in specification and implementation can be done, their parameters must be equal. For all actions $a \in Act$ it is the case that

$$\forall e_a{:}E_a.(\mathcal{I}(d) \wedge c_a(d, e_a)) \Rightarrow f_a(d, e_a) = f'_a(h(d), e_a).$$

6. For all matching actions in specification and implementation, their endpoints must be related. Therefore, for all $a \in Act$ we have

$$\forall e_a{:}E_a.(\mathcal{I}(d) \wedge c_a(d, e_a)) \Rightarrow h(g_a(d, e_a)) = g'_a(h(d), e_a).$$

When the matching criteria are proven, the general equality theorem says that implementation and specification are branching bisimilar.

Theorem 12.1.1 (General equality theorem). Let X and Y be defined by equations (12.1) and (12.2). Let $\mathcal{I}$ be an invariant for X. If $h : D \to D'$ satisfies the matching criteria defined above, then:

$$\mathcal{I}(d) \Rightarrow \quad \tau{\cdot}\tau_{int}(X(d)) = \tau{\cdot}Y(h(d)).$$

This theorem also holds for weak bisimulation equivalence and then the τ at the left can be omitted. This situation is comparable to the situation with the KFAR rules in section 9.7.

Generally, this theorem is used for a concrete initial state d_0 for which the invariant is valid (i.e., $\mathcal{I}(d_0) = true$). In this case if there are no outgoing internal steps from d_0 in the implementation, the conclusion of the theorem can be strengthened to $\tau_{int}(X(d_0)) = Y(h(d_0))$ by omitting the leading τ's at both sides. This is valid in both weak and branching bisimulation.

Example 12.1.2. In figure 12.3 two processes are depicted, namely an implementation at the left and a specification at the right. In the implementation there are two cones ($\{s_1, s_2\}$ and $\{s_3\}$) with as respective focus points the states s_2 and s_3. There is a state mapping h that maps states s_1 and s_2 to state s_4, and state s_3 to s_5. Note that all mapping criteria are valid, showing that both the specification and implementation are branching bisimilar.

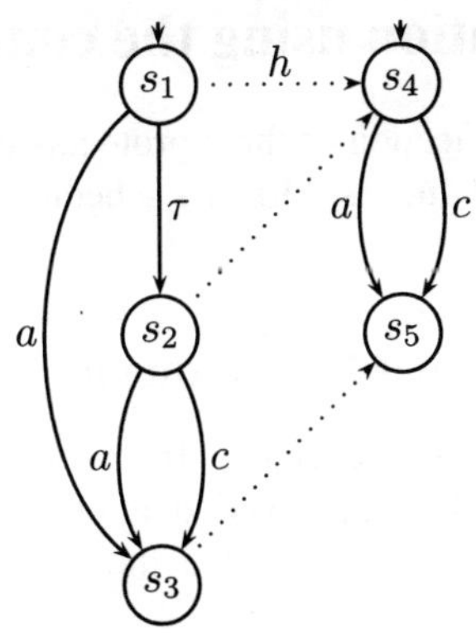

Figure 12.3: A simple pair of a specification and an implementation

Exercise 12.1.3. Let

$$\begin{aligned} X(n{:}\mathbb{N}) = \; & (n|_3{\approx}0){\rightarrow}a{\cdot}X(n{+}1) \\ & +(n|_3{\approx}1){\rightarrow}b{\cdot}X(n{+}1) \\ & +(n|_3{\approx}2){\rightarrow}int{\cdot}X(n{+}1), \\ Y(c{:}\mathbb{B}) = \; & c \rightarrow a{\cdot}Y(\mathit{false}) \\ & +\neg c \rightarrow b{\cdot}Y(\mathit{true}). \end{aligned}$$

What is a suitable focus condition for X with an associated well-founded measure? Give a state mapping $h : \mathbb{N} \rightarrow \mathbb{B}$ such that the matching criteria are satisfied. Prove that the matching criteria are satisfied.

Exercise 12.1.4. Let

$$\begin{aligned} X(n{:}\mathbb{N}) = \; & \textstyle\sum_{m:\mathbb{N}}(n{\approx}3m){\rightarrow}a{\cdot}X(n{+}1) \\ & +\textstyle\sum_{m:\mathbb{N}}(n{\approx}3m{+}1){\rightarrow}b{\cdot}X(n{+}1) \\ & +\textstyle\sum_{m:\mathbb{N}}(n{\approx}3m{+}2){\rightarrow}int{\cdot}X(n{+}1), \\ Y(c{:}\mathbb{B}) = \; & c \rightarrow a{\cdot}Y(\mathit{false}) + \neg c \rightarrow b{\cdot}Y(\mathit{true}). \end{aligned}$$

Transform the first process such that the cones and foci theorem can be applied directly.

Exercise 12.1.5. Let

$$\begin{aligned} X(n{:}\mathbb{N}) = \; & \textstyle\sum_{m:\mathbb{N}}(n{\approx}3m) \rightarrow a{\cdot}X(n+2) \\ & +\textstyle\sum_{m:\mathbb{N}}(n{\approx}3m{+}1) \rightarrow d{\cdot}X(n+1) \\ & +\textstyle\sum_{m:\mathbb{N}}(n{\approx}3m{+}2) \rightarrow int{\cdot}X(n+1), \\ Y = \; & a{\cdot}Y. \end{aligned}$$

Transform the first process such that the cones and foci theorem can be applied. Give a state mapping $h : \mathbb{N} \rightarrow \mathit{Nil}$ where Nil is a sort containing only one element. Formulate an adequate invariant $\mathcal{I} : \mathbb{N} \rightarrow \mathbb{B}$, valid for $n = 0$ and use it to show that the matching criteria hold.

12.2 Protocol verification using the cones and foci

In this section we present the verification of three protocols using the cones and foci technique, namely two unbounded queues, Milner's scheduler, and the alternating bit protocol.

12.2.1 Two unbounded queues form a queue

Consider the two unbounded buffers of example 10.3.4. The two connected queues have the behavior defined by the following linear equation, where the communication action c_2 is pre-hidden to int. We consider this to be the implementation.

$$\begin{aligned} X(q_1, q_2{:}List(D)) = \; & \textstyle\sum_{d:D} r_1(d)\cdot X(d \rhd q_1, q_2) \\ & + (q_2 \not\approx [])\to s_3(rhead(q_2))\cdot X(q_1, rtail(q_2)) \\ & + (q_1 \not\approx [])\to int\cdot X(rtail(q_1), rhead(q_1) \rhd q_2). \end{aligned}$$

The claim is that the behavior of this process is equal to that of a single queue. So, the specification is characterized by

$$\begin{aligned} Y(q{:}List(D)) = \; & \textstyle\sum_{d:D} r_1(d)\cdot Y(d \rhd q) \\ & + (q \not\approx [])\to s_3(rhead(q))\cdot Y(rtail(q)). \end{aligned}$$

In order to prove the two queues equal, we need to indicate a state mapping between the two queues of X and the single queue in Y. The queue q must be equal to the concatenation of the queues q_1 and q_2. This is formalized by introducing the state mapping $h : List(D) \times List(D) \to List(D)$ defined by

$$h(q_1, q_2) = q_1 {+\!\!+} q_2.$$

As the implementation X cannot exhibit an infinite number of int steps, we can take the focus points X to be those states where no int action is possible. That is,

$$FC(q_1, q_2) = q_1 \approx [].$$

It turns out that an invariant is not necessary for this verification. The matching criteria now say that we must show that:

1. The process equation X is int-well-founded. This has been shown in example 10.3.4.

2. The state mapping is preserved under internal steps:

$$q_1 {+\!\!+} q_2 = rtail(q_1) {+\!\!+} (rhead(q_1) \rhd q_2).$$

3. Every visible action Y must be mimicked in a focus point of X:

r_1: $\forall d{:}D. q_1 \approx [] \land true \Rightarrow true.$
s_3: $q_1 \approx [] \land q_1 {+\!\!+} q_2 \not\approx [] \Rightarrow q_2 \not\approx [].$

4. Every visible action in the implementation must be possible in the related state in the specification

   r_1: $\forall d{:}D.true \Rightarrow true.$

   s_3: $q_2 \not\approx [] \Rightarrow (q_1 \mathbin{+\!\!+} q_2) \not\approx [].$

5. The parameters of actions in implementation and specification must match:

   r_1: $\forall d{:}D.d = d.$

   s_3: $q_2 \not\approx [] \Rightarrow rhead(q_2) = rhead(q_1 \mathbin{+\!\!+} q_2).$

6. The endpoints of actions must be related.

   r_1: $\forall d{:}D.(d \triangleright q_1) \mathbin{+\!\!+} q_2 = d \triangleright (q_1 \mathbin{+\!\!+} q_2).$

   s_3: $q_2 \not\approx [] \Rightarrow q_1 \mathbin{+\!\!+} rtail(q_2) = rtail(q_1 \mathbin{+\!\!+} q_2).$

Note that most of the properties are trivial. Others must be proven using induction on the lengths of queues. From the general equality theorem we draw the conclusion that

$$\tau{\cdot}\tau_{\{int\}}(X(q_1, q_2)) \;=\; \tau{\cdot}Y(q_1 \mathbin{+\!\!+} q_2).$$

As there in no internal step possible in the implementation in the initial state (with $q_0 = []$ and $q_1 = []$), we can even conclude:

$$\tau_{\{int\}}(X([], [])) = Y([]).$$

12.2.2 Milner's scheduler

In section 10.2.16 the behavior of a scheduler was calculated for n individual cyclers. Here we show one of the two main properties of the scheduler, namely that the scheduler performs subsequent $on(k)$ actions for increasing k. This behavior is described by

proc $X(k, n{:}\mathbb{N}^+) = on(k){\cdot}X(k|_n{+}1, n);$

Thus, the theorem that we want to prove in branching bisimulation is

$$\boxed{X(1, n) = \tau_{\{d,off\}}(Scheduler(n, \lambda m{:}\mathbb{N}.if(m{\approx}1, 2, 1)))}$$

The scheduler calculated in section 10.2.16 is

$$\begin{aligned}
&Scheduler(n{:}\mathbb{N}^+, f{:}\mathbb{N}^+{\to}\mathbb{N}^+) = \\
&\quad \textstyle\sum_{k:\mathbb{N}^+}(f(k){\approx}2){\to}on(k){\cdot}Scheduler(k, f[k{\to}3]) + \\
&\quad \textstyle\sum_{k:\mathbb{N}^+}(f(k){\approx}3){\to}off(k){\cdot}Scheduler(k, f[k{\to}5]) + \\
&\quad \textstyle\sum_{k:\mathbb{N}^+}(f(k){\approx}4){\to}off(k){\cdot}Scheduler(k, f[k{\to}1]) + \\
&\quad \textstyle\sum_{k:\mathbb{N}^+}(f(k|_n{+}1){\approx}1 \wedge f(k){\approx}3 \wedge k{\leq}n){\to}d(k){\cdot} \\
&\qquad\qquad Scheduler(n, f[k|_n{+}1{\to}2][k{\to}4]) + \\
&\quad \textstyle\sum_{k:\mathbb{N}^+}(f(k|_n{+}1){\approx}1 \wedge f(k){\approx}5 \wedge k{\leq}n){\to}d(k){\cdot} \\
&\qquad\qquad Scheduler(n, f[k|_n{+}1{\to}2][k{\to}1]).
\end{aligned} \tag{12.3}$$

In order to apply the cones and foci theorem, we must make the sum operators in front of the visible actions equal. Therefore, we rewrite the linear process equation for X to the equivalent:

$$\textbf{proc } X(k', n{:}\mathbb{N}^+) = \textstyle\sum_{k:\mathbb{N}^+}(k{\approx}k') {\rightarrow} on(k) {\cdot} X(k|_n{+}1, n);$$

using a reverse application of the sum elimination theorem.

First we observe that there are two relevant invariants for the scheduler. The first one is that for all $j > n$, it is the case that $f(j) = 1$. The second one is that there is exactly one unique $j \le n$ such that $f(j) \in \{2, 3, 5\}$. Using this latter invariant we define $N(f)$ as follows:

$$N(f) = \begin{cases} k & \text{if } f(k) = 2 \text{ for some } k, \\ k|_n{+}1 & \text{if } f(k) \in \{3, 5\} \text{ for some } k. \end{cases}$$

The state mapping $h(n, f) = \langle N(f), n\rangle$ and the focus condition is $FC(n, f) = \forall j{:}\mathbb{N}^+.(j{\approx}N(f) \vee f(j){\approx}1)$. The matching criteria become:

1. All cyclers are forced to do an on step within a finite number of steps. Therefore, there cannot be a loop of internal steps in the scheduler.

2. This case deals with preservation of the state mapping by internal steps. It can be split into a number of cases for all internal summands:

   - $\forall k{:}\mathbb{N}^+.(f(k){\approx}3 \Rightarrow N(f) = N(f[k{\rightarrow}5]))$.
   - $\forall k{:}\mathbb{N}^+.(f(k){\approx}4 \Rightarrow N(f) = N(f[k{\rightarrow}1]))$.
   - $\forall k{:}\mathbb{N}^+.(f(k|_n{+}1{\approx}1) \wedge f(k){\approx}3 \wedge k{\le}n \Rightarrow N(f){=}N(f[k|_n{+}1{\rightarrow}2][k{\rightarrow}4]))$.
   - $\forall k{:}\mathbb{N}^+.(f(k|_n{+}1{\approx}1) \wedge f(k){\approx}5 \wedge k{\le}n \Rightarrow N(f){=}N(f[k|_n{+}1{\rightarrow}2][k{\rightarrow}1]))$.

3. $\forall k{:}\mathbb{N}^+.(N(f) = k \wedge FC(n, f) \Rightarrow f(k){\approx}2)$.

4. $\forall k{:}\mathbb{N}^+.(f(k){\approx}2 \Rightarrow N(f) = k)$.

5. $\forall k{:}\mathbb{N}^+.(f(k){\approx}2 \Rightarrow k = k)$.

6. $\forall k{:}\mathbb{N}^+.(f(k){\approx}2 \Rightarrow N(f)|_n{+}1 = N(f[k{\rightarrow}3]) \wedge n = n)$.

These matching criteria can straightforwardly be checked. Note that the invariants are made valid by the initial state. Also note that as the focus condition is valid in the initial state, and there are no internal steps possible for states where the focus condition holds, the initial τ's that come with the cones and foci theorem can be omitted and equality holds in both weak and branching bisimulation.

12.2.3 The alternating bit protocol

We consider the specification given in section 7.1 of the alternating bit protocol. This sections ends with equation (7.1) saying that the behavior of the alternating bit protocol ABP is equal to that of a simple buffer B. Here we prove this equation using the cones and foci technique.

The first step is to linearize the behavior of $\Upsilon_{\{c_2,c_3,c_5,c_6,i\}}(ABP)$, namely, the behavior of the alternating bit protocol where the internal actions are pre-hidden, i.e., renamed to the visible internal action int. The result of linearization is the following process equation:

$$
\begin{array}{l}
X(s_S{:}\mathbb{N}^+, d_S{:}D, b_S{:}\mathbb{B}, s_R{:}\mathbb{N}^+, d_R{:}D, b_R{:}\mathbb{B}, s_K{:}\mathbb{N}^+, d_K{:}D, b_K{:}\mathbb{B}, s_L{:}\mathbb{N}^+, b_L{:}\mathbb{B}) = \\
\quad \sum_{d:D}(s_S{\approx}1) \to r_1(d){\cdot}X(s_S{=}2, d_S{=}d) + \\
\quad (s_S{\approx}2 \wedge s_K{\approx}1) \to int{\cdot}X(s_S{=}3, s_K{=}2, d_K{=}d_S, b_K{=}b_S) + \\
\quad (s_K{\approx}2) \to int{\cdot}X(s_K{=}3) + \\
\quad (s_K{\approx}2) \to int{\cdot}X(s_K{=}4) + \\
\quad (s_R{\approx}1 \wedge s_K{\approx}3 \wedge b_R{\not\approx}b_K) \to int{\cdot}X(s_R{=}4, s_K{=}1) + \\
\quad (s_R{\approx}1 \wedge s_K{\approx}3 \wedge b_R{\approx}b_K) \to int{\cdot}X(s_R{=}2, d_R{=}d_K, s_K{=}1) + \\
\quad (s_R{\approx}1 \wedge s_K{\approx}4) \to int{\cdot}X(s_R{=}4, s_K{=}1) + \\
\quad (s_R{\approx}2) \to s_4(d_R){\cdot}X(s_R{=}3) + \\
\quad (s_R{\approx}3 \wedge s_L{\approx}1) \to int{\cdot}X(s_R{=}1, b_R{=}\neg b_R, s_L{=}2, b_L{=}b_R) + \\
\quad (s_R{\approx}4 \wedge s_L{\approx}1) \to int{\cdot}X(s_R{=}1, s_L{=}2, b_L{=}\neg b_R) + \\
\quad (s_L{\approx}2) \to int{\cdot}X(s_L{=}3) + \\
\quad (s_L{\approx}2) \to int{\cdot}X(s_L{=}4) + \\
\quad (s_S{\approx}3 \wedge s_L{\approx}3 \wedge b_S{\approx}b_L) \to int{\cdot}X(s_S{=}1, b_S{=}\neg b_S, s_L{=}1) + \\
\quad (s_S{\approx}3 \wedge s_L{\approx}3 \wedge b_S{\not\approx}b_L) \to int{\cdot}X(s_S{=}2, s_L{=}1) + \\
\quad (s_S{\approx}3 \wedge s_L{\approx}4) \to int{\cdot}X(s_S{=}2, s_L{=}1).
\end{array}
$$

The process *ABP* and the linear process X are related by

$$
\begin{array}{l}
\Upsilon_{\{c_2,c_3,c_5,c_6,i\}}(ABP) = \\
X(s_S{=}1, b_S{=}true, s_R{=}1, b_R{=}true, s_K{=}1, s_L{=}1).
\end{array}
\tag{12.4}
$$

For this linear process we can establish the following invariant properties that can straightforwardly be proven.

1. Out of $s_S{\approx}3$, $s_R{\approx}1$, $s_K{\approx}1$, $s_L{\approx}1$ exactly one does not hold.
2. $(s_K{\approx}2 \vee s_K{\approx}3) \Rightarrow b_S{\approx}b_K \wedge d_S{\approx}d_K$.
3. $(s_L{\approx}2 \vee s_L{\approx}3) \Rightarrow (b_L{\not\approx}b_R)$.
4. $s_S{\approx}1 \Rightarrow (b_S{\approx}b_R)$.
5. $(s_R{\approx}2 \vee s_R{\approx}3) \Rightarrow (d_S{\approx}d_R \wedge b_S{\approx}b_R)$.

The buffer can be described by the linear equation

$$
\begin{array}{rl}
B(d_B{:}D, b_B{:}\mathbb{B}) = & \sum_{d:D} b_B \to r_1(d){\cdot}B(d, false) \\
& + \neg b_B \to s_4(d_B){\cdot}B(d_B, true).
\end{array}
$$

Note that the sum operators of the visible actions match neatly, which means that we can directly apply the cones and foci method. The state mapping must map the sizable state vector of X to that of B. We select the contents of the buffer to be that of the sender. Thus, the state mapping maps d_S to d_B. Invariant 2 guarantees when the data is delivered in the implementation $s_4(d_R)$, that $d_R = d_S$.

The Boolean d_B is true when the buffer can read and false when it can write. In the implementation, reading is possible after data is delivered via $s_4(d_R)$, although some internal activity is needed before reading is actually possible. After the action $s_4(d_R)$, it is the case that $s_R{\approx}3$. At the next step of R, the variable s_R is set to 1 and the bit b_R is flipped (see the 9th summand of X). Using invariant 5 we see that from that point $b_S{\not\approx}b_R$. The bits are only made equal again when the reader receives an acknowledgment, in summand 13 of X, setting s_S to 1, indicating that it is ready to read. The situation where the alternating bit protocol is (eventually) willing to read is characterized by:

$$s_R{\approx}3 \lor b_S{\not\approx}b_R \lor s_S{\approx}1.$$

Thus, the state mapping becomes:

$$h(s_S, d_S, b_S, s_R, d_R, b_R, s_K, d_K, b_K, s_L, b_L) = \langle d_S, s_R{\approx}3 \lor b_S{\not\approx}b_R \lor s_S{\approx}1\rangle.$$

The focus condition is the situation where external actions are done. In this case we define the focus condition to be:

$$FC(s_S, s_R) = s_S{\approx}1 \lor s_R{\approx}2$$

as these are the situations where the process can read and write.

It is now straightforward to write down the matching criteria. We omit stating the invariant in each criterion as this would make the criteria unreadable:

1. It is tricky to provide a decreasing measure on the state space. It is more effective to look at the transition system of the ABP in figure 12.4. There it can be seen that there is always an internal step bringing one closer to the focus point, i.e., the situation where an r_1 or an s_4 must be done.

2. In this case we must show that no internal step has any effect on the state mapping h. As there are 13 internal steps, we must check the following 13 cases. The first part of each case is to show that the first part of the state mapping, d_S, does not change. This is trivial and therefore omitted, as d_S is only changed in the first summand with visible action s_4. Therefore, below we only concentrate on the second part. The cases where the right-hand side of the implication is the identity are omitted; we only deal with summands (2), (5), (6), (7), (9), (10), (13), (14), and (15).

$$
\begin{array}{l}
s_S{\approx}2{\land}s_K{\approx}1 \Rightarrow (s_R{\approx}3{\lor}b_S{\not\approx}b_R{\lor}s_S{\approx}1 = s_R{\approx}3{\lor}b_S{\not\approx}b_R{\lor}3{\approx}1).\\
s_R{\approx}1{\land}s_K{\approx}3{\land}b_R{\not\approx}b_K \Rightarrow (s_R{\approx}3{\lor}b_S{\not\approx}b_R{\lor}s_S{\approx}1 = 4{\approx}3{\lor}b_S{\not\approx}b_R{\lor}s_S{\approx}1).\\
s_R{\approx}1{\land}s_K{\approx}3{\land}b_R{\approx}b_K \Rightarrow (s_R{\approx}3{\lor}b_S{\not\approx}b_R{\lor}s_S{\approx}1 = 2{\approx}3{\lor}b_S{\not\approx}b_R{\lor}s_S{\approx}1).\\
s_R{\approx}1{\land}s_K{\approx}4 \Rightarrow (s_R{\approx}3{\lor}b_S{\not\approx}b_R{\lor}s_S{\approx}1 = 4{\approx}3{\lor}b_S{\not\approx}b_R{\lor}s_S{\approx}1).\\
s_R{\approx}3{\land}s_L{\approx}1 \Rightarrow (s_R{\approx}3{\lor}b_S{\not\approx}b_R{\lor}s_S{\approx}1 = 1{\approx}3{\lor}b_S{\not\approx}\neg b_R{\lor}s_S{\approx}1).\\
s_R{\approx}4{\land}s_L{\approx}1 \Rightarrow (s_R{\approx}3{\lor}b_S{\not\approx}b_R{\lor}s_S{\approx}1 = 1{\approx}3{\lor}b_S{\not\approx}b_R{\lor}s_S{\approx}1).\\
s_S{\approx}3{\land}s_L{\approx}3{\land}b_S{\approx}b_L \Rightarrow (s_R{\approx}3{\lor}b_S{\not\approx}b_R{\lor}s_S{\approx}1 = s_R{\approx}3{\lor}\neg b_S{\not\approx}b_R{\lor}1{\approx}1).\\
s_S{\approx}3{\land}s_L{\approx}3{\land}b_S{\not\approx}b_L \Rightarrow (s_R{\approx}3{\lor}b_S{\not\approx}b_R{\lor}s_S{\approx}1 = s_R{\approx}3{\lor}b_S{\not\approx}b_R{\lor}2{\approx}1).\\
s_S{\approx}3{\land}s_L{\approx}4 \Rightarrow (s_R{\approx}3{\lor}b_S{\not\approx}b_R{\lor}s_S{\approx}1 = s_R{\approx}3{\lor}b_S{\not\approx}b_R{\lor}2{\approx}1).
\end{array}
$$

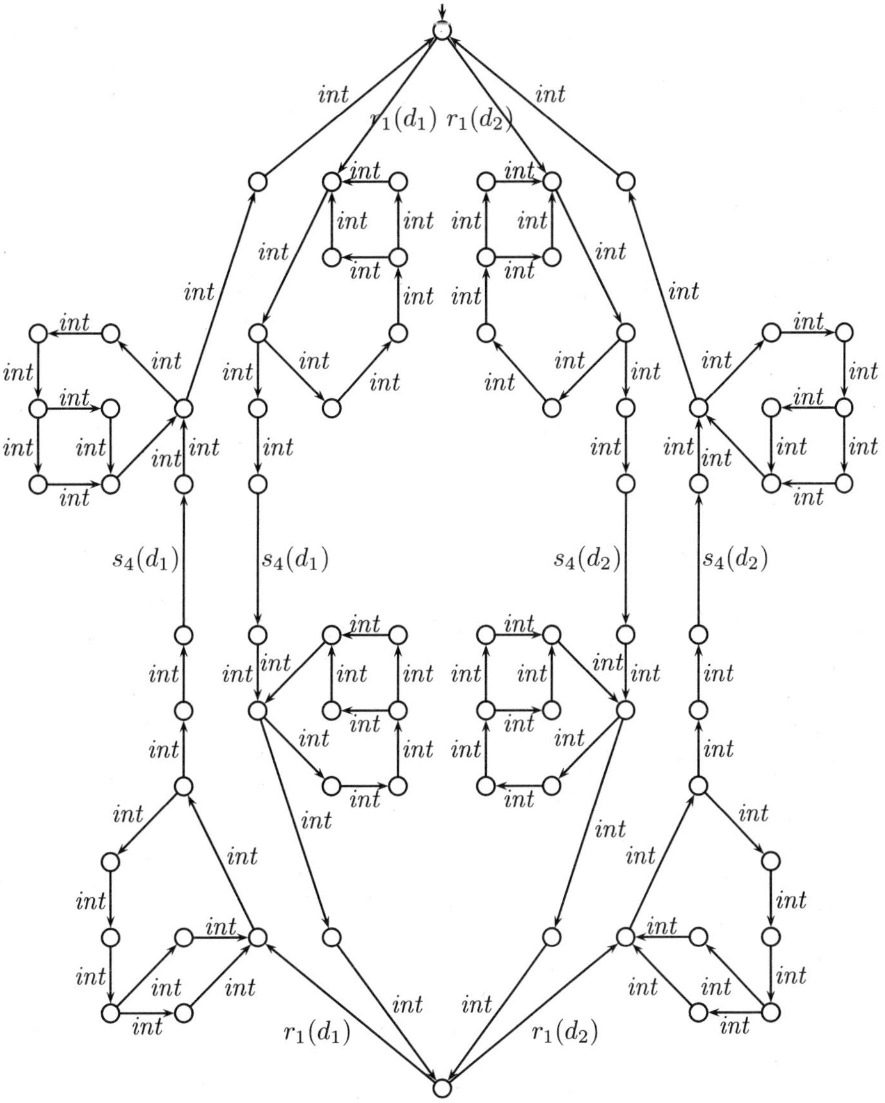

Figure 12.4: The state space of the alternating bit protocol

Almost all cases are trivial to prove. For instance, in the first case using that the condition provides that $s_S{\approx}2$, the right-hand side reduces to $s_R{\approx}3 \vee b_S{\not\approx}b_R = s_R{\approx}3 \vee b_S{\not\approx}b_R$, which is the identity.

The criterion for summand (9) reduces to

$$s_R{\approx}3 \wedge s_L{\approx}1 \Rightarrow (\mathit{true} = b_S{\not\approx}\neg b_R \vee s_S{\approx}1).$$

From invariant 1 it follows that $s_S{\approx}1$, making the right-hand side equal to *true*.

The case for summand (13) leads to the proof obligation

$$s_S{\approx}3 \wedge s_L{\approx}3 \wedge b_S{\approx}b_L \Rightarrow (s_R{\approx}3 \vee b_S{\not\approx}b_R = \mathit{true}).$$

From invariant 3 it follows that $b_L{\not\approx}b_R$. Together with the condition it follows that $b_S{\not\approx}b_R$, from which it is obvious that the proof obligation holds.

3. r_1. Using the focus condition this criterion becomes:

$$(s_S{\approx}1 \vee s_R{\approx}2) \wedge (s_R{\approx}3 \vee b_S{\not\approx}b_R \vee s_S{\approx}1) \Rightarrow s_S{\approx}1.$$

Suppose that the conditions would warrant the conclusion that $s_S{\not\approx}1$. Then from the first part of the condition $s_R{\approx}2$. From the second part it follows that $b_S{\not\approx}b_R$. But this is in contradiction with invariant 5.

s_4. We must show that

$$(s_S{\approx}1 \vee s_R{\approx}2) \wedge \neg(s_R{\approx}3 \vee b_S{\not\approx}b_R \vee s_S{\approx}1) \Rightarrow s_R{\approx}2.$$

From the second part of the condition it follows that $s_S{\not\approx}1$. From the first part we then conclude $s_R{\approx}2$.

4. r_1. This matching criterion is trivial to prove: $s_S{\approx}1 \Rightarrow (s_R{\approx}3 \vee b_S{\not\approx}b_R \vee s_S{\approx}1)$.

s_4. In this case the matching criterion is $s_R{\approx}2 \Rightarrow \neg(s_R{\approx}3 \vee b_S{\not\approx}b_R \vee s_S{\approx}1)$. Thus, $s_R{\approx}2$ must imply $s_R{\not\approx}3$, $b_S{\approx}b_R$, and $s_S{\not\approx}1$. The first case is trivial and the second case follows immediately from invariant 5. The last case is a direct consequence of invariant 1.

5. r_1. In this case we have a trivial matching criterion $s_S{\approx}1 \Rightarrow d = d$.

s_4. This matching criterion is a direct consequence of invariant 5 $s_R{\approx}2 \Rightarrow d_R = d_S$.

6. r_1. For this case we must prove equality for the first and the second argument of the buffer. So, this becomes:

$$s_S{\approx}1 \Rightarrow d = d,$$
$$s_S{\approx}1 \Rightarrow s_R{\approx}3 \vee b_S{\not\approx}b_R \vee 2{\approx}1 = \mathit{false}.$$

The first case is trivial. The second follows immediately from invariant 4 and 1.

s_4. In this case we must show

$$s_R{\approx}2 \Rightarrow d_S = d_S,$$
$$s_R{\approx}2 \Rightarrow 3{\approx}3 \vee b_S{\not\approx}b_R \vee s_S{\approx}1 = true.$$

which is fully trivial.

This finishes checking the matching criteria. Therefore, using the general equality theorem 12.1.1, we can conclude for state vectors where the invariant holds that:

$$\tau{\cdot}\tau_{\{int\}}(X(s_S, d_S, b_S, s_R, d_R, b_R, s_K, d_K, b_K, s_L, b_L)) =$$
$$\tau{\cdot}B(d_S, s_R{\approx}3 \vee b_S{\not\approx}b_R \vee s_S{\approx}1).$$

Hence, using equation (12.4), we can conclude for any d_S that

$$\tau{\cdot}B(d_S, true) = \tau{\cdot}\tau_{\{int\}}(\Upsilon_{\{c_2,c_3,c_5,c_6,i\}}(ABP)) = \tau{\cdot}\tau_{\{c_2,c_3,c_5,c_6,i\}}(ABP).$$

As a final touch, because ABP does not start with an internal action, we can even conclude for any $d_S{:}D$:

$$B(d_S, true) = \tau_{\{c_2,c_3,c_5,c_6,i\}}(ABP).$$

12.3 Historical notes

The cones and foci method was devised alongside attempts to prove the sliding window protocol in an algebraic fashion. It was provided for weak and branching bisimulation in [89]. The cones and foci theorem works well to prove correctness for most distributed algorithms and protocols, but the sliding window protocol required even more, see the verification in chapter 13. The original cones and foci technique has been improved by Fokkink and Pang [62], which also allows the use of time. The cones and foci technique has been used to verify various protocols, such as [81] (which was inspired by [46] claiming that no techniques were available to verify this protocol, also leading to an I/O-automaton verification in [174]), [168] and [10].

The cones and foci theorem is not suited in the case where the correctness of the protocol cannot be formulated as implementation equals specification, where equals refers to branching or weak bisimulation. In I/O automata, simulation equivalence is often used, using forward simulation relations and history variables to ease verification [115]. In case trace equivalence is required prophecy variables and backward simulations can be of use [2, 115].

13

★Verification of Distributed Systems

This chapter contains the verification of three more complex distributed algorithms using cones and foci. The first one is the *tree identify protocol*, which is a leader election protocol for a tree shaped network. Here we only consider the simple case without contention. The proof is taken from [168], where the more complex verification can also be found.

The second verification regards the sliding window protocol, as already introduced in section 7.2. This proof is a simplification of the proof in [10], which was a real tour de force. Fortunately, the proof in section 13.2 in no way reflects the hardship of finding the proof. The sliding window protocol is interesting for two reasons. In the first place it relies heavily on modulo calculations. In the second place, the sliding window protocol is the workhorse for the internet, and so everybody is continuously using this protocol.

The third verification is about the distributed summing protocol. This verification was published as [81]. The interesting aspect of this algorithm is that it is highly nondeterministic. This actually prompted some authors to claim that such nondeterministic algorithms cannot be proven correct in any effective and precise manner. Section 13.3 shows that this is not true.

13.1 Tree identify protocol

In this section we concentrate on the tree identify phase (TIP) of the IEEE1394 or Firewire protocol [107]. This is a rather simple protocol to determine a leader in a network that does not contain cycles. We assume that the nodes communicate directly with each other. The protocol and the proof are taken from [168]. This article [168] also contains a variant of the TIP protocol where the communication between the nodes is asynchronous. This introduces new problems, for which a root contention phase is required. In our setting, root contention does not occur.

We assume a network consisting of a collection of nodes and connections between nodes. The aim of the TIP is to establish a single leader of the network. This is done by establishing parent-child relations between connected nodes. Every node tries to establish exactly one node as its parent. As the network does not contain cycles, every node will ultimately have at most one parent, and exactly one node has no parent at all. This last node becomes the leader in the network.

In order to establish parent-child relations, a node sends a *parent request* to a neighboring node, asking that node to become its parent. A parent request from node i to node j is represented by the action $s(i,j)$, which communicates with the read action $r(i,j)$ to $c(i,j)$.

Each node keeps track of the neighbors from which it has not yet received a parent request. Initially this list contains all neighbors. If a node i is the parent of all its neighbors except for some node j, then i sends a parent request to j. In the case where a node received parent requests from all its neighbors, it is the only parent-less node in the network, and it declares itself the root of the network.

Below, the specification of a single node is given. The process $Node(i,p,s)$ represents node i in state s, with p as the set of possible parents.

$$
\begin{aligned}
\textbf{proc } & \mathit{Node}(i{:}\mathbb{N}^+, p{:}\mathit{Set}(\mathbb{N}^+), s{:}\mathbb{N}) = \\
& \textstyle\sum_{j:\mathbb{N}^+}(j \in p \wedge s \approx 0) \rightarrow r(j,i) \cdot \mathit{Node}(i, p - \{j\}, 0) + \\
& \textstyle\sum_{j:\mathbb{N}^+}(p \approx \{j\} \wedge s \approx 0) \rightarrow s(i,j) \cdot \mathit{Node}(i, \emptyset, 1) + \\
& (p \approx \emptyset \wedge s \approx 0) \rightarrow \mathit{leader}(i) \cdot \mathit{Node}(i, \emptyset, 1).
\end{aligned}
$$

The initial configuration S consists of the parallel composition of the node processes for the nodes $1,\ldots,n$ in state 0. The function $p_0 : \mathbb{N}^+ \rightarrow \mathit{Set}(\mathbb{N}^+)$ contains the neighbors. Initially, $p_0(i)$ contains the neighbors of node i.

$$
\textbf{proc } S = \tau_{\{c\}} \nabla_{\{c,leader\}} \Gamma_{\{r|s \rightarrow c\}} (\mathit{Node}(1, p_0(1), 0) \parallel \cdots \parallel \mathit{Node}(n, p_0(n), 0));
$$

Example 13.1.1. The network

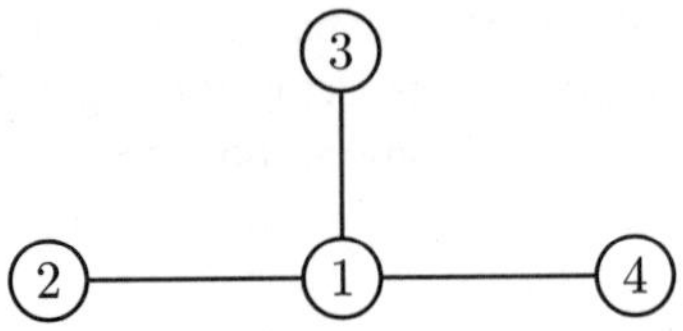

is described by

$$
\begin{aligned}
\textbf{proc } S = \; & \tau_{\{c\}} \nabla_{\{c,leader\}} \Gamma_{\{r|s \rightarrow c\}} \\
& (\mathit{Node}(1, \{2,3,4\}, 0) \parallel \mathit{Node}(2, \{1\}, 0) \parallel \\
& \mathit{Node}(3, \{1\}, 0) \parallel \mathit{Node}(4, \{1\}, 0));
\end{aligned}
$$

The external behavior of this system is given in figure 13.1.

Exercise 13.1.2. Explain why the τ-transitions in the external behavior depicted in Figure 13.1 are not inert.

Exercise 13.1.3. Consider the network

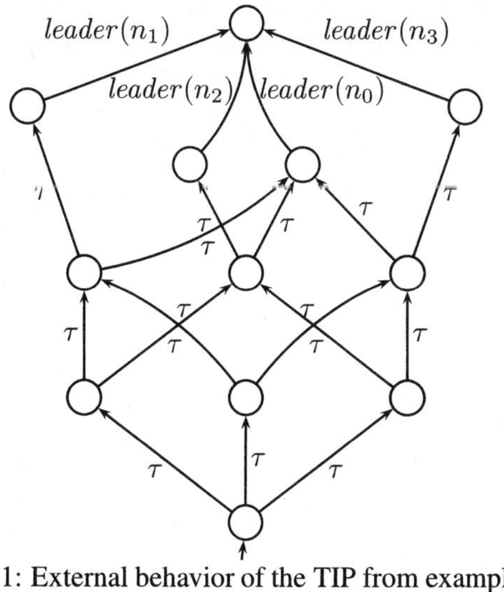

Figure 13.1: External behavior of the TIP from example 13.1.1

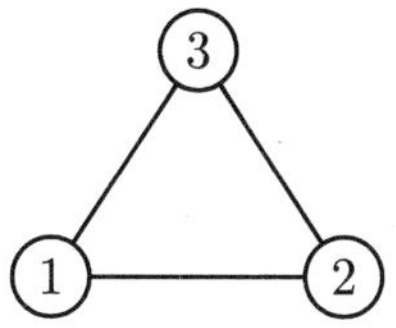

Give a specification of this network. Explain why in this case no root will be elected.

13.1.1 The correctness of the tree identify protocol

In this section we prove using the cones and foci technique that for all connected networks that are free of cycles, the tree identify protocol selects a single leader. For this purpose, a network is specified using the prehide operator.

proc $S_{TIP} = \Upsilon_{\{c\}} \nabla_{\{c,leader\}} \Gamma_{\{r|s \to c\}}(Node(1, p_0(1), 0) \| \cdots \| Node(n, p_0(n), 0));$

It is assumed that for all i and j

1. p_0 only contains nodes. If $i \in p_0(j)$ then $i \leq n$,
2. p_0 is symmetric, i.e., if $i \in p_0(j)$, then $j \in p_0(i)$,
3. All nodes are connected. I.e., for all nodes i and j there is a sequence of nodes $i = i_1, \ldots, i_m = j$ such that $i_k \in p_0(i_{k+1})$ for all $1 \leq k < m$, and
4. The network has no cycles. There are no infinite sequences $i_1, i_2, \ldots$ where $i_{k-1} \neq i_{k+1}$ for all $k > 1$.

The aim of this section is to show that the external behavior of this process, for any connected network without cycles, is $\tau \cdot leader \cdot \delta$. We use the equation for *Node* from the previous section, but remove the parameter of the action *leader*.

As we use the cones and foci method, it is necessary to write the specification as a linear process:

proc $Spec(b{:}\mathbb{B}) = b \rightarrow leader\cdot Spec(false)$;

Thus, we want to prove that $\tau\cdot S_{TIP} = \tau\cdot Spec(true)$.

As a first step, we use the parallel expansion in section 10.2.3, to transform S_{TIP} to a single linear process equation. This equation is given below where S_{TIP} is equal to $Y(n, p_0, \lambda i{:}\mathbb{N}^+.0)$.

$$
\begin{aligned}
&\textbf{proc } Y(n{:}\mathbb{N}^+, p{:}\mathbb{N}^+\rightarrow Set(\mathbb{N}^+), s{:}\mathbb{N}^+\rightarrow\mathbb{N}) = \\
&\qquad \textstyle\sum_{i,j:\mathbb{N}^+}(j{\in}p(i)\wedge p(j){\approx}\{i\}\wedge s(i){\approx}0\wedge s(j){\approx}0\wedge i{\not\approx}j\wedge i{\leq}n\wedge j{\leq}n) \rightarrow \\
&\qquad\qquad int\cdot Y(n, p[i{\rightarrow}p(i){-}\{j\}, j{\rightarrow}\emptyset], s[j{\rightarrow}1])+ \\
&\qquad \textstyle\sum_{i:\mathbb{N}^+}(p(i){\approx}\emptyset\wedge s(i){\approx}0\wedge i{\leq}n) \rightarrow leader\cdot Y(n, p, s[i{\rightarrow}1]);
\end{aligned}
$$

In order to apply the cones and foci theorem, the sum operators in the summands with visible actions need to be the same. Concretely, this means that the sum operator in front of the *leader* action needs to be replaced. We find that the equation for Y can be rewritten to:

$$
\begin{aligned}
&\textbf{proc } Y'(n{:}\mathbb{N}^+, p{:}\mathbb{N}^+\rightarrow Set(\mathbb{N}^+), s{:}\mathbb{N}^+\rightarrow\mathbb{N}) = \\
&\qquad \textstyle\sum_{i,j:\mathbb{N}^+}(j{\in}p(i)\wedge p(j){\approx}\{i\}\wedge s(i){\approx}0\wedge s(j){\approx}0\wedge i{\not\approx}j\wedge i{\leq}n\wedge j{\leq}n) \rightarrow \\
&\qquad\qquad int\cdot Y'(n, p[i{\rightarrow}p(i){-}\{j\}, j{\rightarrow}\emptyset], s[j{\rightarrow}1])+ \\
&\qquad (\exists i{:}\mathbb{N}^+.p(i){\approx}\emptyset\wedge s(i){\approx}0\wedge i{\leq}n) \rightarrow leader\cdot Y'(n, p, \lambda i{:}\mathbb{N}^+.1);
\end{aligned}
$$

We prove the correctness of this step using CL-RSP with invariants. For this purpose, we first list four invariants for Y, which are universally quantified over all positive numbers i and j:

1. If $j{\in}p(i)$ then $j{\leq}n$.
2. If $j{\in}p_0(i)$ then $j{\in}p(i) \vee s(j){=}1$.
3. If $s(j){=}1$ then $p(j){=}\emptyset$.
4. If $j{\in}p(i)$ then $j{\in}p_0(i)$.

We skip the proof that these are indeed invariants, as it is straightforward. Note that the invariants are valid in the initial state of the process, when $p = p_0$ and $s = \lambda i{:}\mathbb{N}^+.0$.

The following lemma says that if $p(i){=}\emptyset$, then all other processes j are not a candidate anymore to declare themselves a leader, i.e., $s(j){=}1$. Hence, this means that $s[i{\rightarrow}1]{=}\lambda i{:}\mathbb{N}^+.1$, from which it is immediately obvious that $Y(n, p, s){=}Y'(n, p, s)$.

Lemma 13.1.4. Provided the invariants 2 and 3 above hold, we find that for all positive numbers i and j:

$$(p(i) = \emptyset \wedge j \neq i) \Rightarrow s(j) = 1.$$

Proof. Consider two nodes i and j. By connectedness, there are distinct nodes $i = i_1, i_2, \ldots, i_m = j$ with $i_{k+1}{\in}p_0(i_k)$ for $k = 1, \ldots, m{-}1$. We derive, by induction on k, that $s(i_k) = 1$ for all $1{<}k{\leq}m$. In particular $s(i_m) = 1$, proving this lemma.

We start with the base case $k{=}2$. As $i_2{\in}p_0(i_1)$ and $p(i_1){=}\emptyset$, invariant 2 yields that $s(i_2){=}1$.

For the induction step, consider $k{>}2$. We know that $i_k{\in}p_0(i_k)$ and by the induction hypothesis $s(i_{k-1}) = 1$. So, $p(i_k) = \emptyset$ by invariant 3. Using invariant 2 we derive that $s(i_k) = 1$. □

We now performed the groundwork to make the essential step in proving implementation and specification equal to each other.

Lemma 13.1.5. For all $n{:}\mathbb{N}^+$, $p{:}\mathbb{N}^+{\to}Set(\mathbb{N}^+)$ and $s{:}\mathbb{N}^+{\to}\mathbb{N}$ for which the invariants hold, we find:

$$\tau{\cdot}\tau_{\{int\}}(Y'(n,p,s)) = \tau{\cdot}Spec(h(n,p,s))$$

where the state mapping $h : \mathbb{N}^+ \times (\mathbb{N}^+{\to}Set(\mathbb{N}^+)) \times (\mathbb{N}^+{\to}\mathbb{N}) \to \mathbb{B}$ is defined by

$$h(n,p,s) = \exists i{:}\mathbb{N}^+.(i{\le}n \wedge s(i){\approx}0).$$

Proof. In order to prove this theorem we must check the matching criteria. Note that only the third criterion is not trivial.

1. As by the invariant 1, each set $p(i)$ contains a finite number of elements, this number is reduced by 1 in each int step. Namely, for some positive numbers i and j, the condition says $j{\in}p(i)$ and in the result after the int j is removed from the set $p(i)$. Therefore, only a finite sequence of consecutive int steps is possible.

2. The second matching criterion yields the following awkward looking proof requirement.

$$\begin{array}{l}\forall i,j{:}\mathbb{N}^+.(j{\in}p(i) \wedge p(j){\approx}\{i\} \wedge s(i){\approx}0 \wedge s(j){\approx}0 \wedge i{\not\approx}j \wedge i{\le}n \wedge j{\le}n \wedge \\ \qquad \exists i'{:}\mathbb{N}^+.(i'{\le}n \wedge s(i'){\approx}0)) \;\Rightarrow\; \exists i''{:}\mathbb{N}^+.(i''{\le}n \wedge s[j{\to}1](i''){\approx}0).\end{array}$$

   But actually, the proof of this requirement is trivial by taking i'' equal to i. In this case we must show $i{\le}n$ (which is a premise), and $s[j{\to}1](i){\approx}0$. But as one premise says that $i{\not\approx}j$, this is equal to $s(i){\approx}0$, which is also a premise.

3. Note that all other matching criteria regard the $leader$ action only. For the third matching criterion we need to define the focus condition. As there are no infinite sequences of internal steps, we can take the negation of the condition for the internal step as the focus condition:

$$\begin{array}{l}FC(n,p,s) = \\ \forall i,j{:}\mathbb{N}^+.(j{\notin}p(i) \vee p(j){\not\approx}\{i\} \vee s(i){\not\approx}0 \vee s(j){\not\approx}0 \vee i{\approx}j \vee i{>}n \vee j{>}n).\end{array}$$

   The third criterion now says:

$$FC(n,p,s) \wedge \exists i{:}\mathbb{N}^+.(i{\le}n \wedge s(i){\approx}0) \Rightarrow \exists i'{:}\mathbb{N}^+.(p(i'){\approx}\emptyset \wedge s(i'){\approx}0 \wedge i'{\le}n).$$

   We prove this by taking i' equal to i. Hence, the only nontrivial conjunct that we must prove in the right-hand side of the implication is $p(i){\approx}\emptyset$. In order to obtain a contradiction, assume $p(i) \neq \emptyset$. We show that we can construct an infinite sequence $i_1, i_2, \ldots$ such that $i_{k-1} \neq i_{k+1}$ for all $k{>}1$ where each i_k has the property that $\{i_{k-1}, i_{k+1}\}{\subseteq}p(i_k)$. Note that this contradicts that p_0 has no cycles (invariant 4), proving that $p(i) = \emptyset$.

First we show that this property holds for i_2. Take $i_1{=}i$. As $p(i){\neq}\emptyset$, there is a $j{\leq}n$ such that $j{\in}p(i)$. From the focus condition and invariant 2 it follows that $p(j){\neq}\{i\}$. Take $i_2 = j$. Suppose $p(j){=}\emptyset$. Then $s(i){=}1$ via invariant 2, which is a contradiction. Hence, there is an $\ell{:}\mathbb{N}^+$ with $\ell{\neq}i$ and $\{\ell, i\}{\subseteq}p(j)$. Take $i_3{=}\ell$.

Now assume that the sequence above has been constructed up to some i_{k-1} for $k{>}2$. We show that the sequence can be extended up to i_k. Note that $i_k{\in}p(i_{k-1})$ and hence $i_k{\in}p_0(i_{k-1})$. By symmetry of p_0 it also holds that $i_{k-1} \in p_0(i_k)$. By invariant 2, $i_{k-1}{\in}p(i_k)$. Thus, $s(i_k){=}0$. By the focus condition it follows that $p(i_k){\neq}\{i_{k-1}\}$. Therefore, there is an additional node, call it i_{k+1}, such that $\{i_{k-1}, i_{k+1}\}{\subseteq}p(i_k)$, which is what we had to prove.

4. The fourth matching criterion is trivial by taking i' to be equal to i.

$$(\exists i{:}\mathbb{N}^+.p(i){\approx}\emptyset \wedge s(i){\approx}0 \wedge i{\leq}n) \Rightarrow \exists i'{:}\mathbb{N}^+.(i'{\leq}n \wedge s(i'){\approx}0).$$

5. The fifth matching criterion need not be checked, as the action *leader* has no parameter.

6. The sixth matching criterion is

$$(\exists i{:}\mathbb{N}^+.p(i){\approx}\emptyset \wedge s(i){\approx}0 \wedge i{\leq}n) \Rightarrow \exists i'{:}\mathbb{N}^+.(i'{\leq}n \wedge s[i{\to}1](i'){\approx}0) = \mathit{false}.$$

This is straightforward by taking i' equal to i. The expression $s[i{\to}1](i'){\approx}0$ in the right-hand side of the implication then becomes $s[i{\to}1](i){\approx}0$, which is equivalent to $1{\approx}0$, i.e., false. This proves the last criterion.

□

We can now wrap up the work and perform the final steps in the correctness proof of the tree identify protocol

Theorem 13.1.6 (Correctness of the tree identify protocol).

$$\tau{\cdot}\tau_{\{int\}}(S_{TIP}) = \tau{\cdot}\mathit{leader}{\cdot}\delta$$

Proof. Collecting the results provided in this section we get

$$\begin{array}{l}
\tau{\cdot}\tau_{\{int\}}(S_{TIP}) = \\
\tau{\cdot}\tau_{\{int\}}(Y(n, p_0, \lambda i{:}\mathbb{N}^+.0)) = \\
\tau{\cdot}\tau_{\{int\}}(Y'(n, p_0, \lambda i{:}\mathbb{N}^+.0)) \stackrel{13.1.5}{=} \\
\tau{\cdot}\mathit{Spec}(h(n, p_0, \lambda i{:}\mathbb{N}^+.0)) = \\
\tau{\cdot}\mathit{Spec}(\mathit{true}) = \\
\tau{\cdot}\mathit{leader}{\cdot}\delta.
\end{array}$$

Actually, if the network consists of a single node, then no parent requests are exchanged, so in that special case the external behavior is $\mathit{leader}{\cdot}\delta$. □

13.2 Sliding window protocol

In section 7.2, a unidirectional sliding window protocol is modeled and it is stated that it behaves as a bounded first-in-first-out buffer. More precisely, it is claimed that for any $n{:}\mathbb{N}^+$ and $q, q'{:}DBuf$:

$$\tau.FIFO([], 2n) = \tau.\tau_I(SWP(q, q', n))$$

where $I = \{c_2, c_3, c_4, c_5, i\}$.

In this section we prove this equation. This proof proceeds in three steps. First the description of the sliding window protocol is linearized. Then an alternative linear process is given which is almost the same as the linearized SWP, except that it does not use modulo calculation for the sequence numbers. We prove that this nonmodulo variant has the same behavior as the SWP. Finally, we show that the nonmodulo SWP is equal to the bounded buffer. We start out with some useful rules for modulo calculations.

13.2.1 Some rules for modulo calculation

Calculations with expressions involving the modulo operator $x|_n$ is very much simplified using the following properties (contributed to Gauß [178]).

1. $(x|_{nm})|_n = x|_n$;
2. $(x|_n + y)|_n = (x + y)|_n$;
3. $(x|_n \cdot y)|_n = (x \cdot y)|_n$;
4. $x|_n = x$ if $0 \leq x < n$;
5. $x|_n < n$.
6. $x = n(x \text{ div } n) + x|_n$.

Exercise 13.2.1. Prove $(1{+}x|_n)|_n = (1{+}x)|_n$.

Exercise 13.2.2. Show that $2013^{2013}|_5 = 3$.

13.2.2 Linearization

In this section we give the results of linearizing the sliding window protocol. First we provide the straightforward linearizations of the channels K and L from section 7.2.

$$
\begin{aligned}
\textbf{proc } K(d_K{:}D, k_K{:}\mathbb{N}, s_K{:}\mathbb{N}^+) = {} & s_K{\approx}1 \to \textstyle\sum_{d:D,k:\mathbb{N}} r_2(d,k)\cdot K(d,k,2)\\
& + s_K{\approx}2 \to j\cdot K(d_K,k_K,1)\\
& + s_K{\approx}2 \to j\cdot K(d_K,k_K,3)\\
& + s_K{\approx}3 \to s_3(d_K,k_K)\cdot K(d_K,k_K,1);
\end{aligned}
$$

$$
\begin{aligned}
L(k_L{:}\mathbb{N}, s_L{:}\mathbb{N}^+) = {} & s_L{\approx}1 \to \textstyle\sum_{k:\mathbb{N}} r_5(k)\cdot L(k,2)\\
& + s_L{\approx}2 \to j\cdot L(k_L,1)\\
& + s_L{\approx}2 \to j\cdot L(k_L,3)\\
& + s_L{\approx}3 \to s_6(k_L)\cdot L(k_L,1);
\end{aligned}
$$

As the protocols S and R are already linear, the following linearization of the sliding window protocol can easily be calculated.

$$
\begin{aligned}
\textbf{proc } & \mathit{SWP}(\ell, m{:}\mathbb{N}, q{:}\mathit{DBuf}, d_K{:}D, k_K{:}\mathbb{N}, s_K{:}\mathbb{N}^+,\\
& \qquad k_L{:}\mathbb{N}, s_L{:}\mathbb{N}^+, \ell'{:}\mathbb{N}, q'{:}\mathit{DBuf}, b{:}\mathit{BBuf}, n{:}\mathbb{N}^+)\\
= {} & \textstyle\sum_{d:D} m{<}n \to r_1(d)\cdot \mathit{SWP}(m{=}m{+}1, q{=}q[((\ell+m)|_n){=}d]) && (1)\\
& + \textstyle\sum_{k:\mathbb{N}} k{<}m \wedge s_K{\approx}1 \to \mathit{int}\cdot\\
& \qquad \mathit{SWP}(d_K{=}q((\ell+k)|_n), k_K{=}(\ell+k)|_{2n}, s_K{=}2) && (2)\\
& + s_K{\approx}2 \to i\cdot \mathit{SWP}(s_K{=}1) && (3)\\
& + s_K{\approx}2 \to i\cdot \mathit{SWP}(s_K{=}3) && (4)\\
& + s_K{\approx}3 \to \mathit{int}\cdot \mathit{SWP}(q'{=}\mathit{if}((k_K{-}\ell')|_{2n}{<}n, q'[(k_K|_n){\to}d_K], q'),\\
& \qquad \mathit{if}((k_K{-}\ell')|_{2n}{<}n, b[k_K|_n{\to}\mathit{true}], b), s_K{=}1) && (5)\\
& + b(\ell'|_n) \to s_4(q'(\ell'|_n))\cdot \mathit{SWP}(\ell'{=}(\ell'{+}1)|_{2n}, b{=}b[\ell'|_n{=}\mathit{false}]) && (6)\\
& + s_L{\approx}1 \to \mathit{int}\cdot \mathit{SWP}(k_L{=}\mathit{nextempty}_{\mathit{mod}}(\ell', b, n, n), s_L{=}2) && (7)\\
& + s_L{\approx}2 \to i\cdot \mathit{SWP}(s_L{=}1) && (8)\\
& + s_L{\approx}2 \to i\cdot \mathit{SWP}(s_L{=}3) && (9)\\
& + s_L{\approx}3 \to \mathit{int}\cdot \mathit{SWP}(\ell{=}k_L, m{=}m{-}(k_L{-}\ell)|_{2n}, s_L{=}1); && (10)
\end{aligned}
$$

The int in summand (2) comes from a c_2, the one in summand (5) stems from c_3, the one in summand (7) comes from c_5, and the one in summand (6) from c_6.

The following lemma relates the sliding window protocol as defined in section 7.2 to the linear variant given above.

Lemma 13.2.3. For all $q, q'{:}\mathit{DBuf}$, $k_K, k_L{:}\mathbb{N}$, $d_K{:}D$, $n{:}\mathbb{N}^+$ it holds that

$$\Upsilon_U(\mathit{SWP}(q,q',n)) = \mathit{SWP}(0,0,q,d_K,k_K,1,k_L,1,0,q',\mathit{empty},n)$$

where $U = \{c_2, c_3, c_5, c_6\}$.

13.2.3 Getting rid of modulo arithmetic

For the verification of the sliding window protocol the modulo calculation turns out to be a nuisance. Therefore, it is convenient to introduce an intermediate linear process M, which is obtained from that of the sliding window protocol by removing all wrapping of indices modulo n or modulo $2n$. This means that the sequence numbers and the indices ℓ and ℓ' can increase indefinitely. Furthermore, the data and Boolean buffers are assumed to be of unbounded size, as their positions are all used.

It is actually an understatement that the introduction of M is for convenience only. As it stands, it is not known whether a direct equivalence proof of SWP and $FIFO$ exists, without the use of an intermediate specification.

Obtaining the linear process M from that of SWP is at most places quite straightforward, except for summand (5). Here condition $(k_K - \ell')|_{2n}{<}n$ is replaced by $\ell' \leq k_K \wedge k_K{<}\ell' + n$. This last condition can be much easier understood than the corresponding condition in the sliding window protocol. It says that the value k_K must occur in the range $[\ell', \ell' + n\rangle$ of expected values in the receiver. This is actually also what $(k_K - \ell')|_{2n}{<}n$ says, but the encoding using modulo calculations is much trickier.

Note that in summand (6) it is not recorded that places in buffer b are freed again. As all indices in the buffer are monotonously increasing, this information is not of much use anymore.

In summand (7) the function $nextempty$ is used. This is the modulo free variant of the function $nextempty_{mod}$. Its definition is much easier. It gives the index of the first free position in b starting at position i within the first m next steps. Its definition for all $i, m{:}\mathbb{N}$, and $b{:}BBuf$ is

eqn $nextempty(i, b, m) = if(b(i) \wedge m{>}0, nextempty(i{+}1, b, m{-}1), i);$

Therefore, the defining equation of M is given by:

$$
\begin{array}{lr}
\textbf{proc}\ M(\ell, m{:}\mathbb{N}, q{:}DBuf, d_K{:}D, k_K{:}\mathbb{N}, s_K{:}\mathbb{N}^+, & \\
\qquad\qquad\qquad k_L{:}\mathbb{N}, s_L{:}\mathbb{N}^+, \ell'{:}\mathbb{N}, q'{:}DBuf, b{:}BBuf, n{:}\mathbb{N}^+) & \\
\quad = \sum_{d:D} m{<}n \rightarrow r_1(d)\cdot M(m{=}m{+}1, q{=}q[(\ell+m)\rightarrow d]) & (1)\\
\quad + \sum_{k:\mathbb{N}} k{<}m \wedge s_K{\approx}1 \rightarrow int\cdot M(d_K{=}q(\ell+k), k_K{=}(\ell+k), s_K{=}2) & (2)\\
\quad + s_K{\approx}2 \rightarrow i\cdot M(s_K{=}1) & (3)\\
\quad + s_K{\approx}2 \rightarrow i\cdot M(s_K{=}3) & (4)\\
\quad + s_K{\approx}3 \rightarrow int\cdot M(q'{=}if(\ell'{\leq}k_K \wedge k_K{<}\ell'{+}n, q'[k_K{\rightarrow}d_K], q'), & \\
\qquad\qquad b{=}if(\ell'{\leq}k_K \wedge k_K{<}\ell'{+}n, b[k_K{=}true], b), s_K{=}1) & (5)\\
\quad + b(\ell') \rightarrow s_4(q'(\ell'))\cdot M(\ell'{=}\ell'{+}1) & (6)\\
\quad + s_L{\approx}1 \rightarrow int\cdot M(k_L{=}nextempty(\ell', b, n), s_L{=}2) & (7)\\
\quad + s_L{\approx}2 \rightarrow i\cdot M(s_L{=}1) & (8)\\
\quad + s_L{\approx}2 \rightarrow i\cdot M(s_L{=}3) & (9)\\
\quad + s_L{\approx}3 \rightarrow int\cdot M(\ell{=}k_L, m{=}m{+}\ell - k_L, s_L{=}1); & (10)
\end{array}
$$

For M, a number of invariants represents the relations between the parameters of the process M. The proof of these invariant properties is straightforward. For this proof note that $\ell'{\leq}\ell + m$ and $k_L{\leq}\ell' + n$ follows from invariant 2 by definition from $nextempty$. Invariant 4 is only used to prove the validity of other invariants. Note that it is not at all trivial, if at all possible, to translate the invariant properties to the linear process SWP with the modulo calculation.

Lemma 13.2.4. The following invariants hold for M.

1. $m \leq n$

2. $\ell \leq k_L \leq nextempty(\ell', b, n) \leq \ell + m$

3. $\ell' - n \leq k_K < \ell + m$

4. $\forall i{:}\mathbb{N}.b(i) \Rightarrow i < \ell + m$

5. $\forall i{:}\mathbb{N}.b(i) \Rightarrow i < k_K + n$

6. $q(k_K) = d_K$

7. $\forall i{:}\mathbb{N}.b(i) \Rightarrow q(i) = q'(i)$

All invariants have a very clear intuition. Invariant 1 expresses that as m is the number of elements in q, it can at most be n. Invariant 2 expresses two properties. The first is that $nextempty(\ell', b, n)$ is confined between ℓ and $\ell{+}m$. In the protocol, ℓ can only be increased via an acknowledgment to $nextempty(\ell', b, n)$ and $nextempty(\ell', b, n)$ can only be increased via a message with index k_K, which never exceeds $\ell{+}m$. The second property says is that the value of k_L in the acknowledgment is always between ℓ and $nextempty(\ell', b, n)$. This is self evident as ℓ is only increased by getting the value of k_L, and k_L is only changed by assigning $nextempty(\ell', b, n)$ to it. All these variables are increasing.

Invariant 3 says that k_K lies between between $\ell'{-}n$ and $\ell{+}m$. Whenever a message is sent, k_K gets a value from ℓ up to $\ell + m$. While k_K is in transit, the value of ℓ' will always stay below $\ell + m$. In other words, $\ell'{-}n$ will stay below k_K.

Invariant 4 says that messages that have been transferred to R have sequence numbers lower than $\ell + m$. Hence, positions in buffer q at higher positions are not filled and $b(j) = \mathit{false}$ for $j > \ell + m$.

Invariant 5 says that if data with sequence number k_K is sent over channel K, a message with a sequence number of $k_K{-}n$ or lower will no longer be sent. Conversely, if there is a message in transit with sequence number k_K, the highest sequence number that a message in K ever had was below $k_K{+}n$.

Invariant 6 says that the contents of channel K matches the contents of q at position k_K. Similarly, invariant 7 says that the contents of buffers q and q' match for those positions that are filled.

We first show that the linearization of the SWP in which modulo calculation is used, is equal to the linear process M. This is proven using the cones and foci theorem, by taking M (with the largest state space) as the implementation and SWP as the specification. For the state mapping from the state variables of M to the state variables of SWP we introduce the auxiliary function mod. It takes the elements from a buffer q from a position ℓ to $\ell{+}n$ and maps these circularly onto the first n elements of a new buffer. The function mod is depicted in figure 13.2 and defined as follows:

Definition 13.2.5. For an arbitrary value $d_0{:}D$, the function mod is defined (for both $q{:}DBuf$ and $q{:}BBuf$) by:

$$mod(q, \ell, n) = \lambda k{:}\mathbb{N}.\mathit{if}(k{<}n, q(\ell{+}(k{-}\ell)|_n), d_0).$$

The following properties characterize precisely what the mod function is supposed to do:

Lemma 13.2.6. Let $q{:}DBuf$ or $q{:}BBuf$, $i{<}n$ and $(j{-}\ell)|_n = j{-}\ell$.

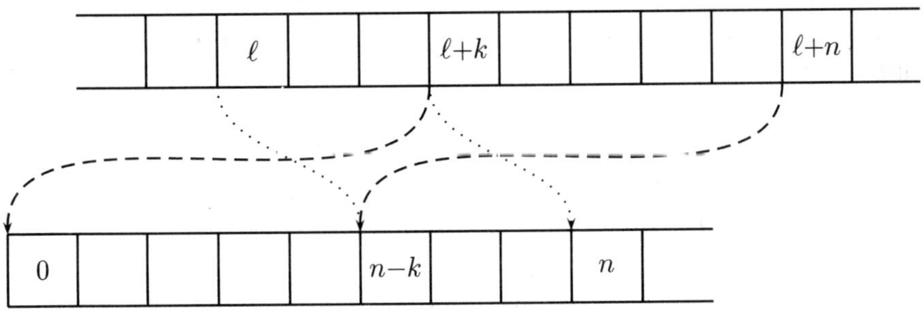

Figure 13.2: A visual representation of the function *mod* (with $\ell{+}k|_n = 0$)

1. $mod(q, \ell, n)((\ell{+}i)|_n) = q(\ell{+}i)$.
2. $mod(q[j{\to}d], \ell, n) = mod(q, \ell, n)[j|_n{\to}d]$.

Proof. The proofs are direct applications of the definition of *mod*.

1. $$\begin{array}{rcl} mod(q,\ell,n)((\ell{+}i)|_n) & = & if((\ell{+}i)|_n{<}n, q(\ell{+}((\ell{+}i)|_n{-}\ell)|_n), d_0) \\ & = & q(\ell{+}(\ell{+}i{-}\ell)|_n) \\ & = & q(\ell{+}i|_n) \\ & = & q(\ell{+}i). \end{array}$$

2. Expanding the definition of *mod* yields:

$$\begin{array}{l} \lambda k{:}\mathbb{N}.if(k{<}n, if(\ell + (k{-}\ell)|_n{\approx}j, d, q(\ell{+}(k{-}\ell)|_n)), d_0) = \\ \qquad \lambda k{:}\mathbb{N}.if(k{\approx}j|_n, d, if(k{<}n, q(\ell{+}(k{-}\ell)|_n), d_0)). \end{array}$$

If $k \geq n$ both sides yield d_0. So, we need to show that for all $k < n$:

$$if(\ell + (k{-}\ell)|_n{\approx}j, d, q(\ell{+}(k{-}\ell)|_n)) = if(k{\approx}j|_n, d, q(\ell{+}(k{-}\ell)|_n)).$$

This boils own to proving that $\ell + (k - \ell)|_n = j$ is equivalent to $k = j|_n$.

$\Rightarrow$) $j|_n = (\ell{+}(k{-}\ell)|_n)|_n = (\ell{+}(k{-}\ell))|_n = k|_n = k$.

$\Leftarrow$) $\ell + (k{-}\ell)|_n = \ell + (j|_n{-}\ell)|_n = \ell{+}(j{-}\ell)|_n = \ell + (j - \ell) = j$.

□

Using this definition we can state and prove the equality between SWP and M.

Lemma 13.2.7. For all variables $\ell, m, k_K, k_L, \ell'{:}\mathbb{N}$, $q, q'{:}DBuf$, $d_K{:}D$, $s_K, s_L, n{:}\mathbb{N}^+$ and $b{:}BBuf$ it holds that:

$$\begin{array}{l} SWP(\ell|_{2n}, m, mod(q,\ell,n), d_K, k_K|_{2n}, \\ \qquad s_K, k_L|_{2n}, s_L, \ell'|_{2n}, mod(q',\ell',n), mod(b,\ell',n), n) = \\ M(\ell, m, q, d_K, k_K, s_K, k_L, s_L, \ell', q', b, n) \end{array}$$

Proof. We use the cones and foci theorem to show that the SWP implements M. We use the following state mapping where at the left of the assignment we find the name for the variable in SWP in terms of variables of M at the right-hand side:

$$\begin{array}{lll} \ell := \ell|_{2n} & m := m & q := mod(q,\ell,n) \\ d_K := d_K & k_K := k_K|_{2n} & s_K := s_K \\ k_L := k_L|_{2n} & s_L := s_L & \ell' := \ell'|_{2n} \\ q' := mod(q',\ell',n) & b := mod(b,\ell',n) & n := n \end{array}$$

We find the following nontrivial matching criteria. Note that as there are no τ's, it is not necessary to prove τ-convergence. Moreover, there are no matching conditions of category 2.

3 and 4 (s_4). We must show that $b(\ell') = mod(b,\ell',n)(\ell'|_n)$. This follows directly from lemma 13.2.6.1.

6 (s_4). We must show that $b(\ell')$ implies $q'(\ell') = mod(q',\ell',n)(\ell'|_n)$. Use lemma 13.2.6.1 again.

6 (r_1). We must show for all $d{:}D$ that

$$mod(q[\ell{+}m{\to}d],\ell|_{2n},n) = mod(q,\ell,n)[(\ell|_{2n}{+}m)|_n{\to}d]$$

provided $m{<}n$. The right-hand side can be written as:

$$\begin{array}{l} mod(q,\ell,n)[(\ell|_{2n}{+}m)|_n{\to}d] = \\ \lambda k{:}\mathbb{N}.if(k{\approx}(\ell{+}m)|_n, d, if(k{<}n, q(\ell{+}(k{-}\ell)|_n), d_0) = \\ \lambda k{:}\mathbb{N}.if(k{<}n, if(k{\approx}(\ell{+}m)|_n, d, q(\ell{+}(k{-}\ell)|_n), d_0). \end{array}$$

The left-hand side can be expanded to

$$\begin{array}{l} mod(q[(\ell{+}m){\to}d],\ell,n) = \\ \lambda k{:}\mathbb{N}.if(k{<}n, if(\ell{+}(k{-}\ell)|_n{\approx}\ell{+}m, d, q(\ell{+}(k{-}\ell)|_n), d_0). \end{array}$$

Obviously, both resulting expressions are equal if $k = (\ell{+}m)|_n$ iff $\ell{+}(k{-}\ell)|_n = \ell{+}m$ provided that $k < n$. We prove this by implication in both directions.

⇒) Suppose $k = (\ell + m)|_n$. Then

$$\ell + (k-\ell)|_n = \ell + (\ell + m - \ell)|_n = \ell + m|_n = \ell + m$$

where in the last step we used that $m < n$.

⇐) If $\ell + (k-\ell)|_n = \ell + m$, then $m = (k-\ell)|_n$. So,

$$(\ell + m)|_n = (\ell + (k-\ell)|_n)|_n = (\ell + k - \ell)|_n = k|_n = k$$

using in the last step that $k < n$.

6 (summand 2). In this case we must show that for all $k{:}\mathbb{N}$ if $k < m$ that the following two properties hold

1. $(\ell + k)|_{2n} = (\ell|_{2n} + k)|_{2n}$, which follows directly by modulo calculation.

2. We must show that $q(\ell{+}k) = mod(q, \ell, n)(\ell|_{2n}{+}k)|_n$. This is lemma 13.2.6.1, which can be applied as $k{<}n$. This follows from invariant 1 and $k{<}m$.

6 (summand 5). In this case we must show that

$$\begin{aligned}&\mathit{if}(\ell'{\leq}k_K \wedge k_K{<}\ell'{+}n, mod(q'[k_K{\to}d_K], \ell', n), mod(q', \ell', n)) = \\ &\qquad \mathit{if}((k_K|_{2n}{-}\ell'|_{2n})|_{2n}{<}n, mod(q', \ell', n)[k_K|_n{\to}d_K], mod(q', \ell', n)).\end{aligned}$$

By invariants 1, 2, and 3 we find that $\ell' - n \leq k_K < \ell + m \leq k_L + m \leq \ell' + n + m \leq \ell' + 2n$. This means that the conditions $\ell' \leq k_K \wedge k_K < \ell' + n$ and $(k_K - \ell')|_{2n} < n$ are equivalent. Moreover, the else parts are the same. By lemma 13.2.6.2 it follows that the then parts are equivalent, too.

6 (s_4). Given that $b(\ell')$ holds, we must show the following two properties:

1. $(\ell'{+}1)|_{2n} = (\ell'|_{2n}{+}1)|_{2n}$, which follows directly from modulo calculation.

2. $mod(b, \ell'{+}1, n) = mod(b, \ell', n)[\ell'|_n{\to}\mathit{false}]$. Expansions of *mod* in this equation yields:

$$\begin{aligned}&\lambda k{:}\mathbb{N}.\mathit{if}(k{<}n, b(\ell'{+}1 + (k{-}\ell'{-}1)|_n), \mathit{true}) = \\ &\qquad \lambda k{:}\mathbb{N}.\mathit{if}(k{\approx}\ell'|_n, \mathit{false}, \mathit{if}(k{<}n, b(\ell'{+}(k{-}\ell')|_n), \mathit{true})).\end{aligned} \tag{13.1}$$

We consider the following three cases:

(a) Suppose $k \geq n$. Both sides yield true and hence equation (13.1) holds.

(b) Suppose $k = \ell'|_n$. The right-hand side of equation (13.1) is false. The left-hand side reduces to $b(\ell' + 1 + (\ell'|_n - \ell' - 1)|_n) = b(\ell' + 1 + n - 1) = b(\ell' + n)$. Using invariant 1 and 4 it follows that $b(\ell' + n) = \mathit{false}$.

(c) If $k{<}n$ and $k{\neq}\ell'|_n$. Equation (13.1) reduces to $b(\ell' + 1 + (k{-}\ell'{-}1)|_n) = b(\ell' + (k - \ell')|_n)$, which are equal.

6 (summand 7). We must show that

$$\mathit{nextempty}(\ell', b, m)|_{2n} = \mathit{nextempty}_{mod}(\ell'|_{2n}, mod(b, \ell', n), m, n)$$

with $m = n$. We show this equation by induction on m, for all b, ℓ', n.

If $m{=}0$, both sides of the equation reduce to $\ell'|_{2n}$. If $m{>}0$, we see that the equation becomes:

$$\begin{aligned}&\mathit{if}(b(\ell'), \mathit{nextempty}(\ell' + 1, b, m - 1), \ell')|_{2n} = \\ &\qquad \mathit{if}(mod(b, \ell', n)(\ell'|_n), \mathit{nextempty}_{mod}((\ell'{+}1)|_{2n}, mod(b, \ell', n), m{-}1, n), \ell'|_{2n}).\end{aligned}$$

As $mod(b, \ell', n)(\ell'|_n) = b(\ell')$, it suffices to show that

$$\mathit{nextempty}(\ell'{+}1, b, m{-}1)|_{2n} = \mathit{nextempty}_{mod}((\ell'{+}1)|_{2n}, mod(b, \ell', n), m{-}1, n).$$

This follows from the induction hypothesis.

6 (summand 10). And finally, we must show that $m + \ell - k_L = m - (k_L - \ell)|_{2n}$. Observe that by invariants 13.2.4.1, and 13.2.4.2, it holds that

$$0 \leq k_L - \ell \leq \ell + m - \ell \leq n.$$

Thus, $k_L - \ell \leq n < 2n$ and hence $(k_L - \ell)|_{2n} = k_L - \ell$, from which the proof obligation follows directly.

□

13.2.4 Proving the nonmodulo sliding window protocol equal to a first-in-first-out queue

We prove that M is branching bisimilar to the FIFO queue of size $2n$, using the cones and foci theorem. For this, it is useful to define the following auxiliary notation:

$$q[i..j\rangle = [q(i), q(i+1), \ldots, q(j-1)].$$

If $j \leq i$, this is the empty queue. Note that if $j \geq i$ then $\#q[i..j\rangle = j - i$.

The state mapping h, which maps the states of M to the states of *FIFO* (see section 7.2), is defined by:

$$\begin{array}{l} h(\ell, m, q, d_K, k_K, s_K, k_L, s_L, \ell', q', b, n) = \\ \quad q'[\ell'..\mathit{nextempty}(\ell', b, n)\rangle \mathbin{++} q[\mathit{nextempty}(\ell', b, n)..\ell{+}m\rangle. \end{array}$$

Intuitively, h collects the data elements in the sending and receiving windows, starting at the first cell in the receiving window (i.e., ℓ') until the first empty cell in this window, and then continuing with the sending window until the first empty cell in that window at position $\ell{+}m$. Note that h is independent of d_K, k_K, s_K, k_L, and s_L; we therefore write $h(\ell, m, q, \ell', q', b, n)$.

The focus points are those states where either the sending window is empty (in which case $\ell{=}m$), or the receiving window is full and all data elements in the receiving window have been acknowledged (meaning that $\ell = \ell' + n$). This exactly characterizes the situation where no internal progress is possible in the sliding window protocol. Therefore, the focus condition for M is defined by the following expression:

$$FC(\ell, m, q, d_K, k_K, s_K, k_L, s_L, \ell', q', b, n) = \ell{\approx}m \lor \ell{\approx}\ell'{+}n.$$

Lemma 13.2.8. For all $\ell, m{:}\mathbb{N}$, $n{:}\mathbb{N}^+$, $q, q'{:}\mathit{DBuf}$ and $d{:}D$ it holds that

$$\tau.\tau_{\{int,i\}}(M(\ell, 0, q, d, 1, m, 1, \ell, q', \mathit{empty}, n)) = \tau.\mathit{FIFO}([], 2n).$$

Proof. First note that the theorem holds for the initial state. According to the cones and foci method, we obtain the following matching criteria. Trivial matching criteria are left out.

1. From any reachable state of M, a focus point can be reached.
2. If $\ell' \leq k_K \land k_K < \ell' + n$ then

$$h(\ell, m, q, \ell', q'[k_K{\to}d_k], b[k_K{\to}\mathit{true}], n) = h(\ell, m, q, \ell', q', b, n).$$

3 (r_1). If $m < n$ then $\#h(\ell, m, q, \ell', q', b, n) < 2n$.

3 (s_4). If $b(\ell')$ then $\#h(\ell, m, q, \ell', q', b, n) > 0$.

4 (r_1). If $(m{\approx}0 \vee \ell{\approx}\ell' + n) \wedge \#h(\ell, m, q, \ell', q', b, n) < 2n$ then $m < n$.

4 (s_4). If $(m{\approx}0 \vee \ell{\approx}\ell' + n) \wedge \#h(\ell, m, q, \ell', q', b, n) > 0$ then $b(\ell')$.

5 (s_4). If $b(\ell')$ then $q'(\ell') = \mathit{head}(h(\ell, m, q, \ell', q', b, n))$.

6 (r_1). If $m{<}n$ then $h(\ell, m{+}1, q[(\ell{+}m){\to}d], \ell', q', b, n) = h(\ell, m, q, \ell', q', b, n){\rhd}d$.

6 (s_4). If $b(\ell')$ then $h(\ell, m, q, \ell' + 1, q', b, n) = \mathit{tail}(h(\ell, m, q, \ell', q', b, n))$.

Below we give the proofs of all these criteria:

1. We show that from any reachable state we can decrease

$$\min(m, \ell' + n - \ell) \tag{13.2}$$

to 0. If this expression has reached 0, a focus point has been reached. Due to invariant 2 and the definition of *nextempty*, the expression $\min(m, \ell' + n - \ell)$ cannot become smaller than 0.

Suppose that we are in a state where $\min(m, \ell' + n - \ell) > 0$. This means that there is unacknowledged data ready to be sent to the receiver ($m{>}0$) and not all data sent to the receiver is received and/or acknowledged ($\ell'{+}n{>}\ell$).

Assume first that $\mathit{nextempty}(\ell', b, n) = \ell$. This means that all data has been acknowledged but data in the sending buffer has not yet been received. In particular the data at position $\ell + 1$ did not arrive. We show that this data can be sent to the other side, causing the situation where $\mathit{nextempty}(\ell', b, n) > \ell$ (and we deal with that later).

Note that in order to send data from the sender to receiver, we need the channel K. The channel can be in one of the following three states: $s_K = 1$, $s_K = 2$, and $s_K = 3$. If $s_K = 1$ (or $s_K = 2$) we can carry out summands (3), (2) (with $k = 0$), (4), and (5) of M. Summand (5) can be carried out as its condition in this case is $\ell' \leq \ell \wedge \ell < \ell' + n$. The first part of this condition holds by definition of *nextempty* as $\ell = \mathit{nextempty}(\ell', b, n) \geq \ell'$. The second part is a direct consequence of the assumption that expression (13.2) is larger than 0. After executing summand (5), $b(\ell) = \mathit{true}$. So, $\mathit{nextempty}(\ell', b, n) > \ell$.

If $s_K = 3$, then the first summand (5) or (6) must be executed, and subsequently, the same sequence as above, also leading to the situation where $\mathit{nextempty}(\ell', b, n) > \ell$.

Now, consider the situation where $\mathit{nextempty}(\ell', b, n) > \ell$. This means that not all data has been acknowledged. For sending the acknowledgment back, channel L must be used. The state variable s_L of channel L can have the values 1, 2, and 3. If $s_L = 1$ (or $s_L = 2$), we can carry out summands (8), (7), (9), and (10) of M and set m to $m + \ell - \mathit{nextempty}(\ell', b, n)$ and ℓ to $\mathit{nextempty}(\ell', b, n)$. As $\ell < \mathit{nextempty}(\ell', b, n)$, the value of m and $\ell' + n - \ell$ are decreased. Hence, expression (13.2) is decreased.

If $s_L = 3$, we can use a similar argument to show that expression (13.2) can be decreased.

2. The expression $h(\ell, m, q, \ell', q'[k_K{\to}d_K], b[k_K{\to}\mathit{true}], n)$ is equal to

$$q'[k_K{\to}d_K][\ell'..\mathit{nextempty}(\ell', b[k_K{\to}\mathit{true}], n)\rangle{+\!\!+}\; q[\mathit{nextempty}(\ell', b[k_K{\to}\mathit{true}], n)..m + \ell\rangle.$$

Or in other words

$$[q'[k_K{\to}d_K](\ell'),\ldots,q'[k_K{\to}d_K](nextempty(\ell',b[k_K{\to}true],n)-1),\\ q(nextempty(\ell',b[k_K{\to}true],n),\ldots,q(\ell+m-1)]). \tag{13.3}$$

This must be equal to $h(\ell,m,q,\ell',q',b,n)$, which can be written as:

$$[q'(\ell'),\ldots,q'(nextempty(\ell',b,n){-}1),\\ q(nextempty(\ell',b,n)),\ldots,q(\ell{+}m{-}1)]. \tag{13.4}$$

As $nextempty(\ell',b[k_K{\to}true],n) \geq nextempty(\ell',b,n)$ the expressions (13.3) and (13.4) are equal if we can show that

$$q'[k_K{\to}d_K](i){=}q(i) \tag{13.5}$$

for all $nextempty(\ell',b,n){\leq}i{<}nextempty(\ell',b[k_K{\to}true],n)$. For $i \neq k_K$ we know that $b(i)$ must hold. So, by invariant 7 we see that equation (13.5) holds.

If $i = k_K$, equation (13.5) boils down to $d_K = q(k_K)$. This is exactly invariant 6.

3 (r_1). We see that $\#h(\ell,m,q,\ell',q',b,n) = m+\ell-\ell' < n+\ell-\ell' < 2n$ where the first inequality follows from the condition and the second from invariants 2 and the definition of $nextempty$.

3 (s_4). If $b(\ell')$ holds, $nextempty(\ell',b,n) > \ell'$. Hence, $\#h(\ell,m,q,\ell',q',b,n) > 0$.

4 (r_1). If $m{\approx}0$ this trivially holds as $n > 0$. If $\ell{\approx}\ell'+n$, we use that

$$\#h(\ell,m,q,\ell',q',b,n) = m+\ell-\ell' < 2n.$$

Therefore, $m+n < 2n$ or in other words $m < n$.

4 (s_4). As $\#h(\ell,m,q,\ell',q',b,n) > 0$, $m+\ell-\ell' > 0$.

- If $m{\approx}0$, it holds that $\ell > \ell'$. By invariant 2 $nextempty(\ell',b,n) \geq \ell > \ell'$. Thus, $b(\ell')$ must hold.
- If $\ell{\approx}\ell'+n$, then $m+\ell-\ell' = m-n > 0$. This contradicts invariant 1.

5 (s_4). If $b(\ell')$ holds, then it follows that $nextempty(\ell',b,n) > \ell'$. Therefore, we find that $head(h(\ell,m,q,\ell',q',b,n)) = q'(\ell')$.

6 (r_1). The expression $h(\ell,m+1,q[(\ell+m){\to}d],\ell',q',b,n)$ equals

$$[q'(\ell'),\ldots,q(nextempty(\ell',b,n)),\ldots,q(\ell+m-1)] \rhd d.$$

This is exactly the same as $h(\ell,m,q,\ell',q',b,n) \rhd d$.

6 (s_4). If $b(\ell')$ holds, it is the case that $nextempty(\ell',b,n){>}\ell'$. So, $h(\ell,m,q,\ell',q',b,n)$ equals

$$[q'(\ell'+1),\ldots,q(nextempty(\ell',b,n)),\ldots,q(\ell+m-1)].$$

This is the same as $tail(h(\ell,m,q,\ell',q',b,n))$.

□

13.2.5 Correctness of the sliding window protocol

We wrap up by combining the previous results into the proof of equality of the sliding window protocol with the FIFO buffer. We restate this identity for the third time. For any $n{:}\mathbb{N}^+$ and $q, q'{:}DBuf$:

$$\tau.FIFO([], 2n) = \tau.\tau_I(SWP(q, q', n))$$

where $I = \{c_2, c_3, c_4, c_5, i\}$.

Proof.

$$\begin{array}{ll}
\tau.\tau_{\{c_2,c_3,c_5,c_6,i\}}(SWP(q,q',n)) = & \text{(Lemma 13.2.3)}\\
\tau.\tau_{\{int,i\}}(SWP(0,0,q,d_K,k_K,1,k_L,1,0,q',empty,n)) = & \text{(Lemma 13.2.7)}\\
\tau.\tau_{\{int,i\}}(M(0,0,q,d_K,k_K,1,k_L,1,0,q',empty,n)) = & \text{(Lemma 13.2.8)}\\
\tau.FIFO([],2n). &
\end{array}$$

□

13.3 Distributed summing protocol

We show the correctness of the distributed summing protocol. In this protocol the numbers distributed over a set of processes must be summed. The protocol is interesting because the way the numbers are summed is completely nondeterministic.

We start with a set of processes that are all connected via some network of bidirectional links (see, e.g., figure 13.3). Each process contains some number, not known to other processes. The algorithm describes how to sum all numbers such that one designated (root) process can output the sum of these numbers.

The algorithm is described as the parallel composition of a (finite) number of processes, indexed by natural numbers. Each process works in exactly the same way, except for the root process, which has number 1. This process differs from the other processes in the sense that it is initially already started, and when it has collected all sums of its neighbors, it issues a $\overline{rep}$ message to indicate the total sum to the outside world, instead of a partial sum to a neighbor.

The overall idea behind the algorithm is that a spanning tree over the links between the processes is constructed with as root the process 1. All partial sums are then sent via this spanning tree to the root.

Initially, a process is waiting for a $start$ message from a neighbor. After it has received the first start message, the process is considered part of the spanning tree and the process by which it is started is called its $parent$. Thereafter it starts all its neighbors except its parent by a $start$ message.

- Those neighbors that were not yet part of the spanning tree will now become part of it with the current process as parent. Eventually, these neighbors will send a partial sum to the current process using an $answer$ message.

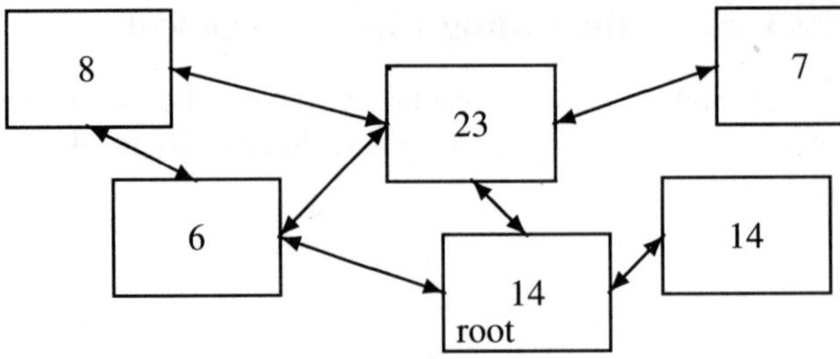

Figure 13.3: A set of distributed processes

- Those neighbors that were already part of the spanning tree ignore the start message. Note however that due to symmetry, these processes will also send a start message to the current process.

After having sent the start messages, each process gets from each neighbor except its parent either a partial sum or a start message. After having received these messages, it adds all received partial sums to its own value, and sends the result as a partial sum to its parent. Eventually, the root process 1 has received all partial sums of its neighbors, and it can report the total sum.

Theorem 13.3.10 says that this simple scheme is correct, i.e., if each process is connected to the root, processes do not have themselves as neighbors and the neighbor relation is symmetric, then the distributed summation algorithm computes the sum of the values of the individual processes. Note that if any of the stated conditions on the topology does not hold, the algorithm either deadlocks, not yielding a result, or it does not sum up all values.

13.3.1 A description in mCRL2

In this section we give a description of the process in mCRL2 and state the correctness criterion. The algorithm is described as the parallel composition of the algorithms for the individual nodes in the network, which are described generically by means of a linear process equation.

The processes of the network interact via matching actions st, $\overline{st}$ (for *start*), ans, $\overline{ans}$ (for *answer*) and the total sum is communicated using a $\overline{rep}$ (for *report*) action. We think of the overbarred action as a sending activity, and a nonoverbarred action as a receiving activity.

Definition 13.3.1. Processes X are described by means of six parameters:

- i: the ID number of the process.
- t: the *total sum* computed so far by the process. Initially, it contains the value that is the contribution of process i to the total sum.
- N: a list of *neighbors* to which the process still needs to send an $\overline{st}$ message. Initially, this list contains exactly all neighbors. We write $rem(j, N)$ to remove

neighbor j from list N. We do not use a set of neighbors, as we use the number of elements in a list, which is not defined for a set.

- p: the index of the initiator, or *parent*, of the process. Variable p is also called the parent link of i.
- w: The number of st and ans messages that the process is still *waiting* for.
- s: the *state* the process is in. The process can be in three states, denoted by 0, 1, and 2. If s equals 0, the process is in its initial state. If s equals 1, the process is active. If s equals 2, the process has finished and behaves as a deadlock.

proc $X(i{:}\mathbb{N}^+, t{:}\mathbb{N}, N{:}List(\mathbb{N}), p, w, s{:}\mathbb{N}) =$

$$\begin{aligned}
&(s{\approx}0) \rightarrow \textstyle\sum_{j:\mathbb{N}} st(i,j)\cdot X(i,t,rem(j,N),j,\#(N){-}1,1)+\\
&\textstyle\sum_{j:\mathbb{N}}(j{\in}N \wedge s{\approx}1) \rightarrow \overline{st}(j,i)\cdot X(i,t,rem(j,N),p,w,s)+\\
&\textstyle\sum_{j,m:\mathbb{N}}(s{\approx}1) \rightarrow ans(i,j,m)\cdot X(i,t+m,N,p,w{-}1,s)+\\
&\textstyle\sum_{j:\mathbb{N}}(s{\approx}1) \rightarrow st(i,j)\cdot X(i,t,N,p,w{-}1,s)+\\
&(i{\approx}1 \wedge N{\approx}[] \wedge w{\approx}0 \wedge s{\approx}1) \rightarrow \overline{rep}(t)\cdot X(i,t,N,p,w,2)+\\
&(i{\not\approx}1 \wedge N{\approx}[] \wedge w{\approx}0 \wedge s{\approx}1) \rightarrow \overline{ans}(p,i,t)\cdot X(i,t,N,p,w,2);
\end{aligned}$$

In line 1 of the definition of X above, process i is in its initial state and an st message is received from some process j, upon which j is stored as the parent and s switches from 0 to 1, indicating that process i has become active. Since it makes no sense to send start messages to one's parent, j is removed from N. The counter w is initialized to the number of neighbors of i, not counting process j. In line 2, a $\overline{st}$ message is sent to a neighbor j, which is thereupon removed from N. In line 3, a sum is received from some process j via an ans message containing the value m, which is added to t, the total sum computed by process i so far. The counter w is decreased. In line 4 an st message is received from neighbor j. The message is ignored, except that the counter w is decreased. In line 5 a $\overline{rep}(t)$ is sent (in case $i = 1$), when process 1 is active, there are no more ans or st messages to be received (formalized by the condition $w = 0$), and an $\overline{st}$ message has been sent to all neighbors (formalized by the condition $N{\approx}[]$). The status variable s becomes 2, indicating that process 1 is no longer active. Line 6 is as line 5 but for processes $i \neq 1$. Now an $\overline{ans}$ message is sent to parent p, containing the total sum t computed by process i.

Next, we define the parallel composition of n copies of the process X in the same way as done in section 10.2.3. The actions st and $\overline{st}$ must communicate, as must ans and $\overline{ans}$. The communications are hidden. The only action that remains visible is $\overline{rep}$.

The t value of the processes are put in a function $\boldsymbol{t}_0$, i.e., $\boldsymbol{t}_0(i)$ indicates the value of t for process i. Similarly, the functions $\boldsymbol{p}$, $\boldsymbol{w}$, and $\boldsymbol{s}$ contain the values of the variables p, w, and s of all processes, respectively.

Definition 13.3.2. We define the process *Impl* as the parallel composition of n processes X, and the process *DSum* as *Impl* with the prehiding, allow, and communication operators applied to it.

$$
\begin{aligned}
&\textbf{proc } \mathit{DSum}(n{:}\mathbb{N}^+, \boldsymbol{t}_0{:}\mathbb{N}^+{\to}\mathbb{N}, \boldsymbol{n}_0{:}\mathbb{N}^+{\to}\mathit{List}(\mathbb{N}^+)) = \\
&\qquad \Upsilon_{\{st^\star, ans^\star\}} \nabla_{\{st^\star, ans^\star, \overline{rep}\}} \Gamma_{\{st|\overline{st}\to st^\star, ans|\overline{ans}\to ans^\star\}} \\
&\qquad\qquad (\mathit{Impl}(k, \boldsymbol{t}_0, \boldsymbol{n}_0, \boldsymbol{p}_0, \boldsymbol{w}_0, \boldsymbol{s}_0)); \\
&\quad \mathit{Impl}(n{:}\mathbb{N}^+, \boldsymbol{t}{:}\mathbb{N}^+{\to}\mathbb{N}, \boldsymbol{n}{:}\mathbb{N}^+{\to}\mathit{Set}(\mathbb{N}), \boldsymbol{p}, \boldsymbol{w}, \boldsymbol{s}{:}\mathbb{N}^+{\to}\mathbb{N}) = \\
&\qquad (n{\approx}1) \to X(1, \boldsymbol{t}(1), \boldsymbol{n}(1), \boldsymbol{p}(1), \boldsymbol{w}(1), \boldsymbol{s}(1)) \\
&\qquad\quad \diamond\ (X(n, \boldsymbol{t}(n), \boldsymbol{n}(n), \boldsymbol{p}(n), \boldsymbol{w}(n), \boldsymbol{s}(n)) \| \mathit{Impl}(n{-}1, \boldsymbol{t}, \boldsymbol{n}, \boldsymbol{p}, \boldsymbol{w}, \boldsymbol{s}));
\end{aligned}
$$

Here, $\boldsymbol{p}_0{=}\lambda i{:}\mathbb{N}^+.1$ (each process considers process 1 as its initiator), $\boldsymbol{w}_0{=}\lambda i{:}\mathbb{N}^+.\#\boldsymbol{n}_0(i)$ ($\boldsymbol{w}_0$ contains the number of neighbors of process i), $\boldsymbol{s}_0{=}\lambda i{:}\mathbb{N}^+.\mathit{if}(i{\approx}1, 1, 0)$ (only the root is initially started).

The distributed summing protocol only works when some requirements on the interconnection of processes are satisfied. With the variable $\boldsymbol{n}_0$ at our disposal, we can formulate these requirements very precisely as follows:

Definition 13.3.3 (Requirements on topology). Let n denote the number of processes in the network. We define $\mathit{goodtopology}(n, \boldsymbol{n}_0)$ as the conjunction of the following properties:

- No process has a link to itself: $\forall i{:}\mathbb{N}^+.i{\notin}\boldsymbol{n}_0(i)$.
- The neighbor relation is symmetric: $\forall i, j{:}\mathbb{N}^+.i{\in}\boldsymbol{n}_0(j) \Leftrightarrow j{\in}\boldsymbol{n}_0(i)$.
- Every process $i \leq n$ is connected to process 1: for all $i{\leq}n$ there are $m{\leq}n$ and $i = i_0, \ldots, i_m = 1$ such that $i_{l+1} \in \boldsymbol{n}_0(i_l)$ for all $0{\leq}l{<}m$.
- $\boldsymbol{n}_0$ only contains valid neighbors: $\forall i, j{:}\mathbb{N}^+.j{\leq}n \land i \in \boldsymbol{n}_0(j) \Rightarrow i \leq n$.

The theorem below states the correctness of the summation algorithm. It says that in a topology as described above, the distributed summation algorithm correctly reports the sum of all values in the processes and halts. The remainder of this section is devoted to proving this theorem. It is repeated and proven as theorem 13.3.10.

Theorem 13.3.4. For all $n{:}\mathbb{N}^+$, $\boldsymbol{t}_0{:}\mathbb{N}^+{\to}\mathbb{N}$ and $\boldsymbol{n}_0{:}\mathbb{N}^+{\to}\mathit{List}(\mathbb{N}^+)$, it holds that:

$$
\mathit{goodtopology}(n, \boldsymbol{n}_0) \Rightarrow \tau{\cdot}\tau_{\{int\}}(\mathit{DSum}(n, \boldsymbol{t}_0, \boldsymbol{n}_0)) = \tau{\cdot}\overline{rep}(\sum_{i=1}^{n} \boldsymbol{t}_0(i)){\cdot}\delta
$$

In the trivial case that the root process 1 has no neighbors, which is equivalent to $n{=}1$, the τ's at the left-hand side and right-hand side of the equation may be omitted.

13.3.2 Linearization and invariants

Using the method of section 10.2.3 it is straightforward to write down a linear process for the network of n processes. The result is given in table 13.1 where the process *L-Impl* is defined. From the technique of linearizing n parallel processes, we can conclude that the following relation between *L-Impl* and *DSum* holds.

$$
\begin{aligned}
&\textit{L-Impl}(n{:}\mathbb{N}^+, \boldsymbol{t}{:}\mathbb{N}^+{\to}\mathbb{N}, \boldsymbol{n}{:}\mathbb{N}^+{\to}\textit{List}(\mathbb{N}), \boldsymbol{p}, \boldsymbol{w}, \boldsymbol{s}{:}\mathbb{N}^+{\to}\mathbb{N}) = \\
&\quad (\boldsymbol{n}(1){\approx}[] \wedge \boldsymbol{w}(1){\approx}1 \wedge \boldsymbol{s}(1){\approx}1) \to \overline{rep}(\boldsymbol{t}(1))\cdot \textit{L-Impl}(\boldsymbol{s}{=}\boldsymbol{s}[1{\to}2]) + \\
&\quad \textstyle\sum_{i,j:\mathbb{N}^+} (\boldsymbol{s}(i){\approx}1 \wedge i \in \boldsymbol{n}(j) \wedge \boldsymbol{s}(j){\approx}1 \wedge i{\not\approx}j \wedge i{\leq}n \wedge j{\leq}n) \to \\
&\qquad int\cdot \textit{L-Impl}(\boldsymbol{n}{=}\boldsymbol{n}[j{\to}rem(i,\boldsymbol{n}(j)), i{\to}rem(j,\boldsymbol{n}(i))], \\
&\qquad\qquad \boldsymbol{p}{=}\boldsymbol{p}[i{\to}j], \boldsymbol{w}{=}\boldsymbol{w}[i{\to}\#\boldsymbol{n}(i){-}1], \boldsymbol{s}{=}\boldsymbol{s}[i{\to}1]) + \\
&\quad \textstyle\sum_{i,j:\mathbb{N}^+} (\boldsymbol{s}(i){\approx}1 \wedge i \in \boldsymbol{n}(j) \wedge \boldsymbol{s}(j){\approx}1 \wedge i{\not\approx}j \wedge i{\leq}n \wedge j{\leq}n) \to \\
&\qquad int\cdot \textit{L-Impl}(\boldsymbol{n}{=}\boldsymbol{n}[j{\to}rem(i,\boldsymbol{n}(j))], \boldsymbol{w}{=}\boldsymbol{w}[i{\to}\boldsymbol{w}(i){-}1]) + \\
&\quad \textstyle\sum_{j:\mathbb{N}^+} (\boldsymbol{n}(j){\approx}[] {\wedge} \boldsymbol{w}(j){\approx}0 {\wedge} \boldsymbol{s}(j){\approx}1 {\wedge} \boldsymbol{s}(\boldsymbol{p}(j)){\approx}1 {\wedge} j{\not\approx}1 {\wedge} j{\not\approx}\boldsymbol{p}(j) {\wedge} j{\leq}n {\wedge} \boldsymbol{p}(j){\leq}n) {\to} \\
&\qquad int\cdot \textit{L-Impl}(\boldsymbol{t}{=}\boldsymbol{t}[\boldsymbol{p}(j){\to}\boldsymbol{t}(\boldsymbol{p}(j)) + \boldsymbol{t}(j)], \boldsymbol{w}{=}\boldsymbol{w}[\boldsymbol{p}(j){\to}\boldsymbol{w}(\boldsymbol{p}(j)){-}1], \boldsymbol{s}{=}\boldsymbol{s}[j{\to}2]).
\end{aligned}
$$

Table 13.1: Linearization of the implementation

Lemma 13.3.5. For all $n{:}\mathbb{N}^+$, $\boldsymbol{t}_0{:}\mathbb{N}^+{\to}\mathbb{N}$ and $\boldsymbol{n}_0{:}\mathbb{N}^+{\to}\textit{List}(\mathbb{N}^+)$ (where $\boldsymbol{p}_0$, $\boldsymbol{w}_0$, and $\boldsymbol{s}_0$ are as in definition 13.3.2), it holds that:

$$\textit{DSum}(n, \boldsymbol{t}_0, \boldsymbol{n}_0) = \textit{L-Impl}(n, \boldsymbol{t}_0, \boldsymbol{n}_0, \boldsymbol{p}_0, \boldsymbol{w}_0, \boldsymbol{s}_0).$$

We provide a number of invariants for *L-Impl*, most of which express that bookkeeping is done properly. The most interesting are invariants 14, 15, and 16. The first of these three implies that process 1 is reachable from each process in state 1 in a finite number of steps by iteratively following parent links (i.e., following variable p). As each process has a unique parent, this is an alternative way of saying that the parent links constitute a tree structure with process 1 as the root (and a self-loop at the root). Invariant 15 expresses that along each such path all processes are in state 1 too, meaning that they are willing to pass partial results along. Invariant 16 expresses that the total sum of the processes is maintained in the processes that are not in state 2. We will see that at a certain moment all processes, except for process 1, are in state 2, which implies that at that moment the total sum is present in process 1.

The invariants mention the functions *Preach*, *Npoint*, *Ppoint*, and $actsum$, which are defined first.

Definition 13.3.6. Let $\boldsymbol{t}$, $\boldsymbol{n}$, $\boldsymbol{p}$, and $\boldsymbol{s}$ be as in definition 13.3.2.

- The function $\textit{Preach}(i, j, \boldsymbol{p}, m)$ expresses that from process i, process j can be reached by following the parent links in $\boldsymbol{p}$. So $\textit{Preach}(i, j, \boldsymbol{p}, m)$ holds if there are $i = i_0, \ldots, i_m = j$ such that, for all $0 \leq l < m, \boldsymbol{p}(i_l) = i_{l+1}$.

- $\textit{Npoint}(i, \boldsymbol{n})$ is the number of sets L in $\boldsymbol{n}$ such that $i \in L$. Intuitively, $\textit{Npoint}(i, \boldsymbol{n})$ is the number of processes that still need to send an $\overline{st}$ message to process i.

- $\textit{Ppoint}(i, \boldsymbol{p}, \boldsymbol{s})$ is the number of processes $j \neq 1$ in the list $\boldsymbol{p}$ such that $\boldsymbol{p}(j) = i$ and $\boldsymbol{s}(j) = 1$. That is, $\textit{Ppoint}(i, \boldsymbol{p}, \boldsymbol{s})$ is the number of active nonroot processes that regard process i as their parent.

- $actsum(\boldsymbol{t}, \boldsymbol{s})$ is the sum of the $\boldsymbol{t}(i)$-values of the processes i that have not terminated yet, i.e., such that $\boldsymbol{s}(i) = 0$ or $\boldsymbol{s}(i) = 1$.

Theorem 13.3.7. The following are invariants of *L-Impl*$(n, \boldsymbol{t}, \boldsymbol{n}, \boldsymbol{p}, \boldsymbol{w}, \boldsymbol{s})$. Here the universal quantification over i and j is left implicit. The conjunction of the invariants is written as $Inv(\boldsymbol{n}_0, \boldsymbol{t}_0, n, \boldsymbol{t}, \boldsymbol{n}, \boldsymbol{p}, \boldsymbol{w}, \boldsymbol{s})$. Note that the initial topology $\boldsymbol{n}_0$ and the initial distribution of values $\boldsymbol{t}_0$ are part of the invariant, although these are not a parameter of *L-Impl*.

1. $\boldsymbol{s}(i) \leq 2$.
2. $\boldsymbol{p}(i) \leq n$.
3. $i \in \boldsymbol{n}(j) \Rightarrow i \leq n$.
4. $i \notin \boldsymbol{n}(i)$.
5. $\boldsymbol{s}(1) \neq 1$.
6. $\boldsymbol{p}(1) = 0$.
7. $\boldsymbol{s}(i) = 0 \wedge j \in \boldsymbol{n}(i) \Rightarrow i \in \boldsymbol{n}(j)$.
8. $\boldsymbol{s}(i) = 0 \wedge i \in \boldsymbol{n}(j) \Rightarrow j \in \boldsymbol{n}(i)$.
9. $\boldsymbol{s}(i) = 0 \Rightarrow \boldsymbol{n}(i) = \boldsymbol{n}_0(i)$.
10. $\boldsymbol{s}(i) = 2 \Rightarrow \boldsymbol{w}(i) = 0 \wedge \boldsymbol{n}(i) = []$.
11. If a process i is in state 0, then it cannot be a parent:
    $\boldsymbol{s}(i) = 0 \Rightarrow \boldsymbol{p}(j) \neq i$.
12. $\boldsymbol{s}(i) = 0 \Rightarrow \boldsymbol{w}(i) = Npoint(i, \boldsymbol{n}) \wedge Npoint(i, \boldsymbol{n}) = \#(\boldsymbol{n}(i)) \wedge Ppoint(i, \boldsymbol{p}, \boldsymbol{s}) = 0$.
13. For every process i, $\boldsymbol{w}(i)$ records exactly the number of messages that are to be received. These can either be st messages or ans messages:
    $\boldsymbol{w}(i) = Npoint(i, \boldsymbol{n}) + Ppoint(i, \boldsymbol{p}, \boldsymbol{s})$.
14. From every process i, process 1 is reachable via parent links in a finite number of steps:
    $\exists m{:}\mathbb{N}.Preach(i, 1, \boldsymbol{p}, m)$.
15. If a process i is in state 1, then its parent is also in state 1: $\boldsymbol{s}(i) = 1 \Rightarrow \boldsymbol{s}(\boldsymbol{p}(i)) = 1$.
16. As long as no $\overline{rep}$ message has been issued by process 1 (i.e., $\boldsymbol{s}(0) \neq 2$), the total sum (i.e., $\sum_{i=1}^{n} \boldsymbol{t}_0(i)$) is present in the processes that are in state 0 or 1: $\boldsymbol{s}(1) \neq 2 \Rightarrow actsum(\boldsymbol{t}, \boldsymbol{s}) = \sum_{i=1}^{n} \boldsymbol{t}_0(i)$.

Proof. The invariants 1 to 12 are easily checked (invariant 6 uses invariant 5). Invariant 13 uses invariants 4, 5, 6, 8, and 12. Invariant 14 uses invariant 11. Invariant 15 uses invariant 13. The last invariant can be proven on its own. □

13.3.3 State mapping, focus points, and final lemma

In order to prove that the distributed summing delivers the correct sum using the cones and foci method, we specify a linear process *L-Spec* describing the specification.

proc $L\text{-}Spec(b{:}\mathbb{B}) = b \rightarrow \overline{rep}(\sum_{i=1}^{n}(\boldsymbol{t}_0))\cdot L\text{-}Spec(\neg b);$

Clearly, $L\text{-}Spec(true) = \overline{rep}(\sum_{i=1}^{n}\boldsymbol{t}_0(i))\cdot\delta$.

Furthermore, we provide a *state mapping* h that specifies how the control variable b of the specification *L-Spec* is constructed out of the parameters $n, \boldsymbol{t}, \boldsymbol{n}, \boldsymbol{p}, \boldsymbol{w}$ and $\boldsymbol{s}$ of the implementation *L-Impl*. We define

$$h(n,\boldsymbol{t},\boldsymbol{n},\boldsymbol{p},\boldsymbol{w},\boldsymbol{s}) = \boldsymbol{s}(1){\approx}1.$$

The intuition behind this definition is as follows. In a configuration s of *L-Impl* that satisfies $\boldsymbol{s}(1) = 1$, $h(s)$ is $true$, so *L-Spec* can perform the $\overline{rep}$ action, after which it halts. *L-Impl* may not be able to perform a matching $\overline{rep}$ action directly, since the computation of the value to be reported has not yet finished (i.e., $\boldsymbol{n}(1) \neq []$ or $\boldsymbol{w}(1) \neq 0$). However, using the fact that *L-Impl* is convergent, we see that after a finite number of internal τ-steps a configuration s' is reached where no τ-step is enabled, $\boldsymbol{s}(1)$ is still 1 (h will be invariant under the τ-steps), but also $\boldsymbol{n}(1) = []$ and $\boldsymbol{w}(1) = 0$. Then the $\overline{rep}$ action can be performed (with the correct value), after which *L-Impl* halts. Conversely, it is easy to verify that if in configuration s *L-Impl* can perform the $\overline{rep}$ action, then $\boldsymbol{s}(1) = 1$, so in configuration $h(s)$ the control variable $b = h(s)$ of *L-Spec* has the value $true$ and the specification *L-Spec* can perform the $\overline{rep}$ action (with corresponding value).

We formalize this intuitive argument, using a *focus condition*, which is a formula that characterizes the configurations of *L-Impl* in which no τ-step is enabled. Such a formula is extracted from the equation characterizing *L-Impl* (see table 13.1) by negating the guards that enable τ-steps in *L-Impl*. As an optimization, we have put the first two negated guards together, and have restricted the focus condition to configurations satisfying the invariant.

$$\begin{aligned} FC(n,\boldsymbol{t},\boldsymbol{n},\boldsymbol{p},\boldsymbol{w},\boldsymbol{s}) = {} & \forall i,j \leq n \\ & (\boldsymbol{s}[i] = 2 \vee i \notin \boldsymbol{n}[j] \vee \boldsymbol{s}[j] \neq 1 \vee i = j)\wedge \\ & (\boldsymbol{n}[j] \neq \emptyset \vee \boldsymbol{w}[j] > 0 \vee \boldsymbol{s}[j] \neq 1 \vee \boldsymbol{s}[\boldsymbol{p}[j]] \neq 1 \vee j = 0). \end{aligned}$$

There are two focus points of the distributed summation algorithm. One is the set of configurations where the algorithm has reported the sum and is terminated, so $\boldsymbol{s}(1) = 2$. The other one contains the configuration s' mentioned above and is characterized by $\boldsymbol{s}(1) = 1$. At that moment the correct sum should be reported. Items 1 and 2 of lemma 13.3.8 below say that all conditions in the process *L-Impl* for issuing a $\overline{rep}$ action are satisfied; so reporting is possible. Item 3 says that in such a case, all other processes are in state 2. Hence, using invariant 16 (i.e., $\boldsymbol{s}(1) \neq 2 \Rightarrow actsum(\boldsymbol{t},\boldsymbol{s}) = \sum_{i=1}^{n}\boldsymbol{t}_0(i)$) we may conclude that the total sum is indeed collected in process 1, i.e., process 1 reports the correct sum.

Lemma 13.3.8. $Inv(\boldsymbol{n}_0,\boldsymbol{t}_0,n,\boldsymbol{t},\boldsymbol{n},\boldsymbol{p},\boldsymbol{w},\boldsymbol{s})$ and $\boldsymbol{s}(1) = 1$ together imply

1. $FC(n,\boldsymbol{t},\boldsymbol{n},\boldsymbol{p},\boldsymbol{w},\boldsymbol{s}) \wedge \boldsymbol{s}(i) = 1 \Rightarrow \boldsymbol{n}(i) = []$.
2. $FC(n,\boldsymbol{t},\boldsymbol{n},\boldsymbol{p},\boldsymbol{w},\boldsymbol{s}) \Rightarrow \boldsymbol{w}(1) = 0$.
3. $goodtopology(n,\boldsymbol{n}_0) \wedge \boldsymbol{w}(1) = 0 \wedge i \neq 1 \Rightarrow \boldsymbol{s}(i) = 2$.

Proof.

1. Toward a contradiction, assume there exists a process i such that $\boldsymbol{s}(i) = 1$ and $\boldsymbol{n}(i) \neq []$, say $j \in \boldsymbol{n}(i)$. By invariant 4 we have $j \neq i$. The first conjunct of $FC(n,\boldsymbol{t},\boldsymbol{n},\boldsymbol{p},\boldsymbol{w},\boldsymbol{s})$ yields that $\boldsymbol{s}(j) = 2$. By invariant 10, $\boldsymbol{w}(j) = 0$, contradicting invariant 13 (remember that $j \in \boldsymbol{n}(i)$).

2. In order to derive a contradiction, assume that $\boldsymbol{w}(1) > 0$. For arbitrary m, we construct a sequence of m processes $1 = i_1, \ldots, i_m$ such that for all $1 \leq l \leq m$, we have $\boldsymbol{s}(i_l) = 1$, $\boldsymbol{w}(i_l) > 0$, $\boldsymbol{p}(i_{l+1}) = i_l$, and if $l \neq 1$, $i_l \neq 1$. Clearly, if $m > n$, there is one element $i_r \neq 1$ which appears twice in the path. Hence, we obtain a cycle in the path starting from i_r that does not contain 1. Therefore, i_1 cannot be reachable via parent links from i_r and in particular from i_m; this contradicts the existence of the current sequence.

   Let a process i_l be given such that $\boldsymbol{w}(i_l) > 0$ and $\boldsymbol{s}(i_l) = 1$. According to invariant 13, at least one of the following should hold.

   - There is some i such that $i_l \in \boldsymbol{n}(i)$. By invariant 4, $i_l \neq i$. By the first part of $FC(n,\boldsymbol{t},\boldsymbol{n},\boldsymbol{p},\boldsymbol{w},\boldsymbol{s})$ it follows that $\boldsymbol{s}(i) \neq 1$. Therefore, either $\boldsymbol{s}(i) = 2$, but this leads to a contradiction using invariant 10 (remember that $\boldsymbol{n}(i) \neq \emptyset$). Or, $\boldsymbol{s}(i) = 0$. By invariant 7, $i \in \boldsymbol{n}(i_l)$. So, by $FC(n,\boldsymbol{t},\boldsymbol{n},\boldsymbol{p},\boldsymbol{w},\boldsymbol{s})$, $\boldsymbol{s}(i_l) \neq 1$. Contradiction.
   - Or there is some i such that $\boldsymbol{p}(i) = i_l$, $i \neq 1$ and $\boldsymbol{s}(i) = 1$. By the second part of $FC(n,\boldsymbol{t},\boldsymbol{n},\boldsymbol{p},\boldsymbol{w},\boldsymbol{s})$, we have $\boldsymbol{w}(i) > 0 \vee \boldsymbol{n}(i) \neq \emptyset$. By item 1 of this lemma, $\boldsymbol{n}(i) = \emptyset$. So $\boldsymbol{w}(i) > 0$. We can take $i_{l+1} = i$.

3. First, assume there is some process $i \neq 1$ such that $\boldsymbol{s}(i) = 1$. Using invariants 13, 15, and 14, it follows that there is a sequence of processes $i = i_1, \ldots, i_m = 1$ such that, for all $0 \leq l < m$, $i_l \neq 1, \boldsymbol{p}(i_l) = i_{l+1}, \boldsymbol{s}(i_l) = 1$ and $\boldsymbol{w}(i_{l+1}) > 0$. In particular $\boldsymbol{w}(1) > 0$, contradicting an assumption.

   Therefore, assume that there is no process $i \neq 1$ such that $\boldsymbol{s}(i) = 1$, but there is some process $i \neq 1$ such that $\boldsymbol{s}(i) = 0$. From the topology requirement it follows that there is a sequence $i = i_1, \ldots, i_m = 1$ such that for all $1 \leq l < m$, $i_{l+1} \in \boldsymbol{n}_0(i_l)$. We show that $\boldsymbol{s}(i_l) = 0$ for all l, $1 \leq l \leq m$. This contradicts the assumption that $\boldsymbol{s}(1) = 1$.

   Note that by assumption $\boldsymbol{s}(i_1) = 0$. Let i_l be such that $\boldsymbol{s}(i_l) = 0$. By invariant 9, it follows that $i_{l+1} \in \boldsymbol{n}(i_l)$. By invariant 13, $\boldsymbol{w}(i_{l+1}) > 0$, so $i_{l+1} \neq 1$ and, by invariant 10, $\boldsymbol{s}(i_{l+1}) \neq 2$. As we have excluded that process i_{l+1} is in state 1, it must hold that $\boldsymbol{s}(i_{l+1}) = 0$, as required.

□

Below we copy the general equality theorem (see theorem 12.1.1) instantiated for the distributed summation algorithm. It says that, given the invariant, implementation *L-Impl* and specification *L-Spec* are equivalent. Its proof requires that the six matching criteria are checked. Given lemma 13.3.8 this is straightforward.

Lemma 13.3.9. Assume $goodtopology(n, \mathbf{n}_0)$.

$$Inv(\mathbf{n}_0, \mathbf{t}_0, n, \mathbf{t}, \mathbf{n}, \mathbf{p}, \mathbf{w}, \mathbf{s}) \Rightarrow \tau{\cdot}L\text{-}Impl(n, \mathbf{t}, \mathbf{n}, \mathbf{p}, \mathbf{w}, \mathbf{s}) = \tau{\cdot}L\text{-}Spec(\mathbf{s}(1){\approx}1)$$

Proof. It suffices to check that the following instances of the matching criteria are implied by the invariant.

1. *L-Impl* in table 13.1 is convergent, i.e., does not admit infinite τ-paths. At each τ-step, either a link in $\mathbf{n}$ is removed, or a process moves from state 1 to state 2. Hence, the sum of the number of links in $\mathbf{n}$ and the number of processes in state 0 or 1 strictly decreases with each τ-step.

2. The following three requirements ensure that the state mapping h is invariant under τ-steps of *L-Impl*.

   (a) $\mathbf{s}(i) = 0 \wedge i \in \mathbf{n}(j) \wedge \mathbf{s}(j) = 1 \wedge i \neq j \wedge i \leq n \wedge j \leq n$ implies $\mathbf{s}(1) = \mathbf{s}[i{\to}1](1)$. We distinguish two cases. If $i \neq 1$, the condition trivially holds because $\mathbf{s}[i{\to}1](1) = \mathbf{s}(1)$. If $i = 1$, one conjunct of the precondition says $\mathbf{s}(1) = 0$. This contradicts invariant 5.

   (b) $\mathbf{s}(i) = 1 \wedge i \in \mathbf{n}(j) \wedge \mathbf{s}(j) = 1 \wedge i \neq j \wedge i \leq n \wedge j \leq n$ implies $\mathbf{s}(1) = \mathbf{s}(1)$. This requirement clearly holds.

   (c) $\mathbf{n}(j) = [] \wedge \mathbf{w}(j) = 0 \wedge \mathbf{s}(j) = 1 \wedge \mathbf{s}(\mathbf{p}(j)) = 1 \wedge j \neq 1 \wedge j \neq \mathbf{p}(j) \wedge j \leq n \wedge \mathbf{p}(j) \leq n$ implies $\mathbf{s}(1) = \mathbf{s}[j{\to}2](1)$. This requirement is also trivially valid, because the assumption explicitly says $j \neq 1$. Hence, $\mathbf{s}[j{\to}2](1) = \mathbf{s}(1)$.

3. Next, we verify that when the $\overline{rep}$ action is enabled in *L-Impl*, it is enabled in *L-Spec*: $\mathbf{n}(1) = [] \wedge \mathbf{w}(1) = 0 \wedge \mathbf{s}(1) = 1$ implies $\mathbf{s}(1) = 1$. This is obviously true.

4. We must show that if *L-Impl* is in a focus point (no internal actions enabled) and *L-Spec* can perform a $\overline{rep}$ action, *L-Impl* can also perform the $\overline{rep}$ action:

   $FC(n, \mathbf{t}, \mathbf{n}, \mathbf{p}, \mathbf{w}, \mathbf{s}) \wedge \mathbf{s}(1) = 1$ implies $\mathbf{n}(1) = [] \wedge \mathbf{w}(1) = 0 \wedge \mathbf{s}(1) = 1$. This is a direct consequence of lemma 13.3.8.2 and lemma 13.3.8.1.

5. We must show that if the $\overline{rep}$ action is enabled in *L-Impl* then the reported sum is equal to the sum reported in *L-Spec*: $\mathbf{n}(1) = [] \wedge \mathbf{w}(n) = 0 \wedge \mathbf{s}(1) = 1$ implies $\mathbf{t}(1) = \sum_{i=1}^{n} \mathbf{t}_0(i)$. By invariant 16 we have $\sum_{i=1}^{n} \mathbf{t}_0(i) = actsum(\mathbf{t}, \mathbf{s})$. By definition, $actsum(\mathbf{t}, \mathbf{s})$ contains the sum of the $\mathbf{t}(i)$ values of all processes i that are not in state 2. By lemma 13.3.8.3, only process 1 is not in state 2. Hence $\sum_{i=1}^{n} \mathbf{t}_0(i) = actsum(\mathbf{t}, \mathbf{s}) = \mathbf{t}(1)$.

6. Finally, we have to show that the h-mapping commutes with the $\overline{rep}$ action, i.e., $\boldsymbol{s}[1\to 2](1) \neq 1$. This is easily seen to hold.

□

Theorem 13.3.10. For all $n{:}\mathbb{N}^+$, $\boldsymbol{t}_0{:}\mathbb{N}^+\to\mathbb{N}$ and $\boldsymbol{n}_0{:}\mathbb{N}^+\to List(\mathbb{N}^+)$, it holds that:

$$goodtopology(n, \boldsymbol{n}_0) \Rightarrow \tau\cdot\tau_{\{int\}}(DSum(n, \boldsymbol{t}_0, \boldsymbol{n}_0)) = \tau\cdot\overline{rep}(\sum_{i=1}^{n} \boldsymbol{t}_0(i))\cdot\delta$$

If $n = 1$, the initial τ's at the left-hand side and the right-hand side of the equation can be omitted.

Proof. Apply lemma 13.3.9 with $\boldsymbol{t}_0$ substituted for $\boldsymbol{t}$, $\boldsymbol{n}_0$ for $\boldsymbol{n}$, $\boldsymbol{p}_0$ for $\boldsymbol{p}$, $\boldsymbol{w}_0$ for $\boldsymbol{w}$, and $\boldsymbol{s}_0$ for $\boldsymbol{s}$. As $goodtopology(n, \boldsymbol{n}_0)$ holds, this substitution reduces the invariant to $true$. Thus we have

$$\tau\cdot L\text{-}Impl(n, \boldsymbol{t}_0, \boldsymbol{n}_0, \boldsymbol{p}_0, \boldsymbol{w}_0, \boldsymbol{s}_0) = \tau\cdot L\text{-}Spec(true).$$

By lemma 13.3.5 and the definition of L-$Spec$ the theorem follows immediately. □

13.4 Historical notes

It is very tedious to design a correct (distributed) algorithm or protocol. This has been recognized very early and several methods to prove them have been proposed. For sequential algorithms Floyd/Hoare logic has been designed [58, 101]. Dijkstra spent a substantial part of his later life to design a calculus to derive correct programs [57]. Also, the I/O-automaton formalism is largely inspired by the desire to prove the correctness of mainly distributed algorithms.

Yet the actual situation is far from optimal in the sense that the majority of algorithms that are published in the literature do not appear to be completely correct. In [9] 26 distributed algorithms were studied, of which 21 were found to be faulty. Often authors fail to imagine corner cases, which they do not treat in the proof. In [67] a round based consensus protocol was investigated wherein the original formulation messages could seep from one round into another, wreaking havoc. Sometimes correct protocols have incorrect proofs. In [52] a round based leader election protocol is defined. The proofs assume that the protocol works in rounds, which is not true, but which can be seen to hold using an argument based on τ-confluence (see [65] for a cones and foci proof).

One of the reasons for this state of affairs is that a proof of a distributed algorithm is unpleasantly detailed, and the true reason why it works is more subtle than people intuitively grasp. Without well-trained systematic and effective proof methodology and notational tools, it is an even harder task. This explains why it took 14 years to find a process-algebraic proof of the sliding window protocol [10] of which the proof here is a compact version. Only when we realized that the proof had to be split into a modulo and a nonmodulo part (inspired by a proof in [167]) could the proof be finished. If the proof methodology is known, more complex protocols can be verified along the same line [10].

Unfortunately, it may take a long time before protocols and distributed algorithms that are published will at large have reliable, even machine-checked proofs. One might, however, start to require that each new algorithm is at least model checked for some limited but realistic instance. Many of the problems that we found while doing laborious manual proofs, could have been revealed easily by model checking a few core behavioral requirements.

14

Verification of Modal Formulas Using Parameterized Boolean Equation Systems

In this chapter, we deal with the question of how to show that modal formulas are valid for the initial state of a linear process. This is done by translating the formula together with the process to a parameterized Boolean equation system (PBES). This system of equations is subsequently solved. Because parameterized Boolean equation systems are quite complex, we first introduce Boolean equation systems (BESs), which are PBESs without data. The relation between BESs and PBESs is comparable to the relation between transition systems and linear processes.

14.1 Boolean equation systems

Given a set of Boolean variables, a Boolean equation system consists of a set of equations, one equation for each variable. The variable occurs at the left-hand side of each equation. The right-hand side consists of an expression possibly involving variables, $true$, $false$, and the conjunction and disjunction operators. Negations are not allowed at the right-hand side. Every equation is preceded by either a μ or a ν to indicate whether a minimal (μ) solution for the equation is sought or whether a maximal (ν) solution is meant. For Booleans, there are only two possible solutions, namely $true$ and $false$, where, by convention, $true$ is largest and $false$ is smallest. We do not write an ordinary equation symbol, but use $\overline{=}$, to indicate that this equality does not have all properties of ordinary equality. The order in which the equations occurs does matter. The equations that occur earlier have higher priority than those that occur later.

One of the simplest conceivable Boolean equation systems is

$$\mu X \overline{=} X.$$

There are two solutions for this equation, namely $X = true$ and $X = false$. Here, we are interested in the smallest (μ) solution, and therefore the solution is $X = \mathit{false}$.

A slightly more complex example is:

$$\nu X = X \vee Y,$$
$$\mu Y = X \wedge Y.$$

The first equation has highest priority, therefore, we first investigate X. We prefer the maximal solution for X, i.e., $X = \mathit{true}$, provided we can solve the second equation with it, and the outcome satisfies the equation for X. Substituting $X = \mathit{true}$ in the second equation leads to

$$\mu Y = \mathit{true} \wedge Y.$$

The minimal solution for this is $Y = \mathit{false}$. Substituting the solutions for X and Y in the first equation makes the first equation true. And therefore, $X = \mathit{true}, Y = \mathit{false}$ is the solution of this Boolean equation system.

Now consider the following slightly altered example:

$$\nu X = Y,$$
$$\mu Y = X \wedge Y.$$

The preferred solution of X is true. As in the previous example, substituting that in the second equation, and finding its minimal solution, leads to the solution $Y = \mathit{false}$. Substituting this solution for the first equation leads to $\mathit{true} = \mathit{false}$, which invalidates the first equation. This means that $X = \mathit{true}$ is not a solution and $X = \mathit{false}$ must be tried as (the only) alternative. Subsequently, we find $Y = \mathit{false}$, which satisfies the first equation and hence the solution is $X = Y = \mathit{false}$.

With more equations, this procedure can be applied recursively. It corresponds to the semantics of Boolean equation systems defined in chapter 15. Every Boolean equation system has a unique solution, which is found in this way. Unfortunately, this and other general known procedures have exponential-time complexity.

The order of the equations in a Boolean equation system is important. Changing the order can change the solution as shown by the following two Boolean equation systems

$$\mu X = Y, \qquad\qquad \nu Y = X,$$
$$\nu Y = X. \qquad\qquad \mu X = Y.$$

The Boolean equation system at the left has solution $(\mathit{false}, \mathit{false})$ for (X, Y), whereas the one at the right, where the order of equations has been reversed, has solution $(\mathit{true}, \mathit{true})$.

It is tempting to think that the solution of a Boolean equation system is determined by the set of all solutions for the equations (obtained without the fixed point operators), and the fixed point operator for each equation. The next example shows that this is not the case. The shape of the right-hand side also plays an important role.

$$\mu X = Y, \qquad\qquad \mu X = Y,$$
$$\nu Y = Y. \qquad\qquad \nu Y = X \wedge Y.$$

The solutions for both systems of equations without fixed point operators are $X = Y = \mathit{true}$ and $X = Y = \mathit{false}$. The fixed point operators for the variables are the

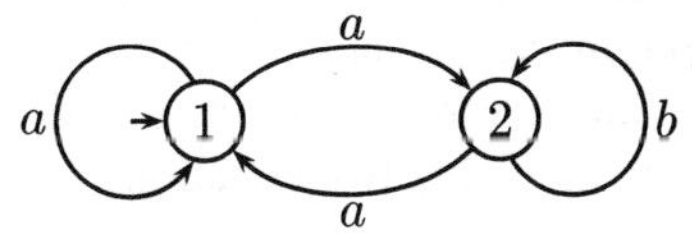

Figure 14.1: A simple transition system

same in the same order. But the solution for the first BES is $X = Y = true$ and the solution for the second is $X = Y = false$.

Exercise 14.1.1. Find solutions for the following Boolean equation systems.

$$\begin{array}{llll} \mu X = Y, & \mu X = X, & \mu X = Y, & \mu X = X, \\ \nu Y = X. & \nu Y = Y. & \nu Y = Y. & \nu Y = X. \end{array}$$

Exercise 14.1.2. Find solutions of the following three BESs.

$$\begin{array}{lll} \mu X_1 = X_1 \wedge X_2, & \nu X_1 = X_1 \wedge X_2, & \nu X_1 = X_1 \vee X_2, \\ \nu X_2 = X_1 \vee X_3, & \mu X_2 = X_1 \vee X_3, & \mu X_2 = X_1 \wedge X_2, \\ \mu X_3 = X_1 \wedge X_2. & \nu X_3 = X_1 \wedge X_2. & \mu X_3 = X_1 \vee X_2. \end{array}$$

14.1.1 Boolean equation systems and model checking

Boolean equation systems are interesting because they can be used to represent and solve the model checking problem. A Boolean equation system can be constructed out of a modal formula and a labeled transition system. The question of whether the formula is valid for the initial state of the transition system is then equivalent to the question of whether the solution of a Boolean equation system is *true* for the first BES variable.

As an example, consider the formula $\mu X.\nu Y.\langle a \rangle X \vee \langle b \rangle Y$. This formula expresses that an infinite sequence of a and b actions exists, where the total number of a's is finite. Now recall that a useful way to view X and Y is as the sets of states where they are valid, and observe that due to the construction $\mu X.\nu Y.\dots$ the "sets" X and Y are equal.

We will find out whether this formula is valid for state 1 of the transition system of figure 14.1 via a translation to a BES. For this purpose we introduce four Boolean variables X_1, X_2, Y_1, and Y_2. The variable X_i represents that X is valid in state i, and Y_i represents that Y is valid in state i. Thus, the solution of X_1 indicates whether our formula holds in the initial state. Now, X_i holds iff Y_i is valid. Moreover, we are interested in the minimal solution of X_i which gives the following two equations:

$$\begin{array}{l} \mu X_1 = Y_1, \\ \mu X_2 = Y_2. \end{array}$$

The equations for Y_i are slightly more complex. Consider Y_1. It is valid if in state 1 either an a can be done and the formula for X holds in the resulting state, or a b is possible ending in a state where Y holds. Inspection of figure 14.1 shows that two a's are possible in state 1, ending in state 1 and 2, respectively, and no b. Thus, Y_1 holds if X_1 is valid or X_2 holds. With the same reasoning for X_2, and applying the maximal fixed point operator we get the following two equations:

$$\nu Y_1 = X_1 \vee X_2 \vee \mathit{false},$$
$$\nu Y_2 = X_1 \vee Y_2.$$

As the outer fixed point symbols are the most important in a modal formula, the equations for the variables for X come before those for Y in the Boolean equation system. There is no required ordering among the variables X_1 and X_2, and among the variables Y_1 and Y_2. The total Boolean equation system becomes:

$$\begin{aligned} &\mu X_1 = Y_1, \\ &\mu X_2 = Y_2, \\ &\nu Y_1 = X_1 \vee X_2 \vee \mathit{false}, \\ &\nu Y_2 = X_1 \vee Y_2. \end{aligned} \tag{14.1}$$

Below, in section 14.3, we define how to translate modal formulas with time and data.

Exercise 14.1.3. Write down the Boolean equation systems that result when checking the following formulas on the transition system in figure 14.1. $\nu X.[\mathit{true}]X \wedge \langle \mathit{true}\rangle \mathit{true}$, $\nu X.\mu Y.\langle a\rangle X \wedge \langle b\rangle Y$ and $\nu X.\mu Y.\langle a\rangle X \vee \langle b\rangle Y$.

14.1.2 Gaussian elimination

First we provide an intuitively appealing way to solve Boolean equation systems, based on two sets of simplification rules. The technique is called *Gaussian elimination*, as it is reminiscent of Gaussian elimination when solving linear equations in linear algebra.[1]

We first look at single equations. Consider the following maximal fixed point equation, where ϕ is an arbitrary right-hand side:

$$\nu X = \phi.$$

This equation can be replaced by

$$\nu X = \phi[X := \mathit{true}]$$

where every occurrence of X can be replaced by true. This replacement will not alter the solutions of the fixed point. This can be understood as follows. If true is a solution for X in $X = \phi$, this gives the required maximal solution for X. In this case $\phi[X := \mathit{true}]$ is true. If true is not a solution for X, then the maximal solution for X must be false.

[1]Carl Friedrich Gauß (1777–1855) was a German mathematician with among others important contributions to statistics, mathematical analysis, astronomy, and optics. At the age of 21 he wrote a book founding modern number theory.

In this case $\phi[X{:=}true]$ also equals $false$. In either case, $\phi[X{:=}true]$ provides the solution for X.

For a minimal fixed point, there is a similar rule with a similar motivation, except that each occurrence of X can be replaced by $false$. Concretely,

$$\mu X{=}\phi$$

can be replaced by

$$\mu X{=}\phi[X{:=}false].$$

We now look at a sequence of Boolean equations. Suppose a Boolean equation system contains the equation

$$\zeta X{=}\phi.$$

Here the symbol ζ is used, to represent either μ or ν. We can replace any occurrence of X in any equation occurring earlier in the sequence by ϕ. We can also substitute ϕ for X if any later equation, if ϕ does not contain free variables (i.e., ϕ is equal to $true$ or $false$).

Gaussian elimination consists of solving a Boolean equation system from bottom to top. If the last equation has the shape

$$\zeta X{=}\phi$$

then replace X in ϕ by either $true$ or $false$ depending on ζ, leading to an equation $\zeta X{=}\phi'$. Subsequently, substitute ϕ' for all occurrences of X in earlier equations. Forget for the moment the equation $\zeta X{=}\phi'$. Now one variable has been removed. Repeat the steps above, until all variables except the initial variable have been removed. The right-hand side of the equation of the initial variable is now either $true$ or $false$ and we know the solution. Forward substitution of variables that are solved in all equations (including those that were forgotten) will give the solutions for all variables.

Applying this to the Boolean equations in equation (14.1) yields the following sequence of steps to solve it.

$$\begin{array}{lclclc}
\mu X_1{=}Y_1 & & \mu X_1{=}Y_1 & & \mu X_1{=}Y_1 & \\
\mu X_2{=}Y_2 & \overset{(1)}{=} & \mu X_2{=}Y_2 & \overset{(2)}{=} & \mu X_2{=}Y_2 & \overset{(3)}{=} \\
\nu Y_1{=}X_1 \vee X_2 & & \nu Y_1{=}X_1 \vee X_2 & & \nu Y_1{=}X_1 \vee X_2 & \\
\nu Y_2{=}X_1 \vee Y_2 & & \nu Y_2{=}X_1 \vee true & & \nu Y_2{=}true &
\end{array}$$

$$\begin{array}{lclclc}
\mu X_1{=}Y_1 & & \mu X_1{=}X_1 \vee X_2 & & \mu X_1{=}X_1 \vee true & \\
\mu X_2{=}true & \overset{(4)}{=} & \mu X_2{=}true & \overset{(5)}{=} & \mu X_2{=}true & \overset{(6)}{=} \\
\nu Y_1{=}X_1 \vee X_2 & & \nu Y_1{=}X_1 \vee X_2 & & \nu Y_1{=}X_1 \vee X_2 & \\
\nu Y_2{=}true & & \nu Y_2{=}true & & \nu Y_2{=}true &
\end{array}$$

$$\begin{array}{lclcl}
\mu X_1{=}true & & \mu X_1{=}true & & \mu X_1{=}true \\
\mu X_2{=}true & \overset{(7)}{=} & \mu X_2{=}true & \overset{(8)}{=} & \mu X_2{=}true \\
\nu Y_1{=}X_1 \vee X_2 & & \nu Y_1{=}true \vee true & & \nu Y_1{=}true \\
\nu Y_2{=}true & & \nu Y_2{=}true & & \nu Y_2{=}true
\end{array}$$

If an equation is temporarily forgotten, it is shown in gray. In steps (1) and (5) a right-hand side variable is replaced by *true* and *false* in accordance with the fixed point symbol. At steps (2), (6), and (9) Boolean simplification rules have been applied. At (3), (4), and (7) backward substitution is used and an equation is forgotten. Finally, at step (8), forward substitution is used.

Note that it is now obvious that the property is true. And indeed there is an infinite sequence of actions starting in the initial state 1, for instance $a{\cdot}b{\cdot}b{\cdot}\cdots$ where a occurs only finitely often.

Although the procedure above looks deceptively simple, it has exponential complexity and it does not work well for larger Boolean equation systems. Solving a Boolean equation system is known to be in NP and co-NP, but it is not NP-hard (nor co-NP-hard). This means that it is possible and even likely that there is a polynomial algorithm to solve a BES, but up to now this algorithm has not been found. However, there are efficient algorithms for subclasses of BESs, in particular when the number of alternations of μ's and ν's is limited or when only disjunctions or conjunctions are used in the right-hand sides of the equations. There are numerous algorithms to solve BESs in general, which, despite their exponential complexity, perform reasonably well in practice.

Exercise 14.1.4. Solve the Boolean equation systems from in exercise 14.1.2 using Gaussian elimination.

Exercise 14.1.5. Solve the following Boolean equation systems that stem from exercise 14.1.3 using Gaussian elimination.

$$
\begin{array}{lll}
\nu X_1 = X_1 \wedge X_2 \wedge \mathit{true} & \nu X_1 = Y_1 & \nu X_1 = Y_1 \\
\nu X_2 = X_1 \wedge X_2 \wedge \mathit{true} & \nu X_2 = Y_2 & \nu X_2 = Y_2 \\
 & \mu Y_1 = (X_1 \vee X_2) \wedge \mathit{false} & \mu Y_1 = X_1 \vee X_2 \vee \mathit{false} \\
 & \mu Y_2 = X_1 \wedge Y_2 & \mu Y_2 = X_1 \vee Y_2
\end{array}
$$

14.2 Parameterized Boolean equation systems

Boolean equation systems have the same disadvantage as labeled transition systems, namely, that they are of a fairly low level. They can become large even for the verification of rather small modal formulas on moderate processes. In order to deal with this problem for LTSs, we introduced linear process equations in which the process behavior is encoded in data parameters. In the same way, we introduce parameterized Boolean equation systems (PBESs) as the concise counterpart of Boolean equation systems.

A parameterized Boolean equation is a fixed point equation of the form

$$\mu X(d_1{:}D_1, \ldots, d_n{:}D_n) = \phi$$

where μ indicates a minimal fixed point, or

$$\nu X(d_1{:}D_1, \ldots, d_n{:}D_n) = \phi$$

where ν indicates that this is a maximal fixed point equation.

Each equation has a unique predicate variable X at its left-hand side that depends on zero or more data variables $d_1, \ldots, d_n$ of sorts $D_1, \ldots, D_n$. We restrict ourselves to a single data variable at the left-hand side in our theoretical considerations.

The right-hand side of each equation is a *predicate formula* containing data terms, Boolean connectives, quantifiers over (possibly infinite) data domains, and data and predicate variables. Predicate formulas ϕ are defined by the following grammar:

$$\phi ::= b \mid X(e) \mid \phi \wedge \phi \mid \phi \vee \phi \mid \forall d{:}D.\phi \mid \exists d{:}D.\phi \mid \mathit{true} \mid \mathit{false}$$

where b is a data term of sort $\mathbb{B}$, X is a predicate variable, d is a data variable of sort D, and e is a data term. Note that negation does not occur in predicate formulas, except as an operator in data terms. This allows us to write predicate formulas of the form $b \rightarrow \phi$, which stand for $\neg b \vee \phi$.

A parameterized Boolean equation system consists of a sequence of zero or more parameterized Boolean equations. Generally, we are interested in the validity of an arbitrary predicate formula in the context of a PBES. This is called the initial expression.

The semantics of a PBES is provided in section 15.4.

Example 14.2.1. Consider a linear process $X(n{:}\mathbb{N}) = (n{<}100) {\rightarrow} a{\cdot}X(n{+}1)$ with initial state $X(0)$. It is a process that can do 100 a's and will then deadlock. Consider the modal formulas $\phi_1 = [\mathit{true}^\star]\langle \mathit{true}\rangle \mathit{true}$ (there is no deadlock, clearly false) and $\phi_2 = \mu Y.[\overline{a}]Y \wedge \langle \mathit{true}\rangle \mathit{true}$ (an a action is inevitable, clearly true). These formulas give rise to the following PBESs. The systematic translation is provided in the next section. We use the convention to write a tilde above the PBES variables to distinguish them from those in the modal formula.

pbes $\nu\tilde{X}(n{:}\mathbb{N}) {=} (n{<}100 {\rightarrow} \tilde{X}(n{+}1)) \wedge n{<}100;$
init $\tilde{X}(0);$

and

pbes $\mu\tilde{Y}(n{:}\mathbb{N}) {=} (\mathit{false} {\rightarrow} \tilde{Y}(n{+}1)) \wedge n{<}100;$
init $\tilde{Y}(0);$

14.3 Translation of modal formulas to parameterized Boolean equation systems

In this section we show how a modal formula and a linear process are translated to a PBES. We start out with the following linear process, omitting time, multi-actions and terminating summands.

proc $X(d{:}D) = \sum_{i \in I} \sum_{e_i : E_i} c_i(d, e_i) \rightarrow a_i(f_i(d, e_i)) {\cdot} X(g_i(d, e_i));$
init $X(d_0);$

Furthermore, we consider a modal formula ϕ. It is convenient for the formulation of the translation that the formula starts with a fixed point symbol. Thus, we consider

$\nu X.\phi$. As any formula ϕ_0 is equivalent to $\nu X.\phi_0$ for any X not occurring in ϕ_0, this is not a restriction.

Now consider every subformula ψ of the modal formula ϕ with the shape

$$\zeta X(x_f{:}D_f{:=}d_f).\psi_0$$

where ζ is either μ or ν. Using α-conversion, we can assume that the variable X is chosen to be unique within the modal formula. Each such subformula is translated to the PBES equation

$$\zeta\tilde{X}(x_f{:}D_f, d{:}D, y_X{:}D_X){=}RHS(\psi_0).$$

The variable (or sequence of variables) x_f stems from ψ, the variable d comes from the linear process and the variable (or the sequence of variables) y_X of sort D_X represents the free variables that occur in ψ. The function RHS is explained below.

The resulting PBES consists of the list of all such equations obtained from ϕ where the equations coming from formulas that are more deeply nested in ϕ occur later in the list.

The function RHS translates the right-hand side of a fixed point equation to the right-hand side of a PBES equation. For most operators the translation follows directly from the syntax. The most interesting case is the translation of the modalities. In the modalities, the predicate $Sat(a_i(f_i(d, e_i)), \alpha)$ is used that expresses that the action $a_i(f_i(d, e_i))$ matches the action formula α.

$$
\begin{array}{ll}
RHS(c) & = c.\\
RHS(\phi \wedge \psi) & = RHS(\phi) \wedge RHS(\psi).\\
RHS(\phi \vee \psi) & = RHS(\phi) \vee RHS(\psi).\\
RHS(\forall x{:}E.\phi) & = \forall x{:}E.RHS(\phi).\\
RHS(\exists x{:}E.\phi) & = \exists x{:}E.RHS(\phi).\\
RHS([\alpha]\phi) & = \bigwedge_{i\in I} \forall e_i{:}E_i.((Sat(a_i(f_i(d, e_i)), \alpha) \wedge c_i(d, e_i))\\
 & \qquad \rightarrow RHS(\phi)[d := g_i(d, e_i)]).\\
RHS(\langle\alpha\rangle\phi) & = \bigvee_{i\in I} \exists e_i{:}E_i.(Sat(a_i(f_i(d, e_i)), \alpha) \wedge c_i(d, e_i)\\
 & \qquad \wedge\, RHS(\phi)[d := g_i(d, e_i)]).\\
RHS(X(d_f)) & = \tilde{X}(d_f, d, y_X).\\
RHS(\mu X(x_f{:}D_f := d_f).\, \phi) & = \tilde{X}(d_f, d, y_X).\\
RHS(\nu X(x_f{:}D_f := d_f).\, \phi) & = \tilde{X}(d_f, d, y_X).
\end{array}
$$

Here, the variable y_X represent the free variables that occur in the body of X. In the last two lines this body is ϕ. In the third but last line, it is the body of X taken from the definition of X that surrounds the occurrence of X that is translated. The variable d in the last three lines comes from the linear process.

Below we define the function Sat that given an action and an action expression yields a Boolean expression that says when the action is allowed by the action expression. Note that the definition is a straightforward inductive definition.

$$
\begin{array}{ll}
Sat(a(d_1,\ldots,d_n),b(d'_1,\ldots,d'_m)) & = \begin{cases} \bigwedge_{i=1}^{n} d_i{\approx}d'_i & \text{if } a{=}b,\ n{=}m \text{ and the sort of each } d_i \text{ equals that of } d'_i, \\ \mathit{false} & \text{otherwise.} \end{cases} \\
Sat(a,c) & = c. \\
Sat(a,\neg\alpha) & = \neg Sat(a,\alpha). \\
Sat(a,\alpha_1 \wedge \alpha_2) & = Sat(a,\alpha_1) \wedge Sat(a,\alpha_2). \\
Sat(a,\alpha_1 \vee \alpha_2) & = Sat(a,\alpha_1) \vee Sat(a,\alpha_2). \\
Sat(a,\forall x{:}D.\alpha) & = \forall y{:}D.(Sat(a,\alpha[x := y])). \\
Sat(a,\exists x{:}D.\alpha) & = \exists y{:}D.(Sat(a,\alpha[x := y])).
\end{array}
$$

Example 14.3.1. Consider a simple lossy channel that reads numbers from a stream and tries to send those to the other side where the data may or may not arrive. Below it is described in linear form. The actions r and s represent reading and delivering the data. The action ℓ stands for losing the data.

act $r, s : \mathbb{N};$
$\quad\ell;$
proc $C(b{:}\mathbb{B}, m{:}\mathbb{N}) = \sum_{m'{:}\mathbb{N}} b {\rightarrow} r(m') {\cdot} C(\mathit{false}, m')$
$\qquad + (\neg b) {\rightarrow} s(m) {\cdot} C(\mathit{true}, m)$
$\qquad + (\neg b) {\rightarrow} \ell {\cdot} C(\mathit{true}, m);$
init $C(\mathit{true}, 0);$

One might want to verify that it is always possible that data is delivered or lost within a finite number of steps. In other words, at any time in the process, one should within a finite number of steps either have the possibility to deliver the data ($s(m)$) or lose the data (ℓ). This can be formulated using the following formula:

$$\nu X.([\mathit{true}]X \wedge \mu Y.([\mathit{true}]Y \vee \langle\ell\rangle \mathit{true} \vee \exists m''{:}\mathbb{N}.\langle s(m'')\rangle \mathit{true})).$$

We translate the linear process and the formula to a BES. Note that the modal formula already starts with a fixed point symbol. There are two subformulas starting with a fixed point symbol, namely, $\nu X.\ldots$ and $\mu Y.\ldots$. These give rise to the following two parameterized Boolean equations, where the one for Y is last as it occurs more deeply nested in the formula.

pbes $\nu \tilde{X}(b{:}\mathbb{B}, m{:}\mathbb{N}) {=} \mathit{RHS}([\mathit{true}]X \wedge \mu Y.(\cdots));$
$\quad\mu \tilde{Y}(b{:}\mathbb{B}, m{:}\mathbb{N}) {=} \mathit{RHS}([\mathit{true}]Y \vee \langle\ell\rangle \mathit{true} \vee \exists m''{:}\mathbb{N}.\langle s(m'')\rangle \mathit{true});$
init $\tilde{X}(\mathit{true}, 0);$

There are no free or bound data variables in the modal formula. The only data parameters that occur in the PBES equations are the variables b and m from the linear process.

The translation of $\mathit{RHS}([\mathit{true}]X \wedge \mu Y.(\cdots))$ goes as follows:

$$
\begin{array}{l}
\mathit{RHS}([\mathit{true}]X \wedge \mu Y.(\cdots)) = \\
\mathit{RHS}([\mathit{true}]X) \wedge \mathit{RHS}(\mu Y.(\cdots)) = \\
\mathit{RHS}([\mathit{true}]X) \wedge \tilde{Y}(b,m).
\end{array}
$$

As the translation of $RHS([true]X)$ is a little more involved, we do this separately. Note that as there are three summands in the linear process, there are three conjuncts in the translation of this box modality.

$$\begin{array}{l} RHS([true]X) = \\ \quad (\forall m':\mathbb{N}.(Sat(r(m'), true) \wedge b) \to RHS(X)[b:=false, m := m']) \wedge \\ \quad ((Sat(s(m), true) \wedge \neg b) \to RHS(X)[b:=true]) \wedge \\ \quad ((Sat(\ell, true) \wedge \neg b) \to RHS(X)[b:=true]). \end{array} \tag{14.2}$$

As $Sat(a, true)$ is $true$ for any action a and $RHS(X)$ becomes $\tilde{X}(b, m)$, equation (14.2) reduces to

$$\begin{array}{l} (\forall m':\mathbb{N}.(true \wedge b) \to \tilde{X}(false, m')) \wedge \\ ((true \wedge \neg b) \to \tilde{X}(true, m)) \wedge \\ ((true \wedge \neg b) \to \tilde{X}(true, m)) \end{array}$$

which we can simplify to

$$\forall m':\mathbb{N}.(b \to \tilde{X}(false, m')) \wedge (\neg b \to \tilde{X}(true, m)).$$

The translation of $RHS([true]X \wedge \mu Y.(\cdots))$ yields

$$\forall m':\mathbb{N}.(b \to \tilde{X}(false, m')) \wedge (\neg b \to \tilde{X}(true, m)) \wedge \tilde{Y}(b, m).$$

In the same way, we can translate $RHS([true]Y \vee \langle \ell \rangle true \vee \exists m'':\mathbb{N}.\langle s(m'') \rangle true)$. The PBES that we obtain in this way is:

$$\begin{array}{ll} \textbf{pbes} & \nu\tilde{X}(b:\mathbb{B}, m:\mathbb{N}) = \forall m':\mathbb{N}.(b \to \tilde{X}(false, m')) \wedge (\neg b \to \tilde{X}(true, m)) \wedge \tilde{Y}(b, m); \\ & \mu\tilde{Y}(b:\mathbb{B}, m:\mathbb{N}) = (\forall m':\mathbb{N}.(b \to \tilde{Y}(false, m')) \wedge (\neg b \to \tilde{Y}(true, m))) \vee \\ & \qquad \neg b \vee \exists m'':\mathbb{N}.\neg b \wedge m \approx m''; \\ \textbf{init} & \tilde{X}(true, 0); \end{array}$$

The translation above can be extended to real-time processes with multi-actions. For multi-actions only a straightforward extension of Sat is required to match a multi-action on an action formula. For time it is required to add an extra parameter u:$\mathbb{R}$ to the resulting PBES that indicates the last time an action took place. For any action in a modality, a condition is added to the PBES that this action takes place after the previously investigated action. For the delay operator it is checked that it is possible to wait sufficiently long, or that the required delay has already passed. As an illustration we give the translations for the box modality and the delay in the timed setting.

$$\begin{array}{lcl} RHS([\alpha']\phi) & = & \bigwedge_{i \in I} \forall e_i:E_i.((Sat(\alpha_i(d, e_i){}^{c}t_i(d, e_i), \alpha') \wedge \\ & & \qquad c_i(d, e_i) \wedge t_i(d, e_i) > u\ ) \to \\ & & \qquad RHS(\phi)[u := t_i(d, e_i)][d := g_i(d, e_i)]), \\ RHS(\Delta^{c}t) & = & (\bigvee_{i \in I \cup J} \exists e_i:E_i.(c_i(d, e_i) \wedge t < t_i(d, e_i))) \vee t \leq u. \end{array}$$

Exercise 14.3.2. Derive the PBESs in example 14.2.1.

Exercise 14.3.3. Consider the process that models objects leaving and entering a room. The number n represents the number of objects in the room.

proc $X(n{:}\mathbb{N}) = \mathit{enter}\cdot X(n{+}1) + (n{>}0) \rightarrow \mathit{leave}\cdot X(n{-}1)$;
init $X(0)$;

Translate the formulas $[\mathit{true}^\star]\langle \mathit{true}\rangle \mathit{true}$ (no deadlock), $\langle \mathit{true}^\star\cdot \mathit{leave}\rangle \mathit{true}$ (there is a path to a *leave* action) and $\nu Y(m{:}\mathbb{N}{:=}0).[\mathit{enter}]Y(m{+}1) \wedge [\mathit{leave}](m{>}0 \wedge Y(m{-}1))$ (it is not possible that more objects leave the room than have entered) to PBESs.

Exercise 14.3.4. Consider the formula

$$\nu X_1(m{:}\mathbb{N}{:=}0).[a]X_1(m{+}1) \wedge \mu X_2(n{:}\mathbb{N}{:=}0).\langle b\rangle X_2(n{+}1) \vee n{\geq}m$$

which says that after any number of a actions it is always possible to do more b actions. Give the PBES to verify that this formula holds for the process $Z = a\cdot Z + b\cdot Z$.

Exercise 14.3.5. Consider the processes $X_1(n{:}\mathbb{N}){=}a^{\varsigma}n\cdot X_1(n{+}1)$, $X_2{=}\sum_{t:\mathbb{R}} a^{\varsigma}t\cdot X_2$. Consider the modal formula $[\mathit{true}^\star]\forall r{:}\mathbb{R}.\Delta^{\varsigma}r$ which says that it is always possible to idle without having to do an action. This formula is invalid for X_1 and valid for X_2. Derive the PBESs for both formulas.

14.4 Techniques for solving parameterized Boolean equation systems

This section provides some techniques to solve a PBES. First we explain how to solve a PBES by translating it to a BES. After that we provide symbolic techniques for solving PBESs, by providing global, and subsequently local transformation rules.

14.4.1 Transforming a parameterized Boolean equation system to a Boolean equation system

A straightforward technique to solve a PBES is to transform it to a BES by instantiating its equations. The obtained BES can then be solved with one of the algorithms for solving BESs, for instance, Gaussian elimination. Note that this parallels generating an LTS from a linear process.

We explain the technique via an example. Consider the following PBES

pbes $\mu X(n{:}\mathbb{N}){=}n{<}2 \wedge X(n{+}1) \wedge Y(n)$;
$\quad\nu Y(n{:}\mathbb{N}){=}n{>}3 \vee Y(n+1)$;
init $X(0)$

We generate the BES by introducing a variable X_0 to represent $X(0)$. By substituting 0 for n we calculate the right-hand side of X_0 and we introduce variables X_1 for $X(1)$ and Y_0 for $Y(0)$. Note that the fixed point symbol is inherited from the PBES equation.

bes $\mu X_0{=}X_1 \wedge Y_0$;

We must now generate the equation for X_1 and Y_0 in a similar fashion. The order of the PBES equations is preserved in the generated BES, where equations stemming from the same PBES equation are grouped. The complete resulting BES becomes

bes $\mu X_0{=}X_1 \wedge Y_0;$
$\mu X_1{=}X_2 \wedge Y_1;$
$\mu X_2{=}\mathit{false};$
$\nu Y_0{=}Y_1;$
$\nu Y_1{=}Y_2;$
$\nu Y_2{=}Y_3;$
$\nu Y_3{=}Y_4;$
$\nu Y_4{=}\mathit{true};$
init $X_0;$

The *false* in this BES is obtained from $2{<}2 \wedge X(3) \wedge Y(2)$ and the *true* stems from $4{>}3 \vee Y(5)$. Observe that it is not necessary to generate BES equations for $X(3)$ and $Y(5)$ as they are eliminated by simple logical operations. Using Gaussian elimination it follows that $X_0 = \mathit{false}$ is the solution of the BES.

It is possible that the generation of a BES from a PBES does not terminate or leads to a huge BES. Simplifying the BES as done above can avoid such excessive generation effort and lead to a solution in a quicker way.

Exercise 14.4.1. Solve the following PBES by translating it to a BES.

pbes $\nu X(n{:}\mathbb{N}){=}X(n{+}1) \wedge Y(n);$
$\mu Y(n{:}\mathbb{N}){=}Y(n);$
init $X(0);$

Exercise 14.4.2. Solve the following PBES.

pbes $\mu X(n{:}\mathbb{N}){=}\forall m{:}\mathbb{N}.(m{<}3 \rightarrow X(m{+}n));$
init $X(0);$

14.4.2 Global solving techniques for parameterized Boolean equation systems

In table 14.1 some global transformation rules for PBESs are given. In these rules we use the symbol $\mathcal{E}$ to indicate a subsequence of Boolean equations. The rules express how a subsequence of a particular shape can be replaced by an equivalent sequence. The set of variables $\mathrm{bnd}(\mathcal{E})$ is defined as the PBES variables occurring at the left-hand side in $\mathcal{E}$, i.e., those that are bound in $\mathcal{E}$. The set of PBES variables $\mathrm{occ}(\phi)$ are those occurring in the formula ϕ. As done elsewhere, ζ and ζ' stand for either μ or ν.

The substitution rule says that it is always possible to substitute backward into a set of fixed point equations. Note that this rule is essential for Gaussian elimination. The migration rule says that two fixed point equations can be exchanged if the first one is solved, i.e., $\mathrm{occ}(\phi) = \emptyset$. In terms of Gaussian elimination, this means that after the first equation is solved, it can be moved to the end of the equations, and using the substitution rule, its right-hand side can be substituted for all occurrences of the variable at the left-hand side.

When we can solve an equation locally, i.e., we can transform each fixed point equation $\zeta X(d{:}D){=}\phi$ into an equation $\zeta X(d{:}D){=}\psi$ where X does not occur in ψ anymore, then each PBES can be solved using the substitution and migration rules. We say that substitution and migration are globally complete.

Substitution ($X, Y \notin \text{bnd}(\mathcal{E})$) $(\zeta X(d{:}D){=}\phi)\mathcal{E}(\zeta' Y(e{:}E){=}\psi) = (\zeta X(d{:}D){=}\phi[Y := \lambda e{:}E.\psi])\mathcal{E}(\zeta' Y(e{:}E){=}\psi)$
Migration ($\text{occ}(\phi){=}\emptyset$ and $X \notin \text{bnd}(\mathcal{E})$) $(\zeta X(d{:}D){=}\phi)\mathcal{E} = \mathcal{E}(\zeta X(d{:}D){=}\phi)$
Switching $(\zeta X(d{:}D){=}\phi)(\zeta Y(e{:}E){=}\psi) = (\zeta Y(e{:}E){=}\psi)(\zeta X(d{:}D){=}\phi)$
Independence ($X \notin \text{occ}(\psi)$ and $Y \notin \text{occ}(\phi)$) $(\zeta X(d{:}D){=}\phi)(\zeta' Y(e{:}E){=}\psi) = (\zeta' Y(e{:}E){=}\psi)(\zeta X(d{:}D){=}\phi)$

Table 14.1: Rules for transforming PBESs

Example 14.4.3. Consider the following PBES

pbes $\nu X(n{:}\mathbb{N}){=}n{>}3 \vee Z(n);$
$\nu Y(n{:}\mathbb{N}){=}n{\leq}3;$
$\mu Z(n{:}\mathbb{N}){=}Y(n);$

Using the migration rule, the equation for Y can be moved after the equation for Z. By subsequent upward substitution of Y, the following equivalent PBES is obtained.

pbes $\nu X(n{:}\mathbb{N}){=}n{>}3 \vee n{\leq}3;$
$\mu Z(n{:}\mathbb{N}){=}n{\leq}3;$
$\nu Y(n{:}\mathbb{N}){=}n{\leq}3;$

By simplifying the right-hand side using ordinary calculation rules, which can always be applied to the right-hand sides, the first equation can be further simplified to $X(n) = \mathit{true}$.

There are more conditions under which it is allowed to manipulate the equations in PBESs. We refer to the switching and independence rules in table 14.1. Although they are not essential for solving a PBES globally, they can turn out to be handy at times.

Example 14.4.4. The nesting depth of a PBES is the number of alternations of μ and ν operators. It is generally seen as a measure of the complexity of a PBES. Using the switching rule, the alternation depth can often be reduced. The PBES at the left below with seven alternations is equivalent to the PBES at the right that is obtained by applying the switching rule only.

$$\begin{array}{ll}
\mu X_0 = X_1 \wedge X_2, & \mu X_0 = X_1 \wedge X_2, \\
\nu X_1 = X_3, & \mu X_2 = X_1 \wedge X_4, \\
\mu X_2 = X_1 \wedge X_4, & \mu X_4 = X_0 \vee X_5, \\
\nu X_3 = true, & \mu X_6 = X_7 \wedge X_0, \\
\mu X_4 = X_0 \vee X_5, & \nu X_1 = X_3, \\
\nu X_5 = X_4 \wedge X_1, & \nu X_3 = true, \\
\mu X_6 = X_7 \wedge X_0, & \nu X_5 = X_4 \wedge X_1, \\
\nu X_7 = X_1 \vee X_5 \wedge X_6. & \nu X_7 = X_1 \vee X_5 \wedge X_6.
\end{array}$$

Exercise 14.4.5. Solve both PBESs from exercise 14.4.4.

14.4.3 Local solving techniques for parameterized Boolean equation systems

In order to apply the techniques from the previous section, it is necessary to transform a fixed point equation $\zeta X(d{:}D){=}\phi$ into an equation of the shape $\zeta X(d{:}D){=}\psi$ where X no longer occurs in ψ. There are several techniques to do this, but there is no general algorithm for this task. Here some of the main techniques are given to solve PBESs locally.

Simplification

Standard rules of logic and arithmetic can always be applied to the right-hand side of a PBES equation.

Example 14.4.6. Consider the following PBES

pbes $\mu X(n{:}\mathbb{N}){=}X(n{+}1) \wedge Y(n);$
$\nu Y(n{:}\mathbb{N}){=}n{>}3 \wedge Z(n);$
$\mu Z(n{:}\mathbb{N}){=}n{<}4;$
init $X(1);$

By backward substitution of Z, the right-hand side of the equation for Y reduces to $n{>}3 \wedge n{<}4$, which is equivalent to *false* as n is a natural number. Substituting $Y(n) =$ *false* in the first equation and solving it yields $X(n) =$ *false* as the solution.

Iterative approximation

In a PBES equation, the solution of the fixed point symbol can be approximated. If the approximation becomes stable, it is the solution to the equation. Consider a minimal fixed point equation

$$\mu X(d{:}D){=}\phi.$$

As it is a minimal fixed point equation, the approximations are inductively defined by

$$X_0(d) = \mathit{false},$$
$$X_{n+1}(d) = \phi[X{:=}X_n].$$

For a maximal fixed point equation, the initial solution is $X_0(d) = true$. The solution is stable if $X_{n+1}(d) = X_n(d)$ for all d. In this case, the fixed point equation can be replaced by $\mu X(d) \!=\! X_n(d)$. Note that X no longer occurs in the right-hand side.

Example 14.4.7. Fixed point approximations can be very useful, as the first approximation is often stable. Consider the following PBES obtained to show that the process $X(n{:}\mathbb{N}) = (n>3) \rightarrow a{\cdot}X(n{+}1) \diamond b{\cdot}X(n^2)$ is deadlock free.

pbes $\nu\tilde{X}(n{:}\mathbb{N}) \!=\! (n>3 \rightarrow \tilde{X}(n{+}1)) \wedge (n \leq 3 \rightarrow \tilde{X}(n^2)) \wedge (n<3 \vee n \geq 3)$;

The first approximation is $X_0(d) = true$. The second is $X_1(d) = (n>3 \rightarrow true) \wedge (n \leq 3 \rightarrow true) \wedge (n<3 \vee n \geq 3)$ which is also equivalent to true. Therefore, the solution for this BES is $X(n) = true$. As we could see right away, for any n the process is deadlock free.

Exercise 14.4.8. Solve the following three PBESs using fixed point approximation.

$\mu X(n{:}\mathbb{N}) \!=\! n \approx 1 \wedge X(n^2 - 37)$.
$\mu X(n{:}\mathbb{N}) \!=\! n \approx 1 \vee X(n{+}1)$.
$\nu X(b{:}\mathbb{B}) \!=\! b \wedge X(\neg b)$.

Patterns

There are situations where fixed point approximation does not work. Some of these situations are quite similar and there are standard ways of eliminating variables from the right-hand side. Such similar situations are referred to as patterns, of which four are given here.

Consider the Boolean equation where f is an arbitrary function

$$\nu X(d{:}D) \!=\! \phi(d) \wedge (\psi(d) \vee X(f(d))).$$

Then this equation is equivalent to

$$\nu X(d{:}D) \!=\! \forall j{:}\mathbb{N}.((\forall i{:}\mathbb{N}.i<j \rightarrow \neg\psi(f^i(d))) \rightarrow \phi(f^j(d))).$$

where f^j is defined by $f^0(d) = d$ and $f^{n+1}(d) = f(f^n(d))$.

For a minimal fixed point pattern, the following is a solution. The Boolean equation

$$\mu X(d{:}D) \!=\! \phi(d) \wedge (\psi(d) \vee X(f(d)))$$

is equivalent to

$$\mu X(d{:}D) \!=\! \exists i{:}\mathbb{N}.\psi(f^i(d)) \wedge (\forall j{:}\mathbb{N}.j \leq i \rightarrow \phi(f^j(d))).$$

Example 14.4.9. Consider a number generating process where a function f determines the next number to be generated.

proc $Generator(n{:}\mathbb{N}) = send(n){\cdot}Generator(f(n))$;
init $Generator(0)$;

The following modal formula expresses that each generated number must be unique

$$[true^\star]\forall m{:}\mathbb{N}.[send(m)\cdot true^\star\cdot send(m)]false.$$

More precisely, it says that a number m cannot be sent twice. The PBES to check this formula on the generator is

pbes $\nu X(n{:}\mathbb{N}){=}X(f(n)) \wedge \forall m{:}\mathbb{N}.(m{\approx}n){\rightarrow}Y(m, f(n));$
$\quad\nu Y(m, n{:}\mathbb{N}) = Y(m, f(n)) \wedge m{\not\approx}n;$
init $X(0);$

The second Boolean equation matches the pattern above by taking $\phi = m{\not\approx}n$ and $\psi = false$. This equation can be replaced by

$$\nu Y(m, n{:}\mathbb{N}){=}\forall j{:}\mathbb{N}.f^j(n){\not\approx}m.$$

Using the substitution rule, as Y no longer occurs on the right-hand side, Y can be eliminated in the first equation, which after some simplification reads

pbes $\nu X(n{:}\mathbb{N}){=}X(f(n)) \wedge \forall m{:}\mathbb{N}.((m{\approx}n){\rightarrow}\forall j{:}\mathbb{N}.f^{j+1}(n){\not\approx}m);$

This equation also fits the pattern. Hence, we can eliminate it using a similar procedure and obtain

pbes $\nu X(n{:}\mathbb{N}){=}\forall j, j'{:}\mathbb{N}.f^{j+1}(f^{j'}(n)){\not\approx}f^{j'}(n);$

If we apply this to the initial value of the PBES, i.e., $n = 0$, we see that the number generator generates unique numbers exactly if $\forall j, j'{:}\mathbb{N}.f^{j+1}(f^{j'}(0)){\not\approx}f^{j'}(0)$. This is exactly what we expect.

There are situations where the pattern above is insufficient. For this the following pattern is given here.

$$\zeta X(d{:}D){=}\phi(d) \wedge \bigwedge_{i=0}^{N-1} (\psi_i(d) \vee X(f_i(d)))$$

is equivalent for $\zeta = \nu$ to

$$\begin{aligned}\nu X(d{:}D){=}&\forall j{:}\mathbb{N}.\forall g{:}\mathbb{N}{\rightarrow}\{0, \ldots, N{-}1\}.\\ &((\forall i{:}\mathbb{N}.i{<}j{\rightarrow}\neg\psi_{g(i)}(f(g, i, d))){\rightarrow}\phi(f(g, j, d))).\end{aligned}$$

For $\zeta = \mu$ it is equivalent to

$$\begin{aligned}\mu X(d{:}D){=}&\exists j{:}\mathbb{N}.\exists g{:}\mathbb{N} \rightarrow \{0, \ldots, N{-}1\}.\\ &((\forall i{:}\mathbb{N}.i{<}j \rightarrow \neg\psi_{g(i)}(f(g, i, d))) \wedge \phi(f(g, j, d))).\end{aligned}$$

Here $f(g, i, d)$ is defined as $f(g, 0, d) = d$ and $f(g, j{+}1, d) = f_{g(j)}(f(g, j, d))$.

Exercise 14.4.10. Eliminate the occurrence of X from the right-hand sides of the following two PBES equations.

$$\mu X(n{:}\mathbb{N}){=}X(n{-}1) \vee n{\approx}0.$$
$$\nu X(n{:}\mathbb{R}){=}X(n/2) \wedge n{<}1.$$

Exercise 14.4.11. Solve the following PBES using patterns.

pbes $\mu X(n{:}\mathbb{N}) = (n{>}6{\rightarrow}X(n{-}1)) \wedge (n{<}2{\rightarrow}X(n{+}7));$
init $X(0);$

Invariants

Just as with processes, invariants are useful to solve PBESs. Consider a PBES consisting of a sequence of n equations ($1 \leq i \leq n$):

$$\zeta_i X_i(d_i{:}D_i) = \phi_i.$$

We call a set of predicate formulas I_i a *PBES invariant* iff for all $1 \leq i \leq n$

$$I_i \wedge \phi_i = I_i \wedge \phi_i[X_j := \lambda d_j{:}D_j.(I_j \wedge X_j)]_{1 \leq j \leq n}.$$

The notation $\phi[X_j := \psi_j]_{1 \leq j \leq n}$ denotes the simultaneous substitution of ψ_j for X_j in ϕ. This definition expresses that if an invariant is valid at the left-hand side of a PBES equation, it is also valid at the occurrence of variables at the right-hand side. The definition intentionally does not have a restriction on an initial state or initial PBES variable. Note that the invariant is independent of the fixed point symbols.

Example 14.4.12. The following PBES has $n|_2{\approx}0$ as an invariant.

pbes $\mu X(n{:}\mathbb{N}){=}n{<}100 \rightarrow X(n{+}2);$

The proof, as shown below, is straightforward.

$$\begin{array}{l}
n|_2{\approx}0 \wedge (n{<}100{\rightarrow}X(n{+}2)) = \\
n|_2{\approx}0 \wedge (n{<}100{\rightarrow}(n|_2{\approx}0{\wedge}X(n{+}2))) = \\
n|_2{\approx}0 \wedge (n{<}100{\rightarrow}((n{+}2)|_2{\approx}0{\wedge}X(n{+}2))).
\end{array}$$

If a PBES has an invariant, it can be added or removed in conjunction with the variables X_i of the right-hand side, without changing the solution for those variables $X_i(d)$, provided that $I_i(d)$ is valid. We show its use by two examples. The first one is traditional in the sense that the invariant is added. The second is quite remarkable, because verification is simplified by removing a property implied by the invariant. It is formulated as an exercise.

Example 14.4.13. Consider the process $X(n{:}\mathbb{Z}) = (n{\not\approx}10){\rightarrow}a{\cdot}X(n{-}1)$ for which we want to know whether the initial state $X(0)$ is deadlock free. We want to check the formula $[\mathit{true}^\star]\langle \mathit{true}\rangle \mathit{true}$. The formula and process lead to the following PBES:

$$\nu X(n{:}\mathbb{Z}) = (n{\not\approx}10{\rightarrow}X(n{-}1)) \wedge (n{\not\approx}10).$$

The predicate $n < 10$ is an invariant of this PBES. Therefore, for those $X(n)$ with $n < 10$, we can solve the PBES

$$\nu X(n{:}\mathbb{Z}) = (n{\not\approx}10{\rightarrow}X(n{-}1)) \wedge (n{<}10).$$

Approximating this PBES leads in two steps to the solution that $X(n) = n{<}10$. Approximation of the first PBES does not terminate in a finite number of steps.

Exercise 14.4.14. Consider the following process which can do a series of $a(n)$ actions with strictly decreasing n.

proc $X(n{:}\mathbb{N}) = \sum_{m:\mathbb{N}}(m<n) \to a(m)\cdot X(m);$
init $\sum_{m:\mathbb{N}} a(m)\cdot X(m);$

The following formula states that the length of the series of actions starting with $a(m)$ is at most m.

$$\forall v{:}\mathbb{N}.[a(v)]\nu Y(j{:}\mathbb{N}{:=}0).([\mathit{true}]Y(j{+}1)\land j{\leq}v).$$

Translate the process and formula to a PBES and solve it. A useful invariant is $j{+}n{\leq}v$.

14.5 Historical notes

The first algorithm to show validity of modal μ-calculus formulas on finite state spaces as defined by [117] was given in [54]. It was improved upon in [40] where binary decision diagrams were chosen as a data structure. The use of Boolean equation systems for this purpose was proposed in [124, 125, 176]. Especially, [124, 125] introduced an extensive theory for Boolean equations, using Gaussian elimination as an algorithm to solve Boolean equation systems and including the observation that Boolean equations and parity games [75, 132, 184] coincide. One of the remarkable open problems is whether there is a polynomial algorithm to solve Boolean equation systems, or equivalently, parity games.

It was observed in [80, 126] that PBESs are the natural environment for establishing the validity of modal formulas with data on linear processes. In [91] a calculus to solve parameterized Boolean equations was defined, from which most rules in this chapter are taken, especially the patterns. Invariants for PBESs were defined in [146].

III

Semantics

15

★Semantics

In this chapter we give a detailed account of the mathematical meaning of data and process constructs in mCRL2, as well as modal formulas and parameterized Boolean equation systems. Hitherto, we have presented the abstract syntax of these constructs, provided some intuitive explanation of their semantics, and presented some properties and algebraic laws, without a formal reasoning regarding their soundness. Providing a formal semantics, i.e., a mapping from the domain of syntactic constructs to a mathematical domain, provides rigorous grounds for these properties and laws. In appendix D the precise syntax of all formalisms that we use in this book is given.

15.1 Semantics of data types

Our language for data types is rather complex and hence, we present its semantics in a stepwise manner. We first define sorts, signatures, expressions, substitutions, and data specifications, and subsequently, provide the abstract data types with a semantics. While doing so, we give constraints on the syntactic constructs to guarantee that they do have a semantics, i.e., they are well-typed. Furthermore, we indicate how the concrete data types of mCRL2 fit into the given framework.

15.1.1 Signatures

An algebraic specification has a signature, which is a set of data types, or sorts, together with the constructors and operations (mappings) defined on them.

Definition 15.1.1 (Signature). A *signature* Σ is a triple $(\mathcal{S}, \mathcal{C}_\mathcal{S}, \mathcal{M}_\mathcal{S})$, where $\mathcal{S}$ is a set of sorts, $\mathcal{C}_\mathcal{S}$ is a set of function symbols over $\mathcal{S}$, called *constructors*, and $\mathcal{M}_\mathcal{S}$ is a set of function symbols over $\mathcal{S}$, called *mappings*. Each function symbol f (i.e., constructor or mapping) has an associated sort, which we call its arity, denoted by $f : D_1 \times \cdots \times D_n \to D$, where $D_1, \ldots, D_n, D$ are sorts in $\mathcal{S}$. A function symbol can occur more than once in $\mathcal{C}_\mathcal{S}$ and $\mathcal{M}_\mathcal{S}$ with different arities.

The formal notions defined before precisely reflect their corresponding syntactic notions in mCRL2: sorts are either basic (built-in) or defined sorts in mCRL2. In an mCRL2 specification, one may also use sort aliasing, i.e., define multiple names for the same sort, and a sort in the signature is the representative for all of its aliases.

Constructors and mappings reflect, respectively, constructors and mappings in the mCRL2 syntax. Constructors are those functions that span up a sort. If there are constructors in a sort, any element of the sort can be denoted using constructors. If there are no constructors, the sort can have elements not denotable by data expressions.

Mappings represent the "other" functions, used for calculating and manipulating data. Apart from the mappings and constructors that are explicitly declared in an mCRL2 specification, standard constructors and mappings are defined for standard sorts. In particular, sorts such as numbers, lists, sets, bags, and structured sorts come equipped with their given constructors and mappings. These can be found in appendix B. For each signature belonging to an mCRL2 specification, the following notions of basic and standard sorts are defined.

Definition 15.1.2 (Basic and standard sorts). The set BS of sorts is called the set of *basic sorts* and it precisely contains the sorts $\mathbb{B}$, $\mathbb{N}^+$, $\mathbb{N}$, $\mathbb{Z}$, and $\mathbb{R}$.

A *standard sort* is either a basic sort, or a sort defined using the function, struct, list, set, or bag mCRL2 constructs. Of particular importance among standard sorts are *function sorts*, which are defined using the mCRL2 function sort construct ($\rightarrow$).

Note that standard sorts need not be constructed from basic sorts. The following example illustrates this.

Example 15.1.3. Consider the following specifications for sorts $Enum_1$, $Enum_2$, Fn_1, and Fn_2.

sort $Enum_1$;
cons $e_1, e_2, e_3 : Enum_1$;

sort $Enum_2 = \textbf{struct } e_1 \mid e_2 \mid e_2$;

sort $Fn_1 = \mathbb{N} \rightarrow Enum_1$;
$\quad Fn_2 = \mathbb{N} \rightarrow Enum_2$;

Sort $Enum_1$ is not a standard sort, while $Enum_2$ is. Both Fn_1 and Fn_2 are standard sorts. They are also function sorts.

An important concept in a data specification is a constructor sort, i.e., a sort D, for which there is at least one constructor in the signature with arity $D_1 \times \cdots \times D_n \rightarrow D$.

Definition 15.1.4 (Constructor sort). Let $\Sigma = (\mathcal{S}, \mathcal{C_S}, \mathcal{M_S})$ be a signature. A sort D in $\mathcal{S_S}$ is called a *constructor sort* iff there is a constructor $f{:}D_1 \times \cdots \times D_n \rightarrow D \in \mathcal{C_S}$.

In constructor sorts all elements can be written by an application of a constructor function symbol. Consider sort $Enum_1$ in example 15.1.3. It is a constructor sort, because $Enum_1$ has explicitly given constructors. The elements of sort $Enum_1$ can be denoted by e_1, e_2, and e_3. But note that we have no evidence that these elements are different. The semantics of the sort $Enum_1$ can be any set with one to three elements; sorts cannot be empty.

Constructor sorts generally have a countable number of elements, but using function sorts this does not have to be the case, as the following specification shows.

sort D;
cons $f : (\mathbb{N}{\rightarrow}\mathbb{N}) \rightarrow D$;

As $\mathbb{N}$ is a sort with a countable number of elements, the sort D can have as many elements as there are function sorts from $\mathbb{N}$ to $\mathbb{N}$, and hence can be uncountable.

As stated before, sorts are not allowed to be empty. Using constructors it is possible to define sorts that can only be empty. We forbid this using the notion of a syntactically nonempty sort.

Definition 15.1.5 (Syntactically nonempty sort). Let $\Sigma = (\mathcal{S}, \mathcal{C_S}, \mathcal{M_S})$ be a signature. A sort $D \in \mathcal{S}$ is inductively defined to be *syntactically nonempty* iff there is a constructor $f{:}D_1{\times}\cdots{\times}D_n{\rightarrow}D \in \mathcal{C_S}$ (for $n{\geq}0$) such that for all $1{\leq}i{\leq}n$, if D_i is a constructor sort, it is syntactically nonempty.

The following example illustrates a violation of the constraint of definition 15.1.5.

Example 15.1.6. Consider the following mCRL2 data specification.

sort D;
cons $f : D \rightarrow D$;

In this case data expressions constructed with f are necessarily infinite: $f(f(f(\cdots)))$. Such expressions do not exist and hence, there are no expressions to represent elements in D. But all elements in D should be written using an expression starting with a constructor symbol. Consequently, the sort D must be empty, which is not allowed. It is efficiently decidable whether a signature is syntactically nonempty.

As mentioned before, the data types in mCRL2 can completely be translated to a signature (following appendix B). The signature that is obtained must be well-typed, meaning that it must satisfy the following properties.

Definition 15.1.7 (Well-typed signature). For a given mCRL2 specification, a data signature $\Sigma = (\mathcal{S}, \mathcal{C_S}, \mathcal{M_S})$ is *well-typed* iff

- $\mathcal{C_S} \cap \mathcal{M_S} = \emptyset$.
- The basic sorts are in $\mathcal{S}$ and constructors and functions defined in appendix B are in $\mathcal{C_S}$ and $\mathcal{M_S}$, respectively. There are not more constructors for basic sorts in $\mathcal{C_S}$ than those indicated in appendix B.
- All standard sorts are in $\mathcal{S}$. Each standard sort in $\mathcal{S}$ has exactly the constructors indicated in appendix B and at least the mappings from appendix B.
- Function sorts are not constructor sorts: if $f{:}D_1{\times}\cdots{\times}D_n{\rightarrow}D \in \mathcal{C_S}$, then D is not a function sort.

- Constructor sorts are syntactically nonempty.

The requirement that for mCRL2 the standard sort specification is precisely that of appendix B is needed to avoid that (by accident) the structure of the built-in data types is changed. If it would be allowed to declare:

cons $one : \mathbb{R}$;

then all real numbers can be represented as one, completely collapsing the data structure. Actually, it would even become inconsistent, making every conceivable proposition about data types true. Similarly, one can add nonstandard elements to the natural numbers, or alter the structure of lists or structured data types. This generally is undesired and very confusing, and therefore forbidden.

Subsorting is a useful means to allow for the definition of a function symbol for a more general sort (e.g., integers) that can be reused for more restrictive sorts (e.g., natural numbers). The following definition captures this notion formally.

Definition 15.1.8 (Subsorting). Given a signature $\Sigma = (\mathcal{S}, \mathcal{C}_\mathcal{S}, \mathcal{M}_\mathcal{S})$, the subsorting relation $\subseteq : \mathcal{S} \times \mathcal{S}$ is the smallest relation satisfying the following constraints:

- for each $D \in \mathcal{S}$, $D \subseteq D$, i.e., subsorting is reflexive,
- for each $D_0, D_1, D_2 \in \mathcal{S}$, if $D_0 \subseteq D_1$ and $D_1 \subseteq D_2$, then $D_0 \subseteq D_2$, i.e., subsorting is transitive,
- $\mathbb{N}^+ \subseteq \mathbb{N}$, $\mathbb{N} \subseteq \mathbb{Z}$, and $\mathbb{Z} \subseteq \mathbb{R}$,
- for each $D_0, D_1 \in \mathcal{S}$, if $D_0 \subseteq D_1$, then $List(D_0) \subseteq List(D_1)$, $Bag(D_0) \subseteq Bag(D_1)$, and $Set(D_0) \subseteq Set(D_1)$, and
- for each $D_1 \times \ldots \times D_n \rightarrow E, D'_1 \times \ldots \times D'_n \rightarrow E' \in \mathcal{D}$, if $D'_i \subseteq D_i$, for each $i \leq n$, and $E \subseteq E'$, then $D_1 \times \ldots \times D_n \rightarrow E \subseteq D'_1 \times \ldots \times D'_n \rightarrow E'$.

We write $D \subset D'$, when $D \subseteq D'$ and $D \neq D'$.

The last bullet in definition 15.1.8 may seem counterintuitive because a function sort is a subsort of another, if the argument sorts are supersorts. The following example illustrates why this is not the case. In this example, we appeal to the substitutability of any element of a subsort in an expression requiring an element of the supersort.

Example 15.1.9. Consider an element of function sort $\mathbb{N} \rightarrow \mathbb{R}$, for example, a function calculating the square root of natural numbers. Such a function can be applied to a positive natural number and the result should be of sort $\mathbb{R}$. In other words, the sort $\mathbb{N} \rightarrow \mathbb{R}$ should intuitively be a subsort of $\mathbb{N}^+ \rightarrow \mathbb{R}$. However, applying a function of sort $\mathbb{N} \rightarrow \mathbb{R}$ to a negative integer does not intuitively make sense and hence, $\mathbb{N} \rightarrow \mathbb{R}$ is not intuitively a subsort of $\mathbb{Z} \rightarrow \mathbb{R}$.

15.1.2 Well-typed data expressions

In this section we formally introduce data expressions and specify when we call an expression well-typed, i.e., allowable in a specification. We are liberal, in the sense that we call an expression well-typed if a reasonable way can be found to type it.

We recapitulate the syntax of data expressions by the following BNF grammar.

$$\begin{array}{rcl} t & ::= & x \mid f \mid [] \mid \{\} \mid \{:\}\ [t,\ldots,t] \mid \{t,\ldots t\} \mid \{t{:}t,\ldots t{:}t\} \mid \\ & & \{t{:}D \mid t\} \mid \lambda x_1{:}D_1,\ldots,x_n{:}D_n.t \mid t(t,\ldots,t) \mid \\ & & \forall x{:}D.t \mid \exists x{:}D.t \mid t \textbf{ whr } x_1 = t,\ldots,x_n = t \textbf{ end}. \end{array}$$

We write the existential and universal quantifier with only one variable, contrary to, for instance, a lambda expression, where expression, and application, because the extension to more variables in the quantifiers does not involve any difficulty or novelty.

We assume the existence of a set of $\mathcal{S}$-typed variables $\mathcal{X}_\mathcal{S}$. In $\mathcal{X}_\mathcal{S}$ there are typed variables of the form $x{:}D$ similar to function symbols. In this case we say x has sort D. In an mCRL2 specification, the set of variable symbols is constantly changing, because variables are locally declared. We take as a ground rule that within any given scope, a variable occurs only once with a unique type in a set of variables. Typically, it is not possible that $\mathcal{X}_\mathcal{S}$ contains both $x{:}\mathbb{N}$ and $x{:}\mathbb{Z}$ at the same time. Of course this does not exclude that in one section the variable x is used of one type and at another place x is used with another type. It is also not allowed that a variable takes the same name as a mapping or a constructor, independent of its type.

There are two issues that may complicate the typing of a data expression: firstly, subsorting implies that a certain expression may belong to various sorts and thus have many types, for example, the constant 0 is a natural number, but also an integer and a real number. Secondly, it is often handy to reuse the same name for a function symbol and override or extend its definition for various sorts of arguments, for example, $+$ is defined on (positive) natural numbers, integers, and reals, and hence $1+1$ can be given multiple types. We use the subsorting relation as a means to give each data expression a unique least type.

To this end, we start with a generic type system for mCRL2 data expressions, which allows for multiple types for each data expression. The type system for data expressions is given in table 15.1. A type judgment is a statement of the form $\mathcal{X}_\mathcal{S} \vdash t : D$, which states that term t is of type D under variable declaration $\mathcal{X}_\mathcal{S}$. We write $\mathcal{X}_\mathcal{S} \vdash t : D' \subseteq D$ as an acronym for $\mathcal{X}_\mathcal{S} \vdash t : D'$ and $D' \subseteq D$. In a type judgment constructors $\mathcal{C}_\mathcal{S}$ and mappings $\mathcal{M}_\mathcal{S}$ are also used, but they are not explicitly listed. We say that a type judgment $\mathcal{X}_\mathcal{S} \vdash t : D$ is provable if it can be derived using the rules in table 15.1. In that case we say that data expression t has type D (in the context of $\mathcal{X}_\mathcal{S}$, $\mathcal{C}_\mathcal{S}$, and $\mathcal{M}_\mathcal{S}$).

Most of the rules are self-explanatory and only a few need further comment. It is worth noting that the empty list (respectively, set and bag) is of type $List(D)$ (resp., $Set(D)$ and $Bag(D)$) for each D. For those constructs that act as a binder, the set of variables $\mathcal{X}_\mathcal{S}$ must be adapted. Consider for instance $\forall x{:}D.t$; first all variables of the shape $x{:}D'$ for any type D' must be removed from $\mathcal{X}_\mathcal{S}$ and then $x{:}D$ is added in order to find a type for t. Note also that in the deduction rule for the **whr end** construct variables x_i are not bound in any t_j. The recursive use of the **whr end** construct is disallowed, for example, in expression $\{x\}$ **whr** $x = x + 1$ **end**, variable x in the right-hand side of $x = x + 1$ must be defined elsewhere in the context and is different from variable x appearing in the left-hand side of the same expression.

Next we give simple examples illustrating the type system.

Example 15.1.10. Consider the following mCRL2 specification:

map $f{:}\mathit{List}(\mathbb{N}) \to \mathit{List}(\mathbb{N})$;
map $f{:}\mathit{List}(\mathbb{B}) \to \mathit{List}(\mathbb{B})$;

and consider the following data expressions:

- $f([])$, and
- $f(x)$ **whr** $x = 0 \triangleright []$ **end**.

Since $[]$ is of type $\mathit{List}(D)$ for each and every D, it follows from the typing rule for term application that $f([])$ is of types $\mathit{List}(\mathbb{N})$ and $\mathit{List}(\mathbb{B})$.

The latter data expression has as the least type $\mathit{List}(\mathbb{N})$ because it follows from the signature of $\triangleright$ that when applied to a first argument of sort $\mathbb{N}$, the result is of type $\mathit{List}(\mathbb{N})$. Concretely, x is of type $\mathit{List}(\mathbb{N})$. Hence, it follows from the typing rules for term application and **whr** that the type of $f(x)$ has the type $\mathit{List}(\mathbb{N})$. In particular it is not of type $\mathit{List}(\mathbb{B})$.

As observed in the previous example, certain data expressions may have several incomparable types and this gives rise to confusion. We define well-typed data expressions as those expressions that have a minimal type defined using a minimal type derivation. First define $\mathcal{X}_S \subseteq \mathcal{X}'_S$ iff

- For all $x{:}D \in \mathcal{X}_S$ there is some $D' \in S$ such that $x{:}D' \in \mathcal{X}'_S$, and
- For all $x{:}D \in \mathcal{X}_S$ and $x{:}D' \in \mathcal{X}'_S$ it holds that $D \subseteq D'$.

In other words, $\mathcal{X}_S \subseteq \mathcal{X}'_S$ if both sets contains the same variables, where those of the second have larger or equal types.

Definition 15.1.11. Let $\mathcal{X}_S$, $\hat{\mathcal{X}}_S$ be two sets of S-typed variables such that $\mathcal{X}_S \subseteq \hat{\mathcal{X}}_S$. Consider two proofs for $\mathcal{X}_S \vdash t : D$ and $\hat{\mathcal{X}}_S \vdash t : \hat{D}$. We say that the first proof is smaller than or equal to the second iff $D \subset \hat{D}$, or $D = \hat{D}$ and the following hold:

- If $t = x$ ($x{:}D \in \mathcal{X}_S$ and $x{:}D \in \hat{\mathcal{X}}_S$), $t = f$ ($f \in \mathcal{C}_S \cup \mathcal{M}_S$), $t = []$, $t = \{\}$, or $t = \{:\}$, then the proofs must be identical.
- If $t = [t_1, \ldots, t_n]$ or $t = \{t_1, \ldots, t_n\}$, then for all $1 \leq i \leq n$, it holds that the proof of the premise $\mathcal{X}_S \vdash t_i : D_i$ in the first proof must be smaller than or equal to the proof of the premise $\hat{\mathcal{X}}_S \vdash t_i : \hat{D}_i$ in the second proof.
- If $t = \{t_1{:}t'_1, \ldots, t_n{:}t'_n\}$, then for all $1 \leq i \leq n$, then in the first proof, the proof of the premise $\mathcal{X}_S \vdash t_i : D_i$ must be smaller than or equal to the proof of the premise $\hat{\mathcal{X}}_S \vdash t_i : \hat{D}_i$ in the second proof, and in the first proof the proof of the premise $\mathcal{X}_S \vdash t'_i : D'_i$ must be smaller than or equal to the proof of the premise $\hat{\mathcal{X}}_S \vdash t'_i : \hat{D}'_i$ in the second proof.

$$\frac{x{:}D \in \mathcal{X}_\mathcal{S},\ \forall_{D'\in\mathcal{S}} x{:}D' \notin \mathcal{C}_\mathcal{S} \cup \mathcal{M}_\mathcal{S}}{\mathcal{X}_\mathcal{S} \vdash x{:}D} \qquad \frac{f : D_1 \times \cdots \times D_n \to D \in \mathcal{C}_\mathcal{S} \cup \mathcal{M}_\mathcal{S}}{\mathcal{X}_\mathcal{S} \vdash f{:}D_1 \times \cdots \times D_n \to D}$$

$$\frac{\forall_{1\le i\le n} \mathcal{X}_\mathcal{S} \vdash t_i{:}D' \subseteq D}{\mathcal{X}_\mathcal{S} \vdash [t_1,\ldots,t_n]{:}List(D)} \qquad \frac{}{\mathcal{X}_\mathcal{S} \vdash []{:}List(D)}$$

$$\frac{\forall_{1\le i\le n} \mathcal{X}_\mathcal{S} \vdash t_i{:}D' \subseteq D}{\mathcal{X}_\mathcal{S} \vdash \{t_1,\ldots,t_n\}{:}Set(D)} \qquad \frac{}{\mathcal{X}_\mathcal{S} \vdash \{\}{:}Set(D)}$$

$$\frac{\forall_{1\le i\le n} \mathcal{X}_\mathcal{S} \vdash t_i{:}D_i \subseteq D, \mathcal{X}_\mathcal{S} \vdash t_i'{:}D_i' \subseteq \mathbb{N}}{\mathcal{X}_\mathcal{S} \vdash \{t_1{:}t_1',\ldots,t_n{:}t_n'\}{:}Bag(D)} \qquad \frac{}{\mathcal{X}_\mathcal{S} \vdash \{:\}{:}Bag(D)}$$

$$\frac{\begin{array}{l}\forall_{D'\in\mathcal{S}} x{:}D' \notin \mathcal{C}_\mathcal{S} \cup \mathcal{M}_\mathcal{S},\\ (\mathcal{X}_\mathcal{S} \setminus \{x{:}D' | D'\in\mathcal{S}\}) \cup \{x{:}D\} \vdash t : \mathbb{B}\end{array}}{\mathcal{X}_\mathcal{S} \vdash \{x{:}D \mid t\}{:}Set(D)} \qquad \frac{\begin{array}{l}\forall_{D'\in\mathcal{S}} x{:}D' \notin \mathcal{C}_\mathcal{S} \cup \mathcal{M}_\mathcal{S},\\ (\mathcal{X}_\mathcal{S} \setminus \{x{:}D' | D'\in\mathcal{S}\}) \cup \{x{:}D\} \vdash t{:}D' \subseteq \mathbb{N}\end{array}}{\mathcal{X}_\mathcal{S} \vdash \{x{:}D \mid t\}{:}Bag(D)}$$

$$\frac{\begin{array}{l}\forall_{1\le i\le n}\forall_{D'\in\mathcal{S}} x_i{:}D' \notin \mathcal{C}_\mathcal{S} \cup \mathcal{M}_\mathcal{S},\\ (\mathcal{X}_\mathcal{S} \setminus \{x_i{:}D_i' \mid 0\le i\le n, D_i' \in \mathcal{S}\}) \cup\\ \quad \{x_i{:}D_i | 1\le i\le n\} \vdash t{:}D\end{array}}{\begin{array}{l}\mathcal{X}_\mathcal{S} \vdash\\ \lambda x_1{:}D_1,\ldots,x_n{:}D_n.t{:}D_1 \times \cdots \times D_n \to D\end{array}} \qquad \frac{\begin{array}{l}\mathcal{X}_\mathcal{S} \vdash t{:}D_1 \times \cdots \times D_n \to D',\\ \forall_{1\le i\le n} \mathcal{X}_\mathcal{S} \vdash t_i{:}D_i' \subseteq D_i\end{array}}{\mathcal{X}_\mathcal{S} \vdash t(t_1,\ldots,t_n){:}D'}$$

$$\frac{\begin{array}{l}\forall_{D'\in\mathcal{S}} x{:}D' \notin \mathcal{C}_\mathcal{S} \cup \mathcal{M}_\mathcal{S},\\ (\mathcal{X}_\mathcal{S} \setminus \{x{:}D' | D'\in\mathcal{S}\}) \cup \{x{:}D\} \vdash t{:}\mathbb{B}\end{array}}{\mathcal{X}_\mathcal{S} \vdash \forall x{:}D.t{:}\mathbb{B}} \qquad \frac{\begin{array}{l}\forall_{D'\in\mathcal{S}} x{:}D' \notin \mathcal{C}_\mathcal{S} \cup \mathcal{M}_\mathcal{S},\\ (\mathcal{X}_\mathcal{S} \setminus \{x{:}D' | D'\in\mathcal{S}\}) \cup \{x{:}D\} \vdash t{:}\mathbb{B}\end{array}}{\mathcal{X}_\mathcal{S} \vdash \exists x{:}D.t{:}\mathbb{B}}$$

$$\frac{\begin{array}{l}\forall_{1\le i\le n} \mathcal{X}_\mathcal{S} \vdash t_i{:}D_i,\\ (\mathcal{X}_\mathcal{S} \setminus \{x_i{:}D' \mid 1\le i\le n, D'\in\mathcal{S}\}) \cup\\ \quad \{x_i{:}D_i \mid 1\le i\le n\} \vdash t{:}D\end{array}}{\mathcal{X}_\mathcal{S} \vdash t \ \mathbf{whr}\ x_1 = t_1,\ldots,x_n = t_n\ \mathbf{end}{:}D}$$

Table 15.1: Type system for mCRL2 data expressions

- If $t = \{x{:}D \mid t'\}$ (both set and bag comprehension), then the proof of the premise $(\mathcal{X}_\mathcal{S} \backslash \{x{:}D' | D' {\in} \mathcal{S}\}) \cup \{x{:}D\} \vdash t' : \mathbb{B}$ in the first proof must be smaller than or equal to the proof of the premise $(\hat{\mathcal{X}}_\mathcal{S} \backslash \{x{:}D' | D' {\in} \mathcal{S}\}) \cup \{x{:}D\} \vdash t' : \mathbb{B}$ of the second proof.

- If $t = \lambda x_1{:}D_1, \ldots, x_n{:}D_n.t'$, then the proof of the premise $(\mathcal{X}_\mathcal{S} \setminus \{x_i{:}D'_i \mid 0{\le}i{\le}n, D'_i \in \mathcal{S}\}) \cup \{x_i{:}D_i | 1{\le}i{\le}n\} \vdash t' : D$ in the first proof must be smaller than or equal to the proof of the premise $(\hat{\mathcal{X}}_\mathcal{S} \setminus \{x_i{:}D'_i \mid 0{\le}i{\le}n, D'_i \in \mathcal{S}\}) \cup \{x_i{:}D_i | 1{\le}i{\le}n\} \vdash t' : \hat{D}$ of the second proof.

- If $t = t'(t_1, \ldots, t_n)$, then for all $1 \le i \le n$ the proof of the premise $\mathcal{X}_\mathcal{S} \vdash t_i : D'_i$ in the first proof must be smaller than or equal to the proof of the premise $\hat{\mathcal{X}}_\mathcal{S} \vdash t_i : \hat{D}'_i$ of the second proof. Moreover, for all $1 \le i \le n$ it holds that $D_i \subseteq \hat{D}_i$, and if for all $1 \le i \le n$ it holds that $D_i = \hat{D}_i$, then the proof of the premise $\mathcal{X}_\mathcal{S} \vdash t' : D_1 \times \cdots \times D_n \to D$ in the first proof must be smaller than or equal to the proof of the premise $\hat{\mathcal{X}}_\mathcal{S} \vdash t' : D_1 \times \cdots \times D_n \to D$ of the second proof.

- If $t{=}\forall x{:}D.t$ or $t{=}\exists x{:}D.t'$, then the proof of the premise $(\mathcal{X}_\mathcal{S} \backslash \{x{:}D' | D' {\in} \mathcal{S}\}) \cup \{x{:}D\} \vdash t' : \mathbb{B}$ in the first proof must be smaller than or equal to the proof of the premise $(\hat{\mathcal{X}}_\mathcal{S} \backslash \{x{:}D' | D' {\in} \mathcal{S}\}) \cup \{x{:}D\} \vdash t' : \mathbb{B}$ in the second proof.

- If $t = t'$ **whr** $x_1 = t_1, \ldots, x_n = t_n$ **end**, then the proof of the premise $(\mathcal{X}_\mathcal{S} \setminus \{x_i{:}D' \mid 1{\le}i{\le}n, D' {\in} \mathcal{S}\}) \cup \{x_i{:}D_i \mid 1{\le}i{\le}n\} \vdash t' : D$ in the first proof must be smaller than or equal to the proof of the premise $(\hat{\mathcal{X}}_\mathcal{S} \setminus \{x_i{:}D' \mid 1{\le}i{\le}n, D' {\in} \mathcal{S}\}) \cup \{x_i{:}\hat{D}_i \mid 1{\le}i{\le}n\} \vdash t' : D$ of the second proof. Moreover, for all $1 \le i \le n$ it must hold that if $D_i = \hat{D}_i$, then the proof of the premise $\mathcal{X}_\mathcal{S} \vdash t_i : D_i$ in the first proof must be smaller than or equal to the proof of the premise $\hat{\mathcal{X}}_\mathcal{S} \vdash t_i : D_i$ in the second proof.

Definition 15.1.12 (Well-typed data expressions). Let $\Sigma = (\mathcal{S}, \mathcal{C}_\mathcal{S}, \mathcal{M}_\mathcal{S})$ be a signature and $\mathcal{X}_\mathcal{S}$ a set of $\mathcal{S}$-typed variable symbols. A data expression t is well-typed with type D (over $\mathcal{X}_\mathcal{S}$, $\mathcal{C}_\mathcal{S}$, and $\mathcal{M}_\mathcal{S}$) when there exists a type judgment $\mathcal{X}_\mathcal{S} \vdash t{:}D$ for some $\mathcal{C}_\mathcal{S}$ and $\mathcal{M}_\mathcal{S}$ provable from the deduction rules of table 15.1 with a unique smallest proof. If $\mathcal{X}_\mathcal{S}$ is not explicitly given, it is assumed that $\mathcal{X}_\mathcal{S}$ is empty.

We illustrate the effects of this definition with a few examples.

Example 15.1.13. Consider the following mCRL2 specification:

map $f : \mathbb{R} \times \mathbb{N} \to \mathbb{B}$;

and consider data expression $f(0,0)$. It follows from the definition of sort $\mathbb{N}$ in appendix B that 0 is a data expression of type $\mathbb{N}$. It follows from the typing deduction rule for term application that $f(0,0)$ is a data expression of type $\mathbb{B}$. There are three possible proofs for a typing of $f(0,0) : \mathbb{B}$, as the first argument can have types $\mathbb{R}$, $\mathbb{Z}$, and $\mathbb{N}$. The proof where the first argument has type $\mathbb{N}$ is the smallest of the three. So, there is a unique smallest proof tree. Hence, $f(0,0)$ is well-typed with type $\mathbb{B}$.

Example 15.1.14. Consider the following mCRL2 specification which is a slight extension compared to the previous example.

map $f : \mathbb{R} \times \mathbb{N} \to \mathbb{B}$;
$f : \mathbb{N} \times \mathbb{R} \to \mathbb{B}$;

In this case the specification $f(0,0)$ is not well-typed. There are two incomparable minimal type derivations for $f(0,0) : \mathbb{B}$.

Example 15.1.15. Consider again a slight variation on the previous example

map $f : \mathbb{R} \times \mathbb{N} \to \mathbb{N}$;
$f : \mathbb{N} \times \mathbb{R} \to \mathbb{R}$;

In this case there are two type derivations namely $f(0,0) : \mathbb{N}$ and $f(0,0) : \mathbb{R}$. As $\mathbb{N} \subseteq \mathbb{R}$ this term is well-typed and has type $\mathbb{N}$.

Example 15.1.16. The following variation shows that there is a major difference between functions that are iteratively applied to function arguments, compared to those being applied to product types.

map $f : \mathbb{R} \to \mathbb{N} \to \mathbb{B}$;
$f : \mathbb{N} \to \mathbb{R} \to \mathbb{B}$;

The term $f(0)(0)$ clearly has type $\mathbb{B}$. There are two type derivations, one where $f(0) : \mathbb{N} \to \mathbb{B}$ and $f(0) : \mathbb{R} \to \mathbb{B}$. As 0 can both have type $\mathbb{N}$ and $\mathbb{R}$ the smallest type yields the smallest type derivation. So, $f(0) : \mathbb{N} \to \mathbb{B}$ and $0 : \mathbb{N}$. In this example $f(0)(0)$ is well-typed, where the function $f : \mathbb{R} \to \mathbb{N} \to \mathbb{B}$ is selected.

Example 15.1.17. Assume the following declarations

map $f : \mathbb{N} \to \mathbb{B}$;
$f : \mathbb{R} \to \mathbb{B}$;
$h : (\mathbb{N} \to \mathbb{B}) \to \mathbb{B}$;
$h : (\mathbb{R} \to \mathbb{B}) \to \mathbb{B}$;

The term $f(0) \wedge h(f)$ is well-typed, where the first f is the one with type $\mathbb{N} \to \mathbb{B}$, whereas the second f is the one with type $\mathbb{R} \to \mathbb{B}$. However, the term $x(0) \wedge h(x)$ **whr** $x = f$ **end** is not well-typed. The two type derivations resulting from the two possible choices for the type of variable x (from the two function symbols f) lead to incomparable proofs. Hence, there is no unique smallest proof for $\emptyset \vdash x(0) \wedge h(x)$ **whr** $x = f$ **end** $: \mathbb{B}$.

If an expression is well-typed and has a smallest type, then we can insert sort transformation operators (e.g., $\mathbb{N}2\mathbb{Z}$) such that each function symbol is applied to terms of which the sorts exactly match the argument types of the function symbol. In this way terms become what we call strongly typed. The advantage of this is that one no longer has to bother about subtyping.

Example 15.1.18. Consider the following two well-typed data expressions where x is a variable of sort $\mathbb{R}$.

$$x + (3 + 0), \quad \{x, y, 5\} \textbf{ whr } y = 17 \textbf{ end}.$$

By adding explicit type information to variables, and by inserting sort transformation functions, these data expressions can be rewritten as follows:

$$x_{\mathbb{R}} + \mathbb{N}2\mathbb{R}(\mathbb{N}^+2\mathbb{N}(3) + 0), \quad \{x_{\mathbb{R}}, \mathbb{N}^+2\mathbb{R}(y_{\mathbb{N}^+}), \mathbb{N}^+2\mathbb{R}(5)\} \textbf{ whr } y_{\mathbb{N}^+} = 17 \textbf{ end}.$$

Exercise 15.1.19. Determine the type(s) of the following expressions and determine whether they are well-typed.

1. $0 + 1$.
2. $\{0, 1, 2/3\}$.
3. $[]$ (the empty list).
4. $\forall l_1{:}\mathit{List}(\mathbb{N}^+).\exists l_2{:}\mathit{List}(\mathbb{N}).l_1{\approx}l_2$.
5. $x{\approx}0$ **whr** $x = \mathit{head}([])$ **end**.
6. $x{\approx}0 \wedge x{\not\approx}\frac{5}{2}$ **whr** $x = \mathit{head}([])$ **end**.

15.1.3 Free variables and substitutions

The lambda operator, the quantifiers, and the **whr** clause are called binders of variables. For instance, the data expression $\lambda x{:}D.t(x)$ is said to bind the variable x in $t(x)$, and variable x is said to be *bound* in $\lambda x{:}D.t(x)$. If a variable occurs in a data expression, and it is not bound, then it is said to occur *freely* (or to be free). For example, x is free and y is bound in $\lambda y{:}\mathbb{N}^+.x{+}y$. The following definition gives a precise account of when we call a variable free in a data expression.

Definition 15.1.20. Let $\Sigma = (\mathcal{S}, \mathcal{C}_{\mathcal{S}}, \mathcal{M}_{\mathcal{S}})$ be a signature and let $\mathcal{X}_{\mathcal{S}}$ be a set of $\mathcal{S}$-typed variables. We inductively define when a variable x is free in a well-typed data expression t of sort D over $\mathcal{X}_{\mathcal{S}}$ as follows:

- The variable x is free in a variable y from $\mathcal{X}_{\mathcal{S}}$ iff x is equal to y.
- The variable x is not free in $[]$, $\{\}$, $\{:\}$ or a function symbol f from $\mathcal{C}_{\mathcal{S}} \cup \mathcal{M}_{\mathcal{S}}$.
- The variable x is free in $[t_1, \ldots, t_n]$ or $\{t_1, \ldots, t_n\}$ iff x is free in some t_i $(1{\leq}i{\leq}n)$.
- The variable x is free in $\{t_1{:}t_1', \ldots, t_n{:}t_n'\}$ iff it is free in some t_i or t_i' $(1{\leq}i{\leq}n)$.
- The variable x is free in $\{y{:}D \mid t\}$ if x is not equal to y and x is free in t.
- The variable x is free in $t(t_1, \ldots, t_n)$ iff it is free in t or it is free in some t_i $(1{\leq}i{\leq}n)$.

- The variable x is free in $\lambda y_1{:}D'_1, \ldots, y_n{:}D_n.t$ iff x is not equal to some y_i for $1{\leq}i{\leq}n$ and x is free in t.

- The variable x is free in $\forall y{:}D'.t$ and $\exists y{:}D'.t$ iff x is not equal to y and x is free in t.

- The variable x is free in t **whr** $y_1{=}t_1, \ldots, y_n{=}t_n$ **end** iff x is free in some t_i $(1{\leq}i{\leq}n)$, or x is free in t and x is not equal to some y_i $(1{\leq}i{\leq}n)$.

Dual to the notion of free variables, the notion of bound variables is defined in the expected manner, for example, if x occurs in term t of the form $\lambda x{:}E.\ldots$, $\forall x{:}E.\ldots$, $\exists x{:}E.\ldots$ or $\ldots$ **whr** $\ldots x{=}p\ldots$ **end**, t, we say that x is bound in t (with type E).

Note that if a variable occurs in an expression, but is not free, it must be bound. Also note that a variable can occur both bound and free in an expression. For example, x is both bound and free in $x + \lambda x{:}\mathbb{N}.x$.

Exercise 15.1.21. Does x occur freely in the following: 1. $x + y$. 2. $\lambda x{:}\mathbb{N}^+.x + y$. 3. $(\lambda x{:}\mathbb{N}^+.x) + x$.

Substitutions, generally written using the letter ξ, are functions that map variables to data expressions. We use a special notation to extend substitutions: substitution $\xi[x{:=}t]$ maps every variable y to $\xi(y)$, except that it maps variable x to t. Substitution $\xi[x_i{:=}t_i]_{1\leq i\leq n}$ maps variables x_i to data expressions t_i and applies ξ to the other variables. If we write $[x{:=}t]$ or $[x_i{:=}t_i]_{1\leq i\leq n}$, we assume that the omitted substitution is the identity mapping. We write the application of such a single substitution to a data expression by placing the substitution after the data expression. We extend the definition of substitutions to more complex data expressions as follows.

Definition 15.1.22. Let $\Sigma = (\mathcal{S}, \mathcal{C}_\mathcal{S}, \mathcal{M}_\mathcal{S})$ be a signature. Let ξ be a substitution. We inductively extend ξ to a function on data expressions as follows. Consider a data expression t:

- If $t = f$ for a function symbol $f \in \mathcal{C}_\mathcal{S} \cup \mathcal{M}_\mathcal{S}$, then $\xi(t) = f$.

- If $t = []$, then $\xi(t) = []$; if $t = \{\}$, then $\xi(t) = \{\}$; and if $t = \{:\}$, then $\xi(t) = \{:\}$.

- If $t = [t_1, \ldots, t_n]$, then $\xi(t) = [\xi(t_1), \ldots, \xi(t_n)]$.

- If $t = \{t_1, \ldots, t_n\}$, then $\xi(t) = \{\xi(t_1), \ldots, \xi(t_n)\}$.

- If $t = \{t_1{:}t'_1, \ldots, t_n{:}t'_n\}$, then $\xi(t) = [\xi(t_1){:}\xi(t'_1), \ldots, \xi(t_n){:}\xi(t'_n)]$.

- If $t = \{x{:}D \mid t'\}$, then $\xi(t){=}\{y{:}D \mid \xi[x{:=}y, y{:=}y](t')\}$, provided that y does not occur freely in t' and $\xi(z)$ for any variable z occurring freely in t'. We assume that we always have sufficiently many fresh variables, such that the required variables y can always be found.

- If $t = t'(t_1, \ldots, t_n)$, then $\xi(t) = \xi(t')(\xi(t_1), \ldots, \xi(t_n))$.

- If $t{=}\lambda x_1{:}D_1, \ldots, x_n{:}D_n.t'$, then

$$\xi(t){=}\lambda y_1{:}D_1, \ldots, y_n{:}D_n.\xi[x_i{:=}y_i, y_i{:=}y_i]_{1\leq i\leq n}(t),$$

  provided all y_i do not occur freely in either t' or $\xi(z)$ for any variable z occurring freely in t'.

- If $t = \forall x{:}D'.t'$ or $t = \exists x{:}D'.t'$, then $\xi(t) = \forall y{:}D'.\xi[x{:=}y, y{:=}y](t')$ or $\xi(t) = \exists y{:}D'.\xi[x{:=}y, y{:=}y](t')$, respectively, provided that y does not occur freely in t' and in $\xi(z)$ for any z occurring freely in t'.

- If $t = t'$ **whr** $x_1{=}t_1, \ldots, x_n{=}t_n$ **end**, then

$$\xi(t) = \xi[x_i{:=}y_i, y_i{:=}y_i]_{1\leq i\leq n}(t') \textbf{ whr } y_1{=}\xi(t_1), \ldots, y_n{=}\xi(t_n) \textbf{ end}$$

  where y_i's are variables that do not occur freely in t' or in $\xi(z)$ for any z free in t'.

Example 15.1.23. We consider the substitution ξ with $\xi(y) = y'$ and apply it to the term $t = \lambda x{:}\mathbb{N}.y{+}x$. In order to do so, we should first rename y in t into a fresh variable. One may choose y' for this purpose, but y' is not sufficiently fresh, because it is free in y' and the result of applying the substitution after renaming would be $\lambda y'{:}\mathbb{N}.y'{+}y'$. This is counterintuitive, as the binder now "captures" the variable substituted for y. Choosing for a sufficiently fresh variable, for example, $z{:}\mathbb{N}$, results in $\lambda z{:}\mathbb{N}.y'{+}z$, which is the intuitive outcome and is very different from the result of choosing insufficiently fresh y'.

Exercise 15.1.24. Apply the following substitutions.

1. $(\lambda x{:}\mathbb{N}.\lambda y{:}\mathbb{N}.x + y + z)[z := u]$.
2. $(\lambda x{:}\mathbb{N}.y)[y{:=}x]$.
3. $(\lambda x{:}\mathbb{N}.\lambda y{:}\mathbb{N}.x)[x{:=}z]$.
4. $(\lambda x, y{:}\mathbb{N}.x)[x{:=}z]$.

15.1.4 Data specifications

Given a signature, we want that certain data expressions are considered to be equal. For instance, we want that $1 + 1$ equals 2. Using a set of conditional equations we define which data expressions are equal to each other. Each condition has the form $c{\rightarrow}t{=}u$ where c is a data expression of type $\mathbb{B}$ and t and u are data expressions with the same type. A typical conditional equation is $x{\geq}y{\rightarrow}max(x, y){=}x$ where x and y are variables. The idea is that whenever an instance of c equals true, then the corresponding instances of t and u are equal. If the condition c is syntactically equal to *true* it is generally omitted. In appendix B, all the basic data types are defined using such conditional equations.

Definition 15.1.25 (Data specification). Let $\Sigma = (\mathcal{S}, \mathcal{C}_\mathcal{S}, \mathcal{M}_\mathcal{S})$ be a signature. We call a tuple $\mathcal{D} = (\Sigma, E)$ a *data specification* where E is a set of *conditional equations*. Each equation in E is of the form $\langle \mathcal{X}_\mathcal{S}, c{\to}t{=}u \rangle$, where $\mathcal{X}_\mathcal{S}$ is a set of typed variables and c, t, and u are data expressions over $\mathcal{X}_\mathcal{S}$.

Definition 15.1.26 (Well-typed data specification). Given a data specification $\mathcal{D} = (\Sigma, E)$, where $\Sigma = (\mathcal{S}, \mathcal{C}_\mathcal{S}, \mathcal{M}_\mathcal{S})$ is a signature. A type derivation associated with $\langle \mathcal{X}_\mathcal{S}, c{\to}\ t = u \rangle \in E$ is a derivation with as three premises, proofs for $\mathcal{X}_\mathcal{S} \vdash c{:}\mathbb{B}$, $\mathcal{X}_\mathcal{S} \vdash t{:}D$, and $\mathcal{X}_\mathcal{S} \vdash u{:}D$, for some type D; such a type derivation associates type D to $\langle \mathcal{X}_\mathcal{S},\ c{\to}\ t{=}u \rangle \in E$. A type derivation associating D to $\langle \mathcal{X}_\mathcal{S},\ c{\to}\ t{=}u\ \rangle \in E$, is smaller than or equal to a second type derivation associating $\hat{D}$ to the same equation iff $D \subset \hat{D}$, or $D = \hat{D}$ and

1. The proof of $\mathcal{X}_\mathcal{S} \vdash c{:}\mathbb{B}$ in the first type derivation is smaller than or equal than the proof of $\mathcal{X}_\mathcal{S} \vdash c{:}\mathbb{B}$ in the second type derivation,
2. The proof of $\mathcal{X}_\mathcal{S} \vdash t{:}D$ in the first type derivation is smaller than or equal to the proof $\mathcal{X}_\mathcal{S} \vdash t{:}D$ in the second type derivation, and
3. The proof of $\mathcal{X}_\mathcal{S} \vdash u{:}D$ in the first type derivation is smaller than or equal to the proof $\mathcal{X}_\mathcal{S} \vdash u{:}D$ in the second type derivation.

The data specification $\mathcal{D}$ is well-typed iff Σ is well-typed and each equation $\langle \mathcal{X}_\mathcal{S},\ c{\to}\ t{=}u \rangle$ in E, has a unique smallest type derivation.

Example 15.1.27. Consider the following mCRL2 data specification:

map $f{:}List(\mathbb{N}) \to List(\mathbb{N})$;
eqn $f([]) = []$

This data specification is well-typed because its only equation can be associated with the minimal type $List(\mathbb{N})$ and the type derivation for this associated type is unique. Note that the empty list is not a well-typed data expression but in the context of the equation, it can be given a unique type.

Example 15.1.28. Assume that we modify the previous example, by adding another function symbol f, as follows.

map $f{:}List(\mathbb{N}) \to List(\mathbb{N})$;
$f{:}List(\mathbb{N}) \to List(\mathbb{B})$;
eqn $f([]) = []$

Then the data specification is no longer well-typed, because the equation can be associated with two types $List(\mathbb{N})$ and $List(\mathbb{B})$, and the corresponding derivations are incomparable.

Example 15.1.29. We slightly modify the previous example, by changing the arity of the second function symbol f, as follows.

map $f{:}List(\mathbb{N}) \rightarrow List(\mathbb{N})$;
$\quad f{:}List(\mathbb{B}) \rightarrow List(\mathbb{N})$;
eqn $f([]) = []$

This data specification is still not well-typed, because although the equation can be associated with only one type, namely, $List(\mathbb{N})$, the two type derivations are incomparable.

15.1.5 Semantics of data types

Data specifications are complex objects, in which variables, sorts, mappings, constructors, equations, and functions play a role. We want to define when two data expressions are or are not equal. This is done using the so-called model class semantics. We first define an applicative D-structure as a collection of sets where each set constitutes the counterpart of a sort. We also show how each data expression can be interpreted as an element in such a set. Subsequently, we define that an applicative D-structure is a model, when all conditional equations are valid. Finally, we define that data expressions are equal iff they are equal in all models. We do not provide the semantics for lists, sets, and bags, as these are provided by the equations in appendix B.

Definition 15.1.30 (Applicative $\mathcal{D}$-structure). Let $\mathcal{D} = (\Sigma, E)$ be a well-typed data specification, with $\Sigma = (\mathcal{S}, \mathcal{C}_\mathcal{S}, \mathcal{M}_\mathcal{S})$. A collection of nonempty sets $\{M_D | D{\in}\mathcal{S}\}$ is called an applicative $\mathcal{D}$-*structure* iff

- $M_\mathbb{B}$ is a set with two distinct elements, denoted by **true** and **false**.
- If $D{=}D_1{\times}\cdots{\times}D_n{\rightarrow}D'$, then M_D contains all functions from $M_{D_1}{\times}\cdots{\times}M_{D_n}$ to $M_{D'}$.

A function $[\![\cdot]\!]$ is called a $\mathcal{D}$-*interpretation* into an applicative $\mathcal{D}$-structure $\{M_D | D \in \mathcal{S}\}$ iff for all $f \in \mathcal{C}_\mathcal{S} \cup \mathcal{M}_\mathcal{S}$ of sort D, it holds that $[\![f]\!] \in M_D$.

We call $\sigma{:}\mathcal{X}_\mathcal{S} \rightarrow \bigcup_{D\in\mathcal{S}} M_D$ a *valuation* if it holds that $\sigma(x) \in M_D$ for all $x{:}D$. We write $\sigma[d/x]$ for a valuation that maps variables according to σ except that it maps x to d. We write $\sigma[d_i/x_i]_{1\leq i\leq n}$ for the valuation σ except that it maps each variable x_i to d_i. Note that a valuation maps variables to semantical values, whereas a substitution maps variables to syntactical expressions.

The interpretation function $[\![\cdot]\!]^\sigma$ is extended to data expressions as follows

- $[\![x]\!]^\sigma = \sigma(x)$ for every variable $x \in \mathcal{X}_D$.
- $[\![f]\!]^\sigma = [\![f]\!]$ for every function symbol $f \in \mathcal{C}_\mathcal{S} \cup \mathcal{M}_\mathcal{S}$.
- $[\![t(t_1, \ldots, t_n)]\!]^\sigma = [\![t]\!]^\sigma([\![t_1]\!]^\sigma, \ldots, [\![t_n]\!]^\sigma)$.
- $[\![\lambda x_1{:}D_1, \ldots, x_n{:}D_n.t]\!]^\sigma = f$ where $f{:}M_{D_1} \times \cdots \times M_{D_n} {\rightarrow} M_D$ is the function satisfying $f(d_1, \ldots, d_n) = [\![t]\!]^{\sigma[d_i/x_i]_{1\leq i\leq n}}$ for all $d_i{:}M_{D_i}$.
- $[\![\forall x{:}D.t]\!]^\sigma =$ **true** iff for all $d{\in}M_D$ it holds that $[\![t]\!]^{\sigma[d/x]} =$ **true**.
- $[\![\exists x{:}D.t]\!]^\sigma =$ **true** iff for some $d{\in}M_D$ it holds that $[\![t]\!]^{\sigma[d/x]} =$ **true**.

- $[\![t \textbf{ whr } x_1{=}t_1,\ldots,x_n{=}t_n \textbf{ end}]\!]^\sigma = [\![t]\!]^{\sigma[[\![t_i]\!]^\sigma/x_i]_{1\leq i\leq n}}$.

If t is a closed data expression, i.e., an expression not containing free variables, the valuation σ does not influence the outcome of $[\![t]\!]^\sigma$ and in such a case we also write $[\![t]\!]$.

Definition 15.1.31 ($\mathcal{D}$-model). Let $\mathcal{D} = (\Sigma, E)$ be a well-typed data specification. An applicative $\mathcal{D}$-structure together with a $\mathcal{D}$-interpretation $[\![\cdot]\!]$ is called a $\mathcal{D}$-*model* iff

- For every equation $c{\to}t{=}u \in E_{\mathcal{S}}$ is holds that for every valuation σ if $[\![c]\!]^\sigma =$ **true** then $[\![t]\!]^\sigma = [\![u]\!]^\sigma$.
- $[\![\mathit{true}]\!]^\sigma =$ **true** and $[\![\mathit{false}]\!]^\sigma =$ **false** for every valuation σ.
- If a basic sort D is a constructor sort (i.e., there is a constructor $f \in \mathcal{C}_{\mathcal{S}}$ of sort $D_1\times\cdots\times D_n{\to}D$), then every element $d \in M_D$ is a constructor element, where a constructor element is inductively defined as follows:
    - Every element $d \in M_D$ is a constructor element if a constructor function $f \in \mathcal{C}_{\mathcal{S}}$ of sort $D_1 \times \cdots \times D_n \to D$ exists such that $d = [\![f]\!](e_1,\ldots,e_n)$ where e_i is either a constructor element of sort D_i, or sort D_i is not a constructor sort.

Definition 15.1.32 (Equality and validity). Let $\mathcal{D} = (\Sigma, E)$ be a well-typed data specification. We say that two data expressions t_1 and t_2 of sort D are *equal*, notation $\models t_1 = t_2$, iff for all $\mathcal{D}$-models consisting of an applicative $\mathcal{D}$-structure $\{M_D | D{\in}\mathcal{S}\}$ and a $\mathcal{D}$-interpretation $[\![\cdot]\!]$ and all valuations σ it holds that $[\![t_1]\!]^\sigma = [\![t_2]\!]^\sigma$. If t is a data expression of sort $\mathbb{B}$, we say that t is *valid*, notation $\models t$ iff $\models t = \mathit{true}$.

Example 15.1.33. Consider the following specification of natural numbers.

sort $\mathit{myNat}, \mathbb{B}$;
cons $\mathit{zero} : \mathit{myNat}$;
  $\mathit{t2}, \mathit{t2p1} : \mathit{myNat} \to \mathit{myNat}$;
map $\mathit{eq} : \mathit{myNat} \times \mathit{myNat} \to \mathit{myNat}$
var $m, n : \mathit{myNat}$;
eqn $\mathit{eq}(\mathit{zero}, \mathit{zero}) = \mathit{true}$;
  $\mathit{eq}(\mathit{zero}, \mathit{t2}(n)) = \mathit{false}$;
  $\mathit{eq}(\mathit{zero}, \mathit{t2p1}(n)) = \mathit{false}$;
  $\mathit{eq}(\mathit{t2}(m), \mathit{t2p1}(n)) = \mathit{false}$;
  $\mathit{eq}(n, m) = \mathit{eq}(m, n)$;

The following collections of sets are possible $\mathcal{D}$-structures for the this data specification:

1. $M_{\mathbb{B}} = \{\textbf{true}, \textbf{false}\}$, $M_{myNat} = \{0, 1, 2, 3, \ldots\}$.
2. $M_{\mathbb{B}} = \{\textbf{true}, \textbf{false}\}$, $M_{myNat} = \{0, 1, 2\}$.
3. $M_{\mathbb{B}} = \{\textbf{true}, \textbf{false}\}$, $M_{myNat} = \{0, 1\}$.
4. $M_{\mathbb{B}} = \{\textbf{true}, \textbf{false}\}$, $M_{myNat} = \{0\}$.

The first two $\mathcal{D}$-structures are also $\mathcal{D}$-models with the $\mathcal{D}$-interpretations given below. The first model consists of the ordinary natural numbers. The mapping *eq* is mapped onto ordinary equality. It is easy to verify that the equations are valid.

$$[\![true]\!]=\mathbf{true},\ [\![false]\!]=\mathbf{false},\ [\![zero]\!]=0,\ [\![eq(n,m)]\!] = [\![n]\!]=[\![m]\!],$$
$$[\![t2(n)]\!]=2[\![n]\!],\ [\![t2p1(n)]\!]=2[\![n]\!]+1.$$

In the second model we change the interpretation of *t2* and *t2p1* into

$$[\![t2(n)]\!] = 2,\ [\![t2p1(n)]\!] = 1.$$

Remarkably, all equations are still valid in the model $\{0, 1, 2\}$, which shows that the indicated equations are insufficient to characterize the natural numbers.

The fourth $\mathcal{D}$-structure cannot be a $\mathcal{D}$-model. Each $\mathcal{D}$-interpretation will have to map $zero$ and $t2(zero)$ to 0. But then it must hold in the model that $true$ and $false$ must also be mapped to the same element as the equations must be valid in the model. In full detail:

$$\begin{aligned}\mathbf{true} &= [\![true]\!] = [\![eq]\!]([\![zero]\!], [\![zero]\!]) \\ &= [\![eq]\!]([\![zero]\!], [\![t2(zero)]\!]) = [\![false]\!] = \mathbf{false}.\end{aligned}$$

The equation $eq(n, m) = eq(m, n)$ is perfectly valid in this specification, but as tools generally use term rewriting applying equations repeatedly from left to right, they will generally end up applying this equation infinitely, often to no avail. For this reason such equations are not used when tool assistance is required to analyze behavioral specifications.

Exercise 15.1.34. Is the third $\mathcal{D}$-structure with two elements in example 15.1.33 a potential $\mathcal{D}$-model?

Exercise 15.1.35. Modify the data specification in example 15.1.33 such that in each $\mathcal{D}$-model the $\mathcal{D}$-interpretations of $zero$, $t2(m)$ and $t2p1(n)$, for each two distinct m and n are all different. Prove that this is indeed the case for the modified specification.

15.2 Semantics of processes

Given that we know now which data expressions are equal and different given a data specification, we define how a process specification gives rise to a timed labeled transition system. First we define what a process specification is.

15.2.1 Processes, action declarations, and process equations

In chapter 4, the syntax of multi-actions has been introduced. The syntax of *process expressions* has only been sketched. Here we provide a definition of process expressions and define when they are well-typed.

Definition 15.2.1 (Action declaration). Let $\Sigma = (\mathcal{S}, \mathcal{C}_\mathcal{S}, \mathcal{M}_\mathcal{S})$ be a signature. An *action declaration* is an expression of the form $a : D_1 \times \cdots \times D_n$ where $n \geq 0$ and all sorts D_i are taken from $\mathcal{S}$.

Definition 15.2.2 (Typing data parameters). Let $\Sigma = (\mathcal{S}, \mathcal{C}_{\mathcal{S}}, \mathcal{M}_{\mathcal{S}})$ be a signature and let $a : D_1 \times \cdots \times D_n$ be an action declaration, $\mathcal{X}_{\mathcal{S}}$ be the set of variable declarations, and t_i, for each $i \leq n$, be a data expression. The typing of $a(t_1, \ldots, t_n)$ over $\mathcal{X}_{\mathcal{S}}$ is a sequence of type derivations $\mathcal{X}_{\mathcal{S}} \vdash t_i{:}D_i' \subseteq D_i$.

A typing of $a(t_1, \ldots, t_n)$ with derivations $\mathcal{X}_{\mathcal{S}} \vdash t_i{:}D_i' \subseteq D_i$ from action declaration $a : D_1 \times \cdots \times D_n$ is smaller than or equal to a typing with $\mathcal{X}_{\mathcal{S}} \vdash t_i{:}\hat{D}_i' \subseteq \hat{D}_i$ from action declaration $a : \hat{D}_1 \times \cdots \times \hat{D}_n$, iff for each $1 \leq i \leq n$, $D_i \subseteq \hat{D}_i$ and the proof of $\mathcal{X}_{\mathcal{S}} \vdash t_i{:}D_i'$ is smaller than or equal to $\mathcal{X}_{\mathcal{S}} \vdash t_i{:}\hat{D}_i'$. We say that an action $a(t_1, \ldots, t_n)$ is well-typed iff there is a unique smallest typing for $a(t_1, \ldots, t_n)$.

Note that the notion of smallest typing derivation also considers multiple action declarations with the same name. The following example illustrates this.

Example 15.2.3. Consider the following action declarations.

act $a : \mathbb{R} \times \mathbb{N};$
$a : \mathbb{N} \times \mathbb{R};$

Then $a(0, 0)$ does not have a smallest typing and is not well-typed. However, $a(0, 1/2)$ does have a unique smallest typing, as there is no typing with the first action declaration.

Definition 15.2.4 (Process expression). Let $\Sigma = (\mathcal{S}, \mathcal{C}_{\mathcal{S}}, \mathcal{M}_{\mathcal{S}})$ be a signature. Process expressions are expressions with the following syntax.

$$\begin{aligned} p ::= {} & \alpha \mid p + p \mid p{\cdot}p \mid \delta \mid c \rightarrow p \mid c \rightarrow p \diamond p \mid \sum_{d:D} p \mid p {}^{c} t \mid t \gg p \mid p \| p \mid p \lfloor\!\lfloor p \mid \\ & p \ll p \mid p | p \mid \Gamma_C(p) \mid \nabla_V(p) \mid \partial_B(p) \mid \rho_R(p) \mid \tau_I(p) \mid \Upsilon_U(p) \mid \\ & X \mid X(u_1, \ldots, u_n) \mid X() \mid X(d_1{=}u_1, \ldots, d_n{=}u_n) \end{aligned}$$

Here, α is a multi-action, c is a Boolean data expression, $d, d_1, \ldots, d_n$ $(n{>}0)$ are variables, t is a data expression of sort $\mathbb{R}$, D is a sort, C is a set of communications, V is a set of multi-action labels, I, U, and B are sets of action labels, R is a set of renamings, X is a process name and $u_1, \ldots, u_n$ are data expressions.

We manipulate with process expressions in the same way that we do with data expressions. We use the special sort $\mathbb{P}$, which is not a data sort, to denote the sort of processes. In data expressions we cannot make reference to processes. In the meta theory, however, we often use functions from data to processes, for example, $f : \mathbb{N} \rightarrow \mathbb{P}$ and sometimes even functions from processes to data as in $g : \mathbb{P} \rightarrow \mathbb{N}$. But note that these are metanotations, and not formally part of the signature and sorts.

Definition 15.2.5 (Process equation). Let $\Sigma = (\mathcal{S}, \mathcal{C}_{\mathcal{S}}, \mathcal{M}_{\mathcal{S}})$ be a signature. A *process equation* is an expression of the form $X(d_1{:}D_1, \ldots, d_n{:}D_n) = p$ where $n{\geq}0$, d_i are variables and D_i are sorts from $\mathcal{S}$.

Definition 15.2.6. Given a set PE of process equations and $\mathcal{X}_{\mathcal{S}}$ a set of typed variables. A typing over $\mathcal{X}_{\mathcal{S}}$ of the process expression $X(t_1, \ldots, t_n)$ is a sequence of type derivations $\mathcal{X}_S \vdash t_i{:}D'_i \subseteq D_i$ for each $1 \leq i \leq n$ provided there is a process equation $X(d_1{:}D_1,\ldots,d_n{:}D_n) = p$ in *PE*.

A typing of $X(t_1,\ldots,t_n)$ with derivations $\mathcal{X}_S \vdash t_i{:}D'_i \subseteq D_i$ from process equation $X(d_1{:}D_1,\ldots,d_n{:}D_n) = p$ is smaller than or equal to a typing of $X(t_1,\ldots,t_n)$ with derivations $\mathcal{X}_S \vdash t_i{:}\hat{D}'_i \subseteq \hat{D}_i$ from process equation $X(\hat{d}_1{:}\hat{D}_1,\ldots,\hat{d}_n{:}\hat{D}_n) = \hat{p}$, iff for each $1 \leq i \leq n$, $D_i \subseteq \hat{D}_i$ and the proof of $\mathcal{X}_S \vdash t_i{:}D'_i$ is smaller than or equal to the proof of $\mathcal{X}_S \vdash t_i{:}\hat{D}'_i$. We say that a process $X(t_1,\ldots,t_n)$ is well-typed iff there is a unique smallest typing for $X(t_1,\ldots,t_n)$.

A process specification consists of a data specification, a set of process equations, an initial process and a set of global variables. The global variables are ordinary free variables in the specification. The major use of global variables is to indicate that at certain points, the values of parameters do not influence the behavior of the processes. These variables are often introduced (and eliminated) in behavior-preserving transformations, such as linearization. Contrary to what the name may suggest, global variables act like constants, and cannot be manipulated during the execution of a process.

Definition 15.2.7. Let $\Sigma = (\mathcal{S}, \mathcal{C}_\mathcal{S}, \mathcal{M}_\mathcal{S})$ be a signature. A *process specification* is a five tuple $PS = (\mathcal{D}, AD, PE, p, \mathcal{X})$ where

- $\mathcal{D}$ is a data specification,
- *AD* is a set of action declarations,
- *PE* is a set of process equations,
- p is a process expression, called the *initial process*, and
- $\mathcal{X}$ is a set of $\mathcal{S}$-typed variables, called the *global variables*.

Definition 15.2.8. Let $\Sigma = (\mathcal{S}, \mathcal{C}_\mathcal{S}, \mathcal{M}_\mathcal{S})$ be a signature. Let $PS = (\mathcal{D}, AD, PE, p, \mathcal{X})$ be a process specification and $\mathcal{X}_\mathcal{S}$ a set of variables. We say that a multi-action α is well-typed over $\mathcal{X}_\mathcal{S}$ iff one of the following items hold:

1. The multi-action α equals τ.
2. The multi-action α is equal to a single multi-action $a(t_1,\ldots,t_n)$ that is well-typed over $\mathcal{X}_\mathcal{S}$.
3. The multi-action α is equal to $\alpha|\beta$ and both α and β are well-typed over $\mathcal{X}_\mathcal{S}$.

Definition 15.2.9. Let $\Sigma = (\mathcal{S}, \mathcal{C}_\mathcal{S}, \mathcal{M}_\mathcal{S})$ be a signature. Let $PS = (\mathcal{D}, AD, PE, p, \mathcal{X})$ be a process specification and let $\mathcal{X}_\mathcal{S}$ be a set of variables. We say that a process expression p is well-typed over $\mathcal{X}_\mathcal{S}$ iff one of the following conditions apply.

1. The process expression p equals a multi-action α, and α is well-typed over $\mathcal{X}_\mathcal{S}$.
2. The process expression p equals $p_1{+}p_2$, $p_1{\cdot}p_2$, $p_1 \| p_2$, $p_1 \mathbin{⌊\!⌊} p_2$, $p_1{\ll}p_2$ or $p_1|p_2$, and p_1 and p_2 are well-typed process expressions over $\mathcal{X}_\mathcal{S}$.

3. The process expression p equals δ.

4. The process expression p is equal to $c\rightarrow p_1$ or $c\rightarrow p_1\diamond p_2$ and c is a well-typed data expression of type $\mathbb{B}$ over $\mathcal{X}_\mathcal{S}$ and p_1 and if present p_2 are well-typed process expressions over $\mathcal{X}_\mathcal{S}$.

5. The process expression p is equal to $\sum_{d:D} p_1$, and D is a sort in $\mathcal{S}$ and p_1 is a well-typed process expression over $(\mathcal{X}_\mathcal{S} \setminus \{d{:}D'|D'{\in}\mathcal{S}\}) \cup \{d{:}D\}$.

6. The process expression p equals $p_1 {}^{\varsigma} t$ or $t{\gg}p_1$, t is a well-typed data expression of type $\mathbb{R}$ over $\mathcal{X}_\mathcal{S}$ and p_1 is a well-typed process expression over $\mathcal{X}_\mathcal{S}$.

7. The process expression p equals $\Gamma_C(p_1)$, p_1 is a well-typed process expression over $\mathcal{X}_\mathcal{S}$, and for each communication $a_1|\cdots|a_n{\rightarrow}a \in C$, it holds that for some $m{\geq}0$ and sorts $D_1, \ldots, D_m$ it is the case that $a_i : D_1 \times \cdots \times D_m \in AD$ for each $i \leq n$, and $a : D_1 \times \cdots \times D_m \in AD$. If $a_1|\cdots|a_n{\rightarrow}a \in C$ and a different $a'_1|\cdots|a'_m{\rightarrow}a' \in C$ then $a_i \neq a'_j$ and $a \neq a'_j$ for all $1 \leq i \leq n$ and $1 \leq j \leq m$.

8. The process expression p equals $\nabla_V(p_1)$ and p_1 is a well-typed process expression over $\mathcal{X}_\mathcal{S}$ and for each multi-action $a_1|\cdots|a_n \in AD$ it holds that each action a_i $(1{\leq}i{\leq}n)$ is declared, i.e., $a_i : D_1{\times}\cdots{\times}D_n \in AD$ for some sorts $D_1, \ldots D_n$. The empty multi-action τ does not occur in V.

9. The process expression p equals $\partial_B(p_1)$, $\tau_B(p_1)$, or $\Upsilon_B(p_1)$, p_1 is a well-typed process expression over $\mathcal{X}_\mathcal{S}$ and for any action $a \in B$, it holds that a is declared, i.e., $a : D_1 \times \cdots \times D_n \in AD$ for some sorts $D_1, \ldots, D_n$.

10. The process expression p equals $\rho_R(p_1)$, p_1 is a well-typed process expression over $\mathcal{X}_\mathcal{S}$ and for any renaming $a{\rightarrow}b \in R$ it holds that $a : D_1 \times \cdots \times D_n \in AD$ and $b : D_1 \times \cdots \times D_n \in AD$ for some $n{\geq}0$ and sorts $D_1, \ldots, D_n$. Furthermore, for each action label a, there is at most one renaming of the shape $a{\rightarrow}b$ that occurs in R.

11. The process expression p equals X and $X = q$ is an equation in PE.

12. The process expression p equals $X(u_1, \ldots, u_n)$ and $X(u_1, \ldots, u_n)$ is well-typed over $\mathcal{X}_\mathcal{S}$.

13. The process expression p equals $X()$ and there is only one equation $X(d_1{:}D_1, \ldots, d_n{:}D_n) = q \in PE$ with process name X and the occurrence of p under investigation is a subprocess of q.

14. The process expression p equals $X(d_1 = t_1, \ldots, d_m = t_m)$, there is only one equation $X(d'_1{:}D_1, \ldots, d'_n{:}D_n) = q \in PE$ with process name X such that the occurrence of p under investigation is a subprocess of q, for each $1{\leq}j{\leq}m$ it holds that d_j is equal to d'_i for some $1{\leq}i{\leq}n$ and t_j is a well-typed expressions of type D_i over $\mathcal{X}_\mathcal{S}$. Furthermore, each d_j is different from $d_{j'}$ for all $1 \leq j < j' \leq m$.

Definition 15.2.10. A process specification $PS = (\mathcal{D}, AD, PE, p, \mathcal{X})$ where $\mathcal{D} = (\Sigma, E)$ and $\Sigma = (\mathcal{S}, \mathcal{C}_\mathcal{S}, \mathcal{M}_\mathcal{S})$, is well-typed iff all of the conditions below are fulfilled.

1. $\mathcal{D}$ is well-typed.

2. For each action declaration $a : D_1 \times \cdots \times D_n \in AD$ and for all $1 \leq i \leq n$ it holds that $D_i \in \mathcal{S}$.

3. For each process equation $X(d_1{:}D_1, \ldots, d_n{:}D_n) = p \in PE$ and for all $1 \leq i \leq n$ it holds that p is a well-typed expression over $(\mathcal{X} \setminus \{d_i{:}D \mid 1 \leq i \leq n, D \in \mathcal{S}\}) \cup \{d_1{:}D_1, \ldots, d_n{:}D_n\}$, $D_i \in \mathcal{S}$ and d_i do not occur as a function symbol in $\mathcal{C}_{\mathcal{S}}$ or $\mathcal{M}_{\mathcal{S}}$. Furthermore, $d_i \neq d_{i'}$ for all $1 \leq i < i' \leq n$.

4. Any action declaration $a : D_1 \times \cdots \times D_n \in AD$ and process equation $a(d_1{:}D'_1, \ldots, d_m{:}D'_m) = p \in PE$ are nonconvertible, meaning that either $n \neq m$, or if $n = m$ then there is some $1 \leq i \leq m$ such that not $D_i \subseteq D'_i$ and not $D'_i \subseteq D_i$.

5. The (initial) process expression p is well-typed process expression over $\mathcal{X}$.

6. If a variable $d{:}D$ occurs in $\mathcal{X}$, then $D \in \mathcal{S}$ and there is no function symbol d that occurs in $\mathcal{C}_{\mathcal{S}} \cup \mathcal{M}_{\mathcal{S}}$.

Example 15.2.11. Consider the following mCRL2 specification.

act $\mathit{read}, \mathit{max} : \mathbb{N};$
proc $\mathit{Max} = \sum_{x:\mathbb{N}} \mathit{read}(x) \cdot \sum_{y:\mathbb{N}} \mathit{read}(y) \cdot \mathit{max}(\mathit{max}(x, y)) \cdot \mathit{Max};$
$\mathit{Max}(x{:}\mathbb{N}) = \sum_{y:\mathbb{N}} \mathit{read}(y) \cdot \mathit{Max}(\mathit{max}(x, y));$
init $\mathit{Max}(1) + \mathit{Max};$

This specification is well-typed. The two process definitions for Max do not clash since they have a different number of arguments. The function max and the action max do not collide as they are different objects.

15.2.2 Semantical multi-actions

In this section we define semantical multi-actions as multi-actions that have model elements as arguments. We want to define the semantics of a process expression as a timed transition system. In these transition systems, transition labels play an important role. Of course these labels are derived from the (multi-)actions of a process. But it is inconvenient to take data expressions as the arguments of these actions. Consider for instance two transitions with action $a(2)$ and $a(1+1)$. The definitions of behavioral equality, such as bisimulation, do not use a model to compare them, and would therefore not consider these actions equal. If we use semantical actions, both actions are represented by $a(\mathbf{2})$ with $\mathbf{2}$ the model element representing 2 and 1+1.

Definition 15.2.12 (Interpretation of a multi-action). Let $\mathcal{D} = (\Sigma, E)$ be a data specification and $[\![\cdot]\!]^{\sigma}$ a $\mathcal{D}$-model. We inductively define the interpretation of a multi-action α for any data-valuation σ as follows:

- $[\![\tau]\!]^{\sigma} = \tau$.
- $[\![a(t_1, \ldots, t_n)]\!]^{\sigma} = a([\![t_1]\!]^{\sigma}, \ldots, [\![t_n]\!]^{\sigma})$.

- $[\![\alpha|\beta]\!]^\sigma = [\![\alpha]\!]^\sigma | [\![\beta]\!]^\sigma$.

Here $|$ is a new operator on semantical multi-actions that is associative and commutative. In analogy with syntactical multi-actions, we write τ for the empty multi-action but we use letters ω and ϖ for semantical multi-actions in general. The empty (semantical) multi-action is a unit for $|$. That is, $\tau|\omega = \omega|\tau = \omega$.

The semantics of processes is defined using so-called inference rules. In these rules we use several notations on semantical multi-actions. These are provided in the following definitions.

Definition 15.2.13. Let ω be a semantical multi-action. We define:

- $\omega_{\{\}}$ is the set of all actions occurring in ω. In particular $\tau_{\{\}} = \emptyset$, $a_{\{\}} = \{a\}$ and $(\omega|\varpi)_{\{\}} = \omega_{\{\}} \cup \varpi_{\{\}}$.
- Let R be a set of renamings. $R \bullet \omega$ is the semantical multi-action where the labels have been renamed according to R. More precisely: $R \bullet a(d_1, \ldots, d_n) = b(d_1, \ldots, d_n)$ if $a \to b \in R$. Otherwise, the result is just $a(d_1, \ldots, d_n)$. This operator distributes over $|$. A particular renaming operators is $\eta_I(\omega)$ which renames all actions labels in I to int. Furthermore, we use $\theta_I(\omega)$ which removes all actions with labels that occur in I. Strictly speaking, $\theta_I(\omega)$ is not a renaming.
- We write $\underline{\omega}$ for the multi-action ω where all data has been removed. In particular $\underline{a(t_1, \ldots, t_n)} = a$.
- Communication is defined using γ_C. It says that a communication within different actions in a multi-action takes place, exactly when this communication occurs in C and the arguments of these actions have the same data arguments. By defining $\gamma_{C_1 \cup C_2}(\omega) = \gamma_{C_1}(\gamma_{C_2}(\omega))$ we can apply each renaming on its own:

$$\gamma_{\{a_1|\ldots|a_n \to b\}}(\omega) =$$

$$\begin{cases} b(\vec{d})|\gamma_{\{a_1|\ldots|a_n \to b\}}(\varpi) & \text{if actions } a_i(\vec{d}) \text{ occur in } \omega \text{ for all } 1 \leq i \leq n \\ \omega & \text{otherwise} \end{cases}$$

where $\varpi = \omega \setminus (a_1(\vec{d})| \ldots |a_n(\vec{d}))$, i.e., the multi-action ω from which actions $a_i(\vec{d})$ are removed.

15.2.3 Substitution on processes

In order to define the semantics of processes, we need to extend the definitions of free variables and substitutions to process expressions.

Definition 15.2.14. A variable x is free in a process expression p, if one of the following holds.

1. p is of the form $a(t_1, \ldots, t_n)$ and x is free in t_i for some $1 \leq i \leq n$.

2. p is of the form $\alpha|\beta$ and x is free in α or x is free in β.

3. p is of one of the forms $p_1{+}p_2$, $p_1{\cdot}p_2$, $p_1\|p_2$, $p_1 \mathbin{|\!\lfloor} p_2$, $p_1{\ll}p_2$, or $p_1|p_2$, and x is free in p_1 or x is free in p_2.

4. p is of the form $c{\to}p'$, and x is free in c or x is free in p'.

5. p is of the form $c{\to}p_1{\diamond}p_2$, and x is free in c, or x is free in p_1, or x is free in p_2.

6. p is of the form $\sum_{d:D} p'$, x is not d, and x is free in p'.

7. p is of one of the forms $p' {}^{c} t$ or $t{\gg}p'$, and x is free in t or x is free in p'.

8. p is of one of the forms $\Gamma_C(p')$, $\nabla_V(p')$, $\partial_B(p')$, $\tau_B(p')$, $\Upsilon_B(p')$, or $\rho_R(p')$, and x is free in p'.

9. p is of the form $X()$ and x is d_i for some $1{\le}i{\le}n$ where the (only) defining equation for X is given by $X(d_1{:}D_1, \ldots, d_n{:}D_n) = q \in PE$.

10. p is of the form $X(u_1, \ldots, u_n)$ and x is free in u_i for some $1 \le i \le n$.

11. p is of the form $X(d_1{=}t_1, \ldots, d_m{=}t_m)$ and x is free in t_i for some $1 \le i \le m$, or x is equal to some d'_j $(1{\le}j{\le}n)$ and not equal to some d_i $(1{\le}i{\le}m)$ where the (only) defining equation for X is given by $X(d'_1{:}D_1, \ldots, d'_n{:}D_n) = q \in PE$.

Note that there are no free variables in δ, τ and X.

Definition 15.2.15. Let $PS = (\mathcal{D}, AD, PE, p, \mathcal{X})$ be a process specification, and ξ be a substitution on data expressions. We extend the substitution ξ to a process expression p, denoted by $\xi(p)$, inductively as follows.

1. $\xi(\delta) = \delta$, $\xi(\tau) = \tau$ and $\xi(a(t_1, \ldots, t_n)) = a(\xi(t_1), \ldots, \xi(t_n))$.

2. $\xi(\alpha|\beta) = \xi(\alpha)|\xi(\beta)$.

3. $\xi(p_1{+}p_2) = \xi(p_1){+}\xi(p_2)$, $\xi(p_1{\cdot}p_2) = \xi(p_1){\cdot}\xi(p_2)$, $\xi(p_1\|p_2) = \xi(p_1)\|\xi(p_2)$, $\xi(p_1 \mathbin{|\!\lfloor} p_2) = \xi(p_1) \mathbin{|\!\lfloor} \xi(p_2)$, $\xi(p_1{\ll}p_2) = \xi(p_1){\ll}\xi(p_2)$, and $\xi(p_1|p_2) = \xi(p_1)|\xi(p_2)$.

4. $\xi(c{\to}p_1) = \xi(c){\to}\xi(p_1)$ and $\xi(c{\to}p_1{\diamond}p_2) = \xi(c){\to}\xi(p_1){\diamond}\xi(p_2)$.

5. $\xi(\sum_{d:D} p) = \sum_{d':D} \xi[d{:=}d', d'{:=}d'](p)$, provided that d' does not occur freely in p and in $\xi(z)$ for any variable z occurring freely in p.

6. $\xi(p {}^{c} t) = \xi(p) {}^{c} \xi(t)$ and $\xi(t{\gg}p) = \xi(t){\gg}\xi(p)$.

7. $\xi(\Gamma_C(p)) = \Gamma_C(\xi(p))$, $\xi(\nabla_V(p)) = \nabla_V(\xi(p))$, $\xi(\partial_B(p)) = \partial_B(\xi(p))$, $\xi(\tau_B(p)) = \tau_B(\xi(p))$, $\xi(\Upsilon_B(p)) = \Upsilon_B(\xi(p))$, and $\xi(\rho_R(p)) = \rho_R(\xi(p))$.

8. $\xi(X) = X$, $\xi(X(t_1, \ldots, t_n)) = X(\xi(t_1), \ldots, \xi(t_n))$, $\xi(X()) = X()$, and $\xi(X(d_1{=}t_1, \ldots, d_m{=}t_m)) = X(d_1{=}\xi(t_1), \ldots, d_m{=}\xi(t_m))$.

$$\frac{}{\alpha \xrightarrow{[\![\alpha]\!]}_u \checkmark} \qquad \frac{}{\alpha \rightsquigarrow_u} \qquad \frac{}{\delta \rightsquigarrow_u}$$

$$\frac{p \xrightarrow{\omega}_u \checkmark}{p+q \xrightarrow{\omega}_u \checkmark} \qquad \frac{p \xrightarrow{\omega}_u p'}{p+q \xrightarrow{\omega}_u p'} \qquad \frac{p \rightsquigarrow_u}{p+q \rightsquigarrow_u}$$

$$\frac{q \xrightarrow{\omega}_u \checkmark}{p+q \xrightarrow{\omega}_u \checkmark} \qquad \frac{q \xrightarrow{\omega}_u q'}{p+q \xrightarrow{\omega}_u q'} \qquad \frac{q \rightsquigarrow_u}{p+q \rightsquigarrow_u}$$

$$\frac{p \xrightarrow{\omega}_u \checkmark}{p\cdot q \xrightarrow{\omega}_u t_u \gg q} \qquad \frac{p \xrightarrow{\omega}_u p'}{p\cdot q \xrightarrow{\omega}_u p'\cdot q} \qquad \frac{p \rightsquigarrow_u}{p\cdot q \rightsquigarrow_u}$$

$$\frac{p \xrightarrow{\omega}_u \checkmark}{c\rightarrow p \xrightarrow{\omega}_u \checkmark} [\![c]\!]=\textbf{true} \qquad \frac{p \xrightarrow{\omega}_u p'}{c\rightarrow p \xrightarrow{\omega}_u p'} [\![c]\!]=\textbf{true} \qquad \frac{p \rightsquigarrow_u}{c\rightarrow p \rightsquigarrow_u} [\![c]\!]=\textbf{true}$$

$$\frac{p \xrightarrow{\omega}_u \checkmark}{c\rightarrow p\diamond q \xrightarrow{\omega}_u \checkmark} [\![c]\!]=\textbf{true} \qquad \frac{p \xrightarrow{\omega}_u p'}{c\rightarrow p\diamond q \xrightarrow{\omega}_u p'} [\![c]\!]=\textbf{true} \qquad \frac{p \rightsquigarrow_u}{c\rightarrow p\diamond q \rightsquigarrow_u} [\![c]\!]=\textbf{true}$$

$$\frac{q \xrightarrow{\omega}_u \checkmark}{c\rightarrow p\diamond q \xrightarrow{\omega}_u \checkmark} [\![c]\!]=\textbf{false} \qquad \frac{q \xrightarrow{\omega}_u q'}{c\rightarrow p\diamond q \xrightarrow{\omega}_u q'} [\![c]\!]=\textbf{false} \qquad \frac{q \rightsquigarrow_u}{c\rightarrow p\diamond q \rightsquigarrow_u} [\![c]\!]=\textbf{false}$$

Table 15.2: Operational semantics for the basic operators

$$\frac{p[d:=t_e] \xrightarrow{\omega}_u \checkmark}{\sum_{d:D} p \xrightarrow{\omega}_u \checkmark} e\in M_D \qquad \frac{p[d:=t_e] \xrightarrow{\omega}_u p'}{\sum_{d:D} p \xrightarrow{\omega}_u p'} e\in M_D \qquad \frac{p[d:=t_e] \rightsquigarrow_u}{\sum_{d:D} p \rightsquigarrow_u} e\in M_D$$

$$\frac{p \xrightarrow{\omega}_u \checkmark}{p^c t \xrightarrow{\omega}_u \checkmark} u=[\![t]\!] \qquad \frac{p \xrightarrow{\omega}_u p'}{p^c t \xrightarrow{\omega}_u p'} u=[\![t]\!] \qquad \frac{p \rightsquigarrow_u}{p^c t \rightsquigarrow_u} u<[\![t]\!]$$

$$\frac{p \xrightarrow{\omega}_u \checkmark}{t\gg p \xrightarrow{\omega}_u \checkmark} u>[\![t]\!] \qquad \frac{p \xrightarrow{\omega}_u p'}{t\gg p \xrightarrow{\omega}_u p'} u>[\![t]\!]$$

$$\frac{p \rightsquigarrow_u}{t\gg p \rightsquigarrow_u} \qquad \frac{}{t\gg p \rightsquigarrow_u} u<[\![t]\!]$$

Table 15.3: Operational semantics for the summation, bounded initialization, and before operators

$$\frac{q[d_1{:=}t_1,\ldots d_n{:=}t_n] \xrightarrow{\omega}_u \checkmark}{X(t_1,\ldots,t_n) \xrightarrow{\omega}_u \checkmark} \qquad \frac{q[d_1{:=}t_1,\ldots d_n{:=}t_n] \xrightarrow{\omega}_u q'}{X(t_1,\ldots,t_n) \xrightarrow{\omega}_u q'}$$

$$\frac{q[d_1{:=}t_1,\ldots d_n{:=}t_n] \rightsquigarrow_u}{X(t_1,\ldots,t_n) \rightsquigarrow_u}$$

where $X(d_1{:}D_1,\ldots,d_n{:}D_n) = q \in PE$.

$$\frac{q[d_1{:=}u_1,\ldots,d_n{:=}u_n] \xrightarrow{\omega}_u \checkmark}{X(d_1'{=}t_1,\ldots,d_m'{=}t_m) \xrightarrow{\omega}_u \checkmark} \qquad \frac{q[d_1{:=}u_1,\ldots,d_n{:=}u_n] \xrightarrow{\omega}_u q'}{X(d_1'{=}t_1,\ldots,d_m'{=}t_m) \xrightarrow{\omega}_u q'}$$

$$\frac{q[d_1{:=}u_1,\ldots,d_n{:=}u_n] \rightsquigarrow_u}{X(d_1'{=}t_1,\ldots,d_m'{=}t_m) \rightsquigarrow_u}$$

where $X(d_1{:}D_1,\ldots,d_n{:}D_n) = q \in PE$ and

$$u_i = \begin{cases} \xi(t_j) & \text{if } d_i = d_j' \text{ for some } 1 \le j \le m, \\ \xi(d_i) & \text{otherwise.} \end{cases}$$

Table 15.4: Operational semantics for recursion

$$\frac{p \xrightarrow{\omega}_u \checkmark,\ q \rightsquigarrow_u}{p\|q \xrightarrow{\omega}_u t_u{\gg}q} \qquad \frac{p \xrightarrow{\omega}_u p',\ q \rightsquigarrow_u}{p\|q \xrightarrow{\omega}_u p'\|t_u{\gg}q} \qquad \frac{p \xrightarrow{\omega}_u p',\ q \xrightarrow{\varpi}_u q'}{p\|q \xrightarrow{\omega|\varpi}_u p'\|q'}$$

$$\frac{p \rightsquigarrow_t,\ q \xrightarrow{\omega}_u \checkmark}{p\|q \xrightarrow{\omega}_u t_u{\gg}p} \qquad \frac{p \rightsquigarrow_u,\ q \xrightarrow{\omega}_u q'}{p\|q \xrightarrow{\omega}_u t_u{\gg}p\|q'} \qquad \frac{p \rightsquigarrow_u,\ q \rightsquigarrow_u}{p\|q \rightsquigarrow_u}$$

$$\frac{p \xrightarrow{\omega}_u \checkmark,\ q \xrightarrow{\varpi}_u \checkmark}{p\|q \xrightarrow{\omega|\varpi}_u \checkmark} \qquad \frac{p \xrightarrow{\omega}_u p',\ q \xrightarrow{\varpi}_u \checkmark}{p\|q \xrightarrow{\omega|\varpi}_u p'} \qquad \frac{p \xrightarrow{\omega}_u \checkmark,\ q \xrightarrow{\varpi}_u q'}{p\|q \xrightarrow{\omega|\varpi}_u q'}$$

Table 15.5: Operational semantics for the parallel operator

$\dfrac{p \xrightarrow{\omega}_u \checkmark,\ q \rightsquigarrow_u}{p \mathbin{\lfloor\!\lfloor} q \xrightarrow{\omega}_u t_u \gg q}$	$\dfrac{p \xrightarrow{\omega}_u p',\ q \rightsquigarrow_u}{p \mathbin{\lfloor\!\lfloor} q \xrightarrow{\omega}_u p' \| t_u \gg q}$	$\dfrac{p \rightsquigarrow_u,\ q \rightsquigarrow_u}{p \mathbin{\lfloor\!\lfloor} q \rightsquigarrow_u}$
$\dfrac{p \xrightarrow{\omega}_u p',\ q \xrightarrow{\varpi}_u q'}{p \vert q \xrightarrow{\omega \vert \varpi}_u p' \| q'}$	$\dfrac{p \xrightarrow{\omega}_u \checkmark,\ q \xrightarrow{\varpi}_u \checkmark}{p \vert q \xrightarrow{\omega \vert \varpi}_u \checkmark}$	
$\dfrac{p \xrightarrow{\omega}_u \checkmark,\ q \xrightarrow{\varpi}_u q'}{p \vert q \xrightarrow{\omega \vert \varpi}_u q'}$	$\dfrac{p \xrightarrow{\omega}_u p',\ q \xrightarrow{\varpi}_u \checkmark}{p \vert q \xrightarrow{\omega \vert \varpi}_u p'}$	$\dfrac{p \rightsquigarrow_u,\ q \rightsquigarrow_u}{p \vert q \rightsquigarrow_u}$
$\dfrac{p \xrightarrow{\omega}_u \checkmark,\ q \rightsquigarrow_u}{p \ll q \xrightarrow{\omega}_u \checkmark}$	$\dfrac{p \xrightarrow{\omega}_u p',\ q \rightsquigarrow_u}{p \ll q \xrightarrow{\omega}_u p'}$	$\dfrac{p \rightsquigarrow_u,\ q \rightsquigarrow_u}{p \ll q \rightsquigarrow_u}$

Table 15.6: Operational semantics for the auxiliary parallel operators

$\dfrac{p \xrightarrow{\omega}_u \checkmark}{\nabla_V(p) \xrightarrow{\omega}_u \checkmark}\ \underline{\omega} \in V \cup \{\tau\}$	$\dfrac{p \xrightarrow{\omega}_u p'}{\nabla_V(p) \xrightarrow{\omega}_u \nabla_V(p')}\ \underline{\omega} \in V \cup \{\tau\}$	$\dfrac{p \rightsquigarrow_u}{\nabla_V(p) \rightsquigarrow_u}$
$\dfrac{p \xrightarrow{\omega}_u \checkmark}{\partial_B(p) \xrightarrow{\omega}_u \checkmark}\ \underline{\omega}_{\{\}} \cap B = \emptyset$	$\dfrac{p \xrightarrow{\omega}_u p'}{\partial_B(p) \xrightarrow{\omega}_u \partial_B(p')}\ \underline{\omega}_{\{\}} \cap B = \emptyset$	$\dfrac{p \rightsquigarrow_u}{\partial_B(p) \rightsquigarrow_u}$
$\dfrac{p \xrightarrow{\omega}_u \checkmark}{\rho_R(p) \xrightarrow{R \bullet \omega}_u \checkmark}$	$\dfrac{p \xrightarrow{\omega}_u p'}{\rho_R(p) \xrightarrow{R \bullet \omega}_u \rho_R(p')}$	$\dfrac{p \rightsquigarrow_u}{\rho_R(p) \rightsquigarrow_u}$
$\dfrac{p \xrightarrow{\omega}_u \checkmark}{\Gamma_C(p) \xrightarrow{\gamma_C(\omega)}_u \checkmark}$	$\dfrac{p \xrightarrow{\omega}_u p'}{\Gamma_C(p) \xrightarrow{\gamma_C(\omega)}_u \Gamma_C(p')}$	$\dfrac{p \rightsquigarrow_u}{\Gamma_C(p) \rightsquigarrow_u}$
$\dfrac{p \xrightarrow{\omega}_u \checkmark}{\tau_I(p) \xrightarrow{\theta_I(\omega)}_u \checkmark}$	$\dfrac{p \xrightarrow{\omega}_u p'}{\tau_I(p) \xrightarrow{\theta_I(\omega)}_u \tau_I(p')}$	$\dfrac{p \rightsquigarrow_u}{\tau_I(p) \rightsquigarrow_u}$
$\dfrac{p \xrightarrow{\omega}_u \checkmark}{\Upsilon_U(p) \xrightarrow{\eta_U(\omega)}_u \checkmark}$	$\dfrac{p \xrightarrow{\omega}_u p'}{\Upsilon_U(p) \xrightarrow{\eta_U(\omega)}_u \Upsilon_U(p')}$	$\dfrac{p \rightsquigarrow_u}{\Upsilon_U(p) \rightsquigarrow_u}$

Table 15.7: Operational semantics for auxiliary operators

15.2.4 Operational semantics

Given a data model (for a data specification) and a process expression, we associate a timed labeled transition system to the process expression as defined below. The timed labeled transition system is the semantics of a process expression. It gives an "operational" meaning to the process, i.e., defines its timed execution on an abstract machine. In order to obtain a timed labeled transition system with real numbers as time stamps, we further require that the model of sort $\mathbb{R}$ is the set of real numbers.

The timed labeled transitions and idle relations are defined using inference rules in a style commonly referred to as *structural (or structured) operational semantics* (SOS). The inference rules are a particular style of inductive definitions which is especially suited to define the transition and idle relations on some given syntax in terms of the transition and idle relations of its components.

The following example illustrates a subtlety involved in the notion of a substitution on processes. In process assignments there can be a confusion between the names bound using the sum operator with the parameters of the process. Parameters that are not mentioned in a process assignment retain their original value, whereas parameters that are explicitly mentioned in a process assignment can be equal to a variable bound in a sum. Thus, an assignment $x = x$ is not equal to leaving it out when x is bound.

Example 15.2.16. Consider the following mCRL2 specification.

act $a : \mathbb{N}$;
proc $P(x{:}\mathbb{N}) = a(x)\cdot \sum_{x:\mathbb{N}} b(x)\cdot P(x{=}x)$;
$Q(x{:}\mathbb{N}) = a(x)\cdot \sum_{x:\mathbb{N}} b(x)\cdot Q()$;

Intuitively, we expect $P(0)$ to first perform $a(0)$, followed by $b(n)$, $a(n)$, followed by $b(n')$, $a(n')$, and so forth, for natural numbers n and n'. However, $Q(0)$ behaves differently, namely, it performs $a(0)$, $b(n)$, $a(0)$, $b(n')$, $a(0)$, and so on, because the parameter x of Q remains unchanged at the recursive invocation of Q. In the case of $Q(0)$, the substitution of x by the sum operator does not carry over to the continuation defined by $Q()$, while the substitution resulting from the instantiation of x with 0 in $Q(x{:}\mathbb{N})$ does.

In order to deal with this, we assume that parameters and bound variables in process equations are different. This can easily be obtained by renaming the parameters of a process equation to fresh ones. In this case the equation for Q above becomes:

proc $Q(y{:}\mathbb{N}) = a(y)\cdot \sum_{x:\mathbb{N}} b(x)\cdot Q()$;

Definition 15.2.17 (Semantics of a process). Let $PS = (\mathcal{D}, AD, PE, p, \mathcal{X})$ be a process specification and assume without loss of generality that the parameters $d_1, \ldots, d_n$ of each process equation $X(d_1{:}D_1, \ldots d_n{:}D_n) = q$ in PE are different from the variables bound in q. Let $\mathcal{A} = \{M_D | D{\in}\mathcal{S}\}$ be a $\mathcal{D}$-structure and $[\![\cdot]\!]$ a $\mathcal{D}$-model, where $M_{\mathbb{R}}$ are the real numbers and $<: \mathbb{R} \times \mathbb{R} \to \mathbb{B}$ is interpreted as the ordinary $<$ on real numbers. We assume that for each model element $e \in M_D$, there is a syntactic denotation for e, namely t_e. Furthermore, we use a substitution ξ mapping the variables in $\mathcal{X}$ to closed data expressions.

We define the semantics of PS given $\mathcal{A}$, $[\![\cdot]\!]$, and ξ as a timed transition system $A = (S, Act, \longrightarrow, \rightsquigarrow, s_0, T)$ as follows:

- The states S are closed process expressions p' with the syntax given in definition 15.2.4. In addition, there is a special termination state, denoted by $\checkmark$.
- The set Act contains the semantical multi-actions.
- The transitions are inductively defined by the operational rules in tables 15.2, 15.3, 15.4, 15.5, 15.6, and 15.7. The transition relation is generally denoted by $p' \xrightarrow{\omega}_u p''$ or $p' \xrightarrow{\omega}_u \checkmark$. Note that the processes are syntactic and the actions and time stamps are semantic. As processes are well-typed, there is only one candidate for the process equation $X(\vec{d}{:}\vec{D}) = q$ in table 15.4. The expressions X and $X()$ fall under the rules in table 15.4 where the argument lists are empty.
- There is an idle relation in each state that expresses that in this state the process can idle up to and including time $t \in \mathbb{R}^{>0}$. It is denoted by $p \rightsquigarrow_t$ and it is also defined by the operational rules in the tables.
- The initial state s_0 is $\xi(p)$.
- The set of terminating states T contains only $\checkmark$, i.e., $T = \{\checkmark\}$.

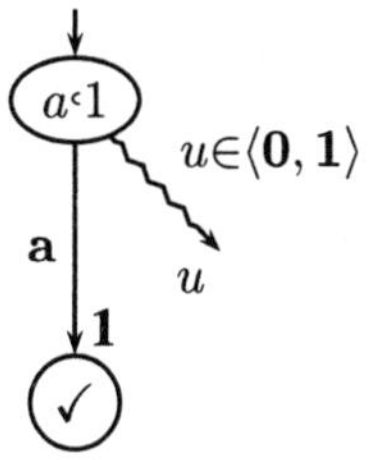

Figure 15.1: The semantics of the process $a{}^{\varsigma}1$

Example 15.2.18. The process $a{}^{\varsigma}1$ has the transition system given in figure 15.1. Only two states are drawn, because only these are relevant in this example. Formally any process p is a state; however, apart from the depicted processes, the rest are not reachable in this case. The two remaining states are $a{}^{\varsigma}1$ and $\checkmark$. The first one is the initial state and the second one is a terminal state. There is a transition $a{}^{\varsigma}1 \xrightarrow{\mathbf{a}}_{\mathbf{1}} \checkmark$. Here the boldface $\mathbf{0}$ and $\mathbf{1}$ are the semantical interpretations of the syntactical numbers 0 and 1, and the boldface $\mathbf{a}$ is the semantical action for the syntactical action a. We only write the boldface numbers and actions here to stress the subtle difference between the syntactical and semantical objects. For standard data types we generally adhere to the standard notation to denote elements in both domains, which might sometimes be confusing. The transition can be derived using the inference rules, as shown below

$$\dfrac{\dfrac{}{a \xrightarrow{\mathbf{a}}_{\mathbf{1}} \checkmark}\ \text{table 15.2}}{a{}^{\varsigma}1 \xrightarrow{\mathbf{a}}_{\mathbf{1}} \checkmark}\ \text{table 15.3}$$

The inference rules used to derive these transitions can be found in the corresponding tables by matching the function symbol in the source of the conclusion. Note that this is the only derivation concerning action transitions of the process $a^{\varsigma}1$. This means that there are no other action transitions possible.

In a similar way we can derive idle transitions $a^{\varsigma}1 \rightsquigarrow_u$ for any $u \in \langle \mathbf{0}, \mathbf{1} \rangle$.

$$\dfrac{\dfrac{}{a \rightsquigarrow_u}\ \text{table 15.2}}{a^{\varsigma}1 \rightsquigarrow_u}\ \text{table 15.3}$$

In previous chapters various process equalities were defined on labeled transition systems. These carry over to processes in the following way. Two processes p and q are equivalent iff the initial states of their transition systems are equivalent for every $\mathcal{D}$-model and substitution of the global variables. They are not equal iff they are not equal for every $\mathcal{D}$-model and substitution. Observe that it is possible that processes p and q are neither equal nor not equal because there are models where they are not equal and there are models were they are equal. This phenomenon is common in logic where it is called contingency.

Exercise 15.2.19. Derive the timed labeled transition systems for $\partial_{\{b\}}(a^{\varsigma}1 + b^{\varsigma}2)$ and $a^{\varsigma}1 \| b^{\varsigma}2$.

15.3 Validity of modal μ-calculus formulas

Given a transition system we define in which states a formula holds. From this we know whether a formula holds in the initial state, and we can even determine whether a formula holds for the initial state of a timed transition system that forms the semantics of a process expression. First, we define the semantics of an action formula by defining which set of timed semantical multi-actions is associated with it.

Definition 15.3.1 (Semantics of action formulas). Let $\Sigma = (\mathcal{S}, \mathcal{C}_\mathcal{S}, \mathcal{M}_\mathcal{S})$ be a signature, $\mathcal{D} = (\Sigma, E)$ a data specification, $\mathcal{A} = \{M_D | D{\in}\mathcal{S}\}$ a $\mathcal{D}$-structure, $[\![\cdot]\!]$ a $\mathcal{D}$-model, and $A = (S, Act, \longrightarrow, \rightsquigarrow, s_0, T)$ a timed transition system where Act consists of semantical multi-actions. Let $Act_t = \{\langle m, t\rangle | m{\in}Act, r{\in}\mathbb{R}^{>0}\}$ be the set of all semantical multi-actions with a time stamp.

Let af be an action expression. We define the interpretation of af, notation $[\![af]\!]^\sigma$ where σ is a valuation, as a set of pairs of a semantical multi-action and a time stamp, inductively by

- $[\![true]\!]^\sigma = Act_t$.
- $[\![false]\!]^\sigma = \emptyset$.
- $[\![t]\!]^\sigma = \begin{cases} Act_t & \text{if } [\![t]\!]^\sigma = \mathbf{true}, \\ \emptyset & \text{otherwise.} \end{cases}$
- $[\![\alpha]\!]^\sigma = \{\langle [\![\alpha]\!]^\sigma, t\rangle \mid t \in \mathbb{R}^{>0}\}$.
- $[\![\overline{af}]\!]^\sigma = Act_t \setminus [\![af]\!]^\sigma$.

- $[\![af \cap af']\!]^\sigma = [\![af]\!]^\sigma \cap [\![af']\!]^\sigma$.
- $[\![af \cup af']\!]^\sigma = [\![af]\!]^\sigma \cup [\![af']\!]^\sigma$.
- $[\![\forall d{:}D.af]\!]^\sigma = \bigcap_{d \in M_D} [\![af]\!]^{\sigma[d/x]}$.
- $[\![\exists d{:}D.af]\!]^\sigma = \bigcup_{d \in M_D} [\![af]\!]^{\sigma[d/x]}$.
- $[\![af{\cdot}u]\!]^\sigma = \{\langle m,t\rangle \mid \langle m,t\rangle \in [\![af]\!]^\sigma,\ t = [\![u]\!]^\sigma,\ t \in \mathbb{R}^{>0}\}$.

Example 15.3.2. Consider actions a and b that have one natural number as argument. A few typical instances of the semantics of action formulas are given below. We write bold numbers to indicate model elements.

$$\begin{array}{l} [\![a(3){\cdot}5]\!]^\sigma = \{\langle a(\mathbf{3}), \mathbf{5}\rangle\}. \\ [\![a(3)|b(5)]\!]^\sigma = \{\langle a(\mathbf{3})|b(\mathbf{5}), t\rangle | t \in \mathbb{R}^{>0}\}. \\ [\![\exists x{:}\mathbb{N}.a(x){\cdot}x]\!]^\sigma = \{\langle a(n), n\rangle | n \in M_{\mathbb{N}}\}. \\ [\![\forall x{:}\mathbb{N}.a(x){\cdot}x]\!]^\sigma = \emptyset. \end{array}$$

Below, we define in which states of a timed transition system a formula holds given a model and an interpretation of the signature in this model. Subsequently, we define that a formula is valid for a process independent of a particular model. We generalize this even further by defining when two formulas are equivalent independent of a model and a particular process.

Definition 15.3.3 (Semantics of modal formulas). Let $\mathcal{D} = (\Sigma, E)$ be a data specification where $\Sigma = (\mathcal{S}, \mathcal{C}_\mathcal{S}, \mathcal{M}_\mathcal{S})$, $\mathcal{A} = \{M_D | D \in \mathcal{S}\}$ a $\mathcal{D}$-structure, $[\![\cdot]\!]$ a $\mathcal{D}$-model, and $A = (S, Act, \longrightarrow, \rightsquigarrow, s_0, T)$ a timed transition system where Act consists of all semantical multi-actions.

Let ϕ be a modal formula. We inductively define the interpretation of ϕ, notation $[\![\phi]\!]^{\sigma,\rho}$, where σ is a valuation and ρ is a logical variable valuation, as a set of states where ϕ is valid, by

- $[\![true]\!]^{\sigma,\rho} = S$.
- $[\![false]\!]^{\sigma,\rho} = \emptyset$.
- $[\![t]\!]^{\sigma,\rho} = \begin{cases} S & \text{if } [\![t]\!]^\sigma = \mathbf{true}, \\ \emptyset & \text{if } [\![t]\!]^\sigma = \mathbf{false}. \end{cases}$
- $[\![\neg\phi]\!]^{\sigma,\rho} = S \setminus [\![\phi]\!]^{\sigma,\rho}$.
- $[\![\phi_1 \wedge \phi_2]\!]^{\sigma,\rho} = [\![\phi_1]\!]^{\sigma,\rho} \cap [\![\phi_2]\!]^{\sigma,\rho}$.
- $[\![\phi_1 \vee \phi_2]\!]^{\sigma,\rho} = [\![\phi_1]\!]^{\sigma,\rho} \cup [\![\phi_2]\!]^{\sigma,\rho}$.
- $[\![\forall x{:}D.\phi]\!]^{\sigma,\rho} = \bigcap_{d \in M_D} [\![\phi]\!]^{\sigma[d/x],\rho}$.
- $[\![\exists x{:}D.\phi]\!]^{\sigma,\rho} = \bigcup_{d \in M_D} [\![\phi]\!]^{\sigma[d/x],\rho}$.
- $[\![\langle af\rangle\phi]\!]^{\sigma,\rho} = \{s \in S \mid$ there are $\langle \alpha, t\rangle \in [\![af]\!]^\sigma$ and $s' \in S$ such that $s \xrightarrow{\alpha}_t s'$ and $s' \in [\![\phi]\!]^{\sigma,\rho}\}$.

- $[\![[af]\phi]\!]^{\sigma,\rho} = \{s \in S \mid \text{for all } \langle \alpha, t\rangle \in [\![af]\!]^{\sigma} \text{ and } s' \in S \text{ if } s \xrightarrow{\alpha}_t s' \text{ then } s' \in [\![\phi]\!]^{\sigma,\rho}\}$.
- $[\![\Delta]\!]^{\sigma,\rho} = \{s \in S \mid s \rightsquigarrow_t \text{ for all } t \in \mathbb{R}^{>0}\}$.
- $[\![\Delta\text{`}u]\!]^{\sigma,\rho} = \{s \in S \mid s \rightsquigarrow_{[\![u]\!]^{\sigma}}\}$.
- $[\![\nabla]\!]^{\sigma,\rho} = \{s \in S \mid \text{not } s \rightsquigarrow_t \text{ for some } t \in \mathbb{R}^{>0}\}$.
- $[\![\nabla\text{`}u]\!]^{\sigma,\rho} = \{s \in S \mid \text{not } s \rightsquigarrow_{[\![u]\!]^{\sigma}}\}$.
- $[\![\mu X(x_1{:}D_1{:=}t_1,\ldots,x_n{:}D_n{:=}t_n).\phi]\!]^{\sigma,\rho} =$
  $\bigcap_{f \in M_{D_1}\times\cdots\times M_{D_n}\to 2^S}\{f([\![t_1]\!]^{\sigma},\ldots,[\![t_n]\!]^{\sigma}) \mid \forall d_1 \in M_{D_1},\ldots,d_n \in M_{D_n}.$
  $f(d_1,\ldots,d_n) = [\![\phi]\!]^{\sigma[d_1/x_1,\ldots,d_N/x_n],\rho[X:=f]}\}$.
- $[\![\nu X(x_1{:}D_1{:=}t_1,\ldots,x_n{:}D_n{:=}t_n).\phi]\!]^{\sigma,\rho} =$
  $\bigcup_{f \in M_{D_1}\times\cdots\times M_{D_n}\to 2^S}\{f([\![t_1]\!]^{\sigma},\ldots,[\![t_n]\!]^{\sigma}) \mid \forall d_1 \in M_{D_1},\ldots,d_n \in M_{D_n}.$
  $f(d_1,\ldots,d_n) = [\![\phi]\!]^{\sigma[d_1/x_1,\ldots,d_n/x_n],\rho[X:=f]}\}$.
- $[\![X(t_1,\ldots,t_n)]\!]^{\sigma,\rho} = \rho(X)([\![t_1]\!]^{\sigma},\ldots,[\![t_n]\!]^{\sigma})$.

We say that ϕ holds in A iff $s_0 \in [\![\phi]\!]^{\sigma,\rho}$ for any σ, ρ, and $[\![\cdot]\!]$.

Definition 15.3.4 (Validity of a modal formula for process specification). Let $PS = (\mathcal{D}, AD, PE, p, \mathcal{X})$ be a process specification and let ϕ be a modal formula. We say that ϕ is valid in PS iff for any $\mathcal{D}$-structure $\mathcal{A}$, $\mathcal{D}$-model $[\![\cdot]\!]$ the timed transition system $A = (S, Act, \longrightarrow, \rightsquigarrow, s_0, T)$ that is the semantics of PS given $\mathcal{A}$ and σ, ϕ holds in A. We say that two modal formulas ϕ and ψ are equivalent iff for all process specifications ϕ is valid iff ψ is valid.

15.4 Semantics of parameterized Boolean equation systems

The semantics of a PBES is a function η that maps predicate variables $\mathcal{X}$ to functions from data to Booleans. First we define the semantics of predicate formulas. Note that this definition strongly resembles (and uses) definition 15.1.30, except that we use an additional interpretation for predicate variables, which is called a predicate environment.

Definition 15.4.1 (Semantics of predicate formulas). Let $\mathcal{D} = (\Sigma, E)$ be a data specification where $\Sigma = (\mathcal{S}, \mathcal{C}_{\mathcal{S}}, \mathcal{M}_{\mathcal{S}})$, $\mathcal{A} = \{M_D | D \in \mathcal{S}\}$ a $\mathcal{D}$-structure, and $[\![\cdot]\!]$ a $\mathcal{D}$-model. Let σ be a valuation and $\eta{:}\mathcal{X} \to (M_D \to M_{\mathbb{B}})$ be a predicate environment. The *interpretation* $[\![\phi]\!]^{\eta\sigma}$ maps a predicate formula ϕ to a Boolean and is inductively defined as follows:

$$\begin{array}{lcl}
[\![true]\!]^{\eta\sigma} & = & \textbf{true} \\
[\![false]\!]^{\eta\sigma} & = & \textbf{false} \\
[\![b]\!]^{\eta\sigma} & = & [\![b]\!]^{\sigma} \\
[\![X(e)]\!]^{\eta\sigma} & = & \eta(X)([\![e]\!]^{\sigma}) \\
[\![\phi_1 \wedge \phi_2]\!]^{\eta\sigma} & = & [\![\phi_1]\!]^{\eta\sigma} \text{ and } [\![\phi_2]\!]^{\eta\sigma} \\
[\![\phi_1 \vee \phi_2]\!]^{\eta\sigma} & = & [\![\phi_1]\!]^{\eta\sigma} \text{ or } [\![\phi_2]\!]^{\eta\sigma} \\
[\![\forall d{:}D.\phi]\!]^{\eta\sigma} & = & \textbf{true} \text{ iff for all } v{\in}M_D \text{ it holds that } [\![\phi]\!]^{\eta(\sigma[v/d])} \\
[\![\exists d{:}D.\phi]\!]^{\eta\sigma} & = & \textbf{true} \text{ iff there is a } v{\in}M_D \text{ such that } [\![\phi]\!]^{\eta(\sigma[v/d])}
\end{array}$$

Consider functions denoted by $M_D{\to}M_{\mathbb{B}}$. The ordering $\sqsubseteq$ on these is defined as $f \sqsubseteq g$ iff for all $d{\in}M_D$, we have $f(d)$ implies $g(d)$. For a set A containing functions $M_D{\to}M_{\mathbb{B}}$, we write $\bigwedge A$ for the *infimum* of the set A and $\bigvee A$ for the *supremum* of the set A. Therefore, $\bigwedge A$ is a function that returns false for any element iff there is a function in A returning false on this element. Similarly, $\bigvee A$ is the function returning true iff there is a function in A returning true.

The *semantics* of an equation system is defined in the context of a predicate environment η and a data environment σ.

Definition 15.4.2 (Semantics of an equation system). Let $\mathcal{D} = (\Sigma, E)$ be a data specification where $\Sigma = (\mathcal{S}, \mathcal{C_S}, \mathcal{M_S})$, $\mathcal{A} = \{M_D | D{\in}\mathcal{S}\}$ a $\mathcal{D}$-structure, and $[\![\cdot]\!]$ a $\mathcal{D}$-model. Let σ be a valuation and $\eta{:}\mathcal{X} \to (M_D \to M_{\mathbb{B}})$ be a predicate environment. The *solution* of an equation system $\mathcal{E}$ is inductively defined as follows:

$$\begin{array}{rcl}
[\epsilon]^{\eta\sigma} & = & \eta, \\
[(\zeta X(d{:}D){=}\phi)\mathcal{E}]^{\eta\sigma} & = & [\mathcal{E}]^{\eta[\zeta X(d:D).\phi([\mathcal{E}]^{\eta\sigma})/X]}
\end{array}$$

where $\zeta X(d{:}D).\phi([\mathcal{E}]^{\eta\sigma})$ is defined as (ζ is either μ or ν)

$$\begin{array}{l}
\mu X(d{:}D).\phi([\mathcal{E}]^{\eta\sigma}) = \bigwedge\{\psi{:}M_D{\to}M_{\mathbb{B}} | \lambda v{\in}M_D.[\![\phi]\!]^{([\mathcal{E}]^{\eta[\psi/X]\sigma[v/d]})\sigma[v/d]}{=}\psi\}, \\
\nu X(d{:}D).\phi([\mathcal{E}]^{\eta\sigma}) = \bigvee\{\psi{:}M_D{\to}M_{\mathbb{B}} | \psi{=}\lambda v{\in}M_D.[\![\phi]\!]^{([\mathcal{E}]^{\eta[\psi/X]\sigma[v/d]})\sigma[v/d]}\}.
\end{array}$$

This definition is complex and requires explanation. The expression $\mu X(d{:}D).\phi([\mathcal{E}]^{\eta\sigma})$ stands for the smallest function ψ satisfying roughly $\psi(d) = \phi[\psi/X]$. The equality $\psi(d) = \phi[\psi/X]$ appears in the context of the PBES $\mathcal{E}$ in which X can occur. The function ψ must be incorporated in $\mathcal{E}$ also, and the resulting predicate environment must be substituted in ϕ. This explains the use of $[\![\phi]\!]^{[\mathcal{E}]\eta[\psi/X]}$. In order to make this expression of the same type as ψ, lambda abstraction is applied over a value v. This value is substituted for d in σ. The explanation for $\nu X(d{:}D).\phi([\mathcal{E}]^{\eta\sigma})$ is the same, except that it is the largest fixed point.

As an illustration consider the equation system $(\nu X{=}Y)(\mu Y{=}X)$. Assume that some predicate environment η and some data environment σ are given. According to the semantics, the solution of this process is given by

$$[\mu Y{=}X]^{\eta[\nu X.Y([\mu Y=X]^{\eta\sigma})/X]}.$$

The expression $\nu X.Y([\mu Y{=}X]^{\eta\sigma})$ is the largest value b such that if it is substituted for X in $\mu Y{=}X$, it is equal to the smallest solution of this equation, which is of course

b. Therefore, b can be either **true** or **false**. The largest choice is **true**. So, for a given predicate environment η, the solution is $\eta[\mathbf{true}/X][\mathbf{true}/Y]$.

Exercise 15.4.3. Show that the solution for $(\mu Y{=}X)(\nu X{=}Y)$ is $\eta[\mathbf{false}/X][\mathbf{false}/Y]$.

Using the semantics of a PBES we can define when we consider two PBESs to be equal, which is exactly the case if they have the same solution for all predicate variables. This allows us to formulate manipulation rules to transform PBESs into each other.

Definition 15.4.4 (System equivalence and system ordering). Let $\mathcal{E}, \mathcal{E}'$ be equation systems. We write $\mathcal{E} \sqsubseteq \mathcal{E}'$ iff for all predicate environments η, all substitutions σ, and all equation systems $\mathcal{F}$ with $\mathrm{bnd}(\mathcal{F}) \cap (\mathrm{bnd}(\mathcal{E}) \cup \mathrm{bnd}(\mathcal{E}')) = \emptyset$, it holds that $([\mathcal{E}\mathcal{F}]^{\eta\sigma})(X) \sqsubseteq ([\mathcal{E}'\mathcal{F}]^{\eta\sigma})(X)$ for all predicate symbols X in $\mathrm{bnd}(\mathcal{F}) \cup \mathrm{bnd}(\mathcal{E}) \cup \mathrm{bnd}(\mathcal{E}')$. We write $\mathcal{E} = \mathcal{E}'$ iff both $\mathcal{E} \sqsubseteq \mathcal{E}'$ and $\mathcal{E}' \sqsubseteq \mathcal{E}$.

The relation $=$ on PBESs satisfies all properties of an equation. In particular, it satisfies congruence, i.e., if $\mathcal{F}$ is a PBES and $\mathcal{E} = \mathcal{E}'$, then $\mathcal{F}\mathcal{E} = \mathcal{F}\mathcal{E}'$ and $\mathcal{E}\mathcal{F} = \mathcal{E}'\mathcal{F}$. The preorders also satisfy the congruence properties.

15.5 Soundness and completeness

We say that two process expressions p and q are equal, iff for all models the roots of their timed transitions systems are strongly bisimilar. The axioms in tables 4.2, 8.1, 5.1, 5.2, 5.3, 5.4, 5.5, 5.6, 5.7, 4.3, 4.4, 4.5 and 5.8 all respect strong bisimulation unless it is explicitly stated that they are applicable to other equivalences, in which case these are respected. This means that if two expressions are transformed into each other by applying one of the axioms in the aforementioned tables, then the timed labeled transition systems associated with these process expressions are bisimilar (behavioral equivalent). We say that the axioms are *sound* with respect to the equivalence. All the axioms in the tables are sound with respect to the indicated equivalence, which is strong bisimulation by default.

We say that a set of axioms are *ground-complete* if two closed process expressions, i.e., processes with no free occurrence of variables, that have equivalent timed labeled transition systems can be transformed to each other by applying axioms and inference rules. The aforementioned axioms are ground-complete for strong bisimulation and the addition of the given axioms for the different notion of equivalences is known to make them ground-complete for the respective notion of behavioral equivalence. Also, for timed strong bisimilarity, the provided axioms are sound and ground complete.

The axioms in tables 6.1 and 6.2 are sound for the equivalence on modal formulas. This means that if the axioms are applied to transform a modal formula, then the original and the result are valid for exactly the same transition systems.

15.6 Historical notes

The type system for the data specifications is inspired by the classical type systems, to which [150] provides an excellent introduction. Our type system is inspired by the investigation into type systems for mCRL2 data types defined in [111]. Subsorting with common elements between subsorts and supersorts is a complicating factor, which is often avoided by assuming different copies of the common elements, for example, by adding explicit typing. We find it awkward to force the specifier to specify the sort of common elements such as empty lists, and hence, ended up with a more complicated type system.

In the early years of algebraic specification, the initial algebra approach has been the standard approach to defining their semantics. Here, we use the model class semantics, due to [182], which does not assume distinctness of different constructor terms. The style of operational semantics used in this chapter is due to Plotkin [154], Hennessy [97], and Milner [135].

IV

Appendixes

Appendix A

Brief Tool Primer

The mCRL2 toolset consists of a versatile collection of tools. This chapter gives a short introduction into their use. There are many tools available in the toolset and all tools have more options than what is treated here. We refer to `www.mcrl2.org` for more information in this regard. Each tool also has a help flag (`--help`, `-h`) providing a short summary about its purpose and an overview of its options.

The toolset provides access to various transformations, reductions, and analysis techniques. In order to analyze large behavioral models, the right tools must be applied in the right order depending on the case at hand. Therefore the toolset is structured as a set of individual tools instead of a single push-button tool. For instance, in order to compare mCRL2 models using a notion of behavioral equivalence, first the mCRL2 models are transformed into linear processes using the tool `mcrl22lps`, then state spaces of the linear processes are generated using the tool `lps2lts`, and finally, the tool `ltscompare` is used to compare the two state spaces. As another example, in order to simulate an mCRL2 model, first the mCRL2 model is transformed into a linear process using the tool `mcrl22lps`, and subsequently, the tool `lpsxsim` is applied to the linearized process.

A.1 Using the GUI or the command line interface

There are two ways to use the toolset. The first one is through the use of the graphical interface `mcrl2-gui` which is depicted in figure A.1. The first step is to right-click on a filename in the file browser at the left. A list of tools will pop up that can be applied to analyze or transform the file. For an mCRL2 specification, the only option is to select the transformation tool `mcrl22lps`. It shows up in the window at the right where all its options are listed. After selecting the right options, the `Run` button must be pressed to run the tool. The output appears both in the window at the right and if applicable, as a new file in the window at the left. At the bottom, the command corresponding to the tool is printed. Note that it is possible to start an editor from mcrl2-gui provided the operating system has associated an editor to the corresponding file type.

The second way to use the tools is by running them from the command line. These

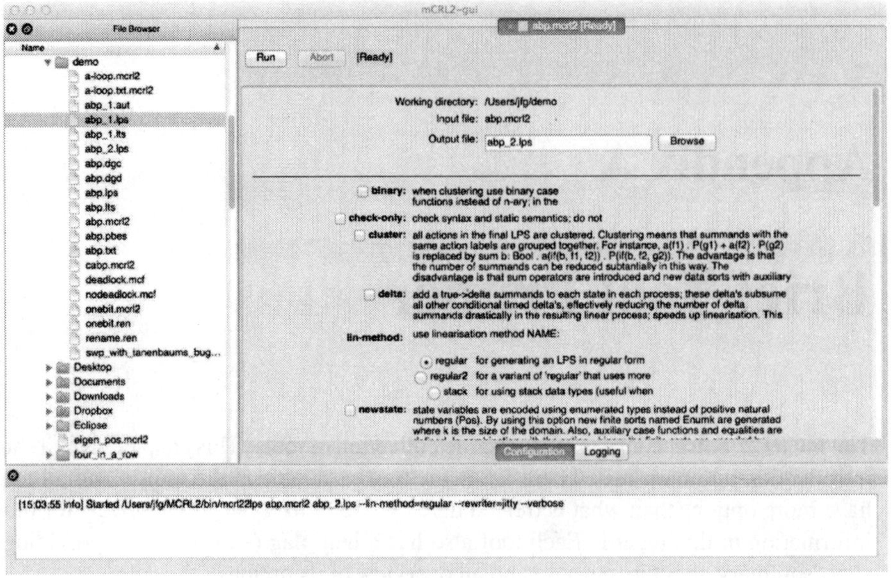

Figure A.1: The mCRL2 graphical user interface

commands are exactly the same as those available in the graphical interface. In the explanation below we use the command line.

A.2 A simple running example

As a running example, we take the switching buffer explained in section 5.3 and depicted in figure 5.3 on page 75. It consists of a one-place buffer X that can temporarily save information in a one-place store B. The buffer stores data of data type D, containing two elements d_1 and d_2. In plain text format the buffer is described as follows. We assume that this description resides in a file `buffer.mcrl2`.

```
sort D=struct d1 | d2;

act r1, s2, s3, r3, c3: D;
proc X=sum d:D.(r1(d)+r3(d)).(s2(d)+s3(d)).X;
     B=sum d:D.r3(d).s3(d).B;

init hide({c3},allow({r1,s2,c3},comm({r3|s3->c3},X||B)));
```

A.3 Linearization

In order to analyze this file, it must first be transformed to a linear process. This is achieved by the linearizer tool which is invoked using the following command:

```
mcrl22lps buffer.mcrl2 buffer.lps
```

The linear process is stored in a compressed format in `buffer.lps`. This file can be transformed to textual format using the pretty print command `lpspp`, and the tool `lpsinfo` provides some elementary information about the linear process. Note that many linearized processes have a section where so-called `glob` variables are declared. These are variables that, once instantiated, do not influence the behavior of the process. Delayed instantiation of such 'glob' variables is often useful because by using linear process transformation tools, one can eliminate more data parameters from the process.

Using the `-v` or `--verbose` option the linearizer provides some information about its progress. The linearizer uses the algorithms described in section 10.2. This means that it can linearize the parallel composition of sequential processes. It cannot linearize processes where the parallel operators (||, `allow`, `hide`, `comm`) occur in the scope of recursion, alternative composition, and sequential composition.

There are different strategies to linearize a process. By default the linearizer tries to obtain a form that is most convenient for further manipulations, which is the regular form obtained by using the `regular` flag. However, this will not always terminate. Using the `regular2` option or the `stack` option generates more complex linear processes, but `regular2` terminates more often than `regular` and `stack` terminates always.

The specification of the switching buffer has the typical shape of an mCRL2 specification. Particularly, it is a good strategy to put hiding `hide`) at the outermost level of the parallel composition. It is a bad strategy to use the internal action `tau` inside specifications. It is better to introduce a special action, such as `skip`, use it instead of a `tau`, and hide it at the outermost level using `hide({skip}, ...)`.

A.4 Manipulating the linear process

After a process is linearized, it can be simulated using `lpsxsim` and `lpssim`. A state space can be generated using the `lps2lts` command. A typical way to use `lps2lts` is given below:

```
lps2lts -v -rjitty buffer.lps buffer.aut
```

The flag `-rjitty` instructs the tool to use the default just-in-time rewriter. There is a just-in-time compiling rewriter (use `-rjittyc`), which is much faster, but is not available on all platforms. The use of other flags can be very useful depending on the situation. We only mention here `--cached`, which at the expense of using more memory can dramatically speed up the generation of a state space if there are sum operators in the linear process.

The resulting state space is written to the file `buffer.aut`. If no output file is specified, the state space is generated but not stored. This is, for instance, useful to see how large the resulting state space is. The tool `ltsinfo` provides basic information about the generated transition system. The generated state space file can have one of the three extensions: `.aut`, `.lts`, or `.fsm`. The `.aut` format is fast to generate, noncompressed and human-readable. This format is used by other toolsets, such as [69]; it only contains transitions and it does not store information about states. The `.fsm` and `.lts` formats save state information. The `.lts` format even stores mCRL2 data types and action declarations, which are used by several other tools. Unfortunately, the `.lts` format is very slow to generate.

When generating a labelled transition system, it is possible to check for states with deadlocks, divergences, or certain outgoing transitions. It can, for instance, be checked whether an *error* action occurs in a transition system. Traces to such states can be saved and inspected using the `tracepp` tool.

It can be useful to transform a linear process before using it to generate a state space or to prove modal formulas. The tool `lpsconstelm` can be used to remove parameters that are constant throughout any run of a process. The tool `lpsparelm` removes parameters that do not influence the behavior of the linear process. This often leads to a substantial reduction of the state space. The tools `lpssumelm` and `lpssuminst` remove sum operators from the linear process. The former tool applies the sum elimination lemma from section 9.4 and the latter instantiates the variables in the sum by replacing it with sequences of summands. All these tools preserve strong bisimulation.

A special reduction tool is `lpsconfcheck`. It tries to prove for each `tau`-summand of the linear process whether it is confluent, and if proven, replaces it by `ctau`. This adapted linear process can be used in `lps2lts` using the `-c` flag to generate a state space while applying τ-prioritization.

A particularly useful transformation tool is `lpsactionrename`. It allows us to rename actions based on the parameters occurring in these actions. Suppose there are many $report(id, v)$ actions and we are only interested in these actions for $id = 1$, then this tool can, for instance, be used to rename all other *report* actions into τ.

A.5 Manipulating and visualizing state spaces

Transition systems can be reduced and compared with respect to several behavioral equivalences using the tools `ltsconvert` and `ltscompare`. An effective way to get insight into the behavior of a process is to hide all but its essential actions, and to reduce the behavior modulo a notion of behavioral equivalence, for instance, branching bisimulation. Applying weak trace reduction tends to reduce small state spaces even further, but often blows up larger state spaces. Note that `ltsconvert` has an option to hide actions before applying a reduction. In `ltscompare` there is a useful feature to create a counter example if two labeled transition systems are not equal.

A transition system can be transformed back to a linear process using the tool `lts2lps`. A typical use is to generate a transition system, reduce it modulo some equivalence and then translate it back to a linear process for further processing or composition with other reduced processes.

There are several tools to visualize a labeled transition system. The basic tool is `ltsgraph` which draws a transition system in either 2D or 3D (figure A.2 at the left).

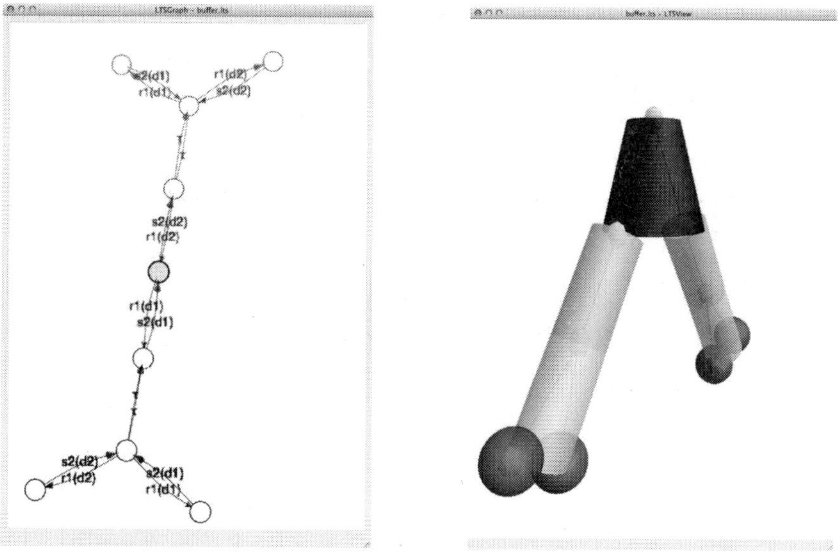

Figure A.2: Visualizations by ltsgraph and an ltsview.

It is possible to drag states and transition labels by hand to obtain an ideal picture. It also has a spring-based algorithm to do the positioning automatically. States and labels that should remain in place can be fixed to the canvas by right clicking on them. Note that `ltsgraph` is very useful to visualize small state spaces.

The tool `ltsview` has been developed to visualize large state spaces. It has been used to obtain insightful pictures of transition systems with up to 10^6 states. The one-place buffer has been depicted by `ltsview` in figure A.2 at the right. The transition system is first transformed to a tree shape by grouping those states that have a common substate into clusters [92]. The tree is then depicted, where the clusters are drawn proportionally to the number of states they contain. When there are many states and transitions it is not useful to draw them all. But after zooming into certain parts of the figure, drawing and inspecting individual states and transitions can be very helpful. Note that state information is only available when drawing a transition system in `.lts` and `.fsm` formats. It is possible to color the visualized state space based on several criteria such as the transition labels, the values of variables in states, or the depth of the tree. It is also possible to simulate the behavior, giving a visual clue where one resides in the behavior of a transition system.

The third visualization tool is called `diagraphica` and it allows for visualization of the dependencies among the valuations of data variables in states [158]. First, one selects some variables from the state vector. All states with the same values for these variables are grouped. This tool is particularly useful to inspect the flow of data or to detect invariants. The tool `diagraphica` also allows us to perform animated simulations and visualize time series. In figure A.3, the result of applying `diagraphica`

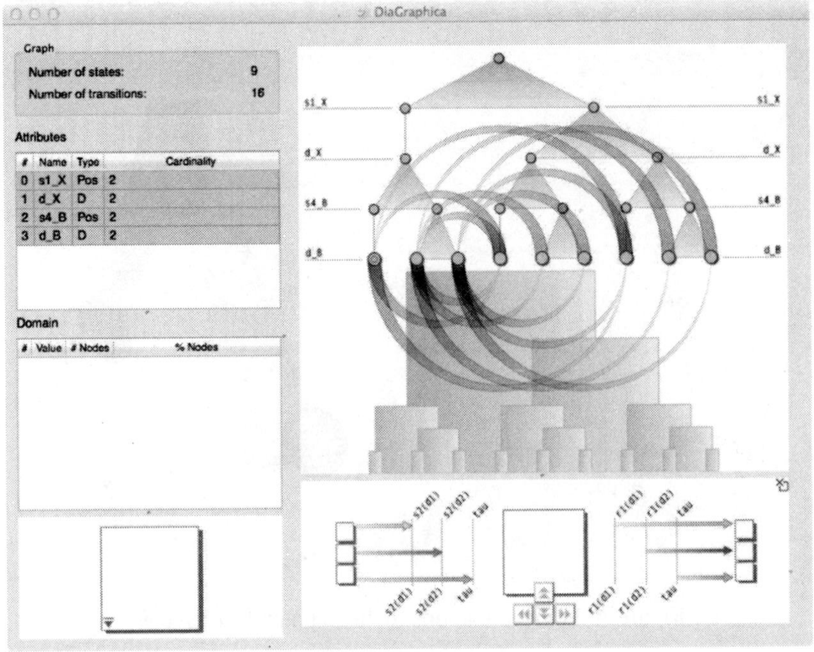

Figure A.3: State space visualization using the diagraphica tool

to the oneplace buffer is depicted.

A.6 Solving modal formulas and manipulating PBESs

In order to verify modal formulas on linear processes and transition systems, these need to be transformed to parameterized boolean equation systems. For this purpose, the tools `lps2pbes` and `lts2pbes` are available. In order to check that the buffer is deadlock free, the following formula can be formulated and put in a file `nodeadlock.mcf`:

```
[true*]<true>true
```

Using the following command, it can be transformed to a PBES.

```
lps2pbes -f nodeadlock.mcf buffer.lps buffer.pbes
```

In this command, the option `-f` is followed by the filename which contains the modal formula to be checked. The resulting PBESs can be printed using `pbespp` and solved using `pbes2bool` and `pbespgsolve`. Both tools first translate the PBES to a boolean equation system. The tool `pbes2bool` applies an adapted form of Gaussian-elimination, whereas `pbespgsolve` uses parity game solvers to solve the

BES. When there are many alternating fixed points in the BES, then pbespgsolve is more useful. With very few alternations of fixed points, pbes2bool is more effective. It has the additional advantage that it can already solve the BES during generation using the --strategy option, which tries to partially solve the PBES while it is being generated. It can also generate counterexamples that, although hard to interpret, are sometimes the only way to detect why a certain modal formula does not hold. Counterexamples are given in terms of a tree of instantiations of PBES variables. In order to interpret them, it is useful to note that the variables in a PBES closely match those in the corresponding linear process.

In order to solve the PBES that represents deadlock freedom of the buffer, it suffices to execute:

```
pbes2bool buffer.pbes
```

Another interesting question about the buffer is whether it delivers the messages in sequence. Such a property can be formulated as follows.

```
nu X(q:List(D)=[]).
    forall d:D.[r1(d)]X(d|>q) &&
    forall d:D.[s2(d)](X(rtail(q)) && val(d==rhead(q))) &&
    [tau] X(q)
```

Assume that this formula is put in the file in_sequence.mcf. The following sequence of commands will show that this formula is not valid.

```
mcrl22lps -v buffer.mcrl2 buffer.lps
lps2pbes -f in_sequence.mcf buffer.lps in_sequence.pbes
pbes2bool -v -c -s2 in_sequence.pbes
```

The -c flag requests a counter example and the -s2 flag optimizes the generation of a BES by eliminating all BES variables that become *true* or *false* while generating the BES. The generated counterexample is

```
1: X([],1,d1,1,d1)
  3: Subst:false   X([d1],2,d1,1,d1)
    5: Subst:false   X([d1],1,d1,2,d1)
      8: Subst:false   X([d2, d1],2,d2,2,d1)
```

The first list in the counterexample corresponds with the list q in the formula. The next four parameters correspond to the state vector of the linear process. By inspecting the state vector for instance using one of the simulators lpssim or lpsxsim, it is clear that this counterexample shows that first d1 and then d2 is read, after which d2 is delivered, while the last element in the list was d1.

Parameterized boolean equation systems are even more amenable to reductions than linear processes. Applying the right transformation before solving a PBES can lead to a huge improvement in the time required to solve the PBES. As for linear processes, there is a tool pbesconstelm to eliminate constant parameters from a PBES, pbesparelm to remove unused parameters from a PBES, and pbesrewr to simplify a PBES by rewriting it. This last tool also has the option to eliminate quantifiers from a PBES. A strengthened version of pbesparelm is pbesstategraph which tries to set variables to default values or even eliminate those data variables by analyzing the data flow graph of the PBES.

A PBES can be transformed to a BES using `pbesinst`. Although this is not as useful as transforming a linear process to a transition system, it can still be of help, for instance to see the structure of a BES. A BES can be printed using `bespp` and solved using `bessolve`. As for all other main formats there is a tool `besinfo` that provides elementary information about a BES.

Appendix B

Equational Definition of Built-In Data Types

The definition of predefined data types is given in this appendix. Each data type is described by conditional equations of the shape $c \to l = r$ where c is the condition, l is the left-hand side of an equation, and r the right-hand side. The equations are used as rewrite rules. When a term t matches l by selecting appropriate values for the variables in l, and the condition c with instantiated variables rewrites to $true$, t is replaced by r, again with the proper instantiation of the variables.

As a general rule, all internal functions and sorts that cannot be accessed directly in an mCRL2 specification start with an @ symbol.

For all sorts, a function if (if), equality ($\approx$), inequality ($\not\approx$), and comparison operators ($<$, $\leq$, $\geq$, $>$) are defined. This includes the basic sorts and all function sorts constructed out of them, used within a specification. As their definitions are all the same, we provide their declarations and definition as a template for an arbitrary sort S. Note that for concrete sorts, there are additional equations for $\approx$. For example, $\mathit{true}{\approx}\mathit{false} = \mathit{false}$. The equation $\mathit{if}(x{\approx}y, x, y) = y$ is called *Bergstra's axiom* and is used to show that $=$ and $\approx$ coincide. Although very useful for manual verification, this equation is of no use to tools. Therefore, it is not generated for the use in tools.

map $\approx, \not\approx, <, \leq, \geq, > : S \times S \to \mathbb{B}$; $\quad\mathit{if} : \mathbb{B} \times S \times S \to S$; **var** $x, y : S$; $\quad b : \mathbb{B}$;	**eqn** $x{\approx}x = \mathit{true}$; $x{\not\approx}y = \neg(x{\approx}y)$; $\mathit{if}(\mathit{true}, x, y) = x$; $\mathit{if}(\mathit{false}, x, y) = y$; $\mathit{if}(b, x, x) = x$; $\mathit{if}(x{\approx}y, x, y) = y$; $x{<}x = \mathit{false}$; $x{\leq}x = \mathit{true}$; $x{>}y = y{<}x$; $x{\geq}y = y{\leq}x$;

B.1 Bool

The Booleans have a straightforward definition. They contain the constructors *true* and *false*. The semantics of the language mCRL2 prescribes that *true* and *false* are different. Adding an equation such that $true = false$ is derivable, makes a specification semantically inconsistent and as everything can be derived, such as specification is of little use.

sort $\mathbb{B}$; **cons** $true, false : \mathbb{B}$; **map** $\neg : \mathbb{B} \to \mathbb{B}$; $\wedge, \vee, \Rightarrow: \mathbb{B}\times\mathbb{B}\to\mathbb{B}$;	**var** $b : \mathbb{B}$; **eqn** $\neg true = false$; $\neg false = true$; $\neg\neg b = b$; $b \wedge true = b$; $b \wedge false = false$; $true \wedge b = b$; $false \wedge b = false$; $b \vee true = true$; $b \vee false = b$; $true \vee b = true$; $false \vee b = b$; $b \Rightarrow true = true$; $b \Rightarrow false = \neg b$;	$true \Rightarrow b = b$; $false \Rightarrow b = true$; $true{\approx}b = b$; $false{\approx}b = \neg b$; $b{\approx}true = b$; $b{\approx}false = \neg b$; $false{<}b = b$; $true{<}b = false$; $b{<}false = false$; $b{<}true = \neg b$; $false{\leq}b = true$; $true{\leq}b = b$; $b{\leq}false = \neg b$; $b{\leq}true = true$;

B.2 Positive numbers

The internal representation of numbers is such that each number has its own unique representation with constructors, and the representation is logarithmic, in the sense that for a number n the representation requires $O({}^2\log(n))$ constructors (just as in the ordinary decimal or binary notation of numbers). In order to achieve this, we first define positive numbers and build all other numbers on the basis of these.

For positive numbers ($\mathbb{N}^+$), the number one is represented by the constructor $@c1$. Larger numbers are constructed using $@cDub(b, n)$ with b a Boolean and n a natural number. Its meaning is

$$@cDub(b, n) = \begin{cases} 2n + 1 & \text{if } b \text{ is } true, \\ 2n & \text{if } b \text{ is } false. \end{cases}$$

When a rewriter is used, the data terms of mCRL2 are translated to this internal representation. For example, a number 2 is translated to $@cDub(false, @c1)$ and 5 becomes $@cDub(true, @cDub(false, @c1))$. When numbers are displayed, they are converted back to standard decimal notation.

sort $\mathbb{N}^+$;
cons $@c1 : \mathbb{N}^+$;
$@cDub : \mathbb{B} \times \mathbb{N}^+ \rightarrow \mathbb{N}^+$;
map $max, min : \mathbb{N}^+ \times \mathbb{N}^+ \rightarrow \mathbb{N}^+$;
$succ, @pospred : \mathbb{N}^+ \rightarrow \mathbb{N}^+$;
$+ : \mathbb{N}^+ \times \mathbb{N}^+ \rightarrow \mathbb{N}^+$;
$@addc : \mathbb{B} \times \mathbb{N}^+ \times \mathbb{N}^+ \rightarrow \mathbb{N}^+$;
$\cdot : \mathbb{N}^+ \times \mathbb{N}^+ \rightarrow \mathbb{N}^+$;
var $b, c : \mathbb{B}$;
$p, q, r : \mathbb{N}^+$;
eqn $@c1 \approx @cDub(b, p) = false$;
$@cDub(b, p) \approx @c1 = false$;
* $succ(p) \approx c1 = false$;
* $@c1 \approx succ(q) = false$;
* $succ(p) \approx @cDub(c, q) = p \approx @pospred(@cDub(c, q))$;
* $@cDub(b, p) \approx succ(q) = @pospred(@cDub(b, p)) \approx q$;
$@cDub(b, p) \approx @cDub(c, q) = b \approx c \wedge p \approx q$;
$p < @c1 = false$;
$@c1 < @cDub(b, p) = true$;
$@cDub(b, p) < @cDub(c, q) = if(c \Rightarrow b, p < q, p \leq q)$;
* $@c1 < succ(q) = true$;
* $succ(p) < @cDub(c, q) = p < @pospred(@cDub(c, q))$;
* $@cDub(b, p) < succ(q) = @cDub(b, p) \leq q$;
$@c1 \leq p = true$;
$@cDub(b, p) \leq @c1 = false$;
$@cDub(b, p) \leq @cDub(c, q) = if(b \Rightarrow c, p \leq q, p < q)$;
* $succ(p) \leq @c1 = false$;
* $succ(p) \leq @cDub(c, q) = p < @cDub(c, q)$;
* $@cDub(b, p) \leq succ(q) = @pospred(@cDub(b, p)) \leq q$;
$max(p, q) = if(p \leq q, q, p)$;
$min(p, q) = if(p \leq q, p, q)$;
$succ(@c1) = @cDub(false, @c1)$;
$succ(@cDub(false, p)) = @cDub(true, p)$;
$succ(@cDub(true, p)) = @cDub(false, succ(p))$;

There is an auxiliary mapping $@addc(b, p, q)$ which is useful as it makes rewriting of addition slightly more efficient. The expression $@addc(b, p, q)$ represents $p+q$ if b is false and $p+q+1$ if b is true. The equations for $@addc$ are given next. Rules marked with * are needed for enumeration over lists where typically expressions of the shape $succ(succ(\#l)) < M$ need to be rewritten to *false*. Here $\#l$ is the length of a list l where l is a variable and M is a constant natural number indicating the maximal length under consideration. For this purpose, the predecessor function $@pospred$ on positive numbers has been introduced. The rules marked with * are not required to rewrite closed expressions (expressions without variables) to normal form.

$$
\begin{array}{ll}
* & @pospred(@c1) = @c1; \\
* & @pospred(@cDub(false, @c1)) = @c1; \\
* & @pospred(@cDub(false, @cDub(b, p))) = \\
  & \quad @cDub(true, @pospred(@cDub(b, p))); \\
* & @pospred(@cDub(true, p)) = @cDub(false, p); \\
  & p + q = @addc(false, p, q); \\
  & @addc(false, @c1, p) = succ(p); \\
  & @addc(true, @c1, p) = succ(succ(p)); \\
  & @addc(false, p, @c1) = succ(p); \\
  & @addc(true, p, @c1) = succ(succ(p)); \\
  & @addc(b, @cDub(c, p), @cDub(c, q)) = @cDub(b, @addc(c, p, q)); \\
  & @addc(b, @cDub(false, p), @cDub(true, q)) = @cDub(\neg b, @addc(b, p, q)); \\
  & @addc(b, @cDub(true, p), @cDub(false, q)) = @cDub(\neg b, @addc(b, p, q)); \\
  & @c1 \cdot p = p; \\
  & p \cdot @c1 = p; \\
  & @cDub(false, p) \cdot q = @cDub(false, p \cdot q); \\
  & p \cdot @cDub(false, q) = @cDub(false, p \cdot q); \\
  & @cDub(true, p) \cdot @cDub(true, q) = \\
  & \quad @cDub(true, @addc(false, p, @addc(false, q, @cDub(false, p \cdot q))));
\end{array}
$$

B.3 Natural numbers

The sort $\mathbb{N}$ represents the natural numbers. An auxiliary sort $@NatPair$ is used for efficient implementation of the *div* and *mod* functions.

Natural numbers are constructed out of the positive numbers using the constructors $@c0$, representing 0, and $@cNat(p)$ which interprets a positive number p as the natural number with the same value.

There are quite a number of auxiliary functions, all preceded with the @ sign. The function $@dub(b, n)$ equals $2n$ if b is *false* and $2n + 1$ if b is *true*. The function $@gtesubtb(b, p, q)$ represents $max(0, p-q)$ if b is *false*, and $max(0, p-q-1)$ if b is *true*. The function $@even(n)$ determines whether n is even. The functions starting with sz, standing for *swap_zero*, are required for bags and are explained in section B.8.

The div and mod (notation $n|_p$) functions are characterized by efficient but complex equations. Essentially there is one function $@dm(n, p)$ that calculates the pair $@cPair(n \text{ div } p, n|_p)$. The abbreviation $@dm$ stands for *divmod.* Div and mod are obtained by taking the first (using $@first$) or last (using $@last$) element of this pair. Divmod is calculated by $@gdm$ which has as property that

$$@gdm(@cPair(m, n), b, q) = \begin{cases} @cPair(2m, @dub(b, n)) & \text{if } m < p, \\ @cPair(2m{+}1, @dub(b, n){-}p) & \text{if } m \geq p. \end{cases}$$

Likewise, $@ggdm$ has the property that

$$@ggdm(m, n, p) = \begin{cases} @cPair(2n, m) & \text{if } m < p, \\ @cPair(2n{+}1, m{-}p) & \text{if } m \geq p. \end{cases}$$

sort $\mathbb{N}$;
$@NatPair$;
cons $@c0 : \mathbb{N}$;
$@cNat : \mathbb{N}^+ \to \mathbb{N}$;
$@cPair : \mathbb{N} \times \mathbb{N} \to @NatPair$;
map $Pos2Nat : \mathbb{N}^+ \to \mathbb{N}$;
$Nat2Pos : \mathbb{N} \to \mathbb{N}^+$;
$max : \mathbb{N}^+ \times \mathbb{N} \to \mathbb{N}^+$;
$max : \mathbb{N} \times \mathbb{N}^+ \to \mathbb{N}^+$;
$max, min : \mathbb{N} \times \mathbb{N} \to \mathbb{N}$;
$succ : \mathbb{N} \to \mathbb{N}^+$;
$pred : \mathbb{N}^+ \to \mathbb{N}$;
$@dub : \mathbb{B} \times \mathbb{N} \to \mathbb{N}$;
$+ : \mathbb{N}^+ \times \mathbb{N} \to \mathbb{N}^+$;
$+ : \mathbb{N} \times \mathbb{N}^+ \to \mathbb{N}^+$;
$+ : \mathbb{N} \times \mathbb{N} \to \mathbb{N}$;
$@gtesubtb : \mathbb{B} \times \mathbb{N}^+ \times \mathbb{N}^+ \to \mathbb{N}$;
$\cdot : \mathbb{N} \times \mathbb{N} \to \mathbb{N}$;
$div : \mathbb{N} \times \mathbb{N}^+ \to \mathbb{N}$;
$\_|\_ : \mathbb{N} \times \mathbb{N}^+ \to \mathbb{N}$;
$exp : \mathbb{N}^+ \times \mathbb{N} \to \mathbb{N}^+$;
$exp : \mathbb{N} \times \mathbb{N} \to \mathbb{N}$;
$@even : \mathbb{N} \to \mathbb{B}$;
$@sz : \mathbb{N} \times \mathbb{N} \to \mathbb{N}$;
$@sz\_add : \mathbb{N} \times \mathbb{N} \times \mathbb{N} \times \mathbb{N} \to \mathbb{N}$;
$@sz\_min : \mathbb{N} \times \mathbb{N} \times \mathbb{N} \times \mathbb{N} \to \mathbb{N}$;
$@sz\_monus : \mathbb{N} \times \mathbb{N} \times \mathbb{N} \times \mathbb{N} \to \mathbb{N}$;
$@first, @last : @NatPair \to \mathbb{N}$;
$@dm : \mathbb{N}^+ \times \mathbb{N}^+ \to @NatPair$;
$@gdm : @NatPair \times \mathbb{B} \times \mathbb{N}^+ \to @NatPair$;
$@ggdm : \mathbb{N} \times \mathbb{N} \times \mathbb{N}^+ \to @NatPair$;
var $b, c : \mathbb{B}$;
$p, q : \mathbb{N}^+$;
$n, n', m, m' : \mathbb{N}$;

eqn $@c0 \approx @cNat(p) = false$;
$@cNat(p) \approx @c0 = false$;
$@cNat(p) \approx @cNat(q) = p \approx q$;
$n < @c0 = false$;
$@c0 < @cNat(p) = true$;
$@cNat(p) < @cNat(q) = p < q$;
$@c0 \leq n = true$;
$@cNat(p) \leq @c0 = false$;
$@cNat(p) \leq @cNat(q) = p \leq q$;
$Pos2Nat(p) = @cNat(p)$;
$Nat2Pos(@cNat(p)) = p$;
$max(p, @c0) = p$;
$max(p, @cNat(q)) = if(p \leq q, q, p)$;
$max(@c0, p) = p$;
$max(@cNat(p), q) = if(p \leq q, q, p)$;
$max(m, n) = if(m \leq n, n, m)$;
$min(m, n) = if(m \leq n, m, n)$;
$succ(@c0) = @cNat(@c1)$;
$succ(@cNat(p)) = succ(p)$;
$pred(@c1) = @c0$;
$pred(@cDub(true, p)) = @cNat(@cDub(false, p))$;
$pred(@cDub(false, p)) = @dub(true, pred(p))$;
$@dub(false, @c0) = @c0$;
$@dub(true, @c0) = @cNat(@c1)$;
$@dub(b, @cNat(p)) = @cNat(@cDub(b, p))$;
$p + @c0 = p$;
$p + @cNat(q) = @addc(false, p, q)$;
$@c0 + p = p$;
$@cNat(p) + q = @addc(false, p, q)$;
$@c0 + n = n$;
$n + @c0 = n$;
$@cNat(p) + @cNat(q) = @cNat(@addc(false, p, q))$;

$@gtesubtb(false, p, @c1) = pred(p)$;
$@gtesubtb(true, p, @c1) = pred(Nat2Pos(pred(p)))$;
$@gtesubtb(b, @cDub(c, p), @cDub(c, q)) = @dub(b, @gtesubtb(b, p, q))$;
$@gtesubtb(b, @cDub(false, p), @cDub(true, q)) = @dub(\neg b, @gtesubtb(true, p, q))$;
$@gtesubtb(b, @cDub(true, p), @cDub(false, q)) = @dub(\neg b, @gtesubtb(false, p, q))$;
$@c0 \cdot n = @c0$;
$n \cdot @c0 = @c0$;
$@cNat(p) \cdot @cNat(q) = @cNat(p \cdot q)$;

$$
\begin{array}{l}
exp(p, @c0) = @c1;\\
exp(p, @cNat(@c1)) = p;\\
exp(p, @cNat(@cDub(false, q))) = exp(p{\cdot}p, @cNat(q));\\
exp(p, @cNat(@cDub(true, q))) = p{\cdot}exp(pcdotp, @cNat(q));\\
exp(n, @c0) = @cNat(@c1);\\
exp(@c0, p) = @c0;\\
exp(@cNat(p), n) = @cNat(exp(p, n));\\
@even(@c0) = true;\\
@even(@cNat(@c1)) = false;\\
@even(@cNat(@cDub(b, p))) = \neg b;\\
@c0 \operatorname{div} p = @c0;\\
@cNat(p) \operatorname{div} q = @first(@dm(p, q));\\
@c0|_p = @c0;\\
@cNat(p)|_q = @last(@dm(p, q));\\
@monus(@c0, n) = @c0;\\
@monus(n, @c0) = n;\\
@monus(@cNat(p), @cNat(q)) = @gtesubtb(false, p, q);\\
@sz(m, @c0) = m;\\
@sz(@c0, n) = n;\\
@sz(@cNat(p), @cNat(p)) = @c0;\\
p{\not\approx}q \rightarrow @sz(@cNat(p), @cNat(q)) = @cNat(q);\\
@sz\_add(@c0, @c0, m, n) = m{+}n;\\
@sz\_add(@cNat(p), @c0, m, @c0) = m;\\
@sz\_add(@cNat(p), @c0, m, @cNat(q)) =\\
\qquad @sz(@cNat(p), @sz(@cNat(p){+}m, @cNat(q)));\\
@sz\_add(@c0, @cNat(p), @c0, n) = n;\\
@sz\_add(@c0, @cNat(p), @cNat(q), n) =\\
\qquad @sz(@cNat(p), @cNat(q){+}@sz(@cNat(p), n));\\
@sz\_add(@cNat(p), @cNat(q), m, n) =\\
\qquad @sz(@cNat(p){+}@cNat(q)), @sz(@cNat(p), m){+}@sz(@cNat(q), n);\\
@sz\_min(@c0, @c0, m, n) = min(m, n);\\
@sz\_min(@cNat(p), @c0, m, @c0) = @c0;\\
@sz\_min(@cNat(p), @c0, m, @cNat(q)){=}min(@sz(@cNat(p), m), @cNat(q));\\
@sz\_min(@c0, @cNat(p), @c0, n) = @c0;\\
@sz\_min(@c0, @cNat(p), @cNat(q), n) = min(@cNat(q), @sz(@cNat(p), n));\\
@sz\_min(@cNat(p), @cNat(q), m, n) =\\
\qquad @sz(min(@cNat(p), @cNat(q)),\\
\qquad\qquad min(@sz(@cNat(p), m), @sz(@cNat(q), n)));\\
@sz\_monus(@c0, @c0, m, n) = @monus(m, n);\\
@sz\_monus(@cNat(p), @c0, m, @c0) = m;\\
@sz\_monus(@cNat(p), @c0, m, @cNat(q)) =\\
\qquad @sz(@cNat(p), @monus(@sz(@cNat(p), m), @cNat(q)));\\
@sz\_monus(@c0, @cNat(p), @c0, n) = @c0;\\
@sz\_monus(@c0, @cNat(p), @cNat(q), n) =\\
\qquad @monus(@cNat(q), @sz(@cNat(p), n));\\
@sz\_monus(@cNat(p), @cNat(q), m, n) =\\
\qquad @sz(@monus(@cNat(p),\\
\qquad\qquad @cNat(q)), @monus(@sz(@cNat(p), m), @sz(@cNat(q), n)));
\end{array}
$$

$@cPair(m,n){\approx}@cPair(m',n') = m{\approx}m' \wedge n{\approx}n';$
$@cPair(m,n) < @cPair(m',n') = m{<}m' \vee (m{\approx}m' \wedge n{<}n');$
$@cPair(m,n) \leq @cPair(m',n') = m{<}m' \vee (m{\approx}m' \wedge n{\leq}n');$
$@\mathit{first}(@cPair(m,n)) = m;$
$@last(@cPair(m,n)) = n;$
$@dm(@c1,@c1) = @cPair(@cNat(@c1),@c0);$
$@dm(@c1,@cDub(b,p)) = @cPair(@c0,@cNat(@c1));$
$@dm(@cDub(b,p),q) = @gdm(@dm(p,q),b,q);$
$@gdm(@cPair(m,n),b,p) = @ggdm(@dub(b,n),m,p);$
$@ggdm(@c0,n,p) = @cPair(@dub(\mathit{false},n),@c0);$
$p{<}q{\rightarrow}@ggdm(@cNat(p),n,q){=}@cPair(@dub(\mathit{false},n),@cNat(p));$
$q{\leq}p{\rightarrow}@ggdm(@cNat(p),n,q){=}@cPair(@dub(\mathit{true},n),@gtesubtb(\mathit{false},p,q));$

B.4 Integers

The sort of integers contains the positive and negative numbers and it is denoted as $\mathbb{Z}$. Integers are constructed out of both natural and positive numbers using two constructors. The integer $@cInt(n)$ for a natural number n represents the integer with value n. The integer $@cNeg(p)$ for a positive number p represents the integer $-p$. This construction is intentionally asymmetric to guarantee that there is only one constructor term representing 0.

The definitions of the operations on integers is straightforward. The only auxiliary function is $@dub(b,n)$ which represents $2n$ if b is false, and $2n+1$ if b is true.

sort $\mathbb{Z}$; **cons** $@cInt : \mathbb{N} \rightarrow \mathbb{Z}$; $@cNeg : \mathbb{N}^+ \rightarrow \mathbb{Z}$; **map** $Nat2Int : \mathbb{N} \rightarrow \mathbb{Z}$; $Int2Nat : \mathbb{Z} \rightarrow \mathbb{N}$; $Pos2Int : \mathbb{N}^+ \rightarrow \mathbb{Z}$; $Int2Pos : \mathbb{Z} \rightarrow \mathbb{N}^+$; $max : \mathbb{N}^+ \times \mathbb{Z} \rightarrow \mathbb{N}^+$; $max : \mathbb{Z} \times \mathbb{N}^+ \rightarrow \mathbb{N}^+$; $max : \mathbb{N} \times \mathbb{Z} \rightarrow \mathbb{N}$; $max : \mathbb{Z} \times \mathbb{N} \rightarrow \mathbb{N}$; $max, min : \mathbb{Z} \times \mathbb{Z} \rightarrow \mathbb{Z}$; $abs : \mathbb{Z} \rightarrow \mathbb{N}$; $- : \mathbb{N}^+ \rightarrow \mathbb{Z}$;	$pred, - : \mathbb{N} \rightarrow \mathbb{Z}$; $-, succ, pred : \mathbb{Z} \rightarrow \mathbb{Z}$; $@dub : \mathbb{B} \times \mathbb{Z} \rightarrow \mathbb{Z}$; $- : \mathbb{N}^+ \times \mathbb{N}^+ \rightarrow \mathbb{Z}$; $- : \mathbb{N} \times \mathbb{N} \rightarrow \mathbb{Z}$; $+, -, \cdot : \mathbb{Z} \times \mathbb{Z} \rightarrow \mathbb{Z}$; $div : \mathbb{Z} \times \mathbb{N}^+ \rightarrow \mathbb{Z}$; $\_\vert\_ : \mathbb{Z} \times \mathbb{N}^+ \rightarrow \mathbb{N}$; $exp : \mathbb{Z} \times \mathbb{N} \rightarrow \mathbb{Z}$; **var** $x, y : \mathbb{Z}$; $b : \mathbb{B}$; $n, m : \mathbb{N}$; $p, q : \mathbb{N}^+$;

eqn

$@cInt(m) \approx @cInt(n) = m \approx n;$
$@cInt(n) \approx @cNeg(p) = false;$
$@cNeg(p) \approx @cInt(n) = false;$
$@cNeg(p) \approx @cNeg(q) = p \approx q;$
$@cInt(m) < @cInt(n) = m < n;$
$@cInt(n) < @cNeg(p) = false;$
$@cNeg(p) < @cInt(n) = true;$
$@cNeg(p) < @cNeg(q) = q < p;$
$@cInt(m) \leq @cInt(n) = m \leq n;$
$@cInt(n) \leq @cNeg(p) = false;$
$@cNeg(p) \leq @cInt(n) = true;$
$@cNeg(p) \leq @cNeg(q) = q \leq p;$
$Nat2Int(n) = @cInt(n);$
$Int2Nat(@cInt(n)) = n;$
$Pos2Int(p) = @cInt(@cNat(p));$
$Int2Pos(@cInt(n)) = Nat2Pos(n);$
$x - y = x + (-y);$

$abs(@cInt(n)) = n;$
$abs(@cNeg(p)) = @cNat(p);$
$max(p, @cInt(n)) = max(p, n);$
$max(p, @cNeg(q)) = p;$
$max(@cInt(n), p) = max(n, p);$
$max(cNeg(q), p) = p;$
$max(m, @cInt(n)) = if(m \leq n, n, m);$
$max(n, @cNeg(p)) = n;$
$max(@cInt(m), n) = if(m \leq n, n, m);$
$max(@cNeg(p), n) = n;$
$max(x, y) = if(x \leq y, y, x);$
$min(x, y) = if(x \leq y, x, y);$
$-p = @cNeg(p);$
$-@c0 = @cInt(@c0);$
$-@cNat(p) = @cNeg(p);$
$-@cInt(n) = -n;$
$-@cNeg(p) = @cInt(@cNat(p));$

$succ(@cInt(n)) = @cInt(@cNat(succ(n)));$
$succ(@cNeg(p)) = -pred(p);$
$pred(@c0) = @cNeg(@c1);$
$pred(@cNat(p)) = @cInt(pred(p));$
$pred(@cInt(n)) = pred(n);$
$pred(@cNeg(p)) = @cNeg(succ(p));$
$@dub(b, @cInt(n)) = @cInt(@dub(b, n));$
$@dub(false, @cNeg(p)) = @cNeg(@cDub(false, p));$
$@dub(true, @cNeg(p)) = -@dub(true, pred(p));$
$@cInt(m) + @cInt(n) = @cInt(m+n);$
$@cInt(n) + @cNeg(p) = n - @cNat(p);$
$@cNeg(p) + @cInt(n) = n - @cNat(p);$
$@cNeg(p) + @cNeg(q) = @cNeg(@addc(false, p, q));$
$q \leq p \rightarrow p - q = @cInt(@gtesubtb(false, p, q));$
$p < q \rightarrow p - q = -@gtesubtb(false, q, p);$
$n \leq m \rightarrow m - n = @cInt(@monus(m, n));$
$m < n \rightarrow m - n = -@monus(n, m);$
$@cInt(m) \cdot @cInt(n) = @cInt(m \cdot n);$
$@cInt(n) \cdot @cNeg(p) = -(cNat(p) \cdot n);$
$@cNeg(p) \cdot @cInt(n) = -(@cNat(p) \cdot n);$
$@cNeg(p) \cdot @cNeg(q) = @cInt(@cNat(p \cdot q));$
$@cInt(n) \text{ div } p = @cInt(n \text{ div } p);$
$@cNeg(p) \text{ div } q = @cNeg(succ(pred(p) \text{ div } q));$
$@cInt(n)|_p = n|_p;$
$@cNeg(p)|_q = Int2Nat(q - succ(pred(p)|_q));$
$exp(@cInt(m), n) = @cInt(exp(m, n));$
$@even(n) \rightarrow exp(@cNeg(p), n) = @cInt(@cNat(exp(p, n)));$
$\neg @even(n) \rightarrow exp(@cNeg(p), n) = @cNeg(exp(p, n));$

B.5 Reals

The reals are much more complex than the integers, because there are an uncountable number of reals. The data type $\mathbb{R}$ that we specify provides an approximation of the "real" real numbers in the sense that it allows the real numbers as a model. We cannot provide constructors for $\mathbb{R}$, as this would incorrectly imply that there would only be a countable number of reals, although technically this can be circumvented if the constructors employ function types. We can explicitly construct reals of the shape

$$\frac{x}{p}$$

where x is an integer and p a positive number. Therefore, $\frac{1}{4}$, $\frac{-17}{23}$, or in fact any rational number, is a denotable real. The equations are such that in a normal form $\frac{x}{p}$, x and p have no common divisor.

sort $\mathbb{R}$;
map $@cReal : \mathbb{Z} \times \mathbb{N}^+ \to \mathbb{R}$;
$Pos2Real : \mathbb{N}^+ \to \mathbb{R}$;
$Nat2Real : \mathbb{N} \to \mathbb{R}$;
$Int2Real : \mathbb{Z} \to \mathbb{R}$;
$Real2Pos : \mathbb{R} \to \mathbb{N}^+$;
$Real2Nat : \mathbb{R} \to \mathbb{N}$;
$Real2Int : \mathbb{R} \to \mathbb{Z}$;
$min : \mathbb{R} \times \mathbb{R} \to \mathbb{R}$;
$max : \mathbb{R} \times \mathbb{R} \to \mathbb{R}$;
$abs : \mathbb{R} \to \mathbb{R}$;
$- : \mathbb{R} \to \mathbb{R}$;
$succ : \mathbb{R} \to \mathbb{R}$;
$pred : \mathbb{R} \to \mathbb{R}$;
$+ : \mathbb{R} \times \mathbb{R} \to \mathbb{R}$;
$- : \mathbb{R} \times \mathbb{R} \to \mathbb{R}$;
$\cdot : \mathbb{R} \times \mathbb{R} \to \mathbb{R}$;
$exp : \mathbb{R} \times \mathbb{Z} \to \mathbb{R}$;
$/ : \mathbb{N}^+ \times \mathbb{N}^+ \to \mathbb{R}$;
$/ : \mathbb{N} \times \mathbb{N} \to \mathbb{R}$;
$/ : \mathbb{Z} \times \mathbb{Z} \to \mathbb{R}$;
$/ : \mathbb{R} \times \mathbb{R} \to \mathbb{R}$;
$floor : \mathbb{R} \to \mathbb{Z}$;
$ceil : \mathbb{R} \to \mathbb{Z}$;
$round : \mathbb{R} \to \mathbb{Z}$;
$@redfrac : \mathbb{Z} \times \mathbb{Z} \to \mathbb{R}$;
$@redfracwhr : \mathbb{N}^+ \times \mathbb{Z} \times \mathbb{N} \to \mathbb{R}$;
$@redfrachlp : \mathbb{R} \times \mathbb{Z} \to \mathbb{R}$;
var $.m, n : \mathbb{N}$;
$p, q : \mathbb{N}^+$;
$x.y : \mathbb{Z}$;
$r, s : \mathbb{R}$;

eqn $@cReal(x,p) \approx @cReal(y,q) = x \cdot @cInt(@cNat(q)) \approx y \cdot @cInt(@cNat(p))$;
$@cReal(x,p) < @cReal(y,q) = x \cdot @cInt(@cNat(q)) < y \cdot @cInt(@cNat(p))$;
$@cReal(x,p) \leq @cReal(y,q) = x \cdot @cInt(@cNat(q)) \leq y \cdot @cInt(@cNat(p))$;
$Int2Real(x) = @cReal(x, @c1)$;
$Nat2Real(n) = @cReal(@cInt(n), @c1)$;
$Pos2Real(p) = @cReal(@cInt(@cNat(p)), @c1)$;
$Real2Int(@cReal(x, @c1)) = x$;
$Real2Nat(@cReal(x, @c1)) = Int2Nat(x)$;
$Real2Pos(@cReal(x, @c1)) = Int2Pos(x)$;
$min(r,s) = if(r<s, r, s)$;
$max(r,s) = if(r<s, s, r)$;
$abs(r) = if(r < @cReal(@cInt(@c0), @c1), -r, r)$;
$-@cReal(x,p) = @cReal(-x, p)$;

$$
\begin{array}{l}
succ(@cReal(x,p)) = @cReal(x+@cInt(@cNat(p)),p);\\
pred(@cReal(x,p)) = @cReal(x-@cInt(@cNat(p)),p);\\
@cReal(x,p) + @cReal(y,q) =\\
\quad @redfrac(x{\cdot}@cInt(@cNat(q))+y{\cdot}@cInt(@cNat(p)),@cInt(@cNat(p{\cdot}q)));\\
@cReal(x,p) - @cReal(y,q) =\\
\quad @redfrac(x{\cdot}@cInt(@cNat(q))-y{\cdot}@cInt(@cNat(p))),@cInt(@cNat(p{\cdot}q));\\
@cReal(x,p){\cdot}@cReal(y,q) = @redfrac(x{\cdot}y,@cInt(@cNat(p{\cdot}q)));\\
y{\not\approx}@cInt(@c0) \rightarrow @cReal(x,p)/@cReal(y,q) =\\
\quad @redfrac(x{\cdot}@cInt(@cNat(q)),y{\cdot}@cInt(@cNat(p)));\\
p/q = @redfrac(@cInt(@cNat(p)),@cInt(@cNat(q)));\\
n{\not\approx}@c0 \rightarrow m/n = @redfrac(@cInt(m),@cInt(n));\\
y{\not\approx}@cInt(@c0) \rightarrow x/y = @redfrac(x,y);\\
exp(@cReal(x,p),@cInt(n)) = @redfrac(exp(x,n),@cInt(@cNat(exp(p,n))));\\
x{\not\approx}@cInt(@c0) \rightarrow exp(@cReal(x,p),@cNeg(q)) =\\
\quad @redfrac(@cInt(@cNat(exp(p,@cNat(q)))),exp(x,@cNat(q)));\\
floor(@cReal(x,p)) = x \text{ div } p;\\
ceil(r) = -floor(-r);\\
round(r) = floor(r+@cReal(@cInt(@cNat(@c1)),@cDub(false,@c1)));\\
@redfrac(x,@cNeg(p)) = @redfrac(-x,@cInt(@cNat(p)));\\
@redfrac(x,@cInt(@cNat(p))) = @redfracwhr(p,x \text{ div } p,x|_p);\\
@redfracwhr(p,x,@c0) = @cReal(x,@c1);\\
@redfracwhr(p,x,@cNat(q)) =\\
\quad @redfrachlp(@redfrac(@cInt(@cNat(p)),@cInt(@cNat(q))),x);\\
@redfrachlp(@cReal(x,p),y) = @cReal(@cInt(@cNat(p))+y{\cdot}x,Int2Pos(x));
\end{array}
$$

B.6 Lists

Lists over some sort D are denoted by $List(D)$. Lists consist of an empty list [] or an element d where n is a number including the constructor [], which is the empty list, and $d \triangleright s$ which prefixes an element d to the list s. The abbreviation $[d_1, d_2, \ldots, d_n]$ stands for the list $d_1 \triangleright d_2 \triangleright \cdots \triangleright d_n \triangleright []$. The mappings on lists are standard. Their straightforward characterizing equations are given below.

sort $List(D)$; **cons** $[] : List(D)$; $\triangleright : D \times List(D) \rightarrow List(D)$; **map** $in : D \times List(D) \rightarrow \mathbb{B}$; $\# : List(D) \rightarrow \mathbb{N}$; $\triangleleft : List(D) \times D \rightarrow List(D)$; $+\!\!+ : List(D) \times List(D) \rightarrow List(D)$; $. : List(D) \times \mathbb{N} \rightarrow D$; $head : List(D) \rightarrow D$; $tail : List(D) \rightarrow List(D)$; $rhead : List(D) \rightarrow D$; $rtail : List(D) \rightarrow List(D)$;	**var** $d, e : D$; $s, t : List(D)$; $p : \mathbb{N}^+$; **eqn** $[] \approx d \triangleright s = false$; $d \triangleright s \approx [] = false$; $d \triangleright s \approx e \triangleright t = d \approx e \wedge s \approx t$; $[] < d \triangleright s = true$; $d \triangleright s < [] = false$; $d \triangleright s < e \triangleright t = (d \approx e \wedge s < t) \vee d < e$; $[] \leq d \triangleright s = true$; $d \triangleright s \leq [] = false$; $d \triangleright s \leq e \triangleright t = (d \approx e \wedge s \leq t) \vee d < e$;

$in(d, []) = false;$ $in(d, e \triangleright s) = d \approx e \vee in(d, s);$ $\#[] = @c0;$ $\#d \triangleright s = @cNat(succ(\#s));$ $[] \triangleleft d = d \triangleright [];$ $(d \triangleright s) \triangleleft e = d \triangleright (s \triangleleft e);$ $[] \mathbin{+\!\!+} s = s;$ $(d \triangleright s) \mathbin{+\!\!+} t = d \triangleright (s \mathbin{+\!\!+} t);$ $s \mathbin{+\!\!+} [] = s;$	$(d \triangleright s).@c0 = d;$ $(d \triangleright s).@cNat(p) = s.pred(p);$ $head(d \triangleright s) = d;$ $tail(d \triangleright s) = s;$ $rhead(d \triangleright []) = d;$ $rhead(d \triangleright (e \triangleright s)) = rhead(e \triangleright s);$ $rtail(d \triangleright []) = [];$ $rtail(d \triangleright (e \triangleright s)) = d \triangleright rtail(e \triangleright s);$

B.7 Sets

The sort $Set(D)$ for some given sort D contains sets over the elements of D. The sort $Set(D)$ represents actual sets, and not some finite representation of it. Due to the uncountable nature of sets, this is achieved by using functions. Every set is essentially represented by a characteristic function $f : D \to \mathbb{B}$. The expression $f(d)$ is true if d is in the represented set, and false if it is not. Note that for a set comprehension, $\{d{:}D|\phi\}$ the expression $\lambda d{:}D.\phi$ is the characteristic function.

The standard operators can easily be defined by these characteristic functions. For example, set inclusion is just the application of a the characteristic function, and for sets x and y, set union is expressed by $\lambda d{:}D.x(d) \vee y(d)$.

There is one problem when using characteristic functions in the setting of dynamic behavior. Frequently occurring operations during the course of a process are the addition and removal of elements of a set. For example, the set could represent the set of open files. Whenever a file is opened, it is added to the set, and whenever a file is closed, it is removed. Using characteristic functions, the set X to which an element d is added, which is subsequently removed again, is a complex lambda expression which is not equal to x itself. In state space exploration, these two objects, although representing the same set, are different objects and therefore give rise to different states. This renders characteristic functions in their bare form unusable for state space exploration.

The solution that we choose is to represent a set by a pair of a characteristic function f and a finite exception set s. An element d is in the set if $f(s)$ is true iff d is not in s. When adding or removing single elements to or from a the set, these manipulations happen in s. By representing s as an ordered list, it has now become straightforward to bring a set in normal form after such elementary operations. Note that this representation is closed under set complement and that all standard operators are relatively straightforward to be defined on this representation. Note also that this representation allows for arbitrarily complex sets, for example, the set of all prime numbers, and at the same it is very convenient for use in state space analysis tools by allowing normalization to unique normal form representation after removing and deleting individual elements from the list.

When using mCRL2, the set representation is hidden from view. But whenever a set is used, it is translated internally to a characteristic function and an exception set. Whenever these objects are printed, they are transformed back to plain set notation.

sort $Set(D)$; **cons** $@set : (D \to \mathbb{B}) \times FSet(D) \to Set(D)$; **map** $\{\} : Set(D)$; $\in : D \times Set(D) \to \mathbb{B}$; $\overline{} : Set(D) \to Set(D)$; $\cup : Set(D) \times Set(D) \to Set(D)$; $\cap : Set(D) \times Set(D) \to Set(D)$; $- : Set(D) \times Set(D) \to Set(D)$; $@false : D \to \mathbb{B}$; $@true : D \to \mathbb{B}$; $@not : (D \to \mathbb{B}) \to D \to \mathbb{B}$; $@and : (D \to \mathbb{B}) \times (D \to \mathbb{B}) \to D \to \mathbb{B}$; $@or : (D \to \mathbb{B}) \times (D \to \mathbb{B}) \to D \to \mathbb{B}$; **var** $e, d : D$; $s, t : FSet(D)$; $f, g : D \to \mathbb{B}$; $x, y : Set(D)$; **eqn** $\{\} = @set(@false, @fset\_empty)$; $e \in @set(f, s) = f(e) \not\approx @fset\_in(e, s)$; $x \subset y = x \subseteq y \wedge x \not\approx y$; $x \subseteq y = (x \cap y) \approx x$;	$\overline{@set(f, s)} = @set(@not(f), s)$; $x - y = x \cap \overline{y}$; $@false(e) = false$; $@true(e) = true$; $@false \approx @true = false$; $@true \approx @false = false$; $@not(f)(e) = \neg f(e)$; $@not(@false) = @true$; $@not(@true) = @false$; $@and(f, g)(e) = f(e) \wedge g(e)$; $@and(f, f) = f$; $@and(f, @false) = @false$; $@and(@false, f) = @false$; $@and(f, @true) = f$; $@and(@true, f) = f$; $@or(f, g)(e) = f(e) \vee g(e)$; $@or(f, f) = f$; $@or(f, @false) = f$; $@or(@false, f) = f$; $@or(f, @true) = @true$; $@or(@true, f) = @true$;

$$@set(f, s) \approx @set(g, t) = \forall c{:}D.(f(c) \approx g(c) \approx @fset\_in(c, s) \approx @fset\_in(c, t));$$
$$@set(f, s) \cup @set(g, t) = @set(@or(f, g), @fset\_union(f, g, s, t));$$
$$@set(f, s) \cap @set(g, t) = @set(@and(f, g), @fset\_inter(f, g, s, t));$$

The sort $Set(D)$ has one constructor $@set$ that takes a characteristic function and an element of a finite set $FSet(D)$. The auxiliary logical operators (e.g., $@and$) are the logical operators lifted to characteristic functions. The comparison operators $<$ and $\leq$ on sets and finite sets are denoted as $\subset$ and $\subseteq$. All auxiliary functions starting with $@fset$ work on finite sets and are defined below.

The sort $FSet(D)$ represents finite exception sets. Actually, these sets are just ordered lists, although other representation could have been chosen, such as balanced ordered trees. The ordered list is defined as a recursive functional type using **struct**. There is an empty list ($@fset\_empty$) and a list constructor ($@fset\_cons$) prepending an element to the list. Elements are added to the list using a mapping $@fset\_insert$ such that all lists are always ordered. Because an $FSet$ is defined as a struct, equations for equality and the ordering operators are generated as indicated in section B.10 and they are not explicitly listed here.

The other auxiliary functions are $@fset\_cinsert$, which only inserts an element if the second argument is $true$, $@fset\_in$, which checks for membership of an element in a set, and $@fset\_union$, $@fset\_inter$, and $@fset\_diff$, which respectively represent union, intersection, and difference on finite sets. Union and intersection require knowledge of the characteristic functions, which are therefore also a parameter. As in sets, $<$ and $\leq$ on finite sets are denoted as $\subset$ and $\subseteq$.

$$
\begin{array}{ll}
\textbf{sort} & \mathit{FSet}(D) = \textbf{struct}\ @\mathit{fset\_empty} \mid @\mathit{fset\_cons}(D, \mathit{FSet}(D));\\
\textbf{map} & @\mathit{fset\_insert} : D \times \mathit{FSet}(D) \to \mathit{FSet}(D);\\
& @\mathit{fset\_cinsert} : D \times \mathbb{B} \times \mathit{FSet}(D) \to \mathit{FSet}(D);\\
& @\mathit{fset\_in} : D \times \mathit{FSet}(D) \to \mathbb{B};\\
& @\mathit{fset\_union} : (D \to \mathbb{B}) \times (D \to \mathbb{B}) \times \mathit{FSet}(D) \times \mathit{FSet}(D) \to \mathit{FSet}(D);\\
& @\mathit{fset\_inter} : (D \to \mathbb{B}) \times (D \to \mathbb{B}) \times \mathit{FSet}(D) \times \mathit{FSet}(D) \to \mathit{FSet}(D);\\
& @\mathit{fset\_diff} : \mathit{FSet}(D) \times \mathit{FSet}(D) \to \mathit{FSet}(D);\\
\textbf{var} & d, e : D;\\
& f, g : D \to \mathbb{B};\\
& s, t : \mathit{FSet}(D);\\
\textbf{eqn} & @\mathit{fset\_insert}(d, @\mathit{fset\_empty}) = @\mathit{fset\_cons}(d, @\mathit{fset\_empty});\\
& @\mathit{fset\_insert}(d, @\mathit{fset\_cons}(d, s)) = @\mathit{fset\_cons}(d, s);\\
& d{<}e \to @\mathit{fset\_insert}(d, @\mathit{fset\_cons}(e, s)) = @\mathit{fset\_cons}(d, @\mathit{fset\_cons}(e, s));\\
& e{<}d \to @\mathit{fset\_insert}(d, @\mathit{fset\_cons}(e, s)) = @\mathit{fset\_cons}(e, @\mathit{fset\_insert}(d, s));\\
& @\mathit{fset\_cinsert}(d, \mathit{false}, s) = s;\\
& @\mathit{fset\_cinsert}(d, \mathit{true}, s) = @\mathit{fset\_insert}(d, s);\\
& @\mathit{fset\_in}(d, @\mathit{fset\_empty}) = \mathit{false};\\
& @\mathit{fset\_in}(d, @\mathit{fset\_cons}(e, s)) = d{\approx}e \vee @\mathit{fset\_in}(d, s);\\
& @\mathit{fset\_union}(f, g, @\mathit{fset\_empty}, @\mathit{fset\_empty}) = @\mathit{fset\_empty};\\
& @\mathit{fset\_union}(f, g, @\mathit{fset\_cons}(d, s), @\mathit{fset\_empty}) =\\
& \qquad\qquad @\mathit{fset\_cinsert}(d, \neg g(d), @\mathit{fset\_union}(f, g, s, @\mathit{fset\_empty}));\\
& @\mathit{fset\_union}(f, g, @\mathit{fset\_empty}, @\mathit{fset\_cons}(e, t)) =\\
& \qquad\qquad @\mathit{fset\_cinsert}(e, \neg f(e), @\mathit{fset\_union}(f, g, @\mathit{fset\_empty}, t));\\
& @\mathit{fset\_union}(f, g, @\mathit{fset\_cons}(d, s), @\mathit{fset\_cons}(d, t)) =\\
& \qquad\qquad @\mathit{fset\_cinsert}(d, f(d){\approx}g(d), @\mathit{fset\_union}(f, g, s, t));\\
& d{<}e \to @\mathit{fset\_union}(f, g, @\mathit{fset\_cons}(d, s), @\mathit{fset\_cons}(e, t)) =\\
& \qquad\qquad @\mathit{fset\_cinsert}(d, \neg g(d), @\mathit{fset\_union}(f, g, s, @\mathit{fset\_cons}(e, t)));\\
& e{<}d \to @\mathit{fset\_union}(f, g, @\mathit{fset\_cons}(d, s), @\mathit{fset\_cons}(e, t)) =\\
& \qquad\qquad @\mathit{fset\_cinsert}(e, \neg f(e), @\mathit{fset\_union}(f, g, @\mathit{fset\_cons}(d, s), t));\\
& @\mathit{fset\_inter}(f, g, @\mathit{fset\_empty}, @\mathit{fset\_empty}) = @\mathit{fset\_empty};\\
& @\mathit{fset\_inter}(f, g, @\mathit{fset\_cons}(d, s), @\mathit{fset\_empty}) =\\
& \qquad\qquad @\mathit{fset\_cinsert}(d, g(d), @\mathit{fset\_inter}(f, g, s, @\mathit{fset\_empty}));\\
& @\mathit{fset\_inter}(f, g, @\mathit{fset\_empty}, @\mathit{fset\_cons}(e, t)) =\\
& \qquad\qquad @\mathit{fset\_cinsert}(e, f(e), @\mathit{fset\_inter}(f, g, @\mathit{fset\_empty}, t));\\
& @\mathit{fset\_inter}(f, g, @\mathit{fset\_cons}(d, s), @\mathit{fset\_cons}(d, t)) =\\
& \qquad\qquad @\mathit{fset\_cinsert}(d, f(d){\approx}g(d), @\mathit{fset\_inter}(f, g, s, t));\\
& d{<}e \to @\mathit{fset\_inter}(f, g, @\mathit{fset\_cons}(d, s), @\mathit{fset\_cons}(e, t)) =\\
& \qquad\qquad @\mathit{fset\_cinsert}(d, g(d), @\mathit{fset\_inter}(f, g, s, @\mathit{fset\_cons}(e, t)));\\
& e{<}d \to @\mathit{fset\_inter}(f, g, @\mathit{fset\_cons}(d, s), @\mathit{fset\_cons}(e, t)) =\\
& \qquad\qquad @\mathit{fset\_cinsert}(e, f(e), @\mathit{fset\_inter}(f, g, @\mathit{fset\_cons}(d, s), t));\\
& @\mathit{fset\_diff}(s, @\mathit{fset\_empty}) = s;\\
& @\mathit{fset\_diff}(@\mathit{fset\_empty}, t) = @\mathit{fset\_empty};\\
& @\mathit{fset\_diff}(@\mathit{fset\_cons}(d, s), @\mathit{fset\_cons}(d, t)) = @\mathit{fset\_diff}(s, t);\\
& d{<}e \to @\mathit{fset\_diff}(@\mathit{fset\_cons}(d, s), @\mathit{fset\_cons}(e, t)) =\\
& \qquad\qquad @\mathit{fset\_cons}(d, @\mathit{fset\_diff}(s, @\mathit{fset\_cons}(e, t)));\\
& e{<}d \to @\mathit{fset\_diff}(@\mathit{fset\_cons}(d, s), @\mathit{fset\_cons}(e, t)) =\\
& \qquad\qquad @\mathit{fset\_cons}(e, @\mathit{fset\_diff}(@\mathit{fset\_cons}(d, s), t));
\end{array}
$$

B.8 Bags

The sort $Bag(D)$ contains elements of sort D with a multiplicity, i.e., the number of times an element occurs in the bag. Our representation of bags resembles our representation of sets. A bag is constructed using the constructor $@fbag$ of a pair with a characteristic function $f : D \to \mathbb{N}$ that indicates how often an element occurs in the bag, and a finite exception bag s that can override f. The number of times an element d occurs in a bag $@bag(f, s)$ is

$$count(@bag(f,s)) = \begin{cases} f(d) & \text{if } s(d) = 0, \\ 0 & \text{if } f(d) = s(d) > 0, \text{ and} \\ s(d) & \text{if } f(d) \neq s(d), s(d){>}0. \end{cases} \quad \text{(B.1)}$$

Essentially, s overrides f if $s(d) > 0$, except when $s(d) = f(d)$. Then the number of elements is set to 0.

The equations characterizing the mappings on bags make use of the mappings on finite bags as given and explained below. The auxiliary mappings ($@zero$, $@one$, $@add$, $@min$, and $@monus$) behave as their counterparts on natural numbers, except that they apply to each element of a characteristic function simultaneously. The auxiliary functions $@Nat2Bool$ and $@Bool2Nat$ translate characteristic functions for bags to those for sets, and vice versa.

sort $Bag(D)$; **cons** $@bag{:}(D{\to}\mathbb{N}){\times}FBag(D){\to}Bag(D)$; **map** $\{:\} : Bag(D)$; $count : D \times Bag(D) \to \mathbb{N}$; $\in : D \times Bag(D) \to \mathbb{B}$; $\cup : Bag(D) \times Bag(D) \to Bag(D)$; $\cap : Bag(D) \times Bag(D) \to Bag(D)$; $- : Bag(D) \times Bag(D) \to Bag(D)$;	$Bag2Set : Bag(D) \to Set(D)$; $Set2Bag : Set(D) \to Bag(D)$; $@zero : D \to \mathbb{N}$; $@one : D \to \mathbb{N}$; $@add : (D{\to}\mathbb{N}){\times}(D{\to}\mathbb{N}){\to}D{\to}\mathbb{N}$; $@min : (D{\to}\mathbb{N}){\times}(D{\to}\mathbb{N}){\to}D{\to}\mathbb{N}$; $@monus{:}(D{\to}\mathbb{N}){\times}(D{\to}\mathbb{N}){\to}D{\to}\mathbb{N}$; $@Nat2Bool : (D \to \mathbb{N}) \to D \to \mathbb{B}$; $@Bool2Nat : (D \to \mathbb{B}) \to D \to \mathbb{N}$;
var $b, c : FBag(D)$; $e : D$; $f, g : D \to \mathbb{N}$;	$h : D \to \mathbb{B}$; $s : FSet(D)$; $x, y : Bag(D)$;

eqn $\{:\} = @bag(@zero, @fbag\_empty);$
$e \in x = count(e, x) > @c0;$
$x \subset y = x \subseteq y \wedge x \not\approx y;$
$x \subseteq y = (x \cap y) \approx x;$
$@zero(e) = @c0;$
$@one(e) = @cNat(@c1);$
$@zero \approx @one = false;$
$@one \approx @zero = false;$
$@add(f, g)(e) = f(e) + g(e);$
$@add(f, @zero) = f;$
$@add(@zero, f) = f;$

$@min(f, g)(e) = min(f(e), g(e));$
$@min(f, f) = f;$
$@min(f, @zero) = @zero;$
$@min(@zero, f) = @zero;$
$@monus(f, g)(c) =$
$@monus(f(e), g(e));$
$@monus(f, f) = @zero;$
$@monus(f, @zero) = f;$
$@monus(@zero, f) = @zero;$
$@Nat2Bool(f)(e) = f(e) > @c0;$
$@Nat2Bool(@zero) = @false;$
$@Nat2Bool(@one) = @true;$
$@Bool2Nat(@false) = @zero;$
$@Bool2Nat(@true) = @one;$

$@Bool2Nat(h)(e) = if(h(e), @cNat(@c1), @c0);$
$count(e, @bag(f, b)) = @sz(f(e), @fbag\_count(e, b));$
$Bag2Set(@bag(f, b)) = @set(@Nat2Bool(f), @fbag2fset(f, b));$
$Set2Bag(@set(h, s)) = @bag(@Bool2Nat(h), @fset2fbag(s));$
$@bag(f, b) \approx @bag(g, c) =$
$if(f \approx g, b \approx c, \forall d{:}D.count(d, @bag(f, b)) \approx count(d, @bag(g, c)));$
$@bag(f, b) \cup @bag(g, c) = @bag(@add(f, g), @fbag\_join(f, g, b, c));$
$@bag(f, b) \cap @bag(g, c) = @bag(@min(f, g), @fbag\_inter(f, g, b, c));$
$@bag(f, b) - @bag(g, c) = @bag(@monus(f, g), @fbag\_diff(f, g, b, c));$

Finite bags are essentially ordered lists with pairs of an element d of D and a positive number p. The number p indicates how often d occurs in the set. There is no need to indicate that d occurs 0 times in the set, as this can be indicated by removing d from the list.

The auxiliary mapping $@fbag\_insert$ does an ordered insert of an element and a positive occurrence count in the list. The mapping $@fbag\_cinsert$ does the same for a natural occurrence count, by simply not inserting elements with occurrence count 0. The mapping $@bag\_count$ counts how often an element occurs in the list and similarly $@bag\_in$ checks whether this count is larger than 0, which indicates that this element occurs in the bag.

The mappings $@fbag\_join$, $@fbag\_inter$, and $@fbag\_diff$ represent the union, intersection, and difference on bags, respectively. The definition is tricky because the element count as characterized by equation (B.1) must be preserved. The swap zero functions ($@sz$, $@sz\_add$, $@sz\_min$, $@sz\_monus$) are introduced to properly maintain this count.

The auxiliary functions $@fbag2fset$ and $@fset2fbag$ assist in translating bags to sets and sets to bags.

sort $FBag(D) = $ **struct** $@fbag\_empty \mid @fbag\_cons(D, \mathbb{N}^+, FBag(D));$
map $@fbag\_insert : D \times \mathbb{N}^+ \times FBag(D) \to FBag(D);$
$@fbag\_cinsert : D \times \mathbb{N} \times FBag(D) \to FBag(D);$
$@fbag\_count : D \times FBag(D) \to \mathbb{N};$
$@fbag\_in : D \times FBag(D) \to \mathbb{B};$
$@fbag\_join : (D \to \mathbb{N}) \times (D \to \mathbb{N}) \times FBag(D) \times FBag(D) \to FBag(D);$
$@fbag\_inter : (D \to \mathbb{N}) \times (D \to \mathbb{N}) \times FBag(D) \times FBag(D) \to FBag(D);$
$@fbag\_diff : (D \to \mathbb{N}) \times (D \to \mathbb{N}) \times FBag(D) \times FBag(D) \to FBag(D);$
$@fbag2fset : (D \to \mathbb{N}) \times FBag(D) \to FSet(D);$
$@fset2fbag : FSet(D) \to FBag(D);$
var $d, e : D;$
$p, q : \mathbb{N}^+;$
$b, c : FBag(D);$
$s : FSet(D);$
$f, g : D \to \mathbb{N};$
eqn $@fbag\_insert(d, p, @fbag\_empty) = @fbag\_cons(d, p, @fbag\_empty);$
$@fbag\_insert(d, p, @fbag\_cons(d, q, b)) = @fbag\_cons(d, p{+}q, b);$
$d{<}e \to @fbag\_insert(d, p, @fbag\_cons(e, q, b)) =$
$@fbag\_cons(d, p, @fbag\_cons(e, q, b));$
$e{<}d \to @fbag\_insert(d, p, @fbag\_cons(e, q, b)) =$
$@fbag\_cons(e, q, @fbag\_insert(d, p, b));$
$@fbag\_cinsert(d, @c0, b) = b;$
$@fbag\_cinsert(d, @cNat(p), b) = @fbag\_insert(d, p, b);$
$@fbag\_count(d, @fbag\_empty) = @c0;$
$@fbag\_count(d, @fbag\_cons(d, p, b)) = @cNat(p);$
$d{<}e \to @fbag\_count(d, @fbag\_cons(e, p, b)) = @c0;$
$e{<}d \to @fbag\_count(d, @fbag\_cons(e, p, b)) = @fbag\_count(d, b);$
$@fbag\_in(d, b) = @fbag\_count(d, b){>}@c0;$
$@fbag\_join(f, g, @fbag\_empty, @fbag\_empty) = @fbag\_empty;$
$@fbag\_join(f, g, @fbag\_cons(d, p, b), @fbag\_empty) =$
$@fbag\_cinsert(d, @sz\_add(f(d), g(d), @cNat(p), @c0),$
$@fbag\_join(f, g, b, @fbag\_empty));$
$@fbag\_join(f, g, @fbag\_empty, @fbag\_cons(e, q, c)) =$
$@fbag\_cinsert(e, @sz\_add(f(e), g(e), @c0, @cNat(q)),$
$@fbag\_join(f, g, @fbag\_empty, c));$
$@fbag\_join(f, g, @fbag\_cons(d, p, b), @fbag\_cons(d, q, c)) =$
$@fbag\_cinsert(d, @sz\_add(f(d), g(d), @cNat(p), @cNat(q)),$
$@fbag\_join(f, g, b, c));$
$d{<}e \to @fbag\_join(f, g, @fbag\_cons(d, p, b), @fbag\_cons(e, q, c)) =$
$@fbag\_cinsert(d, @sz\_add(f(d), g(d), @cNat(p), @c0),$
$@fbag\_join(f, g, b, @fbag\_cons(e, q, c)));$
$e{<}d \to @fbag\_join(f, g, @fbag\_cons(d, p, b), @fbag\_cons(e, q, c)) =$
$@fbag\_cinsert(e, @sz\_add(f(e), g(e), @c0, @cNat(q)),$
$@fbag\_join(f, g, @fbag\_cons(d, p, b), c));$
$@fbag\_inter(f, g, @fbag\_empty, @fbag\_empty) = @fbag\_empty;$
$@fbag\_inter(f, g, @fbag\_cons(d, p, b), @fbag\_empty) =$
$@fbag\_cinsert(d, @sz\_min(f(d), g(d), @cNat(p), @c0),$
$@fbag\_inter(f, g, b, @fbag\_empty));$

$$
\begin{array}{l}
@\mathit{fbag\_inter}(f, g, @\mathit{fbag\_empty}, @\mathit{fbag\_cons}(e, q, c)) = \\
\quad @\mathit{fbag\_cinsert}(e, @\mathit{sz\_min}(f(e), g(e), @\mathit{c0}, @\mathit{cNat}(q)), \\
\qquad @\mathit{fbag\_inter}(f, g, @\mathit{fbag\_empty}, c)); \\
@\mathit{fbag\_inter}(f, g, @\mathit{fbag\_cons}(d, p, b), @\mathit{fbag\_cons}(d, q, c)) = \\
\quad @\mathit{fbag\_cinsert}(d, @\mathit{sz\_min}(f(d), g(d), @\mathit{cNat}(p), @\mathit{cNat}(q)), \\
\qquad @\mathit{fbag\_inter}(f, g, b, c)); \\
d{<}e \rightarrow @\mathit{fbag\_inter}(f, g, @\mathit{fbag\_cons}(d, p, b), @\mathit{fbag\_cons}(e, q, c)) = \\
\quad @\mathit{fbag\_cinsert}(d, @\mathit{sz\_min}(f(d), g(d), @\mathit{cNat}(p), @\mathit{c0}), \\
\qquad @\mathit{fbag\_inter}(f, g, b, @\mathit{fbag\_cons}(e, q, c))); \\
e{<}d \rightarrow @\mathit{fbag\_inter}(f, g, @\mathit{fbag\_cons}(d, p, b), @\mathit{fbag\_cons}(e, q, c)) = \\
\quad @\mathit{fbag\_cinsert}(e, @\mathit{sz\_min}(f(e), g(e), @\mathit{c0}, @\mathit{cNat}(q)), \\
\qquad @\mathit{fbag\_inter}(f, g, @\mathit{fbag\_cons}(d, p, b), c)); \\
@\mathit{fbag\_diff}(f, g, @\mathit{fbag\_empty}, @\mathit{fbag\_empty}) = @\mathit{fbag\_empty}; \\
@\mathit{fbag\_diff}(f, g, @\mathit{fbag\_cons}(d, p, b), @\mathit{fbag\_empty}) = \\
\quad @\mathit{fbag\_cinsert}(d, @\mathit{sz\_monus}(f(d), g(d), @\mathit{cNat}(p), @\mathit{c0}), \\
\qquad @\mathit{fbag\_diff}(f, g, b, @\mathit{fbag\_empty})); \\
@\mathit{fbag\_diff}(f, g, @\mathit{fbag\_empty}, @\mathit{fbag\_cons}(e, q, c)) = \\
\quad @\mathit{fbag\_cinsert}(e, @\mathit{sz\_monus}(f(e), g(e), @\mathit{c0}, @\mathit{cNat}(q)), \\
\qquad @\mathit{fbag\_diff}(f, g, @\mathit{fbag\_empty}, c)); \\
@\mathit{fbag\_diff}(f, g, @\mathit{fbag\_cons}(d, p, b), @\mathit{fbag\_cons}(d, q, c)) = \\
\quad @\mathit{fbag\_cinsert}(d, @\mathit{sz\_monus}(f(d), g(d), @\mathit{cNat}(p), @\mathit{cNat}(q)), \\
\qquad @\mathit{fbag\_diff}(f, g, b, c)); \\
d{<}e \rightarrow @\mathit{fbag\_diff}(f, g, @\mathit{fbag\_cons}(d, p, b), @\mathit{fbag\_cons}(e, q, c)) = \\
\quad @\mathit{fbag\_cinsert}(d, @\mathit{sz\_monus}(f(d), g(d), @\mathit{cNat}(p), @\mathit{c0}), \\
\qquad @\mathit{fbag\_diff}(f, g, b, @\mathit{fbag\_cons}(e, q, c))); \\
e{<}d \rightarrow @\mathit{fbag\_diff}(f, g, @\mathit{fbag\_cons}(d, p, b), @\mathit{fbag\_cons}(e, q, c)) = \\
\quad @\mathit{fbag\_cinsert}(e, @\mathit{sz\_monus}(f(e), g(e), @\mathit{c0}, @\mathit{cNat}(q)), \\
\qquad @\mathit{fbag\_diff}(f, g, @\mathit{fbag\_cons}(d, p, b), c)); \\
@\mathit{fbag2fset}(f, @\mathit{fbag\_empty}) = @\mathit{fset\_empty}; \\
@\mathit{fbag2fset}(f, @\mathit{fbag\_cons}(d, p, b)) = \\
\quad @\mathit{fset\_cinsert}(d, (f(d) {\approx} @\mathit{cNat}(p)) {\approx} (f(d) {>} @\mathit{c0}), @\mathit{fbag2fset}(f, b)); \\
@\mathit{fset2fbag}(@\mathit{fset\_empty}) = @\mathit{fbag\_empty}; \\
@\mathit{fset2fbag}(@\mathit{fset\_cons}(d, s)) = @\mathit{fbag\_cinsert}(d, @\mathit{cNat}(@\mathit{c1}), @\mathit{fset2fbag}(s));
\end{array}
$$

B.9 Function update

A function update $f[d \rightarrow e]$ for a function $f : S \rightarrow T$ is translated to the internal notation $@\mathit{func\_update}(f, d, e)$. The equations below order the function updates such that a function with updates has a unique normal form, which makes this representation suitable for state space exploration. The last two equations define how functions with updates are applied to arguments. Note that function updates are only defined for functions with one argument.

map $@func\_update : (S \to T) \times S \times T \to (S \to T);$
var $x, y : S; v, w : T; f : S \to T;$
eqn $f(x) \approx v \to @func\_update(f, x, v) = f;$
$@func\_update(@func\_update(f, x, w), x, v) = @func\_update(f, x, v);$
$x > y \to @func\_update(@func\_update(f, y, w), x, v) =$
$@func\_update(@func\_update(f, x, v), y, w);$
$x \not\approx y \to @func\_update(f, x, v)(y) = f(y);$
$@func\_update(f, x, v)(x) = v;$

B.10 Structured sorts

The general form of a structured sort is the following, where $n \in \mathbb{N}^+$ and $k_i \in \mathbb{N}$ with $1 \le i \le n$:

$$
\begin{aligned}
\textbf{struct}\ & c_1(pr_{1,1} : A_{1,1}, \ \ldots, pr_{1,k_1} : A_{1,k_1})?isC_1 \\
\mid\ & c_2(pr_{2,1} : A_{2,1}, \ \ldots, pr_{2,k_2} : A_{2,k_2})?isC_2 \\
& \vdots \\
\mid\ & c_n(pr_{n,1} : A_{n,1}, \ldots, pr_{n,k_n} : A_{n,k_n})?isC_n;
\end{aligned}
$$

A declaration of this form gives rise to the following equations, which are given schematically. If projection functions and recognizers are not mentioned explicitly, they are not generated. The sort name *Struct@n* where n is a number is an arbitrary internal name used to denote this sort.

sort *Struct@n*;
cons $c_i : A_{i,1} \times \cdots \times A_{i,k_i} \to Struct@n$ for all $1 \le i \le n$;
map $isC_i : Struct@n \to \mathbb{B}$ for all $1 \le i \le n$;
$pr_{i,j} : Struct@n \to A_{i,j}$ for all $1 \le i \le n,\ 1 \le j \le k_i$;
var $x_{i,j}, y_{i,j} : A_{i,j}$ for all $1 \le i \le n,\ 1 \le j \le k_i$;
eqn $isC_i(c_i(x_{i,1}, \ldots, x_{i,k_i})) = true$ for all $1 \le i \le n$;
$isC_i(c_j(x_{j,1}, \ldots, x_{j,k_j})) = false$ for all $1 \le i, j \le n$ and $i \ne j$;
$pr_{i,j}(c_i(x_{i,1}, \ldots, x_{i,k_i})) = x_{i,j}$ for all $1 \le i \le n$ and $1 \le j \le k_i$;
$c_i(x_{i,1}, \ldots, x_{i,k_i}) \approx c_i(y_{i,1}, \ldots, y_{i,k_i}) = \bigwedge_{1 \le j \le k_i} x_{i,j} \approx y_{i,j}$ for all $1 \le i \le n$;
$c_i(x_{i,1}, \ldots, x_{i,k_i}) \approx c_j(y_{j,1}, \ldots, y_{j,k_j}) = false$ for all $1 \le i, j \le n$ if $i \ne j$;
$c_i(x_{i,1}, \ldots, x_{i,k_i}) < c_i(y_{i,1}, \ldots, y_{i,k_i}) = x_{i,1} < y_{i,1} \vee (x_{i,1} \approx y_{i,1} \wedge$
$(x_{i,2} < y_{i,2} \vee (\ldots \vee (x_{i,k_i-1} \approx y_{i,k_i-1} \wedge (x_{i,k_i} < y_{i,k_i})) \ldots)));$
$c_i(x_{i,1}, \ldots, x_{i,k_i}) < c_j(y_{j,1}, \ldots, y_{j,k_j}) = true$ if $i < j$;
$c_i(x_{i,1}, \ldots, x_{i,k_i}) < c_j(y_{j,1}, \ldots, y_{j,k_j}) = false$ if $i > j$;
$c_i(x_{i,1}, \ldots, x_{i,k_i}) \le c_i(y_{i,1}, \ldots, y_{i,k_i}) = x_{i,1} < y_{i,1} \vee (x_{i,1} \approx y_{i,1} \wedge$
$(x_{i,2} < y_{i,2} \vee (\ldots \vee (x_{i,k_i-1} \approx y_{i,k_i-1} \wedge (x_{i,k_i} \le y_{i,k_i})) \ldots)));$
$c_i(x_{i,1}, \ldots, x_{i,k_i}) \le c_j(y_{j,1}, \ldots, y_{j,k_j}) = true$ if $i < j$;
$c_i(x_{i,1}, \ldots, x_{i,k_i}) \le c_j(y_{j,1}, \ldots, y_{j,k_j}) = false$ if $i > j$;

Note that the projection function $pr_{i,j}$ applied to another constructor than c_i has no equation, and therefore it cannot be determined to which element of the domain $A_{i,j}$ it is equal.

Appendix C

Plain-Text Notation

In this appendix, we present the machine-readable plain-text equivalent of language constructs introduced throughout the book. We start with the plain-text notation for data types and data expression and proceed with the syntax of processes.

C.1 Data types

C.1.1 Sorts

Sort	*Rich notation*	`Plain notation`
Booleans	$\mathbb{B}$	`Bool`
Positive numbers	$\mathbb{N}^{+}$	`Pos`
Natural numbers	$\mathbb{N}$	`Nat`
Integers	$\mathbb{Z}$	`Int`
Real numbers	$\mathbb{R}$	`Real`
Structured types	$\mathbf{struct} \ldots \mid \ldots.$	`struct ... | ....`
Functions	$D_1 \times \cdots \times D_n \to E$	`D1 # ... # Dn -> E`
Lists	$List(D)$	`List(D)`
Sets	$Set(D)$	`Set(D)`
Bags	$Bag(D)$	`Bag(D)`

C.1.2 Functions for any data type

Operator	*Rich notation*	`Plain notation`
Equality	$\_ \approx \_$	`_ == _`
Inequality	$\_ \not\approx \_$	`_ != _`
Less than or equal	$\_ \leq \_$	`_ <= _`
Less than	$\_ < \_$	`_ < _`
Greater than or equal	$\_ \geq \_$	`_ >= _`
Greater than	$\_ > \_$	`_ > _`
Conditional	$if(\_, \_, \_)$	`if(_,_,_)`

C.1.3 Boolean expressions

Operator	*Rich notation*	Plain notation
True	*true*	`true`
False	*false*	`false`
Negation	$\neg\_$	`!_`
Conjunction	$\_\wedge\_$	`_ && _`
Disjunction	$\_\vee\_$	`_ || _`
Implication	$\_\Rightarrow\_$	`_ => _`
Universal quantification	$\forall\_:\_.\_$	`forall _:_._`
Existential quantification	$\exists\_:\_.\_$	`exists _:_._`

C.1.4 Structured-data expressions

Operator	*Rich notation*	Plain notation
Constructor	$c_i(\_,\ldots,\_)$	`ci(_,...,_)`
Recognizer for c_i	$is\_c_i(\_)$	`is_ci(_)`
Projection (i,j), if declared	$pr_{i,j}(\_)$	`prij(_)`

C.1.5 Numerical expressions

Operator	*Rich notation*	Plain notation
Positive numbers	$\mathbb{N}^+\ (1,2,3,\ldots)$	`Pos,(1,2,3,...)`
Natural numbers	$\mathbb{N}\ (0,1,2,\ldots)$	`Nat,(0,1,2,...)`
Integers	$\mathbb{Z}\ (\ldots,-1,0,1,\ldots)$	`Int,(...,-1,0,1,...)`
Conversion	$A2B(\_)$	`A2B(_)`
Maximum	$\max(\_,\_)$	`max(_,_)`
Minimum	$\min(\_,\_)$	`min(_,_)`
Absolute value	$\mathrm{abs}(\_)$	`abs(_)`
Negation	$-\_$	`-_`
Successor	$succ(\_)$	`succ(_)`
Predecessor	$pred(\_)$	`pred(_)`
Addition	$\_+\_$	`_ + _`
Subtraction	$\_-\_$	`_ - _`
Multiplication	$\_\cdot\_$	`_ * _`
Integer div	$\_\ \mathrm{div}\ \_$	`_ div _`
Integer mod	$\_\mid\_$	`_ mod _`
Exponentiation	$\_^{\_}$	`exp(_,_)`
Real division	$\_/\_$	`_ / _`
Rounding operators	$floor(\_)$, $ceil(\_)$, $round(\_)$	`floor(_)`, `ceil(_)`, `round(_)`

C.1.6 Function expressions

<table>
<tr><th>Operator</th><th>Rich notation</th><th>Plain notation</th></tr>
<tr><td>Function application</td><td>$\_(\_,\ldots,\_)$</td><td><code>_(_,...,_)</code></td></tr>
<tr><td>Lambda abstraction</td><td>$\lambda\_{:}D_0,\ldots,\_{:}D_n.\_$</td><td><code>lambda _:D0,...,_:Dn._</code></td></tr>
<tr><td>Function update</td><td>$\_[\_ \rightarrow \_]$</td><td><code>_[_->_]</code></td></tr>
</table>

C.1.7 List expressions

<table>
<tr><th>Operator</th><th>Rich notation</th><th>Plain notation</th></tr>
<tr><td>Empty list</td><td>$[]$</td><td><code>[]</code></td></tr>
<tr><td>List enumeration</td><td>$[\_,\ldots,\_]$</td><td><code>[_,...,_]</code></td></tr>
<tr><td>Element test</td><td>$\_ \in \_$</td><td><code>_ in _</code></td></tr>
<tr><td>Length</td><td>$\#\_$</td><td><code>#_</code></td></tr>
<tr><td>Cons</td><td>$\_ \triangleright \_$</td><td><code>_ |> _</code></td></tr>
<tr><td>Snoc</td><td>$\_ \triangleleft \_$</td><td><code>_ <| _</code></td></tr>
<tr><td>Concatenation</td><td>$\_ {+\!\!+} \_$</td><td><code>_ ++ _</code></td></tr>
<tr><td>Element at position</td><td>$\_ . \_$</td><td><code>_ . _</code></td></tr>
<tr><td>The first element of a list</td><td>$head(\_)$</td><td><code>head(_)</code></td></tr>
<tr><td>List without its first element</td><td>$tail(\_)$</td><td><code>tail(_)</code></td></tr>
<tr><td>The last element of a list</td><td>$rhead(\_)$</td><td><code>rhead(_)</code></td></tr>
<tr><td>List without its last element</td><td>$rtail(\_)$</td><td><code>rtail(_)</code></td></tr>
</table>

C.1.8 Sets and bags

<table>
<tr><th>Operator</th><th>Rich notation</th><th>Plain notation</th></tr>
<tr><td>Empty set</td><td>$\{\}$</td><td><code>{}</code></td></tr>
<tr><td>Set enumeration</td><td>$\{\_,\ldots,\_\}$</td><td><code>{ _,...,_ }</code></td></tr>
<tr><td>Empty bag</td><td>$\{:\}$</td><td><code>{:}</code></td></tr>
<tr><td>Bag enumeration</td><td>$\{\_:\_,\ldots,\_:\_\}$</td><td><code>{ _:_,...,_:_}</code></td></tr>
<tr><td>Bag/set comprehension</td><td>$\{\_:\_ \mid \_\}$</td><td><code>{ _:_ | _ }</code></td></tr>
<tr><td>Element test</td><td>$\_ \in \_$</td><td><code>_ in _</code></td></tr>
<tr><td>Bag multiplicity</td><td>$count(\_,\_)$</td><td><code>count(_,_)</code></td></tr>
<tr><td>Subset/subbag</td><td>$\_ \subseteq \_$</td><td><code>_ <= _</code></td></tr>
<tr><td>Proper subset/subbag</td><td>$\_ \subset \_$</td><td><code>_ < _</code></td></tr>
<tr><td>Union</td><td>$\_ \cup \_$</td><td><code>_ + _</code></td></tr>
<tr><td>Difference</td><td>$\_ - \_$</td><td><code>_ - _</code></td></tr>
<tr><td>Intersection</td><td>$\_ \cap \_$</td><td><code>_ * _</code></td></tr>
<tr><td>Set complement</td><td>$\overline{\_}$</td><td><code>!_</code></td></tr>
<tr><td>Convert set to bag</td><td>$Set2Bag(\_)$</td><td><code>Set2Bag(_)</code></td></tr>
<tr><td>Convert bag to set</td><td>$Bag2Set(\_)$</td><td><code>Bag2Set(_)</code></td></tr>
</table>

C.2 Processes

<table>
<tr><th>Operator</th><th>Rich notation</th><th>Plain notation</th></tr>
<tr><td>Action</td><td>$a(\ldots)$</td><td>a(...)</td></tr>
<tr><td>Multi-action</td><td>_|_</td><td>_|_</td></tr>
<tr><td>Internal action</td><td>τ</td><td>tau</td></tr>
<tr><td>Process instantiation</td><td>$P(t_1, \ldots, t_n)$</td><td>P(t1,...,tn)</td></tr>
<tr><td>Instantiation assignment</td><td>$P(x_1{=}t_1, \ldots)$</td><td>P(x1=t1,...)</td></tr>
<tr><td>Nondeterministic choice</td><td>_ + _</td><td>_+_</td></tr>
<tr><td>Sequential composition</td><td>_ · _</td><td>_._</td></tr>
<tr><td>Deadlock</td><td>δ</td><td>delta</td></tr>
<tr><td>Conditional statement</td><td>_ → _ ◇ _</td><td>_->_ <>_</td></tr>
<tr><td>Sum</td><td>$\sum_{\_:\_}$ _</td><td>sum _:_. _</td></tr>
<tr><td>At (time stamp)</td><td>_‘_</td><td>_@_</td></tr>
<tr><td>Parallel composition</td><td>_ ∥ _</td><td>_||_</td></tr>
<tr><td>Communication merge</td><td>_|_</td><td>_|_</td></tr>
<tr><td>Left merge</td><td>_ ⫫ _</td><td>_||_ _</td></tr>
<tr><td>Until operator</td><td>_ ≪ _</td><td>_<<_</td></tr>
<tr><td>Communication</td><td>$\Gamma_{\{a|b \to c, \ldots\}}(\_)$</td><td>comm({a|b->c,...},_)</td></tr>
<tr><td>Allow</td><td>$\nabla_{\{a|b, \ldots\}}(\_)$</td><td>allow({a|b,...},_)</td></tr>
<tr><td>Blocking</td><td>$\partial_{\{a, \ldots\}}(\_)$</td><td>block({a,...},_)</td></tr>
<tr><td>Renaming</td><td>$\rho_{\{a \to b, \ldots\}}(\_)$</td><td>comm({a->b, ...},_)</td></tr>
<tr><td>Hiding</td><td>$\tau_{\{a, \ldots\}}(\_)$</td><td>hide({a,...},_)</td></tr>
</table>

C.3 Modal logic

C.3.1 Action formulas

<table>
<tr><th>Operator</th><th>Rich notation</th><th>Plain notation</th></tr>
<tr><td>Unit element (for multiactions)</td><td>τ</td><td>tau</td></tr>
<tr><td>Action</td><td>$a(\ldots)$</td><td>a(...)</td></tr>
<tr><td>Multi-action</td><td>_|_</td><td>_|_</td></tr>
<tr><td>Data expression</td><td>_</td><td>val(_)</td></tr>
<tr><td>All multi-actions</td><td>true</td><td>true</td></tr>
<tr><td>No multi-actions</td><td>false</td><td>false</td></tr>
<tr><td>Complement</td><td>$\overline{\_}$</td><td>!_</td></tr>
<tr><td>Universal quantification</td><td>∀_ : _._</td><td>forall_:_._</td></tr>
<tr><td>Existential quantification</td><td>∃_ : _._</td><td>exists_:_._</td></tr>
<tr><td>Time</td><td>_‘_</td><td>_@_</td></tr>
<tr><td>Intersection</td><td>_ ∩ _</td><td>_&&_</td></tr>
<tr><td>Union</td><td>_ ∪ _</td><td>_||_</td></tr>
<tr><td>Implication</td><td>_ → _</td><td>_=>_</td></tr>
</table>

C.3.2 Regular expressions

Operator	*Rich notation*	Plain notation
None	ε	nil
Concatenation	$\_ \cdot \_$	_._
Choice	$\_ + \_$	_|_
Reflexive and transitive closure	$\_^{*}$	_*
Transitive closure	$\_^{+}$	_+

C.3.3 State formulas

Operator	*Rich notation*	Plain notation
Data expression	$\_$	val(_)
True	*true*	true
False	*false*	false
Negation	$\neg \_$	!_
Conjunction	$\_ \wedge \_$	_&&_
Disjunction	$\_ \vee \_$	_||_
Implication	$\_ \rightarrow \_$	_=>_
Diamond modality	$\langle \_ \rangle \_$	<_>_
Box modality	$[\_]\_$	[_]_
Minimal fixed point	$\mu X.\_$	mu X._
Minimal fixed point	$\mu X(d_1{:}D_1{:=}t_1, \_).\_$	mu X(d1:D1=t1,_)._
Maximal fixed point	$\nu X.\_$	nu X._
Maximal fixed point	$\nu X(d_1{:}D_1{:=}t_1, \_).\_$	nu X(d1:D1=t1,_)._
Existential quantifier	$\exists \_ : \_.\_$	exists _:_ ._
Universal quantifier	$\forall \_ : \_.\_$	forall _:_ ._
Delay	Δ	delay
Timed delay	$\Delta^{c}\_$	delay@_
Yaled	∇	yaled
Timed yaled	$\nabla^{c}\_$	yaled@_

C.4 (Parameterized) Boolean equation systems

Operator	*Rich notation*	Plain notation
Data expression	$\_$	val(_)
Variable instantiation	$X(t_1, \ldots, t_n)$	X(t1,...,tn)
True	*true*	true
False	*false*	false
Negation	$\neg \_$	!_
Conjunction	$\_ \wedge \_$	_&&_
Disjunction	$\_ \vee \_$	_||_
Implication	$\_ \rightarrow \_$	_=>_
Existential quantifier	$\exists \_ : \_.\_$	exists _:_ ._
Universal quantifier	$\forall \_ : \_.\_$	forall _:_ ._

Appendix D

Syntax of the Formalisms

This appendix contains the EBNF description for the syntax of the data, processes, modal formulas, parameterized Boolean equation systems, and action renamings.

D.1 Comments

Comments start with the symbol % and with a new line. Apart from this, tabs, spaces, and new lines are ignored, except that they act as separators between syntactic items.

D.2 Keywords

The following list contains all predefined keywords. These keywords cannot be used as identifiers. The keywords are case sensitive.

`sort` | `cons` | `map` | `var` | `eqn` | `act` | `proc` | `init` | `nil`
`delta` | `tau` | `sum` | `block` | `allow` | `hide` | `rename` | `comm`
`struct` | `Bool` | `Pos` | `Nat` | `Int` | `Real` | `List` | `Set` | `Bag`
`true` | `false` | `whr` | `end` | `lambda` | `forall` | `exists` | `div` | `mod` | `in`

D.3 Conventions to denote the context-free syntax

In the syntax below we use the normal BNF conventions. The syntactic categories are indicated using italics; auxiliary symbols are in roman; and keywords and textual symbols occur in teletype font. A line of the form $A \ ::= \ B$ means that the syntactic category A consists of sequences as indicated in B. The following operators are allowed in B. A question mark indicates that the preceding symbol or category is optional, a $*$ indicates a sequence of 0 or more of the preceding objects, and a $+$ indicates 1 or more occurrences. The bar (|) between two syntactical objects means that either of them is meant. Using round brackets syntactical objects can be grouped. The notation [a − z] indicates the range of letters from a to z. The same applies to [A − Z] and [0 − 9].

If more grammatical rules can be applied, disambiguation takes place by using "Left n" or "Right n." For binary operators, this indicates that the operator is right or left associative. For unary operators, it indicates whether it sticks to the right or left object. The number indicates a priority for parsing. The rule with the highest number will be applied first. As the syntax of mCRL2 is quite complex, some grammatical tricks were required to unambiguously parse input. For instance, there are the syntactical categories *ProcExpr* and *ProcExprNoIf* required to parse expressions using nested conditional operators in processes. This appendix is provided for reference and therefore provided without detailed explanation.

D.4 Identifiers and numbers

Identifiers start with a letter and can consist of letters, numbers, underscores, and primes. Numbers have their normal syntax, with an optional – in front.

Number	::= `0` | `-`? `[1-9][0-9]`∗	number
Id	::= (`[a-z]` | `[A-Z]` | `_`)	identifier
	(`[a-z]` | `[A-Z]` | `[0-9]` | `_` | `'`)∗	
IdList	::= *Id*(`,` *Id*)∗	identifier list

D.5 Sort expressions and sort declarations

SimpleSortExpr	::= `Bool`	Booleans
	| `Pos`	Positive numbers
	| `Nat`	Natural numbers
	| `Int`	Integers
	| `Real`	Reals
	| `List` (*SortExpr*)	List sort
	| `Set` (*SortExpr*)	Set sort
	| `Bag` (*SortExpr*)	Bag sort
	| *Id*	Sort reference
	| (*SortExpr*)	Sort expression with parentheses
	| `struct` *ConstrDeclList*	Structured sort

SortExpr	::= *SimpleSortExpr*	
	| *HashArgs* -> *SortExpr* ;	Function sort
SortExprList	::= (*SortExpr* #)∗ *SortExpr* ;	Product sort
HashArgs	::= *SimpleSortExpr*(# *SimpleSortExpr*)∗ ;	Simple product sort
SortSpec	::= `sort` *SortDecl*+ ;	Sort specification
SortDecl	::= *IdList* ;	List of sort identifiers
	| *Id* = *SortExpr* ;	Sort alias
ConstrDecl	::= *Id* ((*ProjDeclList*))? (? *Id*)? ;	Constructor declaration
ConstrDeclList	::= *ConstrDecl* (| *ConstrDecl*)∗ ;	Constructor declaration list
ProjDecl	::= (*Id* :)? *SortExpr* ;	Domain with optional projection
ProjDeclList	::= *ProjDecl* (, *ProjDecl*)∗ ;	Declaration of projection functions

D.6 Constructors and mappings

<table>
<tr><td>IdsDecl</td><td>::= IdList : SortExpr ;</td><td>Typed parameters</td></tr>
<tr><td>ConsSpec</td><td>::= cons (IdsDecl ;)+ ;</td><td>Declaration of constructors</td></tr>
<tr><td>MapSpec</td><td>::= map (IdsDecl ;)+ ;</td><td>Declaration of mappings</td></tr>
</table>

D.7 Equations

<table>
<tr><td>GlobVarSpec</td><td>::= glob (VarsDeclList ;)+ ;</td><td>Declaration of global variables</td></tr>
<tr><td>VarSpec</td><td>::= var (VarsDeclList ;)+ ;</td><td>Declaration of variables</td></tr>
<tr><td>EqnSpec</td><td>::= VarSpec? eqn EqnDecl+ ;</td><td>Definition of equations</td></tr>
<tr><td>EqnDecl</td><td>::= (DataExpr ->)? DataExpr = DataExpr ; ;</td><td>Conditional equation</td></tr>
</table>

D.8 Data expressions

<table>
<tr><td>VarDecl</td><td>::= Id : SortExpr ;</td><td>Typed variable</td></tr>
<tr><td>VarsDecl</td><td>::= IdList : SortExpr ;</td><td>Typed variables</td></tr>
<tr><td>VarsDeclList</td><td>::= VarsDecl (, VarsDecl)* ;</td><td>Individually typed variables</td></tr>
</table>

<table>
<tr><td>DataExpr</td><td>::= Id</td><td>Identifier</td></tr>
<tr><td></td><td>| Number</td><td>Number</td></tr>
<tr><td></td><td>| true</td><td>True</td></tr>
<tr><td></td><td>| false</td><td>False</td></tr>
<tr><td></td><td>| [ ]</td><td>Empty list</td></tr>
<tr><td></td><td>| { }</td><td>Empty set</td></tr>
<tr><td></td><td>| { : }</td><td>Empty bag</td></tr>
<tr><td></td><td>| [DataExprList]</td><td>List enumeration</td></tr>
<tr><td></td><td>| { BagEnumEltList }</td><td>Bag enumeration</td></tr>
<tr><td></td><td>| { VarDecl | DataExpr }</td><td>Set/bag comprehension</td></tr>
<tr><td></td><td>| { DataExprList }</td><td>Set enumeration</td></tr>
<tr><td></td><td>| (DataExpr)</td><td>Brackets</td></tr>
<tr><td></td><td>| DataExpr [DataExpr->DataExpr]</td><td>Function update; Left 13</td></tr>
<tr><td></td><td>| DataExpr (DataExprList)</td><td>Function application; Left 13</td></tr>
<tr><td></td><td>| ! DataExpr</td><td>Negation, set complement; Right 12</td></tr>
<tr><td></td><td>| - DataExpr</td><td>Unary minus; Right 12</td></tr>
<tr><td></td><td>| # DataExpr</td><td>Size of a list; Right 12</td></tr>
<tr><td></td><td>| forall VarsDeclList . DataExpr</td><td>Universal quantifier; Right 1</td></tr>
<tr><td></td><td>| exists VarsDeclList . DataExpr</td><td>Existential quantifier; Right 1</td></tr>
<tr><td></td><td>| lambda VarsDeclList . DataExpr</td><td>Lambda abstraction; Right 1</td></tr>
<tr><td></td><td>| DataExpr => DataExpr</td><td>Implication; Right 2</td></tr>
<tr><td></td><td>| DataExpr || DataExpr</td><td>Conjunction; Right 3</td></tr>
<tr><td></td><td>| DataExpr && DataExpr</td><td>Disjunction; Right 4</td></tr>
<tr><td></td><td>| DataExpr == DataExpr</td><td>Equality; Left 5</td></tr>
<tr><td></td><td>| DataExpr != DataExpr</td><td>Inequality; Left 5</td></tr>
<tr><td></td><td>| DataExpr < DataExpr</td><td>Smaller; Left 6</td></tr>
<tr><td></td><td>| DataExpr <= DataExpr</td><td>Smaller equal; Left 6</td></tr>
<tr><td></td><td>| DataExpr >= DataExpr</td><td>Larger equal; Left 6</td></tr>
<tr><td></td><td>| DataExpr > DataExpr</td><td>Larger; Left 6</td></tr>
</table>

	| *DataExpr* `in` *DataExpr*	Set, bag, list membership; Left 6
	| *DataExpr* `|>` *DataExpr*	List cons; Right 7
	| *DataExpr* `<|` *DataExpr*	List snoc; Left 8
	| *DataExpr* `++` *DataExpr*	List concatenation; Left 9
	| *DataExpr* `+` *DataExpr*	Addition, set/bag union; Left 10
	| *DataExpr* `-` *DataExpr*	Subtraction, set/bag difference; Left 10
	| *DataExpr* `/` *DataExpr*	Division; Left 11
	| *DataExpr* `div` *DataExpr*	Integer div; Left 11
	| *DataExpr* `mod` *DataExpr*	Integer mod; Left 11
	| *DataExpr* `*` *DataExpr*	Multiplication, set/bag intersection; Left
	| *DataExpr* `.` *DataExpr*	List element at position; Left 12
	| *DataExpr* `whr` *AssignmentList* `end`	Where clause; Left 0

DataExprUnit	::= *Id*	Identifier
	| *Number*	Number
	| `true`	True
	| `false`	False
	| `(` *DataExpr* `)`	Bracket
	| *DataExprUnit* `(` *DataExprList* `)`	Function application; Left 14
	| `!` *DataExprUnit*	Negation, set complement; Right 13
	| `-` *DataExprUnit*	Unary minus; Right 13
	| `#` *DataExprUnit*	Size of a list; Right 13

Assignment	::= *Id* `=` *DataExpr* ;	Assignment
AssignmentList	::= *Assignment* (`,` *Assignment*)* ;	Assignment list
DataExprList	::= *DataExpr* (`,` *DataExpr*)* ;	Data expression list
BagEnumElt	::= *DataExpr* `:` *DataExpr* ;	Bag element with multiplicity
BagEnumEltList	::= *BagEnumElt* (`,` *BagEnumElt*)* ;	Elements in a finite bag

D.9 Communication and renaming sets

ActIdSet	::= { *IdList* } ;	Action set
MultActId	::= *Id* (`|` *Id*)* ;	Multi-action label
MultActIdList	::= *MultActId* (`,` *MultActId*)* ;	Multi-action labels
MultActIdSet	::= { *MultActIdList*? } ;	Multi-action label set
CommExpr	::= *Id* `|` *MultActId* `->` *Id* ;	Action synchronization
CommExprList	::= *CommExpr* (`,` *CommExpr*)* ;	Action synchronizations
CommExprSet	::= { *CommExprList*? } ;	Action synchronization set
RenExpr	::= *Id* `->` *Id* ;	Action renaming
RenExprList	::= *RenExpr* (`,` *RenExpr*)* ;	Action renamings
RenExprSet	::= { *RenExprList*? } ;	Action renaming set

D.10 Process expressions

<table>
<tr><td>ProcExpr</td><td>::= Action</td><td>Action or process instantiation</td></tr>
<tr><td></td><td>| Id (AssignmentList?)</td><td>Process assignment</td></tr>
<tr><td></td><td>| delta</td><td>Delta, deadlock, inaction</td></tr>
<tr><td></td><td>| tau</td><td>Tau, hidden action, empty multi-action</td></tr>
<tr><td></td><td>| block (ActIdSet , ProcExpr)</td><td>Block or encapsulation operator</td></tr>
<tr><td></td><td>| allow (MultActIdSet , ProcExpr)</td><td>Allow operator</td></tr>
<tr><td></td><td>| hide (ActIdSet , ProcExpr)</td><td>Hiding operator</td></tr>
<tr><td></td><td>| rename (RenExprSet , ProcExpr)</td><td>Action renaming operator</td></tr>
<tr><td></td><td>| comm (CommExprSet , ProcExpr)</td><td>Communication operator</td></tr>
<tr><td></td><td>| (ProcExpr)</td><td>Brackets</td></tr>
<tr><td></td><td>| ProcExpr + ProcExpr</td><td>Choice operator; Left 1</td></tr>
<tr><td></td><td>| sum VarsDeclList . ProcExpr</td><td>Sum operator; Right 2</td></tr>
<tr><td></td><td>| ProcExpr || ProcExpr</td><td>Parallel operator; Right 3</td></tr>
<tr><td></td><td>| ProcExpr ||_ ProcExpr</td><td>Leftmerge operator; Right 4</td></tr>
<tr><td></td><td>| DataExprUnit -> ProcExpr</td><td>If-then operator; Right 5</td></tr>
<tr><td></td><td>| DataExprUnit IfThen ProcExpr</td><td>If-then-else operator; Right 5</td></tr>
<tr><td></td><td>| ProcExpr << ProcExpr</td><td>Until operator; Left 6</td></tr>
<tr><td></td><td>| ProcExpr . ProcExpr</td><td>Sequential composition operator; Right 7</td></tr>
<tr><td></td><td>| ProcExpr @ DataExprUnit</td><td>At operator; Left 8</td></tr>
<tr><td></td><td>| ProcExpr | ProcExpr</td><td>Communication merge; Left 9</td></tr>
<tr><td>ProcExprNoIf</td><td>::= Action</td><td>Action or process instantiation</td></tr>
<tr><td></td><td>| Id (AssignmentList?)</td><td>Process assignment</td></tr>
<tr><td></td><td>| delta</td><td>Delta, deadlock, inaction</td></tr>
<tr><td></td><td>| tau</td><td>Tau, hidden action, empty multi-action</td></tr>
<tr><td></td><td>| block (ActIdSet , ProcExpr)</td><td>Block or encapsulation operator</td></tr>
<tr><td></td><td>| allow (MultActIdSet , ProcExpr)</td><td>Allow operator</td></tr>
<tr><td></td><td>| hide (ActIdSet , ProcExpr)</td><td>Hiding operator</td></tr>
<tr><td></td><td>| rename (RenExprSet , ProcExpr)</td><td>Action renaming operator</td></tr>
<tr><td></td><td>| comm (CommExprSet , ProcExpr)</td><td>Communication operator</td></tr>
<tr><td></td><td>| (ProcExpr)</td><td>Brackets</td></tr>
<tr><td></td><td>| ProcExprNoIf + ProcExprNoIf</td><td>Choice operator; Left 1</td></tr>
<tr><td></td><td>| sum VarsDeclList . ProcExprNoIf</td><td>Sum operator; Right 2</td></tr>
<tr><td></td><td>| ProcExprNoIf || ProcExprNoIf</td><td>Parallel operator; Right 3</td></tr>
<tr><td></td><td>| ProcExprNoIf ||_ ProcExprNoIf</td><td>Leftmerge operator; Right 3</td></tr>
<tr><td></td><td>| DataExprUnit IfThen ProcExprNoIf</td><td>If-then-else operator; Right 4</td></tr>
<tr><td></td><td>| ProcExprNoIf << ProcExprNoIf</td><td>Until operator; Left 5</td></tr>
<tr><td></td><td>| ProcExprNoIf . ProcExprNoIf</td><td>Sequential composition operator; Right 6</td></tr>
<tr><td></td><td>| ProcExprNoIf @ DataExprUnit</td><td>At operator; Left 7</td></tr>
<tr><td></td><td>| ProcExprNoIf | ProcExprNoIf</td><td>Communication merge; Left 8</td></tr>
<tr><td>IfThen</td><td>::= -> ProcExprNoIf <> ;</td><td>Auxiliary if-then-else; Left 0</td></tr>
</table>

D.11 Actions

<table>
<tr><td>Action</td><td>::= Id ((DataExprList))? ;</td><td>Action, process instantiation</td></tr>
<tr><td>ActDecl</td><td>::= IdList (: SortExprList)? ; ;</td><td>Declarations of actions</td></tr>
<tr><td>ActSpec</td><td>::= act ActDecl+ ;</td><td>Action specification</td></tr>
</table>

MultAct	::= `tau`	Tau, hidden action, empty multi-action
	| *ActionList*	Multi-action
ActionList	::= *Action* (| *Action*)* ;	List of actions

D.12 Process and initial state declaration

ProcDecl	::= *Id* ((*VarsDeclList*))?=*ProcExpr* ; ;	Process declaration
ProcSpec	::= `proc` *ProcDecl*+ ;	Process specification
Init	::= `init` *ProcExpr* ; ;	Initial process

D.13 Data specification

DataSpec	::= (*SortSpec* | *ConsSpec* | *MapSpec* | *EqnSpec*)+ ;	Data specification

D.14 mCRL2 specification

mCRL2Spec	::= *mCRL2SpecElt** *Init* *mCRL2SpecElt** ;	MCRL2 specification
mCRL2SpecElt	::= *SortSpec*	Sort specification
	| *ConsSpec*	Constructor specification
	| *MapSpec*	Map specification
	| *EqnSpec*	Equation specification
	| *GlobVarSpec*	Global variable specification
	| *ActSpec*	Action specification
	| *ProcSpec*	Process specification

D.15 Boolean equation systems

BesSpec	::= *BesEqnSpec* *BesInit* ;	Boolean equation system
BesEqnSpec	::= `bes` *BesEqnDecl*+ ;	Boolean equation declaration
BesEqnDecl	::= *FixedPointOp* *BesVar* = *BesExpr* ; ;	Boolean fixed point equation
BesVar	::= *Id* ;	BES variable
BesExpr	::= `true`	True
	| `false`	False
	| *BesExpr* => *BesExpr*	Implication; Right 2
	| *BesExpr* || *BesExpr*	Disjunction; Right 3
	| *BesExpr* && *BesExpr*	Conjunction; Right 4
	| ! *BesExpr*	Negation; Right 5
	| (*BesExpr*)	Brackets
	| *BesVar*	Boolean variable
BesInit	::= `init` *BesVar* ; ;	Initial BES variable

D.16 Parameterized Boolean equation systems

PbesSpec	::=	*DataSpec*? *GlobVarSpec*? *PbesEqnSpec* *PbesInit* ;	PBES specification
PbesEqnSpec	::=	`pbes` *PbesEqnDecl*+ ;	Declaration of PBES equations
PbesEqnDecl	::=	*FixedPointOp* *PropVarDecl* = *PbesExpr* `;` ;	PBES equation
FixedPointOp	::=	`mu`	Minimal fixed point operator
	|	`nu`	Maximal fixed point operator
PropVarDecl	::=	*Id* (`(` *VarsDeclList* `)`)? ;	PBES variable declaration
PropVarInst	::=	*Id* (`(` *DataExprList* `)`)? ;	Instantiated PBES variable
PbesInit	::=	`init` *PropVarInst* `;` ;	Initial PBES variable
DataValExpr	::=	`val` `(` *DataExpr* `)` ;	Marked data expression

PbesExpr	::=	*DataValExpr*	Data expression
	|	`true`	True
	|	`false`	False
	|	`forall` *VarsDeclList* `.` *PbesExpr*	Universal quantifier; Right 0
	|	`exists` *VarsDeclList* `.` *PbesExpr*	Existential quantifier; Right 0
	|	*PbesExpr* `=>` *PbesExpr*	Implication; Right 2
	|	*PbesExpr* `||` *PbesExpr*	Disjunction; Right 3
	|	*PbesExpr* `&&` *PbesExpr*	Conjunction; Right 4
	|	`!` *PbesExpr*	Negation; Right 5
	|	`(` *PbesExpr* `)`	Brackets
	|	*PropVarInst*	Propositional variable

D.17 Action formulas

ActFrm	::=	*MultAct*	Multi-action; Left 10
	|	`(` *ActFrm* `)`	Brackets; Left 11
	|	*DataValExpr*	Boolean data expression; Left 20
	|	`true`	True
	|	`false`	False
	|	`!` *ActFrm*	Negation; Right 6
	|	`forall` *VarsDeclList* `.` *ActFrm*	Universal quantifier; Right 0
	|	`exists` *VarsDeclList* `.` *ActFrm*	Existential quantifier; Right 0
	|	*ActFrm* `@` *DataExpr*	At operator; Left 5
	|	*ActFrm* `&&` *ActFrm*	Intersection of actions; Right 4
	|	*ActFrm* `||` *ActFrm*	Union actions; Right 3
	|	*ActFrm* `=>` *ActFrm*	Implication; Right 2

D.18 Regular formulas

RegFrm	::=	*ActFrm*	Action formula; Left 20
	|	`(` *RegFrm* `)`	Brackets; Left 21
	|	`nil`	Empty regular formula
	|	*RegFrm* `.` *RegFrm*	Sequential composition; Right 1
	|	*RegFrm* `+` *RegFrm*	Alternative composition; Left 2
	|	*RegFrm* `*`	Iteration; Right 3
	|	*RegFrm* `+`	Nonempty iteration; Right 3

D.19 State formulas

StateFrm ::= *DataValExpr* Data expression; Left 20
| (*StateFrm*) Brackets; Left 20
| true True
| false False
| mu *StateVarDecl* . *StateFrm* Minimal fixed point; Right 1
| nu *StateVarDecl* . *StateFrm* Maximal fixed point; Right 1
| forall *VarsDeclList* . *StateFrm* Universal quantification; Right 2
| exists *VarsDeclList* . *StateFrm* Existential quantification; Right 2
| *StateFrm* => *StateFrm* Implication; Right 3
| *StateFrm* || *StateFrm* Disjunction; Right 4
| *StateFrm* && *StateFrm* Conjunction; Right 5
| [*RegFrm*] *StateFrm* Box modality; Right 6
| < *RegFrm* > *StateFrm* Diamond modality; Right 6
| ! *StateFrm* Negation; Right 7
| *Id* ((*DataExprList*))? Instantiated PBES variable
| delay (@ *DataExpr*)? Delay
| yaled (@ *DataExpr*)? Yaled

StateVarDecl ::= *Id* ((*StateVarAssignmentList*))? ; PBES variable declaration

StateVarAssignment
::= *Id* : *SortExpr* = *DataExpr* ; Typed variable with initial value

StateVarAssignmentList
::= *StateVarAssignment* (,
StateVarAssignment)* ; Typed variable list

D.20 Action rename specifications

ActionRenameSpec
::= (*SortSpec* |
ConsSpec |
MapSpec |
EqnSpec |
ActSpec |
ActionRenameRuleSpec)+ ; Action rename specification

ActionRenameRuleSpec
::= *VarSpec*? rename
ActionRenameRule+ ; Action rename rule section

ActionRenameRule
::= (*DataExpr* ->)? *Action* =>
ActionRenameRuleRHS ; ; Conditional action renaming

ActionRenameRuleRHS
::= *Action* Action
| tau Tau, hidden action, empty multi-action
| delta Delta, deadlock, inaction

Appendix E

Axioms for Processes

In this appendix all process axioms are grouped together. All axioms are valid in strongly timed bisimulation unless indicated otherwise. Those marked with a ‡ are not valid for timed processes.

MA1	$\alpha \mid \beta = \beta \mid \alpha$
MA2	$(\alpha \mid \beta) \mid \gamma = \alpha \mid (\beta \mid \gamma)$
MA3	$\alpha \mid \tau = \alpha$
MD1	$\tau \setminus \alpha = \tau$
MD2	$\alpha \setminus \tau = \alpha$
MD3	$\alpha \setminus (\beta \mid \gamma) = (\alpha \setminus \beta) \setminus \gamma$
MD4	$(a(d) \mid \alpha) \setminus a(d) = \alpha$
MD5	$(a(d) \mid \alpha) \setminus b(e) = a(d) \mid (\alpha \setminus b(e))$ if $a \not\equiv b$ or $d \not\approx e$
MS1	$\tau \sqsubseteq \alpha = \mathit{true}$
MS2	$a(d) \sqsubseteq \tau = \mathit{false}$
MS3	$a(d) \mid \alpha \sqsubseteq a(d) \mid \beta = \alpha \sqsubseteq \beta$
MS4	$a(d) \mid \alpha \sqsubseteq b(e) \mid \beta = a(d) \mid (\alpha \setminus b(e)) \sqsubseteq \beta$ if $a \not\equiv b$ or $d \not\approx e$
MAN1	$\underline{\tau} = \tau$
MAN2	$\underline{a(d)} = a$
MAN3	$\underline{\alpha \mid \beta} = \underline{\alpha} \mid \underline{\beta}$

A1	$x + y = y + x$
A2	$x + (y + z) = (x + y) + z$
A3	$x + x = x$
A4	$(x + y)\cdot z = x\cdot z + y\cdot z$
A5	$(x\cdot y)\cdot z = x\cdot(y\cdot z)$
A6	$\alpha + \delta = \alpha$
A6‡	$x + \delta = x$
A7	$\delta\cdot x = \delta$
Cond1	$\mathit{true}{\rightarrow}x \diamond y = x$
Cond2	$\mathit{false}{\rightarrow}x \diamond y = y$
THEN	$c{\rightarrow}x = c{\rightarrow}x \diamond \delta{}^{\backprime}0$
THEN‡	$c{\rightarrow}x = c{\rightarrow}x{\diamond}\delta$
SUM1	$\sum_{d:D} x = x$
SUM3	$\sum_{d:D} X(d) = X(e) + \sum_{d:D} X(d)$
SUM4	$\sum_{d:D}(X(d) + Y(d)) = \sum_{d:D} X(d) + \sum_{d:D} Y(d)$
SUM5	$(\sum_{d:D} X(d))\cdot y = \sum_{d:D} X(d)\cdot y$
TI	$t{\gg}x = \sum_{u:\mathbb{R}} u{>}t{\rightarrow}(x{}^{\backprime}u) + \delta{}^{\backprime}t$
TB	$x{\ll}t = \sum_{u:\mathbb{R}} u{<}t{\rightarrow}(x{}^{\backprime}u)$
TB1	$x \ll \alpha = x$
TB2	$x \ll \delta = x$
TB3	$x \ll y{}^{\backprime}t = \sum_{u:\mathbb{R}} u < t \rightarrow (x{}^{\backprime}u) \ll y$
TB4	$x \ll (y + z) = x \ll y + x \ll z$
TB5	$x \ll y\cdot z = x \ll y$
TB6	$x \ll \sum_{d:D} Y(d) = \sum_{d:D} x \ll Y(d)$
M	$x \parallel y = x \lfloor\!\lfloor y + y \lfloor\!\lfloor x + x \mid y$
LM1	$\alpha \lfloor\!\lfloor x = (\alpha \ll x)\cdot x$
LM1‡	$\alpha \lfloor\!\lfloor x = \alpha\cdot x$
LM2	$\delta \lfloor\!\lfloor x = \delta \ll x$
LM2‡	$\delta \lfloor\!\lfloor x = \delta$
LM3	$\alpha\cdot x \lfloor\!\lfloor y = (\alpha \ll y)\cdot(x \parallel y)$
LM3‡	$\alpha\cdot x \lfloor\!\lfloor y = \alpha\cdot(x \parallel y)$
LM4	$(x + y) \lfloor\!\lfloor z = x \lfloor\!\lfloor z + y \lfloor\!\lfloor z$
LM5	$(\sum_{d:D} X(d)) \lfloor\!\lfloor y = \sum_{d:D} X(d) \lfloor\!\lfloor y$
LM6	$x{}^{\backprime}t \lfloor\!\lfloor y = (x \lfloor\!\lfloor y){}^{\backprime}t$

S1	$x \mid y = y \mid x$
S2	$(x \mid y) \mid z = x \mid (y \mid z)$
S3	$x \mid \tau = x$
S4	$\alpha \mid \delta = \delta$
S5	$(\alpha \cdot x) \mid \beta = \alpha \mid \beta \cdot x$
S6	$(\alpha \cdot x) \mid (\beta \cdot y) = \alpha \mid \beta \cdot (x \parallel y)$
S7	$(x + y) \mid z = x \mid z + y \mid z$
S8	$(\sum_{d:D} X(d)) \mid y = \sum_{d:D} X(d) \mid y$
S9	$x {}^{\backprime} t \mid y = (x \mid y) {}^{\backprime} t$
TC1	$(x \mathbin{\lfloor\!\lfloor} y) \mathbin{\lfloor\!\lfloor} z = x \mathbin{\lfloor\!\lfloor} (y \parallel z)$
TC2	$x \mathbin{\lfloor\!\lfloor} \delta = x \cdot \delta$
TC3	$(x \mid y) \mathbin{\lfloor\!\lfloor} z = x \mid (y \mathbin{\lfloor\!\lfloor} z)$
R1	$\rho_R(\tau) = \tau$
R2	$\rho_R(a(d)) = b(d)$ if $a \to b \in R$ for some b
R3	$\rho_R(a(d)) = a(d)$ if $a \to b \notin R$ for all b
R4	$\rho_R(\alpha \mid \beta) = \rho_R(\alpha) \mid \rho_R(\beta)$
R5	$\rho_R(\delta) = \delta$
R6	$\rho_R(x + y) = \rho_R(x) + \rho_R(y)$
R7	$\rho_R(x \cdot y) = \rho_R(x) \cdot \rho_R(y)$
R8	$\rho_R(\sum_{d:D} X(d)) = \sum_{d:D} \rho_R(X(d))$
R9	$\rho_R(x {}^{\backprime} t) = \rho_R(x) {}^{\backprime} t$
T1	$x + \delta {}^{\backprime} 0 = x$
T2	$c \to x = c \to x \diamond \delta {}^{\backprime} 0$
T3	$x = \sum_{t:\mathbb{R}} x {}^{\backprime} t$
T4	$x {}^{\backprime} t \cdot y = x {}^{\backprime} t \cdot (t \gg y)$
T5	$x {}^{\backprime} t = t > 0 \to x {}^{\backprime} t$
TA1	$\alpha {}^{\backprime} t {}^{\backprime} u = (t \approx u) \to \alpha {}^{\backprime} t \diamond \delta {}^{\backprime} \min(t, u)$
TA2	$\delta {}^{\backprime} t {}^{\backprime} u = \delta {}^{\backprime} \min(t, u)$
TA3	$(x + y) {}^{\backprime} t = x {}^{\backprime} t + y {}^{\backprime} t$
TA4	$(x \cdot y) {}^{\backprime} t = x {}^{\backprime} t \cdot y$
TA5	$(\sum_{d:D} X(d)) {}^{\backprime} t = \sum_{d:D} X(d) {}^{\backprime} t$

C1 $\Gamma_C(\alpha) = \gamma_C(\alpha)$	C4 $\Gamma_C(x{\cdot}y) = \Gamma_C(x){\cdot}\Gamma_C(y)$
C2 $\Gamma_C(\delta) = \delta$	C5 $\Gamma_C(\sum_{d:D} X(d)) = \sum_{d:D} \Gamma_C(X(d))$
C3 $\Gamma_C(x{+}y) = \Gamma_C(x){+}\Gamma_C(y)$	C6 $\Gamma_C(x\text{‹}t) = \Gamma_C(x)\text{‹}t$
V1 $\nabla_V(\alpha) = \alpha$ if $\underline{\alpha} \in V \cup \{\tau\}$	V4 $\nabla_V(x+y) = \nabla_V(x) + \nabla_V(y)$
V2 $\nabla_V(\alpha) = \delta$ if $\underline{\alpha} \notin V \cup \{\tau\}$	V5 $\nabla_V(x{\cdot}y) = \nabla_V(x){\cdot}\nabla_V(y)$
V3 $\nabla_V(\delta) = \delta$	V6 $\nabla_V(\sum_{d:D} X(d)) = \sum_{d:D} \nabla_V(X(d))$
	V7 $\nabla_V(x\text{‹}t) = \nabla_V(x)\text{‹}t$
TV1 $\nabla_V(\nabla_W(x)) = \nabla_{V\cap W}(x)$	
E1 $\partial_B(\tau) = \tau$	E6 $\partial_B(x+y) = \partial_B(x) + \partial_B(y)$
E2 $\partial_B(a(d)) = a(d)$ if $a \notin B$	E7 $\partial_B(x{\cdot}y) = \partial_B(x){\cdot}\partial_B(y)$
E3 $\partial_B(a(d)) = \delta$ if $a \in B$	E8 $\partial_B(\sum_{d:D} X(d)) = \sum_{d:D} \partial_B(X(d))$
E4 $\partial_B(\alpha\|\beta) = \partial_B(\alpha)\|\partial_B(\beta)$	E9 $\partial_B(x\text{‹}t) = \partial_B(x)\text{‹}t$
E5 $\partial_B(\delta) = \delta$	E10 $\partial_H(\partial_{H'}(x)) = \partial_{H\cup H'}(x)$
H1 $\tau_I(\tau) = \tau$	H6 $\tau_I(x{+}y) = \tau_I(x) + \tau_I(y)$
H2 $\tau_I(a(d)) = \tau$ if $a \in I$	H7 $\tau_I(x{\cdot}y) = \tau_I(x){\cdot}\tau_I(y)$
H3 $\tau_I(a(d)) = a(d)$ if $a \notin I$	H8 $\tau_I(\sum_{d:D} X(d)) = \sum_{d:D} \tau_I(X(d))$
H4 $\tau_I(\alpha\|\beta) = \tau_I(\alpha)\|\tau_I(\beta)$	H9 $\tau_I(x\text{‹}t) = \tau_I(x)\text{‹}t$
H5 $\tau_I(\delta) = \delta$	H10 $\tau_I(\tau_{I'}(x)) = \tau_{I\cup I'}(x)$
U1 $\Upsilon_U(\tau) = \tau$	U6 $\Upsilon_U(x{+}y) = \Upsilon_U(x) + \Upsilon_U(y)$
U2 $\Upsilon_U(a(d)) = int$ if $a \in U$	U7 $\Upsilon_U(x{\cdot}y) = \Upsilon_U(x){\cdot}\Upsilon_U(y)$
U3 $\Upsilon_U(a(d)) = a(d)$ if $a \notin U$	U8 $\Upsilon_U(\sum_{d:D} X(d)) = \sum_{d:D} \Upsilon_U(X(d))$
U4 $\Upsilon_U(\alpha\|\beta) = \Upsilon_U(\alpha)\|\Upsilon_U(\beta)$	U9 $\Upsilon_U(x\text{‹}t) = \Upsilon_U(x)\text{‹}t$
U5 $\Upsilon_U(\delta) = \delta$	U10 $\Upsilon_U(\Upsilon_{U'}(x)) = \Upsilon_{U\cup U'}(x)$

Failures equivalence	F1‡	$a{\cdot}(b{\cdot}x{+}u) + a{\cdot}(b{\cdot}y{+}v) = a{\cdot}(b{\cdot}x{+}b{\cdot}y{+}u) + a{\cdot}(b{\cdot}x{+}b{\cdot}y{+}v)$
	F2‡	$a{\cdot}x + a{\cdot}(y{+}z) = a{\cdot}x + a{\cdot}(x{+}y) + a{\cdot}(y{+}z)$
Trace equivalence	RDIS	$x{\cdot}(y+z) = x{\cdot}y + x{\cdot}z$
Language equivalence	Lang1‡	$x{\cdot}\delta = \delta$
	RDIS	$x{\cdot}(y+z) = x{\cdot}y + x{\cdot}z$
Weak trace equivalence	RDIS	$x{\cdot}(y+z) = x{\cdot}y + x{\cdot}z$
	WT‡	$\tau{\cdot}x = x$
	W‡	$x{\cdot}\tau = x$

Rooted branching bisimulation	W‡ BRANCH‡	$x \cdot \tau = x$ $x \cdot (\tau \cdot (y + z) + y) = x \cdot (y + z)$
Rooted weak bisimulation	W‡ W2‡ W3‡	$x \cdot \tau = x$ $\tau \cdot x = \tau \cdot x + x$ $x \cdot (\tau \cdot y + z) = x \cdot (\tau \cdot y + z) + x \cdot y$

Rooted timed branching bisimulation
BT1 $a^{c}t \cdot (x + \delta^{c}t'') = a^{c}t \cdot (x \ll t' + x^{c}t' + \tau^{c}t' \cdot (x + \delta^{c}t''))$ if $t < t' < t''$
BT2 Let $M = \sup_{d:D}(t(d) \mid b(d))$. If $t' > M$ and $\forall u \in ActionTimes(y).\ \sup_{d:D}(t(d) \mid t(d) < u \wedge b(d)) = u$ then $a^{c}t \cdot (\sum_{d:D} b(d) \to \tau^{c}t(d) \cdot (x + y + \delta^{c}t') + x) = a^{c}t \cdot (x + y + \delta^{c}t')$

Appendix F

Answers to Exercises

2.1.1 It is not possible to give a precise answer to this question, because the relevant interactions depend very much on a concrete system. A possible answer is the following. CD player: *play*, *stop*, *pause*, *Backward*, *Forward*. Text editor: *insertLetter*, *deleteLetter*, *moreCursorRight*, *moveCursorLeft*, *moveCursorDown*, *saveFile*, *openFile*. Data transfer channel: *sendMessage*, *receiveMessage*, *sendUrgentMessage*, *resetChannel*.

2.2.2

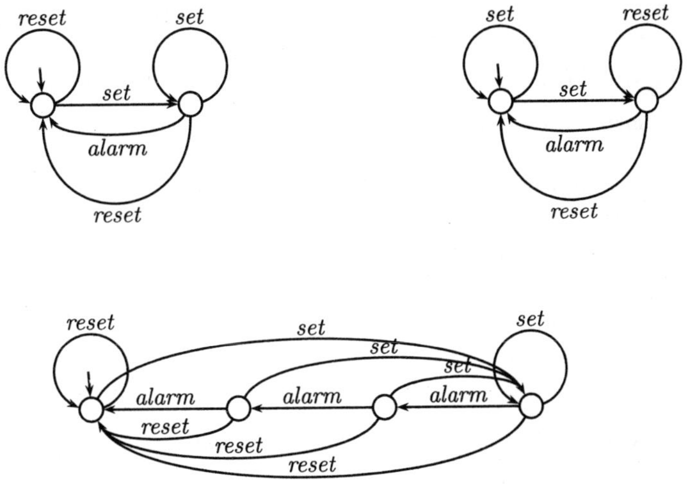

2.2.3 $(\{s_1, s_2\}, \{set, reset, alarm\}, \rightarrow, s_1, \emptyset)$ where

$$\rightarrow = \{(s_1, set, s_2), (s_2, alarm, s_2), (s_2, alarm, s_1), (s_2, reset, s_1)\}.$$

2.3.2 They are all pairwise trace equivalent.

2.3.6 (1) Neither failures nor language equivalent. (2) Language but not failures equivalent. (3) Both failures and language equivalent.

2.3.8 (1) No. (2) Yes. (3) No.

2.3.9 A sequence of a steps can unboundedly be extended in the transition systems to the right if the loop is chosen. None of the finite sequences at the left can mimic that.

2.3.10

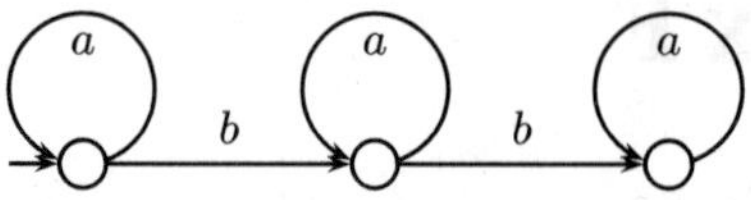

2.3.13 For reflexivity show that $\{\langle s, s\rangle \mid s \in S\}$ is a bisimulation relation. Hence, $s \leftrightarroweq s$ for all s. Likewise, show for symmetry that $\{\langle t, s\rangle \mid s \leftrightarroweq t\}$ is also a bisimulation relation. For transitivity, show that $\{\langle s, u\rangle \mid \exists t \in S. s \leftrightarroweq t \text{ and } t \leftrightarroweq u\}$ is a bisimulation relation.

2.4.6 (1) After doing an a action, branching bisimilar states are reached. (2) After doing the τ-action at the left a state is reached where only b can be done. The only way to mimic this τ-transition is by staying in the root in the diagram in the right. But in this state, an a can be done, which is not possible after doing the τ at the left.

2.4.7 (1) Branching bisimilar. Not rooted branching bisimilar. (2) Rooted branching bisimilar and hence branching bisimilar. (3) Neither rooted nor branching bisimilar.

2.4.8 All τ-transitions in the upper diagrams are inert. None of the τ's in the lower diagrams is inert.

2.4.11 The transition systems in figure 2.11 are rooted weakly bisimilar. The pair in figure 2.12 is not weakly bisimilar.

2.4.12 All pairs are weakly bisimilar. The first pair is not rooted weakly bisimilar. All τ-transitions are inert with respect to weak bisimulation.

2.4.13 Show that the relation $\{\langle s, t\rangle \mid s \leftrightarroweq_b t\}$ is a weak bisimulation relation.

3.1.2 **map** $\geq$: $Nat \times Nat \to \mathbb{B}$;
$<$: $Nat \times Nat \to \mathbb{B}$;
$>$: $Nat \times Nat \to \mathbb{B}$;
var $n, m{:}Nat$;
eqn $n \geq zero = true$;
$zero \geq successor(n) = false$;
$successor(n) \geq successor(m) = n \geq m$;
$successor(n) > zero = true$;
$zero > n = false$;
$successor(n) > successor(m) = n > m$;

3.1.3 **map** $minus, \max, power : Nat \times Nat \to Nat$;
var $m, n{:}Nat$;
eqn $power(successor(m), zero) = successor(zero)$;
$power(m, successor(n)) = times(m, power(m, n))$;
$\max(m, zero) = m$;
$\max(zero, m) = m$;
$\max(successor(n), successor(m)) = successor(\max(n, m))$;
$minus(m, zero) = m$;
$minus(zero, m) = zero$;
$minus(successor(m), successor(n)) = minus(m, n)$;

3.1.4 The first and second equation cause every occurrence of *true* and *false* to be replaced by $even(zero)$ and $even(successor(zero))$, making expressions unreadable. The third equation is even more problematic. It causes a term $even(m)$ for any m to be replaced by $even(successor(successor(m)))$, which is then in turn replaced by

$$even(successor(successor(successor(successor(m))))).$$

This goes on repeatedly, filling up memory and often also the stack, leading to some form of ungraceful termination (crash) of the rewriting tool.

3.1.5 $true = eq(zero, zero) = eq(zero, successor(zero)) = false.$

3.1.6 In both cases apply induction on Nat to m. Use also that it has been shown that $plus(zero, n) = n$.

3.1.7 First prove by induction on n that $less(n, n) = false$. Then $true = less(n, m) = less(n, n) = false$.

3.1.8 **sort** $\mathbb{B}, Nat, List, D;$
cons $[] :\to List;$
$in : D \times List \to List;$
map $append : D \times List \to List;$
$top, toe : List \to D;$
$tail, untoe : List \to List;$
$nonempty : List \to \mathbb{B};$
$length : List \to Nat;$
$+\!\!+ : List \times List \to List;$

var $d, e{:}D, q, q'{:}List;$
eqn $append(d, []) = in(d, []);$
$append(d, in(e, q)) = in(e, append(d, q));$
$top(in(d, q)) = d;$
$toe(in(d, [])) = d;$
$toe(in(d, in(e, q))) = toe(in(e, q));$
$tail(in(d, q)) = q;$
$untoe(in(d, [])) = [];$
$untoe(in(d, in(e, q))) = in(d, untoe(in(e, q)));$
$nonempty([]) = false;$
$nonempty(in(d, q)) = true;$
$length([]) = 0;$
$length(in(d, q)) = successor(length(q));$
$+\!\!+([], q) = q;$
$+\!\!+(in(d, q), q') = in(d, +\!\!+(q, q'));$

3.2.2 $d_1{\approx}d_1 = true$ and $d_2{\geq}d_2 = true$. All others can either be *true* or *false*.

3.2.4 $succ : \mathbb{N}^+ \to \mathbb{N}^+$, $succ : \mathbb{N} \to \mathbb{N}^+$, $succ : \mathbb{Z} \to \mathbb{Z}$, $succ : \mathbb{R} \to \mathbb{R}$. $pred : \mathbb{N}^+ \to \mathbb{N}$, $pred : \mathbb{N} \to \mathbb{Z}$, $pred : \mathbb{Z} \to \mathbb{Z}$, $pred : \mathbb{R} \to \mathbb{R}$.

3.2.5 0 is represented by $@c0$ and 1 by $@cNat(1)$. Suppose $@c0 = @cNat(1)$. Then $true = @c0 \leq @c0 = @cNat(1) \leq @c0 = false$. Contradiction.

3.2.6 $@cNat(cDub(@c1, false))|_{@c1} =$
$@last(@dm(cDub(@c1, false), @c1)) =$
$@last(@gdm(@dm(@c1, @c1), false, @c1)) =$
$@last(@gdm(@cPair(@cNat(@c1), @c0), false, @c1)) =$

$@last(@ggdm(@dub(false, @c0), @cNat(@c1), @c1)) =$
$@last(@ggdm(@c0, @cNat(@c1), @c1)) =$
$@last(@cPair(@dub(false, @cNat(@c1)), @c0)) =$
$@c0.$

3.3.3 $get(i, f) = f(i); assign(b, i, f) = f[i \to b]$.

3.4.4 $if\_then\_else = \lambda b{:}D{\times}D{\to}D, x, y{:}D.b(x, y)$.
$is\_zero = \lambda n{:}(D{\to}D){\to}D{\to}D.\lambda x, y{:}D.n(\lambda z{:}D.y)(x)$.
$is\_zero(\lambda f{:}D{\to}D.\lambda x{:}D.x) = \lambda x, y{:}D.x$.
$is\_zero(\lambda f{:}D{\to}D.\lambda x{:}D.f(x)) = \lambda x, y{:}D.y$.

3.4.1 **sort** $CheckSumType, Data$;
$MessageType =$ **struct** $ack \mid ctrl \mid mes$;
$Message =$ **struct** $frame(MessageType, CheckSumType, Data) \mid$
$frame(MessageType, CheckSumType)$;

3.5.1 **eqn** $map(f, []) = []$;
$map(f, n{\triangleright}L) = f(n) \triangleright map(f, L)$;

3.5.2 **map** $stretch : List(List(D)) \to List(D)$;
var $l : List(D)$;
$L : List(List(D))$;
eqn $stretch([]) = []$;
$stretch(l \triangleright L) = l{+\!\!+}stretch(L)$;

3.5.3 **map** $insert : D \times List(D) \to List(D)$;
var $s, s' : D$;
$L : List(D)$;
eqn $insert(s, []) = [s]$;
$insert(s, s' \triangleright L) = if(s{\approx}s', s \triangleright L, s' \triangleright insert(s, L))$;

or alternately,

var $s, s' : D$;
$L : List(D)$;
eqn $insert(s, []) = [s]$;
$insert(s, s \triangleright L) = s \triangleright L$;
$s{\not\approx}s' \to insert(s, s' \triangleright L) = s' \triangleright insert(s, L)$;

Prove that $insert(s, L)$ will never contains two equal elements assuming that L contains only unique elements. It then follows with induction on the number of $insert$ operations that created lists always contain only unique elements.

Note that the following solution is correct, but taken as a rewrite rule, it will not terminate for open terms. For example, the term $insert(s, L)$ with s and L variables can be rewritten ad infinitum.

map $insert : D \times List(D) \to List(D)$;
var $s : D$;
$L : List(D)$;
eqn $insert(s, L) = if(L{\approx}[], [s], if(s{\approx}head(L),$
$s \triangleright tail(L), head(L) \triangleright insert(s, tail(L))))$;

3.6.1 $\{m{:}\mathbb{N}^+ \mid m{>}1 \wedge \forall n{:}\mathbb{N}^+.2{\leq}n{<}m \Rightarrow m|_n{\not\approx}0\}$.

3.6.2 $\{l{:}List(\mathbb{N}) \mid \forall n{:}\mathbb{N}.(l.n){\approx}0\}$ and $\{l{:}List(\mathbb{N}) \mid \#l{\approx}2\}$.

4.2.3 1. τ. 2. $a(1)|b(2)$. 3. *false*.

4.2.4 The first case can be proven with structured induction on β, where the lemma is proven for all α and γ. Alternately, this case can also be derived from the equation proven in 4.2.1. The second follows as τ can be written as τ, $a(d)$ can be written as $a(d)|\tau$ (using MA3). Using the induction hypothesis $\alpha = a(d)|\alpha'$, we can show $\alpha|\beta = a(d)|(\alpha'|\beta)$ using MA2. In the third case, $\tau\sqsubseteq\tau = true$ and $a(d)|\alpha'\sqsubseteq a(d)|\alpha' \stackrel{\text{MS3}}{=} \alpha'\sqsubseteq\alpha' = true$.

4.3.1 1. $((a+a)\cdot(b+b))\cdot(c+c) \stackrel{\text{A3}}{=} (a\cdot b)\cdot c \stackrel{\text{A5}}{=} a\cdot(b\cdot c)$;

2. $(a+a)\cdot(b\cdot c)+(a\cdot b)\cdot(c+c) \stackrel{\text{A3}}{=} a\cdot(b\cdot c)+(a\cdot b)\cdot(c+c) \stackrel{\text{A5}}{=} (a\cdot b)\cdot c+(a\cdot b)\cdot(c+c) \stackrel{\text{A3}}{=} (a\cdot b)\cdot(c+c)+(a\cdot b)\cdot(c+c) \stackrel{\text{A3}}{=} (a\cdot b)\cdot(c+c) \stackrel{\text{A3}}{=} (a\cdot(b+b))\cdot(c+c)$.

4.3.2 Suppose $x \subseteq y$ and $y \subseteq x$. By definition we have (1) $x+y=y$ and (2) $y+x=x$. Thus we obtain: $x \stackrel{(2)}{=} y+x \stackrel{\text{A1}}{=} x+y \stackrel{(1)}{=} y$.

4.4.1 $x = x+\delta = x+x+y = x+y = \delta$.

4.5.1 $(n>0)\to down + (n>100)\to too\_large\_warning + up$.

4.5.2 1. $true \to x \diamond y = x = \neg true \to y \diamond x$.
$false \to x \diamond y = y = \neg false \to y \diamond x$.

2. $true\vee c' \to x \diamond y = true \to x \diamond y = x = true \to x \diamond (c' \to x \diamond y)$.
$false\vee c' \to x \diamond y = c' \to x \diamond y = false \to x \diamond (c' \to x \diamond y)$.

3. $x+y = x+y+true \to x \diamond y$ and $x+y = x+y+false \to x \diamond y$.

4. if $c = true$, then by the assumption $(c = true \Rightarrow x = y)$ we have $x = y$ and so $c \to x \diamond z = c \to y \diamond z$. if $c = false$, then $c \to x \diamond z = z = c \to y \diamond z$.

4.6.1 $\sum_{n:\mathbb{N}} read(n)\cdot((n < 100) \to forward(n) \diamond overflow)$.

4.6.2 SUM4 resembles A2 expressing that the order in which the sum/choice operators occur does not matter. SUM5 has a clear pendant in A4.

4.7.1 $X = \sum_{m:Message} read(m)\cdot forward(m)\cdot X$.
$X = \sum_{m:Message} read(m)\cdot(empty + forward(m))\cdot X$.

4.7.2 **proc** $CM1 = (get5ct\cdot(get5ct + get10ct) + get10ct)\cdot CM1;$

$$CM1 = \sum_{cream,sugar:\mathbb{B}} ask\_for\_additives(cream, sugar)\cdot serve\_coffee(cream, sugar)\cdot CM;$$

init CM;

4.7.3 **eqn** $multiplicity(i,a,n) = if(n\approx 0, 0, if(a(n-1)\approx i, 1, 0) + multiplicity(i,a,n-1))$;
$equalcontents(a,a',n) = \forall i{:}\mathbb{N}.multiplicity(i,a,n)\approx multiplicity(i,a',n)$;

4.7.4 We specify a coffee machine that pays back to the best of its abilities, but if it has no relevant coins left, it simply stops paying. Note that there are many other conceivable behaviors for this system. The parameter *cash* counts the number of coins in the machine. The parameter *paid* recalls how much is paid. The process name *CM* stands for coffee machine and *RM* for return money. Initially, the coffee machine has three coins of each kind. Note that the state space of this system is infinite, as unbounded numbers of coins can be inserted.

sort $Coin = \textbf{struct}\ coin1 \mid coin5 \mid coin10 \mid coin20 \mid coin50 \mid coin100 \mid coin200;$
map $can\_pay\_back : (Coin{\rightarrow}\mathbb{N}) \times \mathbb{N} \rightarrow \mathbb{B};$
$initial\_cash : Coin{\rightarrow}\mathbb{N};$
$value : Coin \rightarrow \mathbb{N}$
var $cash{:}Coin{\rightarrow}\mathbb{N}; paid{:}\mathbb{N};$
eqn $can\_pay\_back(cash, paid) = \exists c{:}Coin.(value(c) {\leq} paid \rightarrow cash(c){>}0);$
$initial\_cash(c) = 3;$
$value(coin1) = 1;$
$value(coin5) = 5;$
$value(coin10) = 10;$
$value(coin20) = 20;$
$value(coin50) = 50;$
$value(coin100) = 100;$
$value(coin200) = 200;$

proc $CM(cash{:}Coin{\rightarrow}\mathbb{N}, paid{:}\mathbb{N}) =$
$(paid \geq 25) \rightarrow get\_tea{\cdot}CM(cash, paid{-}25)$
$+ (paid \geq 45) \rightarrow get\_coffee{\cdot}CM(cash, paid{-}45)$
$+ \sum_{c:Coin} insert(c){\cdot}CM(cash[c{\rightarrow}(cash(c){+}1)], paid + value(c))$
$+ return\_money{\cdot}RM(cash, paid);$

proc $RM(cash{:}Coin{\rightarrow}\mathbb{N}, paid{:}\mathbb{N}) =$
$(can\_pay\_back(cash, paid))$
$\rightarrow \sum_{c:Coin}((cash(c){>}0){\rightarrow}return(c){\cdot}$
$RM(cash[c{\rightarrow}(cash(c){-}1)], paid{-}value(c)))$
$\diamond\ stop\_to\_pay\_back{\cdot}CM(cash, paid);$

init $CM(initial\_cash, 0);$

4.8.1 1. $a(\tau b + b) \stackrel{\text{A3}}{=} a(\tau(b+b)+b) \stackrel{\text{BRANCH}\ddagger}{=} a(b+b) \stackrel{\text{A3}}{=} ab.$

2. $a(\tau(b+c)+b) \stackrel{\text{BRANCH}\ddagger}{=} a(b+c) \stackrel{\text{A1}}{=} a(c+b) \stackrel{\text{BRANCH}\ddagger}{=} a(\tau(c+b)+c) \stackrel{\text{A1}}{=} a(\tau(b+c)+c).$

3. If $x + y = x$, then $\tau(\tau x + y) = \tau(\tau(x+y)+y) \stackrel{\text{BRANCH}\ddagger}{=} \tau(x+y) = \tau x.$

4.8.2 We only provide the nontrivial cases.
BRANCH‡ $x{\cdot}(\tau{\cdot}(y+z)+y) \stackrel{\text{W2}\ddagger}{=} x{\cdot}(\tau{\cdot}(y+z)+(y+z)+y) \stackrel{\text{A3}}{=} x{\cdot}(\tau{\cdot}(y+z)+(y+z)) \stackrel{\text{W2}\ddagger}{=} x{\cdot}(\tau{\cdot}(y+z)) \stackrel{\text{W}\ddagger}{=} x{\cdot}(y+z).$
W2‡ $\tau{\cdot}x \stackrel{\text{A3}}{=} \tau{\cdot}x+\tau{\cdot}x \stackrel{\text{WT}\ddagger}{=} \tau{\cdot}x+x.$
W3‡ $x{\cdot}(\tau{\cdot}y{+}z) \stackrel{\text{RDIS}}{=} x{\cdot}\tau{\cdot}y{+}x{\cdot}z \stackrel{\text{A3}}{=} x{\cdot}\tau{\cdot}y{+}x{\cdot}z{+}x{\cdot}\tau{\cdot}y \stackrel{\text{RDIS}}{=} x{\cdot}(\tau{\cdot}y{+}z){+}x{\cdot}\tau{\cdot}y \stackrel{\text{W}\ddagger}{=} x{\cdot}(\tau{\cdot}y+z)+x{\cdot}y.$

5.1.1 $a{\cdot}(b{\cdot}c{+}c{\cdot}b + b|c) + c{\cdot}a{\cdot}b + (a|c){\cdot}b.$

5.1.2 Approximately two pages.

5.1.3 $x \parallel y = x \mathbin{\lfloor\!\lfloor} y + y \mathbin{\lfloor\!\lfloor} x + x|y = y \parallel x.$
$x \parallel (y \parallel z) =$
$x \mathbin{\lfloor\!\lfloor} (y \parallel z) + (y \parallel z) \mathbin{\lfloor\!\lfloor} x + x|(y \parallel z) =$
$x \mathbin{\lfloor\!\lfloor} (y \parallel z) + (y \mathbin{\lfloor\!\lfloor} z) \mathbin{\lfloor\!\lfloor} x + (z \mathbin{\lfloor\!\lfloor} y) \mathbin{\lfloor\!\lfloor} x + (y|z) \mathbin{\lfloor\!\lfloor} x + x|(y \mathbin{\lfloor\!\lfloor} z) + x|(z \mathbin{\lfloor\!\lfloor} y) + x|(y|z) =$
$x \mathbin{\lfloor\!\lfloor} (y \parallel z) + y \mathbin{\lfloor\!\lfloor} (x \parallel z) + z \mathbin{\lfloor\!\lfloor} (x \parallel y) + y|(z \mathbin{\lfloor\!\lfloor} x) + x|(y \mathbin{\lfloor\!\lfloor} z) + x|(z \mathbin{\lfloor\!\lfloor} y) + x|(y|z).$
The expression $(x \parallel y) \parallel z$ can similarly be expanded.

5.2.1 1. $c(1)|d$. 2. $c(1)|b(2)$.
3. $(d_1{\approx}e_1 \wedge d_2{\approx}e_2) \to c(d_1, d_2) + (d_1{\not\approx}e_1 \vee d_2{\not\approx}e_2) \to (a(d_1, d_2)|b(e_1, e_2))$.

5.2.2 $c|d$ and $e|b$; e and $c|d$.

5.3.1 The node in the middle is the root node.

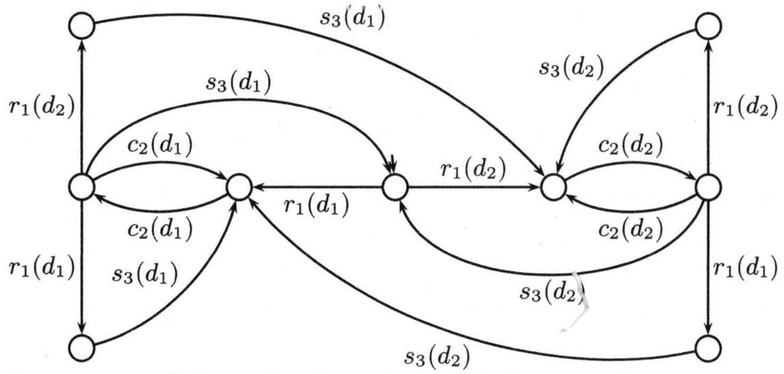

Data elements are read via gate 1 and sent via gate 3 in the same order.

Two shortest execution traces of $\nabla_{\{r_1,c_2\}}(S)$ to a deadlock state are $r_1(d_1)\, c_2(d_1)\, r_1(d_1)$ and $r_1(d_1)\, c_2(d_1)\, r_1(d_2)$.

5.3.2 **act** $r_1, s_2, r_2, c_2, s_3, r_3, c_3, s_4, s_5{:}D$;
proc $X(b{:}\mathbb{B}) = \sum_{d:D} r_1(d)\cdot(b \to s_2(d) \diamond s_3(d))\cdot X(\neg b)$;
$Y = \sum_{d:D} r_2(d)\cdot s_4(d)\cdot Y$;
$Z = \sum_{d:D} r_3(d)\cdot s_5(d)\cdot Z$;
init $\nabla_{\{r_1,s_4,s_5,c_2,c_3\}}(\Gamma_{\{s_2|r_2\to c_2,s_3|r_3\to c_3\}}(X \parallel Y \parallel Z))$;

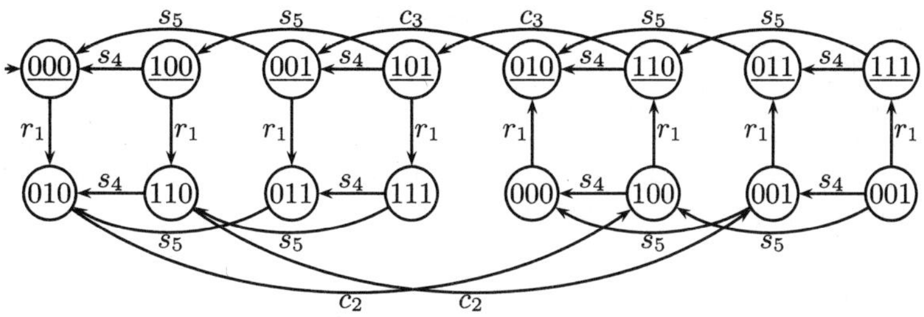

The three bits in the states denote whether there is a datum in the buffer of Y, X, or Z, respectively. In an underlined state the next incoming datum is sent on via gate 2; otherwise via gate 3. The initial state is <u>000</u>.

5.4.1 1. b. 2. $b + b|b$. 3. δ.

5.5.1

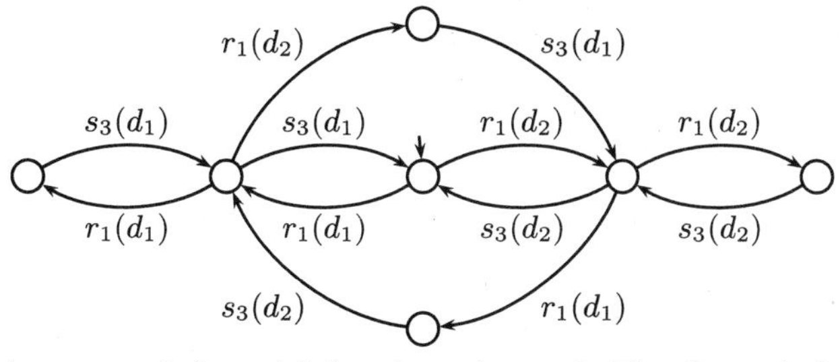

The reduced state space is deterministic and contains no τ's. Therefore, reducing it further using weak bisimulation or weak trace equivalence does not make sense.

5.6.4 $e{\cdot}f + f{\cdot}e$.

6.1.1 1. $\langle a\rangle(\langle b\rangle \mathit{true} \wedge \neg\langle c\rangle \mathit{true})$. 2. $[a]\neg(\langle b\rangle \mathit{true} \vee \langle c\rangle \mathit{true})$. 3. $[b]\mathit{false} \vee [a][b]\mathit{false}$.

6.1.2 Use the identities between modal formulas. The modalities containing c_1 and c_2 can be removed.

6.1.3 $a{\cdot}(b+c)$ and δ.

6.2.1 1. $[\overline{\mathit{error}}^\star]\langle \mathit{true}\rangle \mathit{true}$. 2. $[\mathit{true}^\star{\cdot}a]\langle \mathit{true}^\star{\cdot}(b \cup c)\rangle \mathit{true}$. 3. $[\mathit{true}^\star{\cdot}a{\cdot}\overline{b}^\star]\langle \mathit{true}^\star{\cdot}b\rangle \mathit{true}$.

6.2.2 The first formula says that after a *send* done in the initial state, there is a path on which a *receive* can happen. The second formula says that whenever a *send* happens in a state reachable from the initial state, then there is a path to a *receive*. The latter is generally what one wants to express.

6.2.3 Use the rules in table 6.2. $[R_1{\cdot}(R_2 + R_3)]\phi = [R_1]([R_2]\phi \wedge [R_3]\phi) = [R_1][R_2]\phi \wedge [R_1][R_3]\phi = [R_1{\cdot}R_2{+}R_1{\cdot}R_2]\phi$. The case with the diamond modalities is similar.

6.3.1 The formula $\mu X.[a]X$ is invalid for an a-loop, whereas the formula $\nu X.[a]X$ is valid. As $\nu X.[a]X$ is equivalent to true, there is no transition system for which the minimal fixed point formula holds, and the maximal one does not.

6.3.2 $(a+Y)$ with $Y = b{\cdot}Y$.

6.3.3 The first formula says that after an a the action b must be done within a finite number of steps. The second one says that an action b only needs to be possible after an a within a finite number of steps. The process $a{\cdot}(b+c)$ makes the second formula valid and not the first. The first formula implies the second.

6.3.4 The formula $[\mathit{true}^\star{\cdot}a]\langle \mathit{true}^\star{\cdot}b\rangle \mathit{true}$ equals $\nu X.([\mathit{true}]X \wedge [a]\mu Y.(\langle \mathit{true}\rangle Y \vee \langle b\rangle \mathit{true}))$. The minimal fixed point variable Y can be reached from X, but X not from Y.

6.3.5 The process P with $P = \mathit{send}{\cdot}P + \mathit{receive}{\cdot}\delta$ makes the first formula valid, and the second invalid.

6.3.6 The first formula says that each sequence consisting of only a and b actions ends in an infinite sequence of a's. The second expresses that each sequence of a and b actions contains only finite subsequences of a's. The first formula is valid and the second is not valid for the process P defined by $P = a{\cdot}P$.

6.4.1

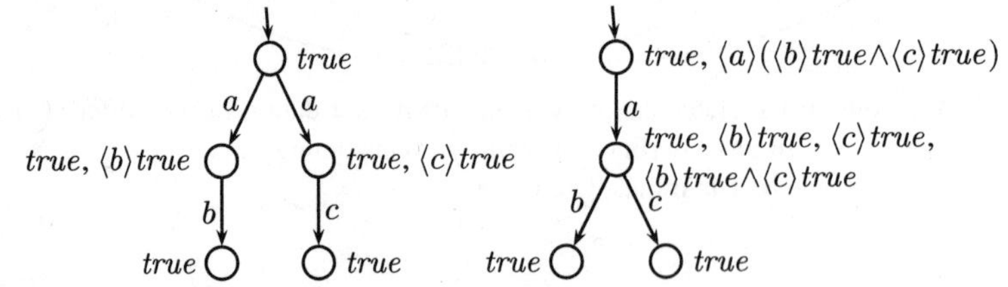

6.4.2 $\langle a\rangle[b]\mathit{false}$, $\langle a\rangle[c]\mathit{false}$, $\langle a\rangle(\langle b\rangle \mathit{true} \wedge \langle c\rangle\langle d\rangle \mathit{true})$.

6.5.1 $\forall n, m{:}\mathbb{N}.[\mathit{true}^\star{\cdot}\mathit{generate}(n)\mathit{true}^\star{\cdot}\mathit{generate}(m)](m{>}n)$.

6.5.2 $\forall f{:}\mathbb{N} \to \mathbb{N}.[\mathit{true}^\star{\cdot}\mathit{deliver}(f)]\forall n{:}\mathbb{N}.f(n{+}1){>}f(n)$.

6.5.3 $\forall p{:}\mathit{Product}.\nu X(n{:}\mathbb{N}{:=}0).$

$$[\overline{\mathit{enter}(p) \cup \mathit{leave}(p)}]X(n) \wedge$$
$$[\mathit{enter}(p)]X(n{+}1) \wedge [\mathit{leave}(p)]X(n{-}1) \wedge$$
$$\mu Y(n'{:}\mathbb{N}{:=}n).((n' \approx 0) \vee ([\overline{\mathit{enter}(p) \cup \mathit{leave}(p)}]Y(n') \wedge$$
$$[\mathit{enter}(p)]Y(n'{+}1) \wedge [\mathit{leave}(p)]Y(n'{-}1) \wedge \langle \mathit{true}\rangle \mathit{true})).$$

7.3.1 Properties 3, 5, and 6 are valid. The others are not valid.

7.3.2 According to requirement 2, the scanner must be manually movable out of the scanning room, meaning that no brake is applied, the motor is off, and the platform is undocked. But this contradicts the first requirement saying that when undocked, the brakes must be applied and the bed is in the outermost position. Most likely it is needed to weaken requirement 2, and rethink the procedure in case of an emergency.

8.1.1 (a) Properly timed LTS, no time deadlock. The idle transition at 3 is superfluous. (b) Proper, two time deadlocks. (c) Improper, as $3.1 < 4$. (d) Proper, one time deadlock in the initial state. The idle transition at 3.1 can be omitted.

8.1.2 

8.2.2 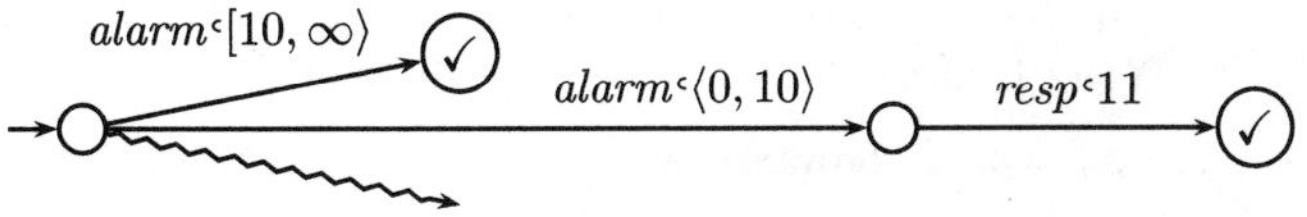

8.2.3 $A_1 = (\{s_1\}, \emptyset, \emptyset, \rightsquigarrow^1, s_1, \emptyset)$ and $A_2 = (\{s_2\}, \emptyset, \emptyset, \rightsquigarrow^2, s_2, \emptyset)$ where $s_1 \rightsquigarrow_t^1$ holds iff $t < 2$ and $s_2 \rightsquigarrow_t^2$ holds iff $t \leq 2$. The second transition system can be drawn using a single $\rightsquigarrow_2$ transition from the initial state. The first one is hard to draw, because there is no largest real number, smaller than 2.

8.3.2 None of the transition systems are timed strongly bisimilar.

8.3.3 The transition systems in (a) and (c) are strongly bisimilar. The transition system in (b) has the option to idle to 2 at which time the $a`2$ can be done no longer.

8.3.7 The τ is an internal step that can take place at any time. Therefore, ignoring the τ does not disable y as there is always a τ that can be chosen to enable it. As both x and y can idle until infinity, the τ cannot disable the behavior of x and y.

8.4.2 **proc** $\mathit{DriftingClock}(t{:}\mathbb{R}) =$

$$\textstyle\sum_{u:\mathbb{R}}(t{+}1{-}\epsilon{\leq}u{\leq}t{+}1{+}\epsilon) \rightarrow \mathit{tick}`u{\cdot}\mathit{DriftingClock}(t{+}1);$$

8.4.3 The coffee machine can be described by

$$\begin{aligned}
\textbf{proc}\ \mathit{CM} = {} & \textstyle\sum_{t:\mathbb{R}} \mathit{coin}`t\cdot \\
& \textstyle\sum_{u`\mathbb{R}}((u \leq t{+}10) \\
& \quad \rightarrow \big(\mathit{selectCoffee}`u \textstyle\sum_{v`\mathbb{R}}(v{\leq}u{+}5) \rightarrow \mathit{coffee}`v + \\
& \qquad \mathit{selectTea}`u \textstyle\sum_{v`\mathbb{R}}(v{\leq}u{+}5) \rightarrow \mathit{tea}`v\big) \\
& \quad \diamond\ \mathit{returnCoin}`u)\cdot \mathit{CM};
\end{aligned}$$

8.4.4 1. Induction on b.

2. $a \overset{\text{A6}}{=} a + \delta = a + \sum_{u:\mathbb{R}} \delta`u \overset{\text{SUM3}}{=} a + \sum_{u:\mathbb{R}} \delta`u + \delta`t = a + \delta + \delta`t = a + \delta`t.$

3. $\delta`4{+}\delta`2 = \delta`4{+}\delta`2`4 = (\delta{+}\delta`2)`4 = (\sum_{t:\mathbb{R}} \delta`t{+}\delta`2)`4 \overset{\text{SUM3}}{=} (\sum_{t:\mathbb{R}} \delta`t)`2 = \delta`2.$

8.4.5 $x`t{\cdot}a`t \overset{\text{T4}}{=} x`t{\cdot}(t{\gg}a`t) \overset{\text{TI}}{=} x`t{\cdot}(\sum_{u:\mathbb{R}} u{>}t{\rightarrow}a`t`u + \delta`t) \overset{\text{TA1}}{=}$ $x`t{\cdot}(\sum_{u:\mathbb{R}} u{>}t{\rightarrow}(t{\approx}u{\rightarrow}a`t{\diamond}\delta`\min(t,u)) + \delta`t) = x`t{\cdot}(\sum_{u:\mathbb{R}} u{>}t{\rightarrow}\delta`t + \delta`t) =$ $x`t{\cdot}\delta`t.$

8.4.6 $a`1{\cdot}c`2{\cdot}b`3.$

8.4.7 Induction on $\mathbb{B}$. If $c = \mathit{false}$, the equation reduces to $x \ll \delta`0 = \delta`0$ which is provable using TB2, TB3, and T5.

8.4.8 $a{}^{\varsigma}1{\cdot}(b{}^{\varsigma}3+\tau{}^{\varsigma}2{\cdot}c{}^{\varsigma}4) =$
$a{}^{\varsigma}1{\cdot}(b{}^{\varsigma}3+\tau{}^{\varsigma}2{\cdot}c{}^{\varsigma}4+\delta{}^{\varsigma}2.1) \stackrel{\text{BT1}}{=}$
$a{}^{\varsigma}1{\cdot}((b{}^{\varsigma}3+\tau{}^{\varsigma}2{\cdot}c{}^{\varsigma}4)\ll 2+(b{}^{\varsigma}3+\tau{}^{\varsigma}2{\cdot}c{}^{\varsigma}4){}^{\varsigma}2+\tau{}^{\varsigma}2{\cdot}(b{}^{\varsigma}3+\tau{}^{\varsigma}2{\cdot}c{}^{\varsigma}4+\delta{}^{\varsigma}2.1)) =$
$a{}^{\varsigma}1{\cdot}(\delta{}^{\varsigma}2+\tau{}^{\varsigma}2{\cdot}c{}^{\varsigma}4+\tau{}^{\varsigma}2{\cdot}(b{}^{\varsigma}3+\delta{}^{\varsigma}2+\delta{}^{\varsigma}2.1)) =$
$a{}^{\varsigma}1{\cdot}(\tau{}^{\varsigma}2{\cdot}c{}^{\varsigma}4+\tau{}^{\varsigma}2{\cdot}b{}^{\varsigma}3) = \cdots =$
$a{}^{\varsigma}1{\cdot}(\tau{}^{\varsigma}2{\cdot}b{}^{\varsigma}3+c{}^{\varsigma}4)$.

8.5.1 $[\mathit{true}^\star](\Delta\vee\langle\mathit{true}\rangle\mathit{true})$. $\langle\mathit{true}^\star\rangle(\nabla\wedge[\mathit{true}]\mathit{false})$.

8.5.2 $[\mathit{true}^\star]\forall p{:}\mathit{Product}, t{:}\mathbb{R}.[\mathit{enter}(p){}^{\varsigma}t]$
$\mu X.([\forall u{:}\mathbb{R}.u{\leq}t+5\wedge \overline{\mathit{leave}(p){}^{\varsigma}u}]X\wedge\langle\mathit{true}\rangle\mathit{true})$.
$\exists m{:}\mathbb{N}.\nu X(n{:}\mathbb{N}{:=}0, \mathit{sum}{:}\mathbb{R}{:=}0).\forall p{:}\mathit{Product}, t, u{:}\mathbb{R}.[\overline{\mathit{enter}(p)\cup\mathit{leave}(p)}^\star\cdot$
$\mathit{enter}(p){}^{\varsigma}t{\cdot}\overline{\mathit{enter}(p)\cup\mathit{leave}(p)}^\star{\cdot}\mathit{leave}(p){}^{\varsigma}u]$
$(X(n{+}1, \mathit{sum}{+}u{-}t)\wedge(n{>}m\Rightarrow\frac{\mathit{sum}}{n}{\leq}3))$.

9.1.4 Assume $p_1 = q_1, \ldots, p_n = q_n$ are provable. We list these assumptions below as items 1 to n.

$1.\quad \Gamma\vdash p_1 = q_1$

$\vdots$

$n.\quad \Gamma\vdash p_n = q_n$
$n{+}1. \Gamma\vdash f = f$ reflexivity
$n{+}2. \Gamma\vdash f\,p_1 = f\,q_1$ congruence using 1 and $n{+}1$
$n{+}3. \Gamma\vdash f\,p_1\,p_2 = f\,q_1\,p_2$ congruence using 2 and $n{+}2$

$\vdots$

$2n.\quad \Gamma\vdash f\,p_1\,p_2\ldots p_{n-1} = f\,q_1\,q_2\ldots q_{n-1}$ congruence using $n{-}1$ and $2n{-}1$
$2n{+}1\Gamma\vdash f\,p_1\,p_2\ldots p_{n-1}\,p_n = f\,q_1\,q_2\ldots q_{n-1}\,q_n$ congruence using n and $2n$

Note that $f\,p_1\,p_2\ldots p_{n-1}\,p_n$ and $f(p_1, p_2, \ldots, p_{n-1}, p_n)$ are alternative ways of writing the same object.

9.1.5 By η-conversion we find $\lambda x{:}D.p = \lambda y{:}D.((\lambda x{:}D.p)y)$. We know using β-conversion that $(\lambda x{:}D.p)y = p[x{:=}y]$. If y does not occur in the context, we are able to derive $\lambda y{:}D.(\lambda x{:}D.p)y = \lambda y{:}D.p[x{:=}y]$. Using transitivity α-conversion follows.

9.2.3 We need to put the condition $d' = e$ in context in order to use it, via the $\Rightarrow$ introduction rule. Then it is necessary to put $\lambda d'{:}D$ around the left and right-hand side using the abstraction rule. But this is not allowed as d' occurs in the context.

9.3.2 α-conversion yields $\lambda d{:}D.X(d) = \lambda e{:}D.X(e)$. Put Σ in front using congruence.

9.3.3 Write p for $\sum_{d:D}\sum_{e:E}X(d,e)$. Note that d and e do not occur freely in p. Assume that the context Γ contains at least SUM1. We derive

1. $\Gamma\vdash\sum_{d:D}x = x$ by start using that SUM1 is in Γ;
2. $\Gamma\vdash\sum_{e:E}x = x$ by start using that SUM1 is in Γ;
3. $\Gamma\vdash\sum_{d:D}p = p$ by substitution using 1;
4. $\Gamma\vdash\sum_{e:E}\sum_{d:D}p = \sum_{d:D}p$ by substitution using 2;
5. $\Gamma\vdash\sum_{e:E}\sum_{d:D}p = p$ by transitivity using 3 and 4.

9.4.2 First note that $x{}^{\varsigma}t \stackrel{\text{T5}}{=} (t{>}0){\rightarrow}x{}^{\varsigma}t$ for any $t{:}\mathbb{R}$. Using lambda abstraction, congruence, and SUM1, it follows that $x = \sum_{t:\mathbb{R}}x{}^{\varsigma}t = \sum_{t:\mathbb{R}}(t{>}0)\rightarrow x{}^{\varsigma}t$.

9.4.3 ($\subseteq$) By SUM3

$$\sum_{d:D} c(d) \rightarrow x = \sum_{d:D} c(d) \rightarrow x + c(e) \rightarrow x = \sum_{d:D} c(d) \rightarrow x + x.$$

So $x \subseteq \sum_{d:D} c(d) \rightarrow x$.

($\supseteq$) If $b = \mathit{true}$ then $b \rightarrow x = x$, and if $b = \mathit{false}$ then $b \rightarrow x = \delta{}^{c}0 \subseteq x$, so $b \rightarrow x \subseteq x$. By substitution of $c(d)$ for b it follows that $c(d) \rightarrow x \subseteq x$ where d does not occur in the context. Then by abstraction, congruence, SUM4, and SUM1 $\sum_{d:D} c(d) \rightarrow x \subseteq x$.

9.5.1 1. $\Gamma \cup \{\mathit{true} = \mathit{true} \Rightarrow x = y\} \vdash \mathit{true} = \mathit{true} \Rightarrow x = y$ start (generalized);

2. $\Gamma \cup \{\mathit{true} = \mathit{true} \Rightarrow x = y\} \vdash \mathit{true} = \mathit{true}$ reflexivity;

3. $\Gamma \cup \{\mathit{true} = \mathit{true} \Rightarrow x = y\} \vdash x = y$ modus ponens using 1 and 2;

4. $\Gamma \cup \{\mathit{true} = \mathit{true} \Rightarrow x = y\} \vdash \lambda z{:}\mathbb{P}.\mathit{true} \rightarrow z = \lambda z{:}\mathbb{P}.\mathit{true} \rightarrow z$ reflexivity;

5. $\Gamma \cup \{\mathit{true} = \mathit{true} \Rightarrow x = y\} \vdash (\lambda z{:}\mathbb{P}.\mathit{true} \rightarrow z)x = (\lambda z{:}\mathbb{P}.\mathit{true} \rightarrow z)y$ congruence using 3 and 4;

6. $\Gamma \cup \{\mathit{true} = \mathit{true} \Rightarrow x = y\} \vdash (\lambda z{:}\mathbb{P}.\mathit{true} \rightarrow z)x = \mathit{true} \rightarrow x$ β-conversion;

7. $\Gamma \cup \{\mathit{true} = \mathit{true} \Rightarrow x = y\} \vdash (\lambda z{:}\mathbb{P}.\mathit{true} \rightarrow z)y = \mathit{true} \rightarrow y$ β-conversion;

8. $\Gamma \cup \{\mathit{true} = \mathit{true} \Rightarrow x = y\} \vdash \mathit{true} \rightarrow x = (\lambda z{:}\mathbb{P}.\mathit{true} \rightarrow z)x$ symmetry from 6;

9. $\Gamma \cup \{\mathit{true} = \mathit{true} \Rightarrow x = y\} \vdash \mathit{true} \rightarrow x = (\lambda z{:}\mathbb{P}.\mathit{true} \rightarrow z)y$ transitivity 5 and 8;

10. $\Gamma \cup \{\mathit{true} = \mathit{true} \Rightarrow x = y\} \vdash \mathit{true} \rightarrow x = \mathit{true} \rightarrow y$ transitivity from 7 and 9;

11. $\Gamma \vdash (\mathit{true} = \mathit{true} \Rightarrow x = y) \Rightarrow \mathit{true} \rightarrow x = \mathit{true} \rightarrow y$ $\Rightarrow$ introduction from 10.

9.5.2 Use induction on c_1, and within that induction on c_2.

9.5.3

$$\frac{\Gamma \vdash \phi[x{:=}@c1], \quad \Gamma \vdash \phi[x{:=}p] \Rightarrow \phi[x{:=}@cDub(b,p)]}{\Gamma \vdash \phi} \text{ induction on } \mathbb{N}^+$$

$$\frac{\Gamma \vdash \phi[x{:=}@c0], \quad \Gamma \vdash \phi[x{:=}@cNat(p)]}{\Gamma \vdash \phi} \text{ induction on } \mathbb{N}$$

$$\frac{\Gamma \vdash \phi[x{:=}@cInt(n)], \quad \Gamma \vdash \phi[x{:=}@cNeg(p)]}{\Gamma \vdash \phi} \text{ induction on } \mathbb{Z}$$

9.5.4 ($\supseteq$) By SUM3

$$\sum_{b:\mathbb{B}} b \rightarrow x \diamond y = \sum_{b:\mathbb{B}} b \rightarrow x \diamond y + \mathit{true} \rightarrow x \diamond y + \mathit{false} \rightarrow x \diamond y = \sum_{b:\mathbb{B}} b \rightarrow x \diamond y + x + y.$$

So $x + y \subseteq \sum_{b:\mathbb{B}} b \rightarrow x \diamond y$.

($\subseteq$) $\mathit{true} \rightarrow x \diamond y = x \subseteq x + y$ and $\mathit{false} \rightarrow x \diamond y = y \subseteq x + y$, so by induction on Booleans $b \rightarrow x \diamond y \subseteq x + y$. Then by abstraction, congruence, SUM4, and SUM1 $\sum_{b:\mathbb{B}} b \rightarrow x \diamond y \subseteq x + y$.

9.5.5 Using SUM3, it can be shown that $X(0) + X(1) + X(2) \subseteq \sum_{n:\mathbb{N}} n \leq 2 \rightarrow X(n)$. Using induction on n, it can be shown that $n \leq 2 \rightarrow X(n) \subseteq X(0) + X(1) + X(2)$. This is intricate, when done precisely using the induction principles. A possibility is to use the induction principle for $\mathbb{N}$, and within that the induction principle for $\mathbb{N}^+$. A more hand waving proof can be given by assuming that either $n \leq 2$ or $n > 2$. In the first case, it is generally known that n can only be 0, 1, or 2, and hence the result follows. In the second case the left-hand side is equal to $\delta@0$ and the proof follows using axiom T1.

9.5.6 To prove the second rule from the first assume some given formula ϕ, for which $\phi(1)$, $\phi(n) \Rightarrow \phi(2n)$ and $\phi(n) \Rightarrow \phi(2n+1)$ can be proven. Define the operator

$$\psi = \lambda n{:}\mathbb{N}.\forall i{:}\mathbb{N}.(2^{n-1} \leq i < 2^n) \rightarrow \phi(i).$$

For ψ it can be shown that $\psi(1)$ and $\psi(n) \Rightarrow \psi(n+1)$. Hence, from rule 1 we conclude that $\psi(n)$ for any n. From this $\phi(n)$ follows.
In order to prove the first rule from the second, define $\psi = \lambda n{:}\mathbb{N}^+.\phi(f(n))$ where $f = \lambda n{:}\mathbb{N}^+.\min(\lceil {}^2\log(n) \rceil, 1)$. Use that $f(2^n) = n$, $f(2n) = 1+f(n)$ for $n > 1$ and $f(2n+1) = 1+f(n)$ for $n > 1$.

9.6.4 Show that X is a solution for Y. So, it must be shown that $X = a{\cdot}a{\cdot}a{\cdot}X + a{\cdot}a{\cdot}X$. Prove this using the defining equation for X and axiom A3.

9.6.5 First show that $Y = Y{\cdot}\delta$ by showing that $Y{\cdot}\delta$ is a solution for Y. This leads to the proof obligation that $Y{\cdot}\delta = a{\cdot}(Y{\cdot}\delta){\cdot}\delta$. It is now straightforward to show that Y is a solution for X by proving $Y = a{\cdot}Y$. This follows from the defining equation for Y by removing the δ at the end.

9.6.6 Show that $\lambda l{:}List(\mathbb{N}).X(\#(l))$ is a solution for Y. Remove the sum operator with SUM1.

9.6.7 Show that $\lambda n{:}\mathbb{N}.X(n|_N)$ is a solution for Y. Use the calculation rules in section 3.2.2.

9.6.8 Show that $\lambda n{:}\mathbb{N}^+.(n{\approx}1 {\rightarrow} X + n{\approx}2 {\rightarrow} b{\cdot}c{\cdot}X + n{\approx}3 {\rightarrow} c{\cdot}X)$ is a solution for Y.

9.6.9 Define an auxiliary process Z by $Z(n{:}\mathbb{N}) = n{\approx}0 {\rightarrow} X {\diamond} \nabla_{\{a,b\}}(b \| Z(n-1))$. Show that Z is a solution for Y by induction on n. If $n = 0$, it must be shown that $Z(0) = a{\cdot}Z(1)$, $Z(1) = a{\cdot}Z(2) + b{\cdot}Z(0)$. If $n = m{+}1$ with $m > 1$, the proof obligation is $Z(m{+}1) = a{\cdot}Z(m{+}2) + b{\cdot}Z(m)$. Note that a required identity, easily provable with RSP, is $Z(m) = \nabla_{\{a,b\}}(Z(m))$. Thus, with RSP, $Y(n) = Z(n)$ and in particular $X = Z(0) = Y(0)$.

9.7.1 The conclusion from KFAR is $\tau{\cdot}\tau_{\{head\}}(X) = \tau{\cdot}\tau_{\{head\}}(tail)$.

9.7.2 $\tau{\cdot}y = \tau{\cdot}y + \delta = \tau{\cdot}\tau{\cdot}y + \delta$. Hence, using the wrong KFAR we can conclude $\tau{\cdot}y = \tau{\cdot}\delta$.

9.7.3 Define $Y_1 = i{\cdot}Y_2 + a_1$ and $Y_2 = i_1{\cdot}Y_1 + a_2$. Using RSP it immediately follows that $\rho_{\{i_1 \rightarrow i\}}(Y_1) = X_1$. Define $Y_1' = i{\cdot}Y_2' + a_1$ and $Y_2' = \tau{\cdot}Y_1' + a_2$. Obviously, $\tau_{\{i_1\}}(Y_1) = Y_1'$. Define $Y_1'' = i{\cdot}Y_2'' + a_1$ and $Y_2'' = \tau{\cdot}Y_1'' + a_1 + a_2$. Using RSP and W2‡ it follows that $Y_1'' = Y_1'$. Define $Y_1''' = i{\cdot}Y_2''' + a_1$ and $Y_2''' = i_1{\cdot}Y_1''' + a_1 + a_2$. Then, $\tau_{\{i_1\}}(Y_1''') = Y_1''$. Define $Y_1'''' = i{\cdot}Y_2'''' + a_1$ and $Y_2'''' = i{\cdot}Y_1'''' + a_1 + a_2$ and $\rho_{\{i_1 \rightarrow i\}}(Y_1''') = Y_1''''$. Wrapping up:

$$\begin{array}{l} \tau_{\{i\}}(X_1) = \tau_{\{i\}}(\rho_{\{i_1 \rightarrow i\}}(Y_1)) = \tau_{\{i\}}(\rho_{\{i_1 \rightarrow i\}}(\tau_{\{i_1\}}(Y_1))) = \\ \tau_{\{i\}}(\rho_{\{i_1 \rightarrow i\}}(Y_1')) = \tau_{\{i\}}(\rho_{\{i_1 \rightarrow i\}}(Y_1'')) = \tau_{\{i\}}(\rho_{\{i_1 \rightarrow i\}}(\tau_{\{i_1\}}(Y_1'''))) = \\ \tau_{\{i\}}(\rho_{\{i_1 \rightarrow i\}}(Y_1''')) = \tau_{\{i\}}(Y_1''''). \end{array}$$

In the same way one can show that $\tau_{\{i\}}(Y_1'''') = \tau_{\{i\}}(Z_1)$ where Z_1 is defined by $Z_1 = i{\cdot}Z_2 + a_1 + a_2$ and $Z_2 = i{\cdot}Z_1 + a_1 + a_2$. It is obvious that Z is a solution for Z_1 and Z_2 when Z is defined by $Z = i{\cdot}Z + a_1 + a_2$, and so, using RSP, $Z = Z_1$. Using KFAR for weak bisimulation $\tau_{\{i\}}(Z) = \tau{\cdot}(a_1{+}a_2)$. Combining all results yields:

$$\tau_{\{i\}}(X_1) = \tau_{\{i\}}(Y_1'''') = \tau_{\{i\}}(Z_1) = \tau_{\{i\}}(Z) = \tau{\cdot}(a_1{+}a_2).$$

This proof follows the outline given in [173] in which it is shown that the cluster fair abstraction rule is provable from KFAR in weak bisimulation. $\tau_{\{i\}}(X_1)$ is not rooted branching bisimilar to $\tau{\cdot}(a_1{+}a_2)$ and therefore they cannot be proven equal using the axioms for branching bisimulation. The actual situation is more severe. Also $\tau{\cdot}\tau_{\{i\}}(X_1) = \tau{\cdot}(a_1{+}a_2)$ is not provable from KFAR in branching bisimulation.

9.8.1 $S = a{\cdot}S + d{\cdot}S_1, \quad S_1 = a{\cdot}S_1 + c{\cdot}S.$

10.1.4 Substitute $\lambda n{:}\mathbb{N}, b{:}\mathbb{B}.b{\to}X \diamond s_2(n){\cdot}X$ in Y.

10.1.5 $Z(n{:}\mathbb{N}^+) = (n{\approx}1){\to}a{\cdot}Z(2) + (n{\approx}2){\to}b{\cdot}Z(1) + (n{\approx}1){\to}b{\cdot}Z(3) +$
$(n{\approx}3){\to}a{\cdot}Z(4) + (n{\approx}4){\to}a{\cdot}Z(2) + (n{\approx}4){\to}a{\cdot}Z(1).$
$Z(n{:}\mathbb{N}^+) = (n{\not\approx}2){\to}a{\cdot}Z((n{+}1)|_4) + (n{<}2){\to}b{\cdot}Z((n{+}2)|_4).$
$Z(n{:}\mathbb{N}, c{:}\mathbb{B}) = \sum_{m:\mathbb{N}} a(m){\cdot}Z(m, \mathit{false}) +$
$\neg c{\to}b(n){\cdot}Z(n, \mathit{true}) + \neg c{\to}b(n^2){\cdot}Z(n, \mathit{true}).$
The equation for Y is unguarded and has no unique solution. It does not define a process.

10.1.8 $X(n{:}\mathbb{N}^+) = (n{\leq}2){\to}a{\cdot}X(n{+}1) + (n{\approx}3){\to}b{\cdot}X(1).$

10.2.9 The process declaration is captured by $Z(\mathit{true})$, where

$$Z(b'{:}\mathbb{B}) = b'{\to}a{\cdot}Z(\mathit{false}) + b'{\to}b{\cdot}Z(\mathit{false}) + \neg b'{\to}d{\cdot}Z(\mathit{true}).$$

10.2.10 $X(pc{:}\mathbb{N}^+) =$
$(pc{\approx}1){\to}a{\cdot}X(2) + (pc{\approx}2){\to}a{\cdot}X(1) + (pc{\approx}2){\to}b{\cdot}X(4) +$
$(pc{\approx}3){\to}b{\cdot}X(4) + (pc{\approx}4){\to}a{\cdot}X(2) + (pc{\approx}4){\to}b{\cdot}X(4);$

10.2.11 $X_1(pc{:}\mathbb{N}^+, n{:}\mathbb{N}) =$
$\sum_{m:\mathbb{N}}(pc{\approx}1){\to}a(m){\cdot}X_1(2, m) +$
$\sum_{m:\mathbb{N}}(pc{\approx}2){\to}a(m){\cdot}X_1(2, m) +$
$(pc{\approx}2){\to}c(n){\cdot}X_1(1, 0);$
$X_2 = \sum_{n:\mathbb{N}} a(n){\cdot}X_2;$
$\mathit{Stack} = \textbf{struct}\ \mathit{empty}?\mathit{isEmpty} \mid \mathit{push}(\mathit{getpc}{:}\mathbb{N}^+, \mathit{getn}{:}\mathbb{N}, \mathit{pop}{:}\mathit{Stack});$
$X_3(s{:}\mathit{Stack}) =$
$\sum_{n:\mathbb{N}}(\mathit{getpc}(s){\approx}1){\to}a(n){\cdot}X(\mathit{push}(2, n, \mathit{pop}(s))) +$
$\sum_{n:\mathbb{N}}(\mathit{getpc}(s){\approx}2){\to}a(n){\cdot}X(\mathit{push}(2, n, \mathit{push}(3, n, \mathit{pop}(s)))) +$
$(\mathit{empty}(\mathit{pop}(s)) \wedge \mathit{getpc}(s){\approx}2){\to}c(n) + 4$
$(\neg\mathit{empty}(\mathit{pop}(s)) \wedge \mathit{getpc}(s){\approx}2){\to}c(n){\cdot}X(\mathit{pop}(s)) + 4$
$(\mathit{empty}(\mathit{pop}(s)) \wedge \mathit{getpc}(s){\approx}3){\to}c(n) +$
$(\neg\mathit{empty}(\mathit{pop}(s)) \wedge \mathit{getpc}(s){\approx}3){\to}c(n){\cdot}X(\mathit{pop}(s));$

10.2.12 $X(pc{:}\mathbb{N}^+) = (pc{\approx}1){\to}a{}^{\backprime}3{\cdot}X(2) + (pc{\approx}2){\to}c{}^{\backprime}4{\cdot}X(1);$
$Y(pc{:}\mathbb{N}^+, n{:}\mathbb{N}) = \sum_{m:\mathbb{N}}(pc{\approx}1){\to}r(m){\cdot}Y(2, m)$
$+ (pc{\approx}2 \wedge n{>}10){\to}a{}^{\backprime}n{\cdot}Y(1, n);$

10.2.14 $B_1(b{:}\mathbb{B}, d{:}D) = \sum_{d':D} b{\to}r_1(d'){\cdot}B_1(\neg b, d') + \neg b{\to}s_3(d){\cdot}B_1(\neg b, d).$
$B_2(b{:}\mathbb{B}, d{:}D) = \sum_{d':D} b{\to}r_3(d'){\cdot}B_2(\neg b, d') + \neg b{\to}s_2(d){\cdot}B_2(\neg b, d).$
$X(b_1{:}\mathbb{B}, d_1{:}D, b_2{:}\mathbb{B}, d_2{:}D) =$
$\sum_{d':D} b_1{\to}r_1(d'){\cdot}X(\neg b_1, d', b_2, d_2) +$
$\neg b_1{\wedge}b_2{\to}\tau{\cdot}X(\neg b_1, d_1, \neg b_2, d_1) +$
$\neg b_2{\to}s_2(d_2){\cdot}X(b_1, d_1, \neg b_2, d_2).$

10.2.15 $S(n, n'{:}\mathbb{N}^+) = \sum_{t:\mathbb{R}}(n{\leq}t \leq n{+}1 \wedge n'{+}0.5{\leq}t{\leq}n'{+}1.5) \to c{}^{\backprime}t{\cdot}S(n{+}2, n'{+}2).$

10.2.17 As no communication can take place, a single C can do an $on(1)$ and an $\mathit{off}(1)$ and it will then deadlock.

10.3.13 We prove that $\mathcal{I}_i$ is an invariant for the LPE X in definition 10.1.1. That is,

$$\mathcal{I}_i(d) \wedge h(d, e) \Rightarrow \mathcal{I}_i(g(d, e)) \text{ for } i = 1, 2.$$

If $i = 1$, then we obtain $\mathit{true}{\wedge}h(d, e) \Rightarrow \mathit{true}$, which is true.
If $i = 2$, then we obtain $\mathit{false}{\wedge}h(d, e) \Rightarrow \mathit{false}$, which is true.

10.3.14 Use the invariant $b_1 \vee b_2 = true$.

11.1.3 $\{s_0 \xrightarrow{\tau} s_1, s_2 \xrightarrow{\tau} s_3\}, \emptyset,$
$\{s_0 \xrightarrow{\tau} s_1, s_2 \xrightarrow{\tau} s_3, s_4 \xrightarrow{\tau} s_5\}, \{s_3 \xrightarrow{\tau} s_5, s_4 \xrightarrow{\tau} s_5\}$.

11.1.4 $\{s_0 \xrightarrow{\tau} s_1\}, \emptyset, \{s_0 \xrightarrow{\tau} s_1\}$.

11.1.7 In order to prove the existence of a unique maximal τ-confluent set of τ-transitions for an infinite state transition system it is necessary to consider an infinite collection of sets U_i ($i \in I$) of τ-confluent sets. It must be shown that U, defined by

$$U = \bigcup_{i \in I} U_i,$$

is τ-confluent.

11.2.6 Prioritizing transition systems 1, 3, and 7 maintains branching bisimulation, in accordance with the theory.

11.3.3 (1) Confluent. (2) Not confluent. (3) Confluent.

12.1.3 $FC(n) = n|_3 \not\approx 2$, $M(n) = n|_3$ and $h(n) = n|_3 \not\approx 1$.

12.1.4 Note that from $n \approx 3m$ it follows that $m \approx n$ div 3 (but not vice versa). Therefore, the condition $n \approx 3m$ is equivalent to $n \approx 3m \wedge m \approx n$ div 3. Applying the sum elimination theorem simplifies the condition to $n \approx 3(m \text{ div } 3)$. This is equivalent to $n|_3 \approx 0$. In this way the first summand of exercise 12.1.3 is obtained. The second and third summand can be obtained in a similar way.

12.1.5 The focus condition for n:N is: $\exists m$:N.$(n = 3m \vee n = 3m + 1)$.

$$\mathcal{I}(n) = \begin{cases} \mathit{true} & \text{if } \exists m{:}\mathbb{N}(n = 3m \vee n = 3m + 2) \\ \mathit{false} & \text{if } \exists m{:}\mathbb{N}(n = 3m + 1) \end{cases}$$

The matching criteria are fulfilled for all n with $\mathcal{I}(n) = true$:

- $n = 3m + 2 \Rightarrow \phi(n) = \phi(n + 1) = nil$;
- $n = 3m \Rightarrow h'_a(\phi(n)) = true$;
- $n = 3m \Rightarrow n = 3m$;
- actions do not carry data parameters;
- $n = 3m \Rightarrow \phi(n + 2) = nil$.

13.1.2 Each τ-transition loses the possibility to execute one of the $leader(n)$-actions at the end.

13.1.3 The network is defined by

$$\textbf{proc } S = \tau_{\{c\}} \nabla_{\{c,leader\}} \Gamma_{\{r|s \to c\}}$$
$$(Node(1, \{2, 3\}, 0) \parallel Node(2, \{1, 3\}, 0) \parallel Node(3, \{1, 2\}, 0));$$

No node can start sending a parent request.

13.2.1 $(1+x|_n)|_n = (x|_n+1)|_n = (x+1)|_n = (1+x)|_n$.

13.2.2 $2013^{2013}|_5 = (2013|_5)^{2013}|_5 = 3^{2013}|_5 = (81^{503} \cdot 3)|_5 = (1^{503} \cdot 3)|_5 = 3|_5 = 3$.

14.1.1 $X = false, Y = false; X = false, Y = true; X = true, Y = true; X = false, Y = false$;

14.1.2 $(false, false, false), (true, true, true), (true, false, true)$.

14.1.3 See exercise 14.1.5.

14.1.4 $(false, false, false), (true, true, true), (true, false, true)$.

14.1.5 Solutions are $X_1 = X_2 = true$; $X_1 = Y_1 = X_2 = Y_2 = false$; $X_1 = X_2 = Y_1 = Y_2 = true$.

14.3.2 See the example.

14.3.3 **pbes** $\nu\tilde{X}_1(n{:}\mathbb{N}){=}\tilde{X}_1(n{+}1) \wedge (n{>}0{\rightarrow}\tilde{X}_1(n{-}1)) \wedge (true{\vee}n{>}0)$;
init $X_1(0)$;

pbes $\nu\tilde{X}_2(n{:}\mathbb{N}){=}\tilde{X}_2(n{+}1) \vee (n{>}0{\wedge}\tilde{X}_2(n{-}1)) \vee false \vee n{>}0$;
init $\tilde{X}_2(0)$;

pbes $\nu\tilde{X}_3(m,n{:}\mathbb{N}){=}\tilde{X}_3(m{+}1,n{+}1) \wedge ((false{\wedge}n{>}0){\rightarrow}\tilde{X}_3(m{+}1,n{-}1)){\wedge}$
$(false{\rightarrow}(m{>}0 \wedge \tilde{X}_3(m{-}1,n{+}1))){\wedge}$
$(n{>}0{\rightarrow}(m{>}0 \wedge \tilde{X}_3(m{-}1,n{-}1)))$;
init $\tilde{X}_3(0,0)$;

14.3.4 $\nu\tilde{X}_1(m{:}\mathbb{N}){=}\tilde{X}_1(m{+}1) \wedge \tilde{X}_2(0,m)$, $\mu\tilde{X}_2(n,m{:}\mathbb{N}){=}\tilde{X}_2(n{+}1,m) \vee n{\geq}m$. Note the free variable m that must be added to the equation of $\tilde{X}_2$. The property is represented by $\tilde{X}_1(0)$.

14.3.5 $\nu\tilde{X}_1(n{:}\mathbb{N},u{:}\mathbb{R}){=}\tilde{X}_1(n{+}1,n) \wedge \forall r{:}\mathbb{R}.(r{<}n{\vee}r{\leq}u)$,
$\nu\tilde{X}_2(u{:}\mathbb{R}){=}\forall t{:}\mathbb{R}.(t{>}u{\rightarrow}\tilde{X}_2(t)) \wedge \forall r{:}\mathbb{R}.(\exists t{:}\mathbb{R}.r{<}t \vee r{\leq}u)$.

14.4.1 The answer is *false*.

14.4.2 The answer is *false*.

14.4.5 $X_0 = false$.

14.4.8 $X(n) = false$; $X(n) = n{\approx}0{\vee}n{\approx}1$; $X(b) = false$.

14.4.10 $\mu X(n{:}\mathbb{N}){=}\exists i{:}\mathbb{N}.n{-}i{\approx}0$, or equivalently $\mu X(n{:}\mathbb{N}){=}true$.
$\nu X(n{:}\mathbb{N}){=}\forall j{:}\mathbb{N}.n/2^j{<}1$, which is equivalent to $\nu X(n{:}\mathbb{N}){=}n{<}1$.

14.4.11 $X(0) = true$.

14.4.14 $\nu Z_1{=}\forall v{:}\mathbb{N}.Z_2(0,v,v)$,
$\nu Z_2(j{:}\mathbb{N},n,v{:}\mathbb{N}){=}(\forall m{:}\mathbb{N}.m{<}n{\rightarrow}Z_2(j{+}1,m,v)) \wedge j{\leq}v$.
Use the invariant $j{+}n{\leq}v$ to remove the condition $j{\leq}v$ from the right-hand side of Z_2. Using iterative approximation it can be seen that the solution for the reduced Z_2 is *true* for initial values satisfying $j{+}n{\leq}v$. Consequently, the solution for Z_1 is $true$.

15.1.19 1. $\mathbb{N}^+$, $\mathbb{N}$, $\mathbb{Z}$ and $\mathbb{R}$. Well-typed of type $\mathbb{N}^+$. 2. Well-typed of type $Set(\mathbb{R})$. 3. Types are $List(D)$ for any type D. Not well-typed. Incomparable minimal types are $List(\mathbb{B})$ and $List(\mathbb{N}^+)$. 4. $\mathbb{B}$. Well-typed. 5. $\mathbb{B}$. Well-typed. 6. $\mathbb{B}$. Well-typed.

15.1.21 1. Yes. 2. No. 3. Yes.

15.1.24 1. $\lambda z_1{:}\mathbb{N}.\lambda z_2{:}\mathbb{N}.z_1{+}z_2{+}u$. 2. $\lambda z{:}\mathbb{N}.x$. 3. $\lambda u{:}\mathbb{N}.\lambda y{:}\mathbb{N}.u$. 4. $\lambda u{:}\mathbb{N}, y{:}\mathbb{N}.u$.

15.1.34 Yes. One can for instance use the following interpretation. Note that *eq* cannot be interpreted as equality.

$$[\![true]\!]{=}\mathbf{true},\ [\![false]\!]{=}\mathbf{false},\ [\![zero]\!]{=}0,\ [\![t2(n)]\!]{=}1,\ [\![t2p1(n)]\!]{=}1.$$
$$[\![eq(n,m)]\!] = \begin{cases} true & \text{if } [\![n]\!]{=}0 \text{ and } [\![m]\!]{=}0, \\ false & \text{otherwise.} \end{cases}$$

15.1.35 It suffices to add the following two equations.

var $m, n : myNat$
eqn $eq(t2(m), t2(n)) = eq(m, n);$
$eq(t2p1(m), t2p1(n)) = eq(m, n);$

15.2.19 The only possible action transition for $\partial_{\{b\}}(a^{c}1 + b^{c}2)$ is action $\mathbf{a}$ at time $\mathbf{1}$ leading to termination. Idle transitions are possible from the initial state for any positive time value less than $\mathbf{2}$.

As for $a^{c}1 \| b^{c}2$, the only initial action transition is $\mathbf{a}$ at $\mathbf{1}$ resulting in $1 \gg b^{c}2$. From the latter state, action $\mathbf{b}$ at $\mathbf{2}$ can follow leading to termination. The initial state affords idle transitions for any time value less than $\mathbf{1}$; the intermediate state can perform idle transitions for any value less than $\mathbf{2}$.

Bibliography

[1] W. van der Aalst and C. Stahl. *Modeling business processes: A Petri net oriented approach.* MIT Press, Cambridge, MA, 2011.

[2] M. Abadi and L. Lamport. The existence of refinement mappings. *Theoretical Computer Science*, 82(2):253–284, 1991.

[3] L. Aceto, A. Ingolfsdottir, K.G. Larsen, and J. Srba. *Reactive systems: modelling, specification and verification*. Cambridge University Press, Cambridge, U.K., 2007.

[4] P. Aczel. *Non-well-founded sets*. CSLI Publications, Stanford, CA, 1988.

[5] A. Aho and J. Ullman. *The theory of parsing, translation, and compiling, Vol. 2: Compiling*. Prentice Hall, Englewood Cliffs, NJ, 1973.

[6] R. Alur and T.A. Henzinger. Logics and models of real time: A survey. In *Real time: Theory in practice*. Lecture notes in computer science, Vol. 600 (pp. 74–106), Springer-Verlag, Berlin, Germany, 1992.

[7] H.R. Andersen, C. Stirling, and G. Winskel. A compositional proof system for the modal μ-calculus. In *Proceedings of the IEEE symposium on logic in computer science (LICS'94)* (pp. 144–153), 1994.

[8] L. Åqvist. Deontic logic. In D. Gabbay and F. Guenthner, (eds.), *Handbook of philosophical logic: Vol. II, Extensions of classical logic*. Kluwer, Dordrecht, The Netherlands, 1994.

[9] M. Atif. *Formal modelling and verification of distributed failure detectors*. Ph.D. thesis. Eindhoven University of Technology, The Netherlands, 2011.

[10] B. Badban, W.J. Fokkink, J.F. Groote, J. Pang, and J.C. van de Pol. Verification of a sliding window protocol in μCRL and PVS. *Formal Aspects of Computing*, 17(3):342–388, 2005.

[11] J.C.M. Baeten. A brief history of process algebra. *Theoretical Computer Science*, 335(2–3):131–146, 2005.

[12] J.C.M. Baeten, T. Basten, and M.A. Reniers. *Process algebra: Equational theories of communicating processes*. Cambridge tracts in theoretical computer science, Vol. 50. Cambridge University Press, Cambridge, U.K., 2010.

[13] J.C.M. Baeten and J.A. Bergstra. Real time process algebra. *Formal Aspects of Computing*, 3:142–188, 1991.

[14] J.C.M. Baeten and J.A. Bergstra. Process algebra with signals and conditions. In M. Broy (ed.), *Proceedings of the Marktoberdorf 1990 summer school on programming and mathematical method*, NATO ASI Series F, Vol. 88 (pp. 273–323). Springer-Verlag, Berlin, Germany, 1992.

[15] J.C.M. Baeten, J.A. Bergstra, and J.W. Klop. On the consistency of Koomen's fair abstraction rule. *Theoretical Computer Science*, 51(1–2):129–176, 1987.

[16] J.C.M. Baeten, J.A. Bergstra, and J.W. Klop. Decidability of bisimulation equivalence for processes generating context-free languages. *Journal of the ACM*, 40(3):653–682, 1993.

[17] J.C.M. Baeten and C.A. Middelburg. *Process algebra with timing*. Springer-Verlag, Berlin, Germany, 2002.

[18] J.C.M. Baeten and W.P. Weijland. *Process algebra*. Cambridge tracts in theoretical computer science, Vol. 18. Cambridge University Press, Cambridge, U.K., 1990.

[19] C. Baier and J.-P. Katoen. *Principles of model checking*. MIT Press, Cambridge, MA, 2008.

[20] J.W. de Bakker and E. de Vink. *Control flow semantics*. MIT Press, Cambridge, MA, 1996.

[21] H.P. Barendregt. Lambda calculi with types. In S. Abramsky, D.M. Gabbay, and T.S.E. Maibaum. *Handbook of logic in computer science* (pp. 117–309). Oxford Science Publications, Oxford, U.K., 1992.

[22] J. Barnes (ed.). *Complete works of Aristotle*. Princeton University Press, Princeton, NJ, 1984.

[23] K.A. Bartlett, R.A. Scantlebury, and P.T. Wilkinson. A note on reliable full-duplex transmission over half-duplex links. *Communications of the ACM*, 12(5):260–261, 1969.

[24] H. Bekič. Towards a mathematical theory of processes. In *Programming languages and their definitions: H. Bekič (1936–1982)*. Lecture notes in computer science, Vol. 177 (pp. 156–167), Springer-Verlag, Berlin, Germany, 1984.

[25] J.A. Bergstra and J.W. Klop. Process algebra for synchronous communication. *Information and Control*, 60(1–3):109–137, 1984.

[26] J.A. Bergstra and J.W. Klop. The algebra of recursively defined processes and the algebra of regular processes. In J. Paredaens (ed.), *Proceedings 11th colloquium on automata, languages and programming (ICALP'84)*, Lecture notes in computer science, Vol. 172 (pp. 82–95). Springer-Verlag, Berlin, Germany, 1984.

[27] J.A. Bergstra and J.W. Klop. Verification of an alternating bit protocol by means of process algebra. In W. Bibel and K.P. Jantke (eds.), *Mathematical methods of specification and synthesis of software systems 1985*, Lecture notes in computer science, Vol. 215 (pp. 9–23), Springer-Verlag, Berlin, Germany, 1986.

[28] Y. Bertot and P. Castéran. *Interactive theorem proving and program development. Coq'Art: The calculus of inductive constructions.* Texts in theoretical computer science. An EATCS Series. Springer-Verlag, Berlin, Germany, 2004.

[29] M.A. Bezem, R.N. Bol, and J.F. Groote. Formalizing process algebraic verifications in the calculus of constructions. *Formal Aspects of Computing*, 9(1):1–48, 1997.

[30] M.A. Bezem and J.F. Groote. Invariants in process algebra with data. In B. Jonsson and J. Parrow (eds.), *Proceedings of the 5th international conference on concurrency theory (CONCUR'94)*, Lecture notes in computer science, Vol. 836 (pp. 401–416), Springer-Verlag, Berlin, Germany, 1994.

[31] M. Bezem, J.W. Klop, and R. de Vrijer (eds.). *Term rewriting systems.* Cambridge tracts in theoretical computer science, Vol. 55. Cambridge University Press, Cambridge, U.K., 2003.

[32] J. Bicarregui, J. Dick, and E. Woods. Quantitative analysis of an application of formal methods. In *Proceedings of the 3rd international symposium on formal methods Europe on industrial benefit and advances in formal methods (FME'96)*, Lecture notes in computer science, Vol. 1051 (pp. 60–73), Springer-Verlag, Berlin, Germany, 1996.

[33] S.C.C. Blom. *Partial τ-confluence for efficient state space generation.* Technical Report SEN-R0123, CWI, Amsterdam, The Netherlands, 2001.

[34] S.C.C. Blom, W.J. Fokkink, J.F. Groote, I.A. van Langevelde, B. Lisser, and J.C. van de Pol. μCRL: A toolset for analysing algebraic specifications. In *Proceedings of the 13th conference on computer aided verification (CAV'01)*, Lecture notes in computer science, Vol. 2102 (pp. 250–254), Springer-Verlag, Berlin, Germany, 2001.

[35] G. von Bochmann. Logical verification and implementation of protocols. In *Proceedings of the 4th ACM-IEEE data communications symposium* (pp. 7-15 – 7-20). IEEE, Piscataway, NJ, 1975.

[36] J.P. Bowen and M. Hinchey. Ten commandments of formal methods... Ten years on. In M. Hinchey and L. Coyle (eds.), *Conquering complexity. Part 3*, (pp. 237–251), Springer-Verlag, Berlin, Germany, 2012.

[37] J.C. Bradfield and C.P. Stirling. Modal logics and mu-calculi: An introduction. In J. Bergstra, A. Ponse, and S. Smolka (eds.), *Handbook of process algebra* (pp. 293–330), Elsevier, Amsterdam, The Netherlands, 2001.

[38] J.J. Brunekreef. Sliding window protocols. In S. Mauw and G.J. Veltink (eds.), *Algebraic specification of communication protocols*. Cambridge tracts in theoretical computer science, Vol. 36. Cambridge University Press, Cambridge, U.K., 1993.

[39] B. Bunch. *Mathematical fallacies and paradoxes*. Van Nostrand Reinhold. New York, NY, 1982.

[40] J.R. Burch, E.M. Clarke, K.L. McMillan, D.L. Dill, and L.J. Hwang. Symbolic model checking: 10^{20} and beyond. *Information and Computation*, 98(2):142–170, 1992.

[41] S.N. Burris and H.P. Sankappanavar. A course in universal algebra. Springer-Verlag, Berlin, Germany, 1981. Also available online `http://www.math.uwaterloo.ca/~snburris` (the millennium edition), 2000.

[42] D.E. Carlson. Bit-oriented data link control. In P.E. Green, Jr (ed.), *Computer network architectures and protocols*, (pp. 111–143). Plenum Press, New York, NY, 1982.

[43] V.G. Cerf and R.E. Kahn. A protocol for packet network intercommunication. *IEEE Transactions on Communications*, 22:637–648, 1974.

[44] K.M. Chandy and J. Misra. *Parallel program design: A foundation*. Addison-Wesley, Reading, MA, 1988.

[45] Z. Chaochen, C.A.R. Hoare, and A.P. Ravn. A calculus of durations. *Information Processing Letters*, 40(5):269–276, 1991

[46] C.-T. Chou. *Practical use of the notions of events and causality in reasoning about distributed algorithms*. CS Report #940035, UCLA, Los Angeles, CA, 1994.

[47] N. Coste, H. Garavel, H. Hermanns, F. Lang, R. Mateescu, and W. Serwe. Ten years of performance evaluation for concurrent systems using CADP. In *Proceedings of the 4th international symposium on leveraging applications of formal methods, verification and validation (ISoLA'2010)*, Part II, Lecture notes in computer science, Vol. 6416 (pp. 128–142), Springer-Verlag, Berlin, Germany, 2010.

[48] D. van Dalen. *Logic and structure*. Second edition. Springer-Verlag, Berlin, Germany, 2008.

[49] M. Dam and D. Gurov. Compositional verification of CCS processes. In *Proceedings of the third Ershov memorial conference*, Lecture notes in computer science, Vol. 1755 (pp. 247–256), Springer-Verlag, Berlin, Germany, 1999.

[50] V. Diekert and G. Rozenberg (eds.). *The book of traces*. World Scientific, Singapore, 1995.

[51] E.W. Dijkstra. *A discipline of programming*. Prentice Hall, Englewood Cliffs, NJ, 1976.

[52] D. Dolev, M. Klawe, and M. Rodeh. An $O(n \log n)$ unidirectional distributed algorithm for extrema finding in a circle. *Journal of Algorithms*, 3:245–260, 1982.

[53] E-LOTOS, ISO/IEC 15437 Standard, 2001.

[54] E.A. Emerson and C.-L. Lei. Efficient model checking in fragments of the propositional mu-calculus. In *Proceedings of the 1st IEEE symposium on logic in computer science (LICS'86)* (pp. 267–278). IEEE Computer Society Press, Piscataway, NJ, 1986.

[55] J. Esparza. A false history of true concurrency: From Petri to tools. In *Proceedings of the 17th international SPIN workshop on model checking software (SPIN'10)*, Lecture notes in computer science, Vol. 6349 (pp. 180–186), Springer-Verlag, Berlin, Germany, 2010.

[56] R. Fagin, J. Halpern, Y. Moses, and M. Yoram. *Reasoning about knowledge*. MIT Press, Cambridge, MA, 2003.

[57] W.H.J. Feijen and A.J.M. van Gasteren. *On a method of multiprogramming*. Monographs in computer science, Springer-Verlag, Berlin, Germany, 2003.

[58] R.W. Floyd. Assigning meanings to programs. In *Proceedings of the American Mathematical Society symposium on applied mathematics*, Vol. 19 (pp. 19–31). 1967.

[59] W.J. Fokkink. *Introduction to process algebra*. Texts in theoretical computer science. An EATCS Series. Springer-Verlag, Berlin, Germany, 2000.

[60] W.J. Fokkink. *Modelling distributed systems*. Texts in theoretical computer science. Springer-Verlag, Berlin, Germany, 2007

[61] W.J. Fokkink, J.F. Groote, and M.A. Reniers. *Modelling distributed systems*. Unpublished, 2006.

[62] W.J. Fokkink and J. Pang. Cones and foci for protocol verification revisited. In A.D. Gordon (ed.), *Proceedings of the 6th conference on foundations of software science and computation structures (FOSSACS'03)*, Lecture notes in computer science, Vol. 2620 (pp. 267–281), Springer-Verlag, Berlin, Germany, 2003.

[63] W.J. Fokkink, J. Pang, and A.J. Wijs. Is timed branching bisimilarity a congruence indeed? *Fundamenta Informaticae*, 87(3–4):287–311, 2008.

[64] N. Francez. *Fairness*. Monographs in computer science. Springer-Verlag, Berlin, Germany, 1986.

[65] L.-å. Fredlund, J.F. Groote, and H.P. Korver. Formal verification of a leader election protocol in process algebra. *Theoretical Computer Science*, 177(2):459–486, 1997.

[66] G. Frege. *Begriffsschrift, eine der arithmetischen nachgebildete Formelsprache des reinen Denkens*. Halle a/S, Verlag von Louis Nebert, 1879.

[67] R. Fuzzati, M. Merro, and U. Nestmann. Distributed consensus, revisited. *Acta Informaticae*, 44(6):377–425, 2007.

[68] H. Garavel. Reflections on the future of concurrency theory in general and process calculi in particular. In C. Palamidessi and F.D. Valencia (eds.), *Proceedings of the LIX colloquium on emerging trends in concurrency theory in honor of professor Robin Milner*, Electronic notes in theoretical computer science, Vol. 209. Elsevier, Amsterdam, The Netherlands, 2008.

[69] H. Garavel, F. Lang, R. Mateescu, and W. Serwe. CADP 2011: A toolbox for the construction and analysis of distributed processes. *International Journal on Software Tools for Technology Transfer*, 15(2):89–107, 2013.

[70] R.J. van Glabbeek. A complete axiomatization for branching bisimulation congruence of finite-state behaviors. In A.M. Borzyszkowski and S. Sokolowski (eds.), *Proceedings of mathematical foundations of computer science (MFCS'93)*, Lecture notes in computer science, Vol. 711 (pp. 473–484), Springer-Verlag, Berlin, Germany, 1993.

[71] R.J. van Glabbeek. The linear time-branching time spectrum II: The semantics of sequential processes with silent moves. In *Proceedings of the 4th international conference on concurrency theory (CONCUR'93)*, Lecture notes in computer science, Vol. 715 (pp. 66–81), Springer-Verlag, Berlin, Germany, 1993.

[72] R.J. van Glabbeek. The linear time-branching time spectrum I: The semantics of concrete, sequential processes. In J.A. Bergstra, A. Ponse, and S.A. Smolka (eds.), *Handbook of process algebra* (pp. 3–99). Elsevier, Amsterdam, The Netherlands, 2001.

[73] R.J. van Glabbeek and W.P. Weijland. Branching time and abstraction in bisimulation semantics. *Journal of the ACM*, 43(3):555–600, 1996.

[74] P. Godefroid and P. Wolper. Using partial orders for the efficient verification of deadlock freedom and safety properties. In *Proceedings of the 3rd international workshop on computer aided verification (CAV'91)*, Lecture notes in computer science, Vol. 575 (pp. 332–342), Springer-Verlag, Berlin, Germany, 1991.

[75] E. Grädel, W. Thomas, and T. Wilke (eds.). Automata, logics, and infinite games: A guide to current research. Lecture notes in computer science, Vol. 2500, Springer-Verlag, Berlin, Germany, 2002.

[76] J.F. Groote. The syntax and semantics of timed μCRL. Technical report SEN-R9709, CWI, Amsterdam, The Netherlands, 1997.

[77] J.F. Groote. A note on n similar parallel processes. In S. Gnesi and D. Latella (eds.), *Second International ERCIM Workshop on Formal Methods for Industrial Critical Systems (FMICS'97)* (pp. 65–75), Cesena, Italy, 1997.

[78] J.F. Groote and H. Hüttel. Undecidable equivalences for basic process algebra. *Information and Computation*, 115(2):354–371, 1994.

[79] J.F. Groote, T.W.D.M. Kouters, and A.A.H. Osaiweran. Specification guidelines to avoid the state space explosion problem. In *Proceedings of 4th IPM international conference fundamentals of software engineering (FSEN 2011)*, Lecture notes in computer science, Vol. 7141 (pp. 112–127), Springer-Verlag, Berlin, Germany, 2012.

[80] J.F. Groote and R. Mateescu. Verification of temporal properties of processes in a setting with data. In A.M. Haeberer (ed.), *Proceedings of the 7th international conference on algebraic methodology and software technology (AMAST'98)*, Lecture notes in computer science, Vol. 1548 (pp. 74–90), Springer-Verlag, Berlin, Germany, 1999.

[81] J.F. Groote, F. Monin, and J. Springintveld. A computer checked algebraic verification of a distributed summation algorithm. *Formal Aspects of Computing*, 17:19–37. Springer-Verlag, Berlin, Germany, 2005.

[82] J.F. Groote and J.C. van de Pol. A bounded retransmission protocol for large data packets: A case study in computer checked verification. In M. Wirsing and M. Nivat (eds.), *Proceedings of the 5th conference on algebraic methodology and software technology (AMAST'96)*, Lecture notes in computer science, Vol. 1101 (pp. 536–550), Springer-Verlag, Berlin, Germany, 1996.

[83] J.F. Groote and J.C. van de Pol. State space reduction using partial τ-confluence. In M. Nielsen and B. Rovan (eds.), *Proceedings of the 25th symposium on mathematical foundations of computer science (MFCS'00)*, Lecture notes in computer science, Vol. 1893 (pp. 383–393), Springer-Verlag, Berlin, Germany, 2000.

[84] J.F. Groote and A. Ponse. Proof theory for μCRL: A language for processes with data. In D.J. Andrews, J.F. Groote, and C.A. Middelburg (eds.), *Semantics of specification languages*, Workshops in Computing (pp. 231–250). Springer-Verlag, Berlin, Germany, 1993.

[85] J.F. Groote and A. Ponse. The syntax and semantics of μCRL. In A. Ponse, C. Verhoef, and S.F.M. van Vlijmen (eds.), *Algebra of communicating processes (ACP'94)*, Workshops in Computing (pp. 26–62). Springer-Verlag, Berlin, Germany, 1995.

[86] J.F. Groote, A. Ponse, and Y.S. Usenko. Linearization of parallel pCRL. *Journal of Logic and Algebraic Programming*, 48(1–2):39–72, 2001.

[87] J.F. Groote and M.A. Reniers. Algebraic process verification. In J.A. Bergstra, A. Ponse, and S.A. Smolka (eds.). *Handbook of process algebra* (pp. 1151–1208). Elsevier, Amsterdam, The Netherlands, 2001.

[88] J.F. Groote and M.P.A. Sellink. Confluence for process verification. *Theoretical Computer Science*, 170(1–2):47–81, 1996.

[89] J.F. Groote and J. Springintveld. Focus points and convergent process operators: A proof strategy for protocol verification. *Journal of Logic and Algebraic Programming*, 49(1–2):31–60, 2001.

[90] J.F. Groote and J.J. van Wamel. The parallel composition of uniform processes with data. *Theoretical Computer Science*, 266:631–652, 2001.

[91] J.F. Groote and T.A.C. Willemse. Parameterised Boolean equation systems. *Theoretical Computer Science*, 343:332–369, 2005.

[92] F. van Ham, H.M.M. van de Wetering and J.J. van Wijk. Interactive visualization of state transition systems. *IEEE Transactions on Visualization and Computer Graphics*, 8(4):319–329, 2002.

[93] M.C.B. Hennessy and A. Ingólfsdóttir. A theory of communicating processes with value passing. *Information and Computation*, 107(2):202–236, 1993.

[94] M.C.B. Hennessy and H. Lin. Unique fixpoint induction for message-passing process calculi. In *Proceedings of the 3rd Australasian theory symposium on computing (CATS'97)* (pp. 122–131). Australia Computer Science Communications, 1997.

[95] M.C.B. Hennessy and R. Milner. On observing nondeterminism and concurrency. In *Proceedings of the 7th colloquium on automata, languages and programming (ICALP'80)*, Lecture notes in computer science, Vol. 85 (pp. 299–309), Springer-Verlag, Berlin, Germany, 1980.

[96] M.C.B. Hennessy and R. Milner. Algebraic laws for nondeterminism and concurrency. *Journal of the ACM*, 32(1):137–161, 1985.

[97] M.C.B. Hennessy and G.D. Plotkin. Full abstraction for a simple parallel programming language. In *Proceedings of the 8th symposium on mathematical foundations of computer science (MFCS'79)*, Lecture notes in computer science, Vol. 74 (pp. 108–120), Springer-Verlag, Berlin, Germany, 1979.

[98] T.A. Henzinger, X. Nicollin, J. Sifakis, and S. Yovine. Symbolic model checking for real-time systems. *Information and Computation*, 111:394–406, 1992.

[99] M.G. Hinchey and J.P. Bowen. *Industrial-strength formal methods in practice*. Springer-Verlag, Berlin, Germany, 1999.

[100] Y. Hirshfeld, M. Jerrum, and F. Moller. A polynomial-time algorithm for deciding bisimulation equivalence of normed basic parallel processes. *Journal of Mathematical Structures in Computer Science*, 6:251–259, 1996.

[101] C.A.R. Hoare. An axiomatic basis for computer programming. *Communications of the ACM*, 12(10):576–585, 1969.

[102] C.A.R. Hoare. Communicating sequential processes. *Communications of the ACM*, 21(8):666–677, 1978.

[103] C.A.R. Hoare. *Communicating sequential processes*. Prentice Hall, Englewood Cliffs, NJ, 1985.

[104] G.J. Holzmann. *Design and validation of computer protocols*. Prentice Hall, Englewood Cliffs, NJ, 1991.

[105] Y.L. Hwong, J.J.A. Keiren, V.J.J. Kusters, S. Leemans, and T.A.C. Willemse. Formalising and analysing the control software of the compact muon solenoid experiment at the Large Hadron Collider. *Science of Computer Programming*, 78(12):2435–2452, 2013.

[106] Y.L. Hwong, T.A.C. Willemse, V.J.J. Kusters, G. Bauer, B. Beccati, U. Behrens, K. Biery, O. Bouffet, J. Branson, S. Bukowiec, E. Cano, H. Cheung, M. Ciganek, S. Cittolin, J.A. Coarasa, C. Deldicque, A. Dupont, S. Erhan, D. Gigi, F. Glege, R. Gomez-Reino, A. Holzner, D. Hatton, L. Masetti, F. Meijers, E. Meschi, R.K. Mommsen, R. Moser, V. O'Dell, L. Orsini, C. Paus, A. Petrucci, M. Pieri, A. Racz, O. Raginel, H. Sakulin, M. Sani, P. Schieferdecker, C. Schwick, D. Shpakov, M. Simon, and K. Sumorok. An analysis of the control hierarchy modelling of the CMS detector control system. *Journal of Physics: Conference Series*, 331(2):022010, 2011.

[107] IEEE Computer Society. *IEEE Standard for a High Performance Serial Bus*. Standard 1394-1995, 1996.

[108] ISO. Information processing systems, open systems interconnection, LOTOS: A formal description technique based on the temporal ordering of observational behavior ISO/TC97/SC21/N DIS8807, 1987.

[109] K. Jensen. *Coloured Petri nets*. Springer-Verlag, Berlin, Germany, 1997.

[110] E.Y.T. Juan and J.J.P. Tsai. *Compositional verification of concurrent and real-time systems*. Kluwer/Springer, Dordrecht, The Netherlands, 2002.

[111] J.J.A. Keiren and M.A. Reniers. *Type checking mCRL2*. Computer Science Report CSR-11-11, Technische Universiteit Eindhoven, The Netherlands, 2011.

[112] A. Kaldewaij. *Programming: The derivation of algorithms*. Prentice Hall, Englewood Cliffs, NJ, 1990.

[113] P.C. Kanellakis and S.A. Smolka. CCS expressions, finite state processes and three problems of equivalence. *Information and Computation*, 86(1):43–68, 1990.

[114] J.P. Katoen, J.C. van de Pol, M.I.A. Stoelinga, and M. Timmer. A linear process-algebraic format with data for probabilistic automata. *Theoretical Computer Science*, 413(1):36–57, 2012.

[115] D.K. Kaynar, N. Lynch, R. Segala, and F.W. Vaandrager. *The theory of timed I/O automata*. Synthesis lectures on distributed computing theory, Morgan Claypool Publishers, San Rafael, CA, 2006.

[116] R. Koymans. *Specifying message passing and time-critical systems with temporal logic*. Lecture notes in computer science, Vol. 651, Springer-Verlag, Berlin, Germany, 1992.

[117] D. Kozen. Results on the propositional μ-calculus. *Theoretical Computer Science*, 27:333–354, 1983.

[118] S.A. Kripke. Semantical considerations on modal logic. *Acta Philosophica Fennica*, 16:83–94, 1963.

[119] C.I. Lewis and C.H. Langford. *Symbolic logic*. Dover Publications, New York, NY, 1959.

[120] J. Loeckx, H.-D. Ehrich, and M. Wolf. *Specification of abstract data types*. Wiley/Teubner, New York, NY, 1996.

[121] S.P. Luttik. *Choice quantification in process algebra*. Ph.D. thesis, University of Amsterdam, The Netherlands, 2002.

[122] N.A. Lynch. *Distributed algorithms*. Morgan Kaufmann, San Mateo, CA, 1996.

[123] W.C. Lynch. Reliable full duplex file transmission over half-duplex telephone lines. *Communications of the ACM*, 11(6):407–410, 1968.

[124] A. Mader. Modal μ-calculus, model checking and Gauß-elimination. In E. Brinksma, R.W. Cleaveland, K.G. Larsen, T. Margaria, and B. Steffen (eds.), *Proceedings of the 1st international workshop on tools and algorithms for construction and analysis of systems (TACAS'95)*, Lecture notes in computer science, Vol. 1019 (pp. 72–88), Springer-Verlag, Berlin, Germany, 1995.

[125] A. Mader. *Verification of modal properties using Boolean equation systems*. Ph.D. thesis, Technical University of Munich, Germany, 1997.

[126] R. Mateescu. Local model-checking of an alternation-free value-based modal mu-calculus. In *Proceedings of the 2nd international workshop on verification, model checking and abstract interpretation (VMCAI'98)*, Pisa, Italy, 1998.

[127] R. Mateescu and M. Sighireanu. Efficient on-the-fly model checking for regular alternation free mu-calculus. *Science of Computer Programming*, 46(3):255–281, 2003.

[128] S. Mauw and J.C. Mulder. Regularity of BPA-systems is decidable. In B. Jonsson and J. Parrow (eds.), *Proceedings of the international conference on concurrency theory (CONCUR '94)*, Lecture notes in computer science, Vol. 836 (pp. 34–47), Springer-Verlag, Berlin, Germany, 1994.

[129] S. Mauw and G.J. Veltink. A process specification formalism. *Fundamentae Informaticae* XIII:85–139, 1990.

[130] S. Mauw and G.J. Veltink (eds.). *Algebraic specification of communication protocols.* Cambridge tracts in theoretical computer science, Vol. 36. Cambridge University Press, Cambridge, U.K., 1993.

[131] J. McCarthy. A basis for a mathematical theory of computation. In *Computer programming and formal systems* (pp. 33–70). North Holland, Amsterdam, 1963.

[132] R. McNaughton. Infinite games played on finite graphs. *Annals of Pure and Applied Logic* 65(2):149–184, 1993.

[133] R. Milner. An approach to the semantics of parallel programs. In *Proceedings of cenvegno di informatica teorica* (pp. 283–302), Pisa, Italy, 1973.

[134] R. Milner. Processes: A mathematical model of computing agents. In H.E. Rose and J.C. Shepherdson (eds.), *Proceedings of the logic colloquium 1973* (pp. 158–173). North Holland, Amsterdam, 1973.

[135] R. Milner. *A Calculus of communicating systems.* Lecture notes in computer science, Vol. 92, Springer-Verlag, Berlin, Germany, 1980.

[136] R. Milner. A complete inference system for a class of regular behaviours. *Journal of Computer System Science*, 28(3):439–466, 1984.

[137] R. Milner. *Communication and concurrency.* Prentice Hall, Englewood Cliffs, NJ, 1989.

[138] F. Moller. *Axioms for concurrency.* Ph.D. thesis. Report CST-59-89, Department of Computer Science, University of Edinburgh, Scotland, U.K., 1989.

[139] F. Moller. The importance of the left merge operator in process algebras. In M. Paterson (ed.), *Proceedings of the international symposium on automata, languages and programming (ICALP'90)*, Lecture notes in computer science, Vol. 443 (pp. 752–764), Springer-Verlag, Berlin, Germany, 1990.

[140] F. Moller and C. Tofts. A temporal calculus of communicating systems. In *Proceedings of the 1st international conference on concurrency theory (CONCUR'90)*, Lecture notes in computer science, Vol. 458 (pp. 401–415), Springer-Verlag, Berlin, Germany, 1990.

[141] U. Montanari. True concurrency: Theory and practice. In *Proceedings of mathematics of program construction*, Lecture notes in computer science, Vol. 669 (pp. 14–17), Springer-Verlag, Berlin, Germany, 1993.

[142] P.D. Mosses (ed.). *CASL reference manual.* Lecture notes in computer science, Vol. 2960, Springer-Verlag, Berlin, Germany, 2004.

[143] X. Nicollin and J. Sifakis. The algebra of timed processes, ATP: Theory and application. *Information and Computation*, 114:131–178, 1994.

[144] T. Nipkow, L.C. Paulson, and M. Wenzel. *Isabelle/HOL: A proof assistant for higher-order logic*. Lecture notes in computer science, Vol. 2283, Springer-Verlag, Berlin, Germany, 2008.

[145] E.P. Northrop. *Riddles in mathematics: A book of paradoxes*. Penguin Books, London, U.K., 1975.

[146] S.M. Orzan and T.A.C. Willemse. Invariants for parameterised Boolean equation systems. *Theoretical Computer Science*, 411(11–13):1338–1371, 2010.

[147] A.A.H. Osaiweran, T. Fransen, J.F. Groote, and B. van Rijnsoever. Experience report on designing and developing control components using formal methods. In D. Giannakopoulou and D. Mery (eds.), *Proceedings of the 18th international symposium on formal methods (FM'2012)*, Lecture notes in computer science, Vol. 7436 (pp. 341–355), Springer-Verlag, Berlin, Germany, 2012.

[148] S. Owre, J.M. Rushby, and N. Shankar. PVS: A prototype verification system. In D. Kapur (ed.), *Proceedings of the 11th conference on automated deduction (CADE'92)*, Lecture notes in computer science, Vol. 607 (pp. 748–752), Springer-Verlag, Berlin, Germany, 1992.

[149] R. Paige and R.E. Tarjan. Three partition refinement algorithms. *SIAM Journal on Computing*, 16(6):973–989, 1987.

[150] B.C. Pierce. *Types and programming languages*. MIT Press, Cambridge, MA, 2002.

[151] D.M.R. Park. Concurrency and automata on infinite sequences. In P. Deussen (ed.), *Proceedings 5th GI (Gesellschaft für Informatik) conference*, Lecture notes in computer science, Vol. 104 (pp. 167–183), Springer-Verlag, Berlin, Germany, 1981.

[152] D.A. Peled. All from one, one for all: Model checking using representatives. In *Proceedings of the 5th international conference on computer aided verification (CAV'93)*, Lecture notes in computer science, Vol. 697 (pp. 409–423), Springer-Verlag, Berlin, Germany, 1993.

[153] C.A. Petri. *Kommunikation mit automaten*. Ph.D. thesis, Institut fuer Instrumentelle Mathematik, Bonn, Germany, 1962.

[154] G.D. Plotkin. A structural approach to operational semantics. *Journal of Logic and Algebraic Programming*, 60–61:17–140, 2004.

[155] A. Pnueli. The temporal logic of programs. In *Proceedings of the 18th annual IEEE symposium on foundations of computer science* (pp. 46–57), IEEE, Piscataway, NJ, 1977.

[156] V.R. Pratt. Semantical considerations on Floyd-Hoare logic. In *Proceedings of 17th IEEE annual symposium on foundations of computer science (FOCS'76)* (pp. 109–121), IEEE, Piscataway, NJ, 1976.

[157] V.R. Pratt. Conference report: Workshop on combining compositionality and concurrency. *Bulletin of European Association for Theoretical Computer Science (BEATCS)*, 35:253–254, 1988.

[158] A.J. Pretorius and J.J. van Wijk. Visual analysis of multivariate state transition graphs *IEEE Transactions on Visualization and Computer Graphics* 12(5):685–692, 2006.

[159] A.N. Prior. *Time and modality*. Oxford University Press, Oxford, U.K., 1957.

[160] G.M. Reed and A.W. Roscoe. A timed model for communicating sequential processes. *Theoretical Computer Science*, 58:249–261, 1988.

[161] D. Remenska, J. Templon, T.A.C. Willemse, H.E. Bal, K. Verstoep, W. Fokkink, P. Charpentier, R. Graciani Diaz, E. Lanciotti, S. Roiser, and K. Ciba. Analysis of DIRAC's behavior using model checking with process algebra. *Journal of Physics: Conference Series*, 396(5):052061, 2012.

[162] M. Roggenbach. CSP-CASL. A new integration of process algebra and algebraic specification. *Theoretical Computer Science*, 354(1):42–71, 2006.

[163] A.W. Roscoe. *Understanding concurrent systems.* Springer-Verlag, Berlin, Germany, 2007.

[164] D. Sangiorgi. Bisimulation in higher-order calculi. *Information and Computation*, 131(2):141–178, 1996.

[165] D. Sangiorgi. *Introduction to bisimulation and coinduction.* Cambridge University Press, Cambridge, U.K., 2011.

[166] D. Sangiorgi. Origins of bisimulation and coinduction. In D. Sangiorgi and J. Ruttn (eds.), *Advanced topics in bisimulation and coinduction* (chapter 1), Cambridge tracts in theoretical computer science, Vol. 52 (pp. 1–37). Cambridge University Press, Cambridge, U.K., 2012.

[167] A.A. Schoone. *Protocols by invariants.* Cambridge international series on parallel computing, Vol. 7. Cambridge University Press, Cambridge, U.K., 1996.

[168] C. Shankland and M.B. van der Zwaag. The tree identify protocol of IEEE 1394 in μCRL. *Formal Aspects of Computing*, 10(5–6):509–531, 1998.

[169] M. Sighireanu. LOTOS NT user's manual (Version 2.7). Technical Report INRIA Rhône-Alpes/VASY, France, 2012.

[170] A.S. Tanenbaum. *Computer networks.* Prentice Hall, Englewood Cliffs, NJ, 1981.

[171] B. Thomsen. Plain CHOCS; A second generation calculus for higher order processes. *Acta Informatica*, 30(1):1–59, 1993.

[172] Y.S. Usenko. *Linearization in μCRL.* Ph.D. thesis, Eindhoven University of Technology, The Netherlands, 2002.

[173] F.W. Vaandrager. *Verification of two communication protocols by means of process algebra*. Technical report CS-R8608. Centrum voor Wiskunde en Informatica, Amsterdam, The Netherlands, 1986.

[174] F.W. Vaandrager. Verification of a distributed summation algorithm. In I. Lee and S.A. Smolka (eds.), *Proceedings of the 6th international conference on concurrency theory (CONCUR'95)*, Lecture notes in computer science, Vol. 962 (pp. 190–203), Springer-Verlag, Berlin, Germany, 1995.

[175] A. Valmari. Stubborn sets for reduced state space generation. In *Proceedings of the 10th international conference on applications and theory of Petri nets (APN'90)*, Lecture notes in computer science Vol. 483 (pp. 491–515), Springer-Verlag, Berlin, Germany, 1990.

[176] B. Vergauwen and J. Lewi. Efficient local correctness checking for single and alternating Boolean equation systems. In S. Abiteboul and E. Shamir (eds.), *Proceedings of the 21st international colloquium on automata, languages and programming (ICALP'94)*, Lecture notes in computer science, Vol. 820 (pp. 302–315), Springer-Verlag, Berlin, Germany, 1994.

[177] J.L.M. Vrancken. The algebra of communicating processes with empty process. *Theoretical Computer Science*, 177(2):287–328, 1997.

[178] R.F.C. Walters. *Number theory: An introduction.* Carslaw Publications, 1987.

[179] M.J. van Weerdenburg. *Process algebra with local communication.* Computer Science Report 05/05, Department of Mathematics and Computer Science, Eindhoven University of Technology, The Netherlands, 2005.

[180] A.N. Whitehead and B. Russell. *Principia mathematica, 3 Vols.* Cambridge University Press, Cambridge, U.K., 1910, 1912, and 1913.

[181] G. Winskel. *Events in computation.* Ph.D. thesis, University of Edinburgh, Scotland, U.K., 1980.

[182] M. Wirsing. *Structured algebraic specifications: A kernel language.* Ph.D. thesis, Institut für Informatik, Technische Universät, München, Germany, 1983.

[183] J. Woodcock, P.G. Larsen, J. Bicarregui, and J. Fitzgerald. Formal methods: Practice and experience. *ACM Computing Surveys*, 41(4):1–36, 2009.

[184] W. Zielonka. Infinite games on finitely coloured graphs with applications to automata on infinite trees. *Theoretical Computer Science*, 200(1–2):135–183, 1998.

Index